The Oxford Centre for Staff and Learning Development

Proceedings of the 2002 10th International Symposium

Improving Student Learning

Improving Student Learning Theory and Practice – 10 years on

Edited by Chris Rust

Published by
THE OXFORD CENTRE FOR STAFF & LEARNING DEVELOPMENT
Oxford Brookes University
Wheatley Campus
Wheatley
Oxford
OX33 1HX

Improving Student Learning 10
Improving Student Learning Theory and Practice 10 years on

ISBN 1 873576 69 2

British Library Cataloguing-in-Publication Data.
A catalogue record for this book is available from the British Library.

Printed 2003

Typeset in Palatino

Printed in Great Britain by
Oxonian Rewley Press Ltd
Oxford

Printed on paper produced from sustainable forests.

Contents

Part IV
Skills development and lifelong learning

Part V
Use of C&IT

Part VI
Learning environments

Part VII
Supporting learners

Part VIII
Meeting the challenge of diversity

Part IX
Implementing and managing change and innovation

Part X
Symposia

Preface

This was a landmark International Improving Student Learning Symposium: the tenth in an annual series started in 1993, and the first held outside the UK, in Brussels. After ten years it seemed to be time to take stock of where the Improving Student Learning movement had got to and what it had achieved.

Over those ten years a total of 412 papers have been published in proceedings. As in previous years the Symposium succeeded in bringing together researchers – who develop theory about student learning and research methodologies for studying student learning – with the developers who use these conceptual and research tools to study and evaluate innovations in student learning in their own contexts. And as in previous years there was a healthy mixture of step-by-step development of conceptual and research tools, and new ideas and new challenges to conventional wisdom.

Papers are organised around eight themes:

- Curriculum and programme design
- Learning and teaching methods
- Skills development and lifelong learning
- The use of C&IT
- Learning environments
- Supporting learners
- Meeting the challenge of diversity
- Implementing and managing change and innovation

There were also four symposia, each containing three or four papers, on the following themes:

- Assessing group practice
- Challenges of diversity – exploring experiences and cultural change
- Student cheating and plagiarism
- Enhancing teaching-learning environments in undergraduate courses

The three keynote presentations each acted to provide linkages and to create coherence in the wide range of papers. There were many first time delegates at the Symposium and the keynotes provided a useful overview of some of the key themes of the preceding symposia.

Graham Gibbs' paper attempted to summarise the achievements of the ISL movement since he launched it with a national project begun in 1990. He summarised additions to theory, presented to ISL Symposia, that were originally derived from phenomenographic research undertaken in the late 1970s. He also analysed the 374 papers published in the first nine years and identified a number of patterns and trends. There is less of a focus on 'second order', 'internal perspective' and phenomenographic research, compared with the early years, and more emphasis on 'first order' and external perspectives, involving cognitive psychology and various theoretical approaches that are not derived from students' own experiences. Unfortunately, there is also still relatively little evidence that taking this research seriously actually improves student learning. Gibbs argued for greater emphasis on competence (both teaching competence of teachers and learning competence of students) rather than focusing exclusively on conceptions and approaches to teaching and learning.

Previous work on teachers' or students' technical skills or what they can be observed to actually do has tended to be undertaken separately from work on the conceptions and understandings that drive what they do. But as Keith Trigwell has argued elsewhere, effectiveness involves both sophisticated conceptions and competence. Gibbs' review of past papers identified instances in which authors have described apparently similar innovations that have diametrically opposed consequences and argued for more theorising about practice – about what it is that makes a pedagogy or method effective in improving student learning. He concluded with an outline of what such a theory might look like, using how assessment supports learning as an example.

Marcia Baxter Magolda presented some vivid video accounts of student learning. The 'acted out' sketches, based on actual examples, illustrated complex connections between a number of themes identified separately at previous symposia, including the development over time of students' conceptions of learning and the way constructivist approaches to teaching and assessment foster student development. This is perhaps what 'constructive alignment' looks like when implemented across all three years of a programme. American literature often uses different language and methodologies to explore what are recognisably the same phenomena that are studied in European and Australasian higher education.

Throughout the ten years of ISL Symposia there has been a mixture of qualitative and quantitative approaches to studying student learning and evaluating the impact of innovations deigned to improve student learning. The keynote by Keith Trigwell and John Richardson emphasised the complementary nature of these approaches within the phenomenographic paradigm. Trigwell outlined the interconnected range of phenomenographic category systems or 'outcome spaces' that have emerged from closely related studies over the past 20 years. John Richardson outlined some of the inventories that use these phenomenographic categories as their conceptual underpinnings, but then use psychometric techniques to build reliable items and robust scales. This enables scale scores to be used to measure the extent to which phenomena are experienced in particular contexts and to identify where different perceptions are related – for example students' perceptions of course contexts being related to students' approaches to study. Once constructed, these inventories can be used to study differences between student groups or between contexts. Student questionnaires without soundly based underpinning conceptual frameworks are seldom valuable, and quantification and measurement have been crucial to establishing the existence of consistent relationships and gaining credibility. Sharing the platform to outline the achievements of the two approaches, Trigwell and Richardson highlighted their interdependence.

Some of the practices that papers have focused on in past symposia are now being theorised and studied in more rigorous ways. For example there have been case-study-like accounts in past symposia of attempts to develop students' generic skills. In the tenth anniversary symposium there were several papers theorising generic skill development, including a paper by Simon Barrie taking a phenomenographic approach to exploring teachers' conceptions of generic skills.

This symposium demonstrated that the Improving Student Learning movement is in good health and I expect it to go from strength to strength over the next ten years.

Chris Rust
Oxford Centre for Staff and Learning Development, Oxford Brookes University

July 2003

1 Ten years of Improving Student Learning

Graham Gibbs
Centre for Higher Education Practice, Open University, UK

Abstract

The Improving Student Learning Symposium grew out of a project started in 1989 to see whether, if you took the student learning research seriously, and made principled changes to courses, it made any difference to the way students learn and to their learning outcomes. That project, and the book that reported its outcomes (Gibbs, 1992) was based on a particular research paradigm and body of work involving only a small sub-set of all the research and theory available. The underlying (phenomenographic) concepts were developed in Sweden and the subsequent (often quantitative) applications developed mainly in Australia, the UK, Holland and Hong Kong.

The 'Improving Student Learning' movement has flourished. The original conceptual framework and associated research paradigms have remained prominent, and have provided a rich supportive framework for varied studies from many countries. Work within this paradigm has added to theory, developed research tools and provided empirical evidence in the last decade. The Symposia have become more international and have helped to create and support a lively research community. However there have been relatively few studies that have demonstrated that taking this research seriously actually makes any difference. Very early research relating students' approach to learning outcomes in small scale experimental studies still provides the main evidence of validity, and arguments about benefit in most papers rely largely on long chains of inference going back to these early studies.

There have been few papers that successfully link the broad tactic of encouraging a deep approach to learning with specific course design, teaching or assessment tactics, leaving most teachers none the wiser about what to do to improve their courses. Other aspects of student learning have frequently been reported, such as learning styles and the application of experiential learning theory, but appear not to provide a coherent or stable framework within which a body of work is developed, and provide almost no evidence of positive impact. American and European speakers at Symposia have aroused interest in alternative conceptual frameworks, especially about assessment, without making much impact on the nature of work reported in subsequent papers. Crucial aspects of student learning such as why they study, how they spend their time and how they respond to assessment and feedback have received surprisingly little attention. This chapter argues that research about improving student learning needs to provide more evidence that student learning has been improved and should move into other areas where there is significant scope for leverage on student learning behaviour. It will offer a starting point for one such area that has been particularly neglected, given the large proportion of teachers' time spent on it: how students learn from formative assessment.

1.1   Introduction

The Improving Student Learning Symposia grew out of a single national scale project. In the late 1980s in the UK, the national quality body for Polytechnics, the Council for National Academic Awards (CNAA), became aware that course documentation they were reviewing contained either no rationale for the choice of teaching and assessment methods or rationales which were not underpinned by any knowledge of theory or evidence about how students learn or awareness of which features of course design affect how students learn. They had tired of reading ill-informed and unjustified explanations about why course designs were as they were. They invited tenders for a research project designed to demonstrate that if you took the student learning research seriously when designing courses, it made a difference to student learning. I secured the contract with a bid based around what was known at that time about students' approaches to study and what influenced students' approach. At that time we already knew a good deal about student learning from a phenomenographic perspective that could help us in this project:

- Students vary not just in the quantity or skill of their studying but in their approach to learning, and particularly in the extent to which they are attempting to reproduce or understand study material

- The extent to which students take a surface or deep approach is readily identifiable with quite short questionnaires

- Individuals vary in their approach between courses, within courses and even within single study tasks, so contexts clearly influence students' approach

- Students vary in their conception of learning and their conception constrains their approach such that students with unsophisticated conceptions of learning are likely to take a surface approach regardless of task demands, while students with more sophisticated conceptions of learning can take a surface or a deep approach, according to context

- What students learn varies not just quantitatively, but qualitatively, and it is possible to characterise outcomes in a limited number of qualitatively different ways, either with reference to different levels of understanding of the specific concepts involved or with reference to a general purpose taxonomy of the structure of learning outcomes

- The way students approach their learning (deep or surface) is closely related to the quality of their learning outcomes. A surface approach is likely to lead to short term recall but little understanding or longer term recall, list-like structures, no conclusions etc

- The extent to which students take a deep or surface approach is closely related to a number of features of the learning context

- These contextual features are readily identifiable using questionnaires

- The features associated with students taking a surface approach are implicit in a number of pedagogic approaches, such as Problem Based Learning

However at that time there was almost no evidence that it was possible to intervene in a course with a clear rationale for changes to features of the course and its pedagogy, so as to induce a deep approach to a greater extent and to produce better quality learning outcomes.

The project advertised for teachers who felt that they had severe quality problems on their courses and who wanted to do something about it and to join the project – in particular, teachers whose students took a surface approach to their studies and who wanted to change their course so as to encourage them to take a deep approach. Over one hundred teachers applied to be involved and eight were selected, to represent a wide range of disciplines and institutional contexts and a wide range of existing problems. These eight teachers then engaged in a two-year process involving:

- Diagnosing what was going wrong with their current course by using existing theory and by collecting evidence from students and other sources using existing research tools

- Selecting tactics that could be justified from the literature to address the problems

- Implementing the new tactics

- Evaluating the impact on students' approach and on learning outcomes

At that time we already had research tools to help with diagnosing problems or evaluating the impact of interventions, such as:

- Inventories from Australia and the UK that measured the extent to which students took a surface or deep approach

- Phenomenographic category systems to help categorise, for example, students' approaches to learning, students' conceptions of learning and students' conceptions of a number of concepts, mainly in science and economics

- The SOLO taxonomy (Biggs and Collis, 1982) for categorising the structure of learning outcomes

- Descriptions of how to conduct this kind of research

The eight action research projects produced a wide range of evidence of:

- The extent to which there were problems with the quality of students' approach and the quality of learning outcomes, before the interventions

- Improvements in students' approach (ie towards a deep approach and away from a surface approach)

- Changes in a positive direction in students' descriptions of how they went about studying, for example with greater engagement and meta-cognitive awareness and control

- Quantitative and qualitative improvements in students' performance on assignments and examinations including improvements in the structure of learning outcomes as measured by the SOLO taxonomy

- Changed perceptions of employers of the characteristics of students emerging from courses

- Changes to other courses as a consequence of successful changes to the courses being studied

The main outcomes of the project were a book (Gibbs, 1992) and an associated conference at which the eight teachers presented how they had improved student learning on their courses. There was such a level of interest in this project that we were encouraged to mount a similar conference the following year at which others could present their action research of a similar kind. The number of presenters and participants grew to such an extent that we had to move to a much larger venue and the Improving Student Learning Symposium was born. The symposium in Brussles in 2002 was the 10th anniversary symposium. Over 2,000 participants have attended over 450 sessions involving papers, seminars, workshops and 'works in progress' and 374 papers have been published in annual proceedings. The titles of the Symposia have been:

1. Improving student learning: theory and practice
2. Improving student learning through assessment and evaluation
3. Using research to improve student learning
4. Improving student learning through course design
5. Improving students as learners
6. Improving student learning outcomes
7. Improving student learning through the disciplines
8. Improving student learning strategically
9. Improving student learning using learning technology

It is worth restating the original rationale for the Symposia lest it be lost in academic drift or a single minded pursuit of status or pre-imminence. It was intended:

- To bring those researchers who developed the theory, concepts and research tools together with those who used them to improve student learning, especially with educational developers and teachers undertaking pedagogic research as a way of improving courses. Over the years the Symposia have included presentations from all the main theorists on whose work the field has been constructed and who are most cited, including Ferenc Marton, John Biggs and Noel Entwistle.

- To focus on student learning rather than on teaching

- To focus on improving student learning, not just on studying student learning

- To build a 'community of practice' that collaborates in improving student learning in a scholarly way

- To build the research capacity of this community so as to be able to undertake more rigorous and telling research

It was always assumed that for teachers who wanted to discuss teaching practice there were more practical conferences and for researchers who wanted to discuss research there were also more prestigious research conferences.

1.2   Developments in theory since 1992

At the first ISL Symposium, John Biggs (1994) summarised the underlying model that had been used to link student and contextual variables, students' approach, and learning outcomes, as in Figure 1. This was based on the '3P' model (presage, process and product) that had been used in earlier quantitative studies. The difference between this model and earlier '3P' models was that all the variables were derived from a phenomenographic perspective. It described learners' internal world as they perceived it; for example: how the learner perceived learning and knowledge (Box 1 eg Saljo, 1982, and Perry 1970); characteristics of the context (Box 2 eg Ramsden and Entwistle, 1981); how students then approached specific learning tasks (Box 3 eg Marton and Saljo, 1997); and the quality of students' understanding of key concepts (Box 4 eg Dahlgren and Marton, 1978). It also described internal relationships between these variables. For example if a student perceives learning to be a matter of passive absorption of information (Box 1) or if they are in context with a heavy workload (Box 2) then they are more likely to adopt a surface approach (Box 3) and this will be associated with a lower level of understanding (Box 4). A '3P' model would have involved student variables from an external perspective in each box, for example school exam results in Box 1, class size in Box 2, study hours in Box 3 and exam results in Box 4. It had proved very difficult to identify consistent or strong relationships between such variables from an external perspective but it proved relatively straightforward to identify strong and consistent relationships between these boxes from an internal perspective.

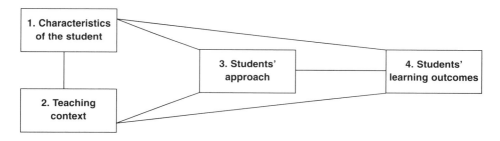

Figure 1.1   Theoretical framework in 1993 (after Biggs, 1994)

Prosser et al (2001) have elaborated on this model to emphasise the importance of students' perceptions of the context rather than the context variables themselves. Student variables and context variables are mediated by students' perceptions and understandings in a way that is related to their approach, as in Fig 2. In this elaborated model all of the elements interact as part of the way students make sense of their studying. For example, in the Linder and Marshall studies discussed below, students' perceptions of their own learning outcomes (Box 4) influenced their understanding of what knowledge consisted of (Box 1).

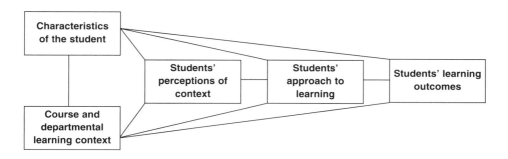

Figure 1.2   Theoretical framework in 2000 – as perceived by the student
               (after Prosser et al 2001)

In the same way that students' conceptions of learning had been shown to relate to their approach to learning, studies in Australia explored teachers' conceptions of teaching and their approaches to teaching. Just as the ASI (Approaches to Studying Inventory) had been developed to measure students' approaches to study in an economical way, so the ATI (Approaches to Teaching Inventory) was developed to measure teachers' approaches (Trigwell et al, 1994). Teachers' approaches were found to relate to students' approaches, and so to student learning outcomes. Just as students' approaches are related to perceived context variables, so features of the perceived teaching context (such as student diversity) were found to relate to teachers' approaches. In addition, studies of the leadership context found variations in the way Heads of Department perceived the support and development of teaching and this, too, contributed to teachers' perceptions of the teaching context and related to teachers' approaches. Figure 3 shows a model about teachers' approaches to teaching that mirrors the model for students' approaches to studying. Other components of students' and teachers' perceptions have been explored, such as teachers and students' perceptions of key skills, which have contributed to and elaborated these underlying models rather than challenging them.

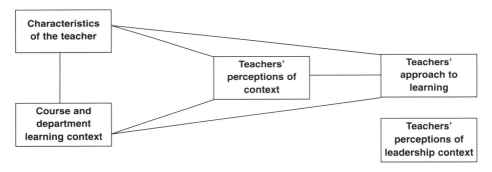

Figure 1.3   Theoretical framework in 2001 as perceived by teachers
(after Prosser et al, 2001)

1.3   Developments in evidence about student learning

Empirical studies relating to these models have provided evidence concerning a number of phenomena:

- Students' approach looks different in different contexts. What a deep approach consists of in different disciplines needs elaborating if it is to make sense. For example a surface approach in music may be revealed by imitation of a teachers' instrumental technique. Cultural differences have been identified, for example in the way Chinese students perceive approaches to study or may memorise in order to understand.

- It is possible to change students' approach both directly and indirectly. A much cited study by Paul Ramsden suggested that changing students' approach through a specially designed study skills programme was unlikely to succeed because students' perceptions of the varied contexts they studied in overrode the influence of the programme. Indeed such programmes may largely succeed in sensitising students to contextual demands. However studies (eg Norton and Dickens, 1995) have shown that it is possible to change students' approach through specially designed programmes that are embedded within the context they study in. There are a number of examples of successfully shifting students' approach by changing the design and demands of courses, as there were in the original action research studies.

- Teachers' approaches to teaching vary in a way characterised as teacher-focused (concerned with transmitting information) or student-focused (concerned with supporting the development by students of concepts). There is no simple one-to-one mapping of teaching techniques to approaches to teaching: for example it is possible to be student focussed about lecturing.

- Teachers' approach is related to students' approach: teachers who have a student-focus are more likely to have students who take a deep approach to studying.

- Teachers' perceptions of the context they teach in are linked to their approach to teaching. Subject matter, class size and student diversity are all related to the extent to which teachers adopt a student focus.

- Just as it is possible to change a students' approach through a study skills programme, so it is possible to change a teachers' approach through a teacher training programme. A teacher training programme has even been demonstrated to change teachers' students' approaches to studying.

- It is possible to improve student performance on assessment tasks by using this framework to make decisions about how to increase the extent to which students take a deep approach.

1.4   Exemplars of attempts to improve student learning

There have been many superb and valuable papers over the years but I have picked out just two rather different studies in order to illustrate the effective use of research to improve student learning. They have been selected because:

- They were both presented by practising teachers rather than by professional researchers and demonstrate the standard of scholarship that can be achieved by practitioners

- Both provided convincing evidence of positive impact on student learning and this, as is discussed below, is not as common as it might be

- Both involved papers at successive Symposia, telling the next stage of unrolling stories of improvement, evaluation and insight

- Both used established theory to explain what was going on and established research tools to study what was going on

Linder and Marshall (1996, 1997) used a range of (mainly American) theory about meta-cognition and culturally relevant learning to develop a wide repertoire of teaching methods specifically for black South African students studying physics. They described and justified their teaching methods with reference to this theory and studied the impact of their use with the ASI, in-depth interviews followed by phenomenographic analysis, and standardised tests of understanding of core physics concepts. They demonstrated marked and rapid changes in students' conceptions of learning, parallel changes in students' conceptions of science concepts and striking improvements in students' performance on tests. Students were improved as learners and their learning outcomes were also improved. Linder and Marshall also contributed to theory by developing the notion of 'epistemological shift' to describe the way their students changed what they thought science itself was, as they developed as learners of physics.

During the symposium on improving student learning outcomes (in 1997) there was a lively debate about outcome-driven curriculum design and assessment and the value to students of specifying learning outcomes in advance. Despite 'clarity of outcomes and standards' being one of the variables that relates closely to the extent to which students take a deep approach (and so included as a scale in the Course Experience Questionnaire, Ramsden 1991) there were concerns that specifying outcomes too tightly would result in students taking a surface approach. Allan (1995, 1996) had been involved in wide scale implementation of the introduction of curricula specified in terms of explicit learning outcomes at the University of Wolverhampton. Her studies showed that the introduction of learning outcome-driven module design:

- Increased the sophistication of students' 'conceptions of learning' (Saljo, 1992). The proportion of students who saw learning as involving 'making sense' increased from 8% to 55%

- Increased constructive alignment (Biggs, 1996) in the form of congruence between students' and teachers' perceptions of high-level goals

Allen went on to study the features of module design that were most important to influencing perceptions of goals.

These were the kinds of studies that the ISL Symposia were established to support and to report.

1.5 Development of a research community

One of the striking features of the ISL Symposia has been the continuity of participation and contribution. As well as a succession of prominent papers from various combinations of Mike Prosser, Keith Trigwell, Paul Ramsden, Elaine Martin and Noel Entwistle, together with colleagues such as Simon Barrie, there has been a long series of contributions from authors such as Lin Norton, Liz McDowell, Eric Meyer, Barbara de la Harpe and Shirley Booth. This has helped to create a stable conceptual and methodological environment which has fostered progressive building on work from preceding years. There have also been a large number of successive presentations from practitioners reporting the application of conceptual frameworks and research tools developed by others, or simply empirical evidence of improved student learning – such as by Margaret Price.

There has also been much evidence of collaboration between teachers within institutions with educational development and research expertise supporting practitioner research. This has taken a highly organised form at the University of Lund where the models outlined above have provided a conceptual and methodological framework for pedagogic research-led teaching improvement programmes involving large numbers of teachers. A similar approach is developing at the University of Oxford. There have also been regular multi-author presentations from institutions such as Sheffield Hallam University, Anglia Polytechnic University, Liverpool Hope University College and Oxford Brookes University

Some years ago Barry Jackson established the ISL mailbase that has been used regularly to collate insights and experience and to debate a range of issues concerning improving student learning.

1.6   Development of research capacity

More than 10% of all the papers presented have concerned the development of methodology and research tools such as questionnaires or phenomenographic category systems. In some years there have been half-day or shorter research methods workshops and conceptual overviews, and some of these have been attended by up to 140 participants. Some of these workshops have been supported by such full handouts that they have been written up as papers and published in proceedings. The papers by Roger Lindsay on experimental design and on interpreting student performance data have been particularly valuable contributions to developing the research capacity of the community. Symposia have also contained, from time to time, 'work in progress' sessions for beginning researchers to present embryonic studies and early data in order to gain guidance. Informal 'research supervisions' from leading research experts has been a valuable feature of symposia for many participants. Jackson (1995) surveyed teachers' attitudes to the use of pedagogic research as a teaching improvement process and found increasing sophistication and positive attitudes that one might not have expected only a few years before.

1.7   A profile of 10 years' papers

The developments described above seem universally positive and encouraging. But has all this research made any difference, and if so, what to?

All 374 published papers from nine Symposia were read and analysed, using the coding template in Appendix 1, in order to obtain an overview of the kind of research undertaken and its focus and blind spots. Seminars, works in progress and workshops were excluded from the analysis.

Each paper was coded:

- By perspective: whether it took an internal, usually phenomenographic, perspective, looking at learning as experienced by participants, or an external, usually cognitive, perspective, where interpretations are made by the researcher using their own concepts and frames of analysis

- By topic: whether the paper was about what students learn, developing teaching methods etc

- By focus: whether the paper was developing theory, developing methodology, developing practice etc

Papers were sometimes multiply coded where they focussed on several things or took more than one perspective.

Before summarising this analysis it is important to highlight that papers published in Improving Student Learning proceedings only represent a proportion of published papers in this field or published papers by the same authors. The authors involved may choose to present at Symposia only a particular kind of their total output. Hence the analysis here may not be representative of research and evidence in this field.

Despite the origins of the Symposia and the dominance of the conceptual frameworks outlined above, only one third of papers took an internal perspective and two thirds took an external perspective (using none of the frameworks described above). The proportion taking an internal perspective declined markedly over the decade, starting at 58% in 1983 and dropping to 11% by 2001. There may have been a much larger proportion of papers that took a broadly student-focussed approach (rather than a teacher focussed approach), but they may have done so using an external perspective – for example studying experiential learning styles.

The majority of papers (61%) have been about the development of practice. Table 1 lists the main focus of papers in rank order. Papers were much more likely to focus on components of courses (such as teaching or assessment methods) than on whole courses or whole programmes and were quite unlikely to focus on the organisational or quality assurance context within which learning takes place. In the current climate where teaching improvement is becoming more strategic and managerial in nature this is worrying.

Focus	% of papers
Development of practice	**61%**
made up of:	
Development of teaching methods	20%
Development of students	13%
Development of assessment methods	13%
Development of courses/modules	8%
Development of programmes	7%
What and how of student learning	**21%**
made up of:	
How students learn	10%
How students differ, or develop over time	6%
What students learn	5%
Teachers	**11%**
made up of:	
How teachers differ, or develop over time	6%
Developing teachers	5%
Systems and contexts	**7%**
made up of:	
Developing departmental or institutional contexts	4%
Quality assurance systems	3%

Table 1.1   Focus of 374 papers

Papers were categorised as presenting evidence of a positive impact on student learning processes and/or their learning outcomes, or as presenting no evidence, evidence of no impact or evidence of a negative impact. Only 13% of papers presented evidence of positive impact: about five papers a year. Of this 13% most presented evidence only of improved learning process (for example students taking a deep approach to a greater extent) with no evidence of improved learning outcome except with reference to other studies of the link between approach and outcome. It might have been expected that taking an internal perspective would make it more difficult to provide evidence of impact but papers taking an external perspective were even less likely to present evidence of impact: only 10% containing such evidence.

It was common for papers to report no difference as a result of an intervention of some kind, or to present unconvincing evidence (for example with no data from a control group or any other kind of data for comparison, or no description of the form of analysis that would aid interpretation of statements from students). A number of papers presented evidence of a negative impact of an intervention designed on a principled basis, and a very small number presented evidence of a spectacularly negative impact (for example Jones and Hassall 1996). On the basis of the evidence presented, an innovator could not be very confident of being able to have a positive impact, or of being able to replicate the positive impact of others.

The likelihood of a paper reporting impact varied between different topic areas. 20% of papers about developing students reported a positive impact, 15% of papers about developing courses and 14% of papers concerning the what students learn or how they learn. Most of the other 86% of papers about the what and how of learning were simply descriptive of differences between students. At the other end of the scale only 5% of papers about developing departmental or institutional contexts contained evidence of impact, only 4% of papers about developing teachers and no papers at all about developing quality assurance systems. In the UK despite the universal use of learning and teaching strategies in institutions they are almost all 'knowledge free zones' demonstrating a remarkable level of ignorance about what makes a difference to the quality of student learning. Very few have any kind of evaluation framework or plans that would be capable of demonstrating impact on student learning. The Improving Student Learning Symposia apparently have little to offer them. A paper presented in 2002 by Mike Prosser and Simon Barrie about quality enhancement systems based on performance indicators derived from student learning research offers some hope of progress here.

The extent to which papers present evidence of positive impact has declined over time, with 18% of papers presented in 1995 ("Using research to improve student learning") containing evidence of impact and 0% of papers in 2001 ("Improving student learning through using learning technology").

Papers were also coded according to their purpose. 58% were concerned with the development of practice, 14% with the development of theory or concepts about learning and teaching and 10% with the development of research tools or methodology. 14% had no clear focus. There was a very uneven pattern across topic areas. For example about half of all papers about how students learn concerned development of theory and concepts, and a further quarter about developing methodology and research tools: a much higher proportion than for papers in other topic areas.

1.8   Conclusions

After a decade there is disappointingly little evidence that all the research and development reported at the Symposia actually makes a positive difference, and the proportion of papers presenting such evidence is declining. In contrast the amount of theory and concept building, and especially description of variation, is increasing. Perhaps this is a higher status activity. There are a large number of atheoretical descriptions of practice with no evidence about impact, especially about the use of information and communications technologies. This lack of evidence of impact is despite the ready availability of a range of well developed and useful research tools and ample accounts of their use. In some topic areas papers rarely use readily available appropriate research tools. For example not one of the many papers about increasing students' reflectiveness makes use of any of the available questionnaires on reflection (eg Kember and Yeung, 2000) to measure any improvement.

The original strong internal theoretical and methodological perspective is being lost. Eclecticism is no bad thing in itself though the coherence of theory and bodies of evidence may suffer. Evidence of impact and the use of an internal perspective have both been strongest when the focus is on research rather than on practice.

There is little focus on the context in which learning takes place: on departments, institutions and quality assurance systems (and this despite Noel Entwistle's (1995) demolition of the Scottish Quality Assurance system from the perspective of what is known about student learning).

1.9   Some questions about key findings

1. Some of the most interesting development since 1992 has involved studies of approaches to teaching, teachers' perceptions of the context of teaching and perceptions of leadership of teaching. There is an appealing logical linkage from leadership, though perceptions of contexts, to teachers' conceptions and approaches to teaching and from there to students' approaches and to student learning outcomes. The implication is that by changing leadership of teaching or changing teaching contexts you could change student learning outcomes. But while there are empirically demonstrated linkages of some kind between adjacent levels in this long logical chain, and sometimes even linkages between three levels, there is as yet no empirical evidence that changing either conceptions of leadership of teaching or perceptions of the context of teaching, has any impact on students' approaches, let alone on their learning outcomes. It seems unlikely that a large proportion of variance in learning outcomes could be explained by variations in conceptions of leadership.

2. Several of the key aspects of teachers' conceptions of context that have been identified in papers concern things that teachers cannot do much about because they relate to broad policy and funding issues that result in more, and more varied, students entering higher education. Studies of the relationship between perceptions of context and teachers' approaches to teaching may simply describe what happens when teachers do not respond appropriately to changed contexts. But teachers can change what they do when faced with these contexts. For example papers have reported a clear relationship between class size and student performance and also between class size and the extent to which students take a surface approach (Gibbs et al). But the same papers also reported exceptions to these patterns where teachers had changed practices and succeeded in supporting a deep approach despite large classes. It is not the case that large classes inevitably lead to a surface approach, though it may be very likely if you persist with using conventional teaching methods designed for small classes. There is a danger that phenomenographic studies, and the quantitative studies that follow them, set the world in aspic. The patterns that have been identified are not immutable. What is more the key variables when the studies were originally undertaken may not be the key variables today. For example excessive workload was identified as a key variable relating to students' approach about twenty years ago at Lancaster University in the UK. Today at Lancaster and elsewhere there seems to be much more of a problem capturing sufficient student time and effort to do enough studying of any kind, in the face of students undertaking part time work, to earn money, and insufficient assessment and feedback, caused by teachers being too busy. It is unclear that the CEQ still measures what are the key variables for higher education in the 21st century. Even if the CEQ were to be still entirely relevant, although it has been used for many years now as a measure of those features of courses that have been found to relate to students' approach there have been no studies reported at the Symposia that show that improved CEQ scores are related to any kind of improved outcome other than students' approach: better retention, happier students, better marks, happier employers, more competent employees or any other measure.

3. Most of the evidence that students' approach relates to outcomes is drawn from studies in the 1970s and early 1980s. We are still largely reliant in the inference that if we change students' approach then we will also improve learning outcomes. Few studies reported at the Symposia have any direct evidence about learning outcomes. Some of the most useful papers report quantitative improvements in student exam marks (for example papers by Margaret Price) following very modest and simple interventions, but such papers are rare.

4. Over the years there have been a substantial number of papers from mainland Europe, particularly Scandinavia, and from the USA. Some of these have presented or utilised quite different explanatory frameworks than those outlined at the start of this paper. For example popular sessions by Tom Angelo at two Symposia were based on the AAHE 'Classroom Assessment' initiative. Although presented using its own terminology and emphases, some shallow digging and cross referencing would have found parallels with the notion of constructive alignment of goals and assessment, with work on the role of feedback in learning, and with constructivism in general as it applies to active learning in the classroom. It included useful insights into how to design assessment so that it measured and valued the outcomes of a deep approach rather than only a surface approach. These presentations left not a ripple in their wake. No studies were presented at subsequent symposia that resembled 'classroom assessment' work or built on insights from this work. A substantial literature has developed in the USA on what happened when 'classroom assessment' was widely implemented. As with many such initiatives practice was varied in focus and quality and the quality of evaluation evidence varied even more. But insights have emerged and they are important. In particular the roles of 'meta-cognitive control' and 'self efficacy' in student learning have been elaborated. These Symposia seem oblivious of this work.

5. There has been conflicting evidence of impact from almost identical interventions. For example, studies of the introduction of campus-based open learning have reported both shifting students to a deep approach and improved marks in one case and shifting students to a surface approach and reduced marks in another case. What seems to be missing here is first, an adequate account of how open learning is meant to improve student learning or second, any awareness that you can implement interventions well or badly.

Taking this second issue first, Keith Trigwell has recently defined excellent teaching in a way that combines the notion of student focused teaching and the notion of competence, in a matrix. Excellence equals doing the right kind of thing but also doing it competently. This emphasis on competence seems long overdue. It seems clear that it is not enough for students to intend to understand (taking a deep approach) they also have to be competent as learners in implementing a deep approach so that they are able to understand. Re-orientation of students cannot be enough in itself. A paper by Chambers and Northedge (2000) reminded us how much difficulty students have with the discourse they are expected to use in the social sciences. It cannot be easy taking a deep approach if you do not know how the discourse, through which you might demonstrate any understanding, actually works. Much of Andy Northedge's and my own early work concerned developing students' competence as learners. Efforts by researchers such as Eric Meyer to develop tools to identify at risk students through analysing their studying then have to intervene to improve these identified students. These interventions are not just about re-orientation, they are about improving competence. The sophistication of these interventions seems seldom to match the sophistication of the original diagnoses. 'Training' of both students and teachers, so that they are competent, seems essential. There have been claims by those undertaking pedagogic research-led change, or organisational change driven by student learning theory, that staff development is unlikely to be an effective lever for improvement and it has become fashionable to mock all training as if it only involved 'tips' or 1950's-style behavioural change. However papers have reported evidence of improvements in teachers' approach, and in students' ratings of teachers, as a result of staff development. If we do not take this issue of competence more seriously then we will continue to implement open learning, and any other methods, well or badly in a random way and with random outcomes.

We don't just need more competence however, but, returning to the first point, we need better theories or models of what competence consists of in relation to specific interventions. We need theories about how teaching and learning methods actually work. What is it about students' revision or teachers' implementation of open learning that makes it work? Or about self assessment, or work based learning, or any of the other interventions reported at the Symposia? These interventions are often presented as if they were self explanatory or as if there was only one possible (implicit) rationale for them. Methods implemented with one rationale may turn out to work, or not work, for completely different reasons. For example papers have reported success with PSI – an American peer tutoring system – but for reasons more to do with the experienced students explaining the hidden curriculum to new students than to do with the original rationale for PSI. Too many papers describe only the surface features of an intervention with little awareness of what is actually going on that might improve student learning.

We have tended to treat the actual mechanisms and tactics of learning and teaching as if they didn't matter. All that is argued to matter is conceptions, perceptions and approaches. I do not believe we will get very far concentrating only on conceptions, perceptions and approaches. But it also seems clear that surface descriptions of practice will not get us far either. I think we need better theories about what teachers and students actually do rather than only about what they perceive or understand. I believe that much of the evidence we need to build such theory already exists and is not much referred to in ISL Symposia. To illustrate what I mean by this I'd like to take the case of assessment. I choose assessment because it seems clear from a range of studies that assessment dominates students' perceptions and their study lives and that in many contexts students only do what is assessed and they do it in such a way that it will meet perceived assessment demands. There seems more scope for leverage over student learning by changing assessment than anything else.

1.10 Towards a theory of the way assessment supports learning

From the point of view of phenomenography what matters about assessment is that it is designed to contribute to constructive alignment. Students should be clear about goals and teaching methods and assessment should be aligned with these goals so that students have perceptions of assessment demands such that they take a deep approach. This view ignores most of the literature available about how assessment affects student learning. The 'appropriate assessment' scale on the CEQ is extraordinarily 'broad brush' and provides teachers with little guidance about what to do. While the item on the CEQ that correlates best with student performance is concerned with feedback from teachers there has been almost no work on feedback reported at the Symposia. Extensive literature on the role of feedback in schools has identified it as the single largest influence on learning outcomes (Black and Wiliam, 1998). In both compulsory and post-compulsory education there is evidence of dramatic changes to learning outcomes resulting from even modest interventions involving feedback.

What follows is a brief list of 'conditions under which assessment supports student learning', derived from a literature review (Gibbs and Simpson, in press). These conditions are not discussed here but merely listed in order to illustrate what a theory about an aspect of teaching might look like. These conditions are intended to be used as a framework by teachers and researchers to evaluate the operation of assessment on a course, and are already being used in the form of a convenient checklist.

Influences of assessment on the volume, focus and quality of studying	
Condition	
1	Sufficient assessed tasks are provided for students to capture sufficient study time
2	Students engage with these tasks, orienting them to allocate appropriate amounts of time and effort to the most important aspects of the course, distributed appropriately across the course.
3	Tackling the assessed task engages students in productive learning activity of an appropriate kind
4	Assessment communicates clear and high expectations for student learning outcomes and achievement
Influences of feedback on learning	
5	Sufficient feedback is provided, both often enough and in enough detail
6	The feedback focuses on learning and on actions under the students' control, rather than on the students themselves and on their characteristics
7	The feedback is timely in that it is received by students while it still matters to them and in time for them to pay attention to further learning or to receive further assistance
8	Feedback is appropriate to the purpose of the assignment and to its criteria for success
9	Feedback is appropriate, in relation to students' understanding of what they are supposed to be doing
10	Feedback is received by students and attended to
11	Feedback is acted upon by students

1.11 Research to explore the impact of assessment on student learning

It is intended to undertake research in a similar way to that undertaken in the study that gave rise to the ISL symposia outlined at the start of this paper. Teams of teachers in varied contexts (a range of science courses at two universities) will be supported to use the above 'conditions' as a framework for reviewing the way students' learning is currently affected by assessment. Pilot interviews have already been used to identify the kind of phenomena they are likely to need to explore in more depth. A range of research tools will be used, taking into account both internal and external perspectives, to identify for example:

- The way students' effort is distributed across the course in relation to assessment demands

- The way perceived demands of assessment relate to the quality of students' engagement with assessment tasks

- The way feedback is provided, perceived and used

The literature will then be used to diagnose problems and also to identify potential tactics to tackle these problems. For example if students are found not to be reading and using feedback (a very common phenomenon) there is literature available on a range of 'two-stage' assignment designs that make it very likely that students will read and use formative feedback from the first stage to improve their understanding and performance measured in a second stage summative assessment, together with evidence that student performance and understanding is improved by such two-stage assignments. There is unlikely to be a simple one-to-one mapping of problems to appropriate tactics but it will probably be possible to list a range of appropriate tactics, each with a clear rationale and supported by empirical evidence, for teachers to select from. The impact of interventions will be evaluated using the same range of methods used for original diagnosis. It is intended to develop an 'Assessment Experience Questionnaire' to make it easy for teachers to diagnose problems with current assessment patterns quickly and easily, and to monitor changes in a controlled way.

Through a series of cycles of evaluation and intervention it is intended to develop:

- Better insights into how assessment supports students learning, resulting in an elaboration of the above 11 'conditions'

- Better research tools that are easy for teachers to use

- A repertoire of assessment tactics designed to address specific assessment problems, with a clear rationale for the operation of each

- Empirical evidence of the impact of these tactics

- Empirical evidence of the extent to which meeting the above conditions supports student learning

- Accounts of successful cycles of evaluation and intervention as models for teachers to emulate in improving their own assessment. These would resemble the case studies in Gibbs (1992).

- Mechanisms to share practice, evidence and explanations amongst the UK's higher education science teaching community through the 'Subject Centres' for Physical Sciences and BioSciences. Funding has been set aside to fund action research supported by these Subject Centres, once research tools, tactics and evidence of impact have been elaborated.

1.12   Aspirations for improving student learning

The first half of this paper was positive about developments in our understanding of how to improve student learning. The second half was more critical, highlighting areas where the paradigms we have been operating within have inherent weaknesses and, in some areas, have not fulfilled their potential. I hope the improving student learning movement, as a whole, continues to flourish and to build a rich and rewarding community within which teachers and researchers together can develop their understanding in a way that leads to real improvements in student learning.

I would like to see:

- A greater emphasis on evidence of impact – both from those developing theory and those developing practice. We need to be more confident that our research and development efforts make a difference.

- More development of theory with clearer implications for practice, and especially clear rationales for interventions. We need to be able to explain why we change things in the particular ways that we do.

- Greater emphasis on what makes interventions to improve student learning actually work. We need to be more competent as innovators and teachers.

And I hope that the movement retains its friendly and interactive 'look and feel' that makes it so distinctive and enjoyable.

References

Allen, J (1996). Learning outcomes in higher education: the impact of outcome-led design on students' conceptions of learning. In Gibbs, G (Eds), *Using research to improve student learning*. Oxford: Oxford Centre for Staff and Learning Development.

Allen, J (1997). Learning outcomes-led modular design: an analysis of the design features which influence students' perceptions of learning. In Rust, C and Gibbs, G (Eds), *Improving student learning through course design*. Oxford: Oxford Centre for Staff and Learning Development.

Biggs, J (1994). Student learning research and theory: where do we currently stand? In Gibbs, G (Ed), *Improving student learning: theory and practice*. Oxford: Oxford Centre for Staff Development.

Biggs, J (1996). Enhancing teaching through constructive alignment. *Higher Education*, **32**, 347–364.

Biggs, JB and Collis, KF (1982). *Evaluating the quality of learning: the SOLO taxonomy*. New York: Academic Press.

Black, P and Wiliam, D (1998). Assessment and classroom learning. Assessment in Education, 5(1), 7–74.

Chambers, E and Northedge, A (2000). Disciplinary differences and commonalities across the humanities and social sciences. In Rust, C (Ed), *Improving student learning through the disciplines*. Oxford: Oxford Centre for Staff and Learning Development.

Dahlgren, LO and Marton, F (1978). Students' conceptions of subject matter: an aspect of learning and teaching in higher education. *Studies in Higher Education*, **3**, 25–35.

Entwistle, N (1995). The use of research on student learning in quality assessment. In Gibbs, G (Ed), *Improving student learning through assessment and evaluation*. Oxford: Oxford Centre for Staff Development.

Gibbs, G (1992). *Improving the quality of student learning*. Bristol: Technical and Educational Services.

Gibbs, G and Simpson, C (in press) Does your assessment support your students' learning? *Journal of Learning and Teaching in Higher Education*.

Jackson, B (1996). Encouraging research into learning in a subject-related context. In Gibbs, G (Ed), *Using research to improve student learning*. Oxford: Oxford Centre for Staff Development.

Jones, C and Hassall, T (1996). The approaches to learning of first year Accounting students: some empirical evidence. In Rust, C & Gibbs, G (Eds), *Improving student learning through course design*. Oxford: Oxford Centre for Staff and Learning Development.

Kember, D, and Yeung, DYP (2000). Development of a questionnaire to measure the level of reflective thinking. *Assessment and Evaluation in Higher Education*, **25**(4), 381–395.

Linder, C and Marshall, D (1996). Introducing and evaluating metacognitive strategies in large class introductory Physics teaching. In Rust, C & Gibbs, G (Eds), *Improving student learning through course design*. Oxford: Oxford Centre for Staff and Learning Development.

Linder, C and Marshall, D (1997). Linking Physics students' development as independent and reflective learners with changes in their conceptions of science. In Rust, C (Ed), *Improving students as learners*. Oxford: Oxford Centre for Staff and Learning Development.

Marton, F and Säljö, R (1997). Approaches to Learning. In Marton, F, Hounsell, D & Entwistle, N (Eds), *The Experience of Learning*. Edinburgh: Scottish Academic Press.

Norton, L and Dickens, TE (1995). Do approaches to learning courses improve students' learning strategies? In Gibbs, G (Ed), *Improving student learning through assessment and evaluation*. Oxford: Oxford Centre for Staff Development.

Perry, WG (1970) *Forms of intellectual and ethical development in the college years*. New York: Holy, Rinehart and Winston.

Prosser, M and Barrie, S (2003). Aligning research on student learning with institutional policies and practices on evaluation and quality assurance. Paper presented at the 10th Improving Student Learning conference. Brusselles, Belgium.

Prosser, M, Ramsden, P, Trigwell, K and Martin, E (2001). Perceptions of teaching and leadership context and its relation to the quality of student learning. In Rust, C (Ed), *Improving Learning Strategically*. Oxford: Oxford centre for Staff and Learning Development.

Ramsden, P (1991). A performance indicator of teaching quality in higher education: the Course Experience Questionnaire. *Studies in Higher Education*, **16**, 129–150

Ramsden, P & Entwistle, NJ (1981). Effects of academic departments on students' approaches to study. *British Journal of Educational Psychology*, **51**, 368–383.

Säljö, R. (1982) *Learning and Understanding*. Goteborg: Acta Universitatis Gothoburgensis.

Trigwell, K, Prosser, M and Taylor, P (1994). Qualitative differences in approaches to teaching first year university science. *Higher Education*, **27**, 75–84.

2 Learners' narratives: real-life stories about constructive-developmental pedagogy

Marcia B Baxter Magolda, Professor, Educational Leadership
Miami University

I appreciate the opportunity to share research on student learning and insights I have obtained from participants in my research. It is their stories I share today as a foundation for our exploration of pedagogy that promotes learning. The stories emerge from two studies. The first is a 16-year longitudinal study of young adults' learning and development. I interviewed these participants annually since they began college in 1986; 101 students began the study, 80 participated through their four years in college, and 39 continue to participate currently. The second is an observation study of three 16-week college courses – zoology, mathematics, and education. I observed all sessions of these courses and interviewed the instructors and selected students. I want to caution you that the stories I share today are particular stories from particular students. They offer one possibility for how learners' assumptions evolve and may or may not be transferable to your contexts. I ask that you listen today with your students in mind so that you can determine whether the perspectives you hear resonate with the perspectives your students hold.

2.1 Constructive-developmental pedagogy

Constructive-developmental pedagogy connects teaching to learners' assumptions about knowledge (Baxter Magolda, 1999). Learners construct knowledge by organising and making meaning of their experience. This construction takes place in the context of their evolving assumptions about knowledge and the learner's role in creating it. However, educators do not always know what learners' assumptions are and how those assumptions affect their learning. Let me give you an example. Chris Snowden, the instructor of the zoology course I observed, expressed his assumptions about knowing and his hopes for his class like this:

> I want my students to appreciate the breadth of zoology and its connections to other disciplines. How do we put together disparate ideas? I'll use my research as examples of how one approaches problems. I want them to understand how information is gained. I want them to appreciate what facts really mean. Tentative facts. That's what all of science is. Subject to change and revision.
> (Baxter Magolda, 1999, p 3)

Ann, one of Chris's students, shared her perspective at the end of the course:

> I take sociology as my minor. It is all opinions, not hard core facts where you are wrong like in zoology. I know he tried to play it off like there is still a lot of research, that it is a really new concept I guess, but still there is some stuff that is [fact] – like freezing cells. I understand what he was trying to do. He was trying to give examples to show what

happened. But if he had just said cryoprotectants whatever, just said the point, I would believe him because he is the teacher. I don't need the proof, it's not like I'm going to argue with him about it.
(Baxter Magolda, 1999, p 3)

Ann's comments reveal that she holds assumptions that differ from those Chris holds. Because she viewed the nature of science as "hard core facts," she interpreted Chris' examples as attempts to prove to her what happened. Although she heard his portrayal of cryobiology as an evolving field, she was convinced that there were facts he could share. Chris, in contrast, viewed science as tentative facts, subject to revision. He was unaware that his effort to get Ann and her peers to appreciate how information is gained conflicted with their interest in getting the right answers. Not knowing the assumptions Ann held about science versus sociology, Chris was unaware of how these affected her learning in his course. Simultaneously, Ann's meaning-making system had no room for the science the way Chris portrayed it. So Ann interpreted it within the framework of her current understanding about knowledge and how it is acquired.

Robert Kegan (1994) noted that much of what contemporary society, including education, expects of students and young adults is "over their heads." That is to say, the expectations require ways of making meaning beyond those learners currently hold. In order to help learners develop the ways of making meaning necessary to meet these expectations, Kegan suggested:

> creating a holding environment that provides both welcoming acknowledgment to exactly who the person is right now as he or she is, and fosters the person's psychological evolution. As such, a holding environment is a tricky, transitional culture, an evolutionary bridge, a context for crossing over. (p 43)

Constructive-developmental pedagogy creates this context for crossing over to more complex assumptions about knowledge.

2.2   Self-authorship

What expectations are we asking college learners to meet? Many educators hope that students will become critical thinkers – able to identify relevant evidence, evaluate it effectively, and make informed judgments within their discipline, develop a coherent sense of self, an appreciation of diversity, and a productive construction of relations with others to guide their adult lives. These hopes are for self-authorship, or the capacity to internally define one's beliefs, identity, and relations with the world (Baxter Magolda, 2001). These expectations are not simply expectations for particular behaviors or skills – they are expectations for how we make meaning of our experience. Developmental theorists suggest that we make meaning of our experience through three interrelated dimensions of development. The epistemological dimension – how do I know? – is grounded in the assumption that what individuals learn and claim to know is grounded in how they construct their knowledge (King & Baxter Magolda, 1996). For example, Ann interprets the knowledge in Chris Snowden's class in the context of her assumption that facts exist in biology. The intrapersonal dimension – who am I? – is grounded in the assumption that how individuals construct knowledge and use their knowledge is closely tied to their sense of self (King & Baxter Magolda, 1996). Ann's assumptions about knowledge are connected to her sense of self – she does not yet have an internal sense of identity that allows her to self-author her perspectives. The interpersonal dimension – what kind of relationships do I want? – is grounded in the assumption that how individuals construct their sense of self is closely tied to how they construct themselves in relation to others (King & Baxter Magolda, 1996). Ann sees Chris as the authority and herself as the recipient of his knowledge, thus she would not consider challenging him. The journey toward self-authorship involves transformations on all three dimensions: from believing external authority to internally defining one's own knowledge and beliefs (epistemological), from external to internal self-definition (intrapersonal), and from acquiring approval to being true to oneself (interpersonal). These transformations underlie the process of moving from how Ann currently makes sense of the world to how we would hope college graduates would make sense of the world.

2.3 Learners' narratives – journeys toward self-authorship

The stories you are about to hear[1] tell one version of how assumptions evolve from external sources of definition to internal ones. Keep in mind that you need to listen carefully to determine if this version resonates with your students in your educational context.

2.3.1 Relying on External Authority.

These first few stories come from learners whose assumptions emphasize external authority. Toni shared her observations about learning as she began college:

> When I first came [to college], I started recording all my classes because I found that most of my exams were based on the lecture. And if I knew my lecture material, I would do well on the exams. Then I found myself spending at least an hour every night recopying my notes and re-listening to the tapes. It just didn't work out because I would get behind. It wasn't worth it, so I stopped doing that. But generally, if I just try to write down things I think are important, I miss out on a lot of information. So I just write down every point that he or she gives me. Not word for word, but every point. (Baxter Magolda, 1992, p 82)

I called Toni's assumptions absolute knowing. She assumes knowledge is certain, the teacher has it, and her role is to acquire it. She held these assumptions as she began college at age 18 (Baxter Magolda, 1992).

Longitudinal participants who started college using absolute knowing encountered contradictions to their assumptions, leading to a transformation to a slightly different way of knowing. Carl and Al expressed this new perspective:

> I don't particularly care for humanities, English or stuff. There's a lot of – the answers are – they can vary. There's no right or wrong answer. I like things where there's a right answer. Like in chemistry, there's a right answer, but in other classes there's not. I guess it could be easier if there's not a right answer, but I feel uneasy in classes like that. (Carl: Baxter Magolda, 1992, p 106)

> You do something like accounting; it's not subjective. But marketing is more subjective. When we analyse a case, there are different ways to go about it. At least from the classes I've had, there's a process you go through to analyse the case. (Al: Baxter Magolda, 1992, pp 106–108)

Carl and Al convey the same sentiments we heard from Ann earlier. Knowledge is certain in some areas, in which case they want the answers. Yet it is uncertain in others, so they want some process for dealing with that uncertainty. This set of assumptions, which I called transitional knowing, was prevalent throughout college in the longitudinal group (Baxter Magolda, 1992).

Learners using absolute or transitional ways of knowing rely on external authorities for knowledge and self-definition. Longitudinal participants who left college using transitional knowing (and some who used more complex ways of knowing) tended to look externally for how to succeed. Mark articulated his plan for success at law school:

> I came here and I tried to figure out what the legal culture figures is success. I knew a Supreme Court clerkship was, so one of my goals was to aim towards that. So I got here to law school and I figured out, "Okay, well, to be a success here you have to get to know some professors who are influential with judges to get a good clerkship, to get in the pipeline, get in the star system here. Also get on Law Review. Write a paper here that you can publish." I thought, "Okay, this is kind of the plan then, step by step." The ultimate plan for success in the legal culture, I mean, go to [this] Law School and do these things, then you've got it made… I would be in the ultimate position to do whatever I want to do because I will have done everything possible, and then I'd be in a position to make a choice that reflected exactly who I was, or at least more clearly. (Baxter Magolda, 2001, p 41)

Mark was still following external formulae. He believed in authority's plans for how "you" know, defined himself through external others, and acted in relationships to acquire approval. His story reveals that although he had developed more complex assumptions about knowing, he had not yet developed an internal sense of self to bring to his decision-making. Thus he relied on external formulae for success.

Using absolute or transitional knowing and following external formulae hold implications for learning. These assumptions lead learners to rely on authority. They do not view themselves as capable of constructing their own understanding or ideas. Unfortunately, learners acquire these assumptions from pedagogy that emphasises passive knowledge acquisition and rewards learners for mimicking authority's knowledge. These ways of knowing conflict with higher education's expectation that learners will critically author their own beliefs in the context of existing knowledge.

2.3.2   Balancing External and Internal Authority.

The next two stories come from learners who are beginning to struggle with the balance of external authority and their own internal voices. Kurt clearly portrayed this struggle:

> I'm the kind of person who is motivated by being wanted, I think. I've gone to a couple of workshops and, either fortunately or unfortunately, I'm the kind of person who gets my self-worth on whether or not other people accept me for what I do or other people appreciate what I'm doing… I'm coming from a position where I get my worth and my value from other people, which is, I think, wrong for me to do. But that's where I am right now. I feel like whether or not I choose to be happy is dependent upon me and only me. If I say, "You made me mad," or the converse, "You made me happy," then I'm giving all of the power that I have to you. The power of choice is mine, I have a choice of how I want to perceive each and every situation in my life… Obviously I'm not to that point yet because I choose to make myself happy and make myself sad on what other people are thinking. (Baxter Magolda, 2001, pp 98–9)

We are hearing from Kurt in his mid-20s. He described the struggle to develop an internal sense of self to use in meeting others in relationships. Longitudinal participants spent most of their twenties in this crossroads trying to integrate their emerging internal voices and external expectations. They questioned the plans they acquired from authority, saw the need to construct their own vision, realised the dilemmas of external self-definition and approval, and were trying hard to cross over to an internal sense of self. This internal sense of self is needed to adopt assumptions about knowing and learning that rely on internal sources.

The struggle between internal and external voice also occurs in the epistemological dimension. Laura reported an important discovery that helped her with this struggle:

> I became very skeptical about what the "truth" was. It's amazing how you can influence statistics. Statistics are supposed to be really the truth. You can't manipulate statistics. But then I learned you really can manipulate statistics to have a point of view to be the truth. So I've come to see that everything's relative; there's no truth in the world – that sort of thing. So I've decided that the only person that you can really depend on is yourself. Each individual has their own truth. No one has the right to decide, "This has to be your truth, too." If everybody is stuck on, "What do the other people think?" then you just waste your whole life. (Baxter Magolda, 1992, pp 136–7)

Laura described the shift from believing that some knowledge is certain to believing it all to be uncertain. She expressed thinking for herself – her internal voice is moving to the foreground and external influence is moving to the background. In the face of this new uncertainty of knowledge, she concluded that everyone can choose her or his own beliefs. This set of assumptions, which I called independent knowing, emerged largely after college for my longitudinal participants.

The struggle to rearrange external and internal influence has important implications for learning. Learners holding these assumptions view facts as tentative and subject to revision; they just do not know how to make judgments about what to believe. They no longer rely on authority, but they are unsure what criteria to use to make knowledge claims. Although they are making progress toward educators' expectations, one more transformation is needed to realise those goals. That transformation is the shift to self-authorship, or the internal capacity to define one's beliefs, identity, and relationships.

2.3.3   Self-Authorship – Achieving Internal Authority

This last set of stories comes from learners who have made the shift to internal authority. Mark, who earlier used external formulas for success in law school, demonstrated a shift to using internal authority in trying to decide whether to marry a woman he had dated since they were teenagers. He described his decision making process:

> As far as personal life, I sit down and I write down things I know, pro and con, "Go into a relationship", "Don't go into a relationship", cost-benefit kind of analysis. Like I said, I don't leave my rationality behind because I think that's really an effective tool. And then I think about all my options, and there's something about it. It carries on its own momentum… So I listen to those feelings, and I come to my room and I sit down and I push all my books away. I grab a sheet of paper or whatever and start writing things down, how I feel. And then when I feel like I've got a handle on those feelings and options, then I talk to the people affected… When you bring other people into it, you push your feelings down just a touch because then you want to be open minded again at that point. And then you talk to people unaffected by it, too, because obviously when people are affected by it they're invested in it… I don't let my feelings rush me into anything because… you're dealing with personal life more – if you do something rash, it can cost you a lot. (Baxter Magolda, 2001, pp 42–3)

Mark's story reveals contextual knowing – finding and judging evidence to make wise decisions, seeking and judging the quality of multiple perspectives, and balancing logic and emotion. He has a process for making his own decisions that makes wise use of external sources of knowledge yet hinges on his internal belief system and identity.

Moving through the crossroads to affirm internal authority in knowing, identity and relationships helped the young adults in the longitudinal study becoming the authors of their own lives. Arriving at the other side of the crossroads yielded an internal self-definition that transformed all three dimensions. Dawn's story of this transformation revealed the connections among the dimensions:

> The more you discover about yourself, the more you can become secure with it. And that obviously leads to greater self-confidence because you become comfortable with who you really are. My confidence level is so much better than it ever has been. I'm more willing to express my ideas and take chances expressing my ideas. "Who cares what people think?" sort of thing. When you're not as self-confident, you're afraid that people are going to laugh at what you think or you're afraid that they're going to think you're stupid – it's all those petty, little things that inhibit us. Whereas when you're confident, you are more willing to say, "This is my opinion; this is why I hold this opinion. You may agree with it or not, but this is what – with my mind I have formulated this opinion and that's how I think and feel". I'm not as afraid to be willing to say that because of what I am this is how I feel. I try not to step on people's toes with my opinions, be offensive about it, but if someone asks me for my opinion or advice or how I think and feel about something, I will definitely tell them. And I think self-awareness too, because you realize that it doesn't really matter if other people agree with you or not. You can think and formulate ideas for yourself and ultimately that's what's important. You have a mind and you can use it. That's probably the most important thing, regardless of the content of what your thoughts and opinions are. It's the fact that you can form an opinion that's more important than the opinion itself. (Baxter Magolda, 2001, pp 151–153)

Dawn's story revealed how her internal self came into being, how it changed her perception and fear of others' appraisals of her, which in turn allowed her to express her own thinking. She acquired the capacity to choose her own beliefs in the context of external knowledge claims. Similarly, she acquired the capacity to choose her own values and identity in the context of external forces. This new capacity enabled her to act in relationships in ways that were true to herself, mutually negotiating how her needs and the needs of others would be met. Longitudinal participants arrived at self-authorship in their late twenties and early thirties.

A few longitudinal participants refined authoring their own lives to create an internal foundation. Sandra's story portrayed this solidification of self-authorship:

> I have a clearer vision of what I really want to do. I have a stronger image of who I am. I'm not so wrapped up in being a counselor, I'm being Sandra. I have a clearer vision of Sandra and the different things that make up who I am. I went from "I am a counselor" to "I do some social work." I am not afraid to say what I believe in and stand for it. I don't make reckless decisions that hurt my lifestyle or self – like quitting my job – but I am able to say, "this is how it is." To help others, you have to maintain self. Now that I'm out of my old job, I recognise the point where I began to lose myself. If it happens again, I see it and don't do it. I don't worry much. I'm confident that I do a good job; I know this. If others disagree, they can find someone else. I have a lot of feedback that I trust is the truth. I've taken charge and get things done. I am more confident. I am able

to recognise signs more quickly now. It sounds nonchalant, but that is how I feel. Some of that was blurry in my old job. I knew some things I wouldn't do, but as we were speeding towards them, I couldn't tell how many I would do. Now I can see the line, and know what I won't do. (Baxter Magolda, 2001, pp 166–168)

The internal foundation gave clarity to Sandra's values and beliefs, allowing her to stand up for them without undue stress, and guided her approach to life. She is grounded in her internal belief system, her internal, coherent sense of self, and in mutuality. This foundation sharpened her vision and focused her behavior.

Achieving self-authorship makes life-long, intentional learning possible. These learners are capable of exploring the complexities of existing knowledge, judging its value, making their own knowledge claims using reasonable evidence, and standing up for what they believe. They are also able to weigh competing knowledge claims and be open to new perspectives if the evidence supports them.

2.4   A framework for promoting self-authorship

In both the longitudinal and observational studies, learners primarily used the externally defined assumptions during college. They encountered the crossroads and independent knowing in their early twenties, and moved into self-authorship only in their late twenties and early thirties. This is consistent with research on college students in the United States (Kegan, 1994; King & Kitchener, 1994). I concluded that this is a result of the teaching/learning environments they encountered because undergraduates in the observation study and young adults in the longitudinal study rapidly shifted to new assumptions when their environments provided adequate challenge and support for doing so.

The courses I observed and many of the environments longitudinal participants encountered after college reveal characteristics that promote learning and self-authorship. Interpreting their stories and synthesising the characteristics they reported yielded a framework of three core assumptions that challenge learners to attempt self-authorship and three principles that support their efforts (Baxter Magolda, 2001). 'Knowledge is complex and socially constructed' challenges learners to view knowledge as uncertain, contextual, and established by agreement among experts. 'Self is central to knowledge construction' challenges learners to view themselves as participants in knowledge construction, thus encouraging the move toward internal authority. 'Authority and expertise are shared mutually in knowledge construction' challenges learners to balance internal and external sources in coming to know. These core assumptions represent challenges that are "over the heads" of learners who are externally focused. Connecting to their external ways of knowing requires creating that context, that culture for crossing over, that Kegan (1994) suggested. That culture is created through the use of three principles to support this developmental transformation. 'Validating learners as knowers' supports them in viewing themselves as capable of constructing knowledge claims. It does not mean validating what they currently know; rather it means affirming that they are capable of thinking, processing information, and participating in the mutual construction of knowledge. 'Situating learning in their experience', or beginning with existing experience or creating relevant experience, helps learners connect to what is being learned, merging it with their current perspectives to arrive at more sophisticated understanding. 'Defining learning as mutually constructing meaning' reinforces the negotiation of external and internal perspectives in arriving at knowledge claims. These three principles collectively engage learners in becoming increasingly sophisticated in their ways of knowing and learning.

Learners' narratives bring this framework to life. Andrew shared his experience:

> In graduate school there was a lot more taking a position and defending it. There were a lot of things where there wasn't exactly a right answer. But you could come up with better answers and explain why you got to them. I had a management class where we were in essence running a business. We ran a simulated airline. There was no one right answer because we had nine groups and nine airlines in the class and all of them chose different philosophies in how they wanted to run their business. And three completely different airlines finished up at the top. In fact, the way our airline did it was different, the teacher said, than any other class had ever done. We just took a completely different approach, yet it was still successful. He even said in the grading of our report that he completely disagreed with it, but it was well argued and reasoned out, and he still gave us an A. I guess I kind of respected that aspect of, you know, "We agree to disagree". I like not always thinking there was one right answer because when you go out and try to deal with a lot of things, there isn't always one right answer. I think too much as an undergraduate we're taught to believe in black and white and there is no grey. And I think there's a lot more grey than there is black and white. You have to reason why you did something. Every time I do something I think through it a little more. Asking that why question a lot more. (Baxter Magolda, 2001, p 197)

In Andrew's graduate programme, knowledge was presented as complex and socially constructed. Multiple perspectives, including students' own perspectives, were welcome and they were invited to construct meaning together. They were invited to bring themselves and their experience into the learning process. As a result of the three core assumptions and three principles permeating his graduate experience, Andrew became adept at working in the grey areas and defending his points of view.

Self as central to learning was a key component of Alice's masters program. She explained the effect of this core assumption on her learning:

> We did a lot of videotaping and audiotaping that were reviewed with the professor and kind of critiqued with different counseling styles. I guess just memorising the concepts and writing them down is one thing, but then practicing them is a whole different ball game. And it helped me to find out which styles felt more natural for me, and it has kind of helped me evolve into what theoretical background that I adhere most strongly to. By doing it some of them really feel better, seem to fit better than others. And the actual doing them on tape really helped in that process, I think.
>
> The hands-on experience through my practicum and internship has made me realise nobody else is in this room with me when I'm doing this counseling session. And so, for me to be clear on these issues, I need to figure them out for myself. Not to say that I'm ever going to figure them out, but to know where I stand on them and to think them through. And I think that's kind of encouraged that process. It's you and your client sitting there. I feel like if I'm not sure where I stand or I'm not clear on what the issues are and what the arguments are both ways and process that myself, then I don't see how I can be of any help at all to this client. So I think that's really encouraged me to do that. I think that I'm more independent. I'm more of a self-thinker. I'm really sorting stuff out for myself instead of just taking notes about everybody else's opinion. (Baxter Magolda, 2001, pp 208–09).

Alice's professors encouraged her to figure out her own counseling philosophy and gave her feedback as she explored options. They presented counseling theories as complex and socially constructed and made it clear that Alice would have to construct her own. Their feedback helped her see that she had to construct it in the context of existing theories, sharing authority and expertise in the process. Working with clients created a context in which to explore what she was learning and what she believed. Through this process, she learned to sort things out for herself.

A third story from an undergraduate student reveals the framework. Rich, a student in the zoology class that I observed, shared this story:

> The whole focus of most of my classes in college have been just regurgitating the facts, with the exceptions of a few like Winter Biology where the base facts were given to you on the ground level and where the actual learning was coming in above and beyond that. The learning was coming in where he would ask, "What do you think about this?" and you couldn't just look on your notes, you couldn't just remember what he said. It is not just blatant memorisation; learning comes into it when you are utilising the ideas towards something new that hasn't been done. That kind of set-up seems to stimulate me more than just being like a computer and storing this information to really do nothing with. This class gave more interest into the applications, what is going on right now, ideas of it, theories on what they don't know. The other classes it was "here is what we know and you have to know it too". There wasn't any fairly mutual exchange between the instructor and the class, no formulations of ideas beyond.
>
> [The lecture] has got to have structure because everybody is not on the same level. And it's got to have a mediator that can guide the group idea in the right direction and that lets certain instances of false knowledge kind of seep into the fact and encourage the idea to come out – but if it is wrong, fine, subtly set it aside so it doesn't get into the collective. It takes some serious skills dealing with people, their collective knowledge. It is the best way to utilise other students', knowledge at least for me. There is a fine line – if I say something that is fundamentally wrong, you have to isolate that response as an instructor and figure out why that student came to that conclusion instead of being like, "No that is the wrong answer". Chris would find out why that came about and steer it over to the rest of the idea: "Okay that is not quite right, but how did you get there? Is this how you got there?" That is what I mean by subtly bringing it back or saying that I would not be wrong if I came out and said something. (Baxter Magolda, 1999, p 122–126)

Rich's report revealed that the complexity of knowledge was in the forefront as the class focused on creating new knowledge from existing information (knowledge as complex and socially constructed). In the formulation of ideas beyond what is currently known, students and instructor struggled together to mutually construct meaning. Yet students were respected (validated as knowers) when they took risks and mutual exploration was the means to straighten out faulty understandings. The interactive lecture format of this course demonstrated that this framework can be effectively implemented in science and in lecture formats. The mathematics course illustrated the use of the framework in a seminar format and the education course revealed its potential in a class of nearly 300 students (Baxter Magolda, 1999).

2.5   Concluding comments

I hope these learners' narratives are useful in considering how your teaching connects to learners' assumptions and provided you with new ideas to explore to promote self-authorship. The framework I advocate is not a technique. It is a pedagogical philosophy about learning, authority, learners, and educators. It demands that we forge genuine partnerships with learners in which we share knowledge construction in all its complexity.

Transforming higher education to promote self-authorship is crucial. Young adults are called upon to manage complex roles in contemporary society. They should not find the crossroads on the horizon at their college graduation but rather have achieved the self-authorship necessary for their success in adult life.

References

Baxter Magolda, MB (1992). *Knowing and reasoning in college: Gender-related patterns in students' intellectual development,* (1st Edn). San Francisco: Jossey-Bass.

Baxter Magolda, MB (1999). *Creating contexts for learning and self-authorship: Constructive-developmental pedagogy,* (1st Edn). Nashville, Tennessee: Vanderbilt University Press.

Baxter Magolda, MB (2001). *Making their own way: Narratives for transforming higher education to promote self-development,* (1st Edn). Sterling, Virginia: Stylus.

Kegan, R (1994). *In over our heads: The mental demands of modern life.* Cambridge, Massachusetts: Harvard University Press.

King, P, and Baxter Magolda, M (1996). A developmental perspective on learning. *Journal of College Student Development,* **37**(2), 163–173.

King, PM and Kitchener, KS (1994). *Developing Reflective Judgment: Understanding and promoting intellectual growth and critical thinking in adolescents and adults.* San Francisco: Jossey-Bass.

Notes

1 The quotes included here were videoclips in the original address. The persons in the video were actors and actresses who verbalized the original words of the study participants. All names are fictitious to protect the anonymity of the participants.

3 Qualitative and quantitative: complementary approaches to research on student learning

Keith Trigwell[1] and John T. E. Richardson[2]
1. University of Oxford; 2. The Open University

3.1 Introduction

A cornerstone of the ISL symposia has been the idea that students show qualitative differences in how they set about their academic studies in higher education. Nowadays, we know a lot more than we did in the past about the nature of those differences and about how we might encourage students to adopt desirable approaches to studying. These gains in our knowledge have come about through the application of both qualitative and quantitative research methods. We have written this paper jointly because we both see qualitative and quantitative methods as contributing collaboratively to research on teaching and learning in higher education. This constructive collaboration runs through the history of the research on approaches to learning that has been a key ingredient of all the ISL symposia. We will use examples of research over the last 25 years to illustrate the contributions made by these two complementary approaches to research on student learning. Nevertheless, we will also point out some areas that seem to have been neglected in the past, and we will suggest some directions for future research.

3.2 Approaches to studying

First, let's return to the very beginning of work on approaches to studying in higher education. Marton (1975) described a study in which he had asked 30 first-year students to read through a newspaper article, to say what they thought the article was about, to say how they had gone about reading the article, and finally to talk about how they approached their academic studies in general. Marton found that the students' accounts of what the article was about could be classified into four different categories that reflected different interpretations or conceptions. These could be ranked in terms of how much they reflected the meaning that the author of the article had originally intended. In other words, there was a hierarchy of learning outcomes.

Marton also found that the students' accounts of how they had gone about reading the article could be classified into two different categories that reflected different 'levels of processing': surface-level processing was aimed at being able to reproduce the text of the article, whereas deep-level processing was aimed at understanding the article's intended meaning. Marton found that the students who had adopted deep-level processing showed qualitatively better outcomes than those who had adopted surface-level processing.

Finally, Marton found that the students' accounts of how they approached their academic studies could be classified into two analogous categories: a surface approach that was based on memorising the course materials for the purposes of academic assessment, and a deep approach that was based upon understanding the meaning of the course materials. Marton claimed that there was an analogous relationship between process and outcome, such that students who adopted a deep approach obtained better examination results.

Subsequent research indicated that the same students might show different approaches to studying in different situations, and, in particular that the use of a deep or surface approach depended on the content, the context, and the perceived demands of particular learning tasks. However, in his original paper, Marton emphasised that different students showed different levels of processing in the same situation. In this case, the use of a deep or surface approach seemed to depend upon the students' having different conceptions of learning and different conceptions of themselves as learners.

Marton (1981) argued that conventional research on learning had adopted a 'first-order' or 'from-the-outside' perspective that tried to describe both the learner and the learner's world in the same terms. He described his own work as adopting a 'second-order' or 'from-the-inside' approach that sought to describe the world as the learner experienced it, and he labelled this approach 'phenomenography'.

3.3   Phenomenographic method

The mole concept in chemistry is an idea that allows chemists to make sense of the relations between the macro 'world' of, for example, mass and volume (things we can see and measure), and the micro 'world' of atoms and molecules (amounts of which need to be known in order to 'do' chemistry). A phenomenographic study of students' experience of the mole concept (Lybeck, Marton, Strömdahl and Tullberg, 1988) is used here to illustrate the features of phenomenography. Following analysis of interviews with 29 students, Lybeck et al. noted that the mole concept was experienced by the group in five qualitatively different ways (see Figure 3.1) The first was as something that is used in calculations but is not real (Conception A). In the second way, the mole concept was seen as something real, but as mass not as number (Conception B). Number, but not as related to mass, was the third way of seeing the mole concept (Conception C). The fourth and fifth ways of seeing do have number as being related to mass, but differ in the extent to which these relations are seen as connecting the macro and micro 'worlds' (Conceptions D and E).

This result is significant for two reasons. First, the variation found in the five conceptions of the mole concept is hierarchical (E is a more complete understanding than A-D, D more than A-C and so on) and the conceptions are logically related, as shown in the linear representation in Figure 1 (the outcome space). All except Conception A see the mole concept as something real, all except A and B see number being involved, and so on. Second, while many students saw that calculations were involved, and that most could do them, many also missed the point of the mole as showing the relations between the macro and micro 'worlds' (Conception E). This limitation in students understanding severely restricts their ability to do, understand and enjoy chemistry. It is a research result that helps to explain to teachers of the mole concept why many of their students are not learning. While this may at first appear to be a surprising statement, most teaching about, or using the mole concept, is focused on calculations. When students do not learn, it is usually assumed that students cannot do the calculations. However, some students who can do the calculations still fail to learn about chemistry because they are unable to grasp the significance of the mole concept as a link between 'worlds'. A change in teaching to focus on the bigger picture (relations between 'worlds') is suggested by this study.

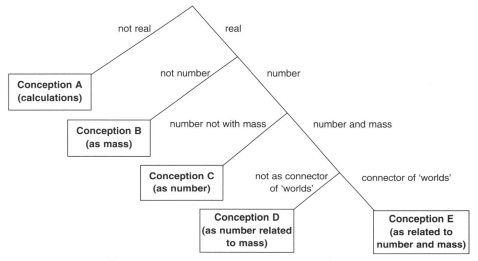

Figure 3.1   Hierarchy and internal relations of conceptions of the mole concept

This outcome space, the map of the structural relations of the variation in the way a group (of students) experience a particular phenomenon (the mole concept), illustrates the power of the phenomenographic approach. Marton (1994) describes phenomenography as: 'the empirical study of the limited number of qualitatively different ways in which we experience … various phenomena in and aspects of the world around us. These differing experiences … are characterised in terms of categories of description, logically related to each other, and forming hierarchies in relation to given criteria. Such an ordered set of categories of description is called the outcome space of the phenomenon … in question. Although different kinds of data can be used, the dominating method for collecting data is the individual interview which is carried out in a dialogical manner. The interviewee is encouraged to reflect on previously unthematised aspects of the phenomena in question. The interviews are transcribed verbatim and the analysis is carried out in an iterative manner on those transcripts. Distinctly different ways of experiencing the phenomenon discussed in the interview are the units of analysis and not the single individuals. The categories of description corresponding to those differing understanding and the logical relations that can be established between them constitute the main results of a phenomenographic study' (p. 4424).

The key elements of phenomenography, and how this approach differs from other research approaches have been described and illustrated elsewhere (Trigwell, 2000; Trigwell and Prosser, 2003). In summary, phenomenography takes a relational (or non-dualist), second-order perspective, aims to describe the key aspects of the variation of the experience of a phenomenon rather than the richness of individual experiences, and produces a limited number of internally related, hierarchical categories of description of the variation (Marton, 1981; 1992; Marton and Booth, 1997; Prosser, 1993; Ashworth and Lucas, 1998; Richardson, 1999; Bowden and Walsh, 2000; see also the Land of Phenomenography website). Phenomenography is a research approach that has significantly increased our understanding of teaching and learning in higher education. In addition to the mole concept, many higher education topic areas have been the subject of phenomenographic studies. A sample is included in table 3.1.

Field	Topic	Reference
biology	photosynthesis	Hazel, Prosser and Trigwell, 2002
chemistry	states of matter	Renström, Andersson and Marton, 1990
	mole concept	Lybeck, et al., 1988
	atomic structure	Keogh, 1991
computing	programming	Booth, 1992
economics		Dahlgren, 1988
geology	mapping	McCracken and Laurillard, 1994
health science	physiotherapy	Abrandt, 1997
	aseptic technique	Davey, 1995
higher education	graduate attributes	Barrie, 2002
mathematics		Crawford et al., 1994
music	instrumental	Reid, 1997
politics	political power	Theman, 1983
physics	electricity and magnetism	Prosser, 1994; Millar, Prosser and Sefton, 1989
	sound	Linder and Erickson, 1989
	mechanics	Johansson, Marton and Svensson, 1985; Prosser and Millar, 1989; Bowden et al. 1992

Table 3.1   Some phenomenographic studies by higher education field

Act	Reference
learning	Marton & Säljö, 1976; Marton, Dall'Alba and Beaty, 1993; Watkins, & Regmi, 1992; Ashwin, 2002; Bailey, 2002
teaching	Samuelowicz & Bain, 1992; Prosser and Trigwell, 1999; Martin & Balla, 1991; Drew & Williams, 2002
leading	Martin et al, (in press)
assessing	Samuelowicz & Bain, 2002
course design	Martin et al., 2000

Table 3.2   Some studies of variation in experience of aspects of learning and teaching

As noted above, a description of qualitatively different approaches to learning (deep and surface: Marton and Säljö, 1976) and conceptions of learning (Säljö, 1979) were outcomes of the earliest studies using (what was then an embryonic form of) this approach. Those results have since been replicated (Entwistle and Ramsden, 1983; Marton, Dall'Alba and Beaty, 1993) and extended to include a focus on the experience of other processes related to learning and teaching (see Table 3.2).

A feature of the outcomes of this research (which derives from its relational origins) is that the categories are descriptions of the relations between people and their context. Individuals are not labelled as deep learners or as student-focused teachers as the approach they adopt or the conception they use may be a function of their perceptions of their environment. What students do in response to one environment may be different to what they do in response to a different environment. Using this perspective, the focus for change in education shifts from characteristics of the student to the students' perceptions of the environment associated with their approach.

So, an awareness of the qualitatively different ways which individuals can experience or respond to an environment is one useful outcome of this approach to research. Another is that the hierarchical internally related outcome space is well-suited for use in the development of studies designed to look at relations between variables, such as between a deep approach to learning and the quality of the learning outcome. For these studies to work, (a) there needs to be a means of identifying and quantifying the variation in the variables being related: if there is no variation there will be no correlation; and (b) the variation needs to be hierarchical. Relations between variables where one or more are not hierarchical are unlikely to be meaningful. The outcome space of a phenomenographic analysis contains a hierarchy of internally-related categories which, if not directly suited to relational studies, offer insight into how such studies might be conducted. Reported studies of this sort are discussed further in the following sections.

3.4 Strengths and weakness of qualitative research

Phenomenographic research has provided us with a vocabulary for talking about the different ways in which students engage with the business of studying in higher education. However, like other qualitative approaches to educational research, phenomenographic studies provide only a limited evidence base. For instance, phenomenographic investigations have typically involved relatively small samples of students (around 30, say). They have generally provided no concrete results about the frequency distributions of approaches, conceptions or orientations to learning or about how those distributions might vary with other characteristics of students, such as their age, gender, academic discipline, educational level, or prior educational experience.

In fact, given the professed concern of qualitative researchers with the individual, the published accounts of phenomenographic research typically provide very little information about the students involved or about how they were selected, recruited or rewarded for their participation in the research. Indeed, in some studies, they might be quite unrepresentative of the populations from which they have been drawn. The small sample sizes also mean that the studies in question would lack statistical power if one wished to test any hypotheses about the relationships between phenomenographic categories and demographic or other characteristics.

To be fair, there are some exceptions to these criticisms. Kember et al. (1990) published a naturalistic study in which they were meticulous in describing their sample of students and how they had been recruited for participation in their study. Their article can be recommended as an example of good practice in the reporting of qualitative research. Van Rossum and Taylor (1987) categorised conceptions of learning in 91 first-year students. Because of the large sample size, they were able to evaluate the relationships between conceptions of learning and demographic characteristics. Van Rossum and Taylor found no difference in the distribution of conceptions of learning between men and women, but they found that older students were more likely than younger students to show more sophisticated conceptions of learning.

Nevertheless, most examples of qualitative research into student learning in higher education have the status of existence proofs. For instance, Säljö (1979) identified five different conceptions of learning among adult learners:

1. Learning as the increase of knowledge.
2. Learning as memorising.
3. Learning as the acquisition of facts, procedures, etc., which can be retained and/or utilised in practice.
4. Learning as the abstraction of meaning.
5. Learning as an interpretative process aimed at the understanding of reality.

In a longitudinal study of Open University students in the United Kingdom, Taylor and Morgan (1986) identified a sixth conception of learning that they initially called 'changing oneself' but which Marton et al. (1993) later called 'changing as a person'. Säljö argued that his taxonomy of learning conceptions represented a developmental sequence, but he did not provide any direct evidence for this claim. In the longitudinal data reported by Marton et al., the sixth conception was seen only during the later years of a student's academic career with the Open University and only in students who had previously exhibited the fifth conception, and so it seems to represent an even more sophisticated conception of learning.

3.5   Strengths and weakness of quantitative research

Students' approaches to studying and their conceptions of learning can also be studied through the responses that they give to quantitative instruments such as inventories and questionnaires. In general, the published accounts of quantitative research tend to be more careful and explicit about the mechanisms by which the samples of students have been obtained; they often provide precise information concerning the distributions of scores in particular samples; and they can be used to assess the relationships between individual differences in studying and background variables such as age, gender, academic subject or educational level. The two instruments that have been most commonly used are Biggs's (1985) Study Process Questionnaire (SPQ) and Entwistle and Ramsden's (1983) Approaches to Studying Inventory (ASI).

The SPQ contains 42 statements, and in each case respondents are asked to say how often the relevant statement is true of them, using a five-point scale. The 42 items are classified under six subscales that reflect the motivational and strategic aspects of three approaches to studying: a surface approach, a deep approach and an achieving approach. The ASI contains 64 statements, and in each case respondents are asked to say whether they agree or disagree with the relevant statement, once again using a five-point scale. The 64 items are classified under 16 subscales that reflect different aspects of four orientations to studying: a meaning orientation, a reproducing orientation, an achieving orientation and a non-academic orientation.

The identification of approaches to studying or conceptions of learning by means of quantitative instruments is not a straightforward matter. It can only be carried out indirectly, by inference from the patterns of responses given by large groups of students. This process relies on technically sophisticated procedures, such as factor analysis or multi-dimensional unfolding analysis, whose detailed implementation remains highly contentious. Nowadays, it is generally recognised that instruments such as the SPQ and the ASI provide a useful means of monitoring individual differences in studying, but also that the instruments themselves are not wholly satisfactory. Richardson (2000) argued that the SPQ was inadequate as a research instrument and in particular that it only measures a generalised surface approach and a generalised deep approach. Biggs, Kember and Long (2001) seem to have acknowledged this by developing a revised version of the SPQ that only measures those two dimensions.

Researchers have also identified problems with the ASI and especially with the subscales intended to measure the achieving orientation and the non-academic orientation. Richardson (1990) suggested that one could use a shortened version of the ASI that contained only the 32 items intended to measure a meaning orientation and a reproducing orientation. Although this version of the ASI has generated some interesting and useful findings, it is not entirely satisfactory. In response to criticisms of the ASI, Entwistle, Tait and McCune (2000) have been developing a Revised Approaches to Studying Inventory (RASI). In its most recent version, this contains 52 items subsumed within 13 subscales that measure different aspects of a deep approach, a surface approach and a strategic approach. This seems to be a more robust instrument that can be recommended for use in future research.

3.6   What have we learned from quantitative research?

As a result of 25 years' quantitative research, we now know a lot more about the differences (or the lack of them) between different groups of students in their approaches to studying.

First, what about gender differences? Richardson and King (1991) concluded from the research evidence that there were no inherent qualitative or quantitative differences between men and women in their approaches to studying in higher education. Nevertheless, gender differences may well arise in particular situations, depending upon the gendered nature of the discipline and the gendered nature of the academic context. Severiens and ten Dam (1997) suggested that apparent gender differences were actually due to differences in gender identity, which can vary among different men and among different women.

Second, what about age differences? There are still stereotypes held by many people in higher education, according to which the predicament and experience of older students are inherently problematic. In fact, the research evidence is quite clear that older students tend to have higher scores than younger students on measures of deep approach and meaning orientation and lower scores than younger students on measures of surface approach and reproducing orientation (Richardson and King, 1998).

Third, what about cultural differences? The evidence suggests that the basic distinction between a meaning orientation and a reproducing orientation emerges across all national systems of higher education, but that it tends to receive a specific interpretation in each system or culture (Richardson, 1994). Richardson (2000) argued that the word 'culture' needs to be understood broadly, so that it might include the culture of the United States, the culture of Access courses in the UK and the culture of people who are deaf. One implication of this is that the responses given to questionnaires on student learning always need to be contextualised and stand in need of analysis and interpretation.

Another issue of both theoretical and practical importance is the difference between students who are successful and those who fail. One would like to think that students who adopt more appropriate or desirable approaches to studying are more likely to complete their courses and are more likely to obtain good marks or grades. Although there is some evidence along these lines, the magnitude of these relationships is not very strong. One important point made by Kember and Harper (1987) is that academic achievement is not a single continuum running from excellence to failure to non-completion, so the predictors of course completion may be different from the predictors of attainment in students who complete their courses.

Trigwell and Prosser (1991) found that in some circumstances a surface approach could be associated with good performance in academic assessments, provided that the teacher demonstrated the relevance of the subject matter, made opportunities for students to ask questions and provided clear assessment criteria. Indeed, Meyer, Parsons and Dunne (1990a, 1990b) found that unsuccessful students do not simply exhibit 'poorer' approaches to studying but fail to exhibit any coherent approaches at all. In other words, academic failure is associated with a disintegration or fragmentation of the normal patterns of studying.

Most recently, Richardson (2000) looked at the difference between students at conventional, campus-based institutions of higher education and those taking courses by distance learning with institutions such as the Open University. He concluded that students in distance education are more likely to exhibit a deep approach or a meaning orientation and less likely to show a surface approach or a reproducing orientation than campus-based students. However, he argued that this was due to differences between the two groups of students in a number of background variables: age and prior education are likely to be particularly important. So, his theoretical conclusion was that there were no inherent differences in approaches to studying related to the two different modes of course delivery.

Quantitative studies looking at relations between variables that have been the subject of phenomenographic studies have also made a substantial contribution to understanding student learning. For example, in addition to the relations between approaches to learning and outcomes mentioned above, van Rossum and Schenk (1984) have shown that students who adopt deep approaches to learning are more likely to report using more complete conceptions of learning. Trigwell and Prosser (1996) report that teachers who adopt teacher-focused, information transmission approaches to teaching are more likely to be working with limiting conceptions of learning and are more likely to constitute a multi-structural (rather than relational) object of study for student learning (Martin, et al., 2000). In all these studies direct use is made of the phenomenographic categories of description, and in all cases (except that of van Rossum and Schenk), the categories were constituted by the authors of the relational study. They all show relations of the form expected.

More recently a range of quantitative relational studies have been conducted using inventories developed from or in conjunction with phenomenographic studies. They show that deep approaches to learning are associated with perceptions of supportive learning environments, higher levels of prior knowledge, more complete conceptions of learning and the subject being learnt, and a higher quality learning outcome (Crawford et al., 1994; Trigwell and Yasukawa, 2000; Trigwell and Ashwin, 2002). They also show evidence of dissonant study orchestrations and dissonance in teaching (Prosser, Trigwell, Hazel and Waterhouse, 2000; Hazel, Prosser and Trigwell, 2002).

3.7 The future for qualitative and quantitative research

The examples of phenomenography and the phenomenographically inspired research described above all have as a central tenet the variation in experience of a group of people. What Marton calls new phenomenography is about the experience of variation – how an individual experiences difference. The focus is on how an individual discerns and learns, and what it is that constitutes the critical aspects that vary that enables the learner to learn more effectively than if less critical aspects were experienced as variant (Marton and Trigwell, 2000). For learning to occur, whether it be in the formal learning contexts established by university teachers, or in the less formal contexts of participation in social practices, there must necessarily be a certain pattern of variation present to experience, and this pattern must be experienced by students. There is no learning without discernment, and there is no discernment without variation. Good teachers help students experience variation by identifying and making use of those aspects of the object of learning that are subject to variation simultaneously.

Future studies may identify, in particular subject areas, those aspects of a topic that, if experienced as being variant, are more likely to lead to the desired understanding. These aspects are what, in the theory of variation, constitute the space of learning (Marton, Runesson & Tsui, in press). In the example we have used in this paper - the mole concept - this space of learning is likely to be derived from the outcome space described in Figure 3.1. The process of helping students conceive of the mole in the form of Conception E will be enhanced if students are able to experience variation between that conception and their own conception of the mole.

In the past, students in higher education have predominantly been young people from middle-class families who have a high level of secondary education. This stereotype is less accurate in countries outside the UK and it has become less accurate within the UK with the broadening of the student population over the last 25-30 years. Nevertheless, we are nowadays encouraged to think of ways of widening participation in higher education by recruiting students from previously underrepresented groups, and this raises interesting issues for future research.

First, what about prior education? In many research studies, students' academic qualifications on admission to higher education have not been found to be related to their approaches to studying, but this may well be because in the past students have been selected on the basis of a relatively narrow range of previous academic experience (Richardson, 2000). In distance education, particularly in institutions that have a relatively open admissions policy, students may begin with no academic qualifications at all or with extensive previous experience of higher education. In this context, the level of prior education seems to be an important determinant of approaches to studying, and this obviously needs to be taken into account when delivering courses to different groups (Richardson, Morgan and Woodley, 1999).

Sometimes, widening participation is interpreted in terms of recruiting more students from ethnic minorities. Whether minority groups are in fact underrepresented in higher education is not easy to judge, because they often have disproportionate numbers of children and young people. In any case, worrying about the representation of students from ethnic minorities tends to distract attention from a potentially more serious issue, that minority students may achieve poorer results. For instance, in the UK, white students are 30% more likely to obtain good degrees (those awarded with first class or upper-second class honours) than students from ethnic minorities. Is this because minority students don't adopt effective approaches to studying, or is it because of racist practices in higher education?

Widening participation is also sometimes interpreted in terms of recruiting more students with disabilities into higher education. From September 2002, universities and colleges in the UK are legally required to provide resources for students with a wide range of disabilities and to anticipate the needs of students with disabilities who may seek admission in the future. Again, it may be hard to tell whether people with disabilities are underrepresented in higher education and, if so, by how much, because the prevalence of many disabilities varies with age and also because students with moderate disabilities may not feel confident about revealing those disabilities to their institutions. Higher education also retains a deficit or medical model of disability that focuses on the competence of the student rather than a social model that focuses on the student's physical context and the attitudes of other people.

There is very little serious research on the experiences of students with disabilities in higher education, and they have certainly been ignored in research on approaches to studying. Richardson and Woodley (1999) compared responses to the ASI given by students with a hearing loss with those given by students who had no reported disability. Although they found statistically significant differences between students with and without a hearing loss, these differences were often very slight in magnitude. More important, they did not conform with stereotypical accounts of deaf people being more concrete and literal in their thinking, but they did conform with the students' own accounts of problems they encountered in teaching situations because of the attitudes and behaviour of teachers and other students.

Even so, there is still no research on approaches to studying in other significant groups of students with disabilities, of whom those with visual impairment and those with dyslexia are perhaps the most obvious. Carrying out research with these student populations raises many technical and methodological problems, but we cannot any longer overlook these populations. Indeed, there may be other groups who are hardly represented at all in higher education but who might be represented in the future. For example, civil rights laws in the United States require that institutions of higher education provide appropriate support services for students with learning disabilities, including those with severe learning disabilities resulting from brain injury or other causes. Accommodating students with learning disabilities is not currently on the agenda in the UK, even given the most generous interpretation of 'widening participation'. But on the argument that what affects North America today will affect Europe tomorrow, we should be alert to this possibility.

More generally, the approaches to studying movement has been predominantly concerned with understanding and appreciating the predicament of all students in higher education, regardless of whether this is achieved through qualitative or quantitative research. Accordingly, people who research student learning should be at the forefront of recognising the varying needs and circumstances of all the groups who make up the student population, both today and tomorrow.

References

Abrandt, M (1997). Learning physiotherapy: The impact of formal education and professional experience. Linköping University, *Studies in Education and Psychology*, No 50.

Ashwin, P (2002). Variation in students' experience of small group tutorials. In Rust, C (Ed), *Improving Student Learning: Theory and Practice – 10 years on*, (this volume Chapter 21). Oxford: Oxford Centre for Staff Development.

Ashworth, P and Lucas, A (1998). What is the 'world' of phenomenography? *Scandinavian Journal of Educational Research*, **42**, 415-31.

Bailey, S, (2002). Student approaches to learning in fashion design, a phenomenographic study. *Art, Design and Communication in Higher Education*, **1**, 81–95.

Barrie, S (2002). Understanding Generic Graduate Attributes. Paper presented at 10th Improving Student Learning conference, Brussels, Belguim.

Biggs, JB (1985). The role of metalearning in study processes. *British Journal of Educational Psychology*, **55**, 185–212.

Biggs, JB, Kember, D and Leung, D (2001). The revised two-factor Study Process Questionnaire: R-SPQ-2F. *British Journal of Educational Psychology*, **71**, 133–149.

Booth, SA (1992). *Learning to Program: A Phenomenographic Perspective*. Göteborg, Acta Universitatis Gothoburgensis.

Bowden, J, Dall'Alba, G, Martin, E, Masters, G, Laurillard, D, Marton, F, Ramsden, P and Stephanou, A (1992). Displacement, velocity and frames of reference: Phenomenographic studies of students' understanding and some implications for teaching and assessment. *American Journal of Physics*, **60**, 262–268.

Bowden, J and Marton, F (1998). *The University of Learning*. London: Kogan Page.

Bowden, J and Walsh, E (Eds), (2000). *Phenomenography*. Melbourne: RMIT Press.

Crawford, K, Gordon, S, Nicholas, J and Prosser, M (1994). Conceptions of mathematics and how it is learned: The perspectives of students entering university. *Learning and Instruction*, **4**, 331–345.

Dahlgren, L.O. (1988). Enduring and short term effects of higher education. Paper presented at the 14th International Congress of Psychology, Sydney.

Dahlgren, LO, and Marton, F (1978). Students' conceptions of subject matter: An aspect of learning and teaching in higher education. *Studies in Higher Education*, **3**, 25–35.

Davies, A and Reid, A (2002). Teachers' and students' conceptions of the professional world. In Rust, C (Ed), *Improving Student Learning: Theory and Practice – 10 years on*, (this volume Chapter 7). Oxford: Oxford Centre for Staff Development.

Davey, J (1995) Aseptic Technique: What and how students of nursing learn. Unpublished Master of Nursing Thesis. University of Sydney.

Drew, L and Williams, C (2002). Variation in the experience of teaching creative practices: the community of practice dimension. In Rust, C (Ed), *Improving Student Learning: Theory and Practice – 10 years on*, (this volume Chapter 10). Oxford: Oxford Centre for Staff Development.

Entwistle, NJ, and Ramsden, P (1983). *Understanding Student Learning*. London: Croom Helm.

Entwistle, N, Tait H, and McCune, V (2000). Patterns of response to an approaches to studying inventory across contrasting groups and contexts. *European Journal of Psychology of Education*, **15**, 33–48.

Hazel, E, Prosser, M and Trigwell, K (2002). Variation in learning orchestration in university biology courses. *International Journal of Science Education*, **24**, 737–751.

Kember, D, Lai, T, Murphy, D, Siaw, I, Wong, J, and Yuen, KS (1990). Naturalistic evaluation of distance learning courses. *Journal of Distance Education*, **5**(1), 38–52.

Kember, D, and Harper, G (1987). Implications for instruction arising from the relationship between approaches to studying and academic outcomes. *Instructional Science*, **16**, 35-46.

Keogh, L (1991). Student conceptions of atomic structure: A phenomenographic study. Unpublished BSc (Hons) dissertation. University of Western Australia.

Johansson, B, Marton, F and Svensson, L (1985). An approach to describing learning as change between qualitatively different conceptions. In West, LHT and Pines, AL (Eds), *Cognitive Structure and Conceptual Change*, New York: Academic Press.

Land of phenomenography http://www.ped.gu.se/biorn/phgraph/welcome.html

Linder, CJ and Erickson, GL (1989). A study of tertiary physics students' conceptualization of sound. *International Journal of Science Education*, **11**, 491–501.

Lybeck, L, Marton, F, Strömdahl, H and Tullberg, A (1988). The phenomenography of the 'Mole Concept' in chemistry. In Ramsden, P (Ed), *Improving Learning: New Perspectives*. London: Kogan Page. 81–108.

Martin, E and Balla, M (1991). Conceptions of teaching and implications for learning. *Research and Development in Higher Education*, **13**, 298–304.

Martin, E,Trigwell, K, Prosser, M and Ramsden, P (2003). Variation in the experience of leadership of teaching in higher education. *Studies in Higher Education*, **28**, 247–259.

Martin, E, Prosser, M, Trigwell, K and Ramsden, P (in press). The perceptions of those who lead and the experience of those being led – some empirical relationships in teaching in higher education. *Studies in Higher Education*.

Marton, F. and Säljö, R. (1976). On qualitative differences in learning: I. Outcome and process. *British Journal of Educational Psychology*, **46**, 4–11.

Marton, F (1975). On non-verbatim learning: I. Level of processing and level of outcome. *Scandinavian Journal of Psychology,* **16**, 273–79.

Marton, F (1981). Phenomenography: Describing conceptions of the world around us. *Instructional Science,* **10**, 177–200.

Marton, F (1992). Phenomenography and 'the art of teaching all things to all men'. *Qualitative Studies in Education,* **5**, 253–267.

Marton, F (1994). Phenomenography. In Husén, T and Postlethwaite, TN (Eds), *The International Encyclopedia of Education.* (2nd Edn) pp 4424–9. Vol 8. Oxford: Pergamon.

Marton, F, Dall'Alba, G, & Beaty, E (1993). Conceptions of learning. *International Journal of Educational Research,* **19**, 277–300.

Marton, F and Booth, S (1997). *Learning and Awareness.* New Jersey: Lawrence Erlbaum Associates.

Marton, F, and Trigwell, K (2000). Variatio est mater studorium. *Higher Education Research and Development,* **19**, 381–395.

Marton, F, Hounsell, D and Entwistle, N (1997). *The Experience of Learning: Implications for Teaching and Studying in Higher Education.* (2nd Edn). Edinburgh, Scottish Academic Press.

Marton, F, Runesson, U and Tsui, A (in press). The space of learning. In Marton, F and Tsui, A (Eds), Classroom discourse and the space of learning. Mahwah, NJ: Lawrence Erlbaum.

McCracken, J and Laurillard, D (1994). A study of conceptions in visual representations: A phenomenographic investigation of learning about geological maps. Paper presented at the Ed-Media World Conference in Educational Multimedia and Hypermedia, Vancouver, Canada.

Meyer, JHF, Parsons, P, and Dunne, TT (1990a). Individual study orchestrations and their association with learning outcome. *Higher Education,* **20**, 67–89.

Meyer, JHF, Parsons, P, and Dunne, TT (1990b). Study orchestration and learning outcome: Evidence of association over time among disadvantaged students. *Higher Education,* **20**, 245–269.

Millar, R, Prosser, M and Sefton, I (1989). Relationship between approach and development in student learning. *Research and Development in Higher Education,* **11**, 49–53.

Prosser, M (1993). Phenomenography and principles and practices of learning. *Higher Education Research and Development,* **12**, 21–31.

Prosser, M (1994). A phenomenographic study of students' intuitive and conceptual understanding of certain electrical phenomena. *Instructional Science,* **22**, 189–205.

Prosser, M and Millar, R (1989). The 'how' and 'what' of learning physics. *The European Journal of Psychology of Education,* **4**, 513–528.

Prosser, M and Trigwell, K (1999). *Understanding Learning and Teaching: The experience in higher education.* Buckingham: Open University Press.

Prosser, M, Trigwell, K, Hazel, E and Waterhouse, F (2000). Students' Experiences of Studying Physics Concepts: The effects of disintegrated perceptions and approaches. *European Journal of Psychology of Education,* **15**, 61–74.

Reid, A (1997). The meaning of music and the understanding of teaching and learning in the instrumental lesson. In Gabrielsson, A (Ed), *Proceedings of the Third Triennial European Society for the Cognitive Sciences of Music Conference.* Uppsala, Uppsala University.

Renström, L, Andersson, B and Marton, F (1990). Students' conceptions of matter. *Journal of Educational Psychology,* **82**, 55—569.

Richardson, JTE (1990). Reliability and replicability of the Approaches to Studying Questionnaire. *Studies in Higher Education,* **15**, 155–168.

Richardson, JTE (1994). Cultural specificity of approaches to studying in higher education: A literature survey. *Higher Education,* **27**, 449–468

Richardson, JTE (1999). The concepts and methods of phenomenographic research. *Review of Educational Research,* **69**, 53–82.

Richardson, JTE (2000). *Researching Student Learning: Approaches to Studying in Campus-Based and Distance Education.* Buckingham: SRHE and Open University Press.

Richardson, JTE, and King, E (1991). Gender differences in the experience of higher education: Quantitative and qualitative approaches. *Educational Psychology,* **11**, 363–382.

Richardson, JTE, and King, E (1998). Adult students in higher education: Burden or boon? *Journal of Higher Education,* **69**, 65–88.

Richardson, JTE, Morgan, A, and Woodley, A (1999). Approaches to studying in distance education. *Higher Education,* **37**, 23–55.

Richardson, JTE, and Woodley, A (1999). Approaches to studying in people with hearing loss. *British Journal of Educational Psychology,* **69**, 533–546.

Säljö, R (1979). Learning about learning. *Higher Education,* **8**, 443–451.

Samuelowicz, K and Bain, JD (1992). Conceptions of teaching held by teachers. *Higher Education,* **24**, 93–112.

Samuelowicz, K and Bain, JD (2002). Identifying academics' orientations to assessment practice. *Higher Education,* **43**, 173–201.

Severiens, S, and ten Dam, G (1997). Gender and gender identity differences in learning styles. *Educational Psychology,* **17**, 79–93.

Taylor, E, and Morgan, AR (1986, April). Developing skill in learning. Paper presented at the Annual Meeting of the American Educational Research Association, Chicago.

Theman, J (1983). *Uppfattningar av polititisk makt* (Conceptions of political power). Göteborg, Acta Universitatis Gothoburgensis.

Trigwell, K (2000). Phenomenography: Discernment and variation. In Rust, C (Ed), *Improving Student Learning Through the Disciplines,* Oxford: Oxford Centre for Staff Development, 75–85.

Trigwell, K and Ashwin, P (2002). Evoked conceptions of learning and learning environments. In Rust, C (Ed), *Improving Student Learning: Theory and Practice – 10 years on,* (this volume Chapter 21). Oxford: Oxford Centre for Staff Development.

Trigwell, K, and Prosser, M (1991). Improving the quality of student learning: The influence of learning context and student approaches to learning on learning outcomes. *Higher Education,* **22**, 251–266.

Trigwell, K and Prosser, M (1996). Changing approaches to teaching: a relational perspective. *Studies in Higher Education,* **21**, 275–84.

Trigwell, K and Prosser, M (2003). Qualitative difference in university teaching. In Tight, M (Ed), *Access and Exclusion, Volume 2,* Elsevier Science Ltd., Amsterdam, 185–216.

Trigwell, K and Yasukawa, K (1999). Learning in a Graduate Attributes-based Engineering Course. *Research and Development in Higher Education,* (http://herdsa.org.au/vic/cornerstones/tocnewcurriculum.html).

Van Rossum, EJ and Schenk, SM (1984). The relationship between learning conception, study strategy and learning outcome. *British Journal of Educational Psychology,* **54**, 73–83.

Van Rossum, EJ, and Taylor, IP (1987, April). The relationship between conceptions of learning and good teaching: A scheme of cognitive development. Paper presented at the Annual Meeting of the American Educational Research Association, Washington, DC.

Watkins, D, and Regmi, M (1992). How universal are student conceptions of learning? A Nepalese investigation. *Psychologia,* **35**, 101–110.

4 Towards disciplinary models of learning

Ursula Lucas[1] and Jan HF Meyer[2]

1.University of the West of England; 2.University of Durham

Key words: conceptions of learning, approaches to learning, Reflections on Learning Inventory (RoLI), disciplines.

Abstract

This paper argues the value of adapting a generic model of student learning (operationalised through the Reflections on Learning Inventory (ROLI) (Meyer, 2000a)) within a subject discipline. The power of this approach lies in its ability to identify those discipline-specific conceptions and approaches that may be related to accumulative or transformative learning processes. The paper draws on experience within economics (Meyer and Shanahan, 2001) and accounting (Lucas 2002a), to make the case for this approach to modelling. The case of accounting is used to provide a detailed example of its potential. The RoLI and a pilot form of the Expectations of Learning Accounting Inventory (ELAcc) were administered to 1,211 students of introductory accounting across five UK universities. The findings, firstly, demonstrate the ways in which different conceptions of the subject of accounting are linked with transformative, accumulative and pathological learning processes and; secondly, indicate that this process of model development may be of value across a range of disciplines.

4.1   Introduction

4.1.1   Towards disciplinary models of learning

Learning is a multivariate process of considerable complexity. Nonetheless, there has been steady progress in recent years towards the development of generic aspects of such a model of learning within higher education (Meyer, 2000a). The aim of such modelling is, ultimately, to inform what interventions might be required to help students improve the quality of their learning processes and achieve improved learning outcomes. Within such modelling learning is assumed to be a purposeful process, driven by a motivation and shaped by an intention. Empirically and conceptually, however, such a model also takes account of the content and context of learning within which variation is revealed. A relatively simple model of student learning, which identifies some key variables and a subset of likely relationships between them, is provided in Figure 4.1[1].

A review of the literature indicates that there is a clear need for further research to be conducted within specific disciplinary settings. Within the Approaches to Studying Inventory (ASI) research there has been speculation amongst researchers that the view of

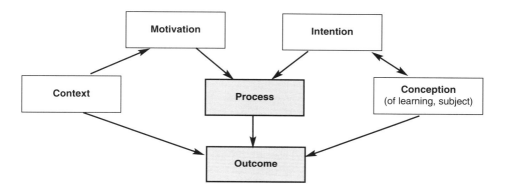

Figure 4.1   A model of variables within learning and likely structural relationships
(adapted from Meyer, 1999)

learning outcome and approach to learning may differ between disciplines (Ramsden, 1984; Meyer et al, 1990; Meyer and Watson, 1991; Eley, 1992). In particular, Meyer and Eley (1999) argue:

> that individual students might well adopt differentiated patterns of learning behaviours that are attributable to the learning contexts shaped by different subjects. That is, perceptions and experiences of learning contexts might be shaped also by the epistemology of a discipline and they might therefore vary considerably from one discipline to another. (p.198).

More recently, work within economics (Meyer & Shanahan, 2001) identified discipline-specific and other aspects of students' 'learning histories' that might affect student learning within economics as follows:

*   Whether English is a first language

*   Preferred or habitual approaches to learning brought on entry to university

*   Prior knowledge of economics (economic misconceptions, economist activity)

*   Prior knowledge or beliefs about learning

Their findings indicate that first year Australian economics students bring with them subject-specific prior knowledge and conceptions of learning as part of their personal learning history; and some of them do so in a form that predisposes them to risk of failure at the very outset of their course. Further, in terms of statistical modelling, their work shows gender-based response differences in terms of both location and structure (Meyer and Shanahan, 2001).

The work within economics was carried out by the development of subscale items specific to economics, together with subscales developed within the Reflections on Learning Inventory (RoLI). The RoLI, still under development (Meyer and Boulton-Lewis, 1999; Meyer, 2000a), operationalises conceptions and processes of learning that traverse an accumulative-transformative emphasis. The power of this approach lies in its ability to identify those discipline-specific conceptions and approaches that may be related to accumulative or transformative learning processes.

4.1.2   Developing a disciplinary model of learning: the case of introductory accounting

The development of a disciplinary model of learning requires the identification of discipline specific aspects that might affect student learning. The emphasis is on the role that prior knowledge factors can play in capturing explanatory variation in epistemological beliefs, conceptions of learning and learning processes. The relative importance of these will clearly differ between disciplines. The search for such factors requires a consideration of the nature of the discipline and a review of previous research in the area.

Within accounting, relatively little research has been conducted into students' beliefs or conceptions of accounting and the extent to which they might impact upon approaches to learning. Some generic inventory studies on approaches to learning (Gow, Kember and Cooper, 1994; Sharma, 1997; Jones and Hassall, 1997; Booth et al, 1999; Byrne et al, 1999) have taken place but they do not cast any light on whether generic inventories are suitable for the discipline of accounting or on how they might be adapted within a discipline-specific context.

However, there is a small, but growing, body of research that provides some insight into students' conceptions of learning introductory accounting. A central issue arising from previous work is that of the negative preconceptions of accounting held by non-accounting students. Several research studies (reviewed by Mladenovic, 2000) show that some introductory accounting students may come to their study of accounting with negative preconceptions of accounting. The power of such stereotypical views of accounting should not be underestimated (Friedman and Lyne, 2001; Fisher and Murphy, 1995). Motivation has been described as "a conscious state of inner arousal (that often involves a degree of affect or emotion towards the object of domain of study)" (Meyer, 1999, p.36). The negative preconceptions of accounting may well be associated with strong emotions about the learning of accounting. One particular attitude reported by non-accounting students (Lucas, 2000) was that the learning of accounting was something to be feared or which caused worry.

For accounting students, preconceptions will inevitably differ. One might expect them to possess positive motivational conceptions of accounting. In this respect prior work in mathematics is of interest. Meyer and Eley (1999) identified explanatory affective sources of variation specific to mathematics. Currently there are indications that the enjoyment scale may be of relevance to accounting, having emerged as an issue within phenomenographic interviews with both lecturers and accounting students (Lucas, 1998). However, it may well be that other motivations exist for students and, if they are not related to an inherent interest in the subject, they may be linked with some of the more negative preconceptions discussed above.

Phenomenographic work on student intentions within accounting has identified relevance to be of central importance (Lucas, 2000). Transformative learning processes are associated with students who have an intention to relate what they learn to aspects of relevance that are intrinsically important to them, whether it be relevance in a career, business or learning within higher education generally. Accumulative learning processes are associated with a sense of detachment, whereby the focus is on passing the subject in order to obtain a qualification (Lucas, 2001). Since non-accounting students are less likely to be less motivated by "love of the subject", it becomes important that they can see the relevance of accounting to either the subject they are studying or to their future career.

Memorisation is also an important issue within the learning process. Within accounting the term "rote-learning" is frequently used in a pejorative sense to denote an inappropriate mode of learning that does not involve understanding. This tendency to rote-learn has been attributed to the dominance of professionally-related textbooks (Zeff, 1989a) and the accreditation requirements of professional accounting bodies (Zeff,1989b; Dewing and Russell, 1998). However, more recently Lucas (2002b) suggests that a key influence on this focus may be the pedagogical uncertainties of accounting educators rather than the external pressures of professional requirements. Recent work by Meyer (2000b) demonstrates that the unqualified use of 'memorising' in studies of student learning is contra-indicated. There are in fact contrasting (deep and surface) forms of 'memorising' representing discrete sources of explanatory variation that can be used to construct finer grained models of student learning in process terms.

The above discussion identifies ways in which key aspects of learning may be affected by the nature of the subject being learnt and the types of students who study that subject. This discussion indicates considerable potential for a further exploration of student learning within the disciplinary context of accounting.

4.2   Developing a model of learning: an illustrative research study

This section describes part of a National Teaching Fellowship project within the discipline of accounting. The ultimate aim of this research study is to construct a multivariate model of student learning, subject-specific to accounting, that is sensitive to individual differences and which can be used for inferential purposes in terms of modelling learning outcomes. As a first stage, a pilot development and trialling of items within the Expectations of Learning Accounting (ELAcc) inventory was conducted in 2000. In that pilot study (Lucas, 2002a), students' responses to subject-specific aspects of prior knowledge and subject-related learning processes were subjected to exploratory factor analyses in order to reduce the dimensionality of the data and obtain insights into latent, and conceptually interpretable, structures. This led to the identification of six subscales which were thought likely to be (a) pertinent to a model of learning within accounting and (b) likely to identify variation between accounting and non-accounting (business) students (detailed in Appendix 1). Further subscales were identified as worthy of further investigation and will be the subject of future work.

Following the parallel example of the previously mentioned work in economics, these six accounting subscales were administered with thirteen RoLI subscales (see Figure 4.2).

The emphasis is on the role that prior knowledge factors can play in capturing explanatory variation in epistemological beliefs, conceptions of learning and learning processes. The development of eleven of these observables[2] is described in Meyer (2000a). In that study, three forms of "memorising" (MAU, MAR, MBU) were found to be independent of one another and to be sensitive to gender-based response differences in terms of both location and structure. These forms of "memorising" are respectively associated in a theoretically congruent manner with "deep"-level processes, learning pathologies, and contrasting conceptions of learning.

The inventory was administered within 5 UK HE Institutions to first year introductory accounting undergraduate students (September/October 2001). These comprised 706 business studies students and 505 accounting students[3]. They completed the inventory at the start of induction or at the first accounting lecture. The metric used within the inventory is described in Appendix 2. A student could score between 0 and 4 for each item, thus permitting a minimum score of 0, or a maximum score of 20, for each subscale.

	ELAcc subscales
Motivation	Enjoyment
Motivation	Lack of interest
Motivation	Worry
Motivation	Relevance to business
Intention	Exam focus
Epistemological belief	Numbers
	RoLI subscales
Not understood factual intake	
Conception of learning	Learning is fact based
Epistemological belief	Knowledge is discrete and factual
Motivation	Learning experienced as duty
Learning process	Memorising before understanding (MBU)
Deep-level process	
Learning process	Memorising with understanding (MWU)
Learning process	Memorising after understanding (MAU)
Learning process	Relating ideas
Conception of learning	Seeing things differently
Learning process	Thinking independently
Learning pathology	
Learning process (anti-process)	Detailed related pathology
Learning process (anti-process)	Fragmentation
Learning process	Memorising as rehearsal (MAR)
Learning process	Learning by example

Figure 4.2   Observables employed in the study.

4.3   Findings

4.3.1   Internal consistency of subscales and the identification of variation

The construction of an inventory entails a laborious process of sifting out items that produce desirable response characteristics and contribute to the construction of a conceptually meaningful subscale. The psychometric performance of items within each subscale was assessed using Cronbach's alpha[4]. Details of Cronbach's alpha, means and standard deviations are provided in Table 4.1.

However, the response distribution within individual items and each subscale also requires review. It is important that statements are worded in such a way as to evoke a good variation in response, whilst at the same time conveying a common meaning with other items within the subscale.

Two of the accounting subscales ('exam focus' and 'relevance') had means that might be deemed to be outside an acceptable range. However, when the means within the separate cohorts of accounting and business students were considered, it was found that 'lack of interest' had a mean of 10 (sd 4.5) for business students and a mean of 5 (sd 5.0) for

ELAcc subscales	Cronbach's Alpha	Mean	Std Deviation
Enjoyment	81	12.9	3.51
Relevance	69	16.0	2.47
Lack of interest	92	7.9	4.87
Worry	88	10.4	4.94
Numbers	88	12.1	3.86
Exam focus	67	4.6	3.04
RoLI subscales			
Learning is fact based	77	12.2	3.48
Knowledge is discrete and factual	55	9.4	2.98
Learning experienced as duty	77	8.0	3.49
Memorising before understanding	87	10.5	4.10
Memorising with understanding	64	14.2	2.67
Memorising after understanding	70	13.3	3.19
Relating ideas	60	14.2	2.64
Seeing things differently	74	14.4	2.93
Thinking independently	69	14.7	2.96
Detailed related pathology	55	8.8	2.94
Fragmentation	64	7.7	2.90
Learning by example	72	9.9	3.75
Memorising as rehearsal	78	11.6	3.95

Note: Values of alpha rounded to two places and multiplied by 100.
    The possible scoring range is 0-20.

Table 4.1   Subscale coefficient, mean and standard deviation

accounting students. This may indicate that this subscale may be a good potential identifier of variation within business students, but not within accounting students. So far as the 'exam focus' and 'relevance' subscales are concerned, whilst there is good internal consistency, they will require further development to support the identification of a wider spectrum of variation. Further analysis on responses to individual items within these subscales, with reference back to the literature, is underway.

4.3.2   Differences in location (means)

This study is concerned with differences in perception between: accounting and business students (Table 4.2), male and female students (Table 4.2), male and female students across degree routes (Table 4.3) and male and female students within degree routes (Table 4.4) . The results of a MANOVA for unbalanced data confirmed a statistically significant overall difference in means attributable to degree route, gender and gender within degree routes (for the test statistics respectively for Wilks' Lambda, Pillais's Trace, Hotelling-Lawley's Trace, Roy's Greatest Root, all $p<0.0001$). This fully justifies a closer study of univariate cases.

There are significant differences between accounting and business students across all the accounting subscales (Table 4.2). Accounting students report higher scores on enjoyment and relevance, but business students report higher scores on worry, numbers, exam focus and lack of interest. These differences also exist between students of the same gender across

	Bus/Acc n=703/503 p value	Inequality	Gender n=648/561 p value	Inequality
Enjoyment	0.000	Acc>Bus	ns	
Relevance to business	0.000	Acc>Bus	ns	
Worry	0.000	Bus>Acc	0.000	F>M
Numbers	0.000	Bus>Acc	0.007	F>M
Exam focus	0.000	Bus>Acc	0.001	M>F
Lack of interest	0.000	Bus>Acc	0.015	M>F
Learning is fact based	0.004	Bus>Acc	ns	
Knowledge is discrete and factual	ns		ns	
Learning experienced as duty	0.024	Acc>Bus	0.010	M>F
Memorising before understanding	0.004	Bus>Acc	ns	
Memorising with understanding	0.033	Acc>Bus	0.000	F>M
Memorising after understanding	ns		0.000	F>M
Relating ideas	ns		0.000	F>Ms
Seeing things differently	ns		0.000	F>M
Thinking independently	0.003	Bus>Acc	ns	
Detailed related pathology	0.000	Bus>Acc	ns	
Fragmentation	0.006	Bus>Acc	0.001	M>F
Learning by example	0.004	Bus>Acc	0.000	M>F
Memorising as rehearsal	0.001	Bus>Acc	0.000	F>M

Table 4.2   Significant differences: accounting and business students and male and female students

	Female Bus/Acc n=332/227 p value	Inequality	Male Bus/Acc n=369/277 p value	Inequality
Enjoyment	0.000	Acc>Bus	0.000	Acc>Bus
Relevance to business	0.000	Acc>Bus	0.000	Acc>Bus
Worry	0.000	Bus>Acc	0.000	Bus>Acc
Numbers	0.000	Bus>Acc	0.000	Bus>Acc
Exam focus	0.000	Bus>Acc	0.000	Bus>Acc
Lack of interest	0.000	Bus>Acc	0.000	Bus>Acc
Learning is fact based	0.001	Bus>Acc	ns	
Knowledge is discrete and factual	ns		ns	
Learning experienced as duty	ns		0.006	Acc>Bus
Memorising before understanding	0.000	Bus>Acc	ns	
Memorising with understanding	ns		ns	
Memorising after understanding	ns		ns	
Relating ideas	ns		0.043	Bus>Acc
Seeing things differently	ns		ns	
Thinking independently	0.008	Bus>Acc	ns	
Detailed related pathology	0.000	Bus>Acc	0.012	Bus>Acc
Fragmentation	0.000	Bus>Acc	ns	
Learning by example	0.050	Bus>Acc	0.045	Bus>Acc
Memorising as rehearsal	0.000	Bus>Acc	ns	

Table 4.3   A comparison of same gender differences across degree routes
Note: tabulated significance levels are rounded to 3 places in both tables 4.2 and 4.3.

	Accounting M/Female n=277/227 p value	Inequality	Business M/Female n=369/332 p value	Inequality
Enjoyment	ns		ns	
Relevance to business	ns		ns	
Worry	0.005	F>M	0.000	F>M
Numbers	ns		0.017	F>M
Exam focus	0.001	M>F	0.052	M>F
Lack of interest	0.002	M>F	ns	
Learning is fact based	ns		0.017	F>M
Knowledge is discrete and factual	0.053	M<F	ns	
Learning experienced as duty	0.004	M<F	ns	
Memorising before understanding	ns		0.002	F>M
Memorising with understanding	0.000	F>M	0.000	F>M
Memorising after understanding	0.000	F>M	0.000	F>M
Relating ideas	0.000	F>M	0.001	F>M
Seeing things differently	0.001	F>M	0.001	F>M
Thinking independently	ns		ns	
Detailed related pathology	0.003	M>F	ns	
Fragmentation	0.000	M>F	ns	
Learning by example	ns		ns	
Memorising as rehearsal	ns		0.000	F>M

Note: tabulated significance levels are rounded to 3 places.

Table 4.4   A comparison of gender differences within degree routes

degree routes (Table 4.3). So far as gender differences are concerned, females on both degree routes report higher scores on worry, but only female business students report higher scores on numbers.

Male students on both degree routes report higher scores on exam focus, but only the male accounting students report higher scores on lack of interest. This latter point may be linked with the higher scores reported by male accounting students on the duty subscale. If learning is conceived of as a duty or moral obligation, then a lack of interest is conceptually consistent.

Within the RoLI subscales, business students score higher across all four of the learning pathology subscales and two (fact based and MBU) of the accumulative subscales. It is interesting to note that business students also score higher on thinking independently. This is not entirely surprising. In the pilot trialling carried out in 2000 (Lucas, 2002a), it was found that business students reported higher scores than accounting students on a subscale which sought to operationalise the concept of the need to question accounting and accountants! They also reported higher scores than accounting students on a subscale which sought to operationalise the concept of accounting as a means of transforming our understanding of business. Clearly, these are subscales which require further investigation in subsequent trials.

Gender differences within the RoLI subscales emerge most clearly from a comparison of gender differences within degree routes (Table 4.4). Female students score higher than males within four of the deep-level process subscales (thinking independently being the exception). It is of note that male gender differences mainly emerge within the accounting degree route, where males score higher on the two anti-process subscales of detail related pathology and fragmentation. This is conceptually coherent with their higher scores for exam focus, lack of interest, duty and knowledge as discrete and factual. Males on both business and accounting score higher than females on exam focus, which is consistent with lower scores on deep-level processes. Interestingly, some of these inequalities (Table 4.2: MAU: F>M; FRAG: M>F; MAR:F>M and Table 4.4: MAU: F>M; RID: F>M; MAR: F>M) are consistent with earlier findings on economics students (Meyer and Shanahan, 2001).

4.3.3   Differences in structure

The comparison of means has led to some interesting observed differences. However, differences in mean scores do not necessarily imply differences in covariance structure. The latter is an essential requirement for structural modelling by either gender or student group. Data were subjected to a number of different exploratory factor analyses. In the analyses that follow, the number of factors initially extracted (three) was, in each case, determined by the number of eigenvalues greater than unity after which solutions were retained as they appeared to be the most conceptually robust of all the solutions considered.

In order to analyse any relationships between variables across groups, it is necessary to establish whether the assumption of a common covariance structure between the groups is admissible. The null hypothesis is that the within-group covariance matrices are equal. In this case the relevant chi-square statistic is significant for accounting students (chi-square = 268.45, df = 190, p = 0.0002) but is not significant for business students (chi-square = 189.38, df = 190, p = 0.49). An analysis of separate factor structures by gender is therefore only justified within the accounting students. Accordingly a gender comparative three-factor structure is presented for these students in Table 4.5.

In terms of common structure, the Factor 1 loadings for male accounting students emphasise transformative learning processes, with negative loadings arising from exam focus and lack of interest and a positive loading from enjoyment. The loadings of duty and example are of interest here. They have formerly been associated with accumulative, rather than transformative, learning processes (Meyer and Boulton-Lewis, 1999). Factor 2 loadings for female accounting students also emphasise transformative learning processes, but without the negative loadings of exam and lack of interest and without the loading of duty. Once again, there is the conceptually surprising loading of learning by example.

Factor 2 for male accounting students emphasises accumulative learning processes with loadings for worry and numbers. Conceptually, one might expect KDF to be related to numbers. Similarly, worry with its associations with "fear of failure" is conceptually coherent within this factor. However, a surprising loading is that of thinking independently, which is usually associated with transformative learning processes. In this respect, a finding in Meyer and Boulton-Lewis (1999) is of interest. Their study compared responses of Australian, Indonesian and South African students for a range of learning conception observables. There was a link between duty, example, and learning is fact-based for the Australian students. However, for the Indonesian students there was an unexpected linkage between thinking independently, duty and learning by example. This is an aspect that requires further exploration. Factor 1 for female accounting students also emphasises accumulative learning processes. However, there is a loading of example and duty which is absent from the male accumulative factor (and is in accord with the findings of Meyer and Boulton-Lewis (1999)).

	F1 Male	F1 Female	F2 Male	F2 Female	F3 Male	F3 Female
FRAG		35			74	52
DRP					50	49
LBEx	36	35		24		
MAR		25	53			34
KDF		81	54			
MBU		55	67			
FACT		77	76			
DUTY	34	40			47	
RID	70			67		
MWU	49			65		
MAU	54		20	53		
SDI	76			74		
IND	35	22	24	30		
REL	44			52	-29	
EXAM	-23	35			49	36
LInt	-28				51	62
WOR			31		40	66
NUM		40	36			
ENJ	46	21		40	-30	-33

Inter-factor correlations	Male		
Female	Factor 1	Factor 2	Factor 3
Factor 1		0.43	0.01
Factor 2	0.15		0.34
Factor 3	0.29	-0.25	

Males n=277, Females n=228
Eigen values (M/F) of the factors are: F1 (6.8/6.3), F2 (3.7/4.9), F3 (1.2/1.62).
All factor loadings multiplied by 100 and rounded. Only loadings with an absolute magnitude>20 printed.
Table 4.5   Exploratory oblique factor solutions: accounting students

And for females both exam and enjoyment load on this factor, whilst they are absent in the male accumulative factor.

A scrutiny of Factor 3, the pathology factor, for both male and female accounting students highlights other differences in their respective accumulative factors. Firstly, whilst fragmentation solely loads on Factor 3 for the males, the loading is split between the accumulative and pathology factors for females. A similar split is apparent for MAR. Duty and relevance (negative loading) load on the pathology factor for males but not for females. There is a conceptually coherent loading of exam focus, worry, numbers and enjoyment (negative) for both males and females within the pathology factor.

The inter-factor correlations for male and female accounting students are also included in Table 4.5. For the female students they indicate a correlation between the accumulative and pathological factor of 0.29, a negative correlation of 0.25 between the transformative factor and pathological factor and a correlation of 0.15 between the accumulative and transformative factor. This does not appear to be unreasonable. However, these gender-based inter-factor correlations vary in one key respect. For the male accounting students there is a correlation of 0.34 between the pathological and accumulative factors, a correlation of 0.01 between the pathological and transformative factors and a correlation of 0.43 between the accumulative and transformative factors. This latter correlation looks odd and may indicate possible structural dissonance (Meyer, 2000c). This requires further investigation.

Table 4.6 presents a three-factor structure for business students. Factor 1 is an accumulative/pathology factor showing loadings on the four pathology subscales and on the four accumulative subscales. There is also a loading on exam focus, which is conceptually coherent. Factor 2 is the transformative factor, but with some interesting loadings in respect of example, MAR, MBU and fact. As might be expected there is a negative loading on exam focus and a positive loading on relevance. More surprising is the loading on numbers. The third factor consists entirely of accounting subscales. It is positively correlated (0.32) with Factor 1 (accumulative/pathological learning processes). This factor can be described as denoting a negative attitude towards the learning of accounting, indicating perceptions of accounting as lacking relevance, being about techniques and numbers and indicating a lack of interest and enjoyment, and worry.

	F1	F2	F3
FRAG	66	-21	
DRP	62		
LBEx	35	23	
MAR	46	21	
KDF	50		
MBU	50	25	
FACT	48	27	
DUTY	55		
RID		64	
MWU		62	
MAU		55	
SDI		62	
IND		49	
REL		42	-21
EXAM	45	-24	27
LInt			88
WOR			58
NUM		25	30
ENJ			-73

n = 706

Eigen values are: F1 (6.6), F2 (4.1), F3 (1.7).

All factor loadings multiplied by 100 and rounded. Only loadings with an absolute magnitude>20 printed.

Inter-factor correlations			
	Factor 1	**Factor 2**	**Factor 3**
Factor 1	1.00	0.29	0.32
Factor 2		1.00	-0.12
Factor 3			1.00

Table 4.6   Exploratory oblique factor solution: business students

4.4   Discussion

This review of differences in location and structure has identified a series of interesting findings which can be used to inform a further review of learning within accounting. Firstly, it is apparent that business studies and accounting students enter their studies with quite different perceptions of accounting, and that these different perceptions can be differentially linked with transformative, accumulative and pathological learning processes in a conceptually consistent manner.

For both male and female accounting students, enjoyment and relevance are linked with transformative learning processes. For business studies students only relevance is so linked. There is also a link between exam focus, lack of interest and worry and pathological learning processes. However, the situation is more complex in the latter area. A clear pathology factor does not emerge as might be expected.

The situation on memorising as rehearsal (MAR) is interesting. It loads on the accumulative factor for male and female business students, and on the pathology factor for female accounting students. For business students it loads on both the accumulative/pathological factor and the transformative factor. MAR items are listed in Appendix 3. Phenomenographic research with lecturers and students (Lucas, 2000 and 2002b) identifies this type of learning process as very common within the learning of accounting, and as one that is not necessarily deemed to be inappropriate by either lecturers or students. It may be that within accounting MAR is not an appropriate way to differentiate between accumulative and transformative learning processes. Further investigation is needed here.

Similarly, learning by example does not load uniquely on either accumulative or transformative factors and does not appear within the pathology factor. Speculatively, it may be that some students may see accounting as a discipline where the epistemology is example-based. Certainly, many students and lecturers see "question practice", or going through examples, as central to learning within accounting (Lucas, 1998). It may be that this model of teaching and learning possesses a previously unacknowledged epistemological power. Further phenomenographic work is needed to investigate this line of enquiry. A further interesting finding is that, for male accounting students, the subscale of duty performs unexpectedly, loading as it does on both transformative and pathological factors. As with learning by example, this is an area which requires further phenomenographic investigation.

For both male and female accounting students, the performance of the subscale of thinking independently is of interest. This loads on the accumulative, as well as the transformative, factor. Speculatively, on a re-reading of the items within this subscale (see Appendix 3), it may be that students are interpreting these statements in a particular way within the context of accounting. Accounting can be seen predominantly as a technique-based subject, where students carry out techniques automatically, where a strategy of "fitting things in" can either be a process of trial and error or a carefully considered logical response. It may be that this subscale requires further review within the context of accounting.

So far as business students are concerned a key finding is the single factor incorporating both accumulative and pathological learning processes and its correlation with the third negative attitude factor. Conceptually, it would not be surprising if such a negative attitude towards accounting was linked with a less than coherent learning approach to the subject of accounting.

4.5 Conclusion

These findings demonstrate that the adaptation of a generic model of student learning within a subject discipline is of value. However, further lines of enquiry are needed. One such line of enquiry will involve further analysis of the data. In particular, cluster analysis will provide an additional model for triangulation purposes. This analytic procedure will exhibit individual differences at a subgroup (cluster) level based on what students have disclosed about themselves via their inventory responses. This is potentially of great interest given the longer-term objective of constructing a modelling insight into how students potentially "at risk" of failure in introductory accounting may be detected. A second line of enquiry requires a reiterative retreat into a more detailed scrutiny of item performance within the accounting (and some of the RoLI) subscales. The conceptually unexpected findings discussed above require a more detailed look at how students may have interpreted items.

These findings demonstrate how a generic model of student learning may be effectively used to support the development of a disciplinary model of learning. Firstly, it provides a means of identifying those discipline-specific conceptions and approaches which may be related to accumulative, transformative or pathological learning processes. Secondly, it also provides an opportunity to identify generic aspects of learning that may, within a discipline, be particularly significant. For example, prior to this study, the conception of learning as a duty had not been identified as a discipline specific belief within accounting. Yet it appears to be significant, particularly as a gender-sensitive aspect of learning. Similarly learning by example requires further investigation.

A more unexpected finding of this study is that the development of a discipline-specific model of learning may cast new light on some aspects of a generic model of learning. For example, thinking independently, which in prior research was indicative of a transformative learning process, appears (speculatively) to be interpreted rather differently by students within accounting. Thus it may be that further research within other disciplines may support a fuller understanding of existing generic models, leading to a virtuous circle of research in this area.

References

Booth, P, Luckett, P, and Mladenovic, R (1999). The quality of learning in accounting education: the impact of approaches to learning on academic performance. *Accounting Education,* **8**(4), 277–300.

Byrne, M, Flood, B and Willis P, (1999). Approaches to Learning: Irish students of accounting. *The Irish Accounting Review* **6**(2), 1–29.

Dewing, IP and Russell, PO (1998). Accounting education and research: Zeff's warnings reconsidered. *British Accounting Review,* **20**(3), 291–312.

Eley, MG (1992) Differential adoption of study approaches within individual students. *Higher Education,* **23**, 231–254.

Fisher, R and Murphy, V (1995). A pariah profession? Some student perceptions of accounting and accountancy, *Studies in Higher Education,* **20**(1), 45–58.

Friedman, AL and Lyne, SR (2001). The beancounter stereotype: towards a general model of stereotype generation. *Critical Perspectives on Accounting,***1**, 423–451.

Gow, L, Kember, D, and Cooper, B (1994). The teaching context and approaches to study of accounting students, *Issues in Accounting Education,* **9**(1), 118–130.

Hinkin. TR (1985). A review of scale development practices in the study of organisations. *Journal of Management* **21**(5), 967–988.

Jones, C & Hassall, T (1997). The approaches to learning of first year accounting students: some empirical evidence. In Rust, C (Ed), *Improving Student Learning: Improving Student Learning Through Course Design*, pp 431–438. Oxford: Oxford Centre for Staff and Learning Development.

Lucas, U (1998). Perceptions of learning and teaching accounting: a phenomenographic study. Sheffield Hallam University, pp 1–296. Unpublished PhD thesis.

Lucas, U (2000). Worlds apart: students' experiences of learning introductory accounting. *Critical Perspectives on Accounting*, **11**, 479–504.

Lucas, U (2001). Deep and surface approaches to learning within introductory accounting: a phenomenographic study. *Accounting Education*, **10** (2) 161–184.

Lucas, U (2002a). Modelling experiences of learning accounting: a search for variation. British Accounting Association Annual Conference, Jersey.

Lucas, U (2002b). Uncertainties and contradictions: lecturers' conceptions of teaching introductory accounting. *British Accounting Review*. 183–204

Meyer, JHF (1999). Assessing outcomes in terms of the 'hidden observables'. In Rust, C (Ed), *Improving Student Learning: Improving Student Learning Outcomes*, pp 25–37. Oxford: Oxford Centre for Staff and Learning Development.

Meyer, JHF (2000a). An overview of the development and application of the Reflections on Learning Inventory (RoLI). Paper presented at the RoLI Symposium, Imperial College, London, September.

Meyer, JHF (2000b). Variation in contrasting forms of 'memorising' and associated variables. *British Journal of Educational Psychology*, **70**, 163–176.

Meyer, JHF (2000c). The modelling of 'dissonant' study orchestration in higher education. *European Journal of Psychology of Education* **XV** (1): 5–18.

Meyer, JHF, Parsons, P, and Dunne, TT (1990). Individual study orchestrations and their association with learning outcomes, *Higher Education*, **20**, 67–89.

Meyer, JHF and Watson, RM (1991). Evaluating the Quality of Student Learning II – study orchestration and the curriculum. *Studies in Higher Education*, **16**, 251–275.

Meyer, JHF and Eley, MG (1999). The development of affective subscales to reflect variation in students' experiences of studying mathematics in higher education. *Higher Education,* **37**, 197–216.

Meyer, JHF and Boulton-Lewis, GM (1999). On the operationalisation of conceptions of learning in higher education and their association with students' knowledge and experiences of learning, *Higher Educational Research and DEvelopment*, **18**(3), 289–302.

Meyer, JHF and Shanahan, M (2001). Making teaching responsive to variation in student learning. In Rust, C (Ed), *Improving Student Learning 8 - Improving Student Learning Strategically,* pp 296–313. Oxford: Oxford Centre for Staff and Learning Development.

Meyer, JHF and Shanahan, M (2001). A triangulated approach to the modelling of learning outcomes in first year economics. *Higher Education Research & Development* **20**(2): 127–145.

Mladenovic, R (2000). An investigation into ways of challenging introductory accounting students' negative perceptions of accounting. *Accounting Education*, *9*(2), 135–154.

Nunnally, JC (1978). *Psychometric Theory*, London: McGraw Hill.

Ramsden, P (1984). The Context of Learning, in Marton, F, Hounsell, D, and Entwistle, N, (Eds), *The Experience of Learning*, pp 144–164. Edinburgh: Scottish Academic Press.

Sharma, DS (1997). Accounting students' learning conceptions, approaches to learning, and the influence of teaching context on approaches to learning. *Accounting Education*, **6**(2), 125–146.

Tait, H, Entwistle, NJ, and McCune, V (1998). ASSIST: a reconceptualisation of the approaches to studying inventory. In Rust, C (Ed), *Improving Student Learning: Improving Students as Learners*, pp 262–271. Oxford: Oxford Centre for Staff and Learning Development.

Zeff, SA (1989a). Does accounting belong in the university curriculum?, *Issues in Accounting Education*, **4**(1), pp 203–210.

Zeff, SA (1989b). Recent trends in accounting education and research in the USA: some implications for UK academics, *British Accounting Review*, **21**(2), 159–176.

Appendix 1   ELAcc and RoLI subscales

ELAcc

Enjoyment (Enj)
I'll enjoy being able to solve problems in accounting

Lack of interest (Lint)
Accounting is a dull subject

Worry (Wor)
I feel worried about learning accounting

Numbers (Num)
The study of accounting mostly involves numbers, figures and formulae

Exam focus (Exam)
In learning accounting I'll aim to get just enough marks to pass the exam

Relevance (Rel)
Learning accounting will help me to understand business better

RoLI

Learning is fact based (Fact)
An accumulative conception of learning directed towards the acquisition and reproduction of facts (learning means collecting all the facts that need to be remembered)

Knowledge is discrete and factual (KDF)
An epistemological belief that knowledge is discrete and factual

Learning is experienced as duty (Duty)
A motivational influence on learning experienced as a moral duty (when I am learning I feel as if I am discharging a moral duty)

Learning by example (LBEx)
My learning has developed as a result of the influence of a particular person

Memorising before understanding (MBU)
Committing to memory material whose meaning is not comprehended (in order to make sense of something I first have to commit it to memory)

Memorising as rehearsal (MAR)
Committing to memory with no intention to understand (I learn things that don't make sense to me by reading them over and over until I can remember them)

Memorising with understanding (MWU)
Committing to memory material which is at the same time comprehended (When I can make sense of something its meaning is remembered at the same time)

Memorising after understanding (MAU)
Committing to memory material whose meaning is comprehended (I need to know the meaning of something before I can commit it to memory)

Relating ideas (RI)
An active, deep-level, process of attempting to relate new ideas to other contexts and experiences or 'mapping' them to see how they fit together

Seeing things differently (SDI)
A transformational conception of learning that involves seeing things from a new perspective (I believe that learning helps me to see things differently from how they looked before)

Thinking independently (Ind)
A conception of learning based on the capacity to think independently (I know that I have learnt something when I can form counter-arguments of my own)

Detail related pathology (DRP)
Over reliance on detail and an inability to integrate it into an overall picture (I have difficulty in fitting together facts and details to form an overall view of something)

Fragmentation (FRAG)
A surface-level lack of an organising principle for processing new information to be learned; such information is perceived to consist, in the absence of any apparent structure, of unconnected 'bits and pieces'

Appendix 2   The inventory metric

If the statement captures what you do, believe, or think, in your studying of accounting:

All of the time or nearly so; alternatively you **definitely agree** with it, then circle 4

About **three quarters of the time**; alternatively you **agree**, but with reservations, then circle 3

About **half the time**; alternatively you are **undecided**, then circle 2

About **one quarter of the time**; alternatively you **disagree** but with reservations, then circle 1

Hardly ever, if at all; alternatively you **definitely disagree**, then circle 0

So please note that in responding to the statements, and depending on how they are worded, things you actively do (eg the fourth statement) are more appropriately responded to in terms of how often you do them on average, while some statements that refer to what you basically think or believe about something (eg the first statement) might be more appropriately responded to in terms of how strongly you agree or disagree with them.

Appendix 3   RoLI subscale items

Thinking independently

I know I have learned something when I can fill the gaps in someone else's argument

I know I have learned something when I can do something without thinking

I know I have learned something when I can fill the gaps in someone else's logic

I know I have learned something when I can carry out a task without guidance

I know I have learned something when I can form counter-arguments on my own

Memorising as rehearsal (MAR)

I have to learn over and over those things that don't make sense to me

I learn things that don't make sense to me by reading them over and over until I can remember them

I learn things whose meanings are not clear by a process of repetition or rehearsal

Saying things over and over to myself is how I remember things whose meaning is not clear to me

I remember things that don't make sense to me by writing them out over and over

Notes

1   Figure 1 shows a simplified version of the model produced by Meyer (1999). It excludes the following variables: capacities, locus, culture and gender.

2   The term 'observable' is used "in preference to the more commonly used term 'variable' to convey the subjective and essentially self-referencing nature of the individual inventory-item response" (Meyer , 2000b, p.167).

3   Small variations in the sample sizes are due to missing data.

4   Nunnally (1978) suggests that a coefficient α value of 0.70 is the minimum standard for a measure producing scores that demonstrate satisfactory internal consistency reliability. However, Tait et al (1998, p.266) propose that an α of 0.50 is acceptable. Hinkin (1995 (1985 in ref)) notes that many scales do not reach the 0.70 α threshold as they comprise too few items, rather than the suggested minimum of five items.

5 From skills to subjects: the reconceptualisation of writing development in higher education

Colleen McKenna

Department of Education and Professional Development, University College London

5.1 Introduction

In the mid-1990s, Jonathan Monroe, director of Cornell University's Writing in the Disciplines programme, visited Queen Mary College, University of London to discuss writing in higher education. His perception, following an initial meeting, was that writing practices in UK Higher Education (HE) were stagnating, locked in a skills-based paradigm:

> ... the consensus among the self-selected group attending their first Writing in the Disciplines workshop was that student writing had since evolved into a mere assessment tool, within the framework of the UK-wide movement towards standardised outcomes, that actively discouraged faculty from focusing on student writing as an integral part of the learning process within and across the disciplines.
>
> The "skills" approach to teaching writing was embedded in a larger culture within higher education in the UK that would need to be challenged from within by faculty committed to restoring student-faculty interaction focused on the process of writing, rather than solely on writing as product, as a means of acculturation into the disciplines. (Monroe, 2001)

For Monroe, skills and outcomes agenda had seriously undermined the development of writing in higher education, and writing practices had to be reclaimed, revalued and even reconceptualised by subject specialists.

The last 5–10 years have seen profound changes in the way in which academic writing is conceptualised in HE in the UK and also worldwide (particularly the US, Europe and South Africa.) This conceptual paper will review several growing areas of research into writing in higher education within the UK and beyond, and consider how such work might have an impact on the teaching of writing in HE. Firstly, three main areas will be explored. These are the academic literacies movement stimulated by Lea and Street, the writing in the disciplines approach developed in the US and increasingly adopted in the UK, and related work on writing and identity by Ivanic and Lillis. All three areas have in common a belief that writing is a social practice rather than merely a skill or activity to be addressed in a remedial context. The growing impact of online communication in higher education will be briefly addressed. Finally, I will raise questions about the implications of theory for practice in writing in higher education.

5.2   Writing as a social practice

Academic literacy is not a neutral, unproblematic skill which students simply have to acquire, but multiple, complex and contested set of social practices which should be given more explicit and critical attention by all members of the academic community. (Roz Ivanic, 1998)

Writing as a social practice embraces a view of writing which foregrounds issues of context. These might be disciplinary, socio-economic, personal, institutional etc. The academic literacies movement stimulated by Mary Lea and Brian Street (2000, 1999, 1997) in the UK moves away from a skills-based, deficit model approach towards a view of writing as an activity which cannot be separated from its context(s), whether they are subject-based, work-based, institutional, personal or indeed a combination of these. The assumption underlying this position is that at university, students must enter into academic subjects and develop an understanding of the conventions, vocabularies and voices associated with that discipline. Literacy therefore involves knowing the language, style and genre of a discipline as well as the surface features of writing. It also involves a fuller awareness of identity and institutional context. Significantly, this approach signals a shift away from thinking about writing as dominated by concerns of grammar, punctuation and paragraph organisation, without, of course, denying that these are significant elements of writing.

Following an ethnographic study into student writing, Lea and Street concluded that students' difficulties with academic writing were often the result of a conflict between competing literacy practices rather than a lack of study skills (Lea and Street 1999, 2000). They proposed an academic literacies framework which describes three models of writing development. The first is a study skills approach which views writing as a transferable skill, largely concerned with surface features, that can be taught separately from the subject curriculum. The underlying assumption here is that once a student masters rules of punctuation and grammar and basic organisation, he/she can write successful essays in any subject. The second model, as Lea and Street define it, sees writing in academia as a process of induction. This is a more subject-based approach which acknowledges that different disciplines have ways of writing which are varied, and that part of the purpose of academic study is to teach students these academic conventions. Finally, the academic literacies model extends beyond this and frames writing as an activity that is embedded in the values, relationships and institutional discourses of the university and also one which is inscribed with power relationships; the writing process requires students to negotiate complex and contested discourses (Lea and Street 1999, 2000). In this sense, it has much to do with Bakhtin's notion of dialogic discourse and the idea that a voice or, more precisely, an utterance is never spoken in a neutral space, but is in fact always uttered against competing and dissenting voices (Bakhtin 1988). (See also Ivanic 1998 and Lillis 2001 for a discussion of Bakhtinian theory in writing development.)

The academic literacies framework views all writing as social practice which cannot be divorced from contextual issues such as the nature of disciplinary discourses, addressivity (role of the reader), power relationships (such as those which exist between student and tutor), student background and institutional practices.   Significantly, they argue that departmental guidelines on writing practices "do not attempt to make a bridge between where students are coming from" and what the discipline demands (Lea and Street 1999).

5.3   Writing in the Disciplines

The Writing in the Disciplines (WiD) model (which has grown out of the Writing Across the Curriculum movement) has become an increasingly popular approach to writing development in the US over the past two decades. It is also informing conversations about writing practice in the UK and has been implemented to varying degrees at Queen Mary, Anglia University and University College London (UCL) (Evison and Mitchell 2002). The WiD ethos views writing as inseparable from the intellectual development of students: writing is the way in which students express and develop subject knowledge and therefore it should be taught as part of the subject curriculum. The WiD programmes in the US stipulate that award-bearing degrees contain writing intensive courses. These courses are governed, in part, by guidelines about the number of words during the course, the re-drafting of work and staff feedback. Class sizes are kept down so that lecturers have dedicated opportunities to engage in written and spoken dialogue with students about their work.

One of the leading US sites of WiD work is Cornell's Knight Institute for Writing in the Disciplines led by Jonathan Monroe.   As with those adopting an academic literacies approach, Monroe argues that the tuition of writing for undergraduates (and postgraduates) should be located within the subject curricula rather than positioned exclusively in the Centre and that it should be treated as part of a student's intellectual progression rather than a surface level concern:

> If writing and the teaching of writing are to be given the priority they deserve, writing must be understood in the most capacious sense, not merely as a matter of mechanical skill, grammar, or style narrowly conceived, but as a matter of profound intellectual importance and resonance, a concern that reaches to the heart of, and indeed informs at all stages, the shapes fields take. (Monroe 2002)

He goes on to argue that "writing" (and the definition of the act is fluid, as he perceives it) is not a fixed subject that can be taught once, but rather an everchanging activity which should be addressed throughout university teaching. His approach to the development of student writing is to initiate and sustain a cross-institutional conversation about writing, and to foster "a sense of shared responsibility for the teaching of writing, and above all for the enhancement of learning through writing, across all disciplines and at all levels of the curriculum" (Monroe 2002).   In particular, Monroe and others have interrogated the relationship between disciplinarity and writing, suggesting that in large part, it is through writing that disciplines are shaped, sustained and re-enacted (Monroe 2002).

One of the questions raised about WiD is the extent to which a discipline can be defined as a body of fixed writing practices. (Monroe, it should be noted, is quick to acknowledge the changing nature of disciplines.) My own experience suggests that within disciplinary teaching and particularly within degree study which involves more than one subject, students often struggle to manage the movement between different discourses. Lea and Street (2000) refer to this as course-switching and found that students struggled with the process.

5.4   Student perspectives: writing and identity

For all its alertness to context, one possible blind spot of the WiD approach is the role of students' identity in shaping writing. One of the features of the academic literacies model and the work of Roz Ivanic and Theresa Lillis is a shift towards student perspective when considering academic writing, such that an awareness of students' backgrounds, their identities, and their process of developing voice in a subject is increasingly taken into account when researching writing practices. Ivanic (1998) considers "discoursal constructions" of identity (that is, the way a writer conveys a sense of self in written texts) with particular reference to adult learners. Lillis (2001), also researching adult learners in HE, offers a critique of institutional discourses on academic writing, arguing that current thinking about literacy undermines a widening participation aim because it ignores the range of cultural and social experiences students bring to their academic writing. Work with mature students who are returning to university has shown that there is often a perceived clash on behalf of the students between a personal sense of identity (which may involve background, age, gender, profession) and an academic identity, and that this tension manifests itself anxieties about writing (Ivanic 1998). Specific work in this area surrounds feedback and students' understanding of terms used in setting and marking written work (Lillis 2001, Ivanic 1998).

Ivanic (1998) argues that "academic discourse communities are constituted by a range of beliefs, assumptions and practices". She suggests that a person's identity "is partly constructed by the membership of and their identification with the values and practices of one or more communities. One of the ways people identify with the community is through the intertextual process of adopting its discourses". At university, students demonstrate an understanding of discourses through writing. Identity, she argues, plays a role here in two ways: 1) it is part of what writers bring to the act of writing and 2) students construct identities through the act of writing. Ivanic's experience is that students who perceive their identities to be outside that of the university struggle to gain access to these discourses.

An example of the potential struggle to integrate academic writing and identity comes from Lillis (2001) who cites the case of a bilingual student from a Yemeni background who had lived all her life and been educated in the UK, but who lacked confidence as a writer in both Arabic and English. She returned to university as a mature student while also working as a bilingual support teacher in a primary school. She told Lillis that "my English and that degree English are totally different... I think I'm going to have to change the way I put words together to form a sentence... I've been thinking about that, about how am I going to do that?" Lillis goes on to describe how, when faced with an essay on language and education, the student tried to interpret the question from her own professional and bilingual perspectives, but found this approach was undermined (and effectively rejected) by the tutor. The student's attempt to assert aspects of her identity in the writing was curtailed and this led to further acts of self-regulation which Lillis was able to observe because of the close working practice she maintained with the student. She argues that it is hard to know how much indirect (and invisible) self-regulation goes on, and in her view, the result is that the student must edit out her self and her experiences and the institution loses out on a potentially new and challenging perspective (Lillis).

5.4.1   "Institutional mystery"

In related work, both Ivanic and Lillis examine the "language"of disciplines and suggest that the discourse of writing is often "hidden" yet taken as being "given" (Lillis 2001). That is, it is assumed that any students entering higher education ought to understand what is meant by words such as "argue", "critical analysis", "be explicit" and more broadly what they are expected to do in, for example, an essay. In reality, it would seem that even students who are quite successful writers struggle to understand what sort of writing is being requested of them. Lillis refers to this as the "institutional practice of mystery" arguing that academics who have been "socialised" into essayist literacy are familiar with it but that students – particularly those from "non-traditional" backgrounds – are often very unsure about conventions and how to go about developing an academic voice. I would go further still and suggest that even "professional" writers who move between disciplines or who become students again can find writing conventions mysterious and difficult to embrace or own.

Lea and Street (2000), who did much of their work with tutors, arrived at a similar position from the perspective of academics. In their study, lecturers described the characteristics of good essay-writing by relying on descriptive terms which are often still unclear to students:

> I need my students to have an introduction which sets the scene and a main body which covers a number of issues highlighted in the introduction and introduces economic theory, application and analysis. Students need to be critical, to evaluate, to try and reach some sort of synthesis and then to simply summarize and conclude. You need a good solid introduction leading into your main body, and each part of your main body will be crafted and it will link with the next. It will have a professional feel about it and will not describe but will critically analyse, and then it will lead into a summary and conclusion.(Lea and Street 2000)

When pressed, the lecturer was unable to elucidate further on terms such as "critically analyse" and "synthesis". Another lecturer struggled even to describe the features or process of strong academic writing: "I know a good essay when I see it but I cannot describe how to write it". (Lea and Street, 2000) This work suggests that even once we are alert to certain contexts, there still exists a metalanguage associated with writing which can be impenetrable, yet is often taken for granted and treated as if it were transparent.

5.5 Writing in online environments

Finally, I wish to touch briefly upon the area of electronic writing which is increasingly part of curricula in higher education. It is now almost impossible to analyse or predict the future of writing in higher education without an awareness of the impact of computer-mediated communication and the internet generally. Jay David Bolter has been writing about online discourse for over a decade. In his text, Writing Space: Computers, Hypertext and the Remediation of Print (second edition), he begins with the question, "Does the advent of the computer announce a revolution in writing, or is the change less significant?" For Bolter, it would seem to be the former, and he points to issues of multimodality (like Kress, 1998; New London Group, 1996; Kress and Van Leeuwen, 2001) and shifts in structure and linearity enabled by hypertext environments as two aspects of computer-based communication which are substantially changing the nature of writing. In terms of the academic essay, he asks, "Why should a writer be forced to produce a single, linear argument or an exclusive analysis of cause and effect, when the writing space allows a writer to entertain and present several lines of thought at once?" He positions this question outside the sole domain of computer-based communication, and draws upon Plato, Wittgenstein, Sontag, Barthes among others as authorities who have challenged the linear argument.

When thinking about online writing, Bolter circumscribes large theoretical positions. What he tends not to do is to scrutinise the disciplinary differences in online writing. Just like the debates underpinning the writing in the disciplines movement, we might usefully ask what role disciplinary knowledge plays in the shaping of online text, and vice-versa.

Mary Lea (2001) goes some way towards answering this question in her recent work on the relationship between online writing in conferencing and essay writing. In particular, she describes how an online discourse community can collectively construct disciplinary knowledge through joint writing that challenges more traditional genres (books, articles etc) for authority. Lea's paper describes an ethnographic study with postgraduate students on the

Open University's "Applications of Information Technology in Open and Distance Education" who were from a range of backgrounds, geographically distributed across the world and who studied the course exclusively on-line.

Significantly, she found that the discourse in the conferencing "messages" and the essays, both of which contributed to the overall assessment, differed in terms of the linguistic conventions used. In particular, a fuller account of authoritative positions used to support arguments was given in the essay than in messages. Furthermore, in online writing, students tended to foreground their own or peers' ideas and opinions at the expense of those of the field's "authorities". Acknowledging that this might in part be due to the relative youth of the online learning field, Lea suggests, nonetheless, that a shift in approaches to knowledge construction was signalled by these differences:

> Students on H802 are involved in the process of disciplinary knowledge construction; they are not merely using the conference to discuss established and authoritative positions explicated in the literature of the field. References to conference messages take on an authority in written assignments normally reserved for established authors; the boundaries of what counts as authoritative subject-based knowledge are being contested in the students' writing. (Lea 2001).

She argues that the use of online conferencing extends the "rhetorical resources" available to students when developing arguments in course assessments. She also suggests that there is an increased reflexivity in the learning experience, comparable to that observed in studies with learning journals (Creme 2000), because students are able to mull over and return to contributions (posted on the online message board) from their peers, a process largely absent from traditional teaching. Particular practices which Lea argues indicate a reflexive approach to learning (and writing) include "leaving a time lag between reading and responding; making meaning in their writing through other students' messages; investing authority in others' messages in written assignments; [and] incorporating messages into written assignments" (Lea 2001).

This work both illustrates and extends theoretical positions in the construction of knowledge in online communities. In effect, Lea is reconceptualising academic writing/meaning making in online environments, particularly participant decisions about what constitutes knowledge and authority in online discourse. Furthermore, she seems implicitly to be embracing a Bakhtinian model of knowledge construction in which multiple voices representing different ideological perspectives create a heteroglossic condition against which other voices must develop.

5.6   Conclusions

This paper was conceived as an attempt to ask what has happened in writing development in higher education over the past decade and it has attempted to explore recent research, which would appear to be characterised by an increased awareness of context – disciplinary, authorial identity, and discourse medium. I will conclude by asking what this means for practice in higher education in terms of where in the curriculum writing is explicitly addressed, and I will briefly consider, by way of example, work at Queen Mary College and University College London.

In 2000, Queen Mary started a WiD programme, instigated by Alan Evison and run by Sally Mitchell. The programme consists of regular seminars (open to all members of staff) and exchange of practice sessions where aspects of writing are discussed with reference to disciplinary contexts. The work has also been characterised by a series of conversations between Mitchell and subject specialists which have resulted in the integration of writing development within departmental teaching (Evison and Mitchell 2002). In at least one case, an entire course curriculum has been rewritten with the teaching of writing relocated to the spine of the course teaching (Fernandez 2002). The programme has received commendation from its academic participants and from external experts in the field (Monroe 2001).

At my own institution, University College London, we began developing a Writing in the Disciplines programme in 2001. There was a strong institutional desire for the provision of centrally run writing courses, so these have been designed to take into account subject and personal context as much as possible. (One course is about writing in academic contexts, and the other is on electronic literacy. See McKenna 2002a and McKenna 2002b.) Additionally, we have set up an institution-wide series of writing workshops for academics, much along the Queen Mary model, and we have undertaken a number of department-based secondments in which subject specialists receive funding to further develop writing provision within their curricula in collaboration with the academic literacies tutor. Furthermore, we have proposed a peer-assisted learning (PAL) project in which postgraduates will work with undergraduates on writing in their disciplines. Wherever possible, we hope this will be tied explicitly to subject teaching (such as a first year seminar). It is intended that the PAL project will provide ongoing support and training for the postgraduate participants as well as a forum in which discussion about writing practices in different disciplines can take place.

In both cases, implementing the theory of context-based writing into practice has been and remains challenging. What can be particularly difficult is to effect a move beyond a notion of writing as a product (that is, a surface, generic skill that remains static as writers move across boundaries) rather than a process. Yet, if practice is to follow what seems to be overwhelming research evidence, then it is important that dialogues about writing across institutions and sectors are instigated and sustained wherever possible.

References

Bakhtin, MM (1988). *The Dialogic Imagination: Four Essays by MM Bakhtin.* Transl. Caryl Emerson and Michael Holquist. Michael Holquist (Ed). Austin: University of Texas Press.

Bolter, JD (2001). *Writing Space: Computers, Hypertext and the Remediation of Print,* (2nd Edn). New Jersey: Lawrence Erlbaum Associates.

Creme, P (2000). The personal in university writing: uses of reflective learning journals. In Lea, M and Stierer, B (Eds), *Student Writing in Higher Education.* Buckingham: SRHE and Open University Press.

Evison, A and Mitchell, S (2002). Developing a profile for writing in the university. Presentation at the *Writing Development in Higher Education* conference. Leicester.

Fernandez, J (2002). Devising and running a writing in the disciplines course. Presentation at the *Writing Development in Higher Education* conference. Leicester.

Ivanic, R (1998). *Writing and Identity: The Discoursal Construction of Identity in Academic Writing.* Amsterdam: John Benjamins.

Kress, G (1998). Visual and verbal modes of representation in electronically mediated communication: the potentials of new forms of text. In Snyder, I *Page to Screen: Taking Literacy into the Electronic Era,* pp 53–79. London: Routledge.

Kress, G and Van Leeuwen, T (2001). *Multimodal Discourse.* Arnold.

Lea, M (2001). Computer conferencing and assessment. *Studies in Higher Education.* **26**(2), 163–79.

Lea, M and Street, B (2000). Student writing and staff feedback in higher education: an academic literacies approach. In Lea, M and Stierer, B (Eds), *Student Writing in Higher Education*. Buckingham: SRHE and Open University Press.

Lea, M and Street, B (1999). Writing as academic literacies: understanding textual practices in higher education. In Candlin,C and Hyland, K (Eds), *Writing: Texts, Processes and Practices*. London: Longman.

Lea, M and Street, B (1997). *Perspectives on Academic Literacies: An Institutional Approach*. Economic and Social Research Council. Swindon.

Lillis, T (2001). *Student Writing: Access, Regulation, Desire*. London: Routledge.

McKenna, C (2002a). What do we mean by electronic literacy? In Rust, C (Ed), *Improving Student Learning Using Learning Technology*, pp 79–88. Oxford: Oxford Centre for Staff Development.

McKenna, C (2002b). Developing a course-unit in electronic literacy: writing in digital environments. In Clark, R and Graal, M (Eds), *Proceedings of Writing Development in Higher Education 2001*, pp169–174. Leicester.

Monroe, J (2001). Global cultures, local writing. In *Journal of Language and Learning Across the Curriculum*.

Monroe, J (2002). *Writing and Revising the Disciplines*. Cornell University Press.

New London Group (1996). A pedagogy of multiliteracies: designing social futures. *Harvard Educational Review*. **66**, 60–92.

6 Fragmentation or cohesion? Students' learning within and across modular undergraduate programmes

Helen Baron
Chester College

Abstract:

Modular undergraduate programmes are well established as the usual curriculum structure in many higher education institutions. Little research has been done to explore the impact of these programme structures upon the students who learn within them, despite frequent assertions that modular programmes fragment students' learning experiences, generating superficial 'pick and mix' programmes which lead to 'rag-bag' degrees awarded through the collection of credits. Modular myths are evident in many academic 'tribes', but what data exists to support or refute them?

The student feedback systems used to help judge the quality of learning in modular systems are often based on questionnaires completed by students responding to the learning experiences offered in each module. How can we understand the whole learning experience of the students, both within and across programmes? Has the development of modularised programmes with multiple sets of delineated outcomes produced fragmented learning, or are students making links across their programmes as they learn, forging new intellectual or skill-based connections? Most research has been undertaken on tutors' perceptions of modular systems: few students have been asked about what synergy or fragmentation they experience across their modular programmes.

A two year case study has taken place in a UK Faculty of Higher Education delivering modular University of Manchester degrees to a thousand students. It tested the 'pick and mix' assertion by exploring student perceptions of their learning across programmes. Data was collected through 310 questionnaires, 22 concept maps and 31 semi-structured interviews. Sampling was based on Approaches to Studying Inventories and grade averages. John Biggs' presage-process-product model of learning, which conceptualises learning as a shifting interactive system, provided a theoretical framework for analysis.

The data gathered from this case study revealed strong patterns of responses that tended to refute the fragmentation assertion. There were significant exceptions to this general tendency, as some students did not perceive coherence in their programmes. Factors promoting cross-programme synergy included individual student characteristics and approaches to learning, inbuilt programme features and the scale of the Faculty's provision. The research thus dents, but does not destroy, assertions of learning fragmentation arising from modular programmes.

6.1   Learning on modular programmes

Modular structures for undergraduate programmes originated in the US, and developed in the UK when the Open University and the University of Stirling pioneered credit-based and unitised-curriculum frameworks. In order to deliver cheaper flexible programmes to larger numbers of students in the 1990s, the majority of UK higher education institutions developed modular programmes which were based on credit accumulation systems. By 1996, 90% of UK institutions had adopted a modular or unitised curriculum, but programme structures and regulations varied considerably (Betts and Smith, 1998). Modularity became the norm not only in the UK higher education sector, but also in further education. Students entering UK higher education now accept modularity as the known curricular norm.

A frequent attack on modular programmes is that they fragment the learning experiences of the students who study upon them. Ashcroft and Foreman-Peck (1995) express the views of many critics about credit accumulation:

> Modular courses can have problems of coherence and fail to provide for an appropriate level of intellectual development. At the extreme, they may degenerate into a pot-pourri approach, with no mechanism to ensure depth and breadth of study. (1995: 140)

The assertion of fragmentation has been a useful source of ammunition for critics of modular programmes. Those who dislike modular schemes for diverse reasons have used the 'pick and mix' attack for decades. Resentment of the growth of student choice and loss of "donnish dominion" (Halsey, 1995), and suspicion of the managerial control that modular schemes promote may have fuelled these attacks. Opponents of modularisation claim that it has created, in the words of one group of educational managers, "'jigsaw' degrees, fragmentation, 'Legoland', 'soundbites', and consequent loss of integration and holism" (Warner 1996: 31). The lack of significant research on the issue has not helped clarify the often polarised debates about learning on modular programmes.

To what extent were pre-modular programmes cohesive? Those wishing to defend traditional disciplinary and departmental control over the HE curriculum may make fragmentation accusations, but some pre-modular curricula may be subject to the same criticism. Roland Barnett (2000) has noted that disciplines in the older universities remain highly classified and separated from each other, so denying students the potential to develop multiple perspectives and the powers of self-critique that such perspectives could offer.

Another false assumption is that modular programmes allow free choice for students who enter an educational cafeteria in which they freely pick up unrelated units. As Quinn (1978) comments,

> The modular system is not analogous to "filling one's 'basket' (mind) with educational 'packets' (modules) at the 'supermarket' (university) and then being given a 'receipt' (degree) as one passes through the 'checkout' (degree ceremony). (1978: 10)

David Robertson (1996) notes that modular frameworks may over-emphasize the detailed components in courses at the expense of the potential synergy of the whole learning experience:

> They can appear to produce a fragmentation of the learning experience, a purposeful separateness... which raises awkward questions about the maintenance of intellectual quality. Put bluntly, students may gain familiarity with the state of the roads but have no idea of their place on the map. (1996: 22–3)

Robertson also notes that the move from courses to modules can help students to develop new intellectual connections, and encourages a broader exposure to a variety of learning experiences in higher education. This move might involve "confrontation with the sovereignty of the academic discipline and its exclusive culture" (1996: 22–23).

Concern in the UK about this issue is also reflected in the US, for as Rothblatt (1991) has pointed out, "no feature of the American modular system so disturbs critics as the absence of coherence in the curriculum" (1991: 138).

What empirical evidence exists to support or deny these assertions? Although student feedback systems form a standard part of modern HE quality systems, little research has been done to explore students' responses to their overall learning experience, as Dai Hounsell (1997) explains:

> Little has been known about how students respond to teaching, how they tackle the everyday demands of learning and studying, or what kinds of difficulties or problems they encounter. In short, the experience of students has been taken for granted rather than systematically explored. (1997: 238)

The 3P model of student learning proposed by Biggs (1999), and Prosser and Trigwell's similar model (1999), provide a basis to explore students' perceptions and possible triggers of synergy.

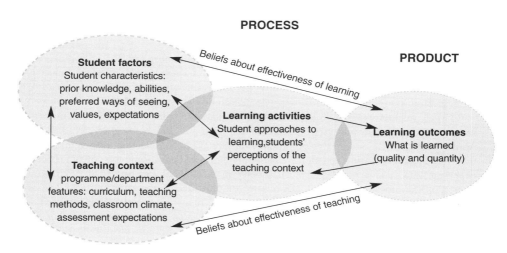

Figure 6.1   The 3P model of teaching and learning (after Biggs 1999)

The model illustrates the shifting interactive elements involved in teaching and learning. It focuses on learning as a process with presage, process and product as three stages, but it is not a rigid sequence: all elements are simultaneously active and influential. They form a learning ecosystem. Both individual student factors and social teaching contexts are acknowledged as important: psychological and socio-cultural factors interrelate and influence learning. Together they determine the learning processes which the students engage in, the approaches they use in their studies, and their learning outcomes. Students adapt and modify their original intentions or expectations as they proceed on modules and programmes; similarly, good teachers actively seek and use student feedback to modify their teaching and assessment.

Because of positive presage factors, some students may be confident and knowledgeable enough at the start of programmes to select and shape coherent learning pathways, but for others it may be very difficult. Students' abilities and past experiences of modular or other curriculum structures will flavour their reaction to present learning. Process factors might include core modules which give students underpinning conceptual frameworks that are statutory in some programmes, but non-existent in others. Product features of the model include what students learn, and their perceptions of their learning.

During and after their programmes, do students perceive their learning as fragmented? Are they building new intellectual connections, or merely collecting credit points towards a degree that has no internal cohesion? These issues have been explored through research in the context of an institution that delivers modular degree programmes to students from a broad range of educational and social backgrounds.

6.2 The case study

The research that was undertaken attempted to clarify the question of synergy or segmentation across complex modular programmes through exploration of students' perceptions of their learning. Prime targets for data were the graduating cohorts of 1999 and 2000 from a small UK Faculty of Higher Education delivering University of Manchester undergraduate and postgraduate degrees. All undergraduate degrees were modular, vocationally orientated and developed theoretical and practical skills, knowledge and experience. Compulsory core modules were studied at all levels of all programmes. The students involved in the case study had completed Joint Honours degrees, with Business as one of their main subjects. Business Studies is now a dominant subject area in many UK modular programmes, and is thus a widely relevant research area. 18% of all UK undergraduate students study Business. (Cooper and Otley, 1998).

A largely qualitative research approach was adopted, but some quantitative data was also sought. Students were interviewed after their final exams but before they received their results and classifications. At this point many might have been reflecting metacognitively on their learning (3P Process), and all were likely to have been considering the outcomes of their exams and assessments (3P Product). Their perceptions on what they had learned across their degree programmes, whether connections were embedded in the curriculum or not, and whether their learning was experienced holistically or not, were sought. Three hundred and ten questionnaires gave a general impression of students' perceptions of whether their learning was holistic or not, 22 concept maps gave an indication of individual learning schemas and 31 semi-structured interviews revealed more detail, "thick description" and individual variations.

In May/June 1999 and 2000 an overview student feedback questionnaire had extra questions inserted to generate data for the study. One hundred and sixty responses were obtained from 234 of the 1999 graduating cohort, a 68% response rate, and 150 responses from the 2000 cohort, a response rate of 60%. The questions are outlined below:

Question 31: *I have been able to make connections in my learning across my degree programme*

Question 32: *The modules I have studied link together to form a connected degree programme*

Question 33:   *Modules such as Work Based Assignment and the Special Management Project helped me to link learning from different degree pathways.*

Sixty-six to seventy-six percent of the responding students agreed or strongly agreed with the three statements. Disagreement ranged from 5% to 16%. Respondents in 2000 were more likely to disagree with the statements than those in 1999, but still gave a clear majority of support. Seventy-four percent of students agreed or strongly agreed with the statement in Question 33 that two specific modules helped them to link their learning. These were a compulsory nine week second level placement with assessment based on learning outcomes negotiated by the student, placement tutor and host organisation, and a Special Management Project designed to connect learning on Joint and Combined Honours degree pathways.

Although the individual students in this case study experienced very different journeys through the levels of their programmes, the questionnaire responses indicated that most appeared to perceive their programmes not as a completely fragmented 'pot pourri' of modules, but as learning experiences with significant links which were inbuilt in their programmes. Questions remain as to why the students who were the exception to this general tendency perceived otherwise.

A significant majority of pilot and main study interviewees also reported that they perceived the programmes they had studied on to be integrated and connected. Twenty-one out of thirrty-one students reported this; two felt their programmes had been fragmented and 8 reported some aspects of their programmes to be connected and some not.

The pilot study interviews revealed that their attitudes toward the structure of their semesterised and modularised pathways of study were predominantly positive:

> The most important thing for me was that my degree did make a cohesive whole, and developed a wider understanding of organisations. (Student D)

> The modular system worked perfectly for me so I wouldn't criticise it in any way. I like the fact that it gives you the choice and it gives you the freedom to say "I've made a mistake, let's try something different". (Student H)

Some students expressed the view that modularity led to over-assessment, particularly at third level. Other students expressed criticism about the lack of study time in a semester: "Twelve weeks sometimes isn't enough to learn, especially in the third year, …you don't have enough time to read around" (Student G). In contrast, a mature student thought that surface learning was the result of lack of student application, not the structure of the degree programme:

> If the student doesn't apply themselves, if they don't do adequate reading and adequate research, doesn't spend enough time reflecting on what they're actually learning, rather than just regurgitating things for exams, if they don't spend time reflecting on what they've learnt…[it's their responsibility]. That's the idea of a degree, and if you're not studying it properly, then I think that would be the case in any degree, whether it was a pure subject or a modular degree or whatever. I think it would be the same. (Student H)

The main study in May/June 2000 focused on five sample groups of students identified through analysis of grade averages and of an Approaches to Study Inventory for Students devised by Noel Entwistle (1988), which provided a practical means of identifying deep, surface and strategic approaches to studying.

Students in the five sample groups produced concept maps that revealed in diagrammatic form their perceptions of what they had learned from the degree programmes they had just completed. These concept maps formed the basis for the 22 main study interviews. Mapping was a highly effective method of both preparing students to talk in interviews about their learning, and illustrating both learning and connections. Diagram 6.2 shows the concept map of a student who viewed their learning as mostly fragmented. Diagram 6.3 is the map of a student who viewed it as mostly connected.

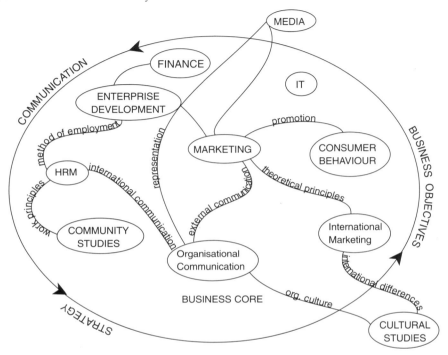

Figure 6.2   Concept map of a student who perceived their learning as mostly fragmented

The dominant impression gained from questionnaire responses, concept maps and interviews was that students did not experience the programmes they studied on as collections of fragmented learning experiences. Several students cited synergy as the major goal of their learning. One wanted to become

> A well rounded complete individual, the idea of being that is the most important factor for me, so you appeal to employers… There's a very high correlation here, between this course, between experience, between personal growth and how you actually become the well rounded complete graduate I think that gives you that job. (Student 1)

This student has created synergy between the traditional ideals of liberal higher education and more utilitarian vocationalism. Student 1 aspires not only to the holism of the "well rounded complete individual", but also to meet the specific demands of employers. Another student also described his learning goal as "becoming a more rounded person with greater understanding" (Student A).

Nine students who perceived their programmes as holistic spoke of it growing to become so as they progressed through their studies:

> You start off with loads and loads of elements, and I think in first year it's really really bitty, and you just think this isn't going to go together, and you're told what to do, you don't get any choice what to do, and in the second year it's a bit funny because you do

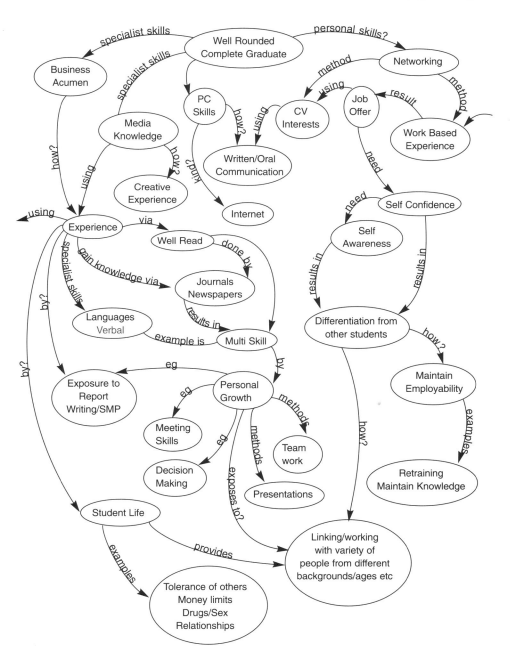

Figure 6.3   Concept map of a student who perceived their learning as mostly holistic

work placement, but then I think suddenly in the third year it does all come together, and you do draw on things from all modules, past experiences and it focuses. (Student 14)

Students who perceived a mixture of synergy and fragmentation often found one pathway of their studies to be holistic, but not the other:

> Modules I felt were a bit splintered, they were a bit too, I don't know, you just seemed to go to one lecture, you do one subject, you go to another lecture which could be your second Sport lecture of the day, you do something entirely different, which isn't linking, you're doing physiology in the morning... in the afternoon you're doing psychology and motivation and things like that. Business, because of the way the subject is, I found it did mix, you did bring in different things that you'd done in different modules... I just found that they were a bit splintered. (Student 11)

This student described her learning as "switching on and off" to disconnected modules and "moving on" in connected ones.

The students who reported predominant fragmentation had presage factors which may have been influential. One reported that she had no clear pathways or career orientation in mind as she selected modules:

> I think I thought of it as different modules. That's how I have thought of the whole degree. And I haven't until now really thought about how they linked. I just thought, which subjects interest me most? I didn't really care if they linked or not, it was just that if I liked them I'm going to do better in them, so that's all my choices. (laughs) To take what I like doing. (Student 15)

Another student reporting fragmentation had generally positive responses to her degree programme. The modular programme allowed her to switch from a Media pathway in her first year to a Business pathway in her final two years. She did, however, reveal that she would have preferred to study Psychology, a subject area not available in the Faculty, rather than Business. Although this student declared her degree to be "so fragmented", she stated that "however, once I started writing down subjects I did think of links between them all" (Student 10).

The three students who reported their programmes as fragmented did, however, cite examples of programme synergy without prompting in their interviews. Their concept maps also illustrated some degree of connection. They drew 12, 15 and 34 cross links within their concept maps respectively.

The majority of students praised the modular system they had experienced, and clearly connected their learning within it. Choice and control were crucial:

> For myself, it's been wonderful, because I've been able to structure what I learn. Obviously in the first year you don't, but you're guided and you sort of pick up what you like and what you don't like... for your third year, you can structure your final degree completely to what you want and what interests you the most. (Student 13)

> You can mould this degree to your own needs and purposes. (Student J)

> It helps you to build on what you already know and what you've already learned: if you choose to take it to a stage higher you can. (Student 20)

Building on "what you already know and what you've already learned" effectively illustrates the relationship between Process and Presage in the 3P model. Using David Robertson's metaphor, these students appear to have some knowledge of both the state of the roads and their place on the map.

Students had varied conceptions of what the links were across their programmes, and what helped create them. The concept maps revealed many skills-based links, with communication, confidence and self management appearing frequently as factors that students thought linked their learning. Although a few students separated their learning into field-based pathways, the majority mingled field, work-based and informal learning freely in their maps.

The findings of this study supported those that emerged from a longitudinal study into the long-term effects of a degree on graduate lives at Oxford Brookes University (Jenkins, Jones and Ward, 2001). Common benefits, including skills development, were evident from both studies, but they also highlit the huge differences in the responses of individual students to their modular programmes

6.3   Forms of synergy in the formal and informal curriculum

Whatever the measures taken to encourage synergy in and across modular programmes, it would be salutary to remember Howard Becker's reminder:

> Students in conventional educational institutions have repeatedly been shown to teach each other how to deal with the constraints, requirements, and opportunities those places embody: how much of the assigned work you really have to do, for example.
> (Becker, 1998:144)

As students enter programmes, their attitudes towards tutors, learning and assessment may be influenced by students from cohorts ahead of them. In this study students observed a wide range of motivation in their friends, and some were open in admitting their own lack of application to study:

> Some students are more dedicated. A lot more focused. Not only that, but you can see that they are trying so hard…they are working so hard… if they haven't been corrupted by being a student for the first two years, once they get to the third year it's like, yes, got to be focused, got to be like that, but I was one of the corrupted ones, (laughs) that's why I don't think, I could have done better. To be quite honest I've enjoyed myself.
> (Student 17)

Students actively construct their experiences of both formal and informal curricula. Whatever the formal curriculum, students will creatively interpret it for their own purposes. A minority of students following the informal curriculum attempt to 'doss' (do minimum work) or 'blag' (bluff their way to better marks or attach themselves to groups where other students will do most of the work). They may or may not connect their learning. The admitted dossers and blaggers interviewed claimed their learning was not fragmented. Their concept maps were unified, and they described connections across their programmes.

Some of the dossers and blaggers were in the 'surface learner' sample group. They may have engaged with fewer ideas and had less material to connect than deep learners, and thus the synergy they reported may be more superficial than that reported by a deep learner. Complexities, subtleties, ambiguities and paradoxes may be more difficult to neatly categorise and link than superficial learning. To compare two metaphors for learning, Lego blocks of standard shapes and sizes are designed to connect, and link without the blocks being changed. Some students spoke of consciously connecting their programme in a neat calculated sequence. Others described their learning as moving through complex and muddy terrain, an image closer to the 3P model.

As well as the possibility of synergy of different depths and complexities being reported, it is possible that it may have been of different types. There are represented in figure 6.4.

Form of Synergy	Examples
Horizontal synergy	Connecting core modules to option modules
Vertical synergy	Connecting through years and levels of a programme
Cross-subject based synergy	Connecting fields on Joint or Combined Honours programmes
Thematically based synergy	In enquiry based learning
Personal skills based synergy	Self management, communication skills
Problem based synergy	Problem-based learning in medicine
Synergy created by the individual learner	Through research for dissertations

Figure 6.4   Possible forms of synergy

All students reporting fragmentation in the case study had limited vertical synergy as they had either switched programmes in the middle of their studies or intercalated. Vertical synergy was most evident in production pathways through degree programmes. As might be expected, Joint Honours students reported much cross-subject synergy which tended to be generated by themselves, rather than by tutors or the curriculum. Within fields, tutors were aware of potential thematic overlaps, but they were largely ignorant about them beyond their academic territory.   Many students reported skills based synergy: finance and IT skills acquired on Business modules being frequently cited as transferable.

6.4   Conclusion

This case study indicates that the 'pick and mix' criticism did not seem to apply for most students on the modular programmes investigated. Inbuilt modules promoting synergy, teaching and assessment methods and the small scale of the Faculty's provision may have helped promote synergy. There was sufficient 'cognitive glue' for the majority of students to connect most of their programmes. Some modular structures, teaching methods and assessment patterns can help establish and develop links with students' previous educational experiences as well as their current ones. Even with synergy-promoting features, however, some students will still find difficulty in developing connections.

Badley and Marshall (1995) assert that the responsibility for designing connecting modules and programmes lies with lecturers and managers:

> It's up to us: we can design and deliver our modules in such a way that students come to adopt a search for understanding and connection (eg with previous knowledge, with other modules, between theory and practice, between argument and evidence) or in such a way that students merely come to complete the requirements of the task or the assessment (by only focusing on unrelated parts and facts, by treating tasks as external impositions, by failing to distinguish between argument and evidence). (1995: 80)

This exhortation is worthy but ignores the complexities of the learning ecosystems that tutors and students engage with. Both the nature, quality and quantity of synergy desired need consideration. Too much synergy might constrain students, too little might lead to curriculum maps that have negative effects rather than positive ones. Different students and different learning contexts need different frameworks and links. The changing forms and content of the higher education curriculum will demand not only an ability to structure programmes so that individual students can absorb knowledge, but also creatively synthesize and generate it within and across modules. This will be a central challenge for the tutors, students and curriculum developers of the future.

References:

Ashcroft, K and Foreman-Peck, L (1995). *The Lecturer's Guide to Quality and Standards in Colleges and Universities.* London: Falmer Press.

Badley, G and Marshall, S (1995). *53 Questions and Answers about Modules and Semesters.* Bristol: Technical and Educational Services.

Barnett, R (1994). *The Limits of Competence.* Buckingham, SRHE and Open University Press.

Barnett, R (2000). Supercomplexity and the Curriculum. *Studies in Higher Education,* **25**, 3.

Becker, H (1998). *Tricks of the Trade: How to Think about Your Research While You're Doing It.* Chicago: University of Chicago Press.

Betts, M and Smith, R (1998). *Developing the Credit-based Modular Curriculum in Higher Education.* London: Falmer Press.

Biggs, J (1999). *Teaching for Quality Learning at University.* Buckingham: SRHE and Open University Press.

Brennan, J and Ramsden, B (1996). UK Higher Education in the 1990s. *Higher Education Digest,* **26**, Autumn 1996.

Cooper, C and Otley, D (1998). The 1996 Research Assessment Exercise for Business and Management. *British Journal of Management,* **9**.

Entwistle, NJ (1988). *Styles of Learning and Teaching.* London: David Fulton.

Eraut, M (1994). *Developing Professional Knowledge and Competence.* London. Falmer Press.

Halsey, AH (1995). *Decline of Donnish Dominion.* Oxford: OUP.

Hounsell, D (1997). Understanding Teaching and Teaching for Understanding. In Marton, F, Hounsell, D and Entwistle, N, *The Experience of Learning: Implications for Teaching and Studying in Higher Education,* (2nd Edn). Edinburgh: Scottish Academic Press.

Jenkins, A, Jones, L, and Ward, A (2001). The Long-term Effect of a Degree on Graduate Lives. *Studies in Higher Education,* **26**(2) 147–161.

Prosser, M and Trigwell, K (1999). *Understanding Learning and Teaching: The Experience in Higher Education.* Buckingham: SRHE and Open University Press.

Quinn, TFJ (1978). A critical appraisal of modular courses and their relevance to the British system of higher education. *British Journal of Educational Technology,* **9**(1), Jan 78.

Robertson, D (1996). The Reconciliation of Academic Disciplines and Modular Frameworks: Student Choice, Knowledge Production and the 'New' Rigidities. *Modular Higher Education in the UK in Focus.* London: HEQC.

Rothblatt, S (1991). The American Modular System. In Berdahl, RO, Moodie, GC, and Spitzberg, IJ (Eds), *Quality and Access in Higher Education: Comparing Britain and the United States.* Buckingham: SRHE and Open University Press.

Schön, DA (1987). *Educating the Reflective Practitioner.* San Francisco: Jossey-Bass.

Scott, P (1995). *The Meanings of Mass Higher Education.* Buckingham: SRHE and Open University Press.

Warner, D (1996). Coherence or chaos? *Managing Higher Education,* **4**, 30–31.

7 Teachers' and students' conceptions of the professional world

Anna Reid[1] and Allan Davies[2]
1. Macquarie University; 2. Centre for Learning and Teaching in Art and Design at The London Institute, Royal College of Art and Wimbledon School of Art

Abstract

In the original 'Improving Student Learning' (ISL) project led by Professor Graham Gibbs in 1991, one of the case studies focused on approaches to learning on a BA (Hons) Graphic Information Design course. The case study, led by Allan Davies, had the modest intention of trying to determine whether a particular curriculum innovation encouraged a deep approach to learning. Our only significant tool then was Biggs SOLO taxonomy. Eleven years later and the innovators have moved on, the course has disappeared and the research context and methodologies have developed. During this period, research has suggested that both teachers and students describe their understanding of teaching and learning according to their perception of the teaching/learning environment (Ramsden, 1992; Prosser & Trigwell, 1999). Studies have identified variation in the way that teachers experience teaching (Samuelowicz & Bain, 1992; Prosser, Trigwell & Taylor, 1994 for example) and variation in the way teachers experience student learning (Bruce & Gerber, 1995).

More recently, Reid (1997) has widened the context of research by examining the relation between the experience of work and teaching/learning within the music discipline. In further research (Reid 1999), relations were found within the music discipline where teachers' and students' experience of one of three defined dimensions was strongly related to the ways in which they understood teaching and learning music. The musicians (and their students) described their experience of the professional world in three hierarchically related ways. This constitution has become known as the 'Music Entity'. In 1999, following a fortuitous meeting at the ISL conference in York, Davies and Reid conducted a joint enquiry, using a phenomenographic approach, to determine the Design Entity (Davies and Reid, 2001). This research focused on discerning the critical differences, or variation, in the way teachers and students experience and understand their subject and its relation to the professional design world. The outcomes of this research have, consequently, begun to impact on student learning through course design and, in particular, assessment. This paper is a comparative study of the research already carried out by the authors in a number of disciplines in which the same focus and methodology has been used.

7.1   Introduction

Research has suggested that both teachers and students describe their understanding of teaching and learning according to their perception of the teaching/learning environment (Ramsden, 1992; Prosser & Trigwell, 1999). Many studies have described variation in the ways that students understand various subject areas (Entwistle & Marton, 1994; Crawford et al, 1994; Petocz & Reid, 2001). The outcomes of that sort of research are the development of learning and teaching environments that focus on the nature of the subject and aim at facilitating a student's understanding of specific topic areas. Some research has looked at the ways in which teachers experience teaching in a variety of different fields (Bond & LeBrun,1996, Samuelowicz & Bain, 1992; Prosser, Trigwell & Taylor, 1994 for example) and variation in the way teachers experience student learning (Bruce & Gerber, 1995). Kember's (1997) meta analysis of these sorts of research studies clearly showed that there were some aspects of commonality between them, that on one side of a continuum the teachers and students were oriented towards a content delivery/acquisition focus and on the other side a learning/understanding focus. The early work by Reid (1997) explored all of these issues in the context of music performance. However, as part of that study she found that students and teachers were aware of a much broader context than simply that provided by a learning institution. Students and teachers described a perception of their professional work and that that perception had a relation to their conception of learning/teaching and the way they went about their learning/teaching.

Research on work-based learning (Garrick & Rhodes, 2000), where students are workers first, has shown that these students focus on the constraints and opportunities provided by the workplace to orient their learning. Students who are workers see that learning contributes to their effectiveness at work and enhances their job satisfaction. This paper explores the way in which students' and teachers' perceptions of professional work provide a broader context for situating their conceptions of teaching/learning within an institutional environment.

We have chosen to describe this exploration by focusing on two 'creative' fields, music and design, as these two professional areas have some obvious similarities. Education in music and design were both shifted in the last century from an orientation where students learned on-the-job in a creative apprenticeship, to learning formalised within an institution. Music and design, which used to be exceedingly practical studies, have become subject to the knowledge revolution and have been institutionalised. However, students intending to become professionals in both areas are often already working in those areas as they study. In essence, students within these fields have a critical understanding of the nature of work in their artistic professions. Finally, the teachers of design and music are often highly regarded practitioners who are intent on propagating their own unique artistry.

7.2   Research in music and design

Data for our studies were collected using an open ended interview protocol (Bowden, 1996; Dortins, 2002). The initial music study focused on students' and teachers' experience of teaching and learning music and resulted in three sets of related categories that described students' conceptions of learning music, students' conceptions of teaching, and teachers' conceptions of teaching and learning. The design of the study was unusual as in the context of learning music performance each student has an individual lesson. Each of the teachers in the study suggested specific students to participate and it was therefore possible to analyse specific student/teacher cases (Reid, 2000). The music study provided evidence of an overarching framework described as the 'Music Entity'. The research in design explored students' understanding of learning design, their understanding of teaching design, and the teachers' understanding of teaching/learning. It also directly explored how students and teachers perceived the nature of work as a designer and the ways in which they thought their learning/teaching may be related to that perception. The plan of the music study has been described in detail elsewhere (Reid, 2000), however in this paper we will describe the specific plan of the design study. The interviews, intended to enable the participants to fully explore their understanding of the design world and how this world is related to their understanding of teaching and learning, were conducted with 17 full time and part time staff from the University of Technology, Sydney and the London Institute. Twenty four first to fourth year students, representing different design specialities, were interviewed. The Australian and British data was treated as a single data set to determine the qualitatively different ways in which the design world is understood by the participants. A second level of data analysis involved the separation of the data into student and staff sets to allow conceptions of learning and teaching to emerge. In this way the 'Design Entity' and the participants' ways of experiencing teaching and learning can be related.

In both of these creative fields, teachers and students identified orientations to their profession that were related to the ways they then thought about their learning/teaching. This orientation has recently become know as the 'Professional Entity' (Reid and Petocz, 2002b) and is a tripartite hierarchy of perceptions of the nature of professional work. Petocz and Reid (2002) have described how in the two contrasting fields of statistics and music, that "the broad descriptor is constant, the specific meaning of each level is defined by the discipline". Here we describe the nature of the disciplinary variation found in design and music and show how the broad descriptor is still constant.

Professional entity	in Music	in Design
Extrinsic technical	Music making is 'outside' the . participant. Music is seen as a combination of technical elements related to an instrument or musical notation.	Being able to apply skills appropriately – . design is about doing
Extrinsic meaning	Here participants describe a more integrated view of music making where the focus is the production of meaningful musical sound for communication.	Being able to meet the needs of society – design is about interpreting
Intrinsic meaning	Here participants describes music as a vehicle for expressing personal artistic truths. The focus of this dimension is on the relation between personal understanding of the world of music and the consequent re-interpretation of it through a communicative process.	Being able to communicate – design is about living

Figure 7.1

Figure 7.1 shows that participants in both design and music described their perceptions of professional work in limiting ways where the art form was considered to consist of the

Students' conceptiona about learning in design	
Conception 1	*Learning design.* Learning is about developing skills, acquiring knowledge and remembering techniques. The students focus on learning enough things so that they can choose the appropriate skill when they get out to work. Design is understood to be about doing something.
Conception 2	*Learning to be a designer.* Learning is about applying and experimenting with skills and techniques. Students recognise the difference between learning at university and work and understand university learning to be preparatory. As in the previous conception design is understood to be about doing something.
Conception 3	*Learning to be part of the design community.* As in the previous conceptions learning is understood to be the acquisition and appropriate application of skills and knowledge. This conception is different because students focus on the social aspects of design, focus their learning on learning as part of a team. Design is understood to be about doing something to solve a problem.
Conception 4	*Learning to innovate and change.* Learning is understood to be discovering about themselves. The focus is on self expression, reflection and integration.

Students' conceptions of learning music	
Conception 1	*Learning an instrument or voice.* In this conception students focus on acquiring the technical skills required of the instrument. They approach their study by rehearsing repetitive physical actions using studies and scales. The outcome of their study is the demonstration of technical skills in an exam situation.
Conception 2	*Learning an instrument or voice and some elements.* Here, students focus on the acquisition of technical skills and some musical elements. Written music is seen as a series of individual technical problems that must be solved. Once technical solutions have been found, musical elements, such as phrasing or dynamics, are added. The outcome of the learning experience is technical proficiency in an exam situation.
Conception 3	*Learning musical meaning.* Here, students reflect on their teachers' advice on technique and stylistic interpretation of music. Technical proficiency on the instrument is seen as a vehicle to enable correct playing of the music. The outcome of the learning experience is to able to play the music with correct technique and musical style in a performance situation.
Conception 4	*Learning to communicate musical meaning.* In this category students see music as a means of communicating with an audience. Written music has an implicit meaning that is expressed by the student using the instrument as a medium. Technique is seen only as a tool through which musical meaning is expressed. The intended outcome of the learning experience is to express the implicit musical meaning of a work to an audience.
Conception 5	*Learning to express personal meaning.* Here students see learning as reflecting on musical knowledge and assimilating musical ideas into a performance that communicates with the audience and expresses personal meaning. The instrument is seen as a vehicle of self expression which is subject to the greater need to express personal meaning through the music. The intended outcome of the learning experience is to communicate personal meaning and interpretation of the music to an audience through performance.

Figures 7.2 and 7.3

technical components. The extrinsic meaning component of both design and music participants described the profession as communicative. The artistic mediums of both sound and vision are intended to communicate something to someone. For the musician this means that the instrumentalist considers professional work to be about communicating the essence of a Mozart Sonata (for instance) to an audience; the professional designer tries to interpret a 'brief' and produce an artefact that fulfils the brief. The most integrated and inclusive view of professional work, the intrinsic meaning dimension, in both cases is about personal commitment to the art form with the musicians focusing on creating and communicating personal meaning through music, and designers trying to 'live' their art form.

Reid has previously described the relations between music students' conceptions of learning music and the Music Entity (1997, 2001) In figures 7.2 and 7.3 we present, in summary form, categories that describe variation in student learning in design and in music.

Finally, (fig 7.4) we describe design teachers' understanding of design. Readers should be aware that Drew (2000) has described categories of design teachers' conceptions of teaching from a different study and that it would be useful to explore the similarities and differences between these two outcome spaces.

Teachers on design	
A	Design is end-product oriented (making)
B	Design is trying to satisfy a lot of other people (problem-solving)
C	Design is being able to identify the problems (functional/aesthetic) that the client faces and being able to present a solution (problem-finding)
D	Design is like orchestration... designer's role to put all the instruments together
E	Design is being open to possibility, a questioning condition (analytical)
F	Design is other ways of seeing (cognitive/creative)
G	Design is understanding people..... and the impact of your design on others (communication)

Figure 7.4

An analysis of the design teachers' interviews suggests that teachers understand learning design in quite different ways from many of the students. Their focus on the client (and what they think the client wants) seems to have a particularly important bearing on the sorts of things they want students to do. This finding lends weight to the view that these ways of understanding learning in design may be related to the Design Entity. For instance, the limiting 'design is end-product oriented' shows an orientation toward the making (technical) components of the entity (extrinsic technical). Similarly categories B and C fit well into the extrinsic meaning view of professional work.

The most limiting of the teachers' conceptions relates to the teacher's intentions to the act of making a product. The learning of skills is a result of this making. Equally, some teachers focus on teaching skills and techniques and often locate the purpose of this within a vocational context. A slightly more sophisticated conception of design is to do with 'client satisfaction'. The focus is on solving the problems that the client has presented. The designer sees the problems, as do the students, in terms of the relationship between aesthetics and functionality. In this limited conception the intention is simply to satisfy the client's wants.

A qualitatively more sophisticated conception relates to the identification of the client's needs. The purpose of the designer is seen to be about finding the actual problems the client is facing and convincing them of it. Success is seen in terms of re-educating the client. The design 'process' is seen by some as being a crucial aspect of successful design. Several design teachers talk about bringing the whole concept together or seeing the designer's role like that of the conductor of an orchestra, ensuring that all the elements of the design process are working in harmony. Some design teachers focus on the critical and analytical aspects of design and claim that successful design is about questioning and looking for possibilities. Here the focus is on the imagination and some teachers talk about design being to do with different or 'other' ways of seeing.

Some teachers see design beyond the relationship with the client and locate the practice of design within a social context with a concern about understanding people and the impact of design on them. The most abstract of the conceptions in the study was articulated as one in which the designer must come to terms with humanity as design as being a core function of the human condition. The success of design is seen to come from a position informed by anthropological perspectives.

7.3   Putting it all together

Whilst many researchers have focused on describing variation in the ways that students and teachers experience learning, teaching or the subject to hand, and then provide sound advances in the development of learning environments, the focus remains on learning/teaching and curriculum that is bound by institutional contexts. The emergence of the music and design entities, and now the knowledge that the Professional Entity is a component of several professional fields, the time is right to further explore the nexus between institutional learning and the world of work. Theory and practice described in the research and outcomes of work-based learning allows us an insight into the autonomy required of professionals in the conduct of their work and also in the conduct of their learning. However, the discovery of the professional entity throws the ideas of the autonomous worker/learner and the 'spoon-fed' university student to the winds. Students forward projection into the world of professional work, their perception of the profession, has an important interaction with the ways in which they go about learning. Similarly, teachers' experience of professional work has long been valued as it is supposed to be able to integrate the critical elements of the workplace within their teaching programme. What happens then when a teacher has a view of work that is 'extrinsic technical'? What happens when a student has a perception of the profession that is 'intrinsic meaning' and then encounters a teacher who does not? One way of exploring some aspects of this particular problem has been the 're-analysis' of our transcripted data.

The initial analysis of both data sets was focused on the identification of categories that defined qualitatively different ways of experiencing learning and teaching in music and design. The same transcripts provided evidence for the music and design entities. Having determined these outcomes, we then went back to individual transcripts to look for evidence that a way of experiencing learning/teaching may be related to a way of experiencing professional work. Reid and Petocz (2002a) used this same technique with their transcripts of statistics students and found that, in most cases, the limiting conceptions of learning sat beside the limiting perceptions of work. In the diagram that follows we show how our design group also 'fit in' with this.

Professional entity	Outside focus		Inside focus
Extrinsic technical Design: doing Music: technical skill	Conception 1: Learning design, learning is about developing skills, acquiring knowledge and remembering techniques. *Conception 1 – Learning an instrument or voice* *Conception 2 – Learning an instrument or voice and some elements*		
Extrinsic meaning Design: Interpreting brief Music: Interpreting score		Conception 2: Learning to be a designer, learning is about applying and experimenting with skills and techniques. Conception 3: Learning to be part of the design community, learning is understood to be the acquisition and application of skills and knowledge. *Conception 3 – Learning musical meaning.* *Conception 4 – Learning to communicate musical meaning.*	
Intrinsic meaning Design: living Music: communicating self			Conception 4: Learning to innovate and change, learning is understood to be discovering about themselves. *Conception 5 – Learning to express personal meaning.*

Figure 7.5

7.4   Using the outcomes of this research

Over the past two years, the outcomes of these research projects have been used to help specialist art and design teachers following a Postgraduate Certificate in Learning and Teaching in Art and Design to reflect on their practice as professional teachers. There have been some interesting spin-offs in this context. Firstly, whilst the outcomes are in concert with Biggs' (Biggs, 1999) notion of constructive alignment, they extend the concept into the professional world. But, as we have seen, students' prior understanding of the professional world has an impact on how they go about studying, therefore an holistic conception of student learning must embrace students' understandings of the professional world. This revelation for many art and design teachers has encouraged them to look more carefully at how students are inducted into their courses, how they cast the learning outcomes for a project or a module, what activities they engage students in to achieve those outcomes and how the assessment of students might be structured to encourage them to move to an intrinsic meaning orientation which embraces conceptions of the world of work. One tutor of animation, when engaging in these outcomes, said, 'The problem is that many students arrive to study animation thinking that it is vitally important to learn how to draw sophisticated characters using state-of-the-art technology. That is their expectation and they are disappointed if it doesn't happen. On the other hand, most employers want animators whose work simply makes them laugh. This can be achieved equally effectively with simple stick drawings'. Here we see a teacher who recognises a significant problem in trying to reconcile the beliefs and expectations of the students with the needs of the industry. He sees that the abilities that the students expect to be developed on the course are fundamentally different from those which are characteristic of the subject of study and those more likely to get them employment.

Using a matrix (Appendix 1) which relates students' conceptions of, and approaches to, learning and teaching with their conceptions of the professional world is also proving useful as an assessment tool for teachers. The matrix, which utilises Biggs' SOLO taxonomy (Biggs & Collis, 1982) along the vertical axis and our outcome space across the horizontal axis, helps to generate criterion referenced descriptors which are hierarchical and developmental. It can be used with students to help them understand the higher order, more meaning oriented objectives of learning on their course whilst having a clear idea of where they stand at the moment.

A further practical outcome of this study is the use of the matrix as a tool for curriculum design (Appendix 2). In establishing the level descriptors, a course team might wish to develop stage and module or project learning outcomes which relate to those in the matrix. The two axes invite course designers to consider the integrated nature of the descriptors, bringing subject conceptions and learning and teaching conceptions together. This profiling methodology provides a richer and more integrated characterisation of the learner at certain stages in their development than might be using differentiated approaches captured in individuated learning outcomes or assessment criteria.

References

Biggs, JB and Collis, KF (1982). *Evaluating the Quality of Learning: The SOLO Taxonomy*. New York: Academic Press.

Biggs, J (1999). *Teaching for Quality Learning at University*. Buckingham: SRHE and Open University Press.

Bond, C and LeBrun, M (1996). Promoting Learning in Law. *Legal Education Review* **17**(1).

Bowden, J (1996). Phenomenographic research – some methodological issues. In Dall'Alba, G and Hasselgren, B (Eds), *Reflections on Phenomenography*, Göteborg Studies in Educational Sciences 109, Sweden.

Bruce, CS and Gerber, R (1995). Towards university lecturers' conceptions of student learning. *Higher Education*, **29**, 443–458.

Crawford, K, Gordon, S, Nicholas, J and Prosser, M (1994). Conceptions of mathematics and how it is learned: perspectives of students entering university. *Learning and Instruction*, **4**, 331–345.

Davies, A and Reid, A (2001). Uncovering Problematics in Design Education: Learning and the Design Entity. In Swann, C. and Young, E. (Eds) *Re-Inventing Design Education in the University: Proceedings of the International Conference*, pp 178–184. School of Design, Curtin University, Perth.

Dortins, E (2002). Reflections on phenomenographic process: Interview, transcription and analysis. In Goody, A, Herrington, J and Northcote, M (Eds), *Quality Conversations: Research and Development in Higher Education*, **25**, 207–213.

Drew, L (2000). A disciplined approach: Learning to practice as design teachers in the University. In Swann, C and Young, E (Eds), *Re-Inventing Design Education in the University: Proceedings of the International Conference.* School of Design, Curtin University, Perth.

Entwistle, N and Marton, F (1994). Knowledge objects: understandings constituted through intensive academic study. *British Journal of Educational Psychology*, **64**, 161–178.

Garrick, J and Rhodes, C (2000). (Eds), *Research and Knowledge at Work: Perspectives, Case-Studies and Innovative Strategies.* London: Routledge.

Kember, D (1997). A reconceptualisation of the research into university academics' conceptions of teaching. *Learning and Instruction*, **7**, 255–275.

Petocz, P and Reid, A (2002). Enhancing learning using generic and specific aspects of knowledge formation. In Goody, A and Ingram, D (Eds), *Spheres of Influence: Ventures and Visions in Educational Development.* Crawley, WA: Organisational and Staff Development Services, The University of Western Australia. [Online] Available at www.csd.uwa.edu.au/ICED2002/publication/.

Petocz P and Reid A, (2001) Students' experience of learning in statistics, *Quaestiones Mathematicae*, Supplement, **1**, 37-45.

Prosser, M and Trigwell, K (1999). *Understanding Learning and Teaching.* Buckingham: SRHE and Open University Press.

Prosser, M, Trigwell, K and Taylor, P (1994). A Phenomenographic Study of Academics' Conceptions of Science Learning and Teaching. *Learning and Instruction*, **4**, 217-232.

Ramsden, P (1992). *Learning to Teach in Higher Education.* London: Routledge.

Reid, A (1997). The Meaning of Music and the Understanding of Teaching and Learning in the Instrumental Lesson. In Gabrielsson, A (Ed), *Proceedings of the Third Triennial European Society for the Cognitive Science in Music Conference.* Uppsala: Uppsala University, **3**, 200 - 205.

Reid, A (1999). Conceptions of Teaching and Learning Instrumental and Vocal Music. PhD Thesis, University of Technology, Sydney.

Reid, A (2000b). Musicians' Experience of the Musical World: Relations with teaching and learning. In Rust, C (Ed), *Improving Student Learning: Improving Learning Through the Disciplines* pp168-184. Oxford: Oxford Centre for Staff Develpment.

Reid, A (2001). Variation in the Ways that Instrumental and Vocal Students Experience Learning Music. *Music Education Research*, **3**, 1, 25–40.

Reid, A and Petocz, P(2002a). Learning about Statistics and Statistics Learning. *Problematic Futures: Educational Research in an Era of Uncertainty*, Australian Association for Research in Education conference. Brisbane.

Reid, A and Petocz, P (2002b). Students Conceptions of Statistics: A Phenomenographic Study, *Journal of Statistics Education*. Volume 11. http://www.amstat.org/publications/jse/jse_index.html

Samuelowicz, K and Bain, JD (1992). Conceptions of teaching held by academic teachers. *Higher Education*, **24**, 93-111.

Appendix 1

Students' conceptions of learning design			
subject learning and teaching	**Extrinsic technical** (doing)	**Extrinsic meaning** (interpreting)	**Intrinsic meaning** (living)
Uni-structural	The outcome is entirely skills focused and is intended to provide the 'right' answer. The student will have relied heavily on the teacher for advice in the belief that the teacher knows the 'right' answer.	The outcome will demonstrate a recognition that design is about problem solving but there will only be one obvious answer. The student will rely on the teacher to confirm the appropriateness of the solution.	The purpose of the design outcome will be seen within a social context but the skills developed will be inappropriate to achieve these ambitions.
Multi-structural	The outcome is about learning lots of skills in preparation for work. The student will be able to provide a list of skills acquired. The student will be reliant on the teacher for advice.	The outcome will demonstrate a recognition that design is about problem solving and there will be several possible distinct answers proposed. The articulation of these outcomes will be predominantly descriptive.	The purpose of the design outcome will be seen within a social context. Several skills will be developed through experimentation but there will be a disjunction between aspiration and fulfilment.
Relational	The outcomes are skills focused with an understanding of the interrelationships and hierarchies of techniques required in the design profession. The student will be motivated to explain their insights to others including their teachers	The outcomes will involve alternative solutions to the problems defined using appropriate skills. It will be clear that transformation of knowledge of the subject is taking place. Skills and knowledge are integrated and the student will regard the teacher as one expert amongst many others who can be drawn upon.	The outcome will be articulated within a social context and relate to the needs of the audience/consumers. Design is seen as identifying and solving problems within a moral and social context
Extended abstract	The outcome will be the application of their knowledge of skills to support design solutions. The student will use their own initiative in seeking to develop and improve techniques and skills in design by using developments within and beyond the design paradigm.	The outcomes will be about searching for solutions beyond the design paradigm. Students will be able to apply their understanding of problem solving in a range of different contexts and identify appropriate skills and techniques. The student will be an independent learner.	Learning is seen as self-discovery. Being a designer is seen as being a change-agent in society. There will be a strong focus on self-expression, reflection and integration of design principles, abilities and social values. The student will be an autonomous learner

Appendix 2

skills ←———————————————————————→ abilities

dependence / autonomy — subject / learning and teaching	Extrinsic technical (doing)	Extrinsic meaning (interpreting)	Intrinsic meaning (living)
Uni-structural			
Multi-structural			
Relational			
Extended abstract			

8 The Kolb Cycle, reflection and all that... what is new?

Elisabet Weedon and John Cowan

UHI Millennium Institute

Keywords: Reflection, Kolb Cycle, capabilities, process analysis, constructivism and social constructivism.

Abstract

This paper examines whether the use of the Kolb cycle as a basis for reflective practice has changed over the past ten years and looks at some of the issues in relation to the use of reflection in Higher Education (HE). The paper starts with an overview of the conference presentation. The discussion engendered by this presentation is then summarised. The final part of the paper considers matters arising out of this discussion. It starts with a brief review of some of the issues in relation to the development of reflective abilities and considers the definition of the word 'reflection'. It then explores the possible need for greater differentiation between different types of reflective activities. The need to evaluate the role of reflection in learning and development is then considered. The conclusion makes some tentative suggestions in terms of possible future directions for HE practitioners in this area.

8.1 Introduction

Our seminar presentation at the 10th ISL conference aimed to contribute to the conference theme in two main ways: by suggesting the extent to which the use of the Kolb Cycle as a basis for reflective practice had changed over the past 10 years; and by engaging colleagues at the conference with us in exploring our suggestions. Our presentation therefore focused on four questions:

What was our practice 10 years ago?

What is it now?

How has it changed?

How is it likely to change further?

For that reason this paper is in three parts:

- An outline of the presentation made to initiate discussion.

- A summary of the points made by the participants, (which have been checked out subsequently with those who left email addresses for that purpose)

- Our own further thoughts, post-conference, arising from the seminar, and written in more traditional format.

8.2   The presentation

In an attempt to ensure a common understanding, the presentation started with a definition of what we saw as useful concepts and terms.   These were constructivism, social constructivism and the Kolb Cycle.

We took constructivism to be that view of learning which sees understanding as actively constructed by the learners themselves, based upon their experiences. As Piaget stated:

> ... thought can neither be a translation nor even a simple continuation of sensory-motor processes in a symbolic form ... it is necessary from the start to reconstruct everything on a new plane. (Piaget, 1950/2001, p 134).

We then took socio-constructivism to be that view of learning which sees understanding as constructed similarly, but with interaction with others being a major factor in the process. We argued that these two definitions stem from Piagetian, neo-Piagetian and Vygotskian (eg Wertsch, 1985) perspectives.

We proposed that the familiar Kolb Cycle (Fig 1) reflects a constructivist approach (eg Kolb, 1984). Beginning either from experiences or from an input generalisation, the learner cycles through reflection into generalisations, and then on via planning for active experimentation (with that generalisation), into the next experiences; and so on to the review of generalisations. For some time this Cycle has informed our own teaching, and, we suggested, that of others concerned for the development of what we prefer to call capabilities.

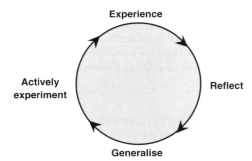

Figure 8.1   The Kolb Cycle

We went on to outline how our own experiences in relation to changes in theoretical underpinnings had impacted on our own practice over the past ten years. One of us (JC) had had 20 years of experience of prompting students to ask, and answer "How do I... ?", with the aim of taking that generalisation straight on into the next similar experience. He has done this in situations where the main interaction for the learner was with the tutor – in activities ranging from the labour-intensive commenting on learning journals to activities with a high student/staff ratio [approximately 130 students to 1 tutor (Cowan, 1998)] working in small tutor-less groups. In that form of activity, interaction between peers was somewhat incidental, and certainly unstructured.

The other of us (EW) had had extensive experience of UK Open University tutoring on courses where the development of capabilities was stressed, and constructivist principles were explicitly emphasised. In this work, her focus had been upon the individual student, and the development of study skills, for the learning materials were centrally produced by course teams. The tutor's role in terms of student learning had thus been mainly supportive and facilitative. Nevertheless, she had had a growing recognition of the role of social interactions in learning, and increasingly sought to develop activities which were structured to take into account the role of others in an individual's learning.

We next presented our impression of what we recalled being around us in 1992, in terms of the approaches being followed to the development of capabilities. We saw:

- The Kolb Cycle in vogue, whatever words those who claimed to follow it placed around the perimeter of Fig 1

- A strong emphasis on asking students to think about how they did the things that were demanded of them

- Focus in this on individual thinking, analysing and answering

- A general vagueness, on the part of both teachers and students, about what reflection entails, its pedagogy and its facilitation

- A tendency for activities to follow a "half-cycle Kolb" (Fig 2), with reflection and generalisation leading straight into the next experiences – and little stress on active experimentation or iteration

- Links to the work of Schön, which anecdotal evidence suggested were made by people who often appeared to refer to texts which they had not read, and which they took to describe the same "reflection" as did Kolb

- Facilitation by the teachers of (by implication) individual thinking

- A constructivist approach, even if those who followed it were unaware of that title

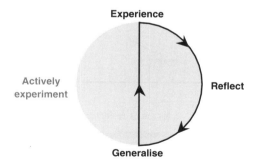

Figure 8.2   The Half Kolb Cycle

We moved from there to what we see as the current situation amongst the leaders in practice, in 2002. Characteristic of such practice, we identified and tried to exemplify from our own practice:

- A separation of "How?" from "How well?", as the questions providing foci for reflection

- Consequent development of activities which we suggested would be more accurately and helpfully described as process analysis and self-evaluation

- A growing stress on, and provision for, active experimentation

- A strong dependence on evaluative reflection, at the outset of any programme for the development of capabilities, and at the end

- Growing recognition of the role and potential of social interactions in learning and development. In this context, we suggest that that those who plan learning and teaching activities are providing, to a greater or lesser extent, for reflection-in-action, on-action, and for-action (Fig 3). Consequently, there is

  - More planned activity between peers – such as group reporting, peer-questioning and group summarising

  - Intermental processes (developing understanding through negotiation for meaning with others) leading into intramental processes.

  - The potential for constructive interactions within a learner's zone of proximal development (eg Wertsch, op cit)

  - Facilitation which depends upon, and harnesses, peer interaction

  - A socio-constructivist approach

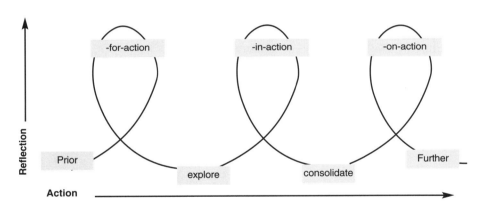

Figure 8.3   The Cowan Diagram – 3 forms of reflection

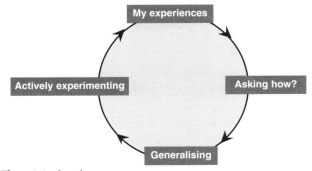

Figure 8.4   The original pedagogy

Hence the original pedagogy (which was described without going outside the personal activity of the reflective and developing learner in Fig 4) has become, for some at least, the developed pedagogy of Fig 5, in which "others" includes both tutors and fellow learners.

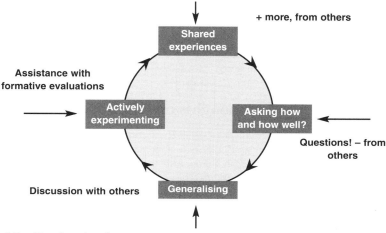

Figure 8.5   Developed pedagogy

8.3   The points made by participants in the conference discussion

The questions we tabled were:
1. Did we describe the status quo reasonably accurately?
2. Have we described the changes over the past ten years fairly?
3. Is socio-constructivism on the increase?
4. One way or another, has facilitation of the development of capabilities advanced in these ten years?

The main themes from the responses of the participants in this seminar (which we have circulated to participants in full, and are available on request) can be summarised as:

Question 1

- The majority of responses supported our description of the 1992 position, with one or two notable dissensions

- There was a sense that the vocabulary used, eg "constructivism" and "Kolb Cycle" may not have been used extensively across the HE sector in 1992. One participant helpfully supported our view that while the terms might not have been used, the practice may nonetheless have reflected the underlying principles of these concepts

Questions 2 to 4

- There has been a growing recognition of social constructivism, but this is patchy

- There is a gulf between researchers in this area and academics; change has occurred but not across the whole of the HE sector

- There is an increasing problem with the growth in number of students and lack of resources, which is hampering change towards a reflective culture in 2002

- The development of capabilities is now more prominent – as evidenced, for example, by portfolio type assessments

This is our summary of the comments made by participants. Those who left an email address were offered the opportunity to comment on the full set of comments as recorded at the conference, but no one chose to suggest amendments or additions. We therefore assume that we have represented the views presented reasonably accurately. In the remainder of this paper, we will explore our own position, post-conference.

8.4   Our own further thoughts on developing capabilities

Following the Dearing (1997) and Garrick (1997) reports there has been considerable emphasis on the development of 'graduateness'. One aspect of this 'graduateness' is the development of capabilities rather than the assimilation of subject-specific content. This emphasis on the development of capabilities has led to an increasing importance being placed on the role of reflection in the process of learning rather than focusing on the product of learning. Recent curriculum development within the new UHI Millennium Institute and other institutions (eg Stewart & Richardson, 2000) has demonstrated this trend with the inclusion of learning journals, reflective journals and logs as part of both the formative and summative assessments in courses. The same is the case for other HE institutions, prompted by the Quality Assurance Agency (QAA) requirements in relation to Personal Development Planning (PDP) which also support this development.

However the seminar presentation and, in particular, the discussion that followed, demonstrated that the inclusion of a capability based curriculum incorporating reflection is a contentious area. This final part of the paper therefore opens with a brief review of some of the issues in relation to the development of reflective abilities, and the very definition of the term 'reflection'. It then explores the possible need for greater differentiation between different types of reflective activities, with different forms and purposes – and, possibly, titles.

The need to evaluate the role of reflection in learning and development is then considered, in relation to examples of our own practice. We recognise that there is a need to evaluate, in some form or another, the extent to which reflection leads to the development of capabilities; this will be explored after an examination of different types of reflection. We would also argue that evaluation of the role of another's input in that process is necessary; however, that will not be considered in this paper. One aspect of this, the role of commenting on students' reflective journals, was considered at last year's conference (Weedon & Cowan, 2001). We conclude with some tentative suggestions of where HE practitioners might best head next in this area.

8.5   Reflection – definitions, distinctions and implications for practice

There is now a considerable literature on reflection. It is clear (Moon, 1999) that reflection has been developed in a range of disciplines and in various cross-disciplinary settings. This has led to a range of studies which are generally unrelated – often with the only common element being reference to the original work of Dewey, Habermas and Schön. It is also perhaps necessary to make a distinction in terms of reflection in relation to practice, such as advocated by Schön (1983); and reflection in relation to the development of capabilities in undergraduate curricula and elsewhere. Reflective practice in relation to work has been particularly emphasised in relation to nursing, teacher training and social work. It could be argued that this differs considerably from the use of reflection within undergraduate courses. Within the former, the emphasis has been on reflection on actual practical experience, whilst the latter focuses on experiences of learning per se.

In addition to the need to make a distinction between at least these two different areas where reflection is being applied, it must also be recognised that there is still no clear definition of the word 'reflection'.

Moon (1999) has suggested that the word "reflection" implies:

> … a form of mental processing with a purpose and/or an anticipated outcome that is applied to relatively complicated or uncomplicated ideas for which there is not an obvious solution.

this being a process which is initiated "in a state of doubt, uncertainty or difficulty" (Moon, op cit). She thus takes us beyond Dewey, for whom reflection was "the kind of thinking that consists in turning a subject over in the mind and giving it serious thought" (Dewey, 1933). Moon further commented on the difficulties surrounding the understanding of the word 'reflection' in that differing interpretations included the following terms: reasoning, thinking, reviewing, problem solving, inquiry, reflective judgement, reflective thinking, critical reflection and reflective practice. Recent thinking, (Clegg et al, 2002) comment on the lack of clarity of Schön's concepts. Kember (2000) reminds us that Mezirow distinguished between non-reflective and reflective action. Our own discussions with colleagues at conferences and workshops across the country has indicated that there is a lack of consensus of the meaning of the term and that for many this has led to a difficulty in incorporating reflective practice into the curriculum. We recognise that this is anecdotal evidence, but it does seem to be supported by the literature.

The practical issues in implementing reflective practice within undergraduate and postgraduate courses are now known and evident in the literature (eg Clegg, et al, op cit and Stewart & Richardson, op cit). Clegg et al focus on implementing reflective practice within continuing professional development (CPD), and examine the tension between action and reflection. They report on two case studies and consider the way in which reflection was used by participants on two different courses. They question the role of reflection as a promoter/driver of change in practice, but interestingly report only their findings from interviews with participants, and do not consider whether the workshop activities which were provided effectively promoted reflective practice. The way that the journaling was supported, for example, through dialogue with another person, is not considered.

In our presentation we had explored the value of the Kolb Cycle as a model within which to consider how we interact with students to encourage reflection on learning. We noted that our earlier use of this model had led us to focus on one half of that circle (see Fig 2), with active experimentation being neglected. We also argued that our earlier use of the model had led us to focus on the individual and not on the interactions which that individual might have had with others in the process of harnessing reflective abilities to further professional development. This is significantly different from the approach of Clegg et al (op cit), who seem to remain focused on the experience for the individual rather than consider the input of others in intermental development of reflective abilities.

8.5.1   Different types and forms of 'reflection'?

The lack of precision in terms of definition of the word reflection as evidenced in the literature leads us to suggest the need to differentiate firmly between different types of reflection. It further prompts us to question:

- The extent to which the Kolb Cycle is relevant to these different types of reflection

- The need to consider the contexts within which different types of reflection might be most appropriate

- The role of others in promoting reflection

- The extent to which different types of learners, or learners at different stages of learning and development, require different types of reflective tasks

We therefore suggest that it is worthwhile to consider several types of reflective activities and their purposes, all of which feature in Moon's analysis (1999), without being as strictly differentiated there as we suggest below.

We find it helpful if not essential in our planning and teaching to differentiate between:

1. **Process analysis**, which occurs when we engage people in thinking about how they do particular tasks which bear a family resemblance to each other, and prompt them to try to generalise. A student is engaged in process analysis when s/he starts to think through precisely how s/he tackles a particular task such as, for example, searching for information on the web or reading a research article. Such analysis could be linked to reflection in action and reflection for action.

2. **Self-evaluation**, which occurs when people formulate judgements about their present performance, usually with intent to bring about improvement or to satisfy themselves that improvement is not needed in the meantime. An example of self-evaluation is the teacher who scrutinises the impact of her feedback on the working of student groups, and judges it less effective than she would have wished. Such self-evaluation can be linked to reflection-on-action and possibly reflection-for-action. Reflection-for-action would be demonstrated if the teacher identified the changes she wished to be able to make in her provision of feedback.

3. **Critical incident analysis**, which differs from the two above in that it examines an episode, for example a teaching session, and encourages the individual to identify any particular aspect of that session which was particularly noteworthy. An exploration of that incident, through reflection, can aid in developing a deeper understanding of a particular aspect of that practice.

4. **Searching for a solution**, which, in total contrast, begins from a carefully considered question which is important to the learner. This question differs from one that may emerge out of a critical incident, in that it is forward looking, and need not necessarily go on to involve process analysis or self-evaluation. It continues into a search for an answer, or part answer, which may be of assistance to the person reflecting. A student in a group project situation would be searching for a solution if s/he took time to think or write about possible answers to the question: "What is the most effective way that I can encourage contributions from the whole group when I next chair a group meeting?"

Finally it is perhaps worth noting the occurrence of a different kind of reflection – one that happens almost by chance, as the result of a particular incident and prompts reflection in its own right. This contrasts with previous types of reflection, in that the starting point is not based on a conscious attempt to reflect, rather that it arises out of a situation, and is usually true reflection-in-action.

5. **Serendipitous reflection**, which begins when, for no reason that we can identify at the time, we suddenly perceive, question, spot another option, or have an insight. Serendipity may come to the aid of an engineering teacher if he suddenly notices that students respond much better to being asked for the "headings" under which they will judge their design – rather than the "criteria" – and wonders what that observation says to him about his practice.

We will now move on to look in some detail at two of these types and purposes of reflection, in our own practice, and to derive from that our use, and non-use of the Kolb Cycle in the future.

8.5.2   Process analysis in practice: an example

Working with project groups, we have facilitated activities in which students are expected to regularly take a short "time out", in which we have pushed them to identify, but in general terms, how they are tackling the tasks they are encountering. Usually they are at first unable even to describe in general terms what sequence their activities have taken, what demands these have entailed, and how they have been making their decisions. We find that, when they begin to arrive at generalisable and detailed summaries, their particular performances tend to improve markedly. The result has usually been that, next time round, they don't need to be persuaded to take time out to think about what they are doing and how they are doing it. They have recognised the usefulness of doing that.

An example of this occurred in a regularly written reflective journal. One of our students was in the habit, required by her course, of keeping a weekly journal to focus on questions of import to her, and to strive to make progress towards an answer by so doing. One week she found herself about to undertake semi-structured interviews – an activity she had considered in theory, but had never experienced. Almost in panic, her question for the week was "What should I do in the interviews, and how on earth can I prepare myself for this?" In that journal, she made considerable progress. A week later, she asked herself what she had learnt from this experience, which she could transfer elsewhere. She described with enthusiasm that she had learnt that it made sense to consider and lay plans, and after putting them into practice, to rush back home, after each interview, to think hard about what had gone well, what had gone less well, and what should be changed – and how she could check the effectiveness of such changes. She did not write in terms of "active experimentation", but she exemplified and reported just that process. In a mere week of facilitated searching for a solution to her question, she had learnt a great deal also about the role of active experimentation, and of repeated and iterative circling round the Cycle.

Process analysis leads to the specification, active experimentation with, and consequent development of generically perceived capabilities.

8.5.3   Searching for a solution in practice: an example

Another student, working to the same remit, chose to engage in an early journal with the questions of current import to her, and to strive to make progress towards and answer by so doing. In an early journal entry, she chose to engage with the question "What do they mean when they ask me to reflect". After a page or so of engaging with this question, she came to the conclusion that reflection was a process which would lead her to having what she described as a "Geronimo" experience. She then posed for herself the consequent question "What should I do, to bring about such useful outcomes for me?" After a page or so of wrestling with this question, she broke off in mid-sentence to note "Wait a minute, wait a minute, I think I feel another Geronimo coming on." It did, and that was a powerful example of reflective searching for (two) solutions to questions which concerned the reflective writer.

In structuring both of these types of reflections we had been minded of the Kolb Cycle in developing the tasks for the students. Yet while in the first example this was relevant, the second hardly led to a generalisation with which the writer could have actively experimented. Analysis of our students' use of reflection in searching for a solution led us to question the extent to which the students did – or indeed could – complete the full cycle. For that reason we have developed structured activities based on process analysis which ask for reflection on undertaking a task, and the subsequent testing out of the conclusion of the reflection, through active experimentation.

8.6 Evaluation of the impact of reflection on learning

As stated above, the role of reflection within the curriculum is contentious. One of the reasons for this is likely to be the difficulty of measuring the impact of reflection on process and its subsequent contribution to a student's learning. It is clear (Kember, 2000) that there has been a proliferation of courses that claim to include reflection on learning or practice This led Kember et al to develop a questionnaire to measure the level of reflective thinking. They argued that development of a questionnaire was essential, as other means of exploring the development of reflective thinking were too time consuming for large numbers of students. The questionnaire developed consisted of sixteen questions based on four different dimensions: habitual action, understanding, reflection and critical reflection. The measurement was based on a five point Likert scale ('definitely agree' to 'definitely disagree'). The statistical evidence suggested that this questionnaire was reliable; however, given the difficulties involved in defining 'reflective thinking' in a precise manner, we suggest that there are grounds for questioning the construct validity of this approach. This reservation is perhaps worthy of further exploration, as might be the development of this questionnaire to allow for some open-ended questions to probe for evidence of the kind of thinking claimed by the students.

In making that last comment, we are aware that our own approach to evaluating the impact of reflection has been somewhat different. We have included in our reflective journalling programmes one (final) submission which asks the students to identify their own development and to evidence these claims from their journals and other work they have undertaken on the module. These submissions seem to us to present more information and evidence of the impact of reflection than the responses to the Kember et al questionnaire. They do evidence and instance the development of capabilities; and this can be linked to reflection in the cases where the students have fully engaged in the tasks. There is also evidence that some students, who have avoided engaging in reflection, have therefore (consistently) claimed that reflection has not helped them in the development of their capabilities. This form of evaluation has provided us with interesting insights and has also prompted us to restructure the tasks more demandingly. For that reason we are now engaging the students explicitly in process analysis tasks rather than in simply writing reflective journals.

The tension between the need for statistically reliable methods of testing, based on a positivist position, and the need for a more qualitative analysis reflecting the phenomenographic stance, is an interesting one. It seems that Schön's initial reason for advocating reflective practice and an acceptance of the usefulness of an activity in what he termed the 'swampy marshlands' (Schön, 1983), was a rejection of the positivist approach. Yet in this quest, an essential quest, for evidence to support interventions in student learning, it seems that some have turned towards psychometric, statistically validated measurement. Maybe there is a need to recognise the complementarity of these two approaches rather than seeing them as conflicting. Thus we argue the desirability of combining the two when aiming to measure the impact of reflection on the development of capability.

8.7 Conclusion

The question which we tabled for consideration during the conference was whether the use of the Kolb Cycle in relation to development of reflective abilities has changed over the past ten years. We started, then, as here, by exploring if our own description of educational practice (in this area) ten years ago was reasonable and whether our subsequent description of the changes which followed was valid. The discussion during our conference presentation offered reasonable support for our stance. Whilst the dialogue was not continued post-conference, our own further thinking was influenced by the contributions of the seminar participants. We have tried to outline that in the final part of this paper.

We conclude that the Kolb Cycle:

- Does provide one model for exploring the development of capabilities through reflective activities

- Needs to incorporate the role of others in promoting development of reflective abilities, at least in relation to development of such abilities amongst undergraduate students

- Offers us a way of exploring deliberately differing interventions at different points of the cycle.

- Is not relevant to all forms of reflection.

We argue that there is a need for considerably more research and exploration of the impact of reflection on learning and on the development of capabilities. Whilst the use of well validated questionnaires to explore any such impact might be one useful tool, it seems that these, unless further developed, will not necessarily provide meaningful evidencing of development.

References

Clegg, S, Tan, J and Saedi, S (2002). Reflecting or acting? Reflective practice and continuing professional development in higher education. *Reflective Practice*, **3**(1) 131–146.

Cowan, J (1998). *On becoming an innovative university teacher: reflection in action*, Buckingham: SRHE and The Open University Press.

Dewey, J (1933). *How we think.* Boston, MA: DC Heath & Co.

Kember, D and Leung, D (2000). Development of a questionnaire to measure the level of reflective thinking. *Assessment and Evaluation in Higher Education*, **25**(4), pp 381–395.

Kolb, DA (1984). *Experiential learning: Experience as the source of learning and development*, New Jersey: Prentice Hall

Moon, J (1999). *Reflection in learning and professional development,* London: Kogan Page.

Piaget, J (2001) *The psychology of intelligence,* London: Routledge.

Recommendations of the National (Dearing) Committee of Inquiry into Higher Education, (1997) HMSO.

Recommendations of the Scottish (Garrick) Committee of the National (Dearing) Committee of Inquiry into Higher Education, (1997) HMSO.

Schön, D (1983) *The reflective practitioner.* New York: Basic Books.

Stewart, S and Richardson, B (2000). Reflection and its place in the curriculum on an undergraduate course: should it be assessed? *Assessment and Evaluation in Higher Education,* **25**(4), pp 369–380.

Weedon, E and Cowan, J (2001) Commenting electronically on students' reflective journals: how can we explore its effectiveness? In Rust, C (Ed), *Improving student learning using learning technology,* Oxford: Oxford Centre for staff and learning development.

Wertsch, J (1985). *Vygotsky and the social formation of mind.* Massachusetts: Harvard University Press

9 Students' experiences of learning to present

Dai Hounsell and Velda McCune

University of Edinburgh

Keywords   learning, oral presentations, students' experiences,

Abstract

This exploratory study sought a fuller understanding of oral presentations as an aspect of undergraduate students' experiences of learning. Semi-structured group interviews were undertaken with 39 students in three honours-level courses in the physical sciences, the social sciences and the humanities. The paper focuses on one of the two principal themes which emerged from the analysis of the interviews: students' experiences of learning how to present effectively. Six sources of influence on the students' experiences are identified: prior experiences of presenting; tutors' guidance and support; the students' experiences both of giving the talk and of handling post-talk questions, comments and discussion; tutors' feedback; and learning from other students' presentations. These influences are seen as mediated by students' emerging grasp of what will be appropriate and feasible for them in presenting effectively, and thus contributing to the evolution of personal styles of presenting.

9.1   Introduction

Undergraduate oral presentations represent an interesting paradox. While their teaching counterpart, the lecture, is still widely and enthusiastically used by large numbers of academic staff in higher education as a means of communicating their subject, the prevalence of oral presentations, though growing, seems substantially lower. Their use in many universities appears to be occasional rather than regular, to vary markedly across subjects and levels, and to be confined to that minority of staff who recognise the benefits to be gained. Similarly, their formal weighting in schemes of assessment is often negligible or zero, presumably reflecting a number of concerns often raised by staff. One is how students' presentations might feasibly be evaluated – a further paradox, this, given the ubiquitousness of questionnaires eliciting students' ratings of teaching. Another concern is, more pointedly, how to ensure that style does not override substance – the problem of the flashy but vacuous presenter. And a third reservation arises from anxieties about how the validity of a grade might be checked or confirmed, given that presentations cannot be held on file unless they are videotaped, which is cumbersome and costly.

Yet while concerns such as these are important, they tend to spring from the standpoints of staff in their roles as assessors and course managers. What has been rather less to the fore, but merits just as much attention, is a students' eye-view of oral presentations. Here we report an exploratory study which aimed to gain a better understanding of students' experiences of learning-to-present.

9.2 Background

A review of the literature on oral presentations in higher education yields only a modest crop of findings, predominantly from small-scale studies of practices in a single course unit or module, and geared in the main to questions of assessment. One cluster of papers (Hay, 1994; Hyland, 1996; Mindham, 1998; Roach, 1999) centres around the generation of criteria to evaluate the quality of student presentations. A second cluster (Lapham and Webster,1999; Cheng and Warren, 1999; MacAlpine, 1999) concentrates on the potential for peer assessment, taking advantage of the fact that students typically give their presentations to an audience which includes their peers. Only Joughin (1999) has attempted a wider set of reflections on oral assessment in general.

In consequence, oral presentations have not been subject to the more searching empirical investigations of students' experiences of learning which have been undertaken on other commonplace undergraduate study activities such as academic reading (Säljö, 1988; Mann, 2000), essay-writing (Hounsell, 1997; Campbell, Smith and Brooker, 1998; McCune, in press), or self-directed projects (Taylor, 1986). We therefore know little about what is entailed in presenting, from the vantage-point of students, and to what extent the pedagogical demands of presenting are similar to, or different from, those of more conventional coursework assignments. Nor do we have a secure grasp of the potential impact of opening up the work of individual students to collective peer display.

In grappling with such questions, our exploratory investigation had its origins in the studies of academic tasks already referred to and a much larger body of experiential and phenomenographic research on students learning (see for example Marton et al, 1997; Bruce and Gerber, 1997; Prosser and Trigwell, 1999). From the outset, however, our intention was not to categorise differences between individuals (eg in their approaches to or conceptions of oral presentations), but rather to try to capture the most salient aspects of the students' collective experiences. In that respect, the research design was more akin to the work of Taylor (1986) on self-directed projects than to that of many more overtly phenomenographic studies.

9.2.1 Research design, samples and settings

The data for the exploratory study were gathered by means of ten semi-structured group interviews with a total of 39 students in course settings in three contrasting subject areas: Humanities (13 students), Social Sciences (14 students), and Physical Sciences (12 students). The three courses concerned were third or final-year Honours-level course units in two Scottish universities. In each course, the students were expected to give a prepared talk and then respond to questions and comments. All of the presentations were linked to written work which was formally assessed. However, the precise requirements varied:

- In the Social Sciences course, 20 minutes was allocated for the talk component and a further 10 minutes for questions and comments. All of the students together with their tutor made up the audience for the presentations, which were linked to an essay which was written up and submitted subsequently.

- In the Physical Sciences course, 15 minutes was allocated for the talk component and 5 minutes for discussion. The presentations were given to a sub-set of the students together with some of their tutors and supervisors, and were based on written reports which the students were required to submit prior to making their presentations.

- The presentations of the students following the Humanities course were not linked to a specified coursework assignment, but were on topics which formed the basis for questions in the later final examinations. The presentations were expected to last for 10–15 minutes, and to lead into tutorial discussion involving all of the students in the group and their tutor.

The group interviews took place as close as was feasible to the time when the presentations were given. Questions raised in the interviews aimed to explore any prior experiences the students had had of oral presentations, within their undergraduate studies or elsewhere; how they had gone about preparing for and delivering their presentations; their experiences of giving the prepared talk component of the presentation and of handling the subsequent discussion; tutor's guidance and feedback; and the students' perceptions of what made for an effective oral presentation.

The ten interviews were tape-recorded and later transcribed in full. All of the transcripts were analysed by both researchers, with the aim of identifying significant issues and concerns associated with the students' experiences. Two principal themes emerged from the analyses: first, the 'sense of audience' displayed by the students in relation to their presentations and the stratagems they pursued to meet their audiences' needs (Hounsell and McCune, 2000); and second, key influences on the students' development of their expertise as presenters, ie learning-to-present. Here we review our findings on that second theme, accompanied by selected extracts from the group interviews. A much fuller substantiation of the findings has been given elsewhere (Hounsell and McCune, 2001).

9.3   Findings on learning-to-present

Our findings are summarised in figure 9.1, which identifies the main influences on the students' development of their expertise as presenters. One set of influences preceded the presentation itself, and comprised the students' prior experiences of presenting together with the guidance they had been given by their tutors on making presentations. A second arose from the experiences, often anxiety-laden, of giving a prepared talk and handling the subsequent discussion, but also extended to what the students were able to learn from observing the presentations of their peers.

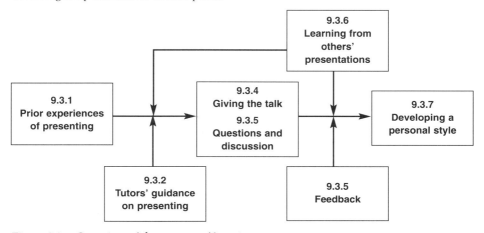

Figure 9.1   Overview of the process of learning to present

The third source of influence was feedback from tutors to students on the quality of their presentations. All of these influences could be seen as having an impact, to greater or lesser degrees, on the development by the students of personal styles of presenting. Each of these influences is now considered in turn, drawing on illustrative extracts from the interviews.

9.3.1 Prior experiences of presenting

Most of the students had had some previous experiences of presenting, whether at school, in earlier university courses, or in employment. For some, that prior experience had been helpful in developing their confidence and introducing them to the skills called for; for others, the experience had been rather more mixed:

> It was a really bad talk we had to give in 2nd year... had to give a talk about our labs and that was so stupid!... They didn't tell you things like, 'Don't put big tables up there', 'Don't put too many graphs up because they're stupid'. And so it ended up being really unenjoyable... And this one was much better because at least we're a bit wiser now. (Physical sciences)

> I've done talks myself individually just for different things... it gives you the confidence so you know that its okay that you'll be able to do it, but apart from that it didn't really help me because it just depends on how well you know the material, I think, and the people as well. Normally I'm far more forthcoming with ideas like audience and eye contact, but today I just felt really embarrassed (Social sciences)

9.3.2 Tutors' guidance on presenting

The pre-presentation guidance given by tutors differed markedly across the three course settings. In the physical sciences, advice in the course handbook was linked to a workshop on giving presentations. Students had reacted to the workshop in contrasting ways: as the two following extracts from the interviews make clear:

> Really what we wanted was reassuring that this is what you should do. We didn't want, 'What you shouldn't do – here's how not to give a talk'. We wanted, 'Here's how to give a talk and be confident about it'. (Physical sciences)

> They advise you, if you are using detailed overheads, don't use more than 5. I had 14 slides, there was actually nothing on each slide, hardly anything. So when I was looking at the screen... I knew where it was going to and I could just talk through the bullet points I had. (Physical sciences)

In social sciences, the course tutor had led a seminar discussion on oral presentations, supported by a handout. The students were not expected to read a formal paper, but should follow a given structure, provide a summary handout, and use visual aids as required. The guidance offered had generally been well-received:

> There was quite detailed advice in the handouts that she gave us, had like websites listed and stuff, it also gave an outline of every section... the sections you should split your presentation up into, what she wanted to see... I found it helpful. (Social sciences)

In the humanities, the course handbook had advised students that their presentations were intended to be starting-points for seminar discussion, that they might find it helpful to write out their presentation in full, and that further advice would be given by tutors.

> They give you, like, a little bit of advice but it's not formal. It's just sort of, 'Don't speak for more than 10 minutes if you can help it' and, 'Just try and make it as interesting as possible'... Some of them say you can bring in handouts and use other materials. (Humanities)

9.3.3   Giving the talk

One of the most striking features of students' interview accounts was the extent to which their levels of anxiety or confidence had coloured their experiences of presenting.

> The first talk was very interesting, but I was just sitting there going, 'It's me next! It's me next!' Being absolutely terrified. (Physical sciences)

> I'm not particularly outgoing and don't enjoy speaking in front of lots of people really. I don't have enough confidence in my own ideas and hopefully that is something I can develop. (Social sciences)

Prior experience could sometimes help to lessen anxiety, as could being able to make one's presentation in a supportive atmosphere. A less congenial setting, however, might have the opposite effect:

> The first minute is the hardest because you hear your own voice out loud in this empty room… it's a really horrible feeling! In that first minute you need your tutor… even if… they go, 'Hmm' or they nod you're like, 'Oh thanks'… it doesn't matter if it wasn't vaguely intelligent what you said, it's just you feel like… everything's going to be alright… But some tutors they just sit and make notes. You feel like you're doing an exam and it's horrible. (Humanities)

Interestingly, levels of anxiety or confidence could rapidly lessen or increase midway through a presentation, but then sometimes return to their previous levels with equal suddenness:

> Sometimes I've started off really nervous with a presentation and then totally kinda got in to my stride. And other times I've started off okay then half way through I can just feel my face go completely red! And once my face has gone red then I know it's just going to get redder! (Humanities)

> Half way through I just go, 'I'm giving a presentation' and then you relax again and then suddenly you run off and lose yourself. (Social sciences)

For some students, there was no substitute for first-hand experience:

> At the end of day you're only going to learn by doing it. (Physical sciences)

> Practice is the only way you're going to get good at presentations. (Social sciences)

9.3.4   Handling questions, comments and discussion

In all three courses, making a presentation entailed not simply giving a prepared talk, but also interacting with the audience. This took varying forms, however. In Physical Sciences, where the presentations were based on written papers students had already submitted, most of the questions came from supervisors, with the apparent aim of testing students' understanding or clarifying points raised. In Social Sciences, students were actively encouraged to raise questions and make comments and suggestions which could feed into the written essays which presenters subsequently submitted. In the Humanities course, by contrast, the principal function of the talk component was to open up questions which could then be pursued in the ensuing tutorial discussion.

But in all three settings, the demands of the discussion component were widely perceived as at least as challenging – and anxiety-provoking – as the talk component, if not more so. The content of a talk could be meticulously prepared in advance, but not so the discussion, for it was difficult to anticipate with any certainty what questions might be asked:

> What I was anxious about was the questions afterwards, because I knew that I could talk for fifteen minutes about a given topic but I didn't know what people were going to ask me. So you have to know your subject fairly well so you can answer their questions. (Social sciences)

> Getting up and giving a talk, it doesn't faze me that much, it's the questions. It's like, oh, what on earth are they going to ask, especially I thought [lecturer] is a very direct questioner and you've just got to know. (Physical sciences)

However, for some, the experience of responding to comments and questions had been a positive one:

> S1: I enjoyed the question bit at the end because I did know more than I had been able to put in my talk and the questions allow you to demonstrate that and stimulate some thinking...
> S2: Yeah, somehow it's a bit more relaxed. (Social sciences)

> Other students have said "I like this point" and "I was thinking this as well about this point", which is useful, you know? And they pick up points which you might not have noticed or sort of skimmed over. (Humanities)

The point was also made that some staff needed to recognise how daunting it was for students to have to handle discussion, and to show greater sensitivity:

> As a tutor, you do lectures and you've got hundreds of people watching you all the time. But if you're a student, you've got twelve of your peers sitting around and if you don't know the answer it's just really tough. Some tutors don't seem to take that into consideration. They just keep talking at you and you're just, like, "I'm sorry, I don't know the answer. I don't know!" And the more they ask the less you know, because the more nervous you get! (Humanities)

9.3.5   Feedback

Students in most subject areas are accustomed to getting written feedback on their coursework, perhaps also with an opportunity to discuss their work with their tutor if they wish. In this study, feedback in the physical sciences and humanities courses was largely informal, and via one-to-one discussions at the student's or tutor's discretion, while in social sciences, each student was given written comments in the week following their presentations. But in all three course settings, there were students who had been given feedback – in some instances, for the first time ever – which they had found helpful, albeit to varying degrees:

> I think it's very important to get the feedback because on another course I'd done the presentation and received really no feedback so you're swimming around wondering, well, you know, are you actually moving in the right direction? I think actually having written feedback as well, and the way it was set out, has been very useful. It's just picked up on your weaknesses but also your strengths as well so giving you some direction on what you really now have to go and focus on. (Social sciences)

> There wasn't much feedback, but [this is] the first talk [I've given where] we've actually been told what the good points were and what the bad points were. It would have been a bit more helpful if we'd had that before. (Physical sciences)

> We can go and see [the tutor], but it's optional, which I think is quite good. So that quite helps, you know, you'll go back to him and he'll tell you what you did wrong or what you did right. (Humanities)

The experiences of other students, particularly in the physical sciences and humanities courses, had been much less positive:

> I'd like to go back and just see, because he didn't ask any questions at the end. It was two other lecturers that asked us, and my supervisor didn't ask anything.
> (Physical sciences)

> I got my essays back through the office, so you don't have that chance to say "What did I get for my presentation?" Whereas, in [another subject], I'd given in my written summary and he gives me it back with a mark just like he would with an essay.
> (Humanities)

9.3.6   Learning from others' presentations

Feedback from tutors has such potentially considerable value in learning-to-write because, formally speaking, it is only the tutor (and perhaps a second marker) who sees the completed assignment. Where an assignment is presented orally, however, what has been produced by a student is on open display. The possibility therefore opens up for students to learn-to-present from observing (and in the process, evaluating the effectiveness of) the presentations of their peers, as in the two examples below:

> S1: You've got hands when you're presenting, it's so good.

> S2: I was noticing that when I was doing [it].

> S1:   No but you used your hands when you were talking about the Northern Hemisphere and the Southern Hemisphere, and it was great because you don't actually have to give all the details of describing… like a diagram, you can point to bits.
> (Physical sciences)

> S1: Your slides were like really packed… [B] had quite a few overheads which had little bits on and [C] just had a load of pictures. I had a load of slides and [D] had a few slides just with bullet points and he talked around them. So really there were five different types of presentation but I think they all came across really well…

> S2: Other people did good. The way [X] did was quite good but I wouldn't say I wanted to do mine like that because I thought the way I did it was quite good. I thought [Y's] was good as well where he stuck [in] his bullet points.
> (Physical sciences)

In another example, a student relates how observing others give their presentations had prompted him not to emulate them, but to try what he felt would be a more productive approach:

> When I've been in tutorials and someone's sort of read out an essay they've written, I don't really pick it up as much because it's too quick. With a presentation I try and do something different… draw sort of conclusions and points just as starter points for further thought I suppose. Yeah, I don't try and necessarily wrap up everything at the end of the presentation like you would an essay. (Humanities)

Equally interestingly, there are indications that a greater attentiveness to the presenting styles of others extends beyond one's fellow-students, to lecturers as presenters. As one student put it:

> It does make you appreciate lecturers as well! I thought it was really easy to stand there and talk about something… It makes me listen a bit more because I think 'Well, they've obviously got this in order for a reason'. (Social sciences)

9.3.7   Towards personal styles of presenting

When these various aspects of students' experiences of presenting are viewed collectively, it becomes evident that, as our model in figure 1 suggested, there is a rich array of potential influences on the development of their expertise in presenting. Students can learn a great deal not only from the more conventional pedagogical 'inputs' of tutors' pre-presentation guidance and post-presentation feedback, but also from their past experiences of presenting, the act of presenting itself (where the challenge encompasses handling questions and discussion as well as giving a prepared talk), and learning from the presentations of others – in the first instance, those of their peers, but extending subsequently to those of their lecturers. But the traffic of influence is not one-way: the students do not merely 'absorb' or 'assimilate' ideas about presenting, but actively develop personal styles of presenting which they themselves judge to be effective and find congenial.   Possibilities or options are weighed and considered, but not necessarily adopted:

> [Lecturer] always… tells you what he's going to say more or less and then elaborates on all the points, which I think is really good for note-taking… So maybe we should be doing that in a mini style in presentations. But I think it doesn't matter so much if it is a little bit more casual, a looser style. (Humanities)

> Some people were coming in to the presentation with blooming overheads… and I was like having this little bit of crumpled paper. Now, I don't think it really matters – you can sort of create your own style. (Humanities)

> Someone did a list of questions that they were going to ask at the beginning and that they went through. I blatantly [hadn't done] that, but I think it's a really good idea, because then people are thinking about it as you go through it. (Social sciences)

However, as with any process of development, students are likely to be at different stages in the evolution of their expertise, and in the degree of confidence with which they can approach the challenges of presenting well. While some are therefore happy to be left to their own devices, others would prefer clear direction:

> I personally don't have the confidence just to sit there with bullet points… some people need the specific structure of an essay in front of them because you haven't been told how to do it therefore you haven't got the confidence… I think you need more guidelines than we actually got. (Humanities)

9.4   Reflections and implications

As our analysis has suggested, when viewed as a learning task, the challenges which oral presentations appear to pose for students are distinctive in a number of respects. Perhaps the most compelling of these, from the student-presenter's point of view at least, is the anxiety which surrounds the giving of a presentation before an audience (albeit of one's 'familiars', to use an old-fashioned but apt term). That anxiety is associated with the challenge of responding to questions and comments as well as that of delivering a prepared talk. To some extent at least, anxiety may be allayed by a supportive environment in which tutor and peers help to make the experience a positive one. Prior practice in giving presentations is also crucial since, as many of the students observed, much of what is entailed in learning-to-present can only be learnt by actually doing it. However, the relevance of the well-known model of learning-from-experience developed by Kolb (Kolb, 1984; Kolb, Boyatzis and Mainemalis, 2001) would appear to be limited, for in that model, experience, observation, reflection and experimentation are readily distinguishable and follow a consistent sequence. In the present study, all of these elements could be pinpointed within the students' accounts of their experiences, but the processes involved seemed more dynamic and the different elements more closely interwoven.

Feedback was also seen as a potentially powerful catalyst in enhancing skills, but did not appear to be as systematically offered as it generally is for more established kinds of assignments. Indeed, many of the students related earlier experiences of giving presentations which had not been accompanied by any feedback at all, which would run counter to long-established theories of learning (Hounsell, 1987). And yet, as the present findings also disclosed, learning from others appears to be a no less potent affordance (Laurillard, 2001) or accelerant to learning. In contrast to assessed essays and reports, oral presentations are an 'on-display' form of assignment: the prepared work is presented publicly rather than submitted privately. While this open display of learning, understandably, generated anxiety and even embarrassment, it did mean that each student had an opportunity of seeing at first hand what his or her peers had prepared and produced. And observing others' presentations could have a number of positive effects. It could prompt reflection on what seemed to work or not work well. It could open up alternative ways of presenting material effectively that were then weighed and considered for their personal relevance and feasibility (ie 'Is this something I could usefully try, and feel comfortable in doing?'), and subsequently perhaps adopted, adapted or rejected. And equally productively, it could prompt an alertness to presentation styles and strategies which was carried over to other contexts such as lectures.

Needless to say, these findings raise implications for university and college teachers whose students are expected to give oral presentations. Some may see in the findings a compelling case for the more formal use of peer feedback – a practice which, as we noted earlier, has often been associated with oral and other kinds of student presentation. But since none of the course settings in our study had made use of peer feedback, we have no evidence to offer of its benefits. Much more pertinently, we would argue, all the elements in the model which our findings have yielded can be seen as potentially powerful affordances to the process of learning-to-present. These include influences such as past experiences of presenting and learning from others as well as more conventional affordances such as tutors' feedback on presentations. The pedagogical challenge is how best to capitalise on each and all of these so that oral presentations are not assignments which, in the experiences of students as learners, are isolated tasks "with no past or future" (Roe, 1974).

Finally, a note of caution is necessary. This exploratory study involved a relatively small number of students in three honours courses, and there was no methodological triangulation: the data came from a single round of group interviews. The findings must therefore be considered tentative and provisional: further research on learning-to-present is sorely needed.

References

Bruce, C and Gerber, R, (Eds), (1997). *Phenomenography in Higher Education*. Special Issue of *Higher Education Research and Development*, **16**(2).

Campbell, J, Smith, D, and Brooker, R (1998). From conception to performance: how undergraduate students conceptualise and construct essays. *Higher Education* 36, pp 449–469.

Cheng, W and Warren, M (1999). Peer and teacher assessment of the oral and written tasks of a group project. *Assessment and Evaluation in Higher Education* **24**(3), pp 301–314.

Hay, I (1994). Justifying and applying oral presentations in geographical education. *Journal of Geography in Higher Education*, **18**(1), pp 43–55.

Hounsell, D (1987). Essay-writing and the quality of feedback. In Richardson, JTE et al, (Eds), *Student Learning: Research in Education and Cognitive Psychology*, pp 109–119. Buckingham: SRHE and Open University Press.

Hounsell, D (1997). Contrasting conceptions of essay-writing. In Marton, F, Hounsell, D and Entwistle, N (Eds), *The Experience of Learning,* pp 106–125. (2nd Rev Edn). Edinburgh: Scottish Academic Press.

Hounsell, D and McCune, V (2000). A sense of audience in oral presentations by undergraduate students. Paper presented at the EARLI Writing 2000 Conference, University of Verona, September 2000.

Hounsell, D and McCune, V (2001). Learning to present: students' experiences and their implications. Paper presented at the Ninth European Conference for Research on Learning and Instruction, 28 August – 1 September 2001, Fribourg, Switzerland.

Hyland, P (1996). Examining action research to improve seminars through assessment. In Gibbs, G (Ed), *Improving Student Learning: Using Research to Improve Student Learning,* pp 207–223. Oxford: Oxford Centre for Staff and Learning Development.

Joughin, G (1999). Dimensions of oral assessment and student approaches to learning. In Brown, S and Glasner, A, (Eds), *Assessment Matters in Higher Education: Choosing and Using Diverse Approaches,* pp 146–156. Buckingham: SRHE and Open University Press.

Kolb, DA (1984). *Experiential Learning: Experience as the Source of Learning and Development.* Englewood Cliffs, NJ: Prentice-Hall.

Kolb, DA, Boyatzis, RE and Mainemalis, C (2001). Experiential learning theory: previous research and new directions. In Sternberg, RJ and Zhang, LF (Eds), *Perspectives on Thinking, Learning and Cognitive Styles,* pp 227–247. Mahwah, NJ and London: LEA.

Lapham, A and Webster, R (1999). Peer assessment of undergraduate seminar presentations: motivations, reflection and future directions. In Brown, S and Glasner, A, (Eds), *Assessment Matters in Higher Education: Choosing and Using Diverse Approaches,* pp 183–190. Buckingham: SRHE and Open University Press.

Laurillard, D (2001). *Rethinking University Teaching: A Conversational Framework for the Effective Use of Learning Technologies.* (2nd Edn). London: RoutledgeFalmer.

MacAlpine, JMK (1999). Improving and encouraging peer assessment of student presentations. *Assessment and Evaluation in Higher Education* **24**, 15–25.

McCune, V (in press). Development of first year students' conceptions of essay writing. *Higher Education.*

Mann, Sarah J (2000). The student's experience of reading. *Higher Education,* **39**(3), pp 297–317.

Marton, F, Hounsell, D and Entwistle, N, (Eds), (1997). *The Experience of Learning.* (2nd Rev Edn). Edinburgh: Scottish Academic Press.

Mindham, C (1998). Peer assessment: report of a project involving group presentations and assessment by peers. In Brown, S, (Ed), *Peer Assessment in Practice,* pp 45–65. Birmingham: SEDA.

Prosser, M, and Trigwell, K (1999). *Understanding Learning and Teaching: The Experience in Higher Education.* Buckingham: Open University Press

Roach, P (1999). Using peer assessment and self-assessment for the first time. In Brown, S and Glasner, A, (Eds), *Assessment Matters in Higher Education: Choosing and Using Diverse Approaches,* pp 191–201. Buckingham: SRHE and Open University Press.

Roe, E (1974). *Assignments.* Brisbane: University of Queensland, Tertiary Education Institute. p 60.

Säljö, R (1988). A text and its meanings: observations on how readers construe what is meant from what is written. In Säljö, R, (Ed), *The Written World: Studies in Literate Thought and Action,* pp 178–194. Berlin: Springer-Verlag.

Taylor, M (1986). Learning for self-direction in the classroom: the pattern of a transition process. *Studies in Higher Education* 11, 55–72.

10 Variation in the experience of teaching creative practices: the community of practice dimension

Linda Drew and Christina Williams
University of Brighton UK

Abstract

This paper explores conceptions of teaching held by academics in departments of art, design and communication and explores links between those conceptions and the communities of practice associated with the subject context.

This paper explores the qualitatively different ways that teachers of creative practices experience their teaching. The study focuses on teachers of practice based subjects in art, design or communication

This paper reports variation between the qualitatively different ways the teachers conceive of teaching in each of the sub-disciplines. The important feature of this analysis is the community of practice dimension, in particular how teaching is perceived as contributing to engaging with the social practices which constitute the particular creative practice.

The community of practice dimension is further explored in relation to how teachers may enhance the experience of learning and the learning environment by developing strategies which address the application of knowledge in practice based settings as well as their activity systems.

10.1   Conceptions of teaching

Much of the work which has examined teachers' conceptions built on research frameworks that also explored students conceptions and approaches to learning. Studies of conceptions of teaching have ranged from the phenomenographic (eg Martin and Balla, 1991; Prosser et al 1994) to those studies of belief orientations (eg Fox, 1983; Kember, 1997). There are however some recurring themes in studies of conceptions of teaching which are well summarised by Kember (1997). At one end of the spectrum there are teachers who focus on information transmission and, at the other end, there are those that focus on changing students' conceptions or understanding of the world (Prosser et al 1994; Samuelowicz and Bain, 1992).

In a study reporting conceptions of learning, Marton, Dall'Alba & Beaty (1993) found the five conceptions of learning identified by Säljö (1979) and they also identified a sixth conception: learning as changing as a person. As conceptions of learning are considered to underlie conceptions of teaching, or certainly to demonstrate a relationship between the two (Prosser et al 1994) it would be not unreasonable to expect that the sixth conception of learning would be related to a conception of teaching. No previous studies appear to discover changing as a person as an element of a conception of teaching. Later in this paper we report a conception of teaching as helping students to change as a person.

Most studies of conceptions of teaching have chosen to focus on traditional university subject disciplines eg sciences and humanities. There are however some studies of conceptions of teaching in practice based disciplines including music (Reid, 2000) and design (Drew, 2000a, 2000b).

In an earlier study of design teachers (Drew, 2000b) five qualitatively different conceptions of design teaching are described as ranging from the teacher as offering something to students, through to the teaching as helping to change students' conceptions. These categories of description illustrate a dimension of the qualitative variation in design teaching. Conception A in this study illustrates that even one-to-one teaching contexts can still been conceptualised in transmission terms, the other four conceptions identified incorporate a degree of student centredness which increases from B to E. Categories D and E also demonstrated a community of practice dimension as a focus for the context of teaching.

The practice-based context of studio teaching can be seen as a student centred approach but, as this study also reports, some teachers in this context hold conceptions of teaching as instructional and teacher focused rather than co-operative and collaborative learning. The quality of this learning environment relates to the context and the conceptions of learning and teaching held by both teacher and student (Reid and Davies, 2000).

10.2 Learning to practice and participation

There is also a significant literature which embraces the sociocultural perspective on practice, particularly emphasising learning to practice in various settings. Learning to practice, whether in workplace or simulated settings is seen as a move towards full participation in a community of practice (Lave and Wenger, 1991; Lave, 1993). These views emphasise social practice as a premise for learning and that 'knowing in practice' arises from participation in that social practice (Billett,1998). The community of practice has been further conceived as constituting smaller units or activity systems (Engeström, 1987) which engage in practice through expansive learning, learning by extension and diversification of activity. Teachers and their learners, engaged in collective work and learning demonstrate all of the principles of the activity system (Engeström, 2001).

Jean Lave describes the social participatory perspective on learning as individuals developing and changing their identities, "… people are becoming kinds of persons" (Lave 1996, p 157). Learning which is the result of participation in social practices means that the participants appropriate ways of seeing the world inherent in those practices. These situational and social factors are a key part of learning to practice (Billett, 2001) and are valued highly by practice-based teachers in this study, who demonstrate related conceptions of teaching.

Lave's study of the apprenticeship of tailors in Liberia during the seventies identifies how the tailors were primarily making ready-to-wear trousers, but the apprentices also learned other important contextual factors about being a tailor:

> …they were learning relations among the major social identities and divisions in Liberian society which they were in the business of dressing. They were learning to make a life, to make a living, to make clothes, to grow old enough, and mature enough to become master tailors, and to see the truth of the respect due to a master of their trade. (Lave, 1996, p 159)

The community of practice dimension is most certainly about "becoming kinds of persons", about developing ways of seeing the world through practice.

10.3 Method

The data is from an interview study of 44 teachers from eight UK Universities and is explored with a phenomenographic approach (Marton and Booth, 1997). The analysis was grouped into three discrete sub-disciplines, fine art (11), design (18) and media (15), through which variation in the practice dimensions could also be discerned. Opportunity sampling was used to identify the eight university departments of art, design and communication. The researchers were able to identify those departments as part of their remit in working for the Learning and Teaching Support Network for Art, Design and Communication. Within each of these departments the participants were selected in such a way as to ensure a spread across subjects and to maximise the variation in possible conceptions of teaching. This paper adopts a second-order perspective on the experience of teaching a practice based subject in art, design and communication departments.

The interviews were semi-structured and consisted of questions designed to encourage the respondent to talk about the way they perceived their teaching role and related strategies and intentions. Each respondent was interviewed for approximately 45 minutes. The interviews were focused on one particular aspect of their teaching eg a specific course, module, unit or project which is practice based (ie with an aim for the students to learn a practice). Their responses were continually followed up with prompts to probe for a better understanding of the meanings behind their statements. Prompts used included:

- What is your role in this teaching situation?
- Could you explain what you mean by that word?
- What do you hope your students will achieve by that?
- What is your intention when you do that?

The interviews were taped and transcribed verbatim, and both researchers read these transcriptions thoroughly, and repeatedly. The aim of phenomenographic analysis is to develop categories of description which illustrate the limited number of qualitatively different ways of experiencing a phenomenon, in this case the experience of teaching a practice based subject in media, fine art and design. In this paper, the lead researcher proposed a provisional analysis of the categories of conceptions in each sub discipline which was then tested and contested by questioning and probing from the co-researcher. This process is seen as an essential part of researcher learning in phenomenography and also ensures internal consistency and validity (Bowden, 2000; Prosser, 2000). The categories were devised by looking for the variation between responses, and the similarities between statements within categories. Then final descriptions were produced to reflect these similarities and differences. The descriptions of the categories were developed using two components – how the explanation is given and what is focused on (Trigwell, 2000, p 74).

The categories of description, described in the next section, are internally related to each other. Categories were sorted into a meaningful order, with the 'lower' less complete conceptions first, moving into 'higher', more complete conceptions. The higher conceptions encompass the lower conceptions and are therefore more complete. This is known as a hierarchy of categories of description; the logical relations between these categories are illustrated in the outcome space. The outcome space is not a full rich description of teaching, rather it is a description of those aspects of teaching that are seen to have qualitative variation. (Table 10.1)

A range of qualitatively different conceptions of teaching in media, fine art and design are identified in this paper. These conceptions are constituted as a hierarchy where the more complete conceptions include some aspects of the more limiting conceptions but not vice versa. The decision to present the categories in terms of increasing sophistication does not necessarily bear any relation to their appropriateness; rather it relates to the perceived need to illustrate the hierarchical relationship which links the categories and their conceptions together. It should be noted that the categories do not necessarily reflect the conceptions of individual teachers. To further illustrate the categories of conceptions a range of quotes are used. It may be difficult in one or two quotes to see the full extent of the variation so the quotes that are used exemplify key aspects of that variation.

10.4   Conceptions of Teaching Creative Practices

For the purposes of this study, creative practice teaching is described in the context of media, fine art and design. These subject areas include teaching the practices of journalism, film making, television and video production, animation and photography, fine art, painting, sculpture, printmaking and related visual arts, graphic design and illustration, interior design and architecture, fashion and textile design. The constant context of each interview was the teachers' practice based teaching as opposed to teaching visual studies for example.

10.4.1   Conception A: Teaching is offering students a range of practical and technical skills

The teacher aims to reinforce technical ability by giving demonstrations and showing individual or groups of students ways of making or doing. The teacher believes that the students need to follow technical topics based on what the teacher feels they need to learn. The emphasis of the learning is on a product or artefact. The intention is to demonstrate or give examples of technical skills.

   Structural aspects of this conception are concerned with the teacher's role, in this case demonstrating, showing or instructing students how to make or do something. There is an emphasis on correct procedures and observing or checking that these are carried out correctly or for the students to demonstrate some technical competence. The focus of the teaching is on technical and practical skills. The teacher feels that they know best what skills to develop or to teach and often refer to content or objectives of the course, rules of the practice or other practical parameters which they feel the students must master before progressing in the subject.

   This teacher discusses the focus of his teaching, to demonstrate a process, observe the students practising it and check they can do it.

> First of all I will demonstrate how to correct, then we move onto something a bit more complicated, I've got these cans of Coke in the studio back there. Then I can show, if I have the camera that way they're all out, with the movement, they're all sharp. Okay that's fine, they're all sharp, but the camera's off thickness, the camera is called a female, you need to get it sharpened over there, we lose light so we have to increase the exposure and so on, just the basics, and then I've got them to do it, and I've got observation sheets which I tick off and they can demonstrate to me that they can actually do it, and I observe and tick off the observation sheet.

Q: And what would you say is your intention with using the observation sheet?

This is just a record for me that they can do it. The course, half of the mark is attendance and successful completion of all of the skills we have to offer, the other half of the course is the final portfolio… so I have to have an actual record that they can actually do it. (Media: PR13)

In this conception the teacher decides what to teach on the basis that they feel the students may not have any useful prior knowledge which they could bring to learning these skills or rules of the practice.

You start to deliver the material, whatever it is, so if you're teaching them 3D objects like spheres and how 3D space works you still have to deliver that material. But the material you deliver is specified, you've got to teach the class, but the actual content you're working with is pre-described. (Media: CU7)

10.4.2 Conception B: Teaching is developing students' critical, practical and technical skills through student interaction

The teacher aims to enable students to develop a critical language by working together in groups or teams to present their own work and to see the work of others. The emphasis of the learning is on peer learning and process. The teacher works with individuals, groups or teams with the intention to enable students to form opinions and ideas.

In this conception the teacher still feels it is important for students to develop practical and technical skills, but the emphasis is on learning with others, sometimes in team or group situations and often with an opportunity for critical debate.

…to encourage the way the group works, the peer group interaction is really important, for example, what student over that side of the group might have a key fabric that somebody over the side of the group might be looking for and if there are not using it then its like, well can you give them they address of that. So it is very much dealing with practical issues and it is also reassuring them, a lot of them really do get unsure and quite worried about this module because it is such a big thing. (Design: NT2)

Teachers often describe their role as facilitating or encouraging the process of learning and of developing confidence in learners. In this conception, teachers are keen to emphasise elements of the process which actively engage with students.

The teaching in this situation is more facilitating that group interaction is happening and the groups are progressing all along certain key dates that they have to meet captured across semester two. So in terms of preparation there is very little note taking or white board writing or handing out lecture notes. The project does not require this, by the time they get to the end of year two the assumption is that they have learnt all that in previous modules and now a synthesis happens. That knowledge comes together. So the teacher, the lecturer is more of a facilitator. In terms of preparation my preparation is more of a psychologist or a facilitator rather than spending two or three nights writing lecture notes to get ready. That doesn't apply in this particular case. So there is not real preparation to say, rather a mental preparation if I could put it that way. You are a facilitator now, you are supervising the process. (Media: CU6)

10.4.3 Conception C: Teaching is developing students' skills and conceptions in the context of professional practice

The teacher encourages students to manage projects involving complex problem solving skills which are set in the context of professional practice. The emphasis of the learning is on peer learning and process. The teacher works with students to develop conceptions with the intention to increase self-awareness, individual and team autonomy and for professional preparation.

In this conception teachers believe that real world scenarios or projects as à simulation of professional practice enable high level learning outcomes including problem solving skills.

> So reflection, there's a kind of debate over whether journalists reflect or not, but we feel its important for students here to play out a lot of ethical situations and scenarios and practical professional situations in a safe environment before they enter the industry, so we do encourage them to reflect, compare and contrast, look at real life journalism and how it compares to what they're doing. (Media: PR15)

> I like to see this as a realistic representation of what the industry is like so that when they go in they won't be too surprised…I think its important that they have if they're going to do a course that's got quite a vocational element to it, it's going to be realistic, and we push them very hard and we give them very difficult situations. I think that we set tight deadlines, we give them the types of responses an editor would give, and that seems to be what they want, they seem to want to be pushed and given a space to play out in. (Media: PR15)

This teacher believes that if students are brought into contact with practising subject experts they can bring a professional context to bear in relation to their work as well as developing ideas and concepts.

> I think one of the things that's most interesting is that when they do come in they're quite gauche and they're very insecure in their ideas, by the end of the module they really should become confident in expressing ideas – visually, orally and intellectually… I think it's because it's a combination of teaching and practice. It's not just one-to-one tutorials. It's also bringing them into contact with experts in the area so that they can actually have a reference point and they can contextualise their ideas in relation to what is actually going on outside. (Design: BN 4)

Some teachers of fine art further described their teaching role as being an artist with students in the role of apprentices to the practice of fine art making. Apprenticeship is seen as a positive experience of being inducted into the fine art social context as well as the extension of practice and making art.

> So my role is in some way as a kind of mediator, but it is as an artist as well, an established artist, but also a shallow artist in a sense. I will talk about them making art, it's an art apprenticeship in a way. That is important I think to form that kind of relationship of shared experiences, knowledge and also the building of experience. It is confidence building and expanding ideas. The possibilities of making work expand is very important. What I try to do is talk about the relevance of materials, as well as appropriate advice. (Fine Art: SI 11)

10.4.4 Conception D: Teaching is helping students change conceptions

The teacher emphasises original research and conceptual thinking skills. The emphasis of the learning is on peer learning and process. The teacher works with students with the intention to improve self-directed research, practice and conceptual skills.

The teacher feels that students should have an ability to relate key concepts to the practice, or to develop practice through critical examination of concepts or theories. Teachers in this conception also stress 'real world' and practice based contexts as in Conception C.

> Well, from the seminar presentation I guess that we are encouraging them to do what I was saying before, to take an area of theoretical work and to apply it to an example or a case study, and they have to learn to critically examine and reflect on that theoretical work in terms of what their thoughts are on that topic. But of course more generally, more generically, I think that they are developing their skills for research and presentation. I think that that's very important in terms of everyone doing this thing, but I mean, these are transferable skills, the ability to take a brief, and come back with a lively and animated presentation on that and to engage other people in it I think is a skill that is essential to a lot of areas in the media practices anyway. So in the seminar I think that that is an important element of it, they are developing still, or researching presentations, and working with colleagues as well. (Media: PR11)

To enable students to change conceptions of the subject, of the world and of their work is seen as an integral part of this conception. These teachers talks about expressing ideas, changing conceptions and also about learning beyond the subject boundaries as an aim for teaching in this subject.

> Ah, to, give them something to think about, some directions or tools, to do a very practical thing, you could say that there are a much wider range of ways of making marks on your territory. For instance, if you look at the practice of that, there are two different ways, now you may not want them to imagine you're a student, you may not want to use those two ways, but they are implications that you are working in a very particular way. You are making a choice to do that, and within that crit, what you are doing dissolves in some way. What often emerges from this is a sense of well, why should I change, and I think that's quite important, to get that out in the open, that they're going to have to face up to go looking for the idea of change in their work. As they come to the end of the course, and at the end of their own practice, not to stay in the same place but to change, and to get used to the idea of change being, on occasion, quite uncomfortable. (Fine Art: FC 7)

10.4.5 Conception E: Teaching is helping students to change as a person

Teachers holding this conception again emphasise original research and conceptual thinking skills and peer learning and process. They differ from those holding Conception D in seeing teaching as a way of enabling students to change themselves as a person or to make changes in their lifeworld.

> ...each student comes away with having achieved something, and achieves something that takes them to another level of their existence, that's a bit ambitious but they have grown whether or not they have learnt anything technical about photography, is of less interest to me, I think they need to move on in their own lives and if they can produce a project with some collaboration with outside agencies or in the wider sense that it might be a scientific institution or a group of young mothers in an organisation, so,

photography is not seen simply a means to an end, but as a real way of shaping how people understand themselves and the world around them. (Media: FC14)

Teachers also express aspects of changing as a person in this conception as relating to their practice, to concepts of creativity and beyond the practice into the student lifeworld.

It's a kind of, liberal art education, you are kind of enabling students to fall on a creative theme, depending on what level they are operating at, and what their ambitions are. You might be producing people who are practitioners in their own right, artists, and people who take that experience back into other fields whether its teaching or curating or other kinds of public art activities. So I think its broader now than it used to be, and I just feel that it's the last traces of liberal art education. It's not geared towards a career or job, but more at developing a person, so that's my view, I think a lot of people would accord with that. (Fine Art: PL 6)

An analysis of these conceptions in terms of their structural and referential components is shown in Table 10.1. This demonstrates the way the categories have a logical ordering within the outcome space. The community of practice dimension is present in conceptions C, D and E.

The structural and referential aspects of the categories of conceptions				
Structural	**Referential**			
Focus of the teaching	Skills	Critical language	Conceptual	Student lifeworld
Giving information to individual students	A			
Developing students through groups (and individuals)		B	C	
Changing students through groups (and individuals)			D	E

Table10.1.   Conceptions of teaching creative practices: outcome space

10.7   Discussion

The conceptions of teaching which are described as demonstrating the community of practice dimension illustrate how teachers see learning as engaging with a practice, by exemplars, stories, narratives and through experience. The process of learning becomes one of apprenticeship to the practice, by engaging with the 'real world' practice and understanding the process through narration, collaboration and social construction (Billett, 2001, 2002; Lave and Wenger, 1991). These teachers' experiences, their own practice and engagement with other practice-based professionals gives a different dimension to the learning, a non-canonical practice (Orr, 1990; Seely Brown and Duguid, 1996).

Janet Wolff's 'The Social Production of Art' (1981) is an attempt to understand the production of art from a sociological perspective. Claiming that 'art is a social product' (p1), she goes on to unravel assumptions about the artist as genius, working in isolation from society, placing such notions firmly in their historical, and socio-economic, contexts. In doing so, she opens up a space in which it becomes possible for us to talk about the production of artists in the 21st century via the processes of higher education, incorporating into this process the beliefs and conceptions held by their teachers about the nature of professional practice. Billett (2001) also agrees that even an artist working in isolation will shape their practice to account for situational factors including physical environments and consideration of the market.

The findings of this study would suggest that teachers of art are drawing on some of these traditional ideas of art as a way of life (rather than 'art as manufacture' (Wolff, 1981, p12) when they talk about professional practice in the context of teaching art to their students. Where teachers of media practice and design talk about industry and commerce in relation to a community of practice, the art teachers tend to discuss this in terms of 'being' or 'becoming' an artist, suggesting that they see art as a way of life rather than a set of skills for employability or as something that can be easily separated from other parts of a student's lived experience.Angela McRobbie further explores the act of producing art 'in the culture society' (1999, p3). Working from Jameson's (1984) claim that culture has become the logic of late capitalism, she investigates cultural practices such as art, fashion and music as 'cultural industries', arguing that these are increasingly important economically and that little is known about the lived experience of such cultural production. She focuses on questions such as 'how do artists make a living within the cultural industries?'

> As students from more diverse backgrounds enter art school, Bourdieu's notion of the artist being able to stay poor in the short term thanks to some small private income in order to achieve success on the longer term is no longer appropriate (Bourdieu, 1993). There has to be some way of being an artist and making a living. (McRobbie, 1999, p8).

She highlights the insecure and negotiable nature of making a living in the culture industries, arguing that 'ducking and diving is no longer the fate of unqualified working-class males but almost surreptitiously has crept up on us all' (p8).

And, interesting here in the context of teachers' conceptions of art's community of practice as a way of being rather than being trained, she suggests that:

> In an aestheticised culture art becomes another transferable skill. Train as an artist to become a DJ. Work nights in a club or bar and get a commission from the promoters to do an installation. Make a video, take photographs etc. Art can now be pursued less grandiosely. (McRobbie, 1999, p8).

Instead of a pedagogy based on institutional teaching cultures, a pedagogy of community (Billett, 2002) is based on participation and access to the activities and requirements of the community. Participation in a community of practice is a key premise to understanding learning to practice, including learning the values and appropriating an identity related to that practice.

What this approach might suggest in relation to teachers of art and their conceptions of their teaching is interesting and generates questions such as:

- What kinds of expectations might we have for learners if teachers see art as life in relation to these new ways of working and making a living in the cultural industries?

- And is this an important distinction if one of the intentions is to encourage an improved learning experience for art students?

References

Billett, S (1998). Situation, social systems and learning. *Journal of Education and Work*, **11**(3), 255–274.

Billett, S (2001). Knowing in practice: re-conceptualising vocational expertise. *Learning and Instruction*, **11**, 431–452.

Billett, S (2002). Workplaces, communities and pedagogy, in Lea, M and Nicoll, K (Eds), *Distributed Learning: Social and cultural approaches to practice*. London: Routledge Falmer

Bourdieu, P (1993).*The Field of Cultural Production*, Polity Press.

Bowden, J (2000). Experience of phenomenographic research: A personal account in Bowden, J and Walsh, E (Eds), *Phenomenography*. Melbourne: RMIT Publishing.

Drew, L (2000a). Do development interventions shape conceptions of teaching in Art and Design? In Rust, C (Ed), *Improving Student Learning: Improving Student Learning through the Disciplines*, pp 230–243. Oxford: Oxford Centre for Staff and Learning Development.

Drew, L (2000b). A disciplined approach: Learning to practice as design teachers in the University, in Swann, C and Young, E (Eds), *Reinventing Design Education in the University*, pp187–193. Curtin University of Technology, Perth, Western Australia.

Engeström, Y (1987). *Learning by Expanding: An Activity Theoretical Approach to Developmental Research*. Helsinki: Orienta-Konsultit Oy.

Engeström, Y (2001). Expansive learning at work: toward an activity theoretical reconceptualisation. *Journal of Education and Work*, **14**, 133–156.

Fox, D (1983). Personal theories of teaching. *Studies in Higher Education*, **8**, 151–163.

Jameson, F (1984). Postmodernism or the cultural logic of late capitalism. *New Left Review*, 146, London.

Kember, D (1997). A reconceptualisation of the research into university academics' conceptions of teaching. *Learning and Instruction*, **7**, 255–275.

Lave, J (1993). The practice of learning. In Chaiklin, S and Lave, J (Eds), *Understanding Practice*, pp 3–32. Cambridge: Cambridge University Press.

Lave, J (1996). Teaching, as learning, in practice. *Mind, Culture and Activity*, **3**, 149–64.

Lave, J and Wenger, E (1991). Situated learning: *Legitimate peripheral participation*. Cambridge: Cambridge University Press.

Martin, E and Balla, M (1991). Conceptions of teaching and implications for learning. In Ross, R (Ed), Teaching for Effective Learning. *Research and Development in Higher Education* **13**. Sydney: HERDSA.

Marton, F and Booth, S (1997). *Learning and awareness*. Mahwah, NJ: Lawrence Erlbaum.

Marton, F Dall'Alba, G and Beaty, E (1993). Conceptions of learning. *International Journal of Educational Research*, **19**, 277–300.

McRobbie, A (1999). *In the Culture Society: Art, Fashion and Popular Music*. London: Routledge.

Orr, S (1987). Narratives at work: Story telling as cooperative diagnostic activity. *Field Service Manager*, **6**, 47–60.

Prosser, M (2000). Using phenomenographic research methodology in the context of research in teaching and learning. In Bowden, J and Walsh, E (Eds), *Phenomenography*. Melbourne: RMIT Publishing.

Prosser, M, Trigwell, K and Taylor, P (1994). A phenomenographic study of academics' conceptions of science learning and teaching. *Learning and Instruction*, **4,** 217–231

Reid, A (2000). Musicians' experience of the musical world: Relations with teaching and learning. In Rust, C (Ed), *Improving Student Learning: Improving Student Learning through the Disciplines,* pp 169–184. Oxford: Oxford Centre for Staff Development.

Reid, A and Davies, A (2000). Uncovering problematics in design education: Learning and the design entity. In Swann, C and Young, E (Eds), *Reinventing Design Education in the University,* pp 179–185. Curtin University of Technology, Perth, Western Australia.

Säljö, R (1979). *Learning in the learner's perspective. 1. Some common-sense conceptions.* Reports from the Department of Education, University of Gothenburg. Gothenburg: Department of Education and Educational Research. University of Gothenburg.

Samuelowicz, K and Bain, JD (1992). Conceptions of teaching held by academic teachers. *Higher Education,* **24,** 93–111.

Seely Brown, J and Duguid, P (1996). Toward a unified view of working, learning and innovation. In Cohen, MD and Sproull, LS (Eds), *Organisational Learning.* Beverly Hills, CA Sage.

Trigwell, K (2000). A phenomenographic interview on phenomenography. In Bowden, J and Walsh, E (Eds), *Phenomenography.* Melbourne: RMIT Publishing

Wolff, J (1981). *The Social Production of Art.* London: Macmillan.

11 Supervisory practices and development programmes to support postgraduate student learning

Gina Wisker, Gillian Robinson, Vernon Trafford, and Mark Warnes,

Anglia Polytechnic University (APU), Cambridge and Essex.

While significant research has been undertaken into undergraduate student learning and the learning and teaching practices which support this (Entwistle and Ramsden, 1983), research into postgraduate student learning and effective support practices is still a relatively new area of investigation.

Action research undertaken with groups of UK originated and Israeli PhD students and International MA/MSc students at APU since 1998 has yielded useful research findings about the perceived success of specific research development programmes, IT and tertiary literacy support and supervisory practices in empowering postgraduate students in their learning. Earlier work reported on the MA/MSc students (Waller, Griffiths, Wu, Wisker 2002).

This paper focuses on the PhD students and on the learning and teaching strategies of both

1) the research development programme and

2) supervisory relationships.

The paper explores action research undertaken with groups of PhD students based in Israel (about 150) from 1997 – 2002. It focuses on postgraduate students' conceptions of research as a form of learning, of which the choice of appropriate research methodology and methods is a key part. In making the learning leap between undergraduate and postgraduate studies, many students experience problems in producing a conceptual framework for their research, specifically in identifying research methods and methodologies which will enable them to achieve their research aims and outcomes. We report here on action research which accompanies, is based on and feeds into research development programmes and supervisory dialogues. These programmes, dialogues and the action research support and empower PhD students throughout their studies from their choice of methodologies and methods to the successful completion of their research. In reporting, we argue the usefulness for the coherence and success in student research of both support practices and action research.

Action research with PhD students involves both quantitative and qualitative methods. At each stage the students are collaborators. The processes and findings are fed back through workshops and supervisory dialogues to help develop further metacognitive awareness via reflection and discussion, and so better enable the learning process .

This paper looks at two specific and crucial points in the research development programme which accompanies and supports postgraduate work. First students' initial development of a conceptual framework and choice of methodologies and methods. Here we consider responses in supervisory dialogues and in focus groups, following methods workshops during the first stage of the research development programme. The paper goes on to look at students' recognition of changes and of the need to change, further develop and clarify both methods and conceptual frameworks during the final (third) stage workshop.

11.1   Introduction

For postgraduate students the choice of conceptual frameworks and research methods is a crucial stage in their work. However, for many this stage poses particular problems. It is not merely the potentially failing postgraduate student who finds difficulties in the early stages of developing a conceptual framework, research questions, the theories to understand, underpin, and interrogate the research objects with these questions, appropriate methodologies and methods to ask the research questions and appropriate analytical frameworks and tools to make sense of what the research and field work data produce. For many students making the transition from undergraduate to postgraduate work, the idea of a research question emerges more as a field of study than an interrogation of that field or a hypothesis related to elements within it. Many students have succeeded both at undergraduate and masters level largely conducting research which involves documentary analysis, accumulation of information with little real questioning of this material in relation to assumptions and a sense of curiosity about the world. Such curiosity, along with risk taking, creativity, a penchant for problem solving and the ability to recognise the need to move between research paradigms, where appropriate is essential for success at postgraduate study. Specifically, this is true of the PhD student whose work is related to professional practice, who connects theory to practice, linking across research disciplines in order to ask fundamental or ground-breaking questions about human behaviours.

11.2   Aims and focus of our research

Action research discussed here aims initially to identify problematic or 'at risk' learning approaches among PhD students which could hamper their likelihood of achieving postgraduate learning outcomes and their PhD, and then to identify effective ways of developing and supporting the work to satisfactory completion of research and achievement of the PhD. Our research accompanies a three stage research development programme, and supervisory dialogues, carried out with cohorts of Israeli PhD students registered at Anglia Polytechnic University from 1997 onwards.

In our work with the Israeli PhD students, we are initially concerned that they can propose, then plan and action a coherent piece of research. This is properly the focus of the first of the three stage research development programme on which all the students are enrolled and which takes place prior to the acceptance of their research proposals but after registration. Towards the end of their research, during the third stage of the research development programme, we are concerned with the cohesion between the elements of their conceptual framework ie between questions, theoretical underpinning, research methodologies and methods, data analysis and findings, and their ability to clearly articulate this conceptual framework throughout their PhD thesis and their viva, a compulsory element of the PhD in the UK system.

This paper focuses on the establishment of a clear conceptual framework at the beginning of the students' PhD research, stage one of the research development programme, and the revisions and clear ability to evidence the conceptual framework in the thesis and mock viva during stage three. Using both quantitative and qualitative research methods in an action research framework, it explores students' problems such as dissonance between research methods and conceptual framework, between approaches, methods and the proposed outcomes of the research, and indicates strategies used to help students overcome such problems. The success in action of such strategies is suggested based on close scrutiny of the students' own reflections on their research which emerge in supervisory dialogues and post-workshop focus groups, and on their final achievement of the PhD.

11.3   Background and theoretical perspectives

For students undertaking a PhD, the planning and preparation stage is crucial. While the process of research and research findings will quite possibly effect some change in the kinds of methods used, and research in itself throws up new ideas, new readings, new discoveries (that is its nature), there needs to be a coherent plan of its direction, what methods and strategies should enable it to reach its object, and a clear conceptual framework underpinning and helping scaffold the whole. If the plan and conceptual frameworks are missing, poorly linked, not cohesive, researchers could suffer from gaps or dissonance between their research methods, conceptual frameworks and research outcomes. Students could fail to address their research objects because methods are inappropriate to the task; could find that new ideas and information cause a problematic deviation, or could experience confusing relativism in which an enormous variety of research questions and data seem impossible to pull into a coherent argument, what Hodge (1995) has defined as 'negative post-modernism'. An initial plan, a clearly developed conceptual framework and appropriately chosen, planned methods are essential, even though the research process itself could well cause the student to change them.

Research methods are the vehicle by which the research is approached, actioned and achieved. They grow from the aim and focus of the research, the questions on which it is based, and a conceptual framework which ensures that questions are asked and actioned through methods which can genuinely help find answers, and that findings can be managed within the framework, can be analysed, interpreted. Without a conceptual framework the richness of any research area becomes that of life itself - immense and confusing.

Established theoretical perspectives on learning inform our action research with the PhD students, based on the conviction that students taking largely accumulation (or surface) approaches are unlikely to achieve postgraduate level learning outcomes largely because they are not involved with postgraduate learning approaches and processes. Students who cannot perceive differences between meaningful and accumulation learning approaches have been identified as 'dissonant' (Meyer and Vermunt 2000) and 'at risk'. Our own earlier work has also indicated that students seeking transformational outcomes but taking largely accumulation approaches are likely to be 'at risk.'

11.4   Transitions: learning levels

Students making the transition to PhD studies from masters work might find the size and scope of the research daunting. They may be unprepared for the complexity of planning, clarity of conceptual framework and so of research methods, the boundaries they need to define around the range of their work, and maintenance of momentum necessary to conduct and complete their project. Some, such as international students moving into different learning cultures, could also meet barriers to their learning at postgraduate level. These could include those of tertiary literacy ie the ability to articulate the complex conceptions and thought processes in a second (or in some cases a fifth) language. Others move into interdisciplinary study and find themselves less well prepared in the research methods of some disciplines than others.

For all these interrelated groups of students, there could be a problematic discrepancy between the learning approaches and research methods they have successfully used in the past and those enabling achievement of research outcomes.

11.5   International postgraduate students

International students who have previously studied in different learning cultures might find the specific expectations of European/US/Australian research paradigms and practices initially alien to their experiences. Making appropriate adjustments will be essential to enable research success in the learning culture in which they undertake PhD study. Any cultural inflections of students' research-as-learning approaches are augmented by inflections of individual learning styles and approaches, motivation, and the shape and outcomes of the study itself. Many of the same cultural conditions which affect undergraduate learning also affect postgraduate learning (See Kiley and Meyer 1998). See also Biggs (1993); Samuelowicz (1987); Hughes and Wisker (1998); Landbeck and Mugler (1994); Bloor and Bloor (1991); Todd (1996); Chen (2001). Students could bring experience of previously rewarded learning approaches which include a reinforcement of, for example, deference to authorities and quantitative, accumulative research methods and approaches. Cultural dissonance could add to difficulties experienced with making the leap between levels of study, and lack of prior experience of the forms and frame of learning interactions such as supervisory relationships could hamper learning. Harris (1995) notes, "it is probably that the experience of being an overseas student itself encourages a cautious serialist approach to learning".

'Cautious serialist' and accumulation approaches might indeed be popular among some international students whose previous learning cultures reward these behaviours, but they are by no means confined to them. Previous work carried out with UK originated PhD and MPhil students (Wisker, 1999) recognises such approaches as common to a number of students from a variety of origins. In extreme cases, some students have not only found it difficult to proceed with their research at each stage, but have failed to complete and gain their awards.

Such approaches might manifest themselves in the desire for very clear guidelines, overly straightforward research questions and methods. This could lead to accumulative approaches (defined as a focus on the acquisition of data, the belief that all knowledge is factual – a surface learning approach) over meaning oriented approaches (defined as a deep approach ie relating new insights and knowledge to relationships with previous learning, and to experience and practice, linking reflection, understanding, learning). Students could have a strong tendency to use previously rewarded, quantitative methods which encourage them to collect large amounts of data without adequate reflection, synthesis or analysis, or adequate connection between the data and its interpretation in relation to research questions.

Such methods might be appropriate when they support the appropriate research of, for example, sports science PhD's using pre- and post-test questionnaires. However, questionnaires, a favourite among quantitative methods, have proved to be a problematic research method unsuitable in the kinds of therapeutic and attitudinal change framework of much of the research carried out by our students. To put it bluntly, reliance upon purely quantitative approaches which encourage acquisition of large amounts of data, often leads to unmanageable and relatively useless masses of data and a large chasm between this data and any of the transformational outcomes, attitudinal or behavioural changes sought in the research itself. Some of these outcomes might be unrealistic and grand beyond the scope of the students' PhDs; others might just be unreachable using questionnaire data and need the more subjective, qualitative research methods which seem less scientifically sound but yield more attitudinal, personal response. These include case studies, interviews, focus groups, and so on.

11.6   Methodology and methods

Action research (Zuber-Skerritt & Ryan, 1994) is the chosen methodology for our research into students' learning, because it enrols and supports the students as collaborators in the research itself. They become more reflective about their own research-as-learning as a result of involvement in the action research and we can learn more about their research strategies and conceptions of research-as- learning because of the direct way in which programme activities, supervisory dialogues and research vehicles each transparently approach the same questions and ideas.

11.6.1   Sample

The students in our Israeli cohorts (1997: n 31, 1998: n 50, 1999: n 14, 2000: n 25, 2001: n 30), the subjects of this study, comprise Jewish, Romanian, Russian, Arab and American, all Israeli. They have the experience of studying within different contexts and learning paradigms to UK based students (Wisker & Sutcliffe, 1999), although an increasing number have undertaken BA and MA studies with APU, and all are required to fulfil the requirements of European research paradigms.

11.6.2   Action research and development programme

Our research work with these students accompanies the research development three stage programme (see figure 11.1) and the supervisory dialogues. These dialogues are conducted by the three 'guardian supervisors' who contribute to the programme, including the programme director. Each guardian supervisor has some responsibility for the whole cohort throughout their research, and each of the three of us have our 'own' PhD students (about 8 each) who are conducting research in areas aligned to our   specialist areas.

This spiral of action research set within the framework of the research and methods training development programme enables students to focus on key stages in their work. They work on the proposal (stage 1), the progress report 'confirmation of candidature' (stage 2) and writing up/ preparing for the viva (stage 3). At each stage a major consideration is exactly how their research methods genuinely enable them to discover what they seek in their work. Results of action research feed directly into workshops, supervisory dialogues and students' and staff reflections. It combines both quantitative and qualitative methods. The quantitative methods enable us to identify patterns of learning approaches and conceptions of research-as-learning across and between cohorts and to identify the results of individuals. The qualitative methods enable us to see how students grapple with, carry out and interpret their research aims and progress, using methodologies, and research methods within their conceptual frameworks. The qualitative research also runs alongside and makes direct use of development and intervention processes of research development workshops and supervisory workshops.

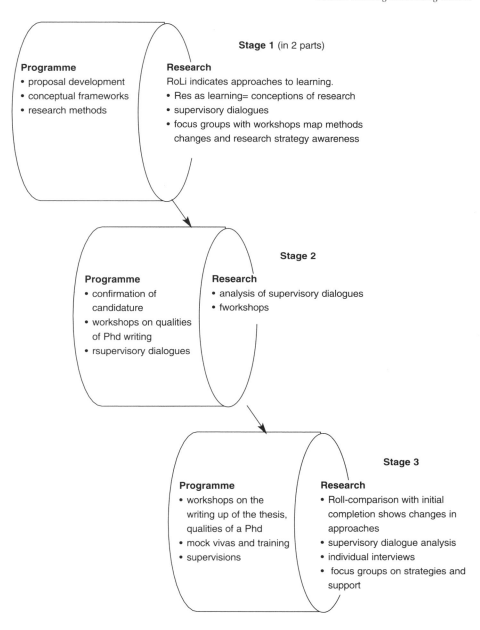

Figure 11.1   Action research cycle accompanying three post graduate research
development programme

11.6.3   Quantitative methods include:

1. The Reflection on Learning Inventory (RoLI, Meyer and Boulton-Lewis 1997). This identifies motivations for learning, intended outcomes, learning approaches, how a student conceptualises learning, and how they know learning has taken place. The RoLI is used with the students during the first and third stages of the research development programme to identify, share, track their approaches to learning and change in these over time. It builds on established theories of students' approaches to learning (Entwistle and Ramsden, 1983) adapting and further developing definitions of surface and deep learning by identifying 'accumulation' as a learning approach favouring (in specific question items) tendencies to see 'knowledge as discrete and factual'; 'understanding based on memory'; identifying 'meaningful learning' as owning the learning, fitting new learning into context, relating it to experience, memorising after understanding; and identifying 'transformation' as related to change outcomes such as changing the world, seeing it differently.

2. The Research-as-learning questionnaire (Wisker 1998) which identifies conceptions of research-as-learning and students' own versions of what they feel their research as learning involves.

    Inventories are analysed using SPSS to identify dissonance and patterns of learning behaviours. Dissonance is defined by a gap or a mismatch; in the case of learning, a mismatch or discrepancy between learning approaches, and between approaches and intended outcomes. Dissonance, it is argued, could lead to problems in achieving graduate learning outcomes (see Meyer & Vermunt 2000) and, we argue, postgraduate learning outcomes. Item averaged mean scores on the three contrasting subscales of the RoLi inventory (accumulation, meaning, transformation) yield information about numbers of students who confuse distinctions between accumulation and meaningful approaches, or who inappropriately take accumulation approaches when seeking largely transformational outcomes (which could leave a gap between results, and any interpretation of findings leading to change.) Items on the RoLi are scored using a Likert scale and include, for example:

    i)   (accumulation oriented items) "I believe that learning is getting all the facts in your head", "I believe that all learning has a discrete and factual nature";

    ii) (meaningful learning items) "I know I have learned something when I can build up a framework about it"; "Learning is about making connections with what you already know";

    iii) (transformational items)"Learning is about empowering oneself"; "When I am learning I feel I am able to make things happen".

11.6.4   Qualitative research methods include:

1. Focus groups as an adjunct to research methods development workshops.

2. Supervisory dialogues in all three stages.
    These are taped and analysed thematically using Nvivo. (for themes, see below) In analysing both supervisory dialogues and focus groups we look for awareness of the appropriateness of methods and conceptual frameworks to research questions and outcomes, and any changes between methods, conceptual frameworks and outcomes over time.

11.7   Results

Postgraduate research-as-learning problems perceived include:

1. Dissonance between aims and approaches resulting in the choice of inappropriate research methods for outcomes sought (often accumulation methods when transformational outcomes are sought);

2. Choice of methodologies and methods which could produce data from which it is difficult to identify coherent and organised meaningful findings. This often involves quantitative methods when outcomes such as qualitative information, feelings, attitudinal change are sought. Also incoherence in the face of amounts of data, identified by Hodge (1995) as negative postmodernism.

Early work with the first cohort of Israeli students in 1997 indicated there was potential dissonance between the research aims and methods of several students. In subsequent cohorts we used the RoLI at the beginning of the students' research to identify conceptions of learning, learning approaches and outcomes. This confirmed what we had suspected and heard in dialogues, helping identify specific dissonance between approaches, largely accumulation in orientation, and outcomes sought, largely transformational, in the case of several students. These results were similar each year (1998-2002 to date) in which we have conducted the research. Many students held the belief that knowledge is factual, memorising precedes understanding, and causality can be identified and mapped. In extreme cases, dissonance is caused by what have been termed 'pathological' learning approaches, ie an adherence to surface learning or accumulation approaches despite the complexity or active nature of the research and despite the level of the work itself (ie postgraduate). Such dissonance could produce frustration and amounts of data that cannot usefully be a genuine contribution to the research.

The Research-as-learning questionnaire developed in 1998 (Wisker) specifically aims to enquire about student conceptions of research and any mismatch between these conceptions and actual research being undertaken. Some students were identified as conceptualising their research as largely knowledge acquisition, the discovery of known facts, beliefs unlikely to lead to the kind of problem solving, risk taking and originality necessary at postgraduate level. Results from this are the focus of future papers.

Analysis of the RoLI showed that students in the 1998-2001groups take a mixture of accumulation and meaning oriented approaches. Some seek transformational outcomes. We identified potential dissonance between their aims and their approaches that could lead to problems with their research.

It is our contention that workshop activities and supervisory dialogues help such students to become aware of potentially problematic consequences of dissonant approaches and to change their approaches, methods and conceptual frameworks to better match approaches to outcomes sought. Dissonance shows itself in the work of individual students, but it is interesting to see patterns of perceptions of research activities emerging within the cohorts, enabling us as facilitators/supervisors to consider where we need to introduce students to other research methods (those which help problem solving, creativity, for example) and where we need to point out pitfalls of chosen research methods and beliefs. Dissonance could produce severe difficulties in managing and interpreting data purposefully, overcoming problems, coming to any coherent conclusions, and making recommendations for change based on conclusions. The Israeli postgraduates are highly motivated, dedicated to effecting positive change in their social and educational contexts within Israel, and often well placed through their work to effect such change, but choice of inappropriate research, methods and

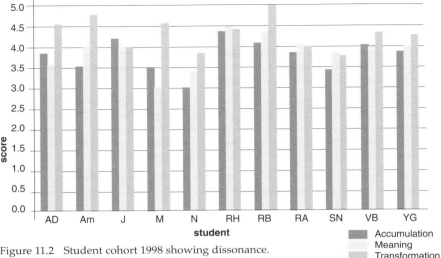

Figure 11.2   Student cohort 1998 showing dissonance.

the mismanagement of conceptual frameworks could endanger their projects at each stage (Wisker and Sutcliffe, 1999; Wisker, Robinson and Trafford 2000).

In the first stage programme, working with students to determine their research aims questions and methods, has enabled us to be more focused on the specific needs of each student. Questionnaire data feeds into that provided by supervisory dialogues, which are taped, transcribed and analysed using NVivo. During the research proposal development programme we have to hand the data from the questionnaires and the supervisions. Taping takes place while we supervise and is transcribed afterwards.

In the third stage programme, completion of the RoLI gives some of the indication of the continuation or overcoming of dissonance.

This shows some dissonance and some development in relation to those students completing in 2001. Eleven individuals with some measure of dissonance were tracked from 1998 to 2001. Following this, six were highlighted and three have been tracked to their final results. In two cases there has been some change in their dissonance ie a reduction in accumulation approaches and in transformational outcomes which indicates a closing of the gap between approaches and methods chosen, and outcomes, so a closer alignment within their conceptual frameworks. To date one of the three students has completed successfully. Some other interesting individual results follow.

Student M increased his accumulation score between 1998-2991 and decreased his meaning score. Unfortunately, he has also been resistant to guidance at all stages in the doctorate (submitted too early against advice and has been referred). A second student , J, exhibited dissonance throughout the 1998-2001 period, slightly reduced accumulation, meaning and transformation scores, and has not been able to complete. A third student, Y, reduced her accumulation scores, reduced her dissonance, maintained transformation scores and gained her PhD.

It is hard to jump to conclusions about this, but there does seem to be a correlation between reduction of accumulation scores (when students are not addressing a purely scientific area of research), reduction in dissonance (ie defined as no distinction between accumulation and meaning score) a tempering of the transformational outcomes (to make them more realistic, some outcomes being beyond the scope of the PhD) and success in the PhD.

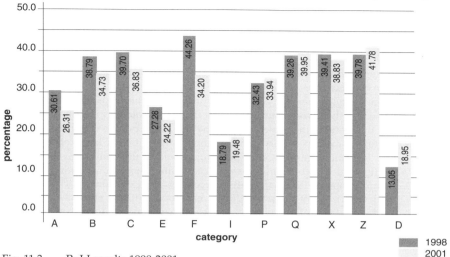

Fig. 11.3   RoLI results 1998-2001

11.7.1   Supervisory dialogues - qualitative findings

In the first stages of the research development programme which runs alongside the action research, we concentrate on clear underpinning and articulation of conceptual frameworks, of which the appropriate choices of research methods is a key element.

In their involvement in supervisory dialogues, students are seen to be empowered and encouraged to develop clear conceptual frameworks for their work. Supervisor questions using a variety of interactions have been identified through thematic analysis based on development from John Heron's 'six category intervention analysis' (1975), thematically analysed using NVivo.

Students need to identify the questions, and methods which will enable them to ask their questions, and they need to recognise the theoretical perspectives which inform their work. They are enabled in doing this through direct questioning, eliciting and supportive comments, and in the supervisory dialogues, some prescription and direction when there is a lack of clarity. It is possible to identify ways in which the supervisor and student work together to scrutinise research methods in relation to the field of study, in order to work out between them how these questions can be asked, which methods and vehicles enable the questions to be asked and findings to be produced and analysed. This is a dynamic and fascinating process.

Our research has produced some interesting examples of first stage dialogues between supervisors and students, and of student discussion arising from research method workshops. Focus groups taped and transcribed following these workshops reflect student discussion about the importance of developing clear conceptual frameworks and identifying appropriate research methodologies and methods. They also indicate ways in which these students learn, and how they work to support each other in the research task over time.

In the third stage of the research development programme, towards the end of their PhD research, students need to revise the whole research process and indicate in the completed thesis and viva how they can clearly identify the conceptual framework and argue it through with external and internal examiners. Dialogues, below, show students and supervisors working out progress at several stages.

The supervisory dialogues:

- pinpoint and ask for logical connections to be made and argued through and
- ask the students to 'tell the story' of the research – a visualisation of its journey.

In (a) logical argument helps some students and (b) metaphors help others. All benefit from being involved in both activities,

Students can see literally where the gaps and fissures, impossible leaps, crossed paths and blank spaces appear in their work, and where they might accumulate so much information which is actually unhelpful in their research task, that the actual process could be swamped.

Study of developmental supervisory dialogues reveal that different kinds of interaction are necessary at different stages in a student's project, and at different stages in a single dialogue. Individual dialogues often involve a variety of interactions, some informing, some eliciting. Our assumptions are that the variety is necessary for discussions which encourage and clarify the development of the project. It is very important that students are clearly aware of requirements, dates, rules and so on, but it is also essential for their work as largely independent learners that they are fully involved creative partners in the inception, clarification, development, progression, reshaping and interpretation of the data. One thought we have is that for ownership, responsibility and for the project to be the student's own, it is preferable to have a high number of eliciting interactions which gradually shape into the student taking control of a project they own and understand, and which is also coherent and likely to succeed. Challenging and clarifying interactions are also necessary in students' work to encourage problematising, creativity, the overcoming of blocks to learning and interpretation, and to encourage a move away from inappropriate decisions and interpretations.

Following taping, transcribing and analysis using NVivo, supervisory questioning themes were divided into ten intervention categories, developing Heron (1975).

- Didactic
- Prescriptive
- Informative
- Confronting
- Tension relieving/social
- Eliciting
- Supporting
- Summarising
- Clarifying
- Collegial exchange

Our own involvement and the shape of the dialogues has been gradually informed by reflecting and focusing our experiences as a staff team, discussing what does and does not seem to work with which student at which stage. The three staff members also have quite different kinds of style in interactions.

Analysing early dialogues with new PhD students who are shaping their proposals yields quite different kinds of interactions from those later on in the student's research. The gender of the supervisor and student is also a factor which will need to be explored through further work.

Stage one

Supervisory dialogues in the summer university, stage 1, take specific shapes designed to help students track through from aims and focus, conceptual framework to research design and methods and then onto the other elements of their work such as ethical considerations, time lines and justification for the level of the award.

Dialogue 1 – students are asked the following questions:

- What is your research question?

- What is your conceptual framework?

A good dialogue is mutually rewarding and leads to productive, directed, useful, owned work.

The following stage one dialogue explores a student's choice of methods, theories and conceptual frameworks to underpin her research. The supervisor elicits and clarifies both the practices and the terminology which aids metacognitive awareness of processes.

Student H:	In order to explore the very nature of management in geriatric hospital, the study will compare the first value regarding leadership and management to the actual managerial behaviours of the managers according to their subordinates.
Supervisor:	You think this is the conceptual framework?[Clarifying and eliciting]
Student H:	Yes.
Supervisor:	So what are the theories that you are working with? [Eliciting]
Student H:	OK, the theory actually, the theory I wanted say later on.
Supervisor:	But it's important now because the theories combine to form your conceptual framework. [Informative]
Student H:	The theory is in leadership and management in organisations.
Supervisor:	So organisational theory? [Eliciting]
Student H:	Yes and…
Supervisor:	And management theory. [Prescribing]
Student H:	Yes, and eh…management in hospitals, especially in geriatric hospitals.
Supervisor:	And you're combining….. [Eliciting]
Supervisor:	Um, maybe rather than learn about, investigate, because what you're actually doing is an investigation, it's a research. Yeah? Why does that come under the conceptual framework? [Clarifying]
Student H:	It's going to be question here.
Supervisor:	That's not your conceptual framework, that's your methodology. [Informative]
Student H:	But, it's a concept.
Supervisor:	What is a concept? [Eliciting]
Student H:	The concept of the research.
Supervisor:	Now, let's start again. (Laugh). The conceptual framework is the theories which are combined to create a framework which you can refer back to when you have your findings and which enable you to conceptualise or make sense of the findings, take meaning from the findings. [Tension relieving, informative]

Dialogues: stage three

Later in the student's final stage three of the development programme, they discuss the results from her questionnaires and the ways in which findings can relate to the original conceptual framework.

Supervisory dialogue: third, final stage

Supervisor: So already it is having an effect? clarifying, supporting

Student H: It is in effect already. So, I believe the results are good, I don't have all the results yet.

Supervisor: But at the moment it looks as though it will have some effect. eliciting

Student H: Yes.

Supervisor:: OK, so I've got three main questions to ask you in this interview and there are questions that for sure will come up in your viva. This is a good time to rehearse. You know the questions, the first one is: how would you justify your contribution to knowledge as having doctoral worthiness. Clarifying, eliciting.

11.7.2   Workshop addressing research methods and conceptual frameworks: first stage.

Supervisory dialogues are not the only opportunity for learning through discussion. Workshops in stage 1 and 3 focus on the development (stage 1) and then the final coherent clarification (stage 3) of the students' conceptual framework underpinning their work.

In an early conceptual frameworks and methods session in stage 1, activities aim to engage students in developing sound conceptual frameworks and appropriate research methods. This workshop involves small groups modelling handling large amounts of data and asking how this could be interpreted. It aims to enable students to consider how they could themselves manage a large amount of data should their research produce this. The session is held in small groups and taped. Results from the session show student reflection on methods. They also show a correlation of the links between choice of methodology and methods, and the ways students might realise difficulties inherent in using research-as-learning approaches producing accumulation of large masses of data somewhat removed from their object or outcomes. Results also indicate students' growing awareness that a variety of approaches might better suit their own research questions and aims than a single, probably quantitatively based, approach. The following comments are taken from the 1998 cohort's discussions, ie the first time we used the exercise.

When really focusing on the question of the focus groups, which aim to encourage a reflection on learning approaches and on disjunction between approach and aims, some of these students have come up with most useful reflections:

> Most of the people agree with it... links between movement. How can we show links? Sometimes the data that we got when collected can lead us to such assumptions that a lot of them... then we have to summarise them... select, decide which assumptions we want to research afterwards, and sometimes we have a previous assumption, and discover after we have collected data, we have a surprise - that nothing conforms to our thinking before, and we have to create absolutely new assumptions... so we need to research what's going on with our (prior) assumptions, then we collect the data... you have to check why it happens. (Student K)

These students discuss links between their previous assumptions and the data, and between both of these and how they might develop findings, draw conclusions. The difficulty of showing links using qualitative methods emerged. The group felt more secure with quantitative methods:

> If they want to use qualitative methods, how can they make the links? How can we show links? If we are making a quantitative sort of research, we can show the links through statistical methods, but if we are doing qualitative work, how can we show links? This belief must lead to a quantitative sort of research. (Student F)

For these students, involvement in questionnaire completion, data analysis discussions, and focus group discussions as part of an initial training/development programme has encouraged them to focus on the gaps and disjunctions between their aims and their methods. It is hoped that they are then more able to take a reflective approach likely to be more open to change and more able to accommodate and respond to the 'surprises' and 'creative' elements of PhD research as well as any clashes in approach and aims (as they meet them) during their research work.

The methods workshop is accompanied by a focus group and precedes the dialogues focusing on conceptual frameworks and methods.

The group work runs for an hour, then students are asked to reflect on the experience and feedback, with one person reporting on the process and the individual case of a person's research methods. In 2000, two of the groups chose to elect a spokesperson who fed back on someone else's methods - which added an extra level of succinctness and clarity to the description. Observation of the group work was fascinating. Students were clearly involved in explaining very precisely and then encouraging questions, suggestions, debates with other students. All of this aimed to help them to define and refine their methods (and change them if necessary). They found overlaps in methods - one group claimed they were all doing case studies - and some real contrasts which helped them to define their own choices. We taped the feedback session, which was very lively and amusing as well as focused. It shows insight into the reasons for the choice of methods and their appropriateness it also shows the way in which co-counselling of supportive peers can enable a student to clarify and focus on their methods. We hope that such support will continue. Sensitive development of support systems could be based on initial programmes of research methods and proposal training.

Some responses indicate cultural difference in research approaches:

F/Speaker: But we talked about connecting the concepts, most of the issues here, we talked about connecting the theories to the methods, because in Israel we used to write the literature and then the research. And then after, in the discussion we connect between the - but we don't really plan the research according to the theoretical.

Tutor: Is that - no? We've got 'yes' nods and 'no' nods. Is that a 'yes' nod? Do the rest of you agree, or not?
(General agreement.)

Some students are working through their research methods to ensure that they fit their aims and conceptual frameworks. One, concentrating on interactions and power in the school, says that discussion with the others in the group has enabled her to think of how the different people involved in her study might interact. She realises she needs to find a way to relate their responses and consider their interactions.

The group work was pronounced most useful as a clarifying procedure, although not everyone was yet fully able to reflect on how useful it could be to their formulation of their research methods:

Most of us were happy with the picture so far although some had some doubts whether the methodologies they are following is going to stay as it is, or there might be some changes. We asked some questions, we listened carefully to the answers. We did not only give positive feedback but we saw what we didn't like, we tried to be objective and we talked about it.

Students participating in the group work session reported a variety of responses. One was visibly seen to have what is called an 'aha!' moment when, through relating her conceptual framework to her research methods, she could see how the whole fitted together. She sat up and looked very pleased and reported that she suddenly could see how it was all working. On tape she commented that the actual process had been revelatory and valuable. There was a visible connection made between the conceptual framework - the whole pattern and shape of her work - and the methods chosen, so that she could see how one - methods - enable the other to be put into action.

Student M:	I also don't know if there's a connection between what we did before with understanding the conceptual framework and what we did now. But for me, it was very fruitful because then it became much… clearer to me. I mean understanding, putting on a sheet of paper the conceptual framework and directly how it applies to the methodology…
Tutor:	So how they follow through.
Student M:	Right, so just one as the cause of the other, and …
Tutor:	Because you had a moment there where visually you went 'ahh'. I don't know if somebody else saw that and I thought 'ooh, a penny's dropped there… '
Student M:	For me it was very good. And also I got, I don't know if it was because of that but I could explain very very clearly and I got feedback about - ah now I understand exactly what you are doing…
Student F:	Discuss it inside first. And it took time and I could see the difference, the changes.
Tutor:	Yes. So by explaining it, it made it clearer - for both of you, yeah?

11.7.3   Case study

Case studies emerge from the workshops and dialogues. D focuses on linking methods to outcomes.

Student D

Student D:	My study is special patients. I am an Art Therapist…
Supervisor:	You can tell us what it is.
Student D:	OK. The methodology? OK. I'm going to send about 300 questionnaires to senior Art Therapists and Supervisors Art Therapists in Israel to check if they have special patients. Some of them might not know about this item, or this subject, as I didn't do a month ago but I knew I had it in hand but I didn't know, I didn't give it a name. So from all the Art Therapists who have special patients - who had, I will prefer someone who had special patients and will give me some perspective about this problem. I will choose 5 of them and I think I'm going to interview them although I - coming to the therapist,

interviewing about the special patient I might go to, into his blood let's say, I don't know how you say it but it's kind of 'wow'. Because in some ways, we talked about it here, the special patient gives meaning to work, gives vision, goal, all our intuition starts working when we work with our special patient, it is very important to us. Some of his biography deals with ours as therapist, so the interviews might be very deep and interesting. And at the end of the tunnel which I'm going through, the moment I'll determine this issue, I think borders will be clearer and therapists will know that this problem exists, how to deal it, maybe some new tools, and that's it, I guess. Thanks. (Clapping).

Student S: This special patient. Is it special to the therapist or is it a special case?

Student D: Special to the therapist. Physio

Supervisor: I like the idea of a tunnel. I think people know what you mean about the long tunnel.

Student D: No light.

Supervisor: No light - yes, lots of light, but maybe not just yet. Thank you.

In this report back, the student develops her conceptual framework and clarifies the need for a variety of methods including questionnaires and interviews to address a sensitive and personal area.

11.7.4   Supervisory dialogues stage 3 final writing up

At this final third stage workshop, students are asked to clarify and defend all aspects and links in their conceptual frameworks and the written thesis.

Supervisor: And at the moment, each one of the chapters is a patchwork text of a lot of historical, real in-depth scholarly historical detail and some more generalisations and not quit enough historicist or feminist theory writing through. Sometimes, that's used to start the chapter but then you get bogged down in the details and the theory then kind of disappears from your analysis. (clarifying, supporting)

Student B: I think part of the problem is because I'm looking at my details as speaking for themselves as an exemplification of the theory.

Supervisor: For the reader, you have to make it really straightforward that that is what you're engaging with. But, I do think that you need to up front that you're taking these three approaches, so that you don't get somebody who's reading it who is just looking for new historicist approach. You have to tell them, no, no, no, I'm doing these three things like you did, I thought that was strong, that's good. Tell them you're doing three things, don't just go for the one because that's not actually the way you're writing, it's not what you want to do. (summarising, prescriptive)

This dialogue supports the student in their work to date and asks them to clarify how their critical approaches help them use their research questions and how explicit this is in the thesis itself. The dialogue encourages the student to make their methods and analysis explicit.

11.8   Conclusion

Our work with cohorts of international postgraduates indicates a need to recognise and develop supportive supervisory practices in relation to culturally inflected learning styles and expectations. We are keen to avoid cultural imperialism which asserts that European modes and research practices are essentially more appropriate or better. Instead, we work with each student to match research methods with their hoped for outcomes, rather than merely attempting to impose those methods with which we are ourselves most familiar per se. This is in alignment with the development of appropriate conceptual frameworks for their research, each of which will be different in relation to the specific research undertaken, and each of which needs to be internally coherent. Empowering and enabling students to conceptualise their research aims and conceptual frameworks, ask questions then proceed to appropriate research methods suggested by the materials, visiting specialists, and workshop activities on the research development programme, guided by our roles as guardian supervisors has proved to be a sound and flexible individually sensitive way of matching outcome to method. Indeed, over the last five years, some of the very creative and transformative, often therapeutic processes, many of the students intend to study and to develop through their research work have caused a creative responsive development of research methods among the group, stretching the descriptions offered by such as Robson (1993), Miles and Huberman (1984), and others.

Students are individuals, and responsiveness to individual differences in learning and need at postgraduate level should inform supervisory practices. The specific issue of matching research methods to the student's research aims, context and their conceptual framework is absolutely crucial in the process of supportive developmental work with students. There is no point in forcing a student to adopt certain methods, just because the supervisor/facilitator is more familiar with them. Nor can they be simply left to use methods which they have found helpful in their lower level, previous study. It is essential that the conceptual framework be clarified and the research methods should match and enable this to work itself through the research process. It is also essential that students understand the implications of their chosen methods - what these can and cannot help them to find out, how sound they are, what disclaimers need to be made, what the boundaries are. And they need to think about processing, analysing and making sense of the information and ideas (and the feelings) which are produced as a consequence of working with the chosen methods. In concentrating on the learning of our diverse Israeli postgraduates, we wished to develop supportive, developmental supervisory practices and programmes to better enable their learning and that of postgraduate students generally, with a specific focus on the establishing of the right research methods to get the research job done.

References

Biggs, J (1993). What do Inventories of Students' Learning Processes Really Measure? A theoretical review and clarification. In *British Journal of Educational Psychology*, **63**, 3–19.

Bloor, M and Bloor, T (1991). Cultural Expectation and Socio-pragmatic Failure in Academic Writing. In Adams, P, Heaton, B, and Howarth, P (Eds), *Socio-Cultural Issues in English for Academic Purposes*, Review of ELT, **1**(2), 1-12.

Chen, JR (2001). The Cross-Cultural Adjustment of Taiwanese Postgraduate Students in England. Unpublished PhD thesis. University of Warwick.

Entwistle, N and Ramsden, P (1983). *Understanding Student Learning*. London: Croom Helm.

Harris, R (1995). Overseas students in the UK University System. *Higher Education*, **29**, 77–92.

Heron, J (1975). *Six category intervention analysis*. London: Tavistock Institute.

Hodge, B (1995). *Monstrous Knowledge: Doing PhDs in the new humanities*. Australian Universities Review, **38**(2) 35-39.

Hughes, S and Wisker, G (1998). Improving the Teaching and Learning Experiences of Overseas Students. In Rust, C (Ed), *Improving Student Learning: Improving Students as Learners*, pp 479–488. Oxford: Oxford Centre for Staff Development.

Landbeck, R and Mugler, F (1994). *Approaches to Study and Conceptions of Learning of Students at the University of the South Pacific*, University of the South Pacific: CELT.

Meyer, JHF and Boulton-Lewis, GM (1997). *Reflections on Learning Inventory*.

Meyer, JHF and Kiley, M (1998). An Exploration of Indonesian Postgraduate Students' Conceptions of Learning. *Journal of Further and Higher Education*, **22**(3), 287–298.

Meyer, JHF and Vermunt, J (2000). Dissonant study orchestration in higher education: manifestation and effects. Introduction to special issue, *European Journal of Psychology of Education*, **15**, 3.

Miles, M, and Huberman, A (1984). *Qualitative Data Analysis: A Sourcebook of New Methods*. London: Sage.

Robson, C (1993). *Real World Research*. Oxford: Blackwell.

Samuelowicz, K (1987). Learning Problems of Overseas Students: Two Sides to a Story. *Higher Education Research and Development*, **6**(2) 121–133.

Todd, L (1996). Supervising Post-graduate Students: Problem or Opportunity? In McNamara, D and Harris, R (Eds), *Quality Teaching in Higher Education for Overseas Students*. London: Routledge.

Waller, S, Griffiths, S, Wu, S, Wisker, G, and Illes, K (2002). Towards the creation of institution-wide support for improving Language for Study Skills for international postgraduate students: providing adequate learning infrastructures including learning technologies and student support. In Rust, C (Ed), *Improving Student Learning Using Learning Technology*. Oxford: Oxford Centre for Staff Development.

Wisker, G. and Sutcliffe, N (1999b). (Eds), *Good Practice Supervising Postgraduates*. Birmingham: SEDA.

Wisker, G, (1999). Recognising (and encouraging the bridging of) Divisions in Postgraduates' Early Research Work. Paper presented to EARLI conference, Goteburg, Sweden.

Wisker, G, Robinson, G and Trafford, V (2000). Postgraduate Learning Styles and Enabling Practices: A Multicultural Action Research Study. Paper published in proceedings of second postgraduate research conference 'Making ends meet' Adelaide.

Zuber-Skerritt, O and Ryan, Y (1994). *Quality in Postgraduate Education*. London: Kogan Page.

12 From practice to theory in developing generic skills

Barbara de la Harpe and Alex Radloff
RMIT University, Melbourne, Australia

12.1 Introduction

For a number of years now attention has increasingly focused on the skills that university graduates develop during their undergraduate study. Concern has been expressed by employer groups worldwide that existing undergraduate programmes are not producing graduates with the kinds of skills that they need in order to be successful in the workplace. There is often a gap between what universities espouse as the outcomes of successful university study and what is actually taught, learned and assessed. More often than not, the emphasis is on discipline content knowledge rather than on skill development or other aspects of learning. More recently pressure has been placed on institutions of higher education by governments, professional bodies and quality agencies to produce graduates who are lifelong learners and equipped for careers in their chosen fields.

In addition, graduates themselves have reported that their undergraduate study has not improved their generic skills. Both employers and graduates report gaps in skill development (AC Nielsen, 2000; Dodridge, 1999; Koehn, 2001; Manninen & Hobrough, 2000). For example, a study of over 1,000 graduates from The London Institute showed that there was a high level of need for career management and enterprise skills and there were gaps in negotiation, networking and self-promotion skills (La Valle, O'Regan & Jackson, 2000). Another study of geography students by Haigh and Kilmartin (1999) found that students valued the opportunity to develop teamwork and public presentation skills, and both they and their teachers agreed that developing skills was an important outcome of university study.

Many universities have recognised that, in order to better meet employer requirements for quality graduates and student expectations, they need to make changes to the curriculum and, necessarily, to how it is taught and what is assessed. In response, a number of institutions around the world, notably in the UK, North America and Australia, have implemented projects, often in response to nationally determined agendas, to promote skill development. As a result, a number of different approaches have been adopted to promote skill development. These have ranged from stand-alone 'bolt-on' courses to courses where skills are highly integrated with the discipline content and are taught and assessed in-context by the subject teacher. In terms of coordination of skills across programmes of study, again, different approaches to what skills are taught and assessed have been reported. These range from skills being highly co-ordinated both horizontally and / or vertically to ad hoc instructor determined integration.

In this paper, we propose a theory that can be used to inform efforts to facilitate skill development. We draw on recent research literature on skill development, current learning theory and accounts of practice, to develop the theory. In doing so, we consider findings from a recent comprehensive study by Bennett, Dunne and Carré (2000) involving 32 university teachers, undergraduate students, 24 graduates in the first years of their employment, recruitment and training managers from 23 companies, and graduate employment schemes from two industries looking at skill acquisition in higher education and work settings. We also use a collection of 17 case studies from institutions in the UK, USA and Australia focusing on issues around skill development and integration (Fallows & Steven, 2000). In addition, we draw on 20 contributions by international researchers on developing core skills in higher education for a learning society (Dunne, 1999). Finally, we use our own experiences including our research on integrating learning support into the curriculum (de la Harpe, 1998) and the development of self-regulated learners (Radloff, 1997), our involvement in the design, development and implementation of a number of institutional projects on supporting skill development (de la Harpe & Radloff, 2001; de la Harpe, Radloff & Wyber, 2000a, 2000b; Soontiens & de la Harpe, 2002; Wyber & de la Harpe, 2000, 2001), and a combined 15 years of experience in professional development with academic staff across disciplines.

12.2   Towards a theory of skill development

A theory can be defined as "a set of concepts and propositions intended to describe and explain some aspect of experience" (Sigelman, 1999, p 11). In our case, the aspect of experience we wanted to make sense of is how institutions ensure that their graduates have developed selected skills during the course of their studies. In other words, we focused on explaining how skill development takes place successfully within a higher education setting.

The theory we propose responds to the concerns expressed about the gap between the rhetoric of skill development and the reality of the paucity of successful implementation programmes. Reasons for this lack of success include the absence of an effective champion or champions for skill development, poorly conceptualised change and implementation strategies, weak implementation of skill development programs and lack of evaluation of outcomes.

Implementing a skill development program "is not a simple and straightforward matter [but] [r]ather… requires careful consideration and skilled management" (Fallows & Steven, 2000, p 228). Generally, it requires knowledge and application of good practice in change and, project management, application of learning theory to skill development, insight, effective management of self and others, and ability to acknowledge the role of feelings at the individual and collective levels. In addition, it requires motivation to change and for recognition and reward to be aligned to activities around skill development. Moreover, it is dependent on both 'knowing and doing', that is, knowing that skills need to be developed and being able actually to undertake the necessary activities to do so.

Our theory-building efforts have involved a series of iterative steps beginning with the listing of all the constructs that we considered pertained to implementing initiatives in skill development such as drivers, consequences, shared understanding, ownership, commitment and feelings. We then ensured that the level of abstraction and analysis were consistent. During this step, it became clear that the level of abstraction and analysis needed to be at the collective rather than at the individual level in line with findings that systemic change or innovation is unlikely to occur if the focus of change is at the individual level. As Bennett, Dunne & Carré (2000, p 169-170) point out,

Evidence from research in schools on achieving effective innovation shows that attempts to change individual teachers is likely to fail unless there is support, and a similar willingness among their colleagues, together with appropriate support of policies within the institution itself… Change efforts can be instigated by individuals… but bottom-up initiatives… although admirable and often groundbreaking, do not provide an effective model for change across an institution, as research on innovation in schools has too often shown.

Thus, the theory proposes that initiatives aimed at developing graduate skills be focused at programme, department or faculty levels rather than at the individual instructor level. The theory also recognises the central role that change management plays in achieving outcomes.

In the next step we grouped and arranged the constructs into a logical order under four phases, namely, need, strategy, implementation and evaluation. We then considered the possible relationships between the constructs and represented these with arrows. Finally, we identified the underlying assumptions required for the theory to work, which are the presence of external drivers, a change agenda, systemic focus on change and consequences.

12.3   Describing the theory

The emergent theory is underpinned by a social constructivist approach to learning, which views learning as involving construction or reconstruction of knowledge through social interaction embedded in a particular cultural setting. Social constructivism is regarded as the most current conceptualisation of the learning process (Derry, 1996; Murphy, 2000; Umass Physics Education Research Group, 1999). The theory encompasses both knowing and doing, recognises the central role of regulation for effective action and takes into account cognition (knowledge and understanding), metacognition (knowledge of and control of self, task and context), motivation (the energisers of behaviour such as drivers and consequences), and affect (feelings associated with actions and thoughts) (Boekaerts, 1997; McKeachie, Pintrich, Lin, & Smith, 1986; Zimmerman, 1994).

As illustrated in Figure 12.1, the theory for skill development at the institutional level is dynamic, is triggered by a driver or drivers and involves an iterative process through four phases, namely need, strategy, implementation and evaluation.

Shared understanding, ownership and commitment

Shared understanding, ownership and commitment are fundamental to the theory. Each of the phases culminates in shared understanding and ownership of, and commitment to, the need for developing student skills inspired by a champion or champions, a strategy for a skill development initiative, implementation of the strategy and evaluation of the outcomes, respectively. Achieving shared understanding, ownership and commitment at each phase is mediated by knowledge of good practice; mediated by knowledge of self, task and the context; and mediated by feelings; and requires planning, monitoring and adapting activities. Appropriate consequences sustain the activities through each phase.

Knowledge of good practice

Knowledge of good practice in getting shared understanding and ownership of, and commitment to, the need, the strategy, the implementation and the evaluation in relation to skill development, is discussed below.

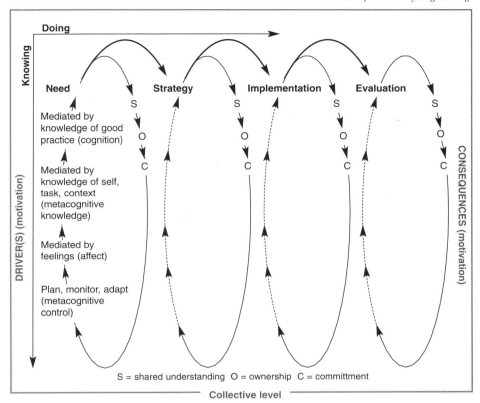

Figure 12.1   Skill development at the institutional level

In terms of the **need** for skill development, knowledge of good practice in change management identifies the central role of champions in articulating the need for skill development. Effective champions for skill development are people in leadership positions who are committed to skill development and are able to influence others to recognise the need for skill development as well. Further, champions must be in a position to provide resources to support skill development initiatives and, when necessary, make changes to organisational practices such as reward and recognition schemes to support the change initiatives (Wolverton, 1998). Champions develop a shared vision and a team approach, and legitimise and endorse change activities. For effective institutional implementation of a skills agenda, Fallows and Steven (2000) point out that one of the key issues to be addressed is the identification of "at least one visible champion" (p 224). Further, it is well recognised that leaders who champion innovation in teaching and learning are fundamental to the success of such innovations (Ramsden, 1998).

In terms of developing a **strategy** for a skill development initiative at the collective level, knowledge of good practice in strategy design and development highlights the importance of the approach, goals, instructor conceptions, and knowledge of how skills are best developed.

The approach to developing skills at the collective level needs to be discipline-based, collaborative, bottom-up as well as top down and in line with the strategic directions of the institution. Such an approach has been shown to be effective in changing staff perceptions and attitudes to their teaching and assessment practices in line with institutional goals (Ramsden, 1998). In addition, strategy development requires management by a project leader working with a team of staff. The project team needs to work in collaboration with instructors to develop the strategy.

Goals are most effective when they are clear, realistic, public, and achievable (Ford & Nichols, 1991). Both short term as well as long-term goals are needed to motivate and direct activities in developing a strategy for skill development.

Instructor conceptions of teaching and how they see their roles as teachers impact on their approach to teaching and assessment, and in turn, on the approach and strategies to learning that their students adopt (Kember, 1998; Prosser & Trigwell, 1999). For effective skill development, instructors need to have or to develop conceptions that are learner-centred and learning-oriented for them to be able to help learners develop their skills (de la Harpe, Radloff & Wyber, 2000a).

Knowledge of how skills are best developed requires that instructors have a good understanding of current theories of learning in order to facilitate skill development. In addition, research on skill development suggests that skills are best developed as part of regular discipline teaching and facilitated by the discipline teacher rather than in stand alone or in 'bolt-on' courses. Moreover, the skills need to be made explicit within the curriculum, and learning outcomes, learning activities and assessment tasks aligned (Biggs, 1999). This approach to skill development is more likely to be effective since, "[w]hen skills remain embedded and implicit within disciplinary study, and are not assessed, students are least likely either to recognise skills or to be eloquent, or even interested, in their description" (Bennett, Dunne & Carré, 2000, p 166).

In terms of **implementation** of a skill development initiative, knowledge of good practice suggests that there needs to be a focus on supporting instructors to contextualise the strategy, to try out new ideas and to share experiences with colleagues (de la Harpe & Radloff, 2000). In addition, it requires a commitment to meeting agreed milestones and documenting progress as part of quality enhancement and assurance.

In terms of **evaluation** of outcomes of a skill development initiative, knowledge of good practice points to the importance of getting feedback about the initiative from key stakeholders including students, instructors and employers on a number of levels. A well known model of evaluation of training and development initiatives (Kirkpatrick, 1998) identifies four levels of evaluation, namely reaction to the programme, learning achieved as a result of participation in the programme, transfer and application of the new learning in different settings and finally, impact of the learning achieved on such factors as performance and productivity. In the context of skill development, this evaluation model can be used to evaluate outcomes of skill development at each of the levels for students, instructors, the project team, support staff, and the champion(s). Graduates and employers can provide valuable information about the fourth level, namely the impact of skill development on graduate performance and on workplace productivity.

Knowledge of self, task and context

Shared understanding, ownership and commitment at each phase as described in the theory namely need, strategy, implementation and evaluation, are **mediated by knowledge of self, task and the context.** At a collective level, this means that there is a high level of insight and awareness of the strengths and weaknesses of the group (the programme, the department, the faculty), an understanding of the key tasks that need to be accomplished during each phase and appreciation of the idiosyncrasies of the context within which the activities are taking place. This metacognitive knowledge informs the way commitment, ownership and shared understanding is achieved in each phase. The importance of metacognitive knowledge for effective action is well documented in the literature on self-regulation of learning (Zimmerman, 1986, 1994).

Feelings

Shared understanding, ownership and commitment are also **mediated by feelings** or affect. The importance of feelings for successful achievement of shared understanding, ownership and commitment of each phase cannot be ignored (Boekaerts, 1993; McCombs & Whistler, 1989). The type and intensity of feelings associated with change initiatives can help or hinder progress and outcomes. Feelings need to be acknowledged and managed as an integral part of the learning and change that is necessary for skill development.

Planning, monitoring and adapting

Finally, achieving shared understanding, ownership and commitment requires **planning, monitoring and adapting** activities. Careful planning of activities, regular monitoring of progress in line with goals, and adapting activities in response to feedback and changed circumstances are important at every phase. Again, metacognitive control is central to effective learning and positive outcomes as evidenced by the literature on self-regulated learning (Zimmerman, 1986,1994).

Drivers and consequences

In the theory, **drivers** and **consequences** provide the motivation for institutional initiatives for skill development. A **driver** is a trigger for action and energises the change process. Most powerful drivers are around crises or major opportunities (Kotter, 1996). Drivers for skill development include for example, government reviews, quality audits, accrediting bodies, significant employer group feedback, student dissatisfaction, opportunity for new funding sources, need to enhance institutional reputation, etc. Drivers relating to skill development need to be significant to influence action because skill development is a complex and challenging concept (Bennett, Dunne & Carré, 2000).

Consequences associated with skill development initiatives at the institutional level may be both positive and negative. Positive consequences may include recognition and rewards such as promotion, conference attendance, additional resources to support teaching, acknowledgement by professional and employer groups, increased demand for places in the programme, and positive student evaluations, etc. Negative consequences may include increased workload, stress associated with new ways of teaching, conflict with peers and student dissatisfaction and resistance to engaging in skill development. Successful implementation of institutional skill development initiatives requires identifying and using effective consequences and ensuring that positive consequences outweigh negative ones.

12.4   Conclusion

The emerging theory described in this paper is based on a synthesis of recurring themes from the now extensive literature on generic skill development and is aimed at informing practice at an institutional level. The theory reflects the complex, evolving, effortful and risky nature of implementing skill development initiatives in the current higher education climate with all its pressures and uncertainties. Further, it highlights the importance of constructive alignment between key variables including:

- need, strategy, implementation and evaluation

- cognition, metacognition, motivation and affect

- drivers and consequences

- knowing and doing

Finally, the theory highlights that the challenge of turning knowing into doing remains at the heart of effective institutional implementation of skill development initiatives. We hope that the theory presented in this paper will help to explain and go some a way towards meeting this challenge.

References

AC Nielsen Research Services. (2000). *Employer satisfaction with graduate skills: Research report.* (Evaluations and Investigations Program Report 99/7). Canberra, ACT: Commonwealth of Australia.

Bennett, N, Dunne, E, and Carré, C (2000). *Skills development in higher education and employment.* Buckingham: SRHE and Open University Press.

Biggs, J (1999). *Teaching for quality learning at university. What the student does.* Buckingham: SRHE and Open University Press.

Boekaerts, M (1993). Being concerned with well-being and with learning. *Educational Psychologist*, **28**(2), 149-167.

Boekaerts, M (1997). Self-regulated learning: A new concept embraced by researchers, policy makers, educators, teachers, and students. *Learning & Instruction*, **2**, 161-186.

de la Harpe, B (1998). *Design, implementation and evaluation of an in-context learning support program for first year Education students and its impact on educational outcomes.* Unpublished doctoral dissertation, Perth: Curtin University of Technology.

de la Harpe, B, and Radloff, A (2000). Supporting skill acquisition: Professional development for academic staff. In Fallows, S and Steven, C (Eds), *Integrating key skills in Higher Education: Employability, transferable skills and learning for life,* pp 165-174. London: Kogan Page.

de la Harpe, B, and Radloff, A (2001). Learning to be strategic about helping staff to increase graduate employability. In Rust, C (Ed), *Improving Student Learning: Improving Student Learning Strategically,* pp 220–226. Oxford: Oxford Centre for Staff Development.

de la Harpe, B, Radloff, A, and Wyber, J (2000a). What do professional skills mean for different disciplines in a business school? Lessons learned from integrating professional skills across the curriculum. In Rust, C (Ed), *Improving Student Learning: Improving student learning through the disciplines,* pp 9-23. Oxford: The Oxford Centre for Staff Development.

de la Harpe, B, Radloff, A, and Wyber, J (2000b). Quality and generic (professional) skills. *Quality in Higher Education*, **6**(3), 231-243.

Derry, S (1996). Cognitive schema theory in the constructivist debate. *Educational Psychologist*, **31**(3/4), 163-175.

Dodridge, M (1999). Generic skill requirements for engineers in the 21st century. *Proceedings – Frontiers in Education Conference*, **3**, (13a9) 9-14.

Dunne, E (Ed) (1999). *The learning society: International perspectives on core skills in higher education*. London: Kogan Page.

Fallows, S, and Steven, C (2000). *Integrating keys skills in higher education: Employability, transferable skills and learning for life*. London: Kogan Page.

Ford, ME and Nichols, CW (1991). Using goal assessments to identify motivational patterns and facilitate behavioral regulation and achievement. In Maehr, ML and Pintrich, PR (Eds), *Advances in motivation and achievement*, **7**, pp 51-84. Greenwich, Connecticut: JAI Press Inc.

Haigh, MJ, and Kilmartin, MP (1999). Student perceptions of the development of personal transferable skills. *Journal of Geography in Higher Education*, **23**(2), 195–206.

Kember, D (1998). Teaching beliefs and their impact on students' approach to learning. In Dart, B and Boulton-Lewis, G (Eds), T*eaching and learning in higher education*, pp 1-25. Camberwell, Victoria: ACER Press.

Kirkpatrick, D (1998). *Evaluating training programs*. New York: Berrett-Koehler.

Koehn, E (2001). Assessment of communications and collaborative learning in Civil Engineering education. *Journal of Professional Issues in Engineering Education and Practice*, **127**(4), 160.

Kotter, JP (1996). *Leading change*. Boston: Harvard Business School Press.

La Valle, I, O'Regan, S, and Jackson, C (2000). The art of getting started: Graduate skills in a fragmented labour market. Institute for Employment Studies Report 364. Eric Document ED436679.

Manninen, J, and Hobrough, J (2000). Skills gaps and overflows? A European perspective of graduate skills and employment in SMEs. *Industry and Higher Education*, **14**(1), 51-57.

McCombs, BL, and Whistler, JS (1989). The role of affective variables in autonomous learning. *Educational Psychologist*, **24**, 277-306.

McKeachie, WJ, Pintrich, PR, Lin, Y, and Smith, DAF (1986). *Teaching and learning in the college classroom. A review of the research literature*. (Technical report No. 86-B-001.0). National Centre for Research to Improve Postsecondary Teaching and Learning, University of Michigan.

Murphy, E (2000). Constructivism: From philosophy to practice [Online]. Available at: http://www.stemnet.nf.ca/~elmurphy/emurphy/cle.html

Prosser, M, and Trigwell, K (1999). *Understanding learning and teaching*. Buckingham: SRHE and Open University Press.

Radloff, A (1997). *A longitudinal study of self-regulation of learning in adult university students*. Unpublished doctoral dissertation, Murdoch University, Western Australia.

Radloff, A, de la Harpe, B, and Wright, L (2001). A strategic approach to helping university teachers to foster student self-directed learning. In Rust, C (Ed), *Improving Student Learning: Improving Student Learning Strategically*, pp 262–270. Oxford: Oxford Centre for Staff Development.

Ramsden, P (1998). *Learning to lead in higher education*. London: Routledge.

Sigelman, CK (1999). *Life-span human development* (3rd Edn). Pacific Grove, CA: Brooks/Cole Publishing.

Soontiens, W, and de la Harpe, B (2002). *Professional skill development in Australian Universities: Is there a bias?* Refereed proceedings of the Higher Education Research and Development Society of Australasia (HERDSA) conference Quality Conversations, Perth, WA.

UMass Physics Education Research Group (1999). *A constructivist view of science education.* [Online]. Available at:
http://www-perg.phast.umass.edu/perspective/Constructivism.html

Wolverton, M (1998). Champions, agents and collaborators: Leadership keys to successful systemic change. *Journal of Higher Education Policy and Management,* **20**(1), 19-30.

Wyber, J, and de la Harpe, B (2000). *Teaching generic skills in context: a quality experience.* Proceedings of the Hong Kong Council for Academic Accreditation (HKCAA) International Conference – New Millenium: Quality & Innovations in Higher Education, Hong Kong, December 4-5.

Wyber, J, and de la Harpe, B (2001). *Professional skills of postgraduate students – enhancement for a career in business.* Refereed proceedings of the HERDSA conference 2000, Toowoomba, Queensland.

Zimmerman, BJ (1986). Becoming a self-regulated learner: Which are the key subprocesses? *Contemporary Educational Psychology,* **11**, 307-313.

Zimmerman, BJ (1994). Dimensions of academic self-regulation: A conceptual framework for education. In Schunk, DH and Zimmerman, BJ (Eds), *Self-regulation of learning and performance. Issues and educational applications* pp 3-21. Hillsdale, New Jersey: Lawrence Erlbaum Associates.

13 Encouraging lifelong learning using information literacy: the development of a theoretical evaluative framework

Nikky Häberle
Cape Technikon, South Africa

13.1 Introduction

Teaching is not so much about the content (information) as it is about teaching students what to do with it (create knowledge). This idea in itself is not new. When striving to improve student learning, the focus is on teaching learners how to learn, and not what to learn. What role does information literacy play in contributing towards improving learning and can it really encourage lifelong learning?

Today's society has been termed the 'information age'. The information explosion in the second half of this century was accelerated by the development and increasing use of technology, particularly the role played by computers. Apart from being able to store vast amounts of information, computers allow for so much more information to be accessible to users. Database systems and the internet increasingly store information electronically that used to be available in traditional print form only. Information technology can be applied to almost any situation and it is this generic usefulness in society that has made it so pervasive. The information explosion is best summed up by Ford (1997: 16):

> In the past three decades, more words have been churned out than in the past five millenniums... it would take a reader eight hours a day for five months to consume just one days' output of technical data.

The problem is that information on its own is passive. It requires interaction and an active and empowered mind to take information and create new knowledge. Gibbs and Habeshaw (1989:17) expressed this idea pertinently after they examined the origin of the word 'knowledge', which has its roots in Greek and ancient Norse and literally translated means 'to have sport with ideas': "Simply giving students information by telling them... will have no impact on their understanding unless they have sport with this information".

Breivik and Gee (1989:13) go one step further and describe information literacy as the new survival skill in the information age. It is this paradigm that set the framework within which the study was based.

13.1.1 A South African Perspective

At the media launch of the National Plan for Higher Education on Monday 5 March 2001, the Minister of Education, Professor Kader Asmal, quoted from president Thabo Mbeki's State of the Nation address at the opening of the 2001 Parliament session (South Africa. Department of Education, 2001). In this address, the president stated that both universities and technikons are expected to play a leading role in contributing to the development of an information society in South Africa.

There are two major challenges facing Higher Education in South Africa:

i   *Transformation*

The democratisation of tertiary education is now in its seventh year and has enabled today's student body to become a multicultural population, one that more accurately represents South Africa's diverse cultures. However, it must be remembered that South Africa faces a unique situation in light of past political agendas and racial discrimination, and learners entering higher education are not a homogenous group. The majority of learners entering tertiary education lack the necessary study skills to cope with the demands of Higher Education. According to the National Commission on Higher Education (South Africa, 1996a: 1) these deficiencies in the educational system are a result of "vast disparities between historically black and historically white institutions in terms of facilities".

In 1995 the Department of Education responded to the challenge by establishing the National Qualification Framework (NQF) to facilitate the democratic transformation of the national education and training system (SAQA, 1997: 6). The NQF was put forward as a mechanism to achieve the educational objectives of transformation and contribution to the development of lifelong learners. The task of implementing the transformation process has been entrusted to the South African Qualification Authority (SAQA). The latter oversees the generation of standards, the design of which is primarily aimed at promoting lifelong learning (SAQA, 1997: 3). Seven critical cross-field outcomes have subsequently been identified for learners in Higher Education. For registration, all seven critical cross-field outcomes have to be incorporated appropriately into the proposed qualification, before it will be considered by SAQA.

ii   *The changing nature of society*

In the 21st century the world has been described as a global village as a result of the increase in flow of goods, services, capital, information, and knowledge across national and international borders. This permeation of trade barriers has led to greater competition amongst providers, forcing higher levels of productivity and efficiency, which in turn encourages the development of technology to provide more goods of better quality at a cheaper cost. This rapid pace of technological advance brought about by globalisation has resulted in both skilled and semi-skilled workers having to engage in lifelong learning if they want to maintain the pace of their competitors and remain at the cutting edge of technological development (Western Cape. Provincial Administration, 2000: 2-4). Failure to engage in lifelong learning would result in potential loss of a competitive edge, loss of business, and on a collective scale – economic decline.

Responding to this changing nature of society requires preparing multi-skilled learners that are able "to think critically and creatively, to pose and solve problems... to become independent and lifelong learners" (Mehl, 1997: 16). The need to develop and provide effective support services for learners has become critical, especially if the government's vision of higher education making a major contribution to the delivery of skilled and socially committed professionals and intellectuals is ever to become a reality.

Furthermore, the African National Congress Education Department reported in its policy framework for education and training that: "Information is of fundamental importance to the process of social and economic development. The quality of life of individuals, communities and nations is increasingly determined by their capacity to absorb, act on and use information. Information resources, skills and literacy are therefore essential elements of lifelong learning" (African National Congress Education Department, 1995: 83).

This is highly significant in particular as the fourth critical outcome listed by SAQA requires learners to be able to "collect, analyse, organise and critically evaluate information" (SAQA, 1997: 7). This aligns with the definition of information literacy as accepted during the course of this study, which "refers to the ability of learners to access, use and evaluate information from different sources, in order to enhance learning, solve problems and generate new knowledge" (Sayed & Karelse, 1997: 13). The aim of information literacy is thus towards encouraging lifelong learning and it is this criteria which SAQA and the NQF listed first as their aim (SAQA, 1997: 3). Information literacy has thus become an integral skill in today's changing society.

In 1997, the Cape Technikon responded to this need by designing a study skills programme for first-year learners called the 'Integrated First Year Experience' (IFYE). The IFYE aligns with the paradigm shift in higher education towards student-centred learning and outcomes-based education, resulting in independent, lifelong learners. An information literacy module forms part of the IFYE programme. In 1997, an updated information literacy initiative was developed at the Cape Technikon using internet-based learning as a means of encouraging self-directed learning, thereby increasing access to knowledge and facilitation of lifelong learners (French et al, 1999: 10).

13.2. The information literacy cycle: a conceptual model of information literacy

The aim was thus to conceptualise the complex nature of information literacy in a local context and thereby also offer a tentative answer as to how information literacy might be integrated into the educational system.

It was felt that a circular model would best represent the concept of information literacy; as with any cycle, there is the implication of an iterative process. This model reflects the goal of information literacy, which is to contribute to an ongoing, life-long, learning experience.

The model consists of three stages, starting with the attitude stage, and circling via the skills stage to the cognitive stage. All three stages are of equal value and can only contribute successfully to the achievement of information literacy when all three stages are linked together and the 'circle' of encouraging information literacy is kept in constant motion.

The model should be viewed beginning in the centre, the focal point remaining always on the learner. This contemporary view of education takes cognisance of the fact that learning is an active process, which involves the quest for knowledge rather than a passive transfer of information. This idea was pertinently expressed by William Butler Yeats (cited in Baer, 1999) when he wrote: 'Education is not the filling of a pail, but the lighting of a fire'.

The lecturer's role has been replaced by that of facilitator who plays essentially a supporting role. Rather than relying solely on the facilitator for information, learners are encouraged, through the facilitator's teaching style, to utilise the many different information sources available, thereby preparing them for active and responsible citizenship in an information society. The permeable circle surrounding the learner in the centre of the model represents the two–way communication that is being encouraged in the 'new' paradigm. Learners are thus no longer solely reliant on the facilitator for information (South Africa. Department of Education, 1997a: 6-7).

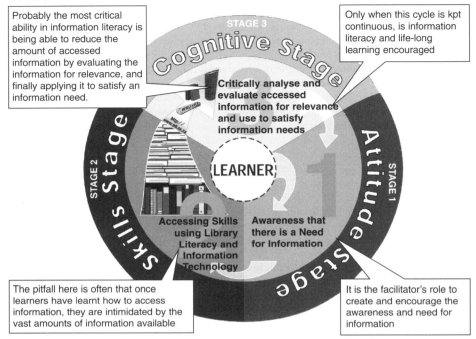

Probably the most critical ability in information literacy is being able to reduce the amount of accessed information by evaluating the information for relevance, and finally applying it to satisfy an information need.

Only when this cycle is kpt continuous, is information literacy and life-long learning encouraged

Critically analyse and evaluate accessed information for relevance and use to satisfy information needs

LEARNER

Accessing Skills using Library Literacy and Information Technology

Awareness that there is a Need for Information

The pitfall here is often that once learners have learnt how to access information, they are intimidated by the vast amounts of information available

It is the facilitator's role to create and encourage the awareness and need for information

Figure 13.1   The Information Literacy Cycle -
A conceptual model of information literacy

Stage 1

Facilitators have the responsibility to adapt their teaching style to create an awareness in their learners that there is a need for information. This may be achieved through relevant subject-specific assignments, which encourages the use of various information sources, such as for example, different sections within the library, the media, government papers, and the Internet, for the successful completion of the assignments.

By awakening an intrinsic interest within the learner, and by integrating the teaching of information literacy into the subject content, and making it relevant to a direct and immediate information need, learners should be more motivated to react positively than if it were offered as an 'add on' with no perceived relevance.

Thus, it is important to start by encouraging a positive attitude towards information literacy by creating an awareness that there is a need for information. Once a positive attitude has been awakened, learners are ready and more intrinsically motivated to learn the skills required to access the information that they require.

Stage 2

It is at this stage that the learner is ready to learn the skills required to be able to access the information that they require. Only now would the teaching of library literacy reach its full potential with learners. The use of information technology and computer literacy, particularly for those learners who have not yet had access to computers, is now of critical importance since it relates to a direct information need (for example, their assignments).

'Knowing how to work a PC, use word-processing software and surf the Internet have become practical, entry-level skills, not key competencies' (Albrecht, 2001: 28).

A slight overlap of the skills and cognitive stage occurs in the model at this stage. It was decided to incorporate library literacy and academic literacy into the 'skills' stage of the conceptual model together with computer literacy even though they each contain a significant cognitive aspect. Together these literacies constitute the skills of the second stage, required towards achieving the broader concept of information literacy.

Stage 3

Once learners have been taught how to access information using the library and the latest information technology they are, however, left with vast amounts of accessed information (represented by the large arrow in the model). The adverse effects of this information overload frightens many learners into aborting their searches for information if they are not readily equipped with probably the most critical ability in information literacy – the cognitive ability to evaluate information for relevance and apply it to satisfy an information need. The 'cognitive stage' of the model represents the higher order cognitive abilities required of the learner; the ability to critically analyse and evaluate the accessed information for relevance, thus eliminating all unnecessary information. With specific reference to the exponential growth rate of information available on the internet, Albrecht (2001: 29) wrote: 'as the sheer quantity of information increases, its quality inevitably decreases. Mass and class are incompatible… and the tendency of the internet to level all information to the same common denominator of mediocrity – make it crucially important to evaluate the quality of what you see, hear, and read'.

Yet information literacy requires even more from the learner, and that is the ability to use and apply the selected information to help solve an educational or social problem. This final stage of the model can only be reached successfully and learners reach their full potential when they have moved through each consecutive stage of the information cycle.

The higher order cognitive skill of evaluating the accessed information for relevance is not restricted only to information found in an academic library and the application of this information to solve a problem is not restricted only to an academic context, but may instead be applied to any information need, be it in an academic, social, economic, or political context.

13.2.1 Information Cycle – information literacy as a life skill:

Once the initial information need has been satisfied, many traditional information literacy initiatives end. However, it is suggested that only once another information need is created, thus keeping the information cycle in constant motion, can the objectives of encouraging information-literate behaviour amongst learners be achieved. It is within the academic environment that facilitators have the opportunity to create such a cycle and the responsibility towards their learners to encourage information-literate behaviour. However, it is only when learners leave the academic environment and proceed to apply their information-literate behaviour to their everyday lives (professional, personal and social), may it be said that the mission of encouraging life-long learners, who will be responsible citizens in an information society, has ultimately been achieved.

13.3   A taxonomic approach to evaluating information literacy

While the importance of information literacy as a fundamental skill amongst learners in the 21st century has been acknowledged and documented on an international scale (Association of College and Research Libraries, 2000), a national scale (via SAQA policy documents), and a provincial scale (Sayed & Karelse, 1997), what is conspicuous in most programmes is the absence of a robust theoretical framework on which the intervention is based. The aim of this study was therefore to develop an evaluative framework that could be applied to a variety of information literacy interventions.

A review of the literature indicated that the majority of information literacy intervention programmes have a tendency to evaluate the ability of their learners in terms of the success of the information literacy programme, generally by means of an information retrieval task (Saracevic & Kantor, 1988: 61-176; Su, 1992: 503-516; Smithson, 1994: 205-221; Nahl-Jakobovits & Jakobovits, 1990: 448-462). These studies focused on the evaluation of the learners, a very important aspect of any educational intervention. However, the focus of this study is on developing an evaluative framework in order to also determine the theoretical adequacy of the information literacy programme from an educational perspective.

The evaluative framework was thus eventually based on a behavioural taxonomic approach using the Taxonomy of Library Skills and Errors (the S&E Taxonomy) developed by Nahl-Jakobovits and Jakobovits (1990) and subsequently the Taxonomy of Behavioural Objectives for Information Literacy (the BO Taxonomy) developed by Nahl-Jakobovits and Jakobovits (1993), see Appendix A and B. Within this behavioural taxonomic approach exist three domains – affective, cognitive, and psychomotor. They developed a system for library user education based on a behavioural taxonomic approach, which is best summed up by Nahl and James (1997: 8) in their description:

> The act of searching as an external psychomotor activity is directed by its cognitive aspect, and driven by its affective... remove the affective process in searching and there is left no need or purpose... remove the cognitive aspect and there is left no strategy or plan... remove the psychomotor and there is left no performance or execution.

This approach was derived from Bloom's "Taxonomy of Educational Objectives" (1973). The taxonomy classifies human behaviour into three domains, adapted from the ancient Hebrew and Greek civilisations according to which the human body is made up of three parts, the soul (affective), the mind (cognitive), and body (psychomotor):

- The affective domain (will), which describes changes in interest, motivation, attitude and feelings

- The cognitive domain (understanding), deals with intellectual abilities and skills

- The psychomotor domain (actions), which includes physical behaviour such as movements, sensations, perceptions and speech

There are three levels that may be attained within each domain – orientation, interaction, and internalisation.

Initially, in 1997, the information literacy module of the IFYE Programme was evaluated using this taxonomic approach. The motivating factor behind the evaluation of the IFYE information literacy module was to determine whether it would be suitable as an implementable intervention at other institutions in the Western Cape. This coincided with the aims of Infolit, an independent project developed in the Western Cape within the framework of the Cape Libraries Project (CALICO). Infolit aimed at focusing on the education of information literacy in the Western Cape, taking into consideration the specific needs of learners in this area (Underwood, 2000). As part of Infolit's drive to promote information literacy, institutions of Higher Education in the Western Cape were invited to submit information literacy pilot projects.

The application of the S&E Taxonomy to the IFYE information literacy module was used to demonstrate that the taxonomic approach, used as a theoretical evaluative framework, had predictive validity. Potential strengths and potential weaknesses predicted by the theoretical analysis manifested themselves during the practical implementation of the module. The theoretical evaluation was cross-validated using interviews with facilitators and learner questionnaires. In 1993, Nahl-Jakobovits and Jakobovits (1993:79) developed the BO Taxonomy based on the same structure as the earlier S&E Taxonomy (1990). This taxonomy extended beyond the boundaries of library use to include the current broader concept of information literacy. What was interesting was the comparison that was made between the two taxonomies.

With the development of the updated and contextually more applicable BO Taxonomy, the analysis was repeated using this new taxonomy. It demonstrated that the taxonomic approach used as a theoretical evaluative framework had construct validity. Thus the initial applications of the two taxonomies demonstrated that the taxonomic approach to the evaluation of information literacy interventions was both practicable and informative. The evaluation also demonstrated that the two taxonomies that were applied had distinct limitations to the context of higher education in South Africa. One of the major drawbacks experienced was that although the S&E Taxonomy proved very useful in the evaluation of the IFYE Module, it focused exclusively on library literacy. The BO Taxonomy on the other hand, focused on information literacy, yet pitched its behavioural outcomes on a level often beyond the reach of South African Higher Education. At the orientation level, for example, first-year learners were required to achieve critical thinking skills and evaluation skills (listed as Critical Exit Level Outcomes on the NQF in the South African Education System).

For this reason the development of a new taxonomy was considered. Before a new taxonomy could be informed the conceptual difficulties experienced with each of the previous taxonomies needed to be addressed.

14.4 The taxonomy of educational outcomes for information literacy in higher education

The conceptual model of information literacy provided the foundation for the development of the new taxonomy. The 'information literacy cycle' informed the design of the new taxonomy – the Taxonomy for Education Outcomes for Information Literacy in Higher Education (the EO Taxonomy) – and consequently, a change in the order of the cognitive and physical (skills) domains is observed in Level 4 of the taxonomy. The new taxonomy is a combination of the S&E Taxonomy and the BO Taxonomy. All three primary domains of the existing taxonomies were incorporated while making substantial changes to the concepts described and the attendant wording of the various outcomes.

	Affective	AE	Cognitive	CE	Physical	PE	Evaluative (E)
Level 1 **Infrastructural** **prerequisites** **Objective:** Provision of adequate resources for information literacy development **Stakeholders:** institution	**A1** Provided with adequate information literacy training and a support infrastructure, facilitators will accept their role in the provision of information literacy education	E1	**C1** Commitment . from the institutional decision-makers for the promotion of information literacy will be evident in all policy forums and policy documentation	E1	**P1** The institution will provide adequate resources and the infrastructure required for the successful implementation of the information literacy intervention	E1	**E1** An evaluation. programme covering all institutional stakeholders involved with promoting the information literacy will be implemented
Level 2 **Orientation** **Objective:** introduction to the concept of information literacy **Stakeholders:** library	**A2** Learners will evidence an awareness of the general need for information in academic and social life	E2	**C2** Learners will acquire information-relevant terminology and be able to comprehend information-relevant distinctions	E2	**P2** Learners will be able to access and retrieve information from the various electronic and non-electronic information sources available in the library	E2	**E2** The library will implement a program to evaluate the effectiveness of the information literacy orientation received by learners on all three domains
Level 3 **Interaction** **Objective:** information access & retrieval **Stakeholders:** facilitators in co-operation with subject librarian	**A3** Learners will be able to confidently identify specific information needs required to complete a subject-specific information retrieval task/ assignment	E3	**C3** Given the subject-specific information retrieval task, learners should be able to formulate appropriate questions and plan an effective search strategy	E3	**P3** Provided with a specific information retrieval task, learners should negotiate search queries and assess the accessed information for relevance	E31	**E3** Stakeholders will jointly evaluate how comprehensively the learners have been engaged with the information literacy interaction in all three domains
	Affective	E4	Physical	E4	Cognitive	E4	Evaluative (E)
Level 4 **Problem solving** **Objective:** Learning to learn **Stakeholders:** facilitators in co-operation with subject librarian	**A4** Learners will respond positively to the challenge of evaluating substantial amounts of accessed information for relevance		**P4** Learners will be able to identify and successfully access multiple information sources relevant to a variety of problems		**C4** Learners will be able to evaluate the information content and apply the information to solve a variety of problems	1	**E4** Stakeholders will jointly evaluate learners' s progress through information literacy interventions, across all three domains

Table 13.1: Taxonomy of educational outcomes for information literacy interventions in higher education

13.4.1   Distinctive features of the new taxonomy

Highly significant is that a new horizontal level was added, which sought to capture the need for adequate orientation to information literacy, something that was implied but not explicit in either of the two taxonomies used.

A further addition was the inclusion of a distinct and separate evaluative domain across all four vertical levels, to accentuate the need to ensure that all levels are appropriately evaluated in terms of the objectives set for them. The absence of any evaluative component that emerged during the analysis of the IFYE Module highlighted the need for such a component.

This vertical dimension was added to the EO Taxonomy to accommodate the self-evaluative component that any educational intervention should contain. This evaluative dimension would place specific emphasis on the competence of the learner, the facilitator, and on the adequacy of the institutional infrastructure at each of the four horizontal levels of the Taxonomy.

The section below reviews the new Taxonomy, and as each level is discussed, the associated evaluative domain is explained in context. In addition, significant departures from the wording or concepts of the original taxonomies upon which this one is based are noted and explained.

Level one: Infrastructural prerequisites

Prior to the development of any educational project an analysis of the infrastructural prerequisites is required. An information literacy needs analysis for learners in the Western Cape has been provided by Sayed (1998). The objective of Level 1 of the new taxonomy is to ensure that adequate resources for information literacy development are provided.

The stakeholders included in this level are those who, although involved with the promotion of the information literacy intervention, are not primarily involved with its development (as compared to the library and its staff, for example). It is therefore important to determine the commitment, availability and adequacy of these infrastructural resources before proceeding with the development of the information literacy intervention.

Level two: Orientation

The objective at level two – orientation – is to introduce learners to the concept of information literacy. Information literacy is a complex literacy comprising of many skills and abilities (including the affective, cognitive and physical domains). It should neither be limited exclusively to library use, as suggested in the S&E Taxonomy, nor should learners be expected to be able to evaluate information (level 1 of the BO Taxonomy) – a higher order cognitive skill – without suitable orientation.

The stakeholders in this level are the academic library and its staff. It appears sensible that the library has the infrastructure and the staff to take on the responsibility of orienting learners to the concept of information literacy.

Level three: Interaction

This level represents the interaction with information that learners should engage with once they have achieved the outcomes necessary for an adequate orientation to the concept of information literacy. This third level of the EO Taxonomy is a synthesis of the behavioural objectives and the library skills and errors identified in the previous taxonomies.

The objective at this level is that learners be able to access and retrieve information. Although many relevant information sources are available in the academic library, learners should be encouraged not to limit themselves only to the academic library. Being able to keep updated with the latest developments and trends through staying in contact with industry is an important example of being information-literate.

The stakeholders at this level of interaction are the facilitators working in co-operation with the subject librarian to ensure that learners are continually encouraged to make use of various information sources (within and outside of the library) through their teaching style. Co-operation from subject librarians ensures that facilitators have a support system that does not leave them feeling as though they are left with an added workload, or de-motivated due to a lack of confidence in their own information literacy ability.

Level four: Problem-solving

The order of the cognitive and physical domain was exchanged to align with the concept of information literacy presented earlier. At this level of the taxonomy higher order cognitive skills are required to be able to apply the accessed and selected information in order to solve a problem and satisfy the information need.

Level 3 of the original S&E Taxonomy and BO Taxonomy – internalisation – was replaced by an entirely new set of educational outcomes. However, 'lifelong information users' and 'lifelong learners' are terms that are synonymous with information literacy and thus the objective of 'learning to learn' remains the same. Although difficult to measure within the short period of time that learners spend in an academic environment, learners may nonetheless be equipped with the attitude, cognitive ability and physical skills necessary to encourage them to become future lifelong learners and information users. The criticism at this point is that these terms come across as being idealistic goals rather than achievable outcomes, which should be measurable and attainable. For this reason the outcomes have been reformulated in terms which are measurable and attainable within the scope of a higher education programme.

The stakeholders on Level 3 are again the facilitators in co-operation with subject librarians. The subject librarian provides the support system for both facilitators and learners in their journey towards information literacy.

With the development of the e-learning information literacy intervention in 2001 it was possible to test this revised taxonomy. Applying the EO Taxonomy to this contemporary information literacy intervention determined the extent to which this new taxonomy could be considered useful as an evaluative framework:

(i) Evaluating information literacy initiatives summatively using the EO Taxonomy would determine to what extent an intervention that has been applied has succeeded in achieving the goals of information literacy from a theoretical point of view.

(ii) Identifying actual weaknesses and programme strengths, would provide the potential for further development of the initiative to eliminate such weaknesses for future implementations.

(iii) Used formatively, the EO Taxonomy would predict, from a theoretical point of view, to what extent an intervention that has not yet been applied would succeed in achieving the goals of information literacy.

(iv) Identifying potential weaknesses and programme strengths, would provide the potential for further development of the initiative to eliminate such weaknesses prior to its implementation.

13.5   Conclusion

As educators we have a responsibility to ourselves and to our learners to keep in touch with the latest developments in our field of study. Our task is to ensure that our learners have successfully achieved the outcomes required for their careers at the time that they exit higher education. As important is that they be equipped with the life skill of information literacy to cope with the rapid developments in their field of study as the information explosion continues to escalate.

This challenge is not one that can be mastered by one stakeholder in isolation, as has been clearly demonstrated by this study. The co-operation and commitment of institutional decision makers, administrators, librarians, facilitators, and ultimately learners is required. Failure to support information literacy will have repercussions on all stakeholders as poor performance of graduates in industry will not only have a negative economic effect on industry, but also reflect poorly on the entire institution, and on a national scale, the entire country.

The area of training both facilitators and librarians to adopt aspects of the others' field of expertise will require further research. It is unrealistic to expect librarians to be adequately prepared to facilitate learners or facilitators when their area of expertise is information science and not education. Conversely, it is unrealistic to expect facilitators to be able to confidently convey complex information literacy skills. Research should focus on developing and implementing such training workshops, which should precede the implementation of any accredited information literacy interventions.

The extent to which the information literacy can be integrated into the academic curriculum in order to be taken seriously by all stakeholders requires further investigation as well as the possibility of linking course-integrated instruction to a measurable exit-level outcome. The implementation of such an approach implies that each learner achieve the problem-solving level represented in the EO Taxonomy at Level 4, within each year of study and this problem-solving behaviour should be encouraged and maintained through constant interaction, and orientation to new relevant information sources – in a constant information literacy cycle.

Finally, the taxonomic approach has provided a method to approach the evaluation of learners in a holistic manner – including affective, cognitive and physical domains. Further research is required into evaluating learners adequately in terms of all three behavioural taxonomic domains, and not just the physical and cognitive domain, as is so often done (by means of an information retrieval task/assignment). Nahl has pioneered research into the extent to which learners' attitudes could be evaluated, particularly as the affective domain is the initiating behavioural domain (Nahl & Tenopir, 1996; Nahl & James, 1997). However, in the South African context this area still requires extensive investigation. Furthermore, the extent of evaluating the higher order cognitive skills in terms of specified outcomes, as presented in this study, similarly requires further investigation.

If institutions are serious about contributing towards the success of improving student learning in higher education, it is time they realised that 'learning is what most adults will do for a living in the 21st century' (Perelman, cited in McCuaig 2000), and accept the challenge to become actively involved in contributing towards creating a lifelong learning culture.

Acknowledgements

The author would like to express her appreciation to Dr Phillip Parsons for comments made on an earlier version of this paper.

The financial assistance of the National Research Foundation (NRF South Africa) towards the research upon which this article is based is hereby acknowledged. Opinions expressed and conclusions arrived at are those of the author and are not necessarily to be attributed to the NRF or the Cape Technikon.

References

African National Congress (ANC) Education Department. (1995). *A Policy Framework for Education and Training*. Manzini: Macmillan.

Albrecht, K (2001). The True Information Survival Skills. *Training & Development*: 24–30, February.

Baer, W (1999). E-Learning: A Catalyst for Competition in Higher Education. *IMP: Information Impacts Magazine.* http://www.cisp.org/imp/june_9906baer.html

Breivik, P and Gee, E (1989). *Information Literacy: Revolution in the Library*. London: Collier Macmillan.

Curzon, S (1995). *Information Competence in the CSU: A Report*. Submitted to the Commission on Learning Resources and Instructional Technology, by the Work Group on Information Competence CLRIT Task 6.1, December.

Ford, D (1997). Data Smog. *Sunday Life*, supplement to The Sunday Argus, 15 June: 16.

Gibbs, G and Habeshaw, T (1989). *Preparing to Teach: An Introduction to Effective Teaching in Higher Education*. Bristol: Technical and Educational Services.

Lenox, M and Walker, M (1993). Information Literacy in the Educational Process. *The Educational Forum*, **57**, 312–324, Spring.

Marchionini, G, (1999). Educating Responsible Citizens in the Information Society. *Educational Technology*, **39**(2), 17–26, March/April.

McCuaig, H (2000). What is E-Learning? In *University of Technology Sydney: E-Learning Courses.* http://learning.uts.edu.au/what/index.html

Mehl, M (1997). SAQA and the NQF: An Outsider's View. *SAQA Bulletin,* **2**(2), 10–18.

Nahl, D and James, L (1997). *Microdescriptors of Library Research: A Longitudinal Study of the Affective, Cognitive and Psychomotor Behaviour of Users.* http://www.soc.hawaii.edu/~leonj/leonpsy/instructor/nsf.html

Nahl-Jakobovits, D and Jakobovits, L (1990). Measuring Information Searching Competence. *College & Research Libraries:* 448-462, September.

Nahl-Jakobovits, D and Jakobovits, L (1993). Bibliographic Instructional Design for Information Literacy: Integrating Affective and Cognitive Objectives. *Research Strategies II*, 7–88, Spring.

Nahl, D and Tenopir, C (1996). Affective and Cognitive Searching Behaviour of Novice End-Users of a Full-Text Database. *Journal of the American Society for Information Science*, **47**(4), 276–286.

Sayed, Y (1998). *The Segregated Information Highway: Information Literacy in Higher Education*. Cape Town: Infolit.

Sayed, Y and Karelse, C (1997). *The Segregated Information-Highway: An Assessment of Information Literacy in Higher Education*. [Summary Report.] Rondebosch, Cape Town Infolit.

South Africa. Department of Education (1997a). *Curriculum 2005: Lifelong Learning for the 21st Century.* Pretoria: CTP Books.
South African Qualification Authority (SAQA) (1997). *SAQA Bulletin*, **1**(1), May/June.
Underwood, P (2000). Origins and Aims. In *Infolit: Information Literacy: A Project of the Adamastor Trust.* http://www.adamastor.ac.za/Academic/Infolit/origins.html
Western Cape. Provincial Administration. Department of Economic Affairs, Agriculture and Tourism. (2000). *Green Paper on Preparing the Western Cape for the Knowledge Economy of the 21st Century.* [Executive Summary]

Appendix A

Taxonomy of Library Skills and Errors (Nahl-Jakobovits & Jakobovits, 1990)

	Affective domain	**Cognitive domain**	**Psychomotor domain**
Level 3 internalizing the library	**A3** *Affective internalization* Demonstrating support for the library perspective on society and self.	**C3** *Cognitive internalization* Acquiring personal and subjective intuition of a scholarly discipline.	**P3** *Psychomotor internalization* Performing cumulative . searches in one's field and promoting the library in one's life
Level 2 Interacting with the library	**A2** *Affective interaction* Demonstrating continuous striving and value preferences favourable to the library and its system.	**C2** *Cognitive interaction* Acquiring objective knowledge of search sequences, their analysis and synthesis.	**P2** *Psychomotor interaction* Negotiating search queries and performing a single, one-time search that meets a current information need.
Level 1 Orienting to the library	**A1** *Affective orientation* Demonstrating willingness to practice library tasks and maintaining selective attention	**C1** *Cognitive orientation* Acquiring representative knowledge and comprehending library-relevant distinctions	**P1** *Psychomotor orientation* Performing physical operations (hands-on experiences, browsing and walking around).

Appendix B

Taxonomy of Behavioural Objectives for Information Literacy
(Nahl-Jakobovits & Jakobovits, 1993)

	Affective	Cognitive	Sensorimotor
Level 1 (Orientation) Critical thinking objective: information evaluation	**A1** Becoming sensitive to the need to evaluate information	**C1** Evaluating the source of the information according to appropriate standards	**S1** Coping in an information society and engaging in learning activities
Level2 (Interaction) Using information information retrieval knowledge objective: information use	**A2** Having the perception of an information need and feeling the excitement of being an independent searcher	**C2** Formulating the questions and planning a search strategy	**S2** Recognizing the provided as suitable to the need and experiencing a sense of well being
Level3 (Internalization) Learning to learn objective: information success	**A3** Attaining the feeling of personal empowerment	**C3** Evaluating the information content and being enlightened by it	**S3** Facilitating one's life through lifelong information seeking and enjoying its rich benefits

14 Learning to learn from online dialogue: are we building cairns or dry stane dykes?

Liz Broumley,

UHI Millennium Institute

14.1 Introduction

The revolutionary potential of using Information and Communications Technology (ICT) to support learning lies not merely in delivering information but in enabling communication and dialogue, which, many would argue, are at the centre of pedagogic effectiveness (for example, Laurillard 1993, Mayes 2000). This facility is particularly significant for distance learning students. When campus-based students use ICT to support their learning they often do not need to take advantage of its potential for dialogue (Crook 2002). Distance learning students however, find that the technology gives them a potential for communication with tutors and peers that has not previously been available (McAteer et al 2002). In order to maximise this potential, both staff and students need to become skilled in using asynchronous communication for learning (Salmon 2000). This paper argues that part of the process of becoming skilled in using asynchronous communications for learning involves using it to develop academic capabilities. This means moving from posting content about a particular topic to integrated, analytical dialogue about that topic; moving from building cairns to dry stane dykes[1].

UHI Millennium Institute (UHI)[2] is one institution that is seeking to develop vibrant learning communities using the potential offered by ICT. The geographic area covered by UHI (the Highlands and Islands of Scotland) includes some of the most geographically remote communities in the UK and covers one fifth of the UK landmass. It is a dispersed, networked institution comprising thirteen partners (FE colleges and research institutions) situated across the region. UHI uses ICT as a means of creating learning opportunities amongst people in these diverse and often remote locations. Feedback from pilot studies has indicated strong support for using ICT to create learning communities within the region, and a significant feature of learning communities was seen as participation in academic discussions online (Broumley & Weedon 2001). The academic year 2001/02 saw the introduction of two new online degree programmes within UHI. Using evidence from transcripts of online discussion and feedback from both tutors and students, this paper examines some of the issues about the role of asynchronous online dialogue in learning in relation to the development of academic capabilities.

14.2 e-dialogues

Much has been written about the value of dialogue for student learning (for example Ramsden 1992, Biggs 1999, Bligh 2000), and of the potential for collaborative learning based on dialogue in e-learning situations (eg Mason & Kaye 1990, Laurillard 1993, Koschmann 1996, Bonk & King 1998, Mayes 2000, McAteer et al 2002). The benefits of e-dialogue are particularly apparent to those who approach e-learning from a social constructivist pedagogy and who see the potential for students to use computer mediated communication to co-produce knowledge through activity (Brown et al 1989, Jones & Asensio 2002). The connectivity provided through e-learning offers a real potential for students in remote areas to build communities of practice (Wenger 1998) which can extend beyond the learning community.

Despite this potential, accounts of experience suggest that student engagement in both asynchronous and synchronous dialogue is often patchy, and may contribute relatively little to the achievement of the specified learning outcomes (Hara & Kling 1999, Bonk 2001). Crook (op cit) suggests that serious revision of our models of learning and teaching may be necessary for successful development of networked learning to become an "arena for community". As part of this revision and to facilitate the realisation of e-learning's potential we need to pay attention to what happens in e-dialogue and how this affects student learning.

A critical issue in developing effective networked learning is the development of new skills by both lecturing staff and students. In early examples of e-learning we often see both groups struggling to adapt their existing face-to-face communication skills to a very different environment, and quite deliberately using strategies such as face-to-face induction to create a 'safe' environment for online collaboration (Nicol et al 2003). For increasing numbers of e-learners face-to-face induction is not a realistic option, irrespective of the pedagogic appropriateness of such an approach. Salmon (op cit) develops a model of e-moderating skills founded on online socialisation, which helps to develop the online social skills that are a necessary part of collaborative learning.

In addition to the development of online communities, feedback from UHI students (internal evaluation studies) highlights the importance to them of interaction that furthers academic understanding. Developing academic discussion involves a range of skills; at first year undergraduate level this might include:

- learning to use the language of the discipline

- relating theory and practice

- communicating ideas effectively

- thinking critically using a range of knowledge sources

- building new knowledge/understanding in collaboration with others

The development of these skills is facilitated by tutors providing models of appropriate discourse, scaffolding, providing feedback and stimulating debate or shared tasks. These issues affect face to face learners too, but the transcripts which are available from online discussion allow analysis that can help in understanding the process of academic discourse which is not easily possible for classroom dialogue (Hillman 1999). This analysis can provide feedback which can help us to move towards more integrated e-dialogue - the dry stane dyke.

14.2.1   e-dialogues in a UHI context

From its inception, UHI has developed networked degrees which can be accessed by students in a variety of locations across UHI. These were supported using a mixture of face to face teaching, video and audio conferencing, email and web-based resources. Degree programmes were developed within frameworks that encouraged a social constructivist approach to the use of technology to support learners (Broumley 1999) and the systematic and progressive development of transferable graduate skills[3]. If UHI is to succeed in developing online degree programmes based on these frameworks then increasing our understanding of the role of e-dialogue in developing academic skills is essential.

The introduction of the first two degree programmes that were designed to be entirely online, with all tutorial interaction taking place through the communication tools of a Virtual Learning Environment (VLE) happened in September 2001. These programmes provided an ideal opportunity to work with tutors and students to investigate the role of online discussions in developing learning communities. This paper focuses on the one of these degrees, the BA Child and Youth Studies (BACYS). It draws students from most parts of the UHI and attracts full- and part-time students, who study the same modules together. As one of UHI's first online degrees the BACYS was being carefully evaluated so questionnaire feedback was available from students and staff. This has provided baseline data on the value students place on e-dialogue. Because the degree draws people from such a wide region and includes both full-time and part-time students there is no joint face-to-face induction for the whole group; although there is local college induction, this is not compulsory.

In creating online resources the course team had consciously encouraged a social constructivist approach to learning, with plenty of opportunities for group participation in learning activities. However, as this was the first time they had worked online, they recognised a need to 'learn how to learn' online and therefore were keen to use evaluation and subsequent research to improve both the student experiences and their own online skills. Therefore one purpose of the present analysis is to contribute to a practical understanding of how e-dialogue can contribute to students' learning online.

We started the investigation with some initial questions:

- How do individuals differ in their online behaviour?

- How do students respond to one another in online discussions?

- How valuable do students find different online activities for learning?

In the process of investigating these, additional questions were identified which are discussed in the final section and will be investigated during academic year 2002/03.

14.2.2   e-dialogue research methodology

To investigate e-dialogue a discussion from one BACYS module was chosen for in-depth analysis. The discussion is from a first semester module and took place in weeks 7-9 of a 15 week module. The particular discussion was chosen because it occurred at a point when the students were becoming accustomed to online discussion and before submission deadlines for assignments were competing for attention. By this time the students had had the opportunity to take part in three previous discussions, therefore, the medium was not new to them. The module itself included students from all parts of the network offering the degree, 43 students started the module and 36 completed. By week 7 all those who dropped out of the module had left. For the students this was their first experience of online learning; the tutor had presented this module once before in a pilot study.

The following data on the discussion were collected:

- Transcript of the discussion

- VLE computer log showing the pattern of participation in discussions during all 15 weeks of the module

- The tutor's reflective account of her interaction during the discussions, based on the transcript.

In addition, evaluative data about online discussions were collected independently by questionnaire from both students and tutor.

The topic of the discussion was Health Promotion, which was introduced by the tutor with two questions:

> Many people are in a position to promote the health of children. Should we expect them to do so (on top of their other work)? If so, how can we ensure that health promotion is on everyone's agenda?

The tutor's objectives for this discussion (as derived from a reflective interview) were to:

- encourage the students to consider their experiences of health promotion in the light of the theoretical course material they had studied so far

- facilitate the development of the analytical skills they would need for their first summative assessment

These objectives were not made explicit to the students, although in previous discussions she had encouraged students to reflect on their own relevant experiences in the light of the material they were studying. The nature of the task was very open ended, students were being asked to contribute their thoughts regarding the question but not produce either an individual or group consensus. The tutor was allowing a relatively unstructured discussion in which students could create new threads.

There are a variety of frameworks to analyse online interactions (eg Sugar and Bonk 1998, Hillman op cit, Chappel et al, 2002); we have used the 'elements' approach (Chappel, ibid). This approach is grounded in learning theory and has been developed from involvement in courses which follow a social constructivist pedagogy and use computer mediated communication as the principle learning environment. The 'elements' approach can be used to provide feedback that facilitates the development of academic and tutoring skills. The approach identifies six discussion elements: organising, facilitating, disseminating, diverging, converging and framing (see table 14.1). It gives a basis for both statistical and reflective analysis that can be used to investigate both student and tutor behaviour. In addition, where student contributions to discussions are assessed, it can provide criteria for assessment[4].

This approach can be used to create a group participation profile and examine individual behaviour, both of which were considered important for this study. It was used to identify individual differences between students and differences between the students and the tutor. The analysis gave an anatomy of the discussion in terms of the types of contribution people made and the context in which these contributions were made in terms of the person to whom the contributor was replying. The analysis tool was selected because it also appeared capable of giving insights into the academic skills being evidenced during the interactions.

In order to help contextualise the analysis, computer logs were used to identify whether the levels of contribution seen in this discussion were typical for these students across the module. In addition, students' responses in the end of semester evaluation to questions on their level of participation in online discussions, the usefulness or otherwise of these discussions, their satisfaction with online tutor support and their view of online discussion in comparison with face to face discussion have been used. The tutor's reflections provide another perspective on the context for the discussion by setting the implicit learning outcomes and giving the moderator's views on the postings in relation to these outcomes.

Element	Description
organisation	Interactions between group members designed to co-ordinate collaborative tasks, including meeting deadlines, planning and scheduling.
facilitation	Setting a collaborative climate for learning through acknowledging, recognising and encouraging others; sharing resources; providing social glue.
dissemination	Proposing an idea, presenting new information or resources, using external resources and experiences; explaining; justifying.
divergence	Opening out discussion; questioning; offering new perspectives on shared thought; prompting exploration of other views; dissonance or disagreement.
convergence	Promoting agreements; summarising; weaving; building on the thoughts of others; identifying areas of consistency and agreement; application of newly constructed meaning.
framing	Framing the understanding of a collaborative task; generalising; theorising; identifying task boundaries; scaffolding.

Table 14.1   Description of the 'elements'   (Adapted from Chappel, ibid)

14.2.3   e-dialogue findings

The answers that emerged to our original research questions were as follows:

How do individuals differ in their online behaviour?

Over the three week period 20 students took part in the discussion, with participation rates that were typical of their contribution rates in other discussions. Figure 14.1 shows the pattern of contribution. There were a total of 67 contributions by 21 contributors (including the tutor). The tutor made 18 contributions or almost 27% of the postings, with 73% of postings from students. Using Salmon's guideline of tutors contributing about 20% of the postings, the tutor's contributions here seem rather high. However it has been suggested that in order to establish frequent participation online it may be necessary for tutors to 'front load' their online tutorial support in the early weeks of a new discussion group (Broumley &

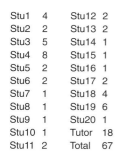
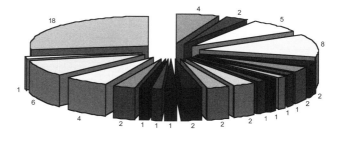

Stu1	4		Stu12	2
Stu2	2		Stu13	2
Stu3	5		Stu14	1
Stu4	8		Stu15	1
Stu5	2		Stu16	1
Stu6	2		Stu17	2
Stu7	1		Stu18	4
Stu8	1		Stu19	6
Stu9	1		Stu20	1
Stu10	1		Tutor	18
Stu11	2		Total	67

Figure 14.1   Number of postings made by each participant

Weedon op cit, Nicol et al op cit). Student feedback also suggests that online tutor presence was valued.

Although 20 students participated, eight only posted once, seven posted twice and five posted four or more times. Between them the five 'frequent posting' students (those posting 4 or more times) contributed 40% of the total postings and 55% of the student postings. This pattern of a sub-set of relatively active participants with a larger number of less frequent contributors is not untypical (Mann, 2002).

Use of the 'elements' approach to analyse contributions provides a richer insight into the e-dialogue than simple frequency statistics on postings. As one posting can contain several elements the total number of elements is greater than the number of postings. The tutor posted 41 separate elements and the students 85. A comparison between the tutor and the students showed that the tutor's postings contained an average of 2.28 elements per posting and the students' 1.76. However what also became apparent was that the students and tutor were making significantly (p <0.02) different types of contribution, as can be seen from figure 14.2.

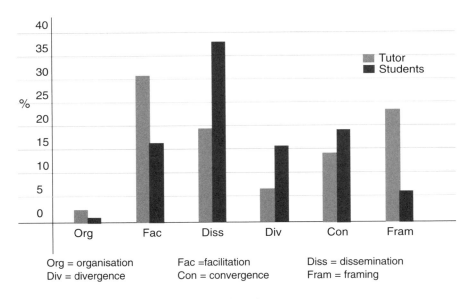

Figure 14.2 Comparison between tutor and students

From the outset the students were more likely than the tutor to post a straightforward dissemination (38% of student contributions) mainly giving information to the rest of the group in answer to the tutor's questions. However this dissemination was often being done with little attempt to build on the contributions of others; the individual contributions were 'on topic' but many did not make explicit reference to other postings even where one posting was a reply to a previous one. In these cases the students appeared to be building cairns, placing a relevantly shaped (on topic) contribution on top of others. It is possible that the students were implicitly acknowledging others, with mental agreement or disagreement, but this wasn't obvious from the written postings.

As the discussion progressed students did make more use of both divergence (16% of student contributions) and convergence (20%), which suggests that there was a growing attempt to inter-relate comments recognising what had preceded them. With this we begin to see some move towards building a dry stane dyke, creating an integrated discussion. Whilst the students made relatively little use of the framing category this was the second most frequent element for the tutor, a finding which reflects student-tutor roles; the tutor was providing the scaffolding and boundaries for the discussion. Neither the tutor nor the students made significant use of the organising category, which perhaps reflects the relatively unstructured nature of the discussion; as the students were not required to come to a group decision organisation was not particularly relevant.

The tutor's preferred element in this discussion was facilitation (32% of her comments). This was something the tutor had used quite extensively from the start of the discussion; interestingly after eight days some of the students began to demonstrate facilitating behaviour too. One interpretation of this is that they were modelling their behaviour on that of the tutor. If this is the case, then good e-dialogue practice by the tutor might make a significant contribution to the development of e-dialogue skills in students.

In order to understand more about the difference between students, the types of posting by 'frequent posters' were compared with the rest. What transpired was a difference in usage of the discussion board; the frequent posters were more likely to post a contribution that had only one element, rather than a multi-element posting. Overall the frequent posters had an average of 1.52 elements per posting compared with an average of 2 for the rest.

When the types of elements used were analysed there was no significant difference between the two groups although frequent posters were slightly less likely to use the divergent, convergent and framing elements than other students, and more likely to use facilitation, as shown in figure 14.3.

What might be emerging are two different patterns of contribution. One pattern was frequent postings giving new information but often only containing one or two elements, another

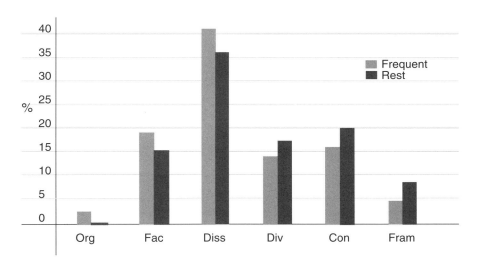

Figure 14.3   Comparison between frequent posters and the rest

showed less frequent but longer (and more reflective) postings, with a greater number of elements, including elements that built on the academic contributions of others.

How do students respond to one another in online discussions?

In order to consider this question it was decided to analyse the elements according to the person to whom the students were responding. This was determined using the computer log detailing the message replied to, and gave three categories:

- a reply to a student
- a reply to the tutor
- the start of a new thread

New threads were started when someone posted a message with a new topic heading, rather than using the reply option to link to a previous posting. The first message in the discussion always starts a new thread, participants can chose whether to reply to another contributor or start a new thread themselves. Diagram 4 shows the distribution of elements in these three categories.

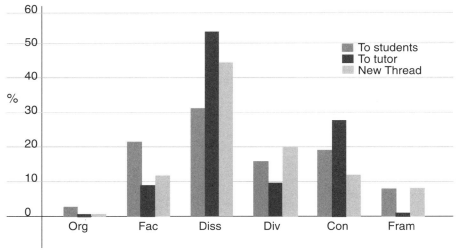

Figure 14.4   Comparison of elements used to students, tutors or when staring a new thread

The observed differences in figure 14.4 are significant, $p < 0.01$. Although the primary type of response is dissemination regardless of who the student is replying to, it appears that students are more likely to use facilitating and divergent responses with peers and fewer disseminations than they do to the tutor. Not only do students present more information to tutors they are also more likely to give convergent responses to tutors than to peers. The framing category is never used in response to the tutor although it occurs in response to peers and when introducing a new thread. In this discussion students introduced thirteen new threads in comparison with three by the tutor.

These patterns of interaction may reflect expectations about the roles of tutors and students. Tutors are expected to provide direction and support for students, and although online dialogue creates a more student-led environment (Nicol et al op cit) the students here were still less likely to organise, facilitate or frame when they responded to the tutor than when they responded to their peers. Similarly they are more willing to express divergence from peers than from the tutor. When the pattern of responses to other students is considered as a whole it suggests that this group of students were developing the academic skills necessary for collaborative learning relationships. They were willing to present new information to support one another and express both agreement and disagreement, they seemed to be beginning to build a more integrative dialogue - a dry stane dyke?

How valuable do students find different online activities for learning?

On the basis of the responses to student evaluation questionnaires we found that for BACYS students as a whole:

- discussions were reported as the most useful online activity

- there was a positive correlation between student satisfaction with tutor support and the frequency of tutor presence online

- 47% of the group thought that online learning was better or much better than face-to-face learning, 34% thought face-to-face was better or much better and 19% had no preference

When responses from students in this module were analysed, it was found that they were even more likely to report that the discussions were helpful, and that they preferred online learning, than were the whole student group. This finding was not known when the module was selected for in-depth study.

The students claimed to value the help they received from others[5]; this first quotation suggests the development of a learning community.

> With so many people working at the same time, any queries I had were resolved by another student in a matter of hours. Everybody went out of his or her way to help other students and if no one knew the answer we'd contact the tutor. I enjoyed the conversations, jokes and answers to queries.

They appreciated the support from tutors:

> … there was high involvement from the tutors on the discussion boards; this was very encouraging, giving a more personal touch as the course can be very isolating.

Interesting discussions themselves became a motivator for students to take part, particularly when they felt they could contribute a different or novel view, rather than simply agreeing with the rest.

But there were drawbacks:

> … I found that if I was away from the computer for any reason when I came back to the discussion I was overwhelmed by the quantity of messages.

> … if someone misreads what you're trying to say… everything can be taken out of context and misconstrued, so had to be vary wary of how sentences are worded.

> [in face-to-face contact] … you can explain through words/body language and expression more clearly and obtain clear, full answers to questions.

Interestingly these last two points may also be true of face-to-face situations, where imprecise verbal comments and non-verbal behaviour can be misinterpreted, leading to similar problems to the ones these students describe. Face-to-face interaction can also suffer from communication breakdown.

Several students mention time as a problem; online discussions take longer, both to participate in physically and to conduct a whole conversation; they impose a cognitive load not found in face to face discussions as people have to reconstruct a dialogue over several days. Finally, students did recognise that they had to learn new skills in order to take part in e-dialogues:

> At the beginning I was apprehensive about using them, although now I am making more of an effort to be part of the conversations.

14.3   Discussion and conclusions

This work began by outlining the importance of e-dialogue in realising the potential of e-learning, and specifically in relation to the potential of ICT for collaborative, social constructivist learning which can create vibrant learning communities and enable students to develop recognised academic skills. On the basis of the data analysed here we have some grounds for optimism; in addition we can identify some practical outcomes, both in terms of feedback to practitioners and for ongoing research. Although this study has provided some initial answers to opening questions, it has also helped to identify further questions, which will become part of the next cycle of action research. The 'elements' approach has helped to identify differences in behaviour between individuals and differences according to who individuals feel they are 'talking' to. It is also helping to identify the types of academic skills students are evidencing online, and suggesting that students may model their behaviour on that of the tutor. For undergraduates learning the language of their discipline this might help encourage appropriate use of academic concepts and procedures. However the methodology is capable of extension using reflective feedback from students as well as from tutors (Tomlie 2001). For the tutor here, the reflective interview proved an important part of her developing e-moderating skills; reflective analysis with students may also prove a useful development process.

A point brought out by the tutor was that for e-dialogue to be effective it might be necessary to make the learning outcomes of the dialogue explicit so students have a clearer idea of what is expected. One way of achieving this might be by incorporating the outcomes into the module design and assessment. This could be done by building on Mayes' classification of three types of learning courseware (op cit). These are: primary courseware (which is largely content), secondary courseware (for example, activities) and tertiary courseware (such as dialogue or personal reflection). If this were combined with Biggs' constructive alignment (op cit), which creates an alignment of learning outcomes, assessment and learning and teaching activities, then having once decided on the learning outcomes and assessment, we can identify the learning and teaching, in terms of Mayes' courseware. We might even consider how to evaluate learning at the design stage. This could help to ensure that e-dialogue maps onto the outcomes and assessment, which could be expressed in the framework shown in table 14.2.

E-dialogues themselves could become part of the courseware; by making dialogues available to other students they may be able benefit from vicarious learning (Mayes 2002). In addition, different types of collaborative activities could be incorporated to give students clear opportunities to acquire a range of academic skills.

Learning outcome	Assessment	Learning and teaching		Evaluation of effectiveness
		Courseware	Learning opportunities	
		Primary		
		Secondary		
		Tertiary		

Table 14.2:   Framework for module design and evaluation

Future research will investigate some of these issues and consider some of the implications for the social aspects of learning which have not been investigated here. Of particular interest are the boundaries for dialogue and the level of disclosure found amongst students, and how these might impact on a developing community of practice. This study has also raised interesting questions about the assumptions which are often made about the differences between e-dialogue and face-to-face dialogue.

In conclusion, this investigation has found evidence of both cairns and dry stane dykes, but is building cairns part of the process of learning to build a dry stane dyke?

Acknowledgements

Sincere thanks go to staff and students on the BA Child and Youth Studies degree for their collaboration, without which none of this work would have been possible, and to Dr Erica McAteer for permission to use the 'elements' approach in this study.

References

Biggs, J (1999). *Teaching for Quality Learning at University*. Buckingham: SRHE and The Open University Press.

Bligh, D (2000). *What's the point in Discussion?* Exeter: Intellect Books,

Bonk, CH and King, KS (1998). *Electronic Collaborators.* New Jersey: Lawrence Erlbaum Associates.

Bonk, CJ (with help from Maher, E.) (2001). *Online teaching in an online world*, (available from http://www.courseshare.com/reports.php)

Broumley, L (1999). *Towards a Learning Strategy for the University of the Highlands and Islands: Report of the LET Working Group*. UHI, Inverness, available at http://www.learn.uhi.ac.uk/LET/LET_Report.html

Broumley, L and Weedon, E (2001). Evaluation of the LINC Project: Learning in Networked Communities. UHI, Inverness, available at http://www.learn.uhi.ac.uk/adapt.htm

Brown, JS, Collings, A and Duguid P (1989). Situated Cognition and the culture of learning, *Educational Researcher*, **18**(1) 32–42.

Chappel, H, MacAteer, E, Harris, R and Marsden, S (2002). Fast coding of online behaviours using an 'Elements' approach, proceedings of the third International Conference on Networked Learning, Sheffield, p55-62.

Crook, C (2002). The campus experience of networked learning. In Steeples, C and Jones, C (Eds), *Networked Learning: Perspectives and Issues*. London: Springer.

Hara, N and Kling, R (1999). Students' Frustrations with a Web-Based Distance Education Course. *First Monday*, **4**(12) (December 1999) available at http://www.firstmonday.dk/issues/issue4_12/hara/index.html

Hillman, DCA (1999). A new method for analyzing patterns of interaction. *American Journal of Distance Education*, **13**(2) 37–47.

Jones, C and Asensio, M (2002). Designs for Networked Learning in Higher Education. In Steeples, C and Jones, C (Eds), *Networked Learning: Perspectives and Issues*. London: Springer.

Koschmann, T (Ed), (1996). CSCL: Theory and practice of an emerging paradigm. Mahwah, NJ: Lawrence Erlbaum Associates.

Laurillard, D (1993). *Rethinking University Teaching*. London: Routledge.

Mann, (2002). Understanding Networked Learning: A Personal Inquiry into an Experience of Adult Learning On-line proceedings of the third International Conference on Networked Learning, Sheffield.

Mason and Kaye (1990). Towards a new paradigm for distance education. In Harasim L (Ed) *Online Education: Perspectives on a New Environment*. New York: Praeger.

Mayes, T (2000). *Pedagogy, Lifelong Learning and ICT,* Scottish Forum on Lifelong Learning Report No. 1, Glasgow.

Mayes, T (2002). Learning from watching others learn. In Steeples, C and Jones, C (Eds) *Networked Learning: Perspectives and Issues*. London: Springer.

McAteer, E, Tolmie, A, Crook, C, Macleod, H and Musselbrook, K (2002). Learning networks and the issue of communication skills. In Steeples, C and Jones, C (Eds), *Networked Learning: Perspectives and Issues*. London: Springer.

Nicol, DJ, Minty, I, and Sinclair, C (in press). The social dimensions of online learning, *Innovations in Education and Teaching International*.

Ramsden, P (1992). *Learning to Teach in Higher Education*. London: Routledge.

Salmon, G (2000). *E-moderating: the key to teaching and learning online*. London: Kogan Page.

Steeples, C and Jones, C (Eds), (2002), *Networked Learning: Perspectives and Issues*. London Springer.

Sugar, B and Bonk, CJ (1998). Student Role Play in the World Forum: Analyses of an Arctic Adventure Learning Apprenticeship. In Bonk, CH and King, KS (Eds), *Electronic Collaborators*. New Jersey: Lawrence Erlbaum Associates.

Tomlie, A (2001). Characteristics of Online Learning Environments: Informing Practice in Networked Learning, SCROLLA Symposium, November 2001

Wenger, E (1998). *Communities of Practice: Learning meaning and identity*. Cambridge: Cambridge University Press.

Notes

1 Both cairns and dry stane dykes are made from uncut stones; a cairn is a pile of stones, often used as a way mark, a dry stane dyke is a wall comprising carefully integrated stones.

2 UHI Millennium Institute is an HEI, which is working towards becoming the University of the Highlands and Islands.

3 Details of UHI's approach to graduate skills can be found at www.pdp.uhi.ac.uk

4 Personal communication Dr E McAteer.

5 The following quotes were made in response to open questions on student evaluation questionnaires

15 Evoked conceptions of learning and learning environments

Keith Trigwell and Paul Ashwin
University of Oxford

Keywords: evoked conceptions, learning approach, deep, surface, learning environments.

Abstract

This paper describes a study designed to explore the idea of evoked conceptions of learning, and the relations between these aspects of students' awareness, their awareness of other environmental variables, and their learning outcomes. An evoked conception of learning is one that students adopt in response to their perceived learning task in a particular context. It may reflect the aims they have for their studies, once they have started that study and experienced that study environment. The results show that when students perceived the learning environment as being more supportive of learning, they are more likely to describe an evoked conception of learning that is more closely aligned with those promoted by the university. They also had higher scores on the deep approach to learning scale, lower scores on the surface approach scale, and expected to gain a higher degree classification. These associations suggest that evoked conceptions, like conceptions of learning and prior experience of learning, are crucial indicators of learning approach and outcome.

15.1 Introduction

How do students conceptualise what is required of them in learning? This question has been investigated from a variety of perspectives. Marton and Säljö (1997) describe qualitatively different ways of conceiving of learning; Perry (1988) describes qualitatively different conceptions of knowledge; Roach, Blackmore and Dempster (2001) describe differences as being adaptive (more open) or adoptive (more regulated); Ramsden (1991) identified variation in the perceived clarity of required goals and standards as a factor related to learning approach; and Marton and Booth (1997) see this conceptualisation as the indirect object of learning, which differs from the act of learning, and what it is that is being learned (the direct object).

The reason for such interest in this topic is the belief that students' conceptions of their academic tasks will, to a large extent, define the nature of the task, and the way that they approach that task. For example, Marton and Säljö (1997) found that when students describe the use of more sophisticated or inclusive conceptions of learning, they are more likely to be also adopting a deep approach to learning than students who conceive of learning in a limited way, such as memorising to pass examinations.

Students may also adopt and use different conceptions according to perceived differences in the context. So it is not so much conceptions of learning per se but those conceptions that are evoked by the students' experience of their unique learning situation, that are likely to be most strongly related to students' approaches to learning, perceptions of their learning environment and learning outcome. An evoked conception of learning is one that students adopt in response to their perceived learning context. It may not be the same as a more generic conception as expressed by students in less situated interviews or in their response on inventories of their conceptions of learning: if students perceive a situation requires it, a less or more sophisticated conception may be evoked. From this perspective, evoked conceptions are seen to be an integral part of the process of learning and are likely to be more strongly related to approaches to learning than generic conceptions of learning.

The study that is reported in this paper has been designed to test whether differences in these evoked conceptions can be measured and, if they can, whether evoked conceptions are related to approaches to learning and learning outcome.

A relational model of student learning that accommodates the relations between the variables in the study is shown in Figure 15.1. It builds on the ideas of situated-ness and awareness (Marton and Booth, 1997; Prosser and Trigwell, 1999). Using this relational model we contend that in any act of learning, evoked prior experiences, perceptions, approaches and outcomes are simultaneously present in a student's awareness, although in some contexts, one or more of these aspects may be more to the foreground of awareness, while other aspects may be more to the background. Evoked conceptions of learning, in this model, are part of the evoked prior experience.

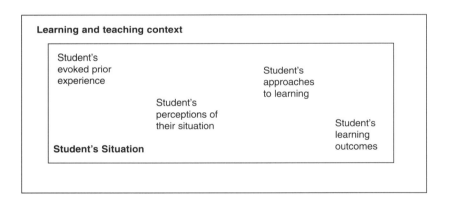

Figure 15.1   A relational model of student learning (Prosser and Trigwell, 1999)

In describing evoked conceptions of learning we have taken as our starting point three separate, but related sets of studies. The qualitative variation in conceptions of learning have been described in two widely quoted research articles, by Säljö (1979), and by Marton, Dall'Alba & Beaty (1993). Five conceptions of learning are reported in both studies: (a) an increase in knowledge; (b) memorising for future use; (c) application; (d) understanding; and (e) seeing things differently. A sixth conception: (f) changing as a person; was reported by Marton, et al. (1993) who also describe learning in the first three conceptions as primarily reproducing, and the last three as primarily seeking meaning.

Two qualitatively different descriptions of aspects of learning (adoptive and adaptive) are also presented by Roach et al. (2001). They note that adaptive learning 'requires higher level thinking in more open situations and is inherently a creative generative and reflective process that requires and develops higher cognitive processes.' Outcomes of adaptive learning would include formation and generation of arguments, reasoning and justification, or synthesis and conceptualisation. Adoptive learning 'is essentially a reproductive process and is appropriate after a situation has been defined'. Outcomes of adoptive learning would include knowledge and practice of techniques and procedures or organisation and structure.

Meyer and colleagues have, since 1995, been developing and testing a 'Reflections on Learning Inventory' (RoLI) that seeks to capture variation in conceptions of learning in a statistical sense (Meyer, 1995, 2000a). This work has parallels with the work we report in this paper, particularly in the manner of the proposed use of the inventory, and in the way RoLI reflects a 'conceptions and process' model of student learning. Meyer (2000b) describes RoLI as a development that 'seeks to underpin a model of student learning that is substantively represented in terms of prior knowledge and process dimensions of variation. These two dimensions of variation are generic; they represent families of observables that are more directly linked as "mechanisms of production" to learning outcomes than other traditional observables such as motivation, intention, perceptions of the learning environment, and so on'. (Meyer, 2000b, p1). In a recent analysis of responses to RoLI, Meyer (2001b) notes that the data, when factor analysed by scale variables, show two factors. The first factor includes four scales: 'learning is fact based', 'knowledge is discrete and factual', 'memorise before understanding', and 'learning motivated by sense of duty'. The second factor includes the 'memorise with understanding', 'memorise after understanding', 'rereading a text', and 'seeing things differently' scales. Each of these groupings is internally conceptually coherent, and qualitatively different to the other.

All three of these studies describe at least two qualitatively different conceptions, or processes, or conceptions and processes, of learning, and have provided a framework for the development of a conceptions of learning scale. However, if, as in this study, the conceptions of learning to be investigated are seen to be evoked by the students' experience of the context, then that context needs to be present in any attempt to capture evoked conceptions. In this respect our approach departs from RoLI which uses generic dimensions of variation. Students' awareness of their context is a crucial component of our definition of evoked conceptions of learning.

In this study, the context is the collegial degree programme at the University of Oxford. It is a context which students are likely to experience quite differently from their prior experience of learning. Students at Oxford are supplied with a very supportive domestic environment, but they are expected to regulate their own learning in accessing an outstanding library and academic staff resource. At the heart of this approach is the tutorial system. It is characterised by students' attendance at a face-to-face tutorial after a lengthy (11–14 hour) preparation time. The tutorials are, in the interest of learning, kept to a minimum, usually about 3 each fortnight (Commission of Inquiry, 1997).

Much has been written about the Oxford tutorial system, and its aims and benefits. For example, Moore (1968) emphasises the ability of this system to cater for individual needs, to support in-depth questioning and to supply immediate feedback. He argues that in the tutorial, knowledge is seen as contested, and that two minds (tutor and student) work on the same problem.

Much less has been written about the students' views of the tutorial system. In an interview study of Oxford students' experience of their learning, one of us (Ashwin, 2002) identified a range of conceptions of the tutorial. One is as described by Moore (as the tutor and student exchanging different points of view on the topic and both coming to a new understanding). Others were more focused on the tutor explaining to the student what the student does not understand, or the tutor showing the student how to see the subject the way the tutor does.

Students' perceptions of the tutorial system are likely to evoke conceptions of learning that are different from conceptions of learning in school. The variation in conceptions of the role of tutorials identified by Ashwin has been used as the starting point for the development of an indicator of variation in evoked conceptions of learning.

We know of no studies involving the concept of evoked conceptions of learning and therefore none that have explored the relations between evoked conceptions of learning and learning approaches and outcomes in higher education. However, similar studies have been conducted into the relations between students' outcomes of learning, their approaches to learning, their perceptions of their learning environment and their prior conceptions of learning (Crawford, et al, 1998) or prior understanding of their subject (Prosser, et al, 2000; Hazel, et al, 2002). In all three of these studies, coherent, but small, relations were found between the four variables. In the two most recent studies, incoherent relations were also observed. Some students who adopted deeper approaches to learning also said they adopted more surface approaches to learning (dissonant learning approaches). As a group they have lower quality outcomes of learning than their colleagues who adopt either a deep or surface approach. The students with dissonant approaches had perceptions of their learning environment that were inconsistent with their adopted learning approaches (incoherent relations). These 'inconsistencies' or incoherent orchestrations, observed among groups of students studying a variety of subjects, have been called dissonant study orchestrations (Meyer, Parsons and Dunne, 1990; Meyer, 2000c).

This study had three aims. First, to explore the concept of qualitatively different evoked conceptions of learning; second, to conduct a study on the relations between evoked conceptions of learning, approaches to learning, perceptions of the learning environment and learning outcomes, and third to search for evidence of dissonant study orchestrations in students studying in a University of Oxford college context.

15.2   Method

A questionnaire containing standard items on approaches to learning, perceptions of the learning environment (Prosser and Trigwell, 1999), and a question on what students anticipated to be their degree classification, was sent to all undergraduate students in the last term of their academic year in one college at the University of Oxford. The questionnaire also included eight new items that were designed to capture students' evoked conceptions of learning.

Typical questionnaire items for learning approaches, perceptions of the learning environment and learning outcomes are shown in table 15.1. All responses were collected on a 5-point Likert scale, except the Anticipated Outcome variable which used a 6-point scale as shown in table 15.1.

Students' evoked conceptions of learning were attained from questionnaire items which asked about the purposes or the types of learning they were considering in various elements of their studies. Ten items were tested in a pilot study conducted the previous year. The content of these items was derived from data collected in interviews with students on their experience of the tutorial system (Ashwin, 2002). The qualitatively different descriptions of the experience of tutorials that constitute the outcomes of Ashwin's study, and the qualitatively different descriptions of the purposes of essays derived from the same interviews, were used to construct items which differed in qualitative terms. The ideas of adaptive and adoptive learning described by Roach et al. (2001) were used to incorporate qualitative variation into single items.

Scales	Example item
Surface approach	Often I feel I am drowning in the sheer amount of material I'm having to cope with in my degree
Deep approach	When I am reading an article or book, I try to find out for myself exactly what the author means
Good teaching	My tutors put a lot of time into commenting on my work
Appropriate workload	I am generally given enough time to understand things I have to learn
Clear goals and standards	The tutors made it clear right from the start what they expect from students
Appropriate assessment	My tutors seem more interested in assessing what I have memorised than what I have understood
Anticipated outcome (6-point scale)	Which of the following degree classifications do you expect: First or upper 2i; 2i; 2ii; 3rd; pass; fail

Table 15.1   Scales (for learning approaches, perceptions of the learning environment and learning outcomes) and example items from each scale

In the pilot study, the items were assembled in two scales to measure aligned and non-aligned evoked conceptions. An aligned evoked learning conception is one that is consistent with what the university describes as the purposes of elements of their studies (for example as set out in the University of Oxford's Commission of Inquiry, 1997). Example items include:

I see the primary purpose of tutorials as being a chance for me to explore my personal understanding of the subject.

In my degree I feel it is more important to find new ways of thinking than it is to gain specific knowledge about the subject areas.

A non-aligned evoked learning conception is one in which the students' view of the purposes of their studies is not consistent with the view expressed by the university. Example items include:

I see the primary purpose of tutorials as being a chance to show my tutors how much I have learned in this subject.

The primary purpose of essays is to present the facts in a clear and concise way.

In preparation for the study reported in this paper, these items were refined, two were removed and five reversed, to produce an aligned evoked conceptions of learning scale containing the eight items shown in table 15.2.

One hundred and fifty five questionnaires were returned. While this total is only 35 percent of the undergraduate population of the college, it is a sufficient return to conduct this study which focuses first on relations between an individual student's structures of awareness of aspects of their learning environment, and second on the variation in these individual orchestrations. This study is not aiming to gather a response which is necessarily representative of the whole population.

Two statistical procedures were used to support the analytical approach adopted. A (principal components) factor analysis of the four learning environment scales ('good teaching'; 'appropriate workload'; 'clear goals and standards'; and 'appropriate assessment')

Number	Scoring Direction	Item
16	Reversed	Tutorials are more about me testing my knowledge than exploring my personal understanding of the subject
25	Normal	In my degree I feel it is more important to find new ways of thinking than it is to gain specific knowledge about the subject areas
32	Reversed	I see my role in tutorials as more about answering my tutor's questions than discussing ideas
45	Reversed	Tutorials are more about me showing my tutors how much I have learned in this subject than developing my understanding
52	Reversed	I see the tutor's role in tutorials as more about explaining ideas than discussing them
56	Normal	In my degree I think it is more important to change my understanding of the subject than to develop in ways that may be attractive to employers
66	Reversed	In my degree I feel it is more important to learn to apply knowledge than it is to find new ways of thinking
68	Normal	I feel that engagement with the primary research literature in my field is a good way for me to learn

Table 15.2   Item number, scoring direction and item for the eight items in the questionnaire making up the aligned evoked conception of learning scale.

showed only one factor with high loadings on all variables. A single 'perceptions of learning environment' scale was produced from a combination of all four of these scales. The scale reliability co-efficient (alpha) for the best seven and eight items was calculated before use was made of the (eight item) Aligned Evoked Conceptions of Learning Scale.

Analyses of the results were conducted using Pearson two-tailed correlations between variables, and a cluster analysis on key variables with all students. For the hierarchical cluster analysis, Ward's method was used to look at relations, for individual students, between evoked conceptions of learning, perceptions of the learning environment, approaches to learning and anticipated learning outcome. All the variables used in the cluster analysis were dichotomised before analysis. Selection of the reported cluster solution was based on the increasing value of the Squared Euclidean Distance between clusters. The cluster analysis was followed by between-group contrasts (of scale means and z-scores) using cluster membership to form the groups (Seifert, 1995).

15.3   Results

The scale reliability co-efficient (alpha) for the eight items making up the Aligned Evoked Conception of Learning Scale was found to be 0.71. The best alpha for a seven-item scale was less than 0.7. Responses (on the 1–5 point scale) fell within a range of 1.73–4.88 with a mean of 3.36 and a standard deviation of 0.57.

The relations between responses on the aligned evoked conception of learning variable and other variables used in the study were explored using correlation and cluster analyses. The outcome of the cluster analysis is shown in table 15.3.

Variable	Cluster	
	1	2
n	41	100
Aligned evoked conception of learning	2.84 (.44)	3.58 (.48)
Surface approach to learning	3.40 (.74)	2.45 (.60)
Deep approach to learning	3.20 (.59)	3.90 (.48)
Perceptions of a supportive learning environment	2.64 (.53)	3.60 (.40)
Anticipated outcome (degree classification)	4.71 (.64)	5.48 (.66)

Table 15.3   Mean (and standard deviations) cluster scale scores for evoked conception of learning, approaches to learning, perceptions of the learning environment and anticipated outcome variables.

(Eleven students in the sample who are exchange students did not expect a degree classification from Oxford and responded 'not applicable' to the item on anticipated outcome). Differences between the two cluster means on all variables are statistically significant at < .001

The two groups of students identified in the cluster analysis show coherent sets of relations between variables. The first group includes 41 students who, on average, have less aligned evoked conceptions of learning than their 100 colleagues in the second cluster. They perceive the environment to be less supportive of their learning, adopt more of a surface approach and less of a deep approach than their colleagues in cluster 2, and report that they expect to receive a degree classification approximately one level of award below that of these colleagues.

Table 15.4 shows the direction and extent of the correlations between the two approaches to learning (surface and deep) the four perceptions of the learning environment variables, and the evoked conception of learning variable.

Perceptions scales	Deep approach	Surface approach
Good teaching	0.43*	-0.49*
Appropriate workload	0.31*	-0.79*
Clear goals and standards	0.29*	-0.36*
Appropriate assessment	0.37*	-0.53*
Aligned evoked conception of learning	0.56*	-0.53*
Pearson, 2-tailed; n=151 (*$p \leq 0.001$)		

Table 15.4   Correlations between the four perceptions of learning environment scales, aligned evoked conception of learning scale and deep and surface approaches to learning scales

All the correlations between a reported deep approach to learning and the five other variables are positive and statistically significant. Conversely, all the correlations between a surface approach to learning and the perceptions variables are negative and statistically significant.

15.4   Discussion

The results reported above are significant in three respects. First, they show coherent and significant relations between evoked conception of learning, approaches to learning, perceived learning environments and learning outcomes. Second, the idea of evoked conception of learning appears to be measurable, meaningful and useful. This paper contains the first report of this concept, and the way it has been defined and used. Third, the cluster analysis results show no evidence of dissonant learning orchestrations among this group of students in this environment.

One of the aims of this study was to investigate the relations between evoked conception of learning, approaches to learning, perceptions of the learning environment and learning outcomes. To do this, evoked conceptions of learning at the University of Oxford had first to be described and then represented in a series of questionnaire items that were able to capture the qualitative differences between the experience of students. This process was conducted through an analysis of the quantitative methods being used to describe variation in conceptions of learning, a study of the Oxford students' experience of their learning environment, and a trial of an earlier version of the scale in a pilot study. Only the results of the implementation of the final (eight-item) version of the scale are reported in this paper.

The aligned evoked conception of learning scale contains items which focus on the University of Oxford tutorial system (the dominant approach used to facilitate learning) but it also includes items on students' perceived purpose of their degree and their engagement with primary research literature as part of their learning. It has an acceptable scale reliability (alpha) of 0.71. Responses on individual items were received across the full 1–5 point range and for the full scale from 1.73 to 4.88 showing that the scale range was valid and discriminatory. Most significantly, as explained further below, the relations between scores on this scale, and those on the other scales used, were strong, and consistently in the direction anticipated by the model proposed in Figure 15.1. This new scale appears to have statistical and face validity and has the potential to be a robust and efficient indicator of a situational component of the students' learning environment.

It is not, however, a scale that can be readily used in a context that is dissimilar to that at the University of Oxford. The very idea of evoked conceptions of learning has a built-in evoked-by-the-context component. While this limits the utility of the scale, it enhances its effectiveness in the contexts for which it has been designed.

The aligned evoked conceptions of learning scale was used at the University of Oxford in conjunction with quantitative indicators of students' approach to learning, their course experience and their assessment of the outcome of that experience. As shown in Tables 15.3 and 15.4, strong relations between these variables are observed. Correlations are high, and all variables in the cluster analysis are aligned. All the results reported are highly statistically significant. As noted above, the directions of these relations and correlations are all as would be anticipated from the model shown in Figure 15.1. Where students in this context perceive their environment to be supportive of learning, and their evoked conceptions of learning are aligned with the broad objectives of that context, they are more likely to adopt a deep approach to learning and expect to achieve a higher quality learning outcome. Where students have a less aligned evoked conception of learning they perceive their environment to be less supportive of learning, are more likely to adopt a surface approach to learning and expect to achieve a lower degree classification on average.

Students at the University of Oxford, like their colleagues in other universities, also vary in the approaches they adopt to learning, and in how they perceive their learning context. Some students who perceive a less appropriate workload, worse teaching, an inappropriate assessment system and unclear goals and standards, adopt more of a surface approach to learning than their colleagues in the same environment. Those adopting the deeper approaches experienced good teaching, clearer goals and standards, more appropriate assessment and a more appropriate workload.

These results described in the paragraph above are consistent with previous studies that have explored relations between these variables (Crawford, et al, 1998; Prosser, et al, 2000; Hazel, et al, 2002). The aspect of the results from this study that is new is the inclusion of students' evoked conceptions of what learning at the University of Oxford entails, and the alignment of the responses on this scale with those on the scales used in the other studies.

Studies of failing students (Meyer, Parsons and Dunne, 1990; Entwistle, Meyer and Tait, 1991) and into the relations between students' outcomes of learning, their approaches to learning, their perceptions of their learning environment and their prior understanding of their subject (Prosser, et al, 2000; Hazel, et al, 2002) show variation in the coherence of their study patterns. In all three studies, students with the least successful outcomes were more likely to have dissonant learning approaches or incoherent relations between their perceptions of their learning environment and their adopted learning approaches. Evidence from the studies by Prosser, et al and Hazel, et al indicates that students' prior understanding is strongly linked to their learning orchestration.

The data collected from students studying in this Oxford college context show no evidence in the cluster analysis of a group of students with dissonant study orchestrations. Both clusters in the preferred solution also contain students who describe coherent learning orchestrations. One explanation for this result is the level of students' prior understanding of their subject matter. The admissions system at Oxford University, which is conducted by interview at the subject level following high achievement at Secondary School level is more likely to result in less variation in prior knowledge than in the cases of the engineering, physics and biology students studied in those cases where dissonance was found.

15.5   Conclusions

This empirical study involving 155 undergraduate students in one collegial context has yielded evidence of a set of relations between the different ways university students think about their learning in a certain context, and their expectations of the outcomes of that learning. This paper contains the first report of the measurement and use of evoked conceptions of learning as part of that context.

Two clusters of students, each with coherent learning orchestrations were identified in the study. The cluster of 100 students who have an evoked conception of learning that is more aligned with the aims of their higher education context (for example, seeing tutorials as being more about the development of understanding than testing knowledge), report that they will achieve, on average, a degree classification almost one level higher than 41 of their colleagues in the other cluster. They also report adopting deeper approaches to learning, and perceive that the learning environment is more supportive of their learning.

As with the studies that led to the use of the Course Experience Questionnaire (CEQ) as an instrument to assist academic development (Ramsden, 1991) there is no evidence that any of the relations between the relevant variables are causal. However, as with the CEQ, the evoked conception of learning scale captures an aspect of students' experience of learning which is related to their approach to learning and their learning outcomes. Changing the environment in ways indicated by the nature of the students' response with the aim of evoking conceptions of learning that are more aligned with objectives may offer another path to improvements in student learning. With this aim in mind, the aligned evoked conception of learning scale is to be used next on a large-scale study of the students' experience of learning across the University of Oxford. Data collected are to be made available to departments, colleges, students and the central administration of the university to facilitate debate on how the environment might be changed.

Acknowledgements

Mark Fricker, Jackie Lewis, Gemma Stevenson and Josh Kern supported the design and implementation of this project. Students at their college supplied the data.

References

Ashwin, P (2002). Variation in students' experience of small group tutorials. In Rust, C (Ed), *Improving Student Learning: Theory and Practice – 10 years on*, (this volume Chapter 21). Oxford: Oxford Centre for Staff Development.

Commission of Inquiry (1997). *Commission of Inquiry Report.* Oxford: University of Oxford.

Crawford, K, Gordon, S, Nicholas, J and Prosser, M (1998). University mathematics students' conception of mathematics. *Studies in Higher Education*, **23**, 87–94.

Entwistle, NJ, Meyer, JHF and Tait, H (1991). Student failure: disintegrated patterns of study strategies and perceptions of the learning environment. *Higher Education*, **21**, 246–261.

Hazel, E, Prosser, M and Trigwell, K (2002). Variation in learning orchestration in university biology courses. *International Journal of Science Education*, **24**, 737–751.

Marton, F, Dall'Alba, G and Beaty, E (1993). Conceptions of learning. *International Journal of Educational Research*, **19**, 277–300.

Marton, F and Booth, S (1997). *Learning and Awareness.* New Jersey: Lawrence Erlbaum Associates.

Marton, F and Säljö, R (1997). Approaches to Learning. In Marton, F, Hounsell, D and Entwistle, NJ (Eds), *The Experience of Learning: Implications for Teaching and Studying in Higher Education.* (2nd Edn), pp39–58. Edinburgh: Scottish Academic Press.

Meyer, JHF (1995). A quantitative exploration of conceptions of learning. *Research and Development in Higher Education*, **18**, 545–550.

Meyer, JHF (2000a). Variation in contrasting forms of 'memorising' and associated observables. *British Journal of Educational Psychology*, **70**, 163–170.

Meyer, JHF (2000b). An overview of the development and application of the Reflections on Learning Inventory (RoLI). Paper presented to an Invitational Symposium.

Meyer, JHF (2000c). The modelling of 'dissonant' study orchestration in higher education. *European Journal of Psychology of Education*, **15**, 5–18.

Meyer, JHF, Parsons, P and Dunne, TT (1990). Individual study orchestrations and their association with learning outcome. *Higher Education*, **20**, 67–89.

Moore, WG (1968). *The Tutorial System and Its Future.* Oxford: Pergamon Press.

Perry, WG (1970). *Forms of Intellectual and Ethical Development in the College Years.* New York: Holt, Rinehart and Winston.

Prosser, M and Trigwell, K (1999). *Understanding Learning and Teaching: The experience in higher education.* Buckingham: SRHE and Open University Press.

Prosser, M, Trigwell, K, Hazel, E and Waterhouse, F (2000). Students' experiences of studying physics concepts: The effects of disintegrated perceptions and approaches. *European Journal of Psychology of Education*, **XV**, 61–74.

Ramsden, P (1991). A performance indicator of teaching quality in higher education: The Course Experience Questionnaire. *Studies in Higher Education*, **16**, 129–150.

Roach, M, Blackmore, P and Dempster, J (2001). Supporting high-level learning through research-based methods: A framework for course development. *Innovations in Education and Teaching International*, **38**, 369–382.

Säljö, R (1979). *Learning in the learner's perspective. I. Some common-sense conceptions.* Reports from the Department of Education, University of Göteborg, No 76.

Seifert, TL (1995). Characteristics of ego- and task-oriented students: A comparison of two methodologies. *British Journal of Educational Psychology*, **65**, 125–138.

16 Procedural approaches to learning: do these provide a viable bridge to a deep approach?

Jennifer Case[1] and Delia Marshall[2]

1 University of Cape Town; 2 University of the Western Cape

Abstract

This paper describes two approaches to learning (in addition to the classic deep and surface approaches) identified in studies of student learning in engineering contexts. The first study (Marshall, 1995) identified the 'procedural deep' approach in a group of engineering foundation programme students in the UK, and the second study (Case, 2000) identified the 'procedural surface' (originally termed algorithmic) approach amongst second year South African chemical engineering students. Both these approaches involve a strategy of focusing on problem solving, but they have respectively deep and surface intentions (the former involving the intention to understand and the latter not). From both studies it was also clear that the approaches students use are adaptations to particular course contexts, and it is suggested that a focus towards a procedural deep objective might preclude the development of a conceptual deep approach (more akin to the classic deep approach).

16.1 Introduction

Many research projects over the last few decades have sought to identify students' approaches to learning in particular course contexts. This paper draws on the findings of two such studies conducted during the 90s in engineering programmes (Case, 2000; Marshall, 1995). What is unusual about these studies is that both sought to identify the approaches present in the particular context, rather than assuming the presence of only classic deep and surface approaches. In addition to these traditional approaches then, Marshall identified a 'procedural deep' approach, and Case identified an 'algorithmic' approach. Both of these approaches have as core strategy a focusing on the solving of problems, but the procedural deep approach involves an intention to understand, while the algorithmic approach does not. This paper compares these two approaches in some detail, and proposes a new characterisation of approaches to learning in science and engineering contexts. The findings also have important implications for teaching practice, and these are discussed.

16.2 Approaches to Learning

Deep and surface approaches to learning were first identified in a well-known series of studies conducted in the late 1970s by Marton and Säljö (1976a; 1976b). These studies examined the way students tackled reading tasks, and identified two qualitatively different 'levels of processing'. Students who used surface-level processing focused on the text itself, trying to memorise as much as possible, while those using deep-level processing aimed to grasp the underlying meaning of the text. The term 'approach to learning', incorporating both what students do (strategy) and why they do it (intention), was subsequently adopted to describe these findings (Marton & Säljö, 1984).

Originally, the term 'approach to learning' referred to how students tackled specific learning tasks within a course (as in Marton and Säljö's study described above). However, other studies began to examine students' approaches to learning at a general course level. Some of the more quantitative course-level research operationalised the concept 'approach to learning' through the development of inventories of students learning, for example, the Approaches to Study Inventory (Entwistle & Ramsden, 1983).

A critical and frequently misunderstood characteristic of approaches to learning as defined in these early studies is that they capture students' responses and adaptations to course contexts, rather than representing innate cognitive characteristics of a student. Clearly a student's choice of approach is to some extent determined by his/her past experience, but this only describes part of the picture. The nature of the course as perceived by students is an important determinant of the choice of approach, as shown clearly in the large scale Entwistle and Ramsden (1983) study.

Research into student approaches to learning over the last two decades has mushroomed, with a large body of work claiming descent from Marton and Säljö's original investigations. Both quantitative and qualitative studies have generally assumed the existence of deep and surface approaches prior to commencing the study, and have proceeded to identify the prevalence of these approaches in their student samples. Some concerns have been voiced that this could lead to a situation where the deep/surface model could cease to be descriptive, and in fact become prescriptive (Bock, 1986; Webb, 1997). Other researchers have also suggested that this bipolar description of approaches to learning may not capture some of the nuances and subtleties in students' learning experiences (Barnett, 1990; Volet & Chalmers, 1992).

Ramsden (1988) posited that deep and surface approaches would have very different manifestations in different academic specialisations, in agreement with the context-dependent nature of approaches as originally formulated by Marton and Säljö. Ramsden suggested that in science contexts a deep approach to a task might initially demand a narrow focus on details, which on its own could appear to be a surface approach. In the humanities he argued that a deep approach would usually involve establishing personal meaning right from the beginning of a task, which might suggest a deep approach. Entwistle (1997) also argues that researchers need to reformulate approaches to learning within different disciplinary contexts.

> The defining features [of deep and surface approaches] also fail to do justice to differences between disciplines. The specific processes involved in seeking deep understanding, as well as the balance betweeen them, must vary across subject areas. Ideally, the idea of a deep approach needs to be reformulated to show how it emerges in a particular course of study, while students need to be shown how they can apply different learning processes (including memorisation) appropriately in seeking conceptual understanding. This is an area of research which is, so far, undeveloped, and needs attention. (Entwistle, 1997, p 216)

Some researchers have taken this injunction to involve redefining the characteristics of deep and surface approaches within particular disciplinary contexts (for example, Chin & Brown, 2000). We would suggest that this needs to be taken a step further, in order to uncover any other approaches that might emerge from detailed studies. As far as we can establish, there are very few examples of work which have sought to do this (especially when compared to the great body of statistical research which presumes the existence of the deep/surface dichotomy in myriad contexts). One important example however is the work of Booth, who investigated students as they were learning to write computer programs (Booth, 1992). Booth identified four distinctly different approaches to learning in this context: an 'expedient' approach in which a previous programme was identified which would suit the purposes of the current task; a 'constructual' approach, where elements from their previously written programs were cobbled together for a solution; an 'operational' approach which focused on what the program was going to have to do; and a 'structural' approach which focused initially on the problem rather than the program specifications. The first two of these approaches Booth considered to be surface approaches, while the latter two approaches she classified as deep.

Both the studies under review in this paper adopted similar research approaches to Booth, in that the broad construct of 'approach to learning' was assumed to have utility and validity, but the specific approaches present in these contexts were identified from the data using grounded theory rather than imported as a priori assumptions. Only once contextual approaches had been identified were these then compared to the classic deep and surface approaches, and classified accordingly.

16.3   The studies

Marshall (1995) conducted a year-long study of thirteen students who were doing a first year engineering foundation course in the UK. Case (2000) followed eleven students who were doing a second year chemical engineering course at a South African university. Both studies drew strongly on data derived from series of individual interviews held with students over the duration of the course, although this was supplemented by other data such as the completed ASI questionnaire in the Marshall study, and completed journal tasks in the Case study. Marshall interviewed students about their learning both at a course-level and a task-level, which correspond roughly to Case's self-reflective and conceptual data categories.

Both the studies were strongly located in the student learning literature. Marshall focused on students' conceptions of learning and approaches to learning, and how these were influenced by the course context. Case used a theoretical framework incorporating approaches to learning, metacognitive development (conceptualised as a shift in approach to learning) and students' perceptions of the educational context. In this paper we will focus on those aspects of both studies in which approaches to learning were identified.

16.4   Approaches identified

Each study identified three approaches to learning, each of which will be described below in terms of strategy and related intention, which are the key descriptors of approaches to learning as mentioned earlier.

Marshall's (1995) approaches to learning were characterised by the extent to which students showed evidence of seeking out relationships – with parts of the task and the whole, or with other related knowledge. These three approaches were:

- 'Surface' approach:
  strategy: no relationships sought out or established, learn by repetition and memorisation of formulae and simple algorithms
  intention: to be able to repeat formulae and use algorithms in tests/exams

- 'Procedural deep' approach:
  strategy: relating of formulae to each other, or parts of algorithms to other parts
  intention: to gain understanding at some future point through familiarity with applications and problem-solving procedures.

- 'Conceptual deep' approach:
  strategy: relating of learning tasks to their underlying concepts or theory
  intention: to gain understanding while doing this.

Case (2000) also identified three approaches to learning, namely

- 'Information-based' approach:
  strategy: memorising information that can be supplied in response to assessment questions
  intention: to be able to supply relevant information during test/exam

- 'Algorithmic' approach:
  strategy: identifying and memorising calculation methods for solving problems
  intention: to be able to solve problems in test/exam

- 'Conceptual' approach:
  strategy: working through problems and consulting textbook, puzzling over gaps in understanding
  intention: to be able to understand key concepts

The similarity between these sets of findings is striking. At each end of the spectrum each study identified approaches that can be seen to roughly equate to the classic deep and surface approaches (although with subtle contextual features). These approaches (as identified in both studies) will hereafter be referred to using Marshall's terminology of 'surface' and 'conceptual deep'. The 'middle' approaches also appear at first glance to be equivalent, and these will be examined in more detail in the following section.

16.5   The algorithmic and procedural deep approaches

Both the procedural deep approach of Marshall and the algorithmic approach identified by Case have at their core a focus on being able to solve problems, which is the standard way of assessing in tertiary science and engineering courses. In both studies it appeared that this approach was prompted to some extent by students' concerns about whether or not they would pass the course tests and examinations. Beyond the common characteristic of a focus on problem solving, however, there are distinct differences in the nature of these two approaches, which will be outlined below.

As noted earlier, Marshall's procedural deep approach was characterised by a relating of formulae to each other, or parts of algorithms to other parts. Students using this approach were able to manipulate more complicated equations, and cope with different 'unknowns', as indicated in the following quote:

> … Not every [test] question is the same; you have to work it out for yourself. When you get to a question you haven't seen before … you can't just do it parrot-fashion.

Students using a procedural deep approach indicated that although this approach did not centrally focus on understanding, their expectation was that in the long run they would gain understanding through practising problems, as indicated in the following quotes:

> …in Maths, I can use differentiation without fully understanding it… Understanding doesn't come until you've used it a lot. (emphasis added)

> I'll just try and learn the methods, and hopefully understand them through use.

On the basis of this long-term focus on understanding, Marshall characterised the procedural deep approach as a form of a deep approach (although not as sophisticated as the conceptual deep approach).

In Case's algorithmic approach, students indicated that they attempted to memorise standard solution methods, in order to be able to apply these to similar problems in the test or examination. The emphasis lay on working through as many problems as possible, and remembering the solution methods given in the memoranda. Some of these students attempted to find one ideal method for solving a particular type of problem. Solving problems was seen as involving a search for the appropriate equation(s) and substituting values to get an answer. An example of a comment coded in Case's study as indicating an algorithmic approach was the following, where a student was reflecting back on his performance in a test:

> And the thing is, I probably didn't understand, not totally, but often I didn't quite have an understanding of the process, I just knew how to do the calculations…

When responding to conceptual questions posed in the course of the interview, the algorithmic approach manifests as a grasping at formulae without an underlying conceptual understanding, which in many cases led to conceptually illogical answers.

The algorithmic approach identified by Case specifically precluded a focus on understanding, and in fact none of the students using this approach even commented that in the long run they thought they would develop understanding through this approach. On this basis, the algorithmic approach was characterised by Case as a form of a surface approach (although more sophisticated than the information-based approach identified in this study).

At this stage it is worth considering how each study might have coded comments from the other study's middle category. In Marshall's study, comments in which students said they "put loads of numbers into formulas" were classified as indicating a surface approach. The same comment would have been classified as an algorithmic approach in Case's study. In Case's study, many of the students indicating that they used a conceptual approach, also said that they worked through problems to develop this understanding. It is likely that Marshall might have classified these comments as indicating a procedural deep approach. In other terms, it appears that Marshall's surface approach encompasses both Case's information-based and algorithmic approaches, while Case's conceptual approach includes both Marshall's procedural deep and conceptual deep approaches. Each study identified a nuanced distinction that the other did not. If however we bring together these two sets of findings, it would appear that two intermediate approaches between the deep and surface poles have been identified, hereafter termed 'procedural surface' (Case's algorithmic approach) and 'procedural deep' (Marshall's category). These two approaches share a common strategy (working through problems) but have differing intentions (to remember solution methods for use in tests, or to gain understanding through application of solution methods). This is represented in Figure 16.1.

| Surface approach (Case & Marshall) | Procedural surface approach (Case) | Procedural deep approach (Marshall) | Conceptual deep approach (Case & Marshall) |

Fig.16.1   Approaches to learning identified in Marshall and Case studies

16.6   Changes in approaches to learning as a response to course context

Over the duration of the course, Marshall noted a convergence towards a procedural deep approach from both directions, ie from surface to procedural and from conceptual to procedural. This convergence appeared to be related to students' perceptions of the course context, which was perceived to emphasise problem-solving procedures over conceptual understanding. For example the following comment from a student:

> The message from the teaching is "Go through the examples and you'll pass the exam".

The convergence to a procedural approach is vividly illustrated in the following discussion between a student (S) and the interviewer (I):

S: My mistake earlier in the year was trying to understand how formulas work – now I just do it, and don't ask why.

I: So your view of learning has changed since I last spoke to you?

S: Yeah. Now I try just to remember things rather than the meaning behind it all.

I: Why?

S: Because I have struggled to understand and it's a waste of time. So I'll just use the formulae and hopefully understand them later.

By contrast, Case noted a general trend towards the adoption of a conceptual approach, although this was incomplete for many students at the end of the course (and only fully implemented in later courses). There was a student who had entered the course with a conceptual approach and reverted to an algorithmic approach, but even she later then attempted to shift back again to a conceptual approach when the limitations of this approach became apparent. This general trend appeared to relate to some extent also to the course context in this case, where the lecturer placed a very strong focus on the development of conceptual understanding (and geared the assessment accordingly).

16.7   Discussion

The identification of two intermediate approaches between the classic deep and surface approaches is a potentially important finding in relation to the process of students' changing their approaches (also termed metacognitive development). Is there maybe some sense in the advice often given to science and engineering students to practice lots of problems and that understanding will come in the long run? The 'surface – procedural surface – procedural deep – conceptual deep' continuum does suggest an interesting route for changing one's approach. Moving from surface to procedural surface involves only a change in strategy but not in intention (moving from memorising information to working on problems). Changing from procedural surface to procedural deep involves changing one's intentions (towards a focus on understanding) but not having to change one's strategy. Finally, the move from procedural deep to conceptual deep involves developing a better strategy in order to accomplish the same intention. In this sense then one could quite possibly argue that the new approaches identified in this paper might well represent some form of a 'bridge' to a deep approach. This is illustrated in Figure 16.2.

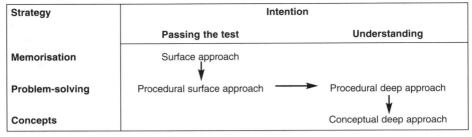

Fig. 16.2   Changes in approaches to learning

It is also patently clear however that the extent of students' changing their approaches depends very strongly on their perceptions of the course context. In this paper we have considered two contexts, one where students perceived that a procedural deep approach was most appropriate, and another in which they perceived that a conceptual deep approach was required. In each instance the majority of students appeared to attempt to tailor their use of approaches accordingly. This raises interesting questions for foundation type courses such as that studied by Marshall, where frequently the course objectives are aimed primarily towards students developing competency in basic skills. Is it advisable for such a course to be focused explicitly on the development of a procedural deep approach (which might involve some students having a move away from a conceptual deep approach towards this)? Given the strong focus in engineering and science courses on the ability to solve problems, often, as evidenced in assessment, given implicitly more importance than understanding concepts, this might be a sensible strategy for helping students to succeed. The danger lies in that students might thereafter struggle to make the appropriate adjustment to a conceptual deep approach when required.

16.8   Conclusion

Drawing on the findings of two studies of student learning, this paper has proposed the identification of two approaches to learning that fall between the deep and surface poles. Both the procedural surface and procedural deep approaches use a strategy that involves working through problems, but they have very different intentions: the latter approach involves an ultimate intention towards understanding while the former does not. The first important implication of these findings is that working through problems may indeed provide a bridge to a deep approach, as students make the transition from a procedural surface to a procedural deep approach. Secondly however, it is clear that such transitions are generally made in response to students' perceptions of course contexts, and a course that focuses towards procedural deep objectives will be unlikely to move students towards a conceptual deep approach.

References

Barnett, R (1990). *The idea of higher education.* London: SRHE and Open University Press.

Bock, HK (1986). Phenomenography: orthodoxy and innovation or innovation and orthodoxy? In Bowden, J (Ed), *Student learning: Research into practice* pp 95–114. Melbourne, Australia: Centre for the Study of Higher Education, University of Melbourne.

Booth, S (1992). *Learning to program: A phenomenographic perspective.* Gothenburg, Sweden: Acta Universitatis Gothoburgensis.

Case, JM (2000). Students' perceptions of context, approaches to learning and metacognitive development in a second year chemical engineering course. Unpublished PhD, Monash University, Melbourne.

Chin, C, & Brown, DE (2000). Learning in science: A comparison of deep and surface approaches. *Journal of Research in Science Teaching,* **37**(2), 109–138.

Entwistle, N (1997). Reconstituting approaches to learning: A response to Webb. *Higher Education,* **33**, 213–218.

Entwistle, NJ and Ramsden, P (1983). *Understanding student learning.* London: Croom Helm.

Marshall, D (1995). The relationship between learning conceptions, approaches to learning and learning outcomes in foundation year engineering students. Unpublished DPhil, University of Oxford, Oxford.

Marton, F, and Säljö, R (1976a). On qualitative differences in learning: I – Outcome and process. *British Journal of Educational Psychology,* **46**, 4–11.

Marton, F, and Säljö, R (1976b). On qualitative differences in learning: II – Outcome as a function of the learner's conception of the task. *British Journal of Educational Psychology,* **46**, 115–127.

Marton, F, and Säljö, R (1984). Approaches to learning. In Marton, F, Hounsell, D, and Entwistle, N (Eds), *The experience of learning* (pp 36–55). Edinburgh, UK: Scottish Academic Press.

Ramsden, P (1988). Studying learning: Improving teaching. In Ramsden, P (Ed), *Improving learning: new perspectives.* pp 13–31. London: Kogan Page.

Volet, SE, and Chalmers, D (1992). Investigation of qualitative differences in university students' learning goals, based on an unfolding model of stage development. *British Journal of Educational Psychology,* **62**, 17–34.

Webb, G (1997). Deconstructing deep and surface: Towards a critique of phenomenography. *Higher Education,* **33**, 195–212.

17 Explaining achievement in higher education

Ellen P. W. A. Jansen and Marjon Bruinsma
University of Groningen

Abstract

In this research project the relation between students' pre-entry characteristics, ratings on courses and reported work discipline, the use of deep information processing strategy, and academic achievement, is investigated. The responses of two cohorts of students in the Arts department of the University of Groningen, the Netherlands, on course evaluation questionnaires, questionnaires on study behaviour are analysed and related to academic achievement outcomes, using a path model. Ability measured by grade point average in secondary education was the most important predictor of achievement, followed by work discipline. Perceived course difficulty and age had an effect on the rating of the quality of the course and instructor. However, the rating of the course and instructor was not related to study outcome, work discipline or deep information processing. Furthermore, gender, ability, perceived difficulty and work discipline had significant effects on student involvement during the course.

17.1   Introduction

Educational effectiveness has always been an important focus of attention in higher educational research. Within this framework for many years, drop out has been seen as a phenomenon to be identified. The question why certain students decide to drop out while others decide to persist has been an starting-point for many studies in higher education (for example, Bean, 1980; Bean & Metzner 1985; Bijleveld, 1993; Jansen, 1996; Pascarella, 1980; Prins, 1997; Tinto, 1975, 1987). These studies have shown that achievement or dropout is the result of interactions between student, departmental and environmental characteristics.

Most of these studies proceed from so-called interactional approaches to explain academic achievement or dropout. The first model that focused on the interactional approach was Spady's model (1971). In his model Spady argued that social integration was, among other things, influenced by study results, 'normative congruence' that is the interaction between complex patterns of ability, aptitude, interests, goals, values and expectations, support by friends and by mutual group values. Dropout was seen as a longitudinal process resulting from a combination of commitment and study results. Spady's model was soon followed by Tinto's models (1975, 1987) who proposed that both student characteristics and its interactions with the social as well as the academic environments influences a students' decision to persist or to withdraw from college.

Other models soon followed these two models, for example, Pascarella (1980) who emphasised the importance of informal contact between student and teacher and Bean (1980

& 1990) who developed a meta-model of dropout, which emphasised the importance of a student's background variables that directly influence social and academic integration as well as environmental variables. Webb (1990) does add to this that most of these explanatory dropout models are not very well applicable to non-campus institutions. Based on research at a non-campus institution he therefore introduced the term 'perceived student/institution fit' instead of the psychological outcomes specified by Bean (1980, 1990) (eg utility, satisfaction, goal commitment, stress) and added the 'term academic self-confidence' to the model.

In the Netherlands these studies were soon elaborated on; for example, Bijleveld (1993) specified a model to explain dropout that stresses both student and departmental characteristics, amount of problem-based learning, amount of interactive teaching methods, spread of study load, and spread of tests. Jansen (1996) looked at the relation between curriculum organisation (eg planning/time tabling, instruction and test/examination) and study achievement at six departments of the University of Groningen. In correspondence with earlier findings (Van der Drift and Vos, 1987; Jansen, 1992; 1993; Joostens and Schoonen, 1987) and in accordance with expectations of the Caroll model (1963) and Creemers (1994), achievement was influenced by measures that affect the student planning behaviour and encourage a positive attitude towards study. The instruction characteristics showed a less clear picture. Prins (1997) used Bijleveld's model, which he extended with variables on academic and social integration of Tinto's model. Prins concluded that study counseling, quality of tests, spread of study load, the number of contact hours and student-centered education influenced the dropout or retention rate. De Jong, U. Roeleveld, J. and Webbink, H.D. (1997a) performed a nation-wide research on study careers in Higher Education. In their 'Amsterdam model of study careers' they integrated the human capital theory and the social integration theory.

Beside the effects of variables on the organisational or departmental level, another missing link in these theories is the role of actual study behaviour. For example, (Berger & Milem, 1999) stated that most of the existing literature on testing the Tinto model has focused on the perceptual components of academic and social integration, while ignoring measures of actual behaviour. They conclude that the results of their study confirm the use of a combined model that accounts for both behavioural and perceptual components to describe the persistence process during the first year of college. According to Berger and Milem (1999) previous research on first-year retention has underestimated the role of involvement or lack of involvement in relation to student persistence.

This paper discusses a model to explain variance in achievement that includes departmental characteristics as well as student pre-entry characteristics and student's study behaviour (see figure 17.1).

We expected direct effects from gender and ability on achievement. For example Jansen (1996), Shah and Burke (1999) and Van den Berg (2002) showed that women and students with higher ability achieved higher results. Furthermore we expected effects from ability on students' work discipline, on perceived difficulty and on student involvement. We expected that students with higher ability in secondary education use the right study strategies or might have more discipline to study. Furthermore, we expected a direct effect from gender on discipline. Studies have shown that female students show more discipline (Macan, Shahani, Dipboye and Phillips, 1990). Beside that, according to our model, older students show higher work discipline than younger students and older students would show higher scores on deep information processing. This last expectation resulted from the idea that older students often

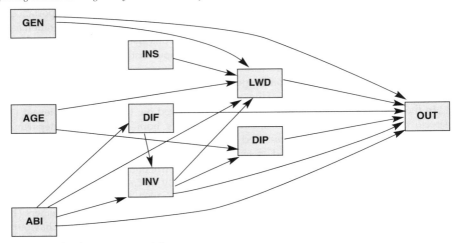

Figure 17.1   The theoretical model

have more study experience and therefore are better disciplined and are better able to use the right or appropriate deep information processing skills.

We expected a relation between the quality of instruction, perceived difficulty, involvement, work discipline and outcome. That is, students who rated the course and instructor positively, would have better results. This assumption is based, among others, on the studies of Perry (for review see Perry, 1997) in which significant effects were reported from instructor expressiveness and lecture content on student ratings of instruction and on student achievement. Furthermore, we expected that students who would rate the course-difficulty as sufficient, and who would be more involved were expected to be more satisfied with their study. Perry (1997) pointed at a relationship between perceived control and instruction. Perceived difficulty can be seen as a proxy of perceived control. According to Perry (1997), students who suffer loss of control are less able to benefit from effective instruction. Therefore we expected students who experienced the course as difficult and time consuming to give lower ratings of the quality of the course and instructor and to be less involved in the course.

Students who are positive about the course and instructor were expected to have a higher score on their work discipline. Because deep information processing is seen as a desired learning strategy, we expected an effect from deep information processing on the outcome variables. And finally, we expected that work discipline be strongly related with student outcome. Work discipline is related to time management behaviour . Macan et al (1990) found significant relations between time management behaviour and self-rated performance and GPA.

In summary this article focuses on the question: "what is the relation between student background characteristics, student ratings of courses, study behaviour and student outcomes like mean grade point average after one year and number of credits after one year?" This main problem is divided in following questions:

- What is the relation between student background characteristics and student ratings?

- What is the relation between student ratings of instruction and their student behaviour in terms of a) work discipline and b) deep information processing, and finally,

- What is the relation between student ratings and achievement in terms of a) grade point average and, b) total number of credits?

17.2   Method

17.2.1   Design and sample

For some years now research projects on the theme 'effectiveness of curriculum and instruction in Higher Education' have been the focus of attention at the University of Groningen. The data used in the study reported here were collected within this framework. In this research project four departments (one from the Faculty of Arts, one from the Faculty of Sciences and two from the Faculty of Economics and Business) participated and data were collected during the college years 1999/2000 and 2000/2001. This paper reports analyses on the students from the department of the Faculty of Arts. Two cohorts of first-year students (N 1999 = 147, male=41, female =106 and N2000 = 149, male=37, female=111) of this department were asked to fill in the questionnaires. Three sorts of data were collected during this year, namely, 1) student ratings of seven courses, which were collected after each course, 2) study behaviour data, which were collected on two occasions, and, 3) study achievement data, which we obtained from the administration system. Each student was asked to fill in their student identification number and because we guaranteed their anonymity, most students did fill in their registration number. This resulted in a rather unique database with data on student ratings, study behaviour and achievement that can be linked on student level.

17.2.2   Variables and instruments

Student ratings of courses

In the Netherlands the tradition of the use of standard questionnaires for student ratings is less widespread than, for example, in the United States. Most institutions and even most departments use their own questionnaire. Sometimes student ratings are collected with standard items but sometimes course specific items are used. Although most questionnaires have their specific subjects the same aspects are globally present in most of them; most of these questionnaires therefore evaluate the same underlying concepts. At the University of Groningen the departments use different forms for evaluating their courses. Fortunately, at the Faculty of Arts all departments use the same form. This form consists of 27 items with most items on a four-point Likert scale that varies from (1) completely agree to (4) completely disagree. The mean response rate was 51.5%.

We analysed the data from the evaluations with a factor analysis, principal components with varimax rotation. This resulted in a four-factor solution that explained 44% of the variance. The first factor 'Course/Instructor' indicates general satisfaction with the course and the instructor. It consisted of eight items that loaded with .35 or more on the factor. Examples of items are: 'The lectures matched the literature' and 'The teacher explained the subject very well.' The second factor 'perceived difficulty' indicates the feeling of being able to succeed in the course. This factor consisted of three items that had factor loadings above or equal to .35. An example of an item is: 'In comparison with other courses the subject matter was …(1: too difficult … 5: too easy). The third factor 'Information' consisted of three items and concerned the information given in advance on subject matter, materials and the assessment syllabus, for example 'When the courses started, there was a handout available'. The final factor consisted of three items that concerned students' involvement. An example item is: I attended … % of the lectures'.

Based on the results of the factor analysis we constructed three indices: course/instructor, difficulty, and, finally, student involvement. The response scale was recoded in the case of negative items. The indices were reduced to a scale from 1 to 4, where 1 is 'good' and 4 is 'bad' (see appendix). Table 17.1 shows the intercorrelations between the three indices.

	course/instructor	difficulty	Involvement
Course/instructor	1.00		
Difficulty	0.23**	1.00	
Involvement	0.06	-0.25**	1.00

*p<0.05, **p<0.01

Table 17.1   Intercorrelations between the evaluation indices

Student variables

We included three student background variables in the model, namely gender, age and ability. These three variables were obtained from the student administrations. Furthermore, two study behaviour variables were included in the study. These variables were obtained via self-report questionnaires. Students filled in a questionnaire on two occasions at the beginning and the end of the first year. The researcher handed out the questionnaire during lectures and tutorials and urgently requested the students to fill in the questionnaire. The questionnaires were collected on the spot. This procedure yielded a total response of 49%. The same procedure yielded on the second occasion a total response of 40%.

The questionnaire consisted of three existing questionnaires of Study Support Groningen and contained items on aspects like low discipline and deep information processing (DIP) (Schouwenburg, 1996; Schouwenburg and Stevens, 1996). Low work discipline is a motivational component in our study and is therefore included. Deep information processing is included because it is seen as a desirable approach to studying. For example, Terenzini (1999, p36) states that "…[Learning] requires time for reflection, consolidation, and internalisation if it is to be long-lasting, "deeper learning". Despite this fact, in reality students content themselves with a more surface approach to learning. This might be related to their own conceptions or motivations to studying, but more importantly this might be related to the teaching or to the assessment procedures. Table 17.2 shows some of the items used in the questionnaire.

Variable	example question
Low work discipline	I work unsystematically
	I am always behind planning
Deep information processing	When I read an complicated text I think of questions about the subject

Table 17.2   Examples of study behaviour questions

Achievement

The administration of the department provided data concerning the number of credits after 12 months and the grades for each course. These grades vary on a scale from 1 to 10, where a 1 is a very bad grade and a 10 an excellent grade. Two outcome measures were computed from this data:

- Grade Point Average (GPA): the grade point average on the seven courses, and

- Total Number of Credits (TNC): this outcome variable consists of the total number of credits a student obtained on the seven courses. In the first year 42 credits are programmed; this is theoretically the equivalent of 1,680 hours of study. If a student succeeded for all the seven courses involved, he or she could earn a maximum of 22 credits.

17.2.3   Model and analyses

The different relations between student background characteristics, instruction characteristics, student behaviour and achievement were analysed by a path model. The model contains three exogene variables, namely gender, age and ability. Furthermore it contains six endogene variables divided in three course characteristics, namely course/ instructor, perceived difficulty and student involvement, two student behaviour characteristics (work discipline and deep information processing) and finally the outcome variables mean grade and total number of credits. We analysed the above mentioned theoretical model using LISREL 8.5 (N=296). Missing values were imputed using the 'expectation-maximisation method' (Dempster, Laird & Rubin, 1977). The two models that included total number of credits and grade point average were analysed with the maximum-likelihood method based on a covariance matrix. We used the root mean square error of approximation (RMSEA) with a cut-off value of .06 and the non-normed fit index (NNFI) with a cut-of value of .96 (Hu & Bentler, 1999) to indicate the fit between the observed data and the hypothesised model.

17.3   Results

Table 17.3 (overleaf) shows the zero-order correlation matrix that was used in the analyses. It shows that deep information processing is not significantly correlated with the outcome variables. Therefore, it is expected that in the model deep information processing will not show strong effects on study outcome. However, because deep information processing is usually seen as a desired way of studying, we decided to incorporate this variable in the model.

17.3.1   Path-models

Table 17.4 (overleaf) shows the fit measures that indicate the fit between the theoretical model and the observed model for the two outcome variables (GPA and TNC) and, secondly, it illustrates the total amount of explained variance by the models. Although the models explain a large amount of variance (49% and 50% respectively), the fit measures do not indicate a good fit. The RMSEA was .10 for both models and the NNFI was .81 and .80.

Based on the expected changes in the model that LISREL modification indices indicate, the model is adjusted. After seven modifications the models show a sufficient fit (see table 17.5).

	gen	abi	age	crs/inst	dif	invol	wrkds	dip	tnc
Gen									
Abi	*0.13*								
Age	*-0.12*	***-0.31***							
crs/in	-0.05	-.003	***-0.18***						
dif	-0.02	-0.05	-0.09	***0.28***					
invol	***-0.19***	***-0.20***	-0.06	0.05	***-0.26***				
wrkds	***0.15***	***-0.41***	-0.08	*0.15*	-0.01	***0.58***			
dip	***-0.21***	-0.01	***-0.37***	0.01	0.10	-0.08	-0.12		
tnc	***0.25***	***0.44***	*-0.17*	-0.11	0.11	***-0.30***	***-0.44***	-0.05	
mgpa	***0.22***	***0.64***	-0.09	***-0.16***	*-0.13*	***-0.31***	***-0.49***	0.01	***0.81***

italic: p<0.05 (2-tailed)   ***bold italic***: p<0.01 (2-tailed)

Table 17.3   legend:

gen   : gender
abi   : ability, grade point average secondary school
age   : age
crs/in : rating course/instructor
dif   : rating perceived difficulty
involv : rating involvement
wrkds   : score low work discipline
dip   : score deep information processing
tnc   : total number of credits on the seven courses
GPA   : Grade Point Average on the seven courses

Table 17.3   Zero order correlations of the variables used in model

	RMSEA	NNFI	explained variance
GPA	0.10	0.81	49%
TNC	0.10	0.80	50%

	RMSEA	NNFI	explained variance
GPA	0.047	0.96	50%
TNC	0.067	0.95	50%

Table 17.4   Fit measures for the theoretical models and explained variance

Table 17.5   Fit measures for the modified models and explained variance

In the following section we start with a discussion of the model with grade point average on the seven courses. This is followed by a contrast with the TNC model.

Table 17.6 shows the significant standardised effects. We expected and found a direct effect from gender on work discipline and GPA. Furthermore, a significant effect from gender on deep information processing and involvement was found. The total standardised effect from gender on GPA was .15. Female students showed better results, rated the course/instructor more positively, and were more involved in the study, used less deep information processing strategies and had a higher work discipline than male students.

Furthermore, not surprisingly, ability showed the largest effect on GPA The total effect was .63, the direct effect .51. Besides that, significant effects were found from ability on involvement, deep information processing, and work discipline. Students with higher ability in secondary education received higher grades at the end of the first year. Moreover, students

	gen	abi	age	crs/in	dif	involv	wrkds	dip
gen								
abi								
age								
crs/in			-0.15		0.27			
dif								
involv	-0.16	-0.23	-0.01		-0.25		0.56	
wrkds	-0.11	-0.47	-0.24		-0.10			
dip	-0.18	0.14	0.40		0.02			
GPA	0.15	0.63	0.05		-0.11		-0.27	

legend:

gen   : gender
abi   : ability, grade point average secondary school
age   : age
crs/in   : rating course/instructor
dif   : rating perceived difficulty
involv   : rating involvement
wrkds   : score low work discipline
dip   : score deep information processing
GPA   : Grade Point Average on the seven courses

Table 17.6   Significant standardised total effects of model with MGPA

with a higher ability were more involved, showed considerably higher work discipline, and used more deep information processing strategies.

The analyses showed a direct effect from age on deep information processing (.40), which implies that older students indicated that they used more deep information processing than younger students did. Furthermore, the analyses yielded a significant effect from age on the course/instructor (direct, -.16), on work discipline (-.24) and a small but significant effects on involvement and GPA. That is, older students showed more discipline, and were more satisfied with the course/instructor. Furthermore, these older students were more involved and showed higher grades.

There were no significant effects from course/instructor on any of the other variables in the model. Perceived difficulty had a relatively large total effect on student involvement (-.25). Students who rated the assignments as less difficult and thought that the study load was in accordance with the number of credits, were more involved. The total effect of difficulty on GPA was moderate (-.11).

The analyses of study behaviour, deep information processing and work discipline showed significant effects from work discipline; that is work discipline showed total effects on involvement (.56), and on GPA (-.27) Students with higher work discipline reported more involvement and received higher grades.

We analysed a model with the alternative achievement outcome, Total Number of Credits after one year (TNC) based on the best fit of the GPA-model. We see the results in table 17.7.

	gen	abi	age	crs/in	dif	invol	wrkds	dip
gen								
abi								
age								
crs/in			-0.15		0.27			
dif								
involv	-0.16	-0.23	-0.11		-0.26		0.52	
wrkds	-0.11	-0.46	-0.21					
dip	-0.18	0.14	0.40					
TNC	0.22	0.58	0.07		0.10		-0.34	

legend:

gen   : gender
abi   : ability, grade point average secondary school
age   : age
crs/in   : rating course/instructor
dif   : rating perceived difficulty
involv   : rating involvement
wrkds   : score low work discipline
dip   : score deep information processing
TNC   : Total number of credits on the seven courses

Table 17.7   Significant standardised total effects of model with TNC

When comparing the GPA model with the TNC model we found no different effects from gender, age, and ability, except that the effect from the last mentioned was higher in the GPA model (.58 versus .63). The explanation is quite obvious: in the GPA-model we look at the obtained grades and not only if someone did pass for a course examination. There is, so to speak, a quality element involved. Students with higher scores in secondary education can be expected to obtain higher grades at university.

Looking at the different rating variables we see the effect of perceived difficulty is positive in the TNC model and negative in the GPA model (.10 versus -.11). And finally, the effect of work discipline on the outcome variable is higher in the TNC model (-.34 versus -.27).

17.4 Discussion

The purpose of this study was to analyse a model that included aspects on student background, ratings, study behaviour and academic achievement. As expected, we found a large effect from ability on achievement. This is in line with earlier findings from, for example, Van der Hulst and Jansen, 2002, Lindblom-Ylänne et al, (1999) and Jansen (1996). However, Lizzio et al, (2002) reported that student's school achievement was a positive but weak predictor of their university achievement. They stressed to interpret this finding cautiously, given the inherent restriction of range. There is a difference in admission policy between Dutch and American universities. In the Netherlands universities are not allowed to select students on their grades from secondary education. There is streaming in Dutch secondary education, that is to say that most students have a VWO-diploma (VWO= Pre-University Education) when they start at university. Although this also causes a restriction of range, maybe there is more variation in grade obtained at secondary school than in the American situation. According to Lizzio et al (2002) student's perceptions of their current learning environment have a stronger influence on study outcome than their mean grade in secondary education. However, our findings point at a strong direct and indirect effect from ability on achievement. These indirect effects went via involvement and work discipline.

The effects from gender on achievement, work discipline and deep information processing were mainly direct. In accordance with other findings, for example Van der Hulst and Jansen (2002), Jansen (1996), De Jong et al. (1997a, 1997b), Shah and Burke (1999) and Van den Berg (2002) we found that female students achieved better results than male students did. The small indirect effects from gender on outcome went via work discipline and involvement. The effect from gender on work discipline was as expected and is in line with Macan et al (1990). They found that women are better time managers than man. The effect from gender on involvement might be related to this discipline. That is, the items for attending lectures, doing assignments in time and spending denominated workload, measured involvement and seems to be related to discipline. Another explanation for the relation between discipline and gender might be that women are more intrinsically motivated than men are (see Prins, 1997).

And finally, the analyses showed that older students had higher scores on deep information processing than younger students. Beside that we found the expected effect from age on work discipline. Furthermore, there were small significant effects from age on involvement and achievement. Younger students showed better results but were less involved. The findings of effects from age on achievement are in line with other studies like Jansen (1996), Shah and Burke (1999), Van der Hulst and Jansen (2002) and Van den Berg (2002). The interpretation of the relation between age and achievement is indistinct. Age can be seen as proxy for ability: older students needed more time for pre-university education, for example because they failed their examination once. Another explanation can be the fact that older students do not receive (enough) financial support for their study, so they have to work and can spend less time at study activities.

A main question in this study concerned the relation between satisfaction with the course/instructor, involvement and perceived difficulty on the one hand, and work discipline and deep information processing on the other hand. In contrast to our expectations, we did not find ability had an effect on the rating of the course/instructor. This is in concordance with the findings of Lizzio et al, (2002) that showed that prior academic achievement had no significant influence on how students evaluate their learning environment. However, students who report perceiving the course as less difficult are more satisfied with the course/instructor. That finding is in line with Perry (1997) who stated that students with high perceived control benefit from effective instruction more than students with low perceived control. A striking finding is that satisfaction with the course/instructor does not have any effect on student's achievement or information processing strategy. This is in contrast with, for example Feldman (1989) who showed significant correlations between different teaching behaviours and achievement. A last finding on the rating outcomes is that students who evaluated the course content and the assignments as difficult attended lectures less frequently and did not complete their assignments in time.

Work discipline showed a large effect on achievement. Students with higher discipline obtained higher grades. Furthermore and not surprisingly, students who attended lectures regularly and completed their assignments on time reported higher discipline. However, it is striking that deep information processing does not affect achievement. This can be a result of the way the students are tested: if the test does not appeal to deep information processing strategies, students will alter their leaning strategy.

Evidently there are some limitations to this study. Firstly, this concerns the use of student ratings forms as indicators of instruction. Hinton (1993), for example, contends that these ratings are poor measures of teaching effectiveness because there is no universally acceptable model of good teaching that can be used for the validation of the constructs in the questionnaires. Other authors, for example, McKeachie (1997) and Centra (1993) are not satisfied with the evaluation forms used because these forms focus mainly on traditional types of instruction like lectures and other teacher-centered methods. And, further, there is an extensive debate about the assumption that course grades are positively related to course evaluation (Theall et al, 2000; Stumpf and Freedman, 1979). However, analyses have shown that this assumption is not applicable to this study (see Jansen and Bruinsma, 2002). Secondly, this study is limited to students within one department and within one university. It seems obvious to replicate this study with more departments and over more universities. However, several studies point at the effects of disciplinary differences (for example Beecher, 1994; Kekäle, 1999, Lindblom-Ylänne and Lonka, 1999). Maybe it is even better to replicate this study for different disciplines and universities separately. Furthermore, departments and even disciplines within departments are free in their choice of evaluations. Some departments do not use questionnaires at all while other departments use different ratings forms. The need for standard questionnaires over different departments, faculties and universities is evident for us as researchers but this idea has, until now, not been widely supported by the departments at our university.

Furthermore, there are a lot of other student characteristics (for example motivation) and course and curricular characteristics that will influence academic achievement. However, in this study we tried to raise a corner of the veil on the relation between student characteristics, the perceived learning environment, and reported study behaviour and academic achievement.

References

Bean, JP (1980). Dropouts and turnover: The synthesis and test of a causal model of student attrition. *Research in Higher Education*, **12**, 155–187.

Bean, JP and Vesper, N (1990). *Quantitative approaches to grounding theory in data.* Using LISREL to develop a local model and theory of student attrition. Paper presented at the Annual Meeting of the American Educational Research Association, Boston.

Bean, JP and Metzner, BS (1985). A conceptual model of non-traditional undergraduate student attrition. *Review of Educational Research*, **55**(4), 485–540.

Beecher, T (1994). The significance of disciplinary differences. *Studies in Higher Education*, **19**(2), 151–161.

Berger, JB and Milem, JF (1999). The role of student involvement and perceptions of integration in a causal model of student persistence. *Research in Higher Education*, **40**(6), 641–664.

Berger, JB and Braxton, JM (1998). Revising Tinto's Interactionalist Theory of Student Departure Through Theory Elaboration: Examining the Role of Organizational Attributes in the Persistence Process. *Research in Higher Education*, **39**(2), 103–119.

Bijleveld, RJ (1993). *Numeriek rendement en studiestaking*. Enschede: Universiteit Twente: CSHOB: proefschrift.

Carroll, JB (1963). A model of school learning. *Teachers College Record*, **64**(8), 723–733.

Centra, J (1993). *Reflective faculty evaluation*. San Francisco, Jossey-Bass.

Creemers, BPM (1994). *The effective classroom*. London: Cassell, School development series.

De Jong , U, Roeleveld, J, Webbink, H.D. (1997a). *Studeren in de jaren negentig. Studiekeuze en studieloopbaan over de periode 1991–1995*. THE Hague: NV SDU (Verder Studeren Series).

De Jong , U, Roeleveld, J, Webbink, H.D. (1997b). *Het Amsterdamse schoolloopbaanmodel*. The Hague, NV SDU.

Dempster, AP, Laird, NM and Rubin, DB (1977) Maximum likelihood estimation from incomplete data via the EM algorithm. Journal of the Royal Statistical Society, Series B, 39, 1–38. In: Little, TD, Schnabel, KU and Baumert, J (Eds), (2000). *Modeling longitudinal and multilevel data: Practical issues, applied approaches, and specific examples*. Mahwah, NJ: Erlbaum Associates.

Feldman, KA (1989). The association between student ratings of specific instructional dimensions and student achievement: refining and extending the synthesis of data from multisection validity studies. *Research in Higher Education*, **30**(6), 583–645.

Hinton, H (1993). Reliability and validity of student evaluations: testing models versus survey research models, *PS: Political Science & Politics*, **26**, 562–569.

Hu, L and Bentler, PM (1999). Cut-off Criteria for Fit Indexes in Covariance Structure Analysis: Conventional Criteria versus New Alternatives. *Structural-Equation-Modeling*, **6**(1), 1–55.

Jansen, EPWA (1992). Kan onderwijsprogrammering studiesnelheid beinvloeden? *Onderzoek van Onderwijs*, **21**(4), 54–55.

Jansen, EPWA (1993a). Curriculum organization and study progress. In Joostens, Th H, Heynen, GWH and Heeve, Al (Eds). *Doability of curricula*. Lisse: Swets & Zeitlinger.

Jansen, EPWA (1993b). Educational programmering related to study-progress. In Koppen, JK and Webler, WD (Ed), *Strategies for increasing access and performance in higher education*. Amsterdam: Thesis publishers.

Jansen, EPWA (1996). *Curriculumorganisatie en studievoortgang*. Groningen: GION (dissertation).

Jansen, EPWA and Bruinsma, M (2002). Student Ratings and Measurement of Study Behavior in a Model for Explaining Study Progress. Paper presented at the Annual Meeting of the American Educational Research Association, New Orleans.

Joostens, ThH. and Schoonen, AJM (1987). Blokken helpt: de farmacie-opleiding aan de RU Groningen. In: van Berkel, HJM, Bax, AE and Schellekens, HMC (Eds) *Differentiatie in het Hoger Onderwijs*. Amsterdam: Versluys.

Kekäle, J (1999). 'Preferred' patterns of academic leadership in different disciplinary (sub)cultures. *Higher Education* **37**(3), 217–238.

Lindblom-Ylänne, S, Lonka, K and Leskinen, E (1999). On the predictive value of entry-level skills for successful studying in medical school. *Higher Education* **37**(3), 239–258.

Lizzio, A, Wilson, K and Simons, R (2002). University students' perceptions of the learning environment and academic outcomes: implications for theory and practice. *Studies in Higher Education*, **27**, 1, 27–52.

Macan, T, Shahani, C, Dipboye, RL and Phillips, A (1990). College students' time management: correlations with academic performance and stress. *Journal of Educational Psychology* **82**(4), 760–768.

McKeachie, W (1997). Student ratings, the validity of use. *American Psychologist*, **52**, 1218–1225.

Pascarella, ET (1980). Student-faculty informal contact and college outcomes. *Review of Educational Research*, **50**(4), 545–575.

Perry, RP (1997). Perceived control in college students: implications for instruction in Higher Education. In Perry, RP and Smart, JC (Eds), *Effective teaching in higher education: research and practice.* New York, Agathon Press.

Prins, J (1997). *Studieuitval in het wetenschappelijk onderwijs. Studentkenmerken en opleidingskenmerken als verklaring voor studieuitval.* Nijmegen: University Press: proefschrift.

Ramsden, P (1991). A performance indicator of teaching quality in higher education: the course experience questionnaire. *Studies in Higher Education*, **16**, 129–150.

Schouwenburg, HC (1996). *Handleiding bij de VSP'94.* (Manual for the Test for Study Problems) Groningen: Studie Ondersteuning.

Schouwenburg, HC and Schilder, AJE (1996). *Handleiding bij de Test voor Diepgaande LeerstofVerwerking DLV'95* (Manual for the Test for Deep Information Processing). Groningen: Studie Ondersteuning.

Spady, W (1971). Dropouts from higher education: Toward an empirical model. *Interchange*, **2**,(3), 38–62.

Stumpf, SA and Friedman, RD (1979). Expected grade covariation with student ratings of instruction: Individual versus class effects. *Journal of educational psychology*, **71**, 293–302.

Terenzini, P (1999). Research and practice in undergraduate education: And never the twain shall meet? *Higher Education*, **38**, 33–48.

Tinto, V (1975). Drop-out from Higher Education: a theoretical synthesis of recent research. *Review of educational research*, **45**(1), 89–125.

Tinto, V (1987). *Leaving College: rethinking causes and cures of student attrition.* Chicago: The University of Chicago.

Theall, M, Scannell, N and Franklin, J, (2000). The eye of the beholder: individual opinion and controversy about student ratings. Electronic Publication.

Webb in Prins, J (1997). *Studieuitval in het wetenschappelijk onderwijs. Studentkenmerken en opleidingskenmerken als verklaring voor studieuitval.* Nijmegen: University Press: proefschrift.

Van den Berg, MN (2002). Studeren? (g)een punt! Een kwantitatieve studie naar studievoortgang in het Nederlandse wetenschappelijk onderwijs in de periode 1996–2000. Amsterdam, Thela Thesis.

Van der Drift, KDJM and Vos, P (1987). *Anatomie van een leeromgeving. Een onderwijseconomische analyse van het universitaire onderwijs.* Lisse: Swets & Zeitlinger.

Van der Hulst, M and Jansen, E (2002), Effects of curriculum organisation on study progress in engineering studies. *Higher Education*, **43**, 489–506.

18 Inquiring into a higher education classroom: insights into the different perspectives of teacher and students

Sarah J. Mann
University of Glasgow

Keywords: classroom research, stimulated recall, social context

Research on higher education has tended to investigate teaching and learning outside the context of the classroom. Qualitative interview and questionnaire-based studies have focused on the relationship between learning approaches and learning outcomes, on student motivations and orientations to learning, on problem-solving strategies, and on student and teacher conceptions of learning and teaching (Prosser & Trigwell, 1999; Marton et al., 1997; Ramsden, 1992; Schmeck, 1988). Some studies have also been undertaken on the impact of departmental context on teaching and learning processes (Ramsden, 1997). Little research has been done on observing and understanding these processes within the actual context of the higher education classroom. Exceptions include Hodgson's study on students' experiences of lectures (Hodgson, 1997) and Martin and Ramsden's study of teachers' intentions, adopted methods and perceived outcomes (Martin & Ramsden, 1998). Studies, such as Anderson, (1995), have also been undertaken on seminars. However, these studies have tended to focus on either the student's perspective or the teacher's perspective with less attention paid to possible inter-relationships between the two perspectives.

18.1   The study

The pilot study reported here sought to understand and illuminate the processes of teaching and learning within higher education by bringing these two different perspectives together through a video and interview based case study of a single higher education classroom.

For the purposes of this paper, I have chosen to focus on the following questions:

- What is the students' experience of learning in this classroom? The teacher's experience of teaching this class?

- What relationship is there between the students' experience and the teacher's experience?

- What does this tell us about what is happening in this classroom and what factors may be contributing to this?

- What are the implications of this analysis for improving student learning?

There were two phases to the data collection. The first phase involved observing and video-recording the class to be investigated. The second phase involved interviews with the relevant teacher and students, focused on retrospective accounts of their experience of the session, prompted by viewing selected video-recordings from the original class.

This method combines classroom observation, stimulated recall and introspection, and open-ended interviewing. It builds on a research design previously adopted by the author (Mann, 2000), which used stimulated recall and open-ended interviews as a means of investigating students' experience of reading. In this case, recall was stimulated by the marking of pauses on the text during reading and the reviewing of these pauses during the interview. Here, recall was stimulated by the viewing of video-recordings of the classroom event.

The process of stimulated recall was first developed by Bloom (1953) for the study of thought processes in lectures and discussions. It was later adopted by Hodgson (1984) in her study of the students' experience of lectures. It has close similarities to Interpersonal Process Recall (IPR), developed by Kagan for the study of supervisor and supervisee experience during counseling sessions (Cashwell, 1994). The process involves the videoing of a counseling session and a follow-up supervision interview in which this video is viewed with the purpose of focusing on the counselor's thoughts and feelings during the counseling interview. This approach has been adapted by George and Cowan (1999) for the purposes of formative evaluation of teaching and learning in higher education.

18.2   The class

The class investigated here was an honours class in one of the Arts disciplines. It was a ten week course taught in the spring term of the academic year in a Scottish university. It consisted of one two-hour class per week for which the students were expected to read a designated text. As a general rule, each session involved a lecture and a discussion. There were 22 students in the class. Most of the students were 4th year honours students (in their last year of study). Three of them were 3rd year honours students. Three of the students were male. The assessment for the 4th year students was a traditional three-hour essay-based exam and for the 3rd years it was an end-of-term essay. During the course, all students were required to submit five one-page summaries and critical reviews of texts of their choice. The best three for each student counted for 50% of their final mark. The course focused on the study of a particular social practice and how it was undertaken in different non-Western cultures.

The class was selected on the basis of 'opportunity sampling' (Woods, 1996, p. 54) where the opportunity to video this class arose serendipitously after discussions with a teacher who was keen to understand what was happening in his classroom.

The teacher (Henry) was a new lecturer at the university, from a non-UK English speaking culture. This was his first experience of teaching in a Scottish context.

The class recorded was in the 9th week of the 10 week course. It was divided into three parts: a lecture and opportunity for discussion on the week's topic; the presentation and discussion of video extracts to provide an example of the week's topic; and a discussion of the reading for that week. There was a short break between the video and reading discussion in which students were asked to get together in small groups to work out how they would tackle the next week's reading. At different times during the class, the teacher asked for questions or comments. Five students contributed questions.

The room was a rectangular seminar room with tables laid out as an open-ended U with the teacher at the front, and students sitting all around the outer edge of the tables. The video was set up at the back of the room. At the end of the class, I asked for volunteers to take part in the research. Only two students contacted me. Student A (Rosie) was 22, in her 4th year, and the daughter of teachers. Student B (Jean) was 20, in her 3rd year and the daughter of a school inspector and nursery teacher. Neither of these two students had asked a question or made a comment in the class. It should be noted that the data offers a partial view of the students' learning experience of this class as it offers insight into the experience of only two students.

18.2.1   The students' and teacher's experience

In this section I present selected quotations from the interview data in order to tell the story of the students' and teacher's individual experience of this particular class. I then offer a summary of each experience. As the interview was conducted on the basis of watching chronologically sequenced excerpts from the original class, the data presented is organised chronologically and gives an insight into how each person experienced the unfolding event. My intention in doing this is to try to preserve as far as possible the essence and vividness of the experience reported.

In order to preserve anonymity, I have given the teacher and students fictional names and taken out of the data any identifying information.

Rosie's experience – 'because if you don't know enough about something'

> It was just taking down facts because the course was covering a wide range of … from different countries which we'd never done anything on before… We had to get through quite a lot in a week. It was quite difficult because we didn't have any visual, we only had one or two incidences of visual sources to look at how….
>
> sometimes we were quite overwhelmed with what he says
>
> it's quite hard to think what to ask, because if you don't know enough about something it's quite difficult to engage with it.
>
> although it's quite relieving when someone does ask a question because there's that horrible silence when he wants you to engage and you just can't because you can't think of a question to ask. Maybe because you don't know enough, maybe because in big groups sometimes you don't have enough confidence to ask about something that you don't know so much about
>
> The thing that struck me, because he had so much subjects from the selected material to get through, he found it quite hard to distil into what we would be interested in so kind of used the question time so that we could pick out things we were interested in…
>
> I hate it when he looks at his watch when no one comments.

What do you feel?

> Like he's really annoyed with us because we are – he said if anyone else wants to respond, he looks around, looks at his watch, so makes you think, can't ask a question …

So you feel a pressure building?

> Definitely, when you have these horrible silences, when no one speaks.
>
> What was quite good about discussing the reading was that we weren't just discussing the subject matter, it wasn't about learning facts, we were analysing the way it was written critically
>
> it's quite hard sometimes to interact and take notes at the same time, especially with something we are unfamiliar with…
>
> but he's a new lecturer so it's quite difficult to adapt to – if you've had people teaching you for 4 years, you know what to expect, how they work and the way it works.

Summary

It seems that Rosie has had a difficult experience in this class. There has been too much to get through and much of it is new and different. She feels a lack of visual information which would have given her a 'picture in her head'. She is also having to adapt to a new teacher and what to expect from him. She hasn't been able to ask a question or comment because 'if you don't know enough about something …' She experiences the silences as 'horrible' and 'hates it' when the teacher looks at his watch. This contributes to her feeling of pressure and inability to contribute. Her focus seems to be on doing what she can to cope with the difficulty of the material and the amount of it. This consists of 'just taking down facts'.

Jean's experience –'I'm so talkative usually in class and I never said a word in this class at all'

I think the one thing that that's struck me so far is that there's so much information that Henry's talking about. I feel a lot of it is absolutely, completely new.

and I didn't get a break in between so at the start of every class you're supposed to be very alert thinking about things, but with the amount of information that's actually being thrown out at you, you do find your concentration slips and you start thinking about other things, and then you get back into it, and then you think, oh God, I've just missed a whole pile of things, oh no, and you try to write down what you remember, but it's really difficult.

I've never found anything so hard in x before. I was just writing it down and thinking, well, if I write it down then maybe I'll grasp it, it's obviously important what he says, so just write it down.

because we can't have a discussion when you don't know what you're talking about, you haven't got any prior knowledge of the article that we had to read.

Did you have a question to ask?

No I didn't, which is unusual, because I am usually quite an active participant in class and the reason was I didn't know what I was talking about, I didn't have an idea, so I decided I would just be quiet and let other people speak

It's quite frustrating because I wanted to be able to discuss things… because there were a number of people who, I got the impression, were very intelligent – I was sort of like left out – I just felt that I wasn't equipped to actually put forward any opinions, or put forward any argument… but I didn't feel I had any kind of grasp on the subject to actually warrant an opinion or for me to actually speak up in class.

I just felt that I was completely in the middle of an ocean and sink or swim… I didn't know what I was doing. It was quite frustrating and in the frustration you turn off, your concentration goes, which is unfortunate.

and they are the only girls that I knew in the class, the rest of them were senior honours… and I was just thinking I do not understand what is going on, oh my God, felt so stupid, and I'm not really.

I think the thing that's quite difficult about this is the discussion is within the whole class.

Seminars are really important because they allow you to form opinions for yourself, not only through arguments and discussion, but listening to other people and to take on their ideas, evaluate them, modify them to your own sentiments, so for people to not say anything then it's pointless.

Summary

Jean also seems to have had a difficult experience in this class. As with Rosie, this is related to the difficulty of the material which she has never found as hard before and the amount of it. She also has to contend with the lack of a break between this and a previous class and the fact that she is only one of four third year students. She is particularly frustrated by the fact that she is normally an active participant in a class, but because of her inability to understand the material and the size of the group, she chooses to 'just be quiet and let others speak'. She judges others to be very intelligent and feels 'left out' and 'so stupid' and yet she says that 'I'm not really'. She tries to cope by 'just writing it down', 'it's obviously important what he says', then 'maybe I'll grasp it'.

Henry's experience – 'that's hard in fact, these scribbling students'

There's not much enthusiasm in this class.

This is my research which I'm bringing to bear, and for me discovering this was wonderful, and the problem is that without having any background in the particulars of the subject matter, they are not able to read this material as new or as interesting.

Just look at them, all their heads to the books, there were no comments. Maybe this is the reticence of students here, but the kinds of things which I'm saying are things which for specialists in the field would be sort of provocative… What gets their goat? That's the question.

I should have talked more about x there. I didn't. It would have been a good moment to have spent on that, but I had a lot of material to present and partly it was because of this overwhelming silence on the part of the students, that I wasn't going to expand, but just rush through this outline.

Just even a small comment could have evoked discussion at that moment, and didn't. That's hard in fact, these scribbling students

I'm really going very far there… because I'm asking questions, saying, please, help me. It's the silence that's…

I'm taking the students very seriously this way and bringing this new material.

How did you feel when you finally got a question?

I felt that I had something to talk about.

… which is a question she should have not asked in fact.

Well, I mean, if another student can answer the question… but it's nice to see they are interacting in any case, that a little bit of peer support and peer tearing down also.

The fact that I turn to the other students to answer these questions, I think from my perspective this is a good thing… I try to keep the illusion of some class discussion at least with a group this big. It seems there are… differences in knowledge, which are really present in this class. There are some students there who are bright, intelligent, read, thought, and others who are struggling

This is already week nine, and these are really week three questions, so I'm finding myself going back to comparisons with x. Very base level comparisons rather than doing the more elaborate analysis, which we could have potentially have done at that moment.

Structurally very awkward moment there… To answer that question I had to do a lot of exposition… So, they could hear my voice, a kind of resigned tone because I realised in order to answer this question, I didn't want to put off, I would have to curtail any discussion at that moment, which was building up around this video... It's too important a question to say, we'll talk about this later.

I've just become completely derailed there, haven't I? My enthusiasm is just drained, my energy is ebbing. I realise that something was asked of me there... I had to be rescued by the students there.

No, she was helping me out at that moment.

That's what I could have done or she could have done if I had been less involved in my own failing at that moment, so you've shown me the low...

Here my energy has picked up... Reminding myself also it's good that she stepped in... reminding myself of who I'm talking to. It was a little boost of confidence that she stepped in there at that moment.

Summary

Henry judges this to be a pretty typical class. He is keen to provoke the students and to take them seriously by presenting his own research. However, he experiences the class as having 'not much enthusiasm' and wonders 'what gets their goat?' He finds 'these scribbling students' hard and also describes the silence as overwhelming. In one instance, he sees the silence and the amount of material he has to present as negatively influencing what he does. His energy and emotions seem to change depending on his judgement of how the class is going and of the kinds of questions and comments he gets from students. These can 'rescue him', provide him with 'structurally awkward moments', give him 'something to talk about', or 'completely derail' him. Some questions he judges as taking the class back to more basic material, inappropriate to this stage in the course. He experiences a difference between those students who are knowledgeable and bright and those who are struggling.

18.2.2 What then is the relationship between the students' experience and the teacher's experience?

George & Cowan (1999, p 61) suggest that the most interesting use of IPR is to uncover the potential mismatches between teachers' and students' experiences. The following discussion summarises what seems to be the relationship between the different experiences and perspectives of these two students and their teacher.

All three participants experience this particular class as difficult. For the students it is primarily the subject matter and hence their inability to contribute questions and participate in discussion. For the teacher, it is the fact that he experiences the class as lacking enthusiasm and motivation, focused on writing notes. He has tried to take the class seriously by sharing his research with them. For him this was a wonderful and exciting experience. Unfortunately the students interviewed find the material so new and difficult that they are unable to engage with it and are reduced to 'just taking down facts'. Although each experience the situation as difficult, the source of difficulty for each is different and unknown to the other.

All three also experience the amount of material dealt with in the class as difficult: 'a lot in a week, so much information, a lot of material to present'. The students respond to this combination of difficulty and amount by just 'writing it down, taking down the facts' and the teacher talks about 'just rushing through, not going to expand'. Although the teacher could be said to be responsible for the amount of material presented, all three participants feel constrained by this and respond in a way that is not supportive of a more engaged and interactive teaching and learning process.

Both Rosie and Henry experience the silences as 'horrible' or 'overwhelming' and Rosie and Jean feel unable to contribute because 'can't ask questions if don't know enough'. From Henry's point of view the silence, combined with the amount of material to present, seems to limit what actions he is able to take as a teacher and stops him expanding a point. By staying with the silence for a while he also feels himself to be 'going very far there'. Rosie experiences this as 'pressure building'. She hates it when he looks at his watch and reads this as the teacher being 'annoyed'. This makes it even harder to ask a question. It is as if each are responding in the only way they can, but in doing so neither can meet each others' needs or expectations.

Another mismatch seems to occur between the teacher's view that some questions asked are basic, as opposed to the students' experience of the material as difficult and therefore presumably needing to ask questions, however 'simple' to support their learning. Linked to this is Jean's experience of not being able to participate in this class when she normally would do so and as a consequence feeling 'left out' and 'so stupid, I'm not really'. There is a sense in which she needs to assert the fact that she isn't stupid and yet she fears that she may well be judged in this way. Implicitly she is right, for Henry comments on the differences between students as 'some who are bright, intelligent, read, thought' and 'others who are struggling'.

Finally, it is not just the students who are struggling and constrained to respond in particular ways. Henry himself, as described above, also experiences the class as a dynamic process in which his actions and experiences are intimately connected with the questions students ask and how he reads their responses to the class. He describes his experience as variously 'derailed', 'enthusiasm is just drained', 'energy is ebbing', 'rescued', 'energy picked up there'.

It seems then that all three experience the situation emotionally as well as cognitively and each of their actions and responses are dynamically related to each others' and their different interpretations of these.

18.3   What does this tell us about the higher education classroom?

This juxtaposition of the teacher's and students' different experiences and perspectives suggests that the following things may be happening in this classroom:

- All three experience this classroom differently, although there is a common experience of difficulty.

- None of the participants seems to be aware of the others' experience. This is particularly so between the teacher and the students. It is as if they are in different worlds.

- All three use 'coping' strategies to deal with the situation.

- All make assumptions and have expectations about what is appropriate behaviour in this particular context, ie an honours seminar.

- Emotion is a significant part of their experience. The extent to which they are able to engage with and behave appropriately in this situation, as they define it, has an impact on their feelings, self-esteem and identity.

- Their experience is dynamic, changing according to how they judge 'things to be going'.

None of them seems to be able to, or sees it as appropriate to, intervene in the situation in such a way that might help it change. It is as if both teacher and students seem to comply with their definition of each others' expectations in such a way that restricts and constrains actions they might each otherwise take which would enrich and enliven the teaching and learning process. In essence, it seems that both teacher and students have become alienated from each other. It is as if there is a fundamental failure of communication between them.

18.4   Implications for improving student learning

At the practical level, these findings support well-documented previous studies and strategies for good teaching (summarised in Toohey, 1999) which suggest that the learning of the students in this case study could be improved by:

- Reducing content

- Linking new information to students' prior knowledge and experience

- Providing students with the opportunity for vicarious experience

- Establishing a supportive learning environment based on agreed ground rules

- Giving students the opportunity to work in small groups

Although implementing such strategies might well contribute to improving the students' learning in this classroom, it is not clear that such strategies would be appropriate to all students or that such strategies would be appropriate throughout the life of the class.

As outlined by Graham Gibbs in his plenary at this year's conference, the Improving Student Learning movement has tended to base its approach on phenomenographic research. This particular research paradigm assumes that how students and teachers conceive of teaching and learning and of the world around them will influence how they act in that world. It also assumes that aligning teaching intentions, intended learning outcomes, teaching methods and assessment practices towards that of developing understanding will itself improve student learning. There is no doubt that such a perspective has contributed very important insights into the teaching and learning process and ways of improving student learning. However, the research described here indicates three significant aspects of classroom-based teaching and learning which are not addressed by this approach. These are the classroom as social context; the failure of communication between the teacher and the students; and the dynamic inter-relationship between the different participants.

However much a teacher changes their conceptions of teaching and adjusts their designs and plans accordingly, they still have to enact these plans in the context of a classroom. The classroom is a complex social situation in which what is taken to be appropriate discursive practices, language and action is governed by particular implicit socio-cultural norms and conventions (Breen, 1985b; van Lier, 1988; Woods, 1996).

As was shown by the data from this study, individual participants find themselves complying with what they take to be the norms governing appropriate action in the classroom, even though it may constrain what they would otherwise wish to do. Thus, the social context of the classroom and the ways in which participants dynamically shape it have to be taken account of in any understanding of how to implement change towards improving student learning1.

This may be where the second feature of teaching and learning in the higher education classroom – the failure of communication – becomes significant. If we assume that teaching and learning processes in the higher education classroom are dynamic and involve an interdependence between teachers and students.and if we assume that how teachers and students act in and experience the classroom will partly be based on the assumptions that they make about each other and about what it is possible to do in the classroom, then it seems essential to any intervention in the classroom to improve student learning, that it addresses the issue of opening up communication between teachers and students. For it is only through teachers and students talking to each other that they will begin to understand each other's perspective and experience. They may thus begin to formulate ways of working together that will enhance both the individual's and the group's capacity to learn and be effective. In this way, students and teachers can check out each other's assumptions and tell each other when something isn't working. The phenomenographic aims of changing conceptions and achieving alignment can be recast as developing understanding and aligning the intentions, experiences and actions of teachers and students through dialogue and negotiation in the classroom.

Acknowledgements

My thanks to the brave teacher and two students who gave of their time and experience to this study.

References

References

Anderson, C (1995). *Learning to Discuss, Discussing to Learn: A Study of Tutorial Groups in a Faculty of Social Science*, PhD thesis, University of Edinburgh.

Bloom, BS (1953). Thought processes in lectures and discussions. *Journal of General Education*, **3**, pp 160-167.

Breen, MP (1985b). The social context for language learning – a neglected situation? *Studies in Second Language Acquisition*, **7**(2), 135-58.

Cashwell, CS (1994). *Interpersonal Process Recall*, ERIC Digest, Report No. EDO-CG-04-10. Greensboro, NC: ERIC Clearinghouse on Counseling and Student Services.

Duranti, A and Goodwin, C (Eds), (1992). *Rethinking Context: Language as an Interactive Phenomenon*. Cambridge: Cambridge University Press.

George, J and Cowan, J (1999). *A Handbook of Techniques for Formative Evaluation - Mapping the Student's Learning Experience*. London: Kogan Page.

Hodgson, VE (1997). Lectures and the experience of relevance. In Marton, F, Hounsell, D and Entwistle, N (1997). *The Experience of Learning: Implications for Teaching and Studying in Higher Education,* (2nd Edn). Edinburgh: Scottish Academic Press.

Mann, SJ (2000). The student's experience of reading, *Higher Education*, **39**, 297–317.

Martin, E & Ramsden, P (1998). Approaches to teaching creative writing. In Dart, B and Boulton-Lewis, G (Eds), *Teaching and Learning in Higher Education*. Melbourne: ACER Press, pp 26-41.

Marton, F, Hounsell, D and Entwistle, N (1997). *The Experience of Learning: Implications for Teaching and Studying in Higher Education,* (2nd Edn). Edinburgh: Scottish Academic Press.

Prosser, M & Trigwell, K (1999). *Understanding Learning and Teaching – The Experience in Higher Education*. Buckingham: SRHE/Open University Press.

Ramsden, P (1997). The context of learning in academic departments. In Marton, F, Hounsell, D & Entwistle, N (1997). *The Experience of Learning: Implications for Teaching and Studying in Higher Education*, (2nd Edn). Edinburgh: Scottish Academic Press.

Ramsden, P (1992). *Learning to Teach in Higher Education*. London: Routledge.

Schmeck, RR (Ed), (1988). *Learning Strategies and Learning Styles, Perspectives on Individual Differences*. New York and London: Plenum Press.

Toohey, S (1999). *Designing Courses for Higher Education*. Buckingham: SRHE / Open University Press.

van Lier, LAW (1988). *The Classroom and the Language Learner*. Applied Linguistics and Language Study, CN Candlin (general editor). London and New York: Longman.

Woods, P (1996). *Researching the Art of Teaching – Ethnography for Educational Use*. London: Routledge.

Note

1 See Duranti & Goodwin (1992) for a discussion of the significance of context, as socially constituted and constitutive, in understanding human action and experience.

19 Relating teaching and research through scholarly understanding of the subject matter

¹**Michael Prosser, ¹Paul Ramsden, ²Elaine Martin, ³Keith Trigwell**
1 The University of Sydney; 2 Victoria University;
3 University of Oxford

19.1 Introduction

This paper addresses aspects of the relation between teaching and research. We draw on our previous work on the relationship between academics' experiences of understanding their subject matter and their teaching. We focus on academics' understanding of subject matter as a critical property of the relationship between research and teaching.

There is conflicting evidence about the relationship between the two primary functions of academic work. Academics the world over assert that there is a positive relation between teaching and research. Equally, students declare their preference for being taught by practising researchers, while universities contend that the two aspects of academic practice enrich each other (Neumann, 1993; Brew and Boud, 1995; Rowland, 1996; Jenkins, Blackman, Lindsay and Paton-Saltzberg, 1998; Brew, 1999; QAA 2001). In addition, it has been argued that global changes in modes of knowledge production imply an increasing use of inquiry-based, transdisciplinary and client-centred curricula which aim to develop research and problem-solving skills in undergraduates (Gibbons, 1998). These would prima facie tend to tighten connections between university teaching and research functions.

Nevertheless, a body of empirical evidence points to little or no relation between teaching and research performance. Ramsden and Moses (1992) reported small negative correlations between teaching and research activity and outputs in Australian higher education. A key meta-analysis based on 58 (principally North American) studies contributing 498 correlations found an overall correlation of 0.06 between measures of teaching (such as student evaluations) and measures of research output (such as publications and competitive grants) (Hattie and Marsh, 1996). There is no available evidence that research productivity among academics is predicted by a strong commitment to teaching, either at individual or aggregate level (Ramsden, 1994).

Existing studies have typically focused on outcome measures of research and teaching. It has been proposed that a more useful comparison would be based on processes and the ways that academic staff experience teaching and research (Elton, 2000; Glassick, et al, 1997; Martin and Ramsden 2000). A simple theory suggests itself from the literature on student learning. When teaching is undertaken as a scholarly endeavour that aims to make student learning possible then it would seem more likely that it is positively associated with research. When teaching is undertaken as the delivery of information, such a relation would seem to be less probable.

To test this hypothesis, we can apply a substantial body of research involving conceptual and methodological developments into the relationships between the experience of university teaching and student learning and more recently the understanding of subject matter and the teaching of that subject matter

Our aim is to explore the relation between teaching and research by examining variations in academics' experience of research, how these variations relate to their experience of teaching, and how the association between these experiences is in turn associated with their experiences of understanding academic subject matter.

19.2   Background

In the present project we propose to address these relationships through a focus on academics' experiences of teaching and research. We use the concepts and methods developed in our earlier research, notably the analysis of both cognitive and affective aspects of variation in the experience of research, teaching and understanding of subject matter, to converge on a problem of practical and theoretical consequence that has so far eluded empirical explanation.

The study builds on a substantial body of research work involving conceptual and methodological developments in relations between university teaching and student learning. In summary, that body of research has established that the way in which university teachers approach their teaching is systematically related to how their students approach their learning, how they themselves conceive and understand teaching and learning, and how they perceive their teaching and leadership environment (Samuelowicz and Bain, 1992; Gow and Kember, 1993; Prosser, Trigwell and Taylor, 1994; Trigwell, Prosser and Taylor, 1994; Kember and Gow, 1994; Trigwell, Ramsden, Martin, and Prosser, 1995; Trigwell and Prosser, 1996a, 1996b; Trigwell, Prosser and Waterhouse, 1999). Student approaches to learning have been shown in a large number of studies to be related to how they perceive their learning environment and to the quality of their learning outcomes (Marton, Hounsell and Entwistle, 1997; Ramsden, 2003; Prosser and Trigwell, 1999).

The essence of the outcomes of this research is that university teachers who approach their teaching with an information transfer and teacher-centred approach are more likely to elicit surface approaches to learning. These approaches are, in turn, associated with lower quality learning outcomes. University teachers who approach their teaching with conceptual change and student-focused approaches are more likely to encourage deep approaches and higher quality learning outcomes.

In our most recent project, we extended this research and showed how qualitative variation in the way academics experienced their understanding of their subject matter related to their experiences of teaching (Martin et al, 2001). We found that student-focused perspectives on university teaching – which our earlier work had already established as being associated with higher quality student learning – were linked to more complex and research-based understandings of subject matter.

For this more recent work we undertook two analyses of the data: a phenomenographic analysis and an analysis of metaphor. These methods complement each other. Both focus on the experience of academic staff. The phenomenographic analysis focuses on the group as a whole and on the range and variation in the way academic staff make sense of teaching and of their subject matter. It also makes explicit the structure of this variation. Analysis of metaphor, however, focuses on the individual experiences of understanding within the sample and offers insight into the richness of personal and affective experience.

In brief, the phenomenographic analysis indicated that student-focused perspectives on university teaching - which our earlier work had already established as being associated with higher quality student learning – appeared to be linked to more complex and research-based understandings of subject matter. At one extreme, subject matter is experienced as a series of facts and/or techniques with little awareness of how it relates to other aspects of the field of study. At the other extreme, the person's focus is on underlying theories and conceptions. There is a strong awareness of how the parts fit to form a whole and how that whole relates to the field or discipline.

The metaphorical analysis helped us to understand the complexity of meaning the subject had for the individual. There are a range of ways in which metaphor is used as an analytical research tool. (Munby 1986; Lakoff and Johnson,1983). Here we develop the work of Munby (1986) and assume that metaphor is used in discourse and thinking to help us make sense of one phenomenon, often an abstract phenomenon, by reference to another more concrete and accessible phenomenon. The use of metaphor appears to be tied to our sensory experience of the world and to the structures that underpin that sensory experience in everyday life. Thus, we can explore the meaning of subject knowledge experienced by an interviewee by attending to the metaphors she or he adopts when talking about subject knowledge. For example, they might describe the subject as a package, or a complex map, or an uncharted landscape – and the adoption of these concrete terms in such an unconscious way gives us subtle insight into their understanding of the subject matter itself.

The analysis emphasised that there is no single simple metaphor used either by individuals or within disciplines; rather there is a 'complex coherence' of metaphors which overall paints a series of detailed pictures, each with a strong sense of structural unity. This variation can be simply characterised by, at one end of the continuum, subject matter being seen as a physical entity – an object. The interviewees' understanding of teaching and learning was always coherent with their understanding of subject matter, so for instance, when subject knowledge was described as an object, then teaching was typically described as giving, and learning as getting, this object. At the other extreme, when subject matter knowledge was seen as an interpretation of a complex set of relationships, then teaching was understood as being about supporting students in their informed interpretation of these relationships. More and less complex interpretations of the meaning of subject knowledge were found across all subject areas; in all cases metaphoric descriptions of understanding of the subject matter were in keeping with metaphoric descriptions of teaching and learning. An equally important outcome was that there was in all cases a strong relationship between the individual level, the metaphoric level, and the group level phenomenographic analysis.

These findings – the relations identified and the success of the methodologies employed – provide the conceptual and empirical basis for our present study of the relationship between teaching and research.

19.3   Conceptual framework

We hypothesise that there is a relationship between the ways academics experience their teaching and experience their research, and that this relationship may be direct or may be mediated through their experience of understanding their subject matter. A direct relationship is shown in Figure 19.1a, and an indirect one is shown in Figure 19.1b.

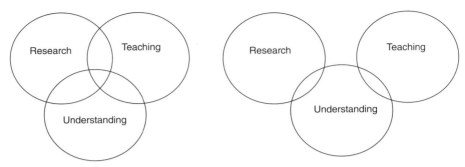

Figures 19.1 a and b   Hypothesised relationships between the experiences of teaching, research and understanding of subject matter

19.3.1   Hypothesised direct relationship

A direct relationship may be one in which an experience of teaching as being about 'a teacher-focused transmission of pieces of knowledge' is related to an experience of research as being about 'the accumulation of facts, procedures, and techniques associated with a certain phenomenon'. On the other hand, an experience of teaching as being about 'student-centred conceptual change' is related to an experience of research as being about 'developing and changing understanding about a phenomenon' – a more inquiry focused perspective.

To explain our theory, the following set of hypothetical data and subsequent analyses of those data provide a detailed example. Table 19.1 shows the hypothetical data.

Academic	Experience of understanding	Experience of teaching	Experience of research
Alex	UA	TA	RA
Brenda	UB	TA	RA
Cliff	UB	TB	RB
Debra	UC	TB	RB
Edward	UC	TC	RC

Table 19.1   Hypothetical data for direct relationship

In this hypothetical study we have interviewed five university teachers and researchers. In analysing the interviews we have identified three sets of categories of description for each of the experiences of understanding subject matter, teaching and research. Suppose the categories in each set form an inclusive hierarchy, with the "C" category being the most inclusive and the "A" category the least inclusive (this is consistent with our present sets of categories for the experience of teaching and understanding subject matter).

For example, these categories may be:

Based upon previous research:

TA: Teacher focus / teacher activity / transferring information

TB: Teacher focus / student activity / acquiring concepts

TC: Student focus / student activity / changing conceptions

Based upon previous research:

UA: Facts & techniques / within one or more fields / internal

UB: Concepts & procedures / within one or more fields

UC: Coherent whole / organising theories / related to other fields

Hypothetical:

RA: Accumulation of facts / procedures / techniques about phenomenon

RB: Developing concepts about a phenomenon

RC: Developing and changing understanding of field of study

Table 19.1 shows how each of the transcripts are categorised in relation to these sets of categories of description. Tables 19.2-4 summarise an analysis of this hypothetical data for a direct relationship between teaching and research

Tables 19.2, 19.3 and 19.4 show substantial direct associations between the experience of teaching and the experience of understanding the subject matter, the experience of research and the experience of understanding the subject matter, and between the experience of teaching and the experience of research respectively. In this hypothetical example, the experience of teaching and research are directly related.

Experience of Teaching	Experience of Understanding		
	UA	UB	UC
TA	Alex	Brenda	
TB		Cliff	Debra
TC			Edward

Table 19.2   Analysis of the hypothetical direct relationship between experience of understanding subject matter and experience of teaching

Experience of Research	Experience of Understanding		
	UA	UB	UC
RA	Alex	Cliff	
RB		Brenda	Edward
RC			Debra

Table 19.3   Analysis of the hypothetical direct relationship between experience of understanding subject matter and experience of research

Experience of Research	Experience of Teaching		
	TA	TB	TC
RA	Alex, Brenda		
RB		Cliff, Debra	
RC			Edward

Table 19.4   Analysis of the hypothetical direct relationship between experience of teaching and experience of research

19.3.2   Hypothesised indirect relationship

An example of how the indirect relationship may be constituted is one in which the experience of teaching is related to the experience of understanding, and the experience of research is related to the experience of understanding, but there is little relationship between the experience of teaching and the experience of research. For example, on the one hand, an experience of teaching as being a teacher-centred transmission of pieces of knowledge may be related to an understanding of the subject matter as being multi-structural, where little relationship is seen between important aspects of the subject matter and between these aspects and the field of study as a whole. An experience of research as being about the accumulation of facts, procedures and techniques about a certain phenomenon may be associated with a similar experience of the understanding of the subject matter.

To explain our theory further, the following set of hypothetical data and subsequent analyses of that data provide a second hypothetical example (Table 19.5).

Academic	Experience of understanding	Experience of teaching	Experience of research
Alex	UA	TA	RA
Brenda	UB	TA	RB
Cliff	UB	TB	RA
Debra	UC	TB	RC
Edward	UC	TC	RB

Table 19.5   Hypothetical data for an indirect relationship between the experience of teaching and the experience of research

In this theoretical study we have again interviewed 5 university teachers and researchers. In analysing the interviews we have identified similar sets of categories of description as for the previous example. Table 19.5 shows how each of the transcripts are categorised in relation to these sets of categories of description.

Tables 19.6, 19.7 and 19.8 summarise an analysis of these data.

Experience of Teaching	Experience of Understanding		
	UA	UB	UC
TA	Alex	Brenda	
TB		Cliff	Debra
TC			Alex

Table 19.6   Analysis of the hypothesised relationship between experience of understanding subject matter and experience of teaching

Experience of Research	Experience of Understanding		
	UA	UB	UC
RA	Alex	Cliff	
RB		Brenda	Edward
RC			Debra

Table 19.7   Analysis of the hypothesised relationship between experience of understanding subject matter and experience of research

Experience of Research	Experience of Teaching		
	TA	TB	TC
RA	Alex	Cliff	
RB	Brenda		Edward
RC		Debra	

Table 19.8   Analysis of the hypothesised indirect relationship between experience of teaching and experience of research

Tables 19.6, 19.7 and 19.8 show direct relationships between the experience of teaching and the experience of understanding the subject matter, the experience of research and the experience of understanding the subject matter, but no direct relationship between the experience of teaching and the experience of research. In this example, the experiences of teaching and research are indirectly related.

In summary, we believe it is possible to trace a relationship between academics' experience of research, experience of teaching and experiences of understanding the subject matter they are teaching and researching. Given the contradictory nature of much of the previous research and analysis of the relationship between teaching and research, the further explication of this relationship from the perspective adopted for this study is expected to have a tangible impact on the theory and practice of scholarly teaching and research in higher education.

From both a practical and policy perspective there is increasing pressure nationally and internationally for academics to develop their practice and scholarship of teaching and research. If academics in higher education are expected to be both scholarly and professional about their teaching and research and to work for continuous improvement, then how they experience the relationship between their teaching and research and how that relationship relates to their scholarly understanding of their subject matter needs to be investigated. Such an investigation will have important consequences for scholarship of teaching and research and the professional development of university academics.

19.3   Methodology

The general plan is to extend the interview and analytical procedures developed in a previous project. Each of 44 Australian and UK academics will be interviewed, in depth, about their experiences of teaching, research and understanding of the subject. The sample will be purposive and include staff from each of the following fields of study: humanities and social sciences, sciences and technology, business and law, health sciences. Purposive sampling will be used to ensure that:

1. there is within field variation in the academics' experience of teaching (approximately equal proportions of academics adopting information transmission and conceptual change approaches);

2. the academics included in the sample are actively engaged in both teaching and research in the same area.

Active involvement in teaching will be characterised by having taught an undergraduate course in the general area of research within the last year. Active involvement in research will be characterised by research being conducted with peer reviewed grant money, or work extending the conclusion of peer reviewed publications.

The interviews will be transcribed and will be analysed using analytical procedures based on metaphoric and phenomenographic methods developed in previous studies.

The phenomenographic perspective, which has been the basis of much of our previous research, seeks to describe the key aspects of the qualitative variation in the way people experience phenomena – in this case teaching, research and the subject matter they are teaching and researching. It assumes that the experience constitutes the relationship between the person and the phenomena. In this case, for example, the experience of, or ways of understanding, the subject matter, relates the academic to the subject matter. It seeks to describe the variation in terms of logically and empirically related decontextualised sets of categories of description. Having identified the categories of description, the transcripts from which the categories are constituted are then classified in terms of these categories.

A metaphoric perspective which is consistent with the phenomenographic perspective, was developed in our previous research. It seeks to explore the individual (as opposed to the group level) experience of subject matter and of teaching and learning, and to reveal the affective as well as cognitive aspect of that experience. We have built on the work of Lakoff and Johnstone (1983, 1999) and adapted the research methods of Munby (1986). From this perspective metaphors describe our experiences of the world and they are tied both to our experiences of the world and our expressions of that world. We come to understand complex, less concrete, phenomena, like ideas or subject matter, by thinking about them in terms of something we know which is concrete. Metaphor, consequently, helps us to make sense of abstract ideas by comparing them to more solid things. Their use in describing our experience is far from arbitrary.

In using metaphor in our analysis we work as a team. First individually, and then in collaboration, we examine the whole transcript for metaphor. In constructing the metaphor fragments for each transcript we list the terms and the frequency with which they are used and we search both for coherence and a lack of coherence within each transcript. Overall, we find a complex range of images and ideas but overwhelmingly there is cohesion in that range and a consistent picture is painted.

The analyses of the relationships between variables will be conducted both quantitatively and qualitatively. Quantitatively we will use a series of crosstabulations and chi-square-based procedures to identify bivariate relationships between the various classifications from the phenomenographic study. Qualitatively, we will use the analysis of metaphors to analyse any coherence or incoherence across the three sets of experiences using similar analytical procedures developed in our previous study. The analysis of metaphors will also form the basis of the development of a number of case studies designed to contextualise the results of the analysis.

19.5   Conclusions

In summary, we believe it is possible to trace a relationship between academics':

- experience of research,
- experience of teaching and
- experiences of understanding the subject matter.

Given the contradictory nature of much of the previous research and analysis of the relationship between teaching and research, the further explication of this relationship from the perspective adopted for this study is expected to have a tangible impact on the theory and practice of scholarly teaching and research in higher education.

Acknowledgments

We wish to acknowledge the support of the Australian Research Council in the funding of this research.

References

Brew, A (1999). Research and teaching: changing relationships in a changing context. *Studies in Higher Education*, **24**, 291-301.

Brew, A and Boud, D (1995). Teaching and research: establishing the vital link with research. *Higher Education*, **29**, 261-273.

Elton, LRB (2000). Turning academics into teachers: a discourse on love. *Teaching in Higher Education*, **5**, 257-260.

Gibbons, M (1998). Higher education relevance in the 21st century, UNESCO World Conference on Higher Education, Paris, Oct 5–9.

Glassick, C, Huber, M, and Maeroff, G (1997). *Scholarship Assessed: Evaluation of the Professoriate.* San Francisco: Jossey-Bass.

Gow, L and Kember, D (1993). Conceptions of teaching and their relation to student learning. *British Journal of Educational Psychology*, **31**, 93-97.

Kember, D and Gow, L (1994). Orientations to teaching and their effect on the quality of student learning. *Journal of Higher Education*, **65**, 117-128.

Hattie, J and Marsh, HW (1996). The relationship between research and teaching: a meta-analysis. *Review of Educational Research*, **66,** 507-142.

Jenkins, A, Blackman, T, Lindsay, R and Paton-Saltzberg, R (1998). Teaching and research: student perspectives and policy implications. *Studies in Higher Education*, **23**, 127-142.

Lakoff, G and Johnson, M (1983). *Metaphors We Live By*. Chicago: University of Chicago Press.

Lakoff, G and Johnson, M (1999). *Philosophy in the Flesh: The Embodied Mind and its Challenge to Western Thought*. New York: Basic Books.

Martin, E and Ramsden, P (2000). Introduction to Scholarship in Teaching. *Higher Education Research and Development*, **19**, 133–137.

Martin, E, Prosser, M, Trigwell, K, Lueckenhausen, G and Ramsden, P (2001). Using Phenomenography and Metaphor to Explore Academics' Understanding of Subject Matter and Teaching. In Rust, C (Ed), *Improving Student Learning Strategically*, pp325–336. Oxford: The Oxford Centre for Staff and Learning Development, .

Marton, F, Hounsell, D and Entwistle, NJ (Eds), (1997). *The Experience of Learning: Implications for Teaching and Studying in Higher Education*. (2nd Edn). Edinburgh: Scottish Academic Press.

Munby, H (1986). Metaphor in the thinking of teachers: an exploratory study. *Journal of Curriculum Studies*, **18**(2), 197–209.

Neumann, R (1993). Research and scholarship: perceptions of senior academic administrators. *Higher Education*, **25**, 97-110.

Prosser, M and Trigwell, K (1999). *Understanding Learning and Teaching: The experience in higher education*. Buckingham: Open University Press.

Prosser, M, Trigwell, K and Taylor, P (1994). A phenomenographic study of academics' conceptions of science teaching and learning. *Learning and Instruction*, **4**, 217-231.

Quality Assurance Agency for Higher Education (2001). Subject review reports. (http://www.qaa.ac.uk/revreps/subjrev/intro.htm)

Ramsden, P (2003). *Learning to Teach in Higher Education*. (2nd Edn). London: Routledge.

Ramsden, P (1994). Describing and explaining research productivity, *Higher Education*, **27**, 207-226.

Ramsden, P and Moses, I (1992). Associations between research and teaching in Australian higher education. *Higher Education*. **23**, 273-295.

Rowland, S (1996). Relationship between teaching and research. *Teaching in Higher Education*, **1**, 7-20.

Samuelowicz, K and Bain, J (1992). Conceptions of teaching held by academic teachers. *Higher Education*, **24**, 93-111.

Trigwell, K and Prosser, M (1996a). Congruence between intention and strategy in science teachers' approach to teaching. *Higher Education*, **32**, 77-87.

Trigwell, K and Prosser, M (1996b). Changing approaches to teaching: A relational perspective. *Studies in Higher Education*, **21**, 275-284.

Trigwell, K, Prosser, M and Waterhouse, F (1999). Relations between teachers' approaches to teaching and students' approaches to learning. *Higher Education*, **37**, 57-70.

Trigwell, K, Prosser, M and Taylor, P (1994). Qualitative differences in approaches to teaching first year university science. *Higher Education*, **27**, 75-84.

Trigwell, K, Ramsden, P, Martin, E and Prosser, M (1995). Teaching approaches and the leadership environment. *Research and Development in Higher Education*, **18**, 722-727.

20 Variation in the conceptions of learning of physiotherapy students in England and Wales: a longitudinal multicentre study

Jenny Morris[1] and Jan HF Meyer[2]

1 Colchester Institute, Colchester, U.K. 2 University of Durham, Durham, U.K.

Abstract

High quality learning is particularly important in vocational education where graduates have to use their learning in ever-changing environments and also be lifelong learners. This longitudinal multicentre study aimed to redress the lack of information on the dynamics of student learning in undergraduate physiotherapy education in England and Wales and enable educators to evaluate the effectiveness of their curriculum design and delivery in facilitating high quality learning. The results of quantitative analysis of the data from the three stages of the study are presented and discussed.

20.1   Introduction

The achievement of high quality learning is important in all graduates, but has an extra relevance in vocational education where the context of practice is continually changing and professions are continuously developing. However, although educators state that it is their hope and intention that graduates leave university with high quality learning, research has found that such outcomes are not always attained (Boulton-Lewis, 1998).

Students' conceptions of what the nature of 'learning' is have strong influences on the way they approach their learning and on the quality of their learning outcomes (Morgan and Beaty, 1997; Prosser and Trigwell, 1999; Meyer and Boulton-Lewis, 1999). It follows that if educators in higher education wish to provide students with educational experiences that foster the acquisition of high quality learning, they need to take account of the variation in students' conceptions of what learning is, both when they enter university and as they progress through it.

The present study reports on the dynamics of student learning in physiotherapy (physical therapy) in order to provide an empirical basis for reflecting on student engagement with their physiotherapy studies.

20.2   Theoretical background

A number of researchers have concluded that students' prior experiences of learning influence both their conceptions of the nature of learning and the way they have approached their learning in the past and that their future learning intentions and behaviours will reflect this (Dart, 1998; Prosser and Trigwell, 1999). In psychometrically operationalised forms

Meyer (1998) describes conceptions of learning as falling into one of two categories - accumulative or transformative. Accumulative conceptions have higher level and generally less desirable quantitative characteristics such as collecting facts, while transformative conceptions are of a higher order qualitative nature and involve the learner in the comprehension of meaning thus perhaps leading to a new way of seeing things and possibly even changing as a person.

Students with accumulative conceptions are likely to use surface approaches to learning. Such approaches are not generally associated with the high quality learning outcomes likely to result from transformative conceptions and a deep approach to learning (Prosser and Trigwell, 1999). Entwistle (1997) and Morgan and Beaty (1997) posit that students' conceptions can change and develop in light of their learning experiences. Entwistle argues that students from school may have quantitative conceptions, but that these broaden and become more qualitative as they progress through university. More generally, data on students' conceptions can also be used to identify students whose conceptions are not in agreement with what the course is expecting of them, including containing a mix of contradictory characteristics, putting them potentially 'at risk' of failure. Appropriate support can then be provided for these students (Meyer and Shanahan, 2001a,b).

Students' conceptions of learning have been investigated using both quantitative and qualitative methods. The Structure of Observed Learning Outcomes (SOLO) taxonomy has been used as a qualitative tool in several studies into students' conceptions of learning. Analysis of student statements has consistently found that the majority of conceptions are of a quantitative nature, even in post-graduate students (Boulton-Lewis, 1995).

The Reflections on Learning Inventory (RoLI) (Meyer and Boulton-Lewis, 1999) is a research instrument specifically designed to quantify students' conceptions of the nature of learning. The domain of this inventory has been largely derived from phenomenographic research findings and, to a lesser extent, other published qualitative sources of variation (Meyer, 2000a). Although still under development, it has been established that the RoLI is able to capture variation in students' contrasting conceptions of learning. It has furthermore been confirmed that variation in contrasting conceptions of learning is associated with variation in conceptually congruent learning processes (Meyer, 1999).

20.3 Methodology

The present study is a longitudinal multicentre one involving students from the 1999 intake at 20 physiotherapy schools in England and Wales. Students completed the RoLI (version 5) at the start of their first, second, and third (final) years of study (referred to as stage 1, stage 2 and stage 3 respectively). Ideally, the RoLI would also have been completed at the end of the final year. However, for logistical reasons, this was not possible. Basic demographic information including age, gender and academic entry route was also requested in the first stage data capture in order to identify possible areas for comparative analysis. In fact the only demographic factor suitable for such analysis was age. Anonymity and confidentiality were assured and a 'no detriment to academic progress' statement was also included in the covering letters.

The RoLI Version 5 contains statements pertaining to the 10 observables in figure 20.1. The observables marked with an asterisk (*) exhibit largely accumulative (quantitative) characteristics while the others display transformative (qualitative) features. In reality, this distinction may not be as clear. In structural and contextualised terms, for example, high scores on INK and REC could conceivably be interpreted as transformative provided they are associated with understanding of knowledge. In process terms high scores on IND, SDI and MAU would normally indicate deep-level learning engagement.

ACC*	Learning conceived as accumulation
REC*	Knowing involves recalling information
MAU	Learning involves memorising after understanding
DUT*	Learning is a duty or moral obligation
FAC*	Learning is fact based
INK*	Learning conceived as increasing knowledge
MBU*	Learning involves memorising before understanding
IND	Knowing involves thinking independently
SDI	Learning conceived as seeing things differently
KDF*	Knowledge is discrete and factual

Figure 20.1   The RoLI Version 5 statements pertaining to the 10 observables

20.4   Results

A total of 742 completed inventories were analysed in stage 1. Stage 2 analysis included 408 matched pairs of responses from both stages, and stage 3 analysis the 237 matched responses for those students who responded in all three stages of the study. In all the stages analyses were undertaken at a group level and differentiated by age (age 1: school leavers < 21 years at start of course, age 2: mature students ≥ 21 years at start of course). Three analytical procedures were employed: exploratory factor analysis, multivariate analysis of variance (MANOVA), and correlation analysis. Factor extraction in all cases is maximum likelihood using squared multiple correlations as communality estimates.

20.4.1   Stage 1

Factor analysis of the whole sample identified two factors (Table 20.1).

Factor 1 contained a strong conceptually consonant accumulative set of observables (compare Meyer and Shanahan, 2001b). Although factor 2 contained a mix of accumulative and transformative observables and appeared to be dissonant (Meyer, 2000b), this factor could be argued to have a largely transforamtive focus, provided that the INK and FAC observables were based on underlying understanding.

A test of homogeneity of covariance structure (Chi-squared = 95.03, p = 0.0007) confirmed that there were statistically significant different covariance structures for the two age groups. The extraction of separate factor structures for each age group is therefore justified and these are presented in Table 20.2.

These analyses identify contrasting patterns of variation between the age groups. For the school leavers, Factor 1 exhibited a consonant accumulative structure, while the Factor 2 solution was dissonant. The mature students exhibited a consonant set of observables in Factor 2. Factor 1 for the older students was dissonant, with a mix of accumulative and

Observables	Factor 1	Factor 2
ACC	.76*	
KDF	.75*	
FAC	.68*	
DUT	.57*	.21
MBU	.50*	
IND		.75*
SDI		.60*
INK		.54*
REC	.35	.46*
MAU		.39

* - values ≥ .45   Values < .20 not included   Inter-factor correlation   0.58

Table 20.1   Whole group factor solution (Stage 1)
Oblique factor loadings
N = 742

Observables	Mature(age 2) Factor 1	School-leaver (age 1)Factor 2	Mature (age 2) Factor 2	School-leaver (age 1)Factor 1
FAC	0.72*			0.75*
INK	0.80*	0.53*		0.21
ACC	0.69*		0.22	0.80*
REC	0.73*	0.39		0.41*
IND	0.44	0.75*		
MAU	0.34	0.38		
SDI	0.26	0.67*		
KDF			0.65*	0.72*
DUT			0.71*	0.58*
MBU		-0.20	0.62*	0.49*

*values ≥ .45   Values < .20 not included   Inter-factor correlations   Age 1   0.56
Age 2   0.51

Table 20.2   Factor structures by age (Stage 1)
Oblique factor loadings
Age 1 (school leavers) N = 504
Age 2 (mature) N = 238

transformative observables. The higher loadings on transformative observables (IND and SDI) in factor 2 for age 1 suggest that this structure, although dissonant, has more virtue than the dissonant structure of factor 1 for age 2 where the high loadings are on accumulative observables (FAC, INK, ACC and REC).

The results of a MANOVA for unbalanced data performed to compare school leavers with mature students confirmed a statistically significant overall difference in means for student age (For Wilks' Lambda, Pillai's Trace, Hotelling-Lawley Trace, Roy's Greatest Root, all p < 0.0001).

Analysis of the univariate cases, thus justified, identified significant differences for age in 3 observables (Table 20.3) The school leavers scores were higher than the mature students on DUT (a measure of motivation) and MAU, and lower on MBU.

Overall, the results for stage 1 posited that, as a whole group, on entry, the students preferentially held quantitative accumulative conceptions of learning The presence of a dissonant factor for both age groups suggests that some of the students held conflicting conceptions of learning which might make study difficult for them and potentially put them at risk of failure.

Observable	Means		F value	Significance
MBU	Age 1 Age 2	11.95 12.99	8.56	0.0035
DUT	Age 1 Age 2	12.42 11.78	5.76	0.0167
MAU	Age 1 Age 2	20.82 19.84	10.20	0.0015

Age 1: School leavers   Age 2: Mature

Table 20.3   Analysis of univariate cases by age (Stage 1)

20.4.2   Stage 2

For this stage of the analysis there were 408 sets of matched data. The differences between the matched mean scores between stage 1 and stage 2 for the group identified a decrease in means in all the observables (Table 20.4), both accumulative and transformative. Observables whose means fell by 0.5 or more were ACC, REC, FAC, INK, KDF and SDI.

Table 20.5 lists the matched mean scores between stage 1 and stage 2 by age and identified a decrease in means in all the observables in both subgroups, but also identifies some notable differences in scores between the two subgroups. Observables with differences equal to or greater than 0.5 are FAC, INK and IND. In all three cases the larger decrease occurred in the mature student group.

However, in this case, a MANOVA identified no overall statistical differences in mean scores attributable to age category (For Wilks' Lambda, Pillai's Trace, Hotelling-Lawley's Trace, Roy's Greatest Root, $p = 0.4814$). The test of homogeneity of within covariance matrices confirmed that non-significant differences were present at stage 2 (Chi-squared = 64.55, $p = 0.18$). Comparative data by age are nevertheless presented in Table 20.5 for the sake of completeness on the grounds that there may well be differences that are educationally of importance because of consistency of pattern in differences rather than the magnitude of differences.

Observables		Means	Standard deviation	Differences in means
ACC	stage 1	17.3	3.0	↓ 0.9
	stage 2	16.4	3.0	
REC	stage 1	20.0	2.6	↓ 0.6
	stage 2	19.4	2.8	
MAU	stage 1	20.6	3.9	↓ 0.3
	stage 2	20.3	4.0	
DUT	stage 1	12.1	3.5	↓ 0.3
	stage 2	11.8	3.3	
FAC	stage 1	17.2	3.4	↓ 1.0
	stage 2	16.2	3.5	
INK	stage 1	21.4	2.2	↓ 0.7
	stage 2	20.7	2.4	
MBU	stage 1	11.8	4.4	↓ 0.3
	stage 2	11.5	4.2	
IND	stage 1	19.0	3.1	↓ 0.3
	stage 2	18.7	3.3	
SDI	stage 1	19.2	3.1	↓ 0.6
	stage 2	18.6	3.3	
KDF	stage 1	13.7	3.1	↓ 0.7
	stage 2	13.0	2.9	

Table 20.4   Matched mean scores for the whole group
(stage 1 and stage 2)
N = 408

Analysis was also undertaken on the differences in means between the stage 1 and stage 2 matched data by age. The MANOVA results identified no overall age effect on the differences between stage 1 and stage 2 data (Wilks' Lambda, Pillai's Trace, Hotelling-Lawley's Trace, Roy's Greatest Root p = 0.1168). There was also no statistically significant difference in covariance structure (Chi-squared = 51.16 p = 0.6221).

Although not strictly statistically justified in overall terms, in response to the presence of noticeably larger changes in mean difference found for age for some observables, analysis of univariate cases was undertaken. This analysis identified two observables exhibiting significant effects (INK and FAC) with IND approaching significance ($p < 0.05$) (Table 20.6).

Despite this, the overall statistically non-significant decrease in mean scores on all observables found at stage 2 posits little change in conceptions of learning during the first year of study.

20.4.3   Stage 3

There were 237 sets of matched data available for analysis. With two exceptions, the matched mean scores followed the same decreasing trend as they did in stage 2 (Table 20.7). It is notable that the observables whose mean scores increased were SDI and IND, observables exhibiting transformative conceptions. In contrast to the differences in means between stages 1 and 2, none of differences in mean scores between stages 2 and 3 exceeded 0.5.

Obs		Mean	sd	Diff	Mean	sd	Diff
ACC	stage 1	17.3	3.0	↓ 0.8	17.3	2.8	↓ 1.0
	stage 2	16.5	2.9		16.3	3.1	
REC	stage 1	20.0	2.5	↓ 0.5	19.7	2.8	↓ 0.7
	stage 2	19.5	2.8		19.0	2.9	
MAU	stage 1	20.7	4.0	↓ 0.4	20.3	3.6	↓ 0.2
	stage 2	20.3	4.0		20.1	4.0	
DUT	stage 1	12.2	3.2	↓ 0.4	11.8	4.1	↓ 0.1
	stage 2	11.8	3.2		11.7	3.7	
FAC	stage 1	17.1	3.4	↓ 0.7	17.4	3.7	↓ 1.7
	stage 2	16.4	3.5		15.7	3.6	
INK	stage 1	21.3	2.1	↓ 0.6	21.6	2.3	↓ 1.1
	stage 2	20.7	2.4		20.5	2.5	
MBU	stage 1	11.7	4.2	↓ 0.3	12.4	4.9	↓ 0.6
	stage 2	11.4	4.1		11.8	4.3	
IND	stage 1	18.9	3.0	↓ 0.1	19.3	3.4	↓ 0.8
	stage 2	18.8	3.3		18.5	3.3	
SDI	stage 1	19.0	3.2	↓ 0.5	19.8	2.7	↓ 0.8
	stage 2	18.5	3.4		19.0	3.0	
KDF	stage 1	13.7	3.1	↓ 0.6	13.6	2.9	↓ 0.6
	stage 2	13.1	2.9		13.0	3.0	

Table 20.5   Matched mean scores by age (stage 1 & stage 2)
School leavers N = 305
Mature N = 103

Observable	Diff in mean		Significance
INK	Age 1	- 0.55	
	Age 2	- 0.16	0.0274
FAC	Age 1	- 0.69	
	Age 2	- 0.73	0.0065
IND	Age 1	- 0.98	
	Age 2	- 0.77	0.0722

Table 20.6   Analysis of univariate cases for differences in means by age between
stage 1 and stage 2

Observables		Means	Standard deviation	Differences in means
ACC	Stage1	17.3	3.0	
	Stage 2	16.4	3.0	↓ 0.9
	Stage 3	16.1	3.1	↓ 0.3
REC	Stage 1	20.0	2.5	
	Stage 2	19.4	2.7	↓ 0.5
	Stage 3	18.9	3.0	↓ 0.5
MAU	Stage 1	20.6	3.8	
	Stage 2	20.5	3.8	↓ 0.1
	Stage 3	20.1	3.9	↓ 0.4
DUT	Stage 1	12.1	3.4	
	Stage 2	11.6	3.4	↓ 0.5
	Stage 3	11.1	3.4	↓ 0.5
FAC	Stage 1	17.2	3.4	
	Stage 2	16.2	3.4	↓ 1.0
	Stage 3	16.0	3.6	↓ 0.2
INK	Stage 1	21.5	2.1	
	Stage 2	20.9	2.2	↓ 0.7
	Stage 3	20.6	2.1	↓ 0.3
MBU	Stage 1	11.6	4.3	
	Stage 2	11.2	4.1	↓ 0.3
	Stage 3	11.2	4.1	↓ 0.1
IND	Stage 1	19.1	3.0	
	Stage 2	18.7	3.2	↓ 0.4
	Stage 3	19.0	3.1	↑ 0.2
SDI	Stage 1	19.3	3.0	
	Stage 2	18.8	3.3	↓ 0.6
	Stage 3	19.1	3.0	↑ 0.4
KDF	Stage 1	13.7	3.0	
	Stage 2	13.0	3.0	↓ 0.7
	Stage 3	12.6	3.1	↓ 0.4

Table 20.7   Matched mean scores for whole group (Stage 1, Stage 2 & Stage 3)
N = 237

Table 20.8 identifies that, with the exception of MBU, the pattern of direction of change of differences in means was the same for both age groups. With reference to the increase in mean scores for SDI and IND, it is noticeable that there was a much larger increase for IND among the mature students than the school leavers, while the increase in means on SDI was the same.

The continued decline in the mean scores on MBU for the school leaver age group is positive (desirable) in theoretical terms. However, the similar direction of change in MAU is contradictory. As MAU is logically linked with SDI and IND in terms of them representing

Obs		School leavers N = 179			Mature N = 58		
		Mean	sd	Diff	Mean	sd	Diff
ACC	stage 1	17.3	3.1		17.5	2.8	
	stage2	16.4	2.9	↓ 0.8	16.6	3.0	↓ 0.9
	stage 3	16.3	3.1	↓ 0.2	15.6	3.2	↓ 0.9
REC	stage 1	20.0	2.6		19.7	2.4	
	stage2	19.6	2.7	↓ 0.5	19.1	2.8	↓ 0.6
	stage 3	19.0	3.0	↓ 0.6	18.7	2.9	↓ 0.5
MAU	stage 1	20.9	3.9		19.8	3.8	
	stage2	20.6	3.8	↓ 0.3	20.3	3.8	↓ 0.5
	stage 3	20.1	3.9	↓ 0.5	20.0	4.0	↓ 0.4
DUT	stage 1	12.1	3.3		11.9	3.9	
	stage2	11.5	3.2	↓ 0.6	11.7	3.8	↓ 0.1
	stage 3	11.1	3.3	↓ 0.4	10.9	4.0	↓ 0.8
FAC	stage 1	17.1	3.5		17.4	3.4	
	stage2	16.2	3.4	↓ 0.8	15.9	3.5	↓ 1.5
	stage 3	16.1	3.7	↓ 0.1	15.6	3.5	↓ 0.4
INK	stage 1	21.4	2.0		21.8	2.3	
	stage2	20.9	2.1	↓ 0.5	20.7	2.4	↓ 1.1
	stage 3	20.6	2.0	↓ 0.3	20.4	2.3	↓ 0.2
MBU	stage 1	11.3	4.0		12.5	5.0	
	stage2	11.0	3.9	↓ 0.2	11.9	4.8	↓ 0.6
	stage 3	10.8	4.0	↓ 0.2	12.1	4.4	↑ 0.2
IND	stage 1	19.0	2.8		19.3	3.3	
	stage2	18.6	3.3	↓ 0.4	18.9	2.9	↓ 0.4
	stage 3	18.7	3.1	≠ 0.1	19.7	2.9	↑ 0.8
SDI	stage 1	19.1	2.9		20.0	2.8	
	stage2	18.6	3.4	↓ 0.5	19.1	3.0	↓ 0.9
	stage 3	19.0	2.9	↑ 0.4	19.5	3.1	↑ 0.4
KDF	stage 1	13.6	3.0		13.7	2.6	
	stage2	13.0	2.9	↓ 0.7	12.8	3.0	↓ 0.9
	stage 3	12.7	3.1	↓ 0.3	12.2	2.9	↓ 0.5

Table 20.8   Matched mean scores by age (Stage 1, Stage 2 & Stage 3)

transformative conceptions, and the mean scores for the latter two observables increased, Pearson correlation co-efficients among these four observables for each age group were undertaken in order to further investigate their inter-relationships. The significant correlations found (p < 0.0001) are listed in Table 20.9. The lack of significant correlation between MBU and any of the other three observables is notable.

		School leavers		Mature		
		N =179		N = 58		
Stage 1	SDI – IND	r = 0.35	p < 0.0001	SDI – IND	r = 0.53	p < 0.0001
	SDI – MAU	r = 0.08	p = 0.2848	SDI – MAU	r = 0.27	p = 0.0406
	SDI – MBU	r = - 0.13	p = 0.0726	SDI – MBU	r = 0.34	p = 0.0099
	IND – MAU	r = 0.24	p = 0.0014	IND – MAU	r = 0.26	p = 0.0487
	IND – MBU	r = 0.08	p = 0.2694	IND – MBU	r = 0.31	p = 0.0168
	MAU – MBU	r = 0.07	p = 0.3424	MAU – MBU	r = 0.18	p = 0.1845
Stage 2	SDI – IND	r = 0.38	p < 0.0001	SDI – IND	r = 0.39	p = 0.0028
	SDI – MAU	r = 0.30	p < 0.0001	SDI – MAU	r = 0.32	p = 0.0155
	SDI – MBU	r = 0.06	p = 0.3895	SDI - MBU	r = 0.10	p = 0.4763
	IND – MAU	r = 0 27	p = 0.0002	IND – MAU	r = 0.40	p = 0.0018
	IND – MBU	r = 0.09	p = 0.2135	IND – MBU	r = 0.02	p = 0.8773
	MAU – MBU	r = 0.06	p = 0.3940	MAU – MBU	r = 0.05	p = 0.6822
Stage 3	SDI – IND	r = 0.37	p < 0.0001	SDI – IND	r = 0.26	p = 0.0516
	SDI – MAU	r = 0.28	p = 0.0002	SDI – MAU	r = 0.33	p = 0.0111
	SDI – MBU	r = 0.05	p = 0.5016	SDI – MBU	r = 0.25	p = 0.0599
	IND – MAU	r = 0.14	p = 0.0680	IND – MAU	r = 0 .27	p = 0.0370
	IND – MBU	r = 0.03	p = 0.6586	IND – MBU	r = 0.16	p = 0.2172
	MAU – MBU	r = - 0.04	p = 0.5503	MAU – MBU	r = 0.13	p = 0.3288

Table 20.9　Correlations by age among MBU, MAU, IND and SDI

Observables		Factor 1	Factor 2	Factor 3
FAC	stage 1	.90*		
ACC	stage 1	.78*		
INK	stage 1	.70*		
REC	stage 1	.67*		
KDF	stage 1	.41		.39
IND	stage 1		.85*	
SDI	stage 1		.45*	
MAU	stage 1		.26	
DUT	stage 1			.69*
MBU	stage 1			.55*

Values < 0.2 not included　　　　*values ≥ 0.45

Inter-factor correlations

	Factor 1	Factor 2	Factor 3
Factor 1	1.00	0.28	0.47
Factor 2	0.28	1.00	0.09
Factor 3	0.47	0.09	1.00

Table 20.10　Whole group factor solution for Stage 1 (Stage 3)
　　　　　　Oblique rotation
　　　　　　N = 237

Exploratory factor analyses were also performed on the stage 3 data to identify any possible structural changes in conceptions of learning across the three stages of the study. On entry to the programme (Table 20.10), this group exhibited a factor structure that was consonant. Factors 1 and 3 were essentially accumulative while Factor 2 was transformative.

Observables		Factor 1	Factor 2	Factor 3
REC	.73*			
INK	stage 2	.73*		
FAC	stage 2	.72*	.21	
ACC	stage 2	.61*	.31	
DUT	stage 2		.68*	
KDF	stage 2	.23	.59*	
MBU	stage 2		.58*	
SDI	stage 2			.76*
IND	stage 2	.23		.47*
MAU	stage 2			.39

Values < 0.2 not included   *values ≥ 0.45
Inter-factor correlations

	Factor 1	Factor 2	Factor 3
Factor 1	1.00	0.56	0.21
Factor 2	0.56	1.00	0.15
Factor 3	0.21	0.15	1.00

Table 20.11   Whole group factor solution for Stage 2 (Stage 3)
Oblique rotation
N = 237

Observables		Factor 1	Factor 2	Factor 3
FAC	stage 3	.78*	.20	
REC	stage 3	.78*		
ACC	stage 3	.70*	.30	
INK	stage 3	.66*		
DUT	stage 3		.75*	
KDF	stage 3		.72*	
MBU	stage 3		.50*	
SDI	stage 3			.80*
IND	stage 3	.40		.41
MAU	stage 3			.34

Values < 0.2 not included   *values ≥ 0.
Inter-factor correlations

	Factor 1	Factor 2	Factor 3
Factor 1	1.00	0.53	0.07
Factor 2	0.53	1.00	0.07
Factor 3	0.07	0.07	1.00

Table 20.12   Whole group factor solution for Stage 3 (Stage 3))
Oblique rotation
N = 237

At stage 2 (Table 20.11) factors 1 and 2 were accumulative and factor 3 transformative. Although the presence of IND in factor 1 suggests the possibility of a dissonant outcome, its low value posits that all the factors can be regarded as consonant.

The stage 3 solution (Table 20.12) demonstrated a similar arrangement as for stage 2. The first two factors were accumulative in nature, although the continued inclusion of a stronger IND continued to be anomalous in factor 1, and factor 3 was transformative.

20.5   Discussion

20.5.1   Stage 1

The factor structure for the whole group factor analysis (Table 20.1) is generally consistent with theoretical expectations that students often enter higher education and exhibit (variation in) predominantly accumulative conceptions of learning (Boulton-Lewis, 1995; Entwistle, 1997; Prosser and Trigwell, 1999).

The structure of the dissonant factor solution for the mature students (Table 20.2) posits that this group exhibited a theoretically more problematic pattern of variation, suggesting the likelihood of a larger numbers of 'at risk' responses contributing to this pattern of variation. Insofar as such a dissonant factor structure represents theoretically undesirable dimensions of variation, there will be students who can be thought of as being represented in an abstract sense in the extreme locations of the factor structure who may be 'at risk' of failure. Potentially weaker academic backgrounds and less confidence in their abilities are possible explanations. Whatever the reasons, these results suggest that additional study support needs to be overtly made available to mature entrants.

Secondly, the finding from the analysis of univariate cases (Table 20.3) that mature students had significantly lower scores on DUT, an outcome which suggests they are more intrinsically than extrinsically motivated agrees with other research into older students. Young (1990) found that, as with other mature students, mature physiotherapy students demonstrate high levels of commitment and motivation because they have often had to make sacrifices and overcome hurdles to gain entry onto courses. Brookfield (2000) also confirms the high intrinsic motivation of mature students. This feature could potentially have a positive effect on academic performance in any otherwise 'at risk' students.

Meyer (1999, 2000c) has demonstrated that the two conceptually contrasting 'memorisation' categories of MBU and MAU are empiricaly distinct. This contrast has implications for the significant differences found for age across these two observables (Table 20.3). The presence and pattern of significant differences for the two memorisation observables poses a challenge to perceived wisdom. Brookfield (2000) argues that older students with greater life experience focus preferentially on understanding material. Prosser and Trigwell (1999) posit that school leavers tend to enter university with quantitative conceptions with a strong emphasis on memorising and reproducing facts. The findings of stage 1 of the study were not in accord with both these widely held perceptions. Whether these findings were unique to this group or are more prevalent in higher education remains an open question in the absence of comparable data. Possible reasons for these findings can however be proposed. It is possible that school leavers' learning experiences at school have a focus on understanding rather than a dominant emphasis on memorisation, but confirmation of this could only be obtained by further investigation on a wide range of school leavers. With regard to mature students, it is possible that they feel inferior in some way compared with younger students who have a long recent history of academic study. Research has shown that mature physiotherapy students do tend to have low levels of self-esteem (Young, 1990). This could lead them to conceive learning at a lower level as quantitative rather than qualitative, even though their life experience suggests that they are likely to be more able than school leavers to use qualitative forms of cognitive processing (Brookfield, 2000).

20.5.2   Stage 2

The most notable feature of the stage 2 results was that the difference in means for the whole group matched scores were all lower than they had been in stage 1 (Table 20.4). Only four observables had differences in means of less than 0.5. In terms of theoretically desirable conceptions, the fall in mean values for the accumulative observables ACC, FAC, REC, INK and KDF were positive. The differences for REC and INK could also be regarded as positive, but this assertion would challenge the optimistic statement made earlier regarding these observables in the results of the stage 1 whole group factor analysis (Table 20.1). The lower values for SDI, and other transformative conceptions are undesirable, but, overall, the trends could be interpreted as encouraging.

The larger fall in mean scores on FAC and INK among the mature students between stages 1 and 2 may suggest that their experience of the first year of their course had demonstrated that any initial lack of confidence felt in their academic abilities was unjustified, resulting in them later holding less strong accumulative conceptions of learning. However, this hypothesis cannot be verified here.

The continuing emphasis on accumulative rather than transformative conceptions in both age groups at the end of the first year of study could be explained by the fact that, although the design of many UK physiotherapy programmes is based on sound educational principles, they still tend to have a strong focus in the first year on biomedical and clinical sciences and physiotherapy skill acquisition. Such a focus would tend to support retention of accumulative conceptions rather than a move towards transformative ones. If this is so, then the falls in value given to some of the accumulative conceptions like ACC (0.9), FAC (1.0), INK (0.7), KDF (0.7) and REC (0.6) by the whole group (Table 20.2) could be viewed as positive. However, it must be noted that the values for SDI, a transformative conception, fell by the same amount as REC.

The large fall in mean values for ACC and FAC in both age groups in stage 2 (Table 20.5) were particularly to be welcomed as it suggested that students' learning experiences had weakened their conception that learning is fact based and merely accumulative, a perception in conflict with the desired quality of learning outcomes. The larger change in the mature students for FAC is particularly positive and agreed with the literature which proposes a stronger leaning towards quantitative than qualitative conceptions in this age group (Brookfield, 2000). However, it must be borne in mind that this possible positive trend is not supported by the results for most of the other observables.

Interpretation of the stage 2 results was not assisted by the fact that no definite temporal patterns in the students' conceptions of learning were identified. Overall, despite the changes discussed, the results from the first two stages of the study appeared to be equivocal.

20.5.3   Stage 3

The pattern of decrease in mean scores for the whole group and the two age groups identified in stage 2 continued in stage 3 (Tables 20.7 and 20.8). The two exceptions of higher scores for IND and SDI were encouraging as they represented desirable transformative conceptions and counter the undesirable fall in scores for these observables which occurred in stage 2. These findings may suggest that, as students progress through the course, their learning experiences are fostering the desired objectives within physiotherapy education, that students become increasingly independent, self-directed learners as they progress through the programme.

The consistent decrease in scores over time on observables which posit accumulative conceptions – ACC, REC, DUT, FAC, INK, KDF – posit an encouraging trend (Table 20.8). The largest decreases in mean scores occurred in the mature group, supporting the suggestion made earlier that this group's dependence on accumulative conceptions might have declined during the course as their self-confidence strengthened. However, the changes identified were small.

The factor analysis of the stage 3 sample (Tables 20.10, 20.11 and 20.12) provides a helpful overview of the temporal developments in the students' conceptions of learning. Except for the presence of IND in (in each case) factor 1 at stages 2 and 3, all the factor structures are consonant.

The design and delivery of physiotherapy programmes in England and Wales has been altered extensively in recent years to incorporate and embed sound educational practices which encourage students to achieve high quality learning. Although the trends identified by the findings were small, it is possible that the desired outcomes might have been achieved by the end of the final year of study. Unfortunately, data relating to the final year could not be obtained and stronger conclusions cannot be drawn.

Overall, the findings of this study demonstrate a strong temporal stability in the respondents' conceptions of learning. Although notable findings were identified at individual stages of the study, these were often not present later. In addition, the often small changes involved made definitive interpretation difficult.

Possible explanations for this stability relate to homogeneity of students and/or curriculum design. The generally high academic entry requirements for admission to physiotherapy education, with an associated restricted focus on required subjects, could mean that physiotherapy students exhibit a narrow, similar range of characteristics. This explanation is likely to be less true for the mature students who tend to have more diverse academic backgrounds than school leavers. Overall, however, the findings for the two age groups were similar. Alternatively, the students' learning experiences may vary little during their physiotherapy education and thus produce little change in conceptions. Physiotherapy programmes in the UK no longer have the marked distinction between basic sciences in the first year and clinically focussed content later on. However, even if a 'smoother' curriculum design were a factor in the stability of the findings, the important message is that this study does not suggest a desirable transition towards transformative conceptions as posited by Entwistle (1997) and Morgan and Beaty (1997).

The absence of findings from similar longitudinal research means that it is not possible to identify whether the pattern of these findings is unique to this student cohort or physiotherapy education or true of other disciplines as well. Morgan and Beaty (1997) provide only limited research evidence to demonstrate that a move from accumulative to transformative conceptions does occur.

19.5.4   Limitations of the study

The limitations of the present study are acknowledged, particularly the lack of data relating to students' final year of study.

Ideally, all those who responded in stage 1 would have participated in the later stages of the study. However, a decline in responses was anticipated, as this is a characteristic of longitudinal studies (Magnusson and Bergman, 1990; Menard, 1991). The multicentre nature of this study also increased the likelihood of this trend as the first author was unable to motivate respondents directly. The reality of decreased numbers of matched responses over time challenges the validity of comparing the results from different stages.

More helpful insights might have been obtained if more than one demographic factor could have been investigated. Although information on gender, route of entry and place of study was obtained in addition to age, small numbers or disproportionate group sizes meant that only age could be usefully analysed.

20.6   Conclusion

This exploratory study identified that the physiotherapy students who participated held very stable conceptions of learning over time. Despite the presence of some encouraging changes, the conceptions which predominated throughout were accumulative rather than transformative. This finding raises questions as to whether students' educational experiences, although largely involving sound educational design, facilitate desired high quality learning. However, more research of this kind is needed before any conclusions can be drawn.

The findings also suggest that some mature physiotherapy students may potentially be at greater risk of failure than their younger counterparts, both on entry and at the end of the first year of study, indicating that ongoing study and learning support should be provided.

References

Boulton-Lewis, GM 1995). The SOLO taxonomy as a means of shaping and assessing learning in higher education, *Higher Education Research and Development*, **14**, 143-154.

Boulton-Lewis, GM (1998). Applying the SOLO taxonomy to learning in higher education. In Dart, B and Boulton-Lewis, GM (Eds), *Teaching and learning in higher education*, Melbourne: ACER.

Brookfield, S (2000). Adult cognition as a dimension of lifelong learning. In Field, J and Leicester, M (Eds), *Lifelong learning: education across the lifespan*, Philadelphia: Falmer Press.

Dart, B (1998). Teaching for improved learning in small classes. In Dart, B and Boulton-Lewis, GM (Eds), *Teaching and learning in higher education*, Melbourne: ACER.

Entwistle, N (1997). Contrasting perspectives on learning. In Marton, F, Hounsell, D and Entwistle, N (Eds), *The experience of learning: implications for teaching and studying in higher education*. (2nd Edn), Edinburgh: Scottish Academic Press.

Magnusson D and Bergman, LR (1990). General issues about data quality in longitudinal research. In Magnusson D and Bergman LR (Eds), *Data quality in longitudinal research*, Cambridge, Cambridge University Press

Menard S (1991). *Longitudinal research, California*, Sage Publications

Meyer, JHF (1998). A medley of individual differences. In Dart, B and Boulton-Lewis, GM (Eds), *Teaching and learning in higher education*, Melbourne: ACER.

Meyer, JHF (1999). Embryonic 'memorising' models of student learning 8th EARLI Conference, Goteborg.

Meyer, JHF (2000a). An overview of the development and application of the Reflections on Learning Inventory (RoLI), RoLI Symposium, London

Meyer, JHF (2000b). An empirical approach to the modelling of dissonant study orchestration in higher education. *European Journal of Psychology of Education*, (special edition), **15**, 5-18.

Meyer, JHF (2000c). Variation in contrasting forms of 'memorising' and associated observables. *British Journal of Educational Psychology*, **70**, 163-176.

Meyer, JHF and Boulton-Lewis, GM (1999). On the operationalisation of conceptions of learning in higher education and their association with students' knowledge and experiences of their learning. *Higher Education Research and Development*, **18**, 289-302.

Meyer, JHF and Shanahan, MP (2001a). A triangulated approach to the modelling of learning outcomes in first-year economics. *Higher Education Research and Development*, **20**, 127-145.

Meyer, JHF and Shanahan, MP (2001b). Making teaching responsive to variation in student learning. In Rust, C (Ed), Improving Student Learning — Improving Student Learning Strategically, pp 296-313. Oxford: Oxford Centre for Staff and Learning Development.

Morgan, A and Beaty, L (1997). The world of the learner In Marton, F, Hounsell, D and Entwistle, N (Eds), *The experience of learning: implications for teaching and studying in higher education,* (2nd Edn), Edinburgh: Scottish Academic Press.

Prosser, M and Trigwell, K (1999). *Understanding learning and teaching: the experience in higher education*, Buckingham: Open University Press.

Young, J. M. (1990). Mature students in physiotherapy undergraduate education. *Physiotherapy*, **76**, 127-131.

21 Variation in students' experiences of small group tutorials

Paul Ashwin
University of Oxford

Abstract:

This study examined students' conceptions of the role of the Oxford tutorial in their learning. An analysis of interviews with 28 students constituted four qualitatively different conceptions of the Oxford tutorial. These ranged from the tutorial involving the tutor explaining to the student what the student did not know, to the tutorial involving the tutor and the student in exchanging different points of view and both coming to a new understanding of the topic under discussion. These different conceptions also appeared to be related to variations in students' views of the role of the work done in preparation for the tutorial, their view of the students' and tutor's roles in the tutorial, and the conception of knowledge that students adopted in relation to the tutorial. The implications of this study are discussed in terms of the relations between students' conceptions of tutorials and their anticipated learning outcomes and its implications for contexts outside of Oxford in terms of students' conceptions of academic tasks.

21.1   The 'Oxford Tutorial'

The Oxford tutorial is part of a learning system that involves a period of intensive study, usually in a library, the preparation of some work, whether an essay or completion of a problem sheet, followed by the tutorial itself. Students usually have about 3 tutorials a fortnight and spend about 13 hours preparing for each tutorial. First years spend less time preparing than final year students (11 hours compared to about 14 hours) and arts and social science students spend longer preparing than science students (about 15 hours compared to 9 hours) (all figures from the Commission of Inquiry 1997).

The size of tutorials varies with 1 tutor working with between 1 and 6 students. The Commission of Inquiry (1997) found that the most common size of tutorial was 2 students but that tutorials in social sciences, sciences and engineering tended to be bigger than those in the arts.

The structure of tutorials vary; tutors have autonomy in deciding how to structure them and what content to focus on in tutorials. However, a general structure appears to be that there will be an interrogation, whether questioning or discussion, of the work that the student(s) have completed in preparation for the tutorial. This work may be handed in beforehand; in the case of an essay may be read out in the tutorial, or the tutor may take in the work at the end of the tutorial or not at all. The discussion usually starts with the student(s) being given the opportunity to ask any questions they have about the subject matter and proceeds from there.

Different commentators have had very different views of the effectiveness of the tutorial. Moore (1968), based on his experience as a tutor at Oxford, emphasised three cardinal principles of the tutorial: catering for the individual, the co-operation between tutor and student and a particular view of knowledge. He argued that the individual nature of the tutorial allows each student to learn at their own pace and to ask any questions they may have. It also allows the tutor to adapt the process to the student's learning needs and to give students immediate feedback on their performance. He argued that the tutorial relationship should be one in which two minds worked on the same problem and that it is an opportunity for intellectual growth for the student and the tutor, in which the student should gradually acquire independence from their tutor. Finally, Moore argued that, in the tutorial, knowledge is seen as contested. The undergraduate has the opportunity to put forward his or her own ideas and present a critical analysis of a particular problem or proposition. Moore felt that his view of the tutorial system was best summed up by Reeves:

> [T]here is no substitute for the individual tutorial, either singly or in pairs. Its function is not to instruct: it is to set the student the task of expressing his thought articulately and then to assist him in subjecting his creation to critical examination and reconstructing it. The charge of spoon-feeding so often levelled against the tutorial method implies a complete misunderstanding of its function. (Dr Marjorie Reeves, Vice-Principal of St Anne's College, Oxford quoted in Moore 1968).

In contrast to the views of Moore and Reeves, Elton (2001) has argued that tutorials at Oxford, as well as Cambridge, are centred around the tutor rather than on the discussion of students' ideas and that they do not normally result in high quality student learning. He argued that "It may be noted that the famous Oxbridge tutorial is firmly teacher centred and, except for the most able students, may not normally lead to deep learning" (Elton 2001).

However, the Oxford tutorial has not been examined from the perspective of students. This study sought to examine the following questions:

- What do students understand to be the role of tutorials in their learning?

- Are there relations between their conceptions of the tutorials and their understanding of the role of the work they complete in preparation for the tutorial?

- Do students' understandings of their own role in the tutorial and the role of the tutor vary with their conceptions of the Oxford tutorial?

- Are the conceptions of knowledge that students adopt in the tutorial related to their conception of the tutorial?

21.2   Method

Twenty-eight undergraduates from a variety of disciplines and years of study were interviewed about their experiences of studying at Oxford. The students were volunteers. They were asked to describe a typical, but actual, week of study. The interviews were then structured around this description, with particular attention paid to the meaning to students of various activities that they engaged in in their studies. In all cases this led to a discussion about the tutorial system.

The interviews were analysed using a phenomenographic approach (Marton and Booth 1997). The focus was on qualitative variation in the ways in which the students experienced tutorials at Oxford. The different meanings that students assigned to tutorials were used to form categories that were formed and reformed. The aim was to offer a hierarchy of empirically grounded and logically consistent categories of description of the different ways in which students experienced tutorials. The analysis was carried out by the author, with a colleague who verified that the categories could be justified from the interviews.

21.3   Results

Four qualitatively different ways of understanding the role of tutorials were constituted in the analysis of the interviews:

1. Tutorials as the tutor explaining to the student what the student does not understand

2. Tutorials as the tutor showing the student how to see the subject in the way that the tutor does

3. Tutorials as the tutor bringing things into relation to each other to help the student develop a new perspective in the wider context of the discipline

4. Tutorials as the tutor and the student exchanging different points of view on the topic and both coming to a new understanding.

These qualitatively different understandings of the tutorial were found to be related to different student understandings of the role of work that was completed in preparation for the tutorial, the role of the student and the tutor in tutorials, and the conception of knowledge that students adopted in the tutorial. These dimensions are included in descriptions of the categories below.

1.   Tutorials as the tutor explaining to the student what the student does not understand

Students adopting this conception saw the purpose of tutorials as being to check their progress and to ensure the efficient transfer of information relevant to the topic[1] that was the subject of the tutorial. The role of the preparation work was for the student to produce an artefact, whether an essay or solutions to a series of problems, that would be used by the tutor to assess how much the student knew, to help the student gain knowledge that they could use in the tutorial and to help them develop an overview of the topic. The students adopting this conception saw their role in the tutorial was to be tested by their tutor, to use the information they had gained to answer the tutor's questions, and to absorb information from the tutor. They saw the tutor's role was to test the student and to provide the student with new information on the topic. Thus under this conception of tutorials, knowledge was seen as accumulative and uncontested.

> Doing the [preparation] work is the important thing, then what you get out of the tutorial is 1) you see whether you've done it right or not, 2) you're learning whether you've done it in an efficient way or whether there's a better way of doing it, 3) you learn whether it's really that relevant or not… So the purpose of them is to make sure you know it, teach you the good ways of doing it, giving you more information, telling you what's relevant, and that's about it. (Fourth year physicist)

> It varies very much between tutor and tutor, some tutors' tutorials are like a lecture, you come away with very organised notes, adding a lot to the information you didn't know before, which is very useful. Other times you leave the tutorial not feeling like you've gained a lot from it. . .[Tutorials are important to ensure] that the information you've got isn't a) wrong, b) one sided or c) too hazy. You sometimes write things that are a little too hazy to prove a case one way or another, and a tutor will usually be able to say 'yes, but don't you think you need to prove that with something else?' or provide you with the proofs for it or against it, which gives you more proof to then write a more coherent essay when it comes to Finals. (Second year historian)

2. *Tutorials as the tutor showing the student how to see the subject in the way that the tutor does*

Students adopting this conception of tutorials considered the purpose of tutorials to be for the student to get to understand the topic in the way that the tutor did. They saw the role of the preparation work was for the student to show the tutor how much they had understood the material that they had studied for the tutorial. They perceived that their role was to discuss the tutor's ideas in relation to the ideas they had gained from their preparatory work, whilst they saw the tutor's role was to ask students questions that took them beyond their initial understanding of the topic and to explain the topic in the way that they viewed it. In this case knowledge was seen as uncontested but it was not seen as accumulative, as understanding of the topic was based on more than an accumulation of facts. It was rather concerned with seeing the material in the correct way.

> [The purpose of tutorials is] to put forward the things that I've discovered from the reading that I've done, to ask questions of areas that I'm not too sure about and to have my knowledge of the subject probed by the tutor through their questions and then have them explain the way that they view it and discuss those interpretations of the particular topics, and then get a better understanding of the topics as a whole, and a much deeper understanding… The tutors tend to explain the slightly more subtle aspects of the different parts of the work that we're investigating. They tend to ask questions, rather leading questions, and then they lead you though the answers that they want you to come to until you come to the conclusion that they hope you do come to, and by then you tend to understand what they're trying to get you to understand and it just gives you a better understanding of the topic. (First year biochemist)

> Basically, I'll ask him a question – often it'll be that he works through it on the board and he just keeps on working through it… I basically write down what he is doing and try to understand what he is doing. Sometimes it's just that I haven't got a picture in my mind of what is happening – I can do all this maths, but I don't have an image, I'm not very good at drawing graphs of these things in my mind and I can't just see what would happen say to a billiard ball in a field and I can't see why it's flying a particular direction, whereas he'll be able to visualise what it's doing. Say I have a big equation, he'll be able to just draw a picture on the board of what is going on and he'll describe why it's moving this way or moving this way. He'll often do a very novel method: say, I've thought of a method of solving something, my method will go round a big circle and his will go straight through and do it in three lines… I get a lot of new ways of thinking about problems out of them basically. I get a lot out of them because I pick up their ways of approaching problems. (Third year physicist)

3. *Tutorials as the tutor bringing things into relation with each other to help the student develop a new perspective in the wider context of the discipline*

Students adopting this conception saw the purpose of tutorials as developing their ideas to gain a new perspective on the topic, and this new perspective may also have been new to the tutor. They saw that the role of preparation work was for them to develop an argument about the topic that was then the focus of the tutorial. They saw their role in the tutorial was to discuss the relations that the tutor developed in relation to the students' preparation work, whilst they saw that the role of the tutor was to develop these relations. Under this conception of the tutorial, knowledge was seen by the student to be contested.

> I see it [the tutorial] as an opportunity really to show off a bit, show him what I can do, and then get his better and more learned ideas for where I could be going in the future.

They are your opportunity to talk to this very wise person, who knows all the answers, and you don't want them giving you the answers, but you want them to make you think differently, and that's what it's about, thinking differently.
(First year English student)

The most scary tutor I ever had was quite terrifying actually. He was very nice but his tutorials, you used to come out of them like you'd forcibly rearranged the ideas in your head, and you'd actually understand it in the end. He'd pick out things you didn't even realise you'd misunderstood and interrogate you about it until you knew what you'd misunderstood. That's what tutors should do really otherwise you don't learn anything from them, so there's not really much point in them teaching you really. They may as well give you a list of books to read for the term and that'll be it. If they don't question you and find out what you haven't understood, then you tend not to learn anything new from them. You might learn new facts, but you won't gain any new understanding. By being asked questions you find out what you have and haven't understood, and are pushed into understanding things yourself, as opposed to just told what your tutor thinks about them… If the tutor asks you a factual question they probably know the answer. If they ask you what you think about something, they generally don't know the answer. Well obviously they don't know what you think about it, but they also don't know what you should think about it. (Second year experimental psychologist)

4. **Tutorials as the tutor and the student exchanging different points of view on the topic and both coming to a new understanding**

Students adopting this conception of tutorials saw that the purpose of tutorials was for the students and tutors to develop their ideas about the topic. As with the third conception, they perceived the role of their preparation work was for them to develop an initial argument about the topic that was then the focus of the tutorial. The role of both student and tutor was to discuss their ideas about the topic in relation to the students' preparatory work, whilst the tutor had an additional responsibility to chair the discussion. Here the relationship between the student and the tutor was seen as more reciprocal, whilst, as with the third conception, knowledge was again seen as contested.

It will often involve a discussion of both the plays' relation to each other and it's basically a discussion where you can either agree or disagree with whoever and it keeps going until the tutor says 'right, that's the end'. In that respect it doesn't particularly have a conclusion to it like an essay would, it just gets you thinking and often leaves you with a different perspective at the end of it, which is pretty much what I would want to get out of it… The whole idea is that it will prompt you to re-think what you've written or to add something new to it. I quite enjoy tutorials because I get to talk… whereas the only thing you get to do with an essay is write, and although that's good for the examiner, it's not quite the same as interacting with them, and you want to be quite argumentative, to persuade people round to your point of view and if you can do that in the tutorial, then it's pretty fulfilling and I quite enjoy that.
(Second year English student)

21.4 Implications

To go back to Moore, Reeves and Elton, it seems that both views of the tutorial are true for some students but not for others. Some students, in accordance with Elton, conceive of the tutorials as a teacher-centred learning environment in which they are instructed by their tutors (conceptions 1 and 2), whilst others agree with Reeves and Moore that it is about students having their ideas subjected to critical examination through which these ideas are reconstructed (conceptions 3 and 4).

Interestingly, students from similar disciplines and years of study were found to have differing conceptions of the Oxford tutorial. Trigwell and Ashwin (2002) used this data on students' conceptions of tutorials to develop items in a questionnaire study that examined students' evoked conceptions of learning. They found that the evoked conceptions of learning (3 and 4) that were more aligned with the University's view of learning, were related positively and significantly to the quality of students' learning (as measured by their approaches to learning), perceptions of their learning environment as supportive, and their anticipated learning outcome. This suggests that students' conceptions of tutorials, that is their understanding of the academic task undertaken as part of the tutorial system, is related to their successful engagement in that system.

This study has implications for teaching and learning situations outside of the Oxford tutorial. Peer learning and ICT systems are often suggested to offer ways of improving students' learning because of the individualised attention that they can offer students. For example, Topping (1996) argues that peer learning in reducing the student-to-peer tutor ratio offers increased 'time on task' and increases students' opportunities to respond to their peer tutor and to have their errors corrected. However, this study suggests that students' conceptions of the academic task that they are engaged in will affect the way they engage in it and the quality of their learning outcomes. Thus, in the case of peer learning and ICT-supported learning, the ways in which students understand these activities will impact on the ways in which they engage in them and the quality of their learning from their involvement in these activities. This suggests that any system of individualised instruction may still need to take account of students' differing conceptions of their academic task and attempt to address them if they are to lead to higher quality student learning.

Notes

1. The words 'topic' and 'material' are used generically in this paper to denote the body of knowledge that is the focus of a particular tutorial.

References:

Elton, L (2001). Research and teaching: conditions for a positive link. *Teaching in Higher Education*, **6**, 43–56.

Commission of Inquiry (1997). Commission of Inquiry Report. Oxford: University of Oxford.

Marton, F and Booth, S (1997). *Learning and Awareness*. New Jersey: Lawrence Erlbaum Associates.

Moore, WG (1968). *The Tutorial System and Its Future*. Oxford: Pergamon Press.

Topping, K (1996). *Effective Peer Tutoring in Further and Higher Education*. Birmingham: Staff and Educational Development Association.

Trigwell, K and Ashwin, P (2002). Evoked Conceptions of Learning and Learning Environments In Rust, C (Ed), Improving Student Learning Theory and Practice – 10 years on, (this volume, Chapter 15). Oxford: Oxford Centre for Staff and Learning Development.

22 Supporting learners of statistics: the difference between personal sense and cultural meaning

Sue Gordon
Mathematics Learning Centre, University of Sydney

Abstract

This paper addresses tensions between the needs of students and expectations in higher education in the context of a service course in statistics. Ways of making visible these tensions and supporting learners are discussed within an activity theory framework. I draw on Leont'ev's (1978) distinction between "personal sense", which has individual, psychological significance, and his notion of "cultural meaning" as collectively or socially endorsed (Leont'ev, 1978, p. 169).

The data concern students' feelings about studying a compulsory statistics course for Psychology, and their conceptions of statistics. The results suggest that a majority of students view statistics as disconnected from other knowledge and irrelevant to their goals and lives. These results are used to underpin issues critical to higher education today.

22.1 Introduction and background

> It practically didn't exist! It was something the government did. Every now and again they took a census. In those days there were no surveys about what brand of coffee you drank. I didn't come up against it until I came here. When I first saw the word 'statistics' in the psychology book, I just blacked it out – I thought I'd worry about it when I came to it.
>
> Alice, a Psychology student, describing statistics

What does "statistics" mean to you? Is your conception of it as a personal tool, useful in your research or work? Alternatively, do you conceive of statistics as something "out there" in society, unrelated to your needs and goals, as Alice's comment above indicates? The focus of this paper is students' meaning making in the context of learning statistics at university. I draw on Leont'ev's (1978) distinction between meaning as cultural or personal. Cultural meanings are connected with the reality of the outside world, the life of society. Personal sense, on the other hand, is connected with the reality of the person's own life, motives and goals. Sometimes there is a mismatch between societal and personal meaning.

The Mathematics Learning Centre where I work assists students at my university with their elementary mathematics and statistics courses. My teaching covers a wide range of topics and is usually on a small group or individual basis. I am particularly involved with second year Psychology students who seek assistance with statistics. The study of statistics is seen as essential to the discipline of Psychology at my university and is included as a compulsory unit of undergraduate study in first and second year. Some Psychology students lack the prerequisite background in mathematics. Many may be termed reluctant learners of statistics, as they do not have an intrinsic interest in the subject.

In order to understand students' learning I draw on activity theory based on the powerful ideas of Vygotsky and Leont'ev (for example, Leont'ev, 1981; Vygotsky, 1978). This theory explains that people actively develop knowledge on the basis of life experiences that are rooted in the ongoing practical and communal life by which societies organise and reorganise themselves. The activity of learning is a process in which people grapple with new information – to make it meaningful, to solve problems and to adapt to new conditions. Activity theory highlights that the ways students learn mathematics or statistics are inseparable from a complex web of personal, social and cultural factors.

Varela, Thompson and Rosch (1991, p 205) describe cognitive capacities as: "paths that exist only as they are laid down in walking". Their metaphor beautifully illustrates the inseparability of personal meaning and setting; the co-emergence of thought and action – knowing as doing.

Students' activities in learning statistics are organised within a dynamic system, which is continually undergoing change and is characterised by interactions including interactions among governments, university boards, teachers and students.

Higher education is currently undergoing major changes. In Australia, a review of higher education by the federal government identifies factors transforming the context of higher education (Department of Education, Science and Training, 2002). These factors include a shift from an elite education system to a mass education system with increasing diversity of students, changing patterns of enrolment, such as increased part time study, impact of information and communication technologies and expectations of graduates held by employers. Moreover, ongoing transformations are altering the focus and very nature of higher education.

> There is an ongoing debate over the 'what' of higher education. This is exemplified by the tension between whether higher education should provide students with a liberal, general education, with a focus on learning for its own sake, or a professionally focused, specialist preparation for the workforce.
> Department of Education, Science and Training (2002, p 2).

Adding to the tensions in the Australian higher education system are an increased dependence of universities on private funding, decreased resources, more emphasis on accountability and substantial changes in the ratio between students and teaching staff – a 38.6% rise in this ratio in the last eight years (Kent, 2002). Systemic changes, such as these are transforming higher education in many countries. They translate into practical terms, defining the resources available to university teachers and impacting on the ways teaching is organised or constrained. For example, a university teacher of statistics perceived that multiple-choice examinations are an undesirable method of assessment but "essential for financial reasons" (Gordon, 1998, p 244).

Engeström (1999) pointed out that if practitioners are able to identify and analyse contradictions and tensions in the system surrounding and shaping their activities they may be able to focus on resolving the contradictions and reorganising the activity "instead of being victimised by changes that roll over them as if forces of a natural catastrophe" (Engeström, 1999 p 68). To do this the tensions must be made visible – recognised – as when a practice is shared and common it becomes invisible.

My starting point is an analysis of empirical data – aspects of my PhD thesis (Gordon. 1998). In the thesis I investigated students' experiences of and orientations to learning statistics as a service course to Psychology. This included investigating students' attitudes to learning statistics, their conceptions of the subject matter, their approaches to learning statistics and how these factors related to attainments on tests and examinations. In this paper I present data to serve as a springboard for examining issues surrounding learning statistics as a service course. What are the tensions and contradictions made visible by the data (Engeström, 1999) and how do we support students' learning in service courses?

22.2   Theoretical framework

Activity theory views human learning as active and purposeful behaviour mediated by interactions and cultural artefacts – tools. The focus of this theory, therefore, is on what the learner does and why he or she so acts, and emphasises the social and cultural arena surrounding an individual's actions. "Activity" encompasses goals and actions both overt and mental. Students' activities determine the quality of their learning and emerging knowledge. As a statistics student explained: "Mathematics is what you make of it. It can be artistic, practical, creative or routine".

The ways students learn statistics reflect their personal stories, their experiences, needs and goals. Teachers of statistics may try to emphasise the usefulness of their subject, but no one can persuade a student of the power of a cultural tool. This discovery depends on the student's experience of its functionality.

In sharp contrast to psychological theories in which cognitive processes are viewed as separate from the emotional domain, activity theory emphasises the inseparability of students' feelings from their thinking. Vygotsky (1962, p 150) describes this inseparability of intellectual processes and affective elements as follows:

> Thought itself is engendered by motivation, ie by our desires and needs, our interests and emotions. Behind every thought there is an affective-volitional tendency, which holds the answer to the last 'why' in the analysis of thinking. A true and full understanding of another's thought is possible only when we understand its affective-volitional basis.

Affective elements operate as invisible dimensions of student learning, neither acknowledged nor valued in higher education. Lerman (1996) argues that the valuing of decontextualised, intellectual processes, divorced from personal elements, is expressive of oppressive discourse. It is this privileging of abstract thought, such as academic mathematics, that is disempowering for some students. Sierpinska & Lerman (1996) refer to the vested interest mathematicians have in maintaining the status of mathematics in society. This idea was passionately expressed by a statistics student (Gordon, 1998). She wrote:

> Maths is an exercise in agony, because the people who teach it make one feel as though maths belongs in a higher plane of evolution. Even though the number system is for everyone, and the concepts are there for everyone, the feeling (especially if you are doing pass options) that you do not deserve to know anything runs rampant.

In the next sections we explore the experience of learning statistics as a service course from the students' perspectives – how they felt about learning it and what their conceptions of statistics were.

22.3   Methodology

Research questions

We focus on the following research questions:

- How did students feel about studying statistics for Psychology?
- What were students' reasons for their willingness or reluctance to study statistics?
- What were the students' conceptions of statistics?
- What were the relationships between students' willingness to study statistics, their conceptions of statistics and their achievements in tests and examinations?
- What issues are exposed for higher education?

Method

A survey on learning statistics was completed by students studying statistics as a compulsory component of second year Psychology at my university. The survey was completed by 279 students, about three quarters of whom were female. The prior level of mathematics studied by the surveyed students was higher than is often assumed for Psychology students. Most had studied calculus at secondary school (over 70%) and almost one quarter of those surveyed had studied mathematics at university (68 students). All the participants had studied a five-week, introductory course in statistics during their first year study of Psychology.

Interestingly, most of the students (57%) expressed an intention to continue studying Psychology at the postgraduate level and only 7% of the participants reported that they intended terminating their study of Psychology after completing second year.

The students completed the survey during a statistics lecture near the end of the first semester, that is, in week 12 of 14 teaching weeks. Hence the survey was completed by the students who attended that lecture, rather than all who were enrolled for statistics. Interviews with selected students were conducted later in the year.

The survey included the following open ended questions:

1. Would you study statistics if it were not a requirement of your psychology course? Please give reasons for your answer.

2. Think about the statistics you've done so far this year.

   a) How do you go about learning it?

   b) What are you trying to achieve?

3. What in your opinion is this statistics course about? Please explain as fully as possible.

Students also completed a questionnaire on their approaches to learning statistics (discussed in Gordon, 1999).

Analysis of open ended questions

Students' responses to the first question listed above were coded as "Yes" or "No" and then classified according to students' reasons for willingness or reluctance to study statistics.

Students' conceptions of statistics were analysed using a phenomenographic approach (Marton, 1986). Phenomenographic research seeks to uncover the subject's own understanding of the phenomenon; in this case students' awareness of the statistics they were studying. The results of phenomenographic analysis are categories of description of the qualitatively different ways students conceive of the phenomenon being investigated. In this investigation the categories describe students' conceptions of statistics indicated by their responses to the survey. The method of categorising written survey responses was based on previous phenomenographic research conducted by colleagues and myself into students' conceptions of mathematics (Crawford, Gordon, Nicholas & Prosser, 1994).

The focus of the categorisation was on responses to the third open-ended question. However, students' responses to all the survey questions were taken into account in order to gain as comprehensive an understanding of the students' perspectives as possible.

A phenomenographic perspective is relational in the sense that a person's experience or awareness of the phenomenon constitutes an internal relationship between the person and the phenomenon (Marton 1988). Svensson (1994, p 12) argues that underpinning the phenomenographic specialisation is an assumption that knowledge is fundamentally a "question of meaning in a social and cultural context". Hence phenomenography as a research tool is consistent with the activity theory framing this investigation, which emphasises the dynamics connecting and transforming individuals, context and subject matter.

The phenomenographic analysis of the data on students' conceptions involved stages of analysis and review. In the first stage, an initial set of categories was identified by an independent researcher and myself. This was achieved by each of us independently reading and classifying the entire set of 279 written responses. We then compared and discussed the categories and agreed on a draft set of categories. In the next stage, each of us, and a third researcher, independently classified 30 of the responses in terms of the draft set of categories. The individual classifications of the three researchers were compared, discussed and reviewed. In this process the categories were clarified and refined and a final set of clear statements of each category was agreed upon. All the survey responses were then classified by two researchers working independently. Finally the classifications were compared and discussed and agreement reached on any classifications that did not match.

22.4   Results

We first focus on the responses to the question:

1. Would you study statistics if it were not a requirement of your psychology course? Please give reasons for your answer.

Seventy three percent of the 249 students surveyed reported that they would not have studied statistics, if they had been given a choice.

Table 22.1 below summarises the categories that emerged most frequently from the responses. Short illustrative excerpts from students' scripts provide examples of responses favouring the learning of statistics and those indicating unfavourable or negative appraisals. Percentages are of 279 (the number of students surveyed) and are rounded to whole numbers, except for percentages less than 1%.

Personal sense		
Category	**Favourable responses**	**Unfavourable responses**
Interest	5 responses (2%)	80 responses (29%)
Excerpts	*It's interesting*	*cause I generally find it dull, boring and tedious*
Affect	13 responses (5%)	37 responses (13%)
Excerpts	*I sort of dig numbers*	*I dislike maths intensely*
Personal relevance	0 responses	21 responses (8%)
Excerpts	–	*No, it is irrelevant to my life*
Confidence	0 responses	20 responses (7%)
Excerpts	–	*Maths of any sort immediately makes me cringe*
Cultural meaning		
Category	**Favourable responses**	**Unfavourable responses**
Necessary for psychology	46 responses (16%)	8 responses (3%)
Excerpts	*It is necessary in the study of psychology*	*I am not sure what relationship there is between statistics and psychology*
General usefulness	19 responses (7%)	1 response (0.4%)
Excerpts	*statistics are used throughout our society ie newspaper reports and it is important to have an understanding of the way in which information is gathered, processed and manipulated*	*No, it is not a practical subject*

Table 22.1   Reasons for willingness or reluctance to study statistics

As can be seen, the most frequently cited reasons were negative and personal, with 29% of the students reporting statistics as boring or tedious ('interest'). The category with the highest positive frequency was 'necessary for psychology' with 16% of the students giving a positive response in this category. Responses in this category indicated that statistics was integral to psychology as a discipline but did not specify why this was so. Responses referring to a specified usefulness of statistics, in society or for a career, were categorised separately, for example, under 'general usefulness'.

Many students gave reasons which fell into more than one category, such as below.

...although I see it is necessary for psychology I find it boring and tedious.

This response was scored as positive in the category 'necessary for psychology' and negative in the category 'interest'.

22.4.1 Distribution of responses according to willingness or reluctance to study statistics

Different reasons were given by students who responded that they would have studied statistics, even if it had not been compulsory to do so ("Yes" students) and those who would not have studied statistics, given a choice ("No" students). The most dramatic differences between these two groups can be seen in the two distributions below (Figure 22.1).

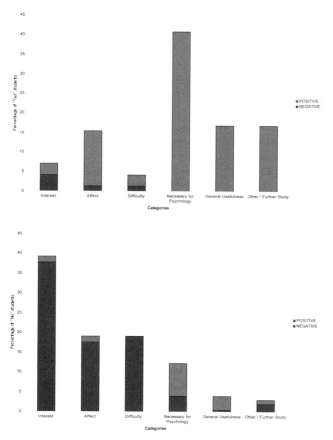

Figure 22.1   Reasons of "Yes" Students and "No" Students

The reasons given by the "Yes" students were mainly that statistics was essential to psychology, or useful – in society generally, or to other study. The reasons given by the "No" students, on the other hand, were dominated by personal, adverse perceptions of statistics or beliefs about its difficulty. Only two of the "Yes" students reported that statistics was interesting, but, unlike the "No" students, this played little part in their appraisals. Hence, rather than reflecting opposite sides of the same coin, the reasons given by students willing to study statistics related primarily to extrinsic factors, while the reasons given by the reluctant majority related mainly to feelings and emotions – the "personal plane" (Lent'ev, 1978).

These findings suggest that the students who expressed positive reasons for studying statistics had "internalised" (Leont'ev, 1981) the institutionally endorsed reasons for doing so, for example the necessity of statistics to psychology as a discipline. Few reported that statistics had "personal sense" (Leont'ev, 1978) for their long term goals or self fulfilment.

22.4.2   Conceptions of statistics

Five categories for students' conceptions of statistics emerged from the phenomenographic analysis. They are: NO MEANING; PROCESSES or algorithms; MASTERY of statistical concepts and methods; a TOOL for getting results in real life and CRITICAL THINKING.

These different ways of conceiving of statistics range from what Reid & Petocz (2002) call "limiting to expansive views". That is, the categories range from the narrowest and most limited to the broadest and most inclusive. If a student's response indicated more than one of these conceptions it was classified in the highest or most expansive category. The categories describe the qualitative differences between one conception of statistics and another. The categories and brief excerpts illustrating the category are summarised below.

Nno meaning (4% of surveys)

Responses in this category indicated conceptions of statistics as an imposed and irrelevant subject. For example, one response to the question "What in your opinion is this statistics course about?" was:

> You tell me, I just learn.

Processes (24% of surveys)

This category expressed conceptions of statistics as being about mechanical techniques or algorithms. In this conception statistical knowledge is viewed as disconnected: for reproduction in assessments. A typical response was:

> ... You don't have to understand how it works, just be able to get the right answer

Mastery (33% of surveys)

This category presented statistics as being about reading and understanding material as presented in class; as information to be accumulated and stored in order to meet the demands of assessments. For example, one student wrote:

> ... I am trying to achieve a basic understanding of the material & concepts & an ability to work out the problems. This will hopefully lead to a good result at the end of the year.

Tool (25% of surveys)

This category indicated conceptions of statistics as a useful tool. Some students indicated statistics as personally useful for example:

> Using statistics to apply it to experiments we will use later on in careers in psychology. A practical course.

Others suggested that it could be applied in real life:

> It is an attempt to give psychology students insight into stats & experimental method, to enable them to do psychological research if they choose to follow psychology as a career.

Critical thinking (3%)

This category was the most "expansive" (Reid & Petocz, 2002). The category indicated conceptions of statistics as providing a perspective on the ways in which data is used to make decisions – a scientific way of thinking and communicating. Responses in this category showed insight into the complexity & limitations of statistical theory.

> Stats is about methodology which is used as a comprehensive form of analysis to interpret and test theories & correlations psychologists create.

22.4.3   Substantiated method.

The majority of students held conceptions of statistics that were fragmented; disconnected from other knowledge and disjoint from their goals and lives. Reid & Petocz (2002) assert that the "importance of developing learning environments that encourage students to use the broader conceptions – to look for meaning in the data and relate this meaning to their own personal situations – cannot be overstated".

Figure 22.2 below shows big differences between the conceptions of students willingly studying statistics and those who were reluctant to study it. The modal category for the conceptions of the "Yes" students was TOOL while for the "No" students the most common category of conception was MASTERY. Almost 60% of the "Yes" students' conceptions were classified in the most expansive two categories, TOOL and CRITICAL THINKING, compared to 18.5% of the "No" students' conceptions in the TOOL category, and none in the CRITICAL THINKING category. Clearly the differences are substantial and are in the expected directions.   These findings indicate strong links between willingness to study statistics and conceptions of it.

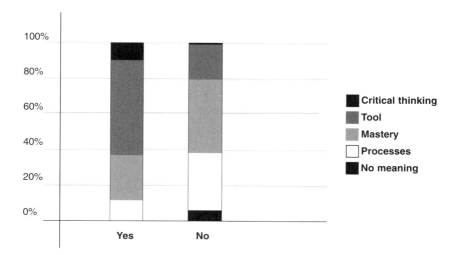

Note: About 10% of responses in each group could not be classified.

Figure 22.2   Bar graph showing percentages of "Yes" and "No" students in each conception category

22.4.5   Performance in assessments

The final mark for statistics was the average of the following four components: the class mark, based on "open-book" tests or quizzes, the examination mark for semester one, and, similarly, the class mark and examination mark for semester two.

The students who expressed willingness to study statistics performed much better than the reluctant learners in the statistics tests and examinations. The mean final mark in statistics for the "Yes" students was 66% compared to 55% attained by the "No" students. The difference between the means was statistically significant ($t=4.1$, $p<0.01$). This difference was not reflected in the overall performances of these two groups in Psychology II, excluding statistics (mean for "Yes students: 67%, mean for "No" students: 66%). Motivation to learn statistics, cannot be divorced from achievement.

22.5   Summary and discussion

The data reported in this paper focussed on Psychology students' feelings about learning a compulsory statistics course and their conceptions of the statistics.

The majority of the students who were surveyed were unwillingly studying statistics at university. They reported learning mechanical procedures or decontextualised statistical concepts and methods. The minority group of students, who expressed a greater willingness to participate in the statistics course, reported more thoughtful and personally meaningful conceptions of statistics. Their increased motivation was reflected in higher marks.

A statistics educator, Cathy, indicated that narrow conceptions of statistics were expected in undergraduate courses. A lack of awareness of the functionality of these skills and processes made it difficult for the students to experience statistical thinking as personally meaningful. She said (Gordon, 1998 p. 248):

> I think that probably they don't have a clear idea yet. They haven't done any research yet and a lot of them aren't even reading the publications in the literature. They're just reading the general text books or whatever, so I think they're not really yet able to have an overview of what it's all about. How they might ever be able to use it.

> Usually they haven't got a clue what to do anyhow, but also any analyses that come up in other areas of the course are more complicated then anything they've covered yet in their actual statistics course. It's hard to coordinate between members of the department.

What is overlooked in this evaluation is the potential for students to develop personally from learning a mathematical subject. Apart from instrumental reasons for teaching statistics – for professional development or to increase their skills in the workforce – this is the opportunity for educators to enhance the mathematical perspectives of these students and so their insights into their worlds. Further, an ability to interpret the statistical information with which we are bombarded is a minimal safeguard against disempowerment. Sandra, a mature learner of statistics summed up most poignantly her feelings about conquering mathematics for the first time in her life. She said:

> It felt very good, it felt a lot like growing up. All my life it felt like I had this dark secret – that I felt really stupid about this area. I'd cover it up so no-one would know. It really felt like growing up.

If we are going to support high quality learning we need to support the learners. Students' experiences and feelings matter.Perhaps we need to think about learning differently. Smith (2001, p.42) offers a reconceptualisation of learning through an ecological metaphor, presenting a gentler, more inclusive view of learning and recognising that learning is "a messy process, punctuated and non-linear, as web-like, fostered by information gathered from new connections which may be from insights from the teacher or other students, journeys into other disciplines or other places, and from a variety of sources"

We could also think about the learning environment differently. The statistics course in this investigation was presented to students in the traditional lecture-tutorial format with assessments being open-book quizzes, assignments and examinations. Research by Mohammad Yusof & Tall, (1999) showed that a mathematics course encouraging cooperative problem solving and reflection changed students' attitudes in a desired direction. That is, changes were from the negative attitudes teachers had come to "expect" from students towards attitudes "preferred" by their teachers.

22.6   Questions

* What is valuable in higher education?

* How do we make visible the invisible – the taken for granted beliefs and perceptions shaping teaching, learning, curriculum and assessment?

* How do we support active learning –which engages students – where a subject is a compulsory such as statistics and may not be perceived as intrinsically interesting?

* Students may see their education as being about specialisation. What scope is there for integrating development of generic skills and knowledge with professional development?

* How do we reconcile the resources available with the need to customise or individualise learning experiences?

* Is mastery of a subject sufficient?

References

Crawford, K, Gordon, S, Nicholas, J and Prosser, M (1994). Conceptions of mathematics and how it is learned: The perspectives of students entering university. *Learning and Instruction*, **4**, 331–345.

Department of Education, Science and Training (2002). Striving for quality: Learning, teaching and scholarship. Department of Education, Science and Training, Canberra, Australia. <http://www.dest.gov.au/crossroads/pubs.htm>

Engeström, Y (1999). Expansive visibilization of work: An activity theory perspective. *Computer Supported Cooperative Work*, **8**, 63–69.

Gordon, S (1998). Understanding Students Learning Statistics: An Activity Theory Approach. Unpublished Doctoral Thesis, The University of Sydney, Sydney. Australian Digital Theses: <http://adt.caul.edu.au/>.

Gordon, S (1999). An Instrument for Exploring Students' Approaches to Learning Statistics. Paper presented at the Annual Meeting of the American Educational Research Association (Montreal, Canada, April 1999). <http://ericae.net/ericdc/ED440142.htm>

Kent, S (2002). Crossroads@cross purposes? Advocate: *Journal of the National Tertiary Education Union*, **9**(2), 16–18.

Leont'ev, A N (1978). *Activity, Consciousness, and Personality*. (M. J. Hall, Trans). Englewood Cliffs, New Jersey: Prentice–Hall.

Leont'ev, A N (1981). The problem of activity in psychology. In Wertsch, JV (Ed), *The Concept of Activity in Soviet Psychology*, pp. 37–71. New York: M. E. Sharpe.

Lerman, S (1996). Intersubjectivity in mathematics learning: A challenge to the radical constructivist paradigm. *Journal for Research in Mathematics Education*, **27**(2), 133–150.

Marton, F (1986). Phenomenography – a research approach to investigating different understandings of reality. *Journal of Thought*, **21**(3), 28–49.

Marton, F (1988). Describing and improving learning. In Schmeck, R (Ed), *Learning Strategies and Learning Styles*, pp 53–82. New York: Plenum Press.

Mohammad Yusof, Y & Tall, D (1999). Changing attitudes to university mathematics through problem solving. *Educational Studies in Mathematics*, **37**, 67–82.

Reid, A & Petocz, P (2002). Students' Conceptions of Statistics: A Phenomenographic Study. *Journal of Statistics Education*, **10**(2), <www.amstat.org/publications/jse/v10n2/reid.html>.

Sierpinska, A & Lerman, S (1996). Epistemologies of mathematics and of mathematics education. In Bishop , AJ (Ed), *International Handbook of Mathematics Education*, pp 827–876. Dordrecht: Kluwer Academic Publishers.

Smith, C (2001). Enactivism – An ecological paradigm for learning. In Gunn, S. and Begg, A. (Eds), *Mind, Body & Society*, pp 35–43. Melbourne, Australia: Department of Mathematics and Statistics, The University of Melbourne.

Svensson, L (1994). Theoretical foundations of phenomenography. In Ballantyne, R and Bruce, C (Eds), *Phenomenography: Philosophy and Practice*. Proceedings of the 1994 Phenomenography Conference, pp 9–20. Brisbane: Centre for Applied Environmental and Social Education Research, Queensland University of Technology.

Varela, F, Thompson, E and Rosch, E (1991). *The Embodied Mind*. Cambridge, Massachusetts: The MIT Press.

Vygotsky, L S (1962). *Thought and Language*. Cambridge, Massachusetts: The M.I.T. Press.

Vygotsky, L S (1978). *Mind in Society*. Cambridge, MA: Harvard University Press.

23 Toward a developmental model of intercultural maturity: an holistic approach to collegiate education

Patricia M King[1] and Marcia Baxter Magolda[2]

1 University of Michigan, 2 Miami University (Ohio)

23.1 Introduction

A commonly cited intended learning outcome of American higher education is for students to gain awareness and understanding of other cultures (Bok, 1986; Bowen, 1980; Rosovsky, 1990) from both contemporaneous and historical perspectives, and both within and beyond our national borders. This long-endorsed outcome has recently been the topic of discussion not only among educators, but also among business leaders, who have argued that a dynamic and highly competitive global market has created a demand for workers who can demonstrate intercultural competencies that allow them to function effectively in an increasingly diverse marketplace. For example, the RAND Institute identified cultural competence as the most critical human resource need in the globalisation of American institutions (Bikson & Law, 1994). Professional organisations have also directed their efforts to issues of diversity-related issues, including intercultural awareness, global appreciation, etc. The Association of American Colleges and Universities (AACU, 1998) has taken a leading role in this effort and has linked discussions of diversity-related educational goals to the goals of liberal learning. In their Statement on Liberal Learning, they note:

> Because liberal learning aims to free us from the constraints of ignorance, sectarianism, and myopia, it prizes curiosity and seeks to expand the boundaries of human knowledge. By its nature, therefore, liberal learning is global and pluralistic. It embraces the diversity of ideas and experiences that characterise the social, natural, and intellectual world. To acknowledge such diversity in all its forms is both an intellectual commitment and a social responsibility, for nothing less will equip us to understand our world and to pursue fruitful lives.

This statement illustrates how educational efforts around issues of diversity can – indeed should – be grounded in fundamental collegiate purposes, linking the attainment of diversity knowledge and skills to broader educational goals and in ways that enable students to apply their skills in new and unforeseen contexts.

Demonstrating one's intercultural skills requires several types of expertise, including knowledge of cultures and cultural practices, complex cognitive skills for decision-making, social skills to function effectively in diverse work groups, and personal attributes that include flexibility and openness to new ideas. Although colleges are in many ways well suited to foster the development of these skills, "they are what corporations find in shortest supply among entry-level candidates" (Bikson & Law, 1994, p. 26). Similarly, students often expect faculty and student affairs staff members to be knowledgeable about and sensitive to intercultural issues, effective in teaching about diversity concepts, and in some settings, to effectively mediate cultural conflict; however, many faculty and staff report that they are unprepared to serve in these roles (Holcomb-McCoy & Myers, 1999; King & Howard-Hamilton, 2003; Talbot & Kocarek, 1997).

In times of increased global interdependence, producing interculturally competent citizens who can engage in informed, ethical decision-making when confronted with problems that involve a diversity of viewpoints is becoming an urgent priority. For example, when a group of Fortune 500 companies filed a brief in support of the University of Michigan's affirmative action policies (Kennelly, Mehrberg, & Hennink, 2000), they noted that students with an appreciation for diversity:

> are better prepared to understand, learn from and collaborate with others from a variety of racial, ethnic and cultural backgrounds; demonstrate creative problem solving by integrating differing perspectives; exhibit the skills required for good teamwork; and demonstrate more effective responsiveness to the needs of all types of consumers.

Educators on many college campuses expect students to show tolerance toward those of other cultural backgrounds and to demonstrate understanding of cultural concepts as they reflect the learning goals of their classes and co-curricular activities. However, persistent reports of racially-motivated hate crimes on college campuses strongly suggest the need to find better ways to help students achieve this desired collegiate outcome. In their discussion of the growing tension on US campuses around multicultural issues, Levine and Cureton (1998) noted that "multiculturalism remains the most unresolved issue on campus [in the US] today" (p 91).

Several scholars have proposed conceptual models to describe intercultural (or multicultural) competencies (eg, Howard-Hamilton, Richardson & Shuford, 1998; Pope and Reynolds, 1997; Storti, 1990). These models provide a useful starting point for identifying the attributes that are associated with this ability. For example, Pope & Reynolds (1997) include among their listing of multicultural skills "the ability to identify and openly discuss cultural differences and issues", to "differentiate between individual differences, cultural differences, and universal similarities", and "to use cultural knowledge and sensitivity to make more culturally sensitive and appropriate interventions" (p 271). However, educators not only need a goal toward which to direct their efforts, but benchmarks that indicate progress toward this goal. Further, when looking at a complex phenomenon such as intercultural competence that includes emotionally- and socially-laden dimensions, they need models that take into account a wide range of factors that affect the development of students' competence. In other words, educators would be well-served by having models that indicate what is required within the individual to demonstrate the attributes that reflect intercultural competence. Existing models rely heavily on the assessment of attitudes; while these are arguably a necessary element, they are not sufficient for the production of competent behavior. Further, the assessment of existing models tends to rely on self-report methodologies, which provides an insufficient approach to measuring this outcome.

These factors have motivated us to look for alternative ways of viewing and describing the development of intercultural competence. The changes in students' intercultural skills being called for today require "genuine development," not just knowing more facts or having more awareness, but achieving a level of individual transformation that enables them to apply their knowledge and skills in a variety of contexts. That is, educators are being asked to produce graduates who see the world, themselves, and their own agency in more sophisticated and enabling ways, and who can appropriately draw upon that understanding as the need arises. While some professors have embraced the idea of education as a transforming process for a long time, for many, this will be a much broader orientation to their educational role. To achieve this ambitious goal, we believe that to be effective, teaching for intercultural competence must be approached in a manner that is holistic in nature (described below) and that acknowledges the developmental pathways students often follow as they move toward the achievement of an educational outcome.

23.2 A more holistic approach to understanding collegiate outcomes

As noted above, intercultural competence is a complex, multi-faceted phenomenon that appears to require a wide variety of attributes; these include having an informed understanding of cultural practices, reasoning abilities that enable one to analyse complex problems and construct solutions, social skills that enable one to enhance conversations among diverse groups, and personal attributes (such as tolerance, openness, and the courage to stand up for one's beliefs) that enhance and support the application of one's knowledge and skills. As this list shows, being interculturally competent requires not just one skill but many, and not just a series of separate skills that develop independently, but skills that are interdependent and mutually reinforcing. Further, we argue that competence is not sufficient as an educational goal, but rather, that educators should direct their efforts toward promoting intercultural maturity. By "maturity," we are referring to the developmental capacity that undergirds the ways learners come to make meaning, that is, the way they approach, understand, and act on their concerns; here, our interest is how they do so in intercultural situations. We elaborate on these ideas below.

We draw our conceptualisation of maturity from the college student and adult development literatures, and in particular, from Kegan's (1994) concept of an individual's "mature capacity" to effectively address life's demands. This broader framework encompasses cognitive, identity, interpersonal development and their interconnections. Kegan argued that development in all three dimensions is required for a person to be able to use one's skills, thus providing what we refer to as an "holistic" framework. Those for whom development in one or more dimensions is not adequate for the complex life tasks they face often report being overwhelmed or "in over their heads" (a point emphasised in the title of his book). This approach is illustrated by the reaction of Christine, whose story is described by King and Baxter Magolda (1996). Christine, a white college student who had grown up in an all-white community, had a friendly interaction with an African-American student, was initially interested in seeing him again, and gave him her phone number. However, she soon learned that neither her sister nor her roommate approved of her dating a Black man and upon further reflection, Christine believed that her parents would disapprove as well. Fearing loss of approval of her family members, Christine decided this friendship was not an option for her. Although Christine's initial reaction was to be open to a friendship with someone of another race, her sense of self was too firmly grounded in the need to do what she thought others expected of her for her to accept his friendship. This story illustrates how factors such as the importance of others' approval and assumptions about how to earn this can affect a person's response in a situation with an intercultural dimension.

According to Kegan (1994), mature individuals would approach and respond differently to such situations because they exemplify what he has termed "self-authorship." He described this way of mentally "organising" (or making meaning of) experiences as follows:

> This new whole is an ideology, an internal identity, a self-authorship than can coordinate, integrate, act upon, or invent values, beliefs, convictions, generalisations, ideals, abstractions, interpersonal loyalties, and intrapersonal states. It is no longer authored by them, it authors them and thereby achieves a personal authority. (p 185, italics in original)

In this new internal identity, individuals act as authors of their lives (not just the stage on which their lives are played out), balancing external influences with their internal voice. Many demands placed on adults in contemporary society "require self-authorship because they require the ability to construct our own visions, to make informed decisions in conjunction with co-workers, to act appropriately, and to take responsibility for those actions" (Baxter Magolda, 2001, p 14). Self-authorship requires complex ways of making meaning of experience, drawing on one's understanding in all three dimensions of development noted above:

- cognitive, evaluating one's own views in light of existing evidence and constructing a reasonable perspective based on available evidence

- interpersonal, taking others' perspectives into account rather than being consumed by them; and

- intrapersonal, possessing an internally generated belief system that regulates one's interpretations of experience and guides one's choices.

Figure 23.1 is a visual representation of these dimensions.

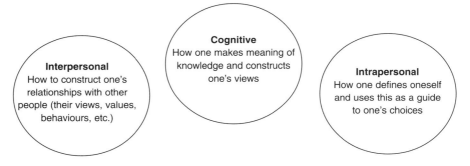

Figure 23.1. Domains of Development

In Figure 23.1, these domains are presented as separate domains of development, which is consistent with much of the research examining each of these aspects of development (cognitive or intellectual development, intrapersonal or identity development, and interpersonal, eg, moral development, respectively).

By contrast, consider Figure 23.2, which shows two additional approaches to conceptualising these domains of development. The "separate domains" model from Figure 23.1 is followed by a visual depiction of a "related domains" approach, which allows for an examination of relationships between and among domains. This second approach is exemplified by King & Kitchener's (1994) longitudinal research on the relationship between intellectual and moral development, in which they presented evidence suggesting that cognitive development may be necessary but not sufficient for moral development and referred to the two models as "different but related" (p 207). They also noted structural similarities between the theories in the two domains (see Kitchener, 1982 and Kitchener & Fischer, 1990 for additional examples), which suggested the kinds of relationships sketched in the third depiction in Figure 23.2, an integrated approach. This approach is bolstered by other empirical evidence indicating that the production of moral behavior requires more than complex cognitive skills. Rest (1986) identified four components that influence whether and how people behave morally: moral sensitivity (awareness of how one's actions affect other people), moral judgment (applying a moral standard, such as fairness to all parties), moral motivation (giving priority to moral over non-moral values such as loyalty or political sensitivity), and moral character (resisting distractions and overcoming frustrations to follow through on a moral plan of action). He noted that these components interact with and affect each other, and that failure to act morally can result from a deficiency in any one component:

> A person who demonstrates great facility at one process is not necessarily adequate in another. We all know people who can render very sophisticated judgments but who never follow through on any course of action; we know people who have tremendous follow-through and tenacity but whose judgment is simple-minded. In short, the psychology of morality cannot be represented as a single variable or process. (p 4)

Similarly, the production of interculturally mature behavior appears to require the self-authored capacities reflected in the cognitive, intrapersonal, and interpersonal domains of development described above.

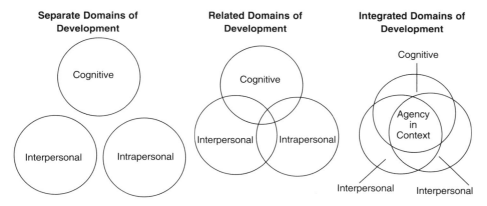

Figure 23.2   Separate, Related and Integrated Perspectives on Domains of Development

Other scholars of human development have also argued that a more holistic approach to educational research and practice is required if we are to be successful in helping students develop the array of skills that will enable them to tackle complex contemporary problems, especially those with an intercultural dimension (Baxter Magolda, 1997, 1999; Jones & McEwen, 2000; Kegan, 1994; Ortiz, 2000; Storti, 1990). Looking at intercultural maturity using a more holistic perspective provides a possible explanation for the ineffectiveness of simpler, more superficial approaches to intercultural competence: perhaps they are ineffective because they fail to consider one or more domains (cognitive, identity, interpersonal) of development. For example, omitting the cognitive component in conflict resolution risks being ineffective with students who see the world in "black and white" terms, and who are thus cognitively unable to analyse an intercultural conflict from the perspective of both parties involved. Similarly, omitting the interpersonal component risks being ineffective with students who decide how to act based on others' expectations, and whose behaviors are thus based on their perceptions of others' views, rather than on the interculturally appropriate criteria that educators may have tried to teach them. The third model depicted in Figure 23.2 illustrates an approach that integrates domains of development, emphasising the overlap (interrelationships) among the three domains of development.

An integrated approach to intercultural competence requires a multi-faceted definition of multicultural competence. Pope and Reynolds (1997) offered one such definition; they identified three groups of multicultural attributes: knowledge (about cultural histories, traditions, values, and practices), skills when interacting with those from other cultures (for examples, skills that reflect one's understanding and respect), and attitudes or awareness that show an appreciation of ways people's actions can reflect their own attitudes, beliefs, values and self-awareness. Similarly, intercultural sensitivity often refers to awareness, knowledge, and appreciation of the "other" where other is identified as a person from a culture different from one's own. This range of attributes illustrates the complexity of the concept. Further, their finding that the factor analysis yielded one factor, not three (Pope & Mueller, 2000; replicated by King and Howard-Hamilton, in press) suggests that these attributes reflect one larger underlying construct rather than three separate sets of attributes.

Examining scholarship on intercultural or multicultural competencies with a holistic lens allows one to identify underlying capacities that may guide (or at least affect) a learner's ability to integrate knowledge, skills, and awareness, and to consistently act in an interculturally mature manner. We argue that the developmental ability that undergirds regarding another culture favorably is the same ability that undergirds one's ability to regard any interpersonal difference favorably. That is, the developmental complexity that allows a learner to understand and accept the general idea of "difference from self" without feeling "threat to self" enables this person to offer positive regard to the "other" across many types of difference, such as race, ethnicity, social class, gender, sexual orientation and religion, among others. While students may be able to learn about cultural differences with or without this foundation in place, they will find it difficult if not impossible to use this knowledge in an intercultural interaction without this foundation. In other words, less complex levels of cognitive and intrapersonal (identity) development may hinder one's ability to use one's intercultural skills.

Our understanding of the interrelationships between and among these dimensions has been informed by many years of collective experience teaching graduate students and researching college student development. In particular, Baxter Magolda's (2001) extensive interviews illuminate these relationships. The following examples were selected to illustrate two aspects of this discussion: a) adults' own descriptions of their self-authorship, and b) how the various elements of self-authorship are interrelated in their descriptions.

Example of a Mature Reflection that Illustrates Self-Authorship.

Evan, a participant in Baxter Magolda's (2001) longitudinal study of young adult development, described what it is like to self-author one's life:

> I told you about this feeling that I had once I became "aware." That is the best word that I can use to describe the difference between how I view my intellectual level now, versus how I felt prior to "noticing" my surroundings and my relationship with the world around me. It was like I woke up one day and things just clicked in my brain and things became clear to me for the first time. The most dramatic difference between before and after was my ability to think, and the subsequent confidence in my abilities and trust in my decisions. I have developed my own approach to solving problems, one which has proven to me to be a good one, and one which has proven to be a good teacher. When it becomes apparent to me that I have relied on this ability, I often try to remember what I did before I began to understand how my mind worked. (Baxter Magolda, 2001, p 121–122)

Evan was refining how his mind worked and simultaneously refining how he thought about himself:

As my personality and sense of self have really begun to develop and become more refined, my ability to direct my life accordingly has become increasingly confident. As I realise who I am, and what is important to me, it becomes easier for me to establish my priorities. Identifying and arranging my priorities has helped me to develop a "road map" for reaching short and long-term goals. Don't get me wrong, I am not trying to predict the future and I by no means know exactly what I want, but I have developed a general idea and use my knowledge as a guide. (Baxter Magolda, 2001, p 122)

Refining who he was also involved refining relationships with others:

I find that I am constantly rebalancing my identity in relationship to others. With my parents' divorce two years ago, and the purchase of my home, I am becoming a central figure in the extended family and have left behind my "youth" oriented identity. At work, my identity continues to grow almost as fast as my personal identity. Since I began with the current crew 2 ½ years ago, I have been titled Asset Manager, Senior Asset Manager, Assistant Vice President, and now Vice President. My identity within the group has changed very much. I owe this to my abilities in being aware of how my mind works and dealing with my personal set of realities. (Baxter Magolda, 2001, p 122–23)

Evan's comments reveal the interweaving of the epistemological, intrapersonal, and interpersonal dimensions of self-authorship. Figuring out how his mind worked answered the epistemological question of "How do I know?" Refining his sense of self answered the intrapersonal question of "Who am I?" This resolution led him to identify and arrange priorities and develop a plan for pursuing them. Evan attributed progress on these two dimensions as central to his evolution in relations with others, both in work and home life. Rebalancing his identity in relation to others answered the interpersonal question of "What kind of relationships do I want to construct?" His experience clearly illustrates the integrated model of development shown in Figure 23.2.

Looking at the interrelationships across dimensions of development can also illustrate the development of intercultural maturity. Lauren, another participant in Baxter Magolda's longitudinal study, worked in various business contexts during her twenties. During this time she was struggling to shift from relying on her parents for direction to making her own choices. By her mid-twenties she had acted on her own internal voice both in career and personal choices. She also reported changes in her relations with others:

I also matured in my relationships because people my age were not plentiful, so I did make some new friends that were older. And, also, different types of friends. In high school and college, everybody I hung around with was like me. You should give everybody an opportunity to be your friend regardless of where they work or where they went to school or if they didn't go to school or if their economic background was different than yours. And I can honestly say that I didn't give the other people a chance [before]. And I don't know why. But coming here opened some doors. You just really realise that everybody's different and everybody's unique in their own way. That doesn't mean that they're less because they don't have a college degree, for example. And I'll tell you, too, I think I'm more appreciative right now because from what I see there are so many other sides and walks of life. Everybody's situation isn't like the situation that I have. So maybe a little bit more open, I guess. (Baxter Magolda, 2001, p 288)

Lauren's experience with people different from herself in age and economic background helped her understand multiple realities. Her shift from external to internal self-definition allowed her to be open to these new realities, leading her to construct relationships with people she would have (and in fact did, as she reports below) avoided.

Example of Reasoning about Intercultural Issues Prior to Self-Authorship.

In contrast to her post-college reasoning, Lauren relied on external authority to define herself during college. Her stance on differences was apparent in this story:

> One thing that living off campus showed me the most is that it's really hard sometimes to live with your friends and be good friends with them at the same time. I lived with my best friend last year, and that might have been a mistake because we fought over trivial matters. But it turned into bigger things. This year, we are in the same house but on different floors. We haven't had a fight yet. It's important to learn that they're your friends; however, you can't eat, breathe, and live twenty-four hours a day with them. (Baxter Magolda, 1992, pp 313–314)

Lauren and her best friend fought about their differences when they lived in the same room, leading Lauren to suspect it might have been a mistake to live together. Lauren's revelation the second year that it was easier to get along with friends when living on different floors or not being together so much conveys that maintaining relationships requires avoiding difference. From the vantage point of external self-definition, others' approval is crucial to maintaining relational bonds. Thus difference threatens relationships. This perspective no doubt contributed to Lauren's focus on building friendships with those who were like her during college. This stance does not reflect the ability to deal effectively with difference – a key aspect of intercultural maturity.

23.3   A holistic approach to integrating identity development theories

There has been a virtual explosion of literature on identity development in the last decade, especially research addressing particular dimensions of identity development, including racial (Helms, 1995; Thompson & Carter, 1997), ethnic (Phinney, 1990), and sexual orientation (Evans & D'Augelli, 1996). While these models tend to focus on culturally distinct differences, they also contain some noteworthy similarities, especially when examined from an holistic, developmental perspective. For example, these theories tend to describe movement from lack of awareness of one's particular identity, through a period of confusion and exploration, to a complex, internally defined perspective on how one's race, ethnicity, or sexual orientation are integrated into one's view of oneself and the world. These common developmental progressions clearly include elements from cognitive, identity, and interpersonal domains. In addition, these theories indicate that intercultural competence requires an internally defined sense of self to avoid feeling threatened by difference (Kegan, 1994). This internal sense of self also supports what is often described as a cognitive skill, acknowledging that people hold multiple perspectives on many issues, including intercultural issues (Baxter Magolda, 2000; Ortiz, 2000), and for defensible reasons (King & Shuford, 1996). In other words, there appear to be overarching theoretical perspectives that in some ways subsume or overlap with theories addressing particular dimensions of identity development.

Juxtaposing these theories with the three dimensions of development yields possibilities for an integrated model of development in general and development in intercultural maturity in particular. For example, at the early phases of development, learners accept authorities' views (epistemological dimension), define themselves through external others (intrapersonal dimension), and act in relationships to acquire approval (interpersonal dimension). In the context of racial, ethnic or sexual orientation identity development, these characteristics are consistent with the lack of awareness of one's particular identity that stems from accepting external (often dominant) perspectives. Dissonance in various aspects of identity development often stems from marginalisation by external others, which can call the validity of external authority into question. As learners struggle through the confusion that comes with realising that all knowledge is not certain and that individuals must consider establishing their own views (epistemological dimension), their reliance on external others for definition (intrapersonal) and seeking others' approval in relationships (interpersonal) is also called into question. The particulars of race, ethnicity, or sexual orientation are intertwined in this confusion and exploration. The need to explore these issues for oneself and move away from accepting authorities' views is consistent with the exploration phases of these layers of identity. In later, more complex phases of development where self-authorship on all three dimensions is achieved, an internally defined perspective on how one's race, ethnicity, or sexual orientation is integrated into one's view of oneself is possible. Table 23.1 summarises these implications for the development of intercultural maturity of students' developmental levels.

We now offer some examples of current research on intercultural maturity that draws on multiple dimensions and illustrates interrelationships among them.

Developmental level	Implications for intercultural maturity
Early	
• Learners accept authority's views (cognitive domain) • Learners define themselves externally through others (intrapersonal domain) • Learners act to acquire approval of others (interpersonal domain)	• Learners exhibit lack of awareness of one's particular identity that stems from accepting external (especially socially-dominant) perspectives
Advanced	
• Learners exhibit self-authorship in all three dimensions	• It is now possible to construct an internally-defined perpective on how one's race , ethnicity and/or sexual orientation is integrated into one's view of oneself.

Table 23.1   How developmental levels affect intercultural maturity

23.3.1   Role of the Cognitive Dimension.

There is cognitive complexity in the presence of diverse worldviews, and complex thinking skills that enable students to understand and accept ambiguity and relativism are necessary. Perry's (1968), Baxter Magolda's (1992), and King and Kitchener's (1994) models all posit that earlier, more simplistic stages of cognitive development involve concrete thinking and a belief in absolute knowledge, whereas later, more complex levels reflect an ability to consider knowledge grounded in context, deriving judgments from personal experiences, evidence from other sources, and from the perspectives of others. This raises the distinct possibility that exposure to culturally different worldviews may lead to greater complexity in thinking, as suggested by King and Shuford (1996) and by Ortiz' (1995) finding that women of colour evidenced higher stages of cognitive development. Intercultural perspective taking, another cognitive task, also has application as students are able to develop the ability to consider both cognitive and affective elements that have an impact on culturally different students (Kappler, 1998; Steglitz, 1993). Further, in a study of intercultural competence in US students abroad, Moore and Ortiz (1999) found that interculturally competent students were critical thinkers who suspended judgment until the evidence was in, and who included a diverse range of knowledge in what they considered as evidence. These findings suggest that there are strong reasons to continue to explore the role of cognitive development in various aspects of intercultural maturity.

23.3.2   Role of the Identity and Interpersonal Dimensions.

The second and third dimensions of intercultural competence involve identity development and the ability to interact effectively with others. Several ethnic identity models have attended to the intersection of race and ethnicity in the development of ego identity (Cross, 1991; Helms, 1995; Phinney, 1992). In these models, individuals at more complex stages of development have considered and integrated their ethnicity into a sense of self that is maintained through interactions with diverse others and in participation in majority-defined and -dominated society. In a campus community where culture is expressed, opportunities for learning are enhanced by students who are successful at integrating their ethnicity into their identity (Ortiz, 1997). For example, Howard-Hamilton (2000) showed how a student's level of racial identity development could affect his or her response to and performance on class assignments that call for analysis of issues that involve racial dynamics. This example, along with the experience of Christine, reported above (King and Baxter Magolda, 1996), illustrates the central role of identity development in achieving intercultural maturity. Since cognitive development is given so much attention as an intended college outcome, research exploring the role of these other dimensions of development on intercultural maturity (or even on cognitive development itself) could provide extremely useful information to those who might not be attuned to the apparent roles of these other aspects of development. An example of this is provided by Derryberry and Thoma (2000), who looked at the relationship between college students' moral development and the quality of their friendships. They found that students with higher scores on moral judgment:

> viewed the diversity of college populations in a positive light, were more open to forming friendships in college, were more likely to enter into a range of activities with their college friends, and were more likely to discuss a range of topics than their peers with lower moral reasoning scores. (p 16)

In other words, the quality of one's friendships (the interpersonal domain) may mediate not only one's use of principled moral reasoning, but also one's openness to diversity experiences. These examples all show the value of a broader theoretical perspective that frames separate dimensions of development in a way that illustrates their interconnectedness.

In this discussion, we have contrasted three approaches to conceptualising and researching domains of development, separate domains, related domains, and integrated domains. Table 23.2 notes implicit theoretical assumptions underlying each approach, along with a description of research strategies used for each approach to investigate intercultural understanding. These strategies may be useful to those who are attempting to document the effectiveness and/or impact of existing campus programme and practices, or of new initiatives designed to promote intercultural maturity.

	Separate domains	Related domains	Integrated domains
Implicit Theoretical Assumptions	There are separate domains of development informed by theories that focus on one domain. Development in each domain evolves independently of development in the others, and is affected by different . sets of educational factors.	There are separate domains of development informed by theories that focus on one domain. However, they may be interrelated, and the extent of these relationships can be examined empirically.	Although the separate domains are articulated as specific to a given aspect of development, the domains share a common foundation in principles of maturity. Further, these common elements and the interrelationships across models can illuminate key insights into educational outcomes.
Research Strategy for Studying Intercultural Understanding	Examine domains of development separately, typically focusing on only one domain (eg, cognitive) and the factors that affect development in this domain (eg, greater cognitive complexity or improvement of perspective-taking skills among students in diversity courses).	Assess development independently across domains (eg, cognitive and identity), and note relationships found. Examine factors affecting development that may be common to both (eg, participation in campus diversity programming).	Assess development both within and across the three domains, with an eye toward interdependent aspects of development Examine factors affecting integration of the three domains (eg, emphasising self as central to knowledge construction).

Table 23.2   Separate, related and integrated perspectives on domains of development

23.4   Educational Implications

We have described a model of intercultural maturity that integrates three major domains of development (cognitive, intrapersonal and interpersonal), and have suggested that an integrative model provides a much more powerful tool for understanding and promoting development than do models that take a "separate" or "related" approach. Further, we have emphasised that the development of intercultural maturity unfolds gradually and in a manner that reflects an individual's maturity in each of the three dimensions. How are these insights reflected in educational practices? Next, we offer several resources that exemplify this approach.

In an exceptionally well-crafted article on multicultural education, Ortiz and Rhoads (2000) proposed a framework for multicultural education that illustrates the power and potential of an integrative, developmental approach. They outline a series of five elements (which they refer to as steps) that are part of an individual's journey toward what we have called intercultural maturity. These are: understanding culture; learning about other cultures; recognising and deconstructing white culture; recognising the legitimacy of other cultures; and developing a multicultural outlook. For each, they list a "cognitive goal" that reflects a more complex understanding of the element; for the first, the goal is "to develop a complex understanding of culture (culture shapes people's lives and people shape culture)" (p. 85). These goals also reflect substantive changes in the ways individuals come to understand ("make meaning") of the notion of culture and how they and others experience both their own and others' cultures. In addition, Ortiz and Rhoads chart beginning and ending ways students might frame the problems being addressed for each element, and discuss educational activities designed to facilitate students' understanding of each of the elements. They also argue that an important educational goal is enthusiasm for learning in general and cultural learning in particular. Many students (especially majority White students) report being afraid to discuss diversity issues, either not feeling comfortable with the language of the topic, or afraid that their comments will be misunderstood and labeled racist; both discourage motivation for cultural learning. This model explicitly starts at a lower threshold of risk to encourage (not shut off) the conversation.

Fernandez (2002) adapted the Ortiz and Rhoads (2000) framework to examine the development of intercultural competence. She looked specifically at students' experiences with culture shock, exploring how these could be used to enhance self-authorship. For each of five developmental steps, she noted specific self-authorship goals, cognitive dissonance caused by culture shock, and the role of the guide in providing support for students trying to understand (make meaning of) their experiences. This framework provides a rich conceptual base for diversity educators who help students navigate cultural immersion experiences to become interculturally mature.

Zúñiga (2003) has worked extensively with intergroup dialogue programmes on college campuses to promote student interaction and understanding among students from different social backgrounds. This approach "combines experiential learning and participatory methods with critical analyses of the social realities that shape relationships between social groups in our society" (p 3). Students from different social identity groups that have a history of conflict meet for sustained face-to-face facilitated conversations. Such groups include men and women; White people, biracial/multi-racial/ethnic people, and people of colour; Blacks, Latinos and Native Americans; lesbians, gay men, bisexual and heterosexual people; working, middle and upper socio-economic class; and, Christians, Muslims and Jews. The dialogues are structured to explore students' own experiences and assumptions as the basis for enabling them to understand more fully the idea of socially constructed group distinctions, and how these are played out in intergroup interactions in the US. As Zúñiga explains:

> By encouraging direct encounter and exchange about contentious issues, especially those associated with issues of social identity and social stratification, the intergroup dialogues invite students to actively explore the meanings of singular (as men or women), or intersecting social identities (as men of colour or white men, as white women or women of colour) and to examine the dynamics of privilege and oppression shaping the relationship between social groups in our society. (p 4)

The class opens by establishing the foundations for dialogue, including introductions and guidelines (eg, no personal attacks, respect confidentiality). At the second stage, the purpose is to develop a shared vocabulary around issues of social identities and social stratification, and then to introduce and explore concepts such as prejudice, in/out group dynamics, discrimination, and privilege, and how each affects intergroup relationships. Not until the third stage are "hot topics" the focus of the dialogue, difficult or controversial issues such as separation/self-segregation on campus, racism on campus. Facilitators encourage students to voice their concerns and raise their questions.

They support the process by posing questions, probing for deeper levels of thinking and feeling, and by inviting participants to fully explore the disagreements and conflicts that ensue in the conversation. To encourage collective thinking and questioning, facilitators invite participants to respond to what others are saying and to build on each other's comments and experiences. In closing each topic, participants are asked to identify questions to ponder or specific actions that can be taken to explore or address a particular issue on campus. (p 16)

The last stage is designed to prepare students for post-dialogue experiences, especially for action planning and for building alliances.

The effects of participation in these dialogues are impressive (see Hurtado, 2001 and Stephan and Stephan, 2001 for details of these studies):

...dialogue participation is linked with positive effects on cognitive outcomes such as knowledge about other groups and discrimination in society, stereotype and prejudice reduction, the development of complex thinking, social awareness of self and others in systems of inequality, and increased understanding about the causes of conflict between social groups. Dialogue participation is also found to reduce anxiety about intergroup contact, and to enhance skills related to communication across differences, conflict exploration, comfort dealing with diversity, and perspective taking. Finally, participation in intergroup dialogues, as a participant or a student facilitator, seems to promote more active involvement in social justice work. (Zúñiga, in press, p 18)

These outcomes are noteworthy not only for diversity education, but as indices of the kinds of broader collegiate outcomes mentioned in the AAC&U (1998) Statement of Liberal Learning noted above. In addition, the three approaches summarised here (Fernandez, 2002; Ortiz and Rhoads, 2000; Zúñiga, in press) are consistent with the calls made by Baxter Magolda (2001, in press) for educators to acknowledge the central role of the self in knowledge construction, identity development, and in building relationships with others. In addition to these examples, Baxter Magolda (2003) describes three other existing programmes in both curricular and co-curricular settings that are designed in ways that foster self-authorship. In each case, students are expected and encouraged to take responsibility for their learning and their behaviors, they are expected to become more knowledgeable about themselves and the world around them, and to develop internal compasses to guide their choices and behaviors, turning to others for information and advice, but taking responsibility for their own decisions and actions. Clearly, being able to act in each of these ways requires development in all three developmental domains noted above (the cognitive, intrapersonal and interpersonal domains). Designing educational programmes that take all three of these dimensions into account allows for a more complete approach to the development of complex outcomes such as intercultural maturity.

23.5   Conclusion

In this paper we have introduced an integrated model of development that we think has great potential for better understanding the nature of intercultural maturity and why efforts to promote it have met with mixed success. We encourage other researchers who are interested in examining intercultural maturity from an integrated perspective to conduct studies that will address the questions raised in the research agenda presented above. This is an ambitious undertaking, an agenda that not only presents interesting conceptual and methodological challenges, but that has taken on an urgency in light of recent national and international events. The need to address intercultural issues personally and with more than one's intellect is not a new insight; in fact, it was captured eloquently in 1947 by Aldous Huxley:

> …proverbs are always platitudes until you have experienced the truth of them. The newly arrested thief knows that honesty is the best policy with an intensity of conviction which the rest of us can never experience. And to realise that it takes all sorts to make a world one must have seen a certain number of the sorts with one's own eyes. There is all the difference in the world between believing academically, with the intellect, and believing personally, intimately, with the whole living self. [Jesting Pilate, 207] [Quoted by Storti, 1990, p 53]

"Believing academically" may be a good first step in the development of intercultural maturity. We propose this integrated framework and identify educational programmes that exemplify its major components as steps toward the end of helping students to gain the maturity to believe personally and "with the whole living self."

References

Association of American Colleges and Universities (1998). Statement on Liberal Learning. Retrieved 8/20/02, www.aacu.org/about/mission

Baxter Magolda, MB (1992). *Knowing and reasoning in college: Gender-related patterns in students' intellectual development*. San Francisco: Jossey-Bass.

Baxter Magolda, M (1997). Facilitating meaningful dialogues about race. *About Campus*, **2**(5), 14–18.

Baxter Magolda, M (1999). *Creating contexts for learning and self-authorship: Constructive-developmental pedagogy*. Nashville, Tennessee: Vanderbilt University Press.

Baxter Magolda, MB (2000). Teaching to promote holistic learning and development. In Baxter Magolda, MB (Ed), Teaching to promote intellectual and personal maturity: Incorporating students' worldviews and identities into the learning process, **82**, 88–98. *New Directions for Teaching and Learning*. San Francisco: Jossey-Bass.

Baxter Magolda, MB (2001). *Journeys into adulthood: Narratives for transforming higher education to promote self-understanding*. Sterling, VA: Stylus Publishing.

Baxter Magolda, MB (in press). Identity and learning: Student affairs' role in transforming higher education. Journal of College Student Development.

Bikson, TK and Law, SA (1994). *Global Preparedness and Human Resources: College and Corporate Perspectives*. Santa Monica, CA: RAND Corporation.

Bowen, H (1980). *Investment in learning: The individual and social value of American h_ner education*. San Francisco: Jossey-Bass, Publishers.

Bok, DC (1986). *Higher learning*. Cambridge MA: Harvard University Press.

Cross, WEJ (1991). *Shades of Black: Diversity in African-American identities*. Philadelphia: Temple University Press.

Derryberry, P and Thoma, S (2000). The friendship effect: Its role in the development of moral thinking in students. *About Campus*, **5**(2), 13–18.

Evans, NJ and DíAugelli, AR (1996). Lesbians, gay men, and bisexual people in college. In Savin-Williams, RC and Cohen, KM (Eds), *The lives of lesbians, gays, and bisexuals: Children to adults*, pp 201–226. Fort Worth, TX: Harcourt Brace.

Fernandez, E (2002). Framing incidents of culture shock: A growth process for intercultural maturity. Unpublished paper, University of Michigan. Available from the author, Center for the Study of Higher and Postsecondary Education, 2117 Education Building, 610 East University Avenue, Ann Arbor, MI 49109.

Fortune 500 corporations file brief in support of diversity in higher education. (2000, October 16). [On-line press release]. Available at: http://www.umich.edu/~urel/admissions/releases/fortune.html

Helms, JE (1995). An update of Helms' white and people of colour racial identity models. In Ponterotto, JG, Casas, JM, Suzuki, LA, and Alexander, CM (Eds), *Handbook of multicultural counselling*. Thousand Oaks, CA: Sage.

Holcomb-McCoy, CC and Myers, JE (1999). Multicultural competence and counselor training: A national survey. *Journal of Counseling and Development*, **77**, 294–302.

Howard-Hamilton, MF (2000). Creating a culturally responsive learning environment for African American students. In Baxter Magolda, MB (Ed), Teaching to promote intellectual and personal maturity: Incorporating students' worldviews and identities into the learning process. *New Directions for Teaching and Learning*, **82**, 45–53. San Francisco: Jossey-Bass

Howard-Hamilton, MF, Richardson, S and Shuford, BC (1998). Promoting multicultural education: A holistic approach. *College Student Affairs Journal*, **18**(1), 5–17.

Hurtado, S (2001). Research and evaluation on intergroup dialogues. In Schoem, D and Hurtado, S (Eds), *Intergroup dialogue: Deliberative democracy in school, college, community and workplace*, pp 22–36. Ann Arbor: The University of Michigan Press.

Jones, SR and McEwen, MK (2000). A conceptual model of multiple dimensions of identity. *Journal of College Student Development*, **41**(4) 405–414.

Kappler, BJ (1998). Refining Intercultural Perspective-Taking. Unpublished doctoral dissertation, University of Minnesota, Minneapolis.

Kegan, R (1994). *In over our heads: The mental demands of modern life*. Cambridge, MA: Harvard University Press.

King, PM and Baxter Magolda, MB (1996). A developmental perspective on learning. *Journal of College Student Development*, **37**(2), 163–173.

King, PM& Howard-Hamilton, MF (in press). An assessment of multicultural competence. NASPA Journal.

King, PM, and Kitchener, KS (1994). *Developing reflective judgment*. San Francisco: Jossey-Bass,.

King, PM and Shuford, BC (1996). A multicultural view is a more cognitively complex view: Cognitive development and multicultural education. *American Behavioral Scientist*, **40**(2), 153–164.

Kitchener, KS (1982). Human development and the college campus: Sequences and tasks. In Hanson, GR (Ed), Measuring student development. *New Directions for Student Services*, **20**, 17–45.

Kitchener, KS and Fischer, KW (1990). A skill approach to the development of reflective thinking. In Kuhn, D (Ed), *Contributions to human development: Developmental perspectives on teaching and learning*, 21 Basel, Switzerland: Karger.

Levine, A and Cureton, JS (1998). *When hope and fear collide*. San Francisco: Jossey-Bass.

Mentkowski, M and Associates (2000). *Learning that lasts: Integrating learning, development, and performance in college and beyond*. San Francisco: Jossey-Bass.

Moore, KA, and Ortiz, AM (1999). The Intercultural Competence Project: Site Visit and Focus Group Report. A Report to the Institute on the International Education of Students. Michigan State University.

Ortiz, AM (1995). Promoting Racial Understanding: A Study of Educational and Developmental Interventions. Paper presented at the annual meeting of the Association for the Study of Higher Education in Orlando, FL, November 1995.

Ortiz, AM (1997). Defining Oneself in a Multicultural World: Ethnic Identity in College Students. Unpublished doctoral dissertation, University of California Los Angeles.

Ortiz, AM (2000). Expressing cultural identity in the learning community: Opportunities and challenges. In Baxter Magolda, MB (Ed), Teaching to promote intellectual and personal maturity: Incorporating students' worldviews and identities into the learning process. *New Directions for Teaching and Learning,*pp 67–79. San Francisco: Jossey-Bass.

Ortiz, AM and Rhoads, RA (2000). Deconstructing whiteness as part of a multicultural educational framework: From theory to practice. *Journal of College Student Development,* **41**(1) 81–93.

Perry, WG (1968). *Forms of Intellectual and Ethical Development in the College Years: A Scheme.* New York: Rinehart and Winston, Inc.

Pettigrew, TF (1998). Intergroup contact theory. *Annual Review of Psychology,* **49**, 65–85.

Phinney, JS (1990). Ethnic identity in adolescents and adults: Review of research. *Psychological Bulletin,* **108** (3), 499–514.

Phinney, JS (1992). The Multigroup Ethnic Identity Measure: A New Scale for Use with Diverse Groups. *Journal of Adolescent Research,* 7(2), 156–176.

Pope, RL and Reynolds, AL (1997). Student affairs core competencies: Integrating multicultural awareness, knowledge, and skills. *Journal of College Student Development,* 38, 266–277.

Pope, RL and Mueller, JA (2000). Development and initial validation of the Multicultural Competence in Students Affairs-Preliminary 2 Scale. *Journal of College Student Development,* **41** (6), 599–607.

Rest, JR (1986). *Moral development: Advances in research and theory.* New York: Praeger

Rosovsky, H (1990). *The university: An owner's manual.* New York: WW Norton & Company, Inc.

Stephan, W and Stephan, CW (2001). *Improving intergroup relations.* Thousand Oaks, CA: Sage.

Storti, C (1990). *The art of crossing cultures.* Yarmouth, ME: Intercultural Press.

Steglitz, I (1993). Intercultural Perspective-Taking: The Impact of Study Abroad. Unpublished doctoral dissertation, University of Minnesota, Minneapolis.

Talbot, DM, and Kocarek, C (1997). Student affairs graduate faculty members' knowledge, comfort, and behaviors regarding issues of diversity. *Journal of College Student Development,* 38, 278–287.

Thompson, CE, and Carter RT (1997). *Racial identity theory: Applications to individual, group, and organizational interventions.* Mahway, NJ: Lawrence Erlbaum Chapter 2, 15–32.

Zúñiga, Ximena (in press). Bridging differences through intergroup dialogue. About Campus.

24 Meeting the challenge of diversity: a cautionary tale about learning styles

Linda Price[1] and John TE Richardson
The Open University

24.1 Introduction

Learning styles are a popular notion that has been explored in educational development as a means of addressing the challenges of student diversity in learning. Learning styles research featured throughout the 1970s, 1980s and 1990s as a theme for understanding and improving learning, particularly in computer-based instruction. As individuals, students have different learning traits, capabilities and motivations, and the nature of their thinking and processing while carrying out a particular task may vary. These individual differences present challenges in educating a student population with such diverse qualities. In order to address some of these issues, educators have explored learning styles to examine some of the variations in learning.

More recently, learning styles have re-emerged as a popular theme in educational web developments as a means of modelling individualised learning based on learning objects that are repackaged to match the specific learners' needs. Within the individual differences theme, some of these innovations have been technological implementations based on learning styles. However, the fundamental question remains: do learning styles provide useful information on student learning that can help improve instructional materials so as to accommodate diversity in learning? We address this question by reviewing the learning styles literature and describing a naturalistic study and two experimental studies in which a learning style inventory was used.

24.2 Learning styles

Research on learning styles began in the early 20th century, but its popularity rose during the 1960s and 1970s (Curry, 1983; Riding and Cheema, 1991). Different perspectives have been reported in the learning styles literature that are neither coherent nor consistent (Curry, 1983; Grigorenko and Sternberg, 1995; Lewis, 1976; Messick, 1987; Miller, 1987; Riding, 1998; Riding and Cheema, 1991). Reviewing the literature is complicated by the fact that researchers use 'learning style' interchangeably with other terms such as 'cognitive control' and 'cognitive style'. For the purposes of this paper, 'learning styles' will encompass all of these terms.

'Learning style' is often used as a metaphor for the range of individual differences that exist in human learning. Jonassen and Grabowski (1993) described learning style as 'applied cognitive styles, removed one more level from pure processing ability' (p 233). Curry (1983) provided a model that illustrates how the different perspectives integrate (see Figure 24.1). She grouped the different perspectives into three 'layers': 'instructional preference', 'information processing style' and 'cognitive personality style'. Curry likened these to progressively deeper layers of an onion, in which the outer layer was most influenced by the environment and the inner layer was the least influenced by the environment. Thus, the inner layer of cognitive personality style is more stable, whereas the outer layer of instructional preference is more transient. Curry's model is useful as a pragmatic way of categorising the different perspectives on learning styles in terms of the degree to which they can be influenced and changed.

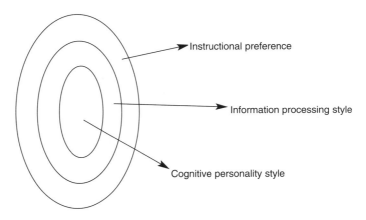

Figure 24.1   Curry's (1983, p. 19) onion model of learning styles

Vermunt's (1998) integrated model (see Figure 24.2) encompasses other aspects of existing research to demonstrate the integration of constructive learning processes that could then be measured by a single instrument, the Inventory of Learning Styles. These processes represent learning styles in different ways. Mental learning models and learning orientations are assumed to be relatively stable, and so these appear to belong to the inner layer of Curry's scheme; in contrast, students' choice of processing and regulating strategies is contextually determined, and so these belong to the outer layers of Curry's scheme. Vermunt's notion of learning style thus serves as an overarching construct that appears to straddle all three of the layers in Curry's onion model (Richardson, 2000, p 162).

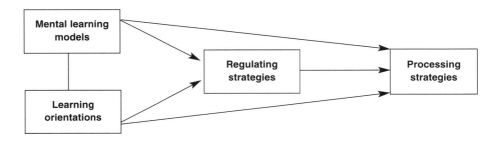

Figure 24.2   Vermunt's (1998, p. 153) model of learning styles

Riding is another researcher who has attempted to provide a model that encompasses previously researched styles (Rayner and Riding, 1997; Riding, 1998; Riding and Cheema, 1991; Riding and Rayner, 1997). Riding's Cognitive Style Analysis (CSA) takes an integrated approach incorporating fundamental elements of style in the development of a learning style model (see Rayner and Riding, 1997; Riding and Cheema, 1991). The Verbal-Imager scale reflects Curry's information-processing style and relates to the processing of external stimuli. The Wholist-Analytic scale, based on Witkin et al's (1977) field-independence style, reflects internal cognitive processing (Riding and Cheema, 1991), and it maps onto Curry's cognitive personality style. This model is useful for examining the different 'layers' in styles of learning.

24.3 Research issues relating to learning styles

Some learning style inventories do not test skill, ability or preferred processing tendency but focus on how the individual thinks they prefer to learn (Jonassen and Grabowski, 1993). The primary use of these results is as a guide for instruction and evaluation. However, the validity of these learning style inventories is based on the assumption that learners can accurately and consistently reflect (a) how they process external stimuli and (b) what their internal cognitive processes are.

Argyris (1976) argued that there was a difference between what an individual reports they are doing (their 'espoused theory') and what they are actually doing (their 'theory in use'). Learning style inventories based on self reports place more reliance on 'espoused theory' than on 'theory in use'. As a research tool, the validity of learning style inventories based on self reports is controversial (Grasha, 1984; Jonassen and Grabowski, 1993). Squires (1981) argued that the lack of concurrent instrument validity may not be due to instrument error but to poor construct definition: constructs that supposedly measure the same construct may actually be measuring different constructs.

There are also different perspectives on the stability of learning styles. Schmeck (1983) conceived learning styles as applied cognitive styles, relatively consistent predispositions to adopt particular learning strategies across different tasks and domains. Witkin et al (1977) also considered learning styles to be relatively stable. However, other researchers have obtained results suggesting that learning styles change over time (Geiger and Pinto, 1991; Goldstein and Chance, 1965; Kolb, 1981; Pinto, Marshall and Boyle, 1994). Moreover, Squires (1981) argued that many studies supporting claims of stability had been conducted on undergraduate students and that their findings might not generalise to the wider population. Laurillard (1978) claimed that learning processes might vary with the task, the materials, the modality of presentation and the environment. Both Squires (1981) and Messick (1987) viewed learning styles as strategies that could be attuned to different tasks and situations.

The stability or variability of learning styles may depend on how they are defined and measured (eg, self reports versus performance in laboratory situations) and their theoretical basis. Grigorenko and Sternberg (1995) distinguished three approaches to measuring learning styles: cognition-centred, personality-centred and activity-centred. Self-report inventories that are based upon personality approaches to learning may often be examining general trends or approaches to learning as opposed to obesvations of behaviour in a specific learning task. In many cases, however, it is simply unclear whether particular instruments are supposed to be measuring general or task-specific variations in learning.

In short, there are reliability, validity, consistency and stability issues to be considered when interpreting results obtained with different measures of learning style. Different learning style inventories may be measuring different layers or levels of a person's approach to learning. In addition, the theoretical basis of different inventories may influence their appropriateness or effectiveness as tools for investigating and understanding variations in learning. Inventories designed to measure general orientations to learning may not be suitable for investigating an individual's approach to learning on a specific task. Certainly, more research is needed before we can be confident that measures of learning style can inform developments in education.

24.4   Overview of the studies

The Open University was founded in 1969 to provide degree programmes by distance learning throughout the UK. It accepts applicants over the normal minimum age of 18 without imposing any formal entrance requirements, subject only to limitations of numbers on specific courses. Originally, nearly all its courses were delivered by specially prepared correspondence materials combined with television and radio broadcasts, video and audio recordings, tutorial support at a local level and (in some cases) week-long residential schools. Nevertheless, in recent years, the Open University has made increasing use of computer-based support, particularly CD-ROMs, dedicated websites and conferencing links.

Honey and Mumford's (1992) Learning Styles Questionnaire (LSQ) was used to examine the relationship between learning style and performance and the relationship between learning style and preference for different instructional representations in computing courses. Study 1 examined whether the LSQ was useful in predicting (a) preference for study mode and (b) attainment in two different modes of delivery of an Open University course in computing: one mode was a traditional (correspondence-based) course supported by other media; the other was an Internet version of the course. Study 2 examined whether the LSQ was useful in predicting students' preferences among instructional representations, and Study 3 examined whether the LSQ was useful in predicting performance, study processes or recall processes when participants were exposed to different representations. The three studies had additional aims, but this paper is concerned only with the value of learning styles in designing educational programmes.

24.5   Study 1

24.5.1   Method

In this study, the LSQ was used to assess whether it was useful in predicting preference for study mode and academic performance. The students were volunteers who were studying an Open University introductory computing course of 9 months' duration. As well as books and other printed items, material on floppy disks was mailed to students at the start of the course.

In the conventional mode of delivery, tutorial support was provided by telephone (or by mail) on a one-to-one basis or through face-to-face group sessions at a regional centre. Students were required to complete assignments throughout the course and to mail them to their tutors. The tutors marked the assignments and forwarded them to the University for administrative handling before they were returned to the students for feedback. In the electronic mode of delivery, tutorial support was provided by electronic mail on a one-to-one basis and through a computer conference on a group basis. Students were also able to contact each other for peer group support. Assignments were submitted electronically through the University to the tutors, who marked and returned them through an electronic assignment handling system.

We shall refer to these two modes of delivery as Mode A and Mode B, respectively. In opting for Mode A or Mode B, it can be assumed that the students were expressing a preference between the two modes of delivery. Samples of students who had registered for the two modes were invited to participate in this study, and Table 24.1 provides basic information concerning the students who agreed to do so. Clearly, the two groups were broadly similar to one another.

		Mode A (conventional)	Mode B (internet)
Sampled students		200	150
Number of respondents		73	59
Response rate		37%	39%
Gender:	female	13 (18%)	16 (27%)
	male	60 (82%)	43 (73%)
Age:	mean	38	38
	standard deviation	8.0	7.2
	minimum	26	22
	maximum	63	55

Table 24.1   Study 1: response rates and student characteristics

At the beginning of the course, the students were asked to complete the LSQ; this was sent by post to students in Mode A and by electronic mail to students in Mode B. The LSQ is intended to measure the respondents' strength of preference for each of four learning styles:

- Activists like new experiences and immediate tasks, thrive on challenge, and are bored by implementation. They learn by doing.

- Reflectors review experiences, analyse thoroughly before concluding, and can postpone decision making. They learn through reflection.

- Theorists are assimilators, tidy and rational, adapting observations into theories. They learn from systems, models, and concepts.

- Pragmatists are 'ideas people', who put theories into practice, like decision making, and problem solving. They learn by practical application of theory.

The LSQ contains 20 statements for each of the four learning styles, and respondents indicate whether they agree or disagree with each statement. The number of 'agree' responses indicates the strength of preference for each learning style, yielding a profile across the four learning styles. The instrument takes about 10 – 15 minutes to complete and about 5 minutes to score, making it ideal for use either electronically or by post.

Students were required to complete eight assignments during the course, yielding an average continuous assessment score. They were also required to take an unseen examination at a regional assessment centre, and the final score for the course was a simple average of the continuous assessment score and the examination score. For further information concerning this study, see Carswell, Thomas, Petre, Price and Richards (2000).

	Mode A conventional (n = 73)	Mode B internet (n = 59)
Activists		
very strong preference	7 (10%)	7 (12%)
strong preference	7 (10%)	7 (12%)
moderate preference	31 (42%)	29 (49%)
low preference	21 (29%)	14 (24%)
very low preference	7 (10%)	2 (3%)
Reflectors		
very strong preference	13 (18%)	13 (22%)
strong preference	19 (26%)	14 (24%)
moderate preference	24 (33%)	13 (22%)
low preference	9 (13%)	11 (19%)
very low preference	8 (11%)	8 (14%)
Theorists		
very strong preference	15 (20%)	6 (10%)
strong preference	13 (18%)	13 (22%)
moderate preference	29 (40%)	17 (29%)
low preference11	(15%)	21 (36%)
very low preference	5 (7%)	2 (3%)
Pragmatists		
very strong preference	6 (8%)	5 (8%)
strong preference	15 (20%)	10 (17%)
moderate preference	24 (33%	)28 (47%)
low preference	17 (23%)	13 (22%)
very low preference	11 (15%)	3 (5%)

Table 24.2   Study 1: LSQ scores in conventional and internet students

24.5.2 Results and discussion

Table 24.2 shows the scores on the LSQ obtained by the respondents who were following the two modes of course delivery. Clearly, the distributions of the two groups are very similar to one another, and so scores on the LSQ did not predict preference for one mode or the other.

Table 24.3 shows the academic performance of the students following the two modes of course delivery. The scores obtained by the students in the two samples were very similar both to one another and to those obtained by the populations of all students taking the course. There was no significant difference between the students following the two modes of course delivery.

Table 24.4 shows the correlation coefficients between the students' overall scores and their scores on the four dimensions of the LSQ. Scores on pragmatism were positively related to academic performance in Mode A but not in Mode B. It might have been predicted, on the

	Study groups		Populations	
	Mode A conventional (n = 73)	**Mode B internet** (n = 59)	**Mode A conventional** (n = 2458)	**Mode B internet** (n = 223)
Coursework	82.4	84.1	83.4	83.2
Examination	64.4	69.9	67.89	68.7
Overall	73.39	77.0	75.6	76.0

Table 24.3   Study 1: mean academic performance (%) in study groups and populations

	Activist	Reflector	Pragmatist	Theorist
Mode A conventional (n = 65)	-0.13	0.08	0.33**	0.18
Mode B internet (n = 53)	-0.06	0.16	0.19	0.21

**p < .01

Table 24.4   Study 1: correlations between LSQ scores and overall academic performance

contrary, that pragmatists (and perhaps activists, too) would have performed better in Mode B, where a more assertive and activity-based form of communication was required. Otherwise, no correlations were significant, and so scores on the LSQ did not consistently predict attainment.

24.6   Study 2

24.6.1   Method

In Study 1, the LSQ did not provide consistent information in predicting either preference for a particular instructional model or the subsequent level of performance on a course. Study 2 was concerned with its value in predicting preference for representations of instructional materials.

The participants were 12 students and 12 academic staff; each group contained six men and six women. The students were recruited from among those studying an introductory course in computing with the Open University who lived within a 60-mile radius of the Milton Keynes campus. They were selected on a first-come, first-served basis and received an honorarium for their participation. The academic staff were volunteers from the Open University's computing department who were experienced in writing distance-learning materials. Table 24.5 shows the age distributions of the two groups of participants; the students showed a wide age range but, not surprisingly, tended to be younger than the academic staff.

The participants were asked to complete the LSQ before arriving at the test session. They were then asked to complete the Group Embedded Figures Test (GEFT), a measure of field independence, and Riding's (1998) CSA. Finally, they were asked to carry out a card-sorting technique (Rugg and McGeorge, 1997) to investigate their preferences among four different representations of four different topics in computing. The scoring scheme shown in Table 24.6 was used to convert their sorting categories into a single measure of their preference for visual representations.

		Age group					
	Gender	Under 25	25-29	30-39	40-49	50-59	60-64
Students	Female	0	2	2	2	0	0
	Male	3	0	2	0	1	0
	Total	3	2	4	2	1	0
Staff	Female	0	0	2	3	1	0
	Male	0	0	1	2	2	1
	Total	0	0	3	5	3	1

Table 24.5   Study 2:: gender and age distributions of participants

Representation type	Weighting
Text alone	1
Structured text (text with tables or bullet points)	2
Mixed (text with tables or bullet points and visual components)	3
Visual (text with visual components)	4

Table 24.6   Study 2: weightings given to preferences for representations: gender and age
distributions of participants

Measure	Students (n = 12)	Staff (n = 10)	Overall (n = 22)
Activist	0.05	0.11	0.16
Reflector	-0.52	0.05	-0.25
Theorist	-0.57	0.16	-0.21
Pragmatist	-0.30	-0.03	-0.12
Field independence	0.08	-0.10	-0.01
Wholist-analyst	-0.04	-0.02	0.00
Verbal-imager	0.07	0.23	0.19

Table 24.7   Study 2: correlations between preference for visual representation and
measures of learning style

24.6.2   Results and discussion

Table 24.7 shows the correlation coefficients between the preference for visual representations
and the other measures of individual differences. None of these correlations coefficients was
statistically significant. This is partly because of the small size of the relevant samples, but it
should be noted that none of the predictor variables showed a relationship that was
consistent between the two groups of participants. Neither the LSQ nor any of the other
instruments for measuring learning styles predicted a preference for particular kinds of
instructional material.

24.7   Study 3

24.7.1 Method

This study was concerned with whether the LSQ was useful in predicting performance when participants studied instructional materials containing different types of visual representation. The participants were 22 students who were taking an introductory course in computing with the Open University. There were 11 men and 11 women, and their ages ranged from 18 to 64.

As in Study 2, the participants completed the LSQ, the CSA and the GEFT. They were then given instructional materials that covered introductory aspects of concurrency. This topic relates to how two or more computing processes run in parallel and was chosen because it is known to be difficult for students of computing. After reading the materials, they were given tests of verbatim, recall and transfer knowledge, following Mayer's (1989) procedures. The verbatim test was a quick 2 minute memory test; in the recall test, students were asked to write down everything they could remember; and the transfer test contained specific questions that examined the participants' ability to apply knowledge. Finally, the participants completed a questionnaire on their mental processes during the study activity and the recall activity.

24.7.2   Results and discussion

Table 24.8 shows the correlation coefficients between the participants' overall test scores and the other measures of individual differences. None of the relationships involving dimensions of the LSQ were statistically significant. The same was true of their scores on the GEFT. However, there was a significant positive relationship between the participants' scores on the retention test and on the Verbal-Imager dimension of the CSA, which measures how an individual prefers to process information. This is probably unsurprising, since the test materials used in this study incorporated different types of visual representation, and so in this case the nature of the task was closely attuned to the nature of the process that was being measured.

Table 24.8 also shows the correlation coefficients between the number of processes reported during the study and recall phases and the other measures of individual differences. None of the relationships were statistically significant. In short, the LSQ did not prove useful in predicting test performance, study processes or recall processes. Indeed, the only measure of learning style that showed such a correlation was the Verbal-Imager dimension of the CSA.

Measure	Performance	Study processes	Recall processes
Activist	0.20	-0.17	-0.09
Reflector	-0.22	0.07	0.12
Theorist	0.25	0.21	0.21
Pragmatist	0.40	0.39	0.20
Field independence	0.20	-0.21	-0.17
Verbal-imager	0.44*	0.22	0.05
Wholist-analytic	0.19	0.07	0.22

*p < .05

Table 24.8   Study 3: correlations between academic performance, number of study processes, number of recall processes and measures of learning style

24.9   Concluding discussion

In the three studies that we have described, Honey and Mumford's (1992) LSQ was not found to be useful in predicting academic performance, preference for particular instructional modes, preference for particular representations, study processes or recall processes. A similar message emerged in the case of the GEFT as an index of field independence and in the case of the CSA. Richardson (1998) argued in a similar manner that field independence was not a useful concept for understanding student autonomy or for predicting academic attainment.

Study 1 used the LSQ to predict general trends towards study in an entire course. Study 2 examined the use of the LSQ to examine learning preferences in a specific context. Study 3 examined the use of LSQ in a task-specific and context-specific episode to predict performance and processes in learning. The results of each of these studies in isolation could be dependent on particular aspects of the design or method. However, the consistently negative pattern of the results makes it unlikely that the results are due to specific features of the studies themselves.

The failure of the LSQ to predict significant outcomes in Studies 2 and 3 might suggest that tests of generalised individual differences are inappropriate for understanding performance in task-specific and context-dependent situations. An analogous point could be made about the GEFT, the CSA and other tasks that have been developed in artificial laboratory situations and may be of limited value in practice-orientated research. On this argument, however, the LSQ would have been expected to provide information about variations in learning across an entire course, but Study 1 failed to confirm this expectation. More generally, the results question the value of measures of individual differences in practice-orientated research (Laurillard, 1978).

The literature on learning styles raises questions about the validity, consistency and stability of the instruments used to measure learning styles. The studies that we have described have reinforced some of these concerns. This leads us to conclude that measures of learning styles may be of limited value in predicting students' preferences and performance. In future research, it may be more useful to examine approaches to learning in situations where students are able to choose among different modes of course delivery and different ways of representing the information that they are expected to learn (see Richardson and Price, 2003).

References

Argyris, C (1976). Theories of action that inhibit individual learning. *American Psychologist*, **31**, 636–654.

Carswell, L, Thomas, PG, Petre, M, Price, BA and Richards, M (2000). Distance education via the Internet: The student experience. *British Journal of Educational Technology*, **31**, 29–46.

Curry, L (1983, April 11–15). An Organization of Learning Styles Theory and Constructs. Paper presented at the 67th Annual Meeting of the American Educational Research Association, Montreal, Quebec.

Geiger, MA and Pinto, JK (1991). Changes in learning style preferences during a three-year longitudinal study. *Psychological Reports*, **69**, 755–762.

Goldstein, AG and Chance, JE (1965). Effects of practice on sex-related differences in performance on Embedded Figures. *Psychonomic Science*, **3**, 361–362.

Grasha, A (1984). Learning styles: The journey from Greenwich Observatory (1976) to the college classroom (1984). *Improving College and University Teaching*, **32**(1), 46–53.

Grigorenko, EL, and Sternberg, RJ (1995). Thinking styles. In Saklofske, DH and Zeidner, M (Eds), *International Handbook of Personality and Intelligence*. New York: Plenum Press.

Honey, P and Mumford, A (1992). *The Manual of Learning Styles* (2nd Edn). Maidenhead: Peter Honey Associates.

Jonassen, DH, Beissner, K and Yacci, M (1993). *Structural Knowledge: Techniques for Representing, Conveying, and Acquiring Structural Knowledge*. Hillsdale, New Jersey: Lawrence Erlbaum Associates.

Jonassen, DH and Grabowski, BL (1993). *Handbook of Individual Differences, Learning, and Instruction*. Hillsdale, New Jersey: Lawrence Erlbaum Associates.

Kolb, DA (1981). Experiential learning theory and the Learning Style Inventory: A reply to Freedman and Stumpf. *Academy of Management Review*, **6**, 289–296.

Laurillard, DM (1978). *A Study of the Relationship Between some of the Cognitive and Contextual Factors in Student Learning*. Unpublished PhD, University of Surrey, Guildford.

Lewis, BN (1976). Avoidance of aptitude-treatment trivialities. In S. Messick (Ed), *Individuality in Learning*. San Francisco: Jossey-Bass.

Mayer, RE (1989). Systematic thinking fostered by illustrations in scientific text. *Journal of Educational Psychology*, **81**, 240-246.

Messick, S (1987). Structural relationships across cognition, personality, and style. In Snow, RE and Farr, NJ (Eds), *Aptitude, Learning and Instruction* pp 35–75 Hillsdale, NJ: Lawrence Erlbaum Associates.

Miller, A (1987). Cognitive styles: An integrated model. *Educational Psychology*, **7**, 251–268.

Pinto, JK, Marshall, AG and Boyle, EJ (1994). A three-year longitudinal study of changes in student learning styles. *Journal of College Student Development*, **35**, 113–119.

Rayner, S, and Riding, RJ (1997). Towards a categorisation of cognitive styles and learning styles. *Educational Psychology*, **17**, 5–27.

Richardson, JTE (1998). Field independence in higher education and the case of distance learning. *International Journal of Educational Research*, **29**, 241–250.

Richardson, JTE (2000). *Researching Student Learning: Approaches to Studying in Campus-based and Distance Education*. Buckingham: SRHE and Open University Press.

Richardson, JTE, and Price, L (in press). Approaches to studying and perceptions of academic quality in electronically delivered courses. *British Journal of Educational Technology*.

Riding, RJ and Rayner, SG (1997). *Learning Styles and Strategies*. Oxford: Carfax.

Riding, RJ (1998). *Cognitive Style Analysis - Research Applications*. Birmingham: Learning and Training Technology.

Riding, RJ and Cheema, I (1991). Cognitive styles: An overview and integration. *Educational Psychology*, **11**, 193–215.

Schmeck, RR (1983). Learning styles of college students. In RF Dillon and RR Schmeck (Eds), *Individual Differences in Cognition* (Vol. 1). New York: Academic Press.

Squires, G (1981). *Cognitive Styles and Adult Learning*. Nottingham: University of Nottingham.

Vermunt, JD (1998). The regulation of constructive learning processes. *British Journal of Psychology*, **68**, 149–171.

Witkin, HA, Moore, CA, Goodenough, RD and Cox, PW (1977). Field-dependent and field-independent cognitive styles and their educational implications. *Review of Educational Research*, **47**, 1–64.

Notes

1 This paper was presented at ISL under Linda Price's former name of Linda Carswell

25 Raising educational research capacity: a discipline-based approach

**Glynis Cousin[1], Mick Healey[2] and Alan Jenkins[3]
with John Bradbeer[4], Helen King[5] and other members of the
Learning to Do Pedagogic Research Group[a]**

1 University of Warwick, 2 University of Gloucestershire,
3 Oxford Brookes University, 4 University of Portsmouth,
5 University of Plymouth

Abstract

Central to the Improving Student Learning (ISL) conference has been the attempt to forge productive links between 'teaching staff' and 'educational research/researchers'. We report initial findings of a project conducted by the Learning and Teaching Support Network (LTSN) Geography, Earth and Environmental Sciences Subject Centre that is seeking to develop and strengthen such links, by having specialist researchers support discipline staff to carry out discipline focused pedagogic research projects.

Our findings include: grounding the research on issues central to the discipline produced high practitioner involvement; and central practitioner concerns in doing such research was more about issues of 'objectivity' and the degree to which such educational research approaches were close to their 'parent' discipline, than competence at particular techniques. The overall conclusion is that specialist researchers working alongside discipline staff to raise their pedagogic research capacity is an effective model.

> The ISL symposia have sought to bring "together those who are primarily researchers into learning in higher education and those who are primarily practitioners concerned more pragmatically with improving their practice".
> (OCSLD, 2002)

> In general, academics in higher education value research above pedagogy. To approach pedagogy through research 'goes with the grain' of academe …
> (Yorke, 2000, 124)

25.1   Introduction

Since the first ISL symposium in 1993 (Gibbs, 1994) there have been many changes in the field of higher educational research and development. One of the more significant changes has been a growth of interest in developing the scholarship of teaching, including staff researching their own teaching (Healey, 2000; 2003; Yorke, 2000). This has led to several institutions establishing policies and practices to build the capacity for research in teaching and learning (eg D'Andrea and Gosling, 2000; O'Connell and Renfrew, 2000). A second change has been the greater importance given to discipline-based approaches (Rust, 2000; Healey and Jenkins, 2003). This paper combines these two trends by focusing on the development of pedagogic research capacity within a discipline context.

There has been emphasis in higher education internationally on the need for developments in learning and teaching to be supported by evidence-based practice. In the UK this has been associated with the publication of the Dearing Report (1997), the founding of the Institute of Learning and Teaching (ILT) (1999), and the establishment of the Higher Education Funding Council of England's (HEFCE) Teaching Quality Enhancement Fund (1999/2000). The establishment of the Economic and Social Research Council (ESRC) Teaching and Learning Research Capacity Building Network (2001) and the emphasis of the third phase of the Teaching and Learning Research Programme (TLRP) on developing research capacity in the areas of post-compulsory education and lifelong learning are further indications of this concern.

Such capacity building may well focus on high-level research with perhaps some focus on disseminating that research to, or even with, practitioners. There is growing interest in developing higher educational research capacity in collaboration with practitioners. This has the strength of ensuring that the research grows out of practice and is likely to shape future practice. However, such research faces the problems of generalisability of local findings and the capacity of classroom practitioners to carry out that research. Arguably one can see such tensions in recent ISL symposia. There is clearly development of high-level research occurring – but the connection to classroom practitioners is perhaps weaker than in the early years of ISL. So general concerns for the ISL 'movement' may well include questions about the effective linkage of high-level research activity with practice-based research and the quality of practitioner based research.

Any concern for quality practitioner based research has to consider disciplinary concerns. Most educational research is generic in character, but to raise the capacity of academics to research their own teaching practices, this needs to be embedded in specific disciplines. It is in their discipline that academics have their principal communities of practice (Wenger 1998). Interest in discipline-based approaches to educational research is international, as witnessed by the activities of the Carnegie Academy for the Advancement of Teaching in the United States and many of the projects funded by The Committee for the Advancement of University Teaching, and its subsequent replacements in Australia. In the UK, the Department for Education and Employment established discipline networks in the mid-1990s. The twenty-four Subject Centres of the LTSN, funded by the Higher Education Funding Councils, which are now actively supporting educational research, followed at the turn of the century. However, if the disciplines are going to engage with educational research effectively they will need to learn from and work with generic educational researchers (Healey and Jenkins, 2003).

These trends provide the context for the LTSN Subject Centre for Geography, Earth and Environmental Sciences (LTSN-GEES) programme, begun in mid-2001, to build the capacity of these related subject areas to undertake research into learning and teaching.

25.2 Raising research capacity in Geography, Earth and Environmental Sciences (GEES): A case study

25.2.1 Choice of topic

The theme of the research programme is 'Enhancing the quality of fieldwork through pedagogic research'. This topic was chosen for three reasons:

1. Fieldwork has a central role in student learning in the GEES subjects - One of the most effective ways to build pedagogic research capacity in a discipline is, we believe, to build that capacity around an issue that is central to the culture, beliefs and practices of that discipline. For on such an issue there is likely to be both intellectual curiosity, a greater willingness to learn from each others' practices, and a concern to act on the results of that research.

2. The fact that fieldwork is as yet little theorised - Despite its central and costly role, to shape effective practice there is a lack of firmly grounded general principles on fieldwork pedagogy that are soundly derived from research investigations. This is well expressed by two earth scientists:

    It has long been recognised by Geoscience educators that field based education provides some of the most valuable and enjoyable educational experiences that our students encounter… but vague beliefs in the value of field-based education are not enough… There are too few [papers] that analyse the educational rationale behind [field]course design and practice, and fewer still with empirical data (Winchester-Seeto & Hart, 2000).

Their view reinforces the views of other writers on the subject (Gold *et al*, 1991; Johnston & Cooke, 2001; Suiter, 2000) about the state of discipline-based pedagogic research and the need to build that capacity around issues of disciplinary concern.

3. Fieldwork lends itself well to a range of pedagogic research methodologies and techniques. In developing research capacity in the three disciplines, it was important that we chose an area that allows for an exploration of a diversity of methodologies and techniques in pedagogic research. The research on fieldwork can rest on a number of techniques (eg focus groups, in-depth interviews, participant observation, large-scale survey, quantitative analysis of web-based support) to support methodologies within qualitative, quantitative or mixed frameworks (eg Cottingham and Healey, 2001). The strengthened expertise colleagues acquire in these research projects can be applied later to other areas of the curriculum.

Hence the aim of the programme is to develop the capacity of the GEES communities to undertake research into teaching and learning through working together on a series of pilot projects, all concerned with enhancing the quality of fieldwork.

25.2.2 Theoretical framework

We planned from the beginning of the programme that all the projects would adopt a common theoretical framework. We needed one that:

1. Is based around a sufficient corpus of theoretical and empirical research to provide a robust platform for capacity building

2. Provides those with little or no experience of pedagogic research with a well-developed literature/knowledge base to inform their particular disciplinary practices and concerns

3. Is applicable to a range of linked projects regarding fieldwork and with the potential to later apply to other learning environments

4. Has the potential to significantly improve the quality of the student learning.

The theory of constructive alignment, we believe, meets these criteria (Biggs, 1999). This theory examines the 'goodness of fit' between the aims of the course, its assessment procedures, the nature of the learning environment, student cultures and motivations and learning styles and approaches. Drawing together a range of the key research frameworks in higher education, it gives the programme a strong theoretical framework that can then be applied to a range of issues on which the three disciplines need theory to guide practice. Further, a common framework supports newcomers to educational research in achieving the necessary capacity to carry out the research, and facilitates effective dissemination (cf Gibbs, 1992).

23.2.3   Methodology and structure

Central to the methodology of the programme is, first, the involvement of members of the GEES communities and, second, the employment of pedagogic research consultants as part of the project team to facilitate raising pedagogic research capacity within a partnership framework. Liz Beaty and Glynis Cousin (then at Centre for Higher Education Development, Coventry University) were persuaded to play the latter role.

We advertised the proposed programme widely within the GEES communities and organised a day workshop to discuss and plan the work in May 2001. We obtained responses from approximately 60 academics working in higher education and one from a member of staff at the Field Studies Council. This was more than we expected. Of these, about half came to the workshop. A similar number became actively involved in the programme's projects. The remainder were invited to act as reviewers and commentators. A mailing list was established to facilitate communication and discussion between the participants. The outcome of the workshop was agreement to focus on four projects. They are:

*   Student views of fieldwork

*   Fieldwork in the curriculum

*   Fieldwork education and technology

*   The impact on the learning and teaching experience of the removal of fieldwork from academic programmes in the GEES subject areas.

Finally, an overview group (Learning to do pedagogic research) was formed to handle the research and evaluation of the project as a whole. The pedagogic research consultants participated in this group alongside colleagues from GEES and the project leaders.

Two subsequent workshops have occurred, the first focused on methodology and research design (two days in September 2001) and the second on data analysis and interpretation (May 2002). A final workshop (January 2003) is planned to discuss publication of the findings, review the lessons learnt and discuss future work.

The remainder of this paper explores the initial findings from the surveys, observations and interviews conducted by the 'Learning to do pedagogic research' group.

25.2.4 Developing capacity – emergent findings

The evidence emerging in relation to the research question set by the 'Learning to do pedagogic research' group ('How far, and in what ways, has the programme succeeded in developing capacity to undertake pedagogic research in the disciplines?'), suggests three conclusions:

1. Strategies for the development of educational research capacity need to vary across the disciplines to reflect differences in disciplinary cultures of inquiry

2. Raising educational research capacity is best encouraged experientially

3. A partnership consisting of subject specialists, educational researchers and internal project evaluators provides a robust model for raising educational research capacity.

Below we discuss each of these issues in turn.

1. *Cultures of inquiry and methodology*

Once pilot project teams had been formed, members were asked to submit responses to a preliminary research skills audit. From sixteen returned forms we found a spread of knowledge in all research methods from discipline-based and/or pedagogic research experiences. Because the subject areas of Geography, Environmental and Earth Sciences involve different cultures of inquiry ranging from the qualitative to the quantitative and from experimental design through to open interviews, this spread did not surprise us. We were aware, however, that the individual respondents would each have different research strengths depending on their subject speciality.

While it is important to avoid over-generalisation, arguably human geographers are more likely to be at home with qualitative research, and earth and environmental scientists with experimental, scientific and quantitative approaches. As one project member noted, 'Most of the methods I use in geography research are transferable and relevant'. Similarly, out of the ten responding to our skills audit indicating experience in experimental design, only one also had knowledge of focus group research or action research.

The audit, though only sufficient in size for indicative findings, was designed to help us to develop a baseline picture about research skills. As the project progressed, interestingly, questions of validity, objectivity and researcher stance emerged as having greater importance than those of research skills or techniques. Notable for instance was the data we gathered from interviews in which we asked participating colleagues for comments on their levels of confidence in doing educational research. A number of the responses expressed anxieties about the credibility of educational research methodology:

> My confidence in performing qualitative research is low... this stems from the fact that I am suspicious of it.

> I am very uncomfortable with 'qualitative' approaches as the reason is that they are frequently an excuse for sloppiness to lead to lack of true representativeness.

> I am concerned about the objectivity and sample size, etc. My scientific background makes me very conscious of experimental design, error analysis, etc.

> [I am] OK on scientific approach, social science methodology approach [is] weaker.

These comments reflect an assumption that educational research is unscientific and entirely qualitative; and that qualitative research designs are less robust than quantitative research. Although it needs to be acknowledged that pedagogic research is a broad church, embracing many methods and methodologies, the sticking point for these subject specialists identifying with a 'scientific approach' does seem to centre on resistance to the qualitative dimension of pedagogic research. The emergent findings from this project suggest that this resistance, or questioning, is best confronted experientially.

2.   *Developing pedagogic research capacity experientially*

Given that most academics are embedded in particular ways of doing research, in the experience of this project, information and discussions about alternatives are an insufficient basis for prompting cross-disciplinary travels. These discussions need to be supported by opportunities to practice. This section describes the processes by which this project has provided such opportunities and support for practice.

The workshops covered three important phases of the projects, namely:

- formulating research questions and project teams, and presenting a theoretical underpinning
- planning educational research designs
- analysing the data gathered.

The illustrative comments in the last section were made around the time of the first workshop. The following, from the second workshop, reveal less anxiety about educational research methodology. By the end of this two-day workshop, each project group, in collaboration with the educational researchers, had clarified its research question and had developed a research design for its exploration. The comments below were made in response to the prompt 'What I learnt about educational research was':

> It is not as difficult as I thought it would be. Some of the methods (action research, etc.) are respectable and appropriate.

> Strengths/weaknesses and appropriateness of research methods.

> How in outline educational methodology works.

> Maybe it's easier than I thought. It does need to be done in my subject area for educational and political reasons.

> Must consider theoretical models and the ways of Biggs.

> The 'meaning' behind all sorts of edu-techno terms. How to deal with non-quantitative information.

These responses tell us something about issues of translation from one culture of inquiry to another. Some of the translation is about breaking down jargon and introducing a theoretical underpinning; some is about demonstrating validity and robustness of design; much, as with many forms of cultural exchange, is about overcoming prejudice. By the time we came to our workshop on data analysis there appeared to be a deeper engagement with these issues. Some of the evidence from this workshop provides us with the most vivid illustration of the usefulness of our experiential learning framework for such an engagement. Workshop participants were asked to rate their confidence on a 1-5 scale against the following statements:

> My data will reveal something worth knowing

I know how to organise and manage the data

I know how to interpret the data

I know how to disseminate the findings

Here we limit ourselves to reporting the findings on the third of these, namely the interpretation of data.

As Fig 25.1 shows, after the workshop, the confidence of delegates about interpreting their data rose dramatically. While we cannot discount the possibility of respondent generosity

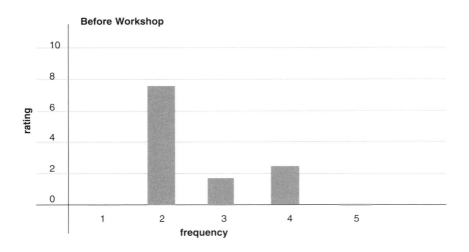

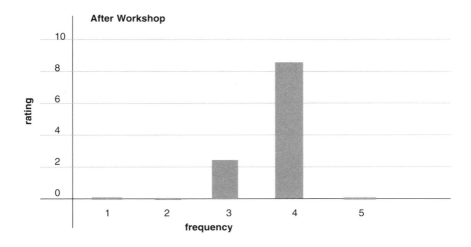

Figure 25.1 Ratings before and after workshop on 'I know how to interpret the data'.

within this evaluation, we have two observations to support the trend these findings suggest (ratings for the other statements also exhibited significant growth in confidence).

Firstly, we had participants work with their own qualitative data as the basis of the workshop. Most groups had adopted a mixed method approach, gathering both quantitative and qualitative data, but many project members expressed uncertainty about the status and weight of the latter. Encouragingly, once we had invited them to segment and label their data on the basis of emergent recurrent themes within the spirit of grounded theory (Glazer and Strauss, 1967), those unfamiliar with the procedures of qualitative data analysis began to appreciate the value of their data. In particular, they began to see that quantitative is not the opposite of qualitative. This simplistic dichotomy neglects the attention qualitative analysis pays to the quantitative in the hunt for patterns, recurrences (of silences and absences as well as of the surfaces) and representativeness.

Generally, participants less familiar with qualitative research came to appreciate that objectivity is reinterpreted rather than abandoned in qualitative research analysis. One group, for instance, wanted to interrogate immediately its data for answers to the question they were seeking to answer. They asked why they were being advised instead to set this pursuit aside and to sort their data descriptively; they were happy with the response that it is important to have a procedure that tries to avoid researchers finding what they are looking for because they are looking for it. This explanation chimed with their own understandings of objectivity, to quote from the field notes of one of the pedagogic research consultants:

> Issues of objectivity were more appreciated when the principles of bracketing and reflexivity were introduced into the explanations of how data organisation and analysis are approached.

Our second observation supports the final issue we want to discuss: the importance of a partnership framework for the development of pedagogic research capacity.

3   *Establishing partnerships for the development of pedagogic research capacity*

As we have noted, the aim was to use the workshops and the pilot research groups as the basis for the establishment of communities of practice of discipline-based educational researchers. In this context, the role of the pedagogic research consultants was to support the generation of conditions for experiential learning within collaborative groups. For this to happen, the educational researchers need to work alongside the groups as brokers as well as trainers. The brokerage involved facilitating understandings about the cultures of inquiry across the subject specialisms and pedagogic research by supporting practical work with cross-disciplinary teams. In this respect, the following field note extracts from observations of the data analysis workshop are of interest:

> There were a number of incidents which suggested the discovery of common ground across research traditions… in talking about validity and qualitative research 'Anne' pointed out that bias is built into any kind of research tradition and cited the cases where different sponsors of environmental research yielded different kinds of findings from the same apparently 'stable' research conditions… 'Ahmed' added to this by talking about the fact that in geology inferences have to be made from the sediments of the past and this has affinities with qualitative depth.

> I think it would be a mistake to bill our day as a 'training day' because although it contained those elements, it also facilitated encounters between different paradigms. The strength of this project overall has been in its ability to encourage different disciplinary areas to engage in creative conversations and to develop research partnerships.

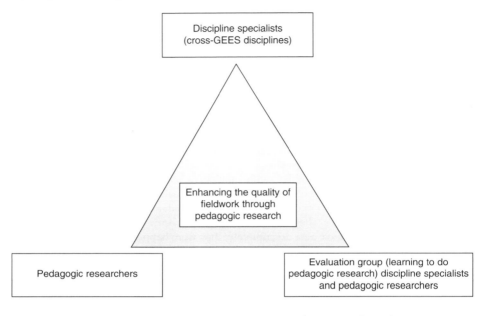

Figure 25.2   Framework for developing pedagogic research capacity through a
partnership model.

Project members' evaluative comments on workshop 2 also supported this view; as one member put it, "I have a refined personal view of its (educational research's) interdisciplinary nature".

In summary, our framework for developing pedagogic research capacity through a partnership model is expressed in Fig 25.2. The corners of the triangle refer to the creation of three overlapping activities between the subject specialists, pedagogic research consultants and an overview group, which undertakes insider evaluation research. The partnership between educational researchers and cross-disciplinary groups of subject specialists has allowed creative connections to be made across cultures of inquiry. These connections have in turn opened up colleagues' receptivity to educational research and their confidence in undertaking it. The overview group embeds a reflective dimension to the project as we hope is in some evidence in this paper.

23.3   Conclusion

Clearly what we have presented are but the preliminary findings of one research project in one UK LTSN Subject Centre; so we are sensitive to avoid generalising too much from this case study. However, we do set our analysis in the general context of ten years of ISL symposia – the aim of which, to bring together researchers into learning in higher education and practitioners, we quoted at the beginning of the paper.

Our approach to bridging the gap between researchers and practitioners, and to developing practice that is more solidly based on educational research, is to:

- Ground that research clearly in the needs and interests of practitioners

- Work with specific disciplinary concerns that matter to those practitioners

- Ensure that such research is methodologically strong by closely involving specialist educational researchers in the project

- Establish an evaluation research group for programmes of research to ensure a reflective dimension

- Recognise that specialist educational researchers play a key role in supporting discipline-based staff in designing their research studies and analysing the results, while ensuring that the key researchers and analysts of that research are the discipline-based specialists.

The initial findings from carrying out this project indicate that the degree to which these discipline-based staff feel both comfortable with, and competent at, carrying out such research is shaped by the extent to which these educational research methodologies differ from their 'home' disciplinary research cultures. Moreover, developing such confidence and competence clearly benefits from staff researching issues of concern to them and their discipline and the support they receive from the educational researchers.

At this stage, when the research from these different projects is still being written up, it is too early to comment on the quality of the research that is produced. Nor as yet can we comment on whether this approach impacts on student learning. We do, however, believe that the preliminary evidence from this project illustrates well the benefits of one of the original purposes of establishing the ISL symposia, namely of bringing together educational researchers and practitioners.

Notes

a. The other members of the group are: Liz Beaty, Jenny Blumhof, Brian Chalkley, Steve Gaskin, Geoff Robinson and Neil Thomas. Adrian Bromage contributed to workshop 2. The project is funded through a £50,000 grant from the LTSN development fund and is supported by a further £12,000 from LTSN-GEES. The authors of this progress report would welcome comments from readers.

Please email: mhealey@glos.ac.uk.

References

Biggs, J (1999). *Teaching for Quality Learning at University*. Buckingham: SRHE and Open University Press.

Cottingham, C & Healey, M (2001). Undergraduate geography fieldcourses: exploring the learning experiences of students, poster presented at International Network for the Learning and Teaching of Geography in Higher Education Symposium, Plymouth, 4 January.

D'Andrea, V & Gosling, D (2000). Promoting research in teaching and learning in higher education: two case studies of multi-disciplinary pedagogic research. Paper presented at ESRC Teaching Learning and Research Programme Conference, Leicester, November. Available at: http://www.TLRP.org/pub/acadpub/Dandrea2000.pdf

Gibbs, G (1992). *Improving Student Learning*. Bristol: Technical and Educational Services.

Gibbs, G (Ed) (1994). *Improving Student Learning: theory and practice*. Oxford: Oxford Centre for Staff Development.

Glazer, B & Strauss, A (1967). *The Discovery of Grounded Theory*. Chicago: Aldine.

Gold, JR, Jenkins, A, Lee, R, Monk, J, Riley, J, Shepherd, I and Unwin, D (1991). *Teaching Geography in Higher Education: A manual of good practice*. Oxford: Basil Blackwell.

Healey, M (2000). Developing the scholarship of teaching in higher education: a discipline-based approach. *Higher Education Research and Development*, **19**(2), 169–187.

Healey, M (2003).The scholarship of teaching: issues around an evolving concept, *Journal on Excellence in College Teaching*, (forthcoming).

Healey, M & Jenkins, A (in press). Discipline-based educational development, in Macdonald, R & Eggins, H (Eds), *The Scholarship of Academic Development*. Milton Keynes: Open University.

Johnston RJ & Cooke R (2001). Standing and Delivering: views from the trenches, *Journal of Geography in Higher Education*, **25**(1), 113–117.

OCSLD (Oxford Centre for Staff and Learning Development) (2002) The 10th Improving Student Learning Symposium (http://www.brookes.ac.uk/services/ocsd/1_ocsld/isl2002/aims.html). Accessed 31 August.

O'Connell, C and Renfrew, A (2000). Fostering research into teaching and learning in a subject-based research environment, paper presented at ESRC Teaching Lerning and Research Programme Conference, Leicester, November. Available at: http://www.TLRP.org/pub/acadpub/Renfrew2000.pdf

Rust, C (Ed) (2000). *Improving Student Learning Through the Disciplines*. Oxford: Oxford Centre for Staff and Learning Development.

Suiter, MJ (2000). Supporting Teaching and Learning in Geoscience: a call for research, paper presented at session on 'Research on Teaching and Learning in Geoscience' at the Geological Society of America Annual Meeting, Reno, Nevada.

Wenger, E (1998). *Communities of Practice: Learning, Meaning and Identity*. Cambridge: Cambridge University Press.

Winchester-Seeto, T & Hart, D (2000). Field teaching – just a nice day in the sun?, paper presented at 3rd International Conference on Geoscience Education, Sydney, Australia.

Yorke, M (2000). A cloistered virtue? Pedagogical researchand policy in UK higher education, *Higher Education Quarterly*, **54**(2), 106-26.

26   The Pedagogical Academy – a way to encourage and reward scholarly teaching

Pernille Hammar Andersson, Thomas Olsson,
Monica Almqvist, Lena Zetterqvist, Anders Axelsson,
Gustaf Olsson and Torgny Roxå
Lund Institute of Technology, Lund University, Sweden

26.1   Introduction

Students entering universities today have a much more diversified educational, social and ethnic background than just ten or fifteen years ago. Universities are faced with new challenges and must develop new strategies to solve different problems but also take advantage of new possibilities. Pedagogical research has increased our knowledge about teaching and student learning in higher education and numerous activities and projects initiated from the government as well as from the universities themselves have started in recent years (Bowden and Marton, 1999).

The pedagogical academy is a novel approach to stimulate and reward scholarly teaching. It has been developed in accordance with widespread views of what a teacher's role is at a university (Boyer, 1990; Kreber, 2000; Trigwell et al, 2000; Biggs, 1999). In this paper we will present and discuss the main ideas behind the pedagogical academy and some important findings and experiences from the implementation of the project.

University lecturers at Lund Institute of Technology (the Faculty of Engineering at Lund University), LTH, may apply for admission to the pedagogical academy. Their teaching skills are assessed and, if they are accepted into the Academy, they receive a certificate declaring that they have attained the grade, "Excellent Teaching Practice (ETP)", and an immediate rise in salary. Moreover, the department to which they belong will receive an increase in their grant.

Lecturers who will be admitted to the Academy are those who can show that they have, over a period of time, and – preferably consciously and systematically – endeavoured to develop themselves as teachers as well as their teaching activities, regardless of the level at which they teach.

26.1.1   Pedagogical development

How can university lecturers be motivated and stimulated to develop their teaching skills? How do we increase lecturers' interest in the scholarship of teaching? An important experience from Lund University is that it is crucial how projects aimed to develop and change teaching activities are initiated and how the objectives are communicated to lecturers at the faculty. Another very important factor is the involvement in such projects by active lecturers from different departments at the faculty.

The Pedagogical Academy has been developed within a larger project at LTH entitled The Breakthrough. The aim of this project is to make LTH a faculty that consciously and systematically strives to develop its teaching and learning culture. It is about changing the paradigm of education from teaching to learning and to create a scholarly teaching environment. An increased dialogue and co-operation about educational issues is very important to stimulate positive development.

Different pedagogical courses about teaching and learning have been available at LTH for about ten years. Many teachers have attended these courses. This has secured a well-established view within the faculty that pedagogy can help teachers improve their teaching and many lecturers now share the same experiences of pedagogical research, methods and terminology. This is the main reason why it is now possible to develop the teaching and learning strategies more systematically at the faculty. Another important reason is that the board and management strongly support and encourage this development.

The Pedagogical Academy has been developed by a group of five lecturers representing different departments at LTH, together with a pedagogical expert (the authors of this paper). This project group is responsible for the development of criteria, instructions and procedures for the assessment of pedagogical competence according to the basic ideas of the Pedagogical Academy.

26.1.2   Aims of the Pedagogical Academy

The main aim of the Academy is to afford status to pedagogical development at LTH. Lecturers and students, present and prospective, should be given a clear signal that LTH is an institute of higher education that systematically strives to improve the quality of its teaching. This will be achieved in the following ways:

- Good, ambitious, quality-conscious lecturers will be rewarded by a certificate of competence and an increase in salary. These lecturers and other ambitious teachers will be a sign that LTH is investing in good teaching and that there are goals at which to aim.

- The departments from which lecturers have been admitted to the Academy will be deemed to have better capacity to provide good teaching. Moreover, if the department in question actively supports its lecturers in applying for and obtaining this certification, it is believed that, in the long run, they will find it easier to recruit and retain good teachers, and thus good students. For this reason, such departments will receive an additional financial contribution for every employee who achieves this certification. This system is based on what today is called docentur, ie achieving the grade of senior lecturer or reader.

- The aim of the system is to initiate positive development, where it is clear that it pays to invest in good, carefully prepared teaching. This in turn will lead to the professionalisation of teaching, ie that good teaching is documented and scrutinized, and thus acts as a springboard for further development.

- The certified lecturers are assumed to be able to contribute to pedagogical development at LTH. This may be realised through active participation in LTH's pedagogical debate and development, and by acting as mentors for younger teachers.

This takes place in line with national and international development regarding the perception of a university lecturer (Boyer, 1990; Healey, 2000; Kreber, 2000; Trigwell, Martin et al., 2000; Abrahamsson, 2001; Fransson and Wahlén, 2001).

26.2   Process of application and acceptance

University lecturers (but not postgraduate students) may apply to the Pedagogical Academy. There are no special demands on how many years the applicant should have lectured or that he or she should use a special pedagogical method. However, the applicant should have a broad experience in higher education and should be able to show that he or she has worked, in a reflecting and open way, to improve the goal of teaching, namely the student's learning.

Lecturers wishing to apply to the Pedagogical Academy should:

* Attend the workshop "How to write a teaching portfolio"

* Submit a teaching portfolio together with a recommendation of their head of department

* Take part in an interview.

26.2.1   The workshop

The workshop "How to write a teaching portfolio" is organised regularly. Lecturers will be admitted to the workshop following a selection process by submitting a short outline of their teaching portfolio. Participation in the workshop is compulsory but it does not guarantee that the lecturer's merits will be approved. The aim of the workshop is to ensure that the portfolio is presented in the required format and to present opportunities for the participants to communicate and share their experiences of teaching and learning.

The workshop consists of four seminars including group discussions mixed with information about the process of application. Two individual consultations with a pedagogical expert are also included.

26.2.2   The teaching portfolio

The method of using portfolios to assess the quality of a lecturer's teaching skills has a long tradition and has been found, through studies, to be very reliable. For further details, see Seldin (1997), Apelgren and Giertz (2001), Karolinska Institute (2001) and Magin (1998).

The portfolio, which is the most important component of the application, consists of three main parts. The first is a CV with a special section dedicated to pedagogical activities. The second is a document of 1–3 pages in length describing the lecturer's personal reflections regarding teaching and learning. This is to be a personal document, focusing on the different aspects of the teaching role, and in this way form what can be referred to as the lecturer's 'personal teaching philosophy'. The third part constitutes a description of what the lecturer has achieved. The examples (4–5 in number) should be related to the second part of the portfolio in such a way that the portfolio constitutes an overview, from which it is evident that the lecturer has reflected on teaching over a period of time and has made the effort to implement his or her ideas in practical teaching. The portfolio is to be related to the six criteria described in section 26.7 below. References, certificates and other documents supporting the claims presented should be enclosed.

26.2.3   The recommendation of the head of department

The intention of this document is to show that the head of department is convinced that the lecturer in question has no shortcomings in his or her relation to the students. Another intention is to provide the head of department with the opportunity to express an opinion on the pedagogical abilities of the applicant.

26.2.4 The interview

The interview is a complement to the recommendation of the head of department and the portfolio submitted by the applicant. The main aim of the interview is to gain an idea of the lecturer's ability to communicate verbally the claims made in the portfolio. It is especially important that the interview is consistent with the portfolio, so that the application is perceived as an integrated whole. The interview also provides an opportunity to clarify confusions arisen during the assessors reading of the portfolio.

26.2.5 Assessment and scrutiny

The qualifications of the applicant are assessed by a group of lecturers (the assessors) working at LTH, and who have themselves been awarded the grade of ETP. These are appointed by the rector of LTH. This group of assessors also includes a representative appointed by the Students' Union at LTH and a pedagogical expert. The assessors read the portfolios and lead the interviews.

The opinion of a scrutiniser will also be appended to the statement of the assessors. This person must also have the grade of ETP. The scrutiniser will have access to the applicant's portfolio and other material submitted, and his or her task is to check the claims made therein. The scrutinizer writes a report which must be available to the assessors before the applicant is interviewed.

The assessors have the right to accept or reject the application. They can also refer it back to the applicant for supplementation. The result of the assessment together with feedback on the application is presented to the applicant at an individual meeting with the pedagogical expert.

26.3 Acceptance

Those applicants whose qualifications have been approved will receive a certificate of "Excellent Teaching Practice", signed by the rector of LTH. The lecturer will also receive an increase in salary, equivalent to that received by those obtaining a senior lectureship or readership (docentur), at present 140 per month. The department at which the lecturer is employed will also receive additional funds.

Once awarded the grade of ETP, a lecturer cannot lose it, but is expected to continue to strive towards improved teaching practices. This places demands on those who have achieved this grade: apart from continuing to work on their own development, they should act as advisers for other lecturers contemplating application to the Academy, and as pedagogical partners in dialogues with others within their department. They should contribute in other ways to vitalising the pedagogical debate, and have the responsibility of spreading information on LTH's Pedagogical Academy. Furthermore, a lecturer who has been awarded the grade of ETP may be called upon in the future to be an assessor or a scrutiniser.

26.7 Criteria for assessment

Communication with students is still the heart of all teaching, but to this are added a number of skills and qualities required for a university lecturer to obtain the grade of ETP. They are: the ability to cooperate with other lecturers, to have open discussions on one's own and other's experiences of teaching, the documentation of experience, regarding teaching as a means of providing students with the requisites for learning instead of a final product, and above all, to have the driving power to scrutinise one's own teaching and its effects with the aim of continuous improvement and thus the students' opportunity to learn.

To assess these skills, six criteria have been formulated. They are supported by the rapidly growing amount of literature on learning and teaching in the university environment (Ramsden, 1992; Bowden and Marton, 1999; Biggs and Collis, 1982; Biggs, 1999; Barr and Tagg, 1995; Ellström, 1996; McKeachie, 1999; Prosser and Trigwell, 1999; Trigwell, 2001). The following criteria are to be made clear in the material submitted for assessment:

1. That the applicant bases his/her work on a learning perspective

2. That the personal philosophy of the applicant constitutes an integrated whole, in which different aspects of teaching are described in such a way that the driving force of the applicant is apparent

3. That a clear development over time is apparent. The applicant should – preferably consciously and systematically – have striven to develop personally and in pedagogical activities

4. That the applicant has shared his or her experience with others, with the intention of vitalising the pedagogical debate

5. That the applicant has cooperated with other lecturers in an effort to develop his or her teaching skills

6. That the applicant is looking to the future by discussing his or her future development, and the development of pedagogical activities.

The term learning perspective in the first criterion is essential to the Pedagogical Academy and the workshop is focused on this subject. Today, there is a great deal of literature available which describes the learning perspective, and empirical research that confirms its advantages regarding the generation of students' learning (Barr and Tagg, 1995; Bowden and Marton, 1999; Ramsden, 1992). This means, briefly, that a lecturer, in the planning, execution and assessment of his or her teaching, focuses more on the students' work in the subject than on his or her own work, ie a focus on the students' encounter with that which is to be learnt. The opposite is usually described as the teaching perspective, where the focus is instead on the teaching, ie the lecturer's work, what he or she does in order for the students to learn something.

The second criterion focuses on the lecturer's own pedagogical philosophy. Applicants should take up aspects of their teaching activities and associated problems. Examples are examinations, motivation, communication, student responsibility, etc. As there are many possible aspects, the lecturer must choose a certain number. The aspects chosen should be connected with each other to reflect an integrated whole. This is equivalent to the fourth level of the SOLO taxonomy, "relational" (Biggs and Collis, 1982), and can thus constitute a description of the lecturer's understanding of what is happening in the teaching situation. This means that the chosen aspects should be organised relative to each other such that it is clear which is of greatest importance, and which is of least importance.

The third criterion perhaps corresponds most clearly to what Boyer (1990) and his followers mean by "Scholarship of Teaching", in the meaning that the lecturer demonstrates that he or she, over time, has worked on developing his or her technique as a teacher. This can be done in a number of ways, but the goal must always be that teaching supports learning. The development of teaching thus means that students learn better. Documentation describing the effects on students' learning should be enclosed.

The research community has demonstrated its ability to make results available for colleagues to scrutinise and build on for a long time. This assumes documentation of activities, the production of data on students' learning performance and a common way of expressing these things. Results from research into "Scholarship of Teaching" show quite clearly that there is a demand from teachers for this kind of quality assurance in teaching (see eg Kreber, 2000), but it also shows that this practice is today the exception rather than the rule (Bain, 1999). Consequently, the fourth criterion is focused on how the applicant can refer to reports, journals, seminars or conferences in which, or at which, he or she has made public his or her experiences, and become engaged in a scrutinising dialogue.

University teaching has been criticised by many for its lack of a connecting thought and context, from the point of view of the students (The Evaluation Office, Lund University, 2000). Furthermore, lecturers maintain that they lack support in their work (The Evaluation Office, Lund University, 1998). We can see nothing but positive effects arising from the cooperation of lecturers at LTH. This also includes experience of managing pedagogic activities. What is especially required in the fifth criterion is examples of cooperation between lecturers in different subjects or giving different courses. However, other activities in which work related to teaching is performed in collaboration with others may also be of importance.

CVs often relate to what a person has done. However, experience is of greatest value as guidance in future achievements and it should be natural for a good teacher to be contemplating ideas about what can be achieved in the future. The portfolio should thus, as described in the sixth criterion, include clear thoughts and ideas on future development, both for the applicant's own work and for the context in which the applicant is working. Another reason is the important role of the Pedagogical Academy to stimulate pedagogical development at LTH.

Finally, and most important, what is being rewarded is not the use of any particular pedagogical method, a special form of teaching or a simple quantitative enumeration of effort. Rather, reward is given to teachers who, in a reflective and open way, have worked to improve students' learning.

26.3   Findings and reflections

The Pedagogical Academy was implemented during the Autumn term of 2001. Each head of department nominated one lecturer from the department to be assessed in the first trial round. In this way, we gained an idea of what a good teacher at LTH is in relation to the given criteria. Furthermore, it provided an opportunity to test the criteria and the procedures. It also provided LTH with a group of ETP lecturers. These lecturers (20 persons) now form the core of the groups that will assess new applicants in the future. In this trial round, the group of lecturers that developed the Pedagogical Academy assessed the pilot group of candidates.

26.3.1   Experience of implementation

Two factors have been found to be critical in the process of implementation of the pedagogical academy. Firstly, a sense of ownership by the academic system itself must be created. This has been secured through the involvement of all the heads of departments and a widespread understanding that the assessment is done by colleagues. It is also very important that lecturers representing different departments at the faculty developed the Academy. Secondly, there must exist a well-established view that pedagogy can help teachers improve their teaching. This is secured through a long tradition of extensive, much appreciated and well attended pedagogical courses.

The findings so far, based on the experiences from the pilot group are:

- The tradition of how a subject is taught seems to affect lecturers a great deal. Teaching at universities is traditionally an individual performance and traditions also affect cooperation and discussion where teaching is concerned

- Many lecturers do not use educational terminology when they describe their teaching. Their own descriptions indicate that they move between different social contexts. Thinking and doing are connected to their research fields and educational terminology is not linked to this. However, the differences between individuals are significant.

- Documentation surrounding scholarly teaching is not systematic. Lecturers are not used to documenting teaching activities mainly because of lack of motivation in the past.

The teaching conditions differ considerably between basic scientific subjects and courses in comparison with applied engineering courses. The size of a course, the number of students attending a course and the position within the curriculum are other factors of major importance.

26.3.2 Evaluation of the Pedagogical Academy

The clearest indication of the success of this project is a high degree of interest among LTH's lecturers in applying to the Academy. The first application to the workshop after the trial round resulted in more than twice the number of applicants than could be admitted.

Attracting interest from outside LTH would be another criterion for success. Other faculties at Lund University, other universities in Sweden and abroad and engineering journals have already shown interest in the Pedagogical Academy. Present and presumptive students and lecturers should be aware that a professional attitude to teaching is encouraged and rewarded at LTH.

An extensive evaluation of the effects of the Academy within the faculty will be performed later.

26.4　Concluding remarks

The pedagogical academy was developed to stimulate and reward scholarly teaching and to afford status to pedagogical development at LTH.

Lecturers wishing to apply to the Pedagogical Academy should attend the workshop "How to write a teaching portfolio", submit a teaching portfolio together with a recommendation of their head of department and take part in an interview. Presently 40 lecturers have participated in the assessment procedure. The project has so far been very successful and some implications and reasons for this are discussed below.

Writing a teaching portfolio has increased many teachers' interest in reaching a better understanding of what actually happens in the process of teaching. It has also increased their interest in developing as teachers.

The focus on pedagogical issues at the faculty has increased. The number of lecturers attending pedagogical courses has risen considerably. The criteria for assessment are used as a starting point for discussions at departments, between lecturers, at conferences and meetings etc. This is especially satisfying in the process of convincing more lecturers to adopt a learning perspective in their teaching activities. The Pedagogical Academy has already stimulated new networks of lecturers sharing a mutual interest and competence in pedagogical issues.

References

Abrahamsson, B (2001). *Careers through promotion and recruiting,* (in Swedish, Stockholm: The National Agency for Higher Education.

Apelgren, K and Giertz B (2001). *Teaching portfolios,* (in Swedish). Uppsala: Uppsala University.

Bain, JD (1999). Introduction to HERD's special issue concerning evaluation for learning. *Higher Education Research & Development,* **18**(2).

Barr, RB and Tagg J (1995). From Teaching to Learning – A New Paradigm for Undergraduate Education. *Change,*(Nov/Dec) pp 13-25.

Biggs, J (1999). *Teaching for Quality Learning at University.* Buckingham: SRHE and Open University Press.

Biggs, JB and Collis KF (1982). *Evaluating the Quality of Learning: The SOLO Taxonomy.* New York: Academic Press.

Bowden, J and Marton F (1999). *The University of Learning.* Kogan Page.

Boyer, EL (1990). *Scholarship Reconsidered. Priorities of the professoriate.* New Jersey: The Carnegie Foundation.

Ellström, PE (1996). Routine and reflection. Prerequisites and prevention of learning in daily work, Life-long Learning, (in Swedish), Ellström, PE, Gustavsson, B and Larsson, S pp 142–179, Lund: Studentlitteratur.

Fransson, A and Wahlén S (2001). *New conditions for learning in higher education.* SOU 2001:1. Stockholm.

Healey, M (2000). Developing the Scholarship of Teaching in Higher Education: a discipline-based approach. *Higher Education Research & Development,* **19**(2).

Karolinska Institute (2001). *Teaching portfolios for lecturers at the Karolinska Institute.* Stockholm.

Kreber, C (2000). How University Teaching Award Winners Conceptualise Academic Work: some further thought on the meaning of scholarship. *Teaching in Higher Education,* **5**(1).

Magin, DJ (1998). Rewarding good teaching: a matter of demonstrated proficiency or documented achievement. *International Journal for Academic Development,* **3**(4)

McKeachie, WJ (1999). *Teaching Tips. Strategies, Research, and Theory for College and University Teachers.* Boston: Houghton Mifflin.

Prosser, M and Trigwell K (1999). *Understanding Learning and Teaching. The Experience in Higher Education.* Buckingham: SRHE and Open University Press.

Ramsden, P (1992). *Learning to Teach in Higher Education.* Routledge.

Seldin, P (1997). *The Teaching Portfolio. A Practical Guide to Improved Performance and Promotion/Tenure Decisions.* Bolton, MA: Anker Publishing Company, Inc.

The Evaluation Office, Lund University (1998). *The Teacher Barometer,* (in Swedish), Lund.

The Evaluation Office, Lund University (2000). *The Student Barometer,* (in Swedish) 2000, Lund.

Trigwell, K, Martin E et al (2000). Scholarship of Teaching: a Model. *Higher Education Research and Development,* **19**(2).

Trigwell, K (2001). Judging University Teaching. *International Journal for Academic Development,* **6**(1).

Cordelia Bryan
Central School of Speech and Drama

One of the greatest changes in higher education over the past 10 years has been the increase in student numbers, necessitating some radical revision to how we assess our students. Despite many improvements in assessment practice which draw on constructivist pedagogic theories of learning, there has been relatively little research into how we assess group practice.

Our research revealed that many tutors would like the idea of dedicating a protocol mark specifically to successful collaboration, although few managed this in reality (Bryan, 2001). Similarly, there was a general desire to allow more time and space for collaborative projects. What tends to happen in reality in many cases is that collaboration is a required strategy for learning (whether in rehearsal and/or performance) rather than an object of assessment in its own right. How well students co-operate, compromise, or negotiate to find creative solutions to problems will affect the final outcome. However, we appear to make little or no distinction (in terms of marks) between those who positively influence the process and those who do not, or who may even affect the process negatively. These team skills, which are so highly prized for life-long learning and sought in applicants by many employers, are often not accredited within HE.

This collection of papers arises out of a three-year consortium project, funded by the Higher Education Funding Council for England's (HEFCE's) Fund for the Development of Teaching and Learning (FDTL), entitled Assessing Group Practice. The consortium is led by Central School of Speech and Drama and includes Dartington College of Arts; Goldsmiths' College; University of Leeds; University of Salford and University of Ulster.

These three papers explore collaborative activity within the performing arts with a view to identifying methods of assessment which can be demonstrated to be fair, robust and practicable. They focus respectively on:

- the importance of group formation on student learning;

- the discourse of assessment: language and ethics in the assessment of group practice; and

- how reflective practice can enhance group work.

All three papers identify and address a range of issues that can contribute in making the assessment of group practice problematic. They draw from a collective pool of research data which explores students' and staff's experience of the assessment of group practice and offer some solutions which may be of interest to colleagues both within and outside the performing arts.

References:

Bryan, C. (2001). Assessing Group Practice unpublished project report.

27 How guided reflection can enhance group work

Cordelia Bryan & Debbie Green
Central School of Speech and Drama

> I developed the notion that community could be a practice, rather than an entity. It is something about the responsibility of the individual to the whole group. By responsibility I don't necessarily mean 'taking care' of the whole group - it is more like each person in the group having a commitment to the individual experience of every member of the group, including themselves.
> Jackie Adkins (2000)

Abstract

It is widely acknowledged by employers and academics that group skills are highly desirable for employment as well as for multifarious life situations. These group skills are, however, rarely defined precisely, and consequently seldom awarded academic credit.

This paper explores collaborative work in the Performing Arts and how the skills and behaviour inherent in this work might be developed and assessed in different contexts, focusing particularly on reflection as the means for students to record and assess their contribution to the group process. Building on the literature, practical approaches, such as teacher-led modeling of structured reflection, are examined, as are methods of 'reflection in the body' to establish a group identity and trust in group work. Reflection is thus seen as a process which challenges the student, rather than one which merely reflects back as one would view an image in a mirror. It is argued that with a raised awareness and a structured approach to reflection in different contexts, students can gain a deeper understanding of the ways in which they have operated and functioned as a group. This in turn empowers the student not only to improve his/her own learning but also to take responsibility for self and the group in the way that Adkins advocates.

27.1 Introduction

Within the performing arts collaboration is, and has always been, common practice. Working together to create a cohesive 'whole' is the very nature of what drama, dance and music is about. However, in higher education we have not fully capitalised upon the invaluable collaborative skills which performing arts students acquire through their study. We know from our daily experience and from surveys of post graduates that performing arts students develop complex collaborative skills which equip them for careers in a wide range of professions and for business. Perhaps it is partially because the performing arts community within HE is confident that collaborative skills are developed and acquired by our students that we have neglected to define them and consequently ignored the potential learning opportunities to be gained from their assessment. More importantly, we have failed to make public the case that performing arts education is the leader in developing these highly sought after transferable skills.

Although this paper focuses on the reflective process, both in the mind and in the body, (and some would argue, one has to have 'done' something in order to be able to reflect upon it) we shall also discuss examples of successful practice where the reflective process has been directly linked to the preparatory stage of work when objectives are negotiated and agreed. In this sense, reflection also encompasses planning and thinking about where one is going, before assessing and evaluating how well one achieved the objectives.

Boud and Walker make a strong case for reflection being highly context-specific (Boud and Walker, 1998). As educators and performers we are reflective practitioners and are thus well placed to model for our students successful ways of reflecting. This paper explores diverse approaches to reflection, drawing on examples provided from within a performing arts consortium project which represents a number of broad based disciplines.

In Assessing Group Practice we have defined assessment in its broadest sense to include feedback of any sort (eg oral, written, self, peer and tutor generated) as well as grades allocated to groups and individuals. Although we are not completely happy with the collaborative process being broken down into a series of skills, we have yet to find another way of describing these complex processes.

27.2 What are collaborative skills and how might they be developed?

Collaborative skills are the skills which students develop in the process of group work, some of which are discussed here. Whilst there are some generic group skills, others are context specific and therefore need to be determined at the outset of any project. Our research revealed a diversity of ways in which collaboration takes place within the performing arts. It revealed few examples, however, where these collaborative skills were specifically graded (Bryan, 2001).

Effective collaboration is likely to encompass various communicative and interactive skills. These include the subtle differences between for example, directing, instructing, requesting, suggesting, clarifying and confirming, and students need to learn when and how to use each. Successful collaboration may require some members to employ skills of persuading, reassuring, motivating, involving, questioning and disagreeing and criticising as conflict can be creative. Not all of these interactive skills will be expressed verbally, yet how well they are developed and employed may, to a large extent, determine the success of a project.

The notion of reflection is embedded within various theoretical frameworks (Brockbank & McGill, 1998; Hutchinson & Allen, 1977; Kember et al., 1999; Moon, 1999; Schon, 1987). Although our research has been within Performing Arts, we have drawn on both management and reflective learning theory and practice. For example, Tuckman and Jenson (1977) identifiy six key stages in group formation - forming, storming, norming, performing, retiring and mourning. Our research accords with Tuckman and Jenson that with a sound understanding of these stages, students are empowered to make their own groups work most effectively by taking the necessary action to counter the challenges as the group moves sequentially through the various stages. Belbin suggests eight key roles for successful groups and provides team members with an inventory to assess their best team roles (Belbin, 1981). We have trailed versions of these models and found that when students gain a realistic understanding of their own strengths, it enables them to participate more positively within the group. For example, students and tutors can choose at the outset of a project, whether the context requires individuals to play to their strengths or whether it is an opportunity to gain experience and exercise some of their less well-developed group roles, thus broadening their personal raft of these transferable skills.

De Bono offers a model where groups use his six metaphorical hats, each of a different colour (De Bono, 1994). His method of parallel thinking was not originally devised for group reflection, however, the authors have experience where it has been used most effectively in rehearsals where no one person has directorial responsibility and where there may be an unproductive struggle for the role of leader by one or more group members. This form of 'thinking action' enables students to contextualise their reflection both individually and in the group. De Bono's method is described here to illustrate how it has been used as an aid to group reflection on process.

Each coloured hat represents a particular mode of thinking. The white hat represents information; the red hat represents feelings and emotions; the yellow hat indicates the 'logical positive' or sunny optimistic; the green hat is for creative effort and 'possibility'; the dark purple hat represents caution, risk assessment and criticism; and the blue hat is for the overarching thinking process or thinking about thinking, traditionally exercised by the chair or facilitator.

The group agrees to use a particular coloured hat, for example, when the white hat is in use, everyone in the group focuses, in parallel, on laying out the information. At no point is there any attempt to disagree, to challenge or to dispute a point. Everyone is thus focused in the same 'direction' and is thinking cooperatively, in parallel. Once all the information is laid out, the group might decide that it is time to use the green hat and to reflect as creatively as possible, again not censoring any ideas at this stage but simply laying them alongside each other.

There are many advantages to using the six hats of De Bono's parallel thinking, in particular the method enables the removal of the ego in discussions. Participants rise above the common temptation to 'knock' any idea which is not their own or to get so carried away with their own idea that they fail to acknowledge that there might be some dangers or drawbacks. Parallel thinking, compared to the more common adversarial discussion which can polarise participants into an early 'either or' situation, enables an atmosphere of cooperation and trust to develop. Subsequent reflection can thus be freed from an often habitual adversarial approach.

Performing arts work requires collaboration most of the time. There is no need to set up simulation exercises as is common practice in business training. The mode of creating a sense of group and complicité is practical, drawing from theatre improvisation and/or games, physical theatre, or dance practice eg weight sharing, physical trust work etc. Within these 'safe' practices and boundaries, courage to commit fully to the group is developed and group reflection can flourish.

Physical work can clearly offer the experience of a group practising being a group; and the link from this physical experience of working with others can be nurtured and related to collaborative work when words become the main medium for communication and expression. If 'give and take', listening and eloquence are present physically can these be transferred into the non-physical situation?

Physical trust work can develop into Contact Improvisation (CI), which is work that demands physical commitment and risk and working intimately with another person. CI, as a dance technique beyond the 'daily' state, is ultimately about interdependence through giving into and using body weight in partnership. By its nature as improvisation, CI is about spontaneity. Through the impulses from the contact, the student develops the ability to 'physically dialogue' with another person. CI demands that the student develops the skill of physically listening to stimuli - receiving and responding and initiating.

Both Moon's and Brockbank and McGill's conditions for reflection include modeling reflection in an emotionally supportive environment that removes the barriers to this mode of learning. Moon argues that group work with reflection is important and that the combination of individual and group reflective practice is most effective (Moon, pp 172-3).

27.3   Some theoretical models explored

Reflection is a mental process with purpose and / or outcome in which manipulation of meaning is applied to relatively complicated or unstructured ideas in learning or to problems for which there is no obvious solution. (Moon, 1999, p161)

This is the definition that Jennifer Moon uses by working through an identification of the nature of reflection and the processes of learning. Her definition is helpful for our purposes as it can encompass all sorts of reflection, both individual and group reflections, on diverse learning situations and contexts. It does not, however, encompass learning through the body, through movement practices. This form of 'reflection' requires constant in-the-moment physical working and only then can the practitioner stand outside the experience and analyse it. Bonnie Bainbridge Cohen, creator of Body-Mind Centering study, explains that

"When the body is experienced from within, the body and mind are not separated but experienced as a whole." She uses the word "'somatization' to engage the kinesthetic experience directly... Through somatization the body cells are informing the brain as well as the brain informing the cells". (Bainbridge Cohen, 1993, p1)

To achieve this holistic approach, the ability to 'dialogue' between the doing and the 'reflection' is developed by the constant 'doing' interspersed with guided reflection. If the philosophical stance of seeing meaning ascribed through the body is followed, the form itself provides the knowing, but, in movement terms, only as long as the doing is allowed to happen unrestricted and unimpeded by the mind - 'the head'. The following are all terms used within movement vocabulary; the mind in the body; the intelligent body; the thinking body; attention and intent aligned with the movement i.e. what is stimulating you and what you want to do in relation to that stimulation integrated with the movement. This is not dissimilar from Schon's notion of reflection-in and reflection-on action (Schön, 1987).

Barnett observed, some 25 years ago, how the notion of reflection was superseding that of criticism within higher education. He argues that this is because reflection carries reflexive and self-monitoring connotations. He warns of the danger of reflection becoming an ideology that requires reflection only at interpretive levels and disregards the potential for empowerment and emancipation. He, like Moon and Cohen, suggests that the reflective process brings to bear a focus upon the individual's own thought and learning development in ways that so-called objective criticism does not. An integration of cognitive and holistic approaches to reflection can thus enable students to reach a state of what he calls 'critical being'. It is from this state of critical being that Barnett believes that students can begin to identify their own strengths and limitations and thus be empowered to develop and move forward (Barnett, 1977).

Whilst Foucault (1980) also proposes that power derives from self-surveillance or 'confession', we would wish to disassociate reflective practice here from any therapeutic sense, instead, suggesting that it is more akin to being honest with oneself - reflection as discourse primarily with self but also within a group context.

Guile and Griffiths (2001) developed the Connective Model to describe the ideal relationship between academic and practical learning. The model involves taking greater account of the context upon student learning which, in their case, was observed in various work situations. They suggest that whilst seeking to empower our students through reflection we may be enhancing their capacity to self-regulate in relation to institutional or workplace norms and values. To encourage students to challenge such notions, their Connective Model seeks to develop in students what they call 'boundary crossing' skills or a capacity to conceptualise their experiences in different ways for differing contexts. They acknowledge that this sort of reflection requires teacher expertise to pose problems, in order to help students analyse their own experiences and arrive at critical understanding of their reality.

Teacher expertise is also central to Brockbank and McGill who argue that the teacher must

a. be aware of process and intentionality about that process and

b. possess an awareness that s/he is modelling the process used.
    (Brockbank and McGill, 1998, p69)

When exploring the deeper realms of personal feelings and beliefs, the teacher needs to draw clear boundaries and adhere to them. Clear guidelines for structured reflection based on an increased awareness of basic group dynamics, such as those which are in development within Assessing Group Practice, can go some way to provide a framework. However, teachers should not underestimate the potential dangers of group reflection on those with low self-esteem.

Maclellan's action research with post graduate trainee teachers concludes that if students are to be autonomous, they must clearly and explicitly intend that their learning be enhanced by reflection in specific ways. The students themselves emphasise that in reflective commentaries they must recognise what the task requires and they must actively construct knowledge to understand the problematic issues (Maclellan, 1999).

Dacre and Mackey reinforce the importance of contextualisation and suggest that reflection must be framed within the expert systems and within the 'narrative traditions' - reflecting on the personal and social narrative of existence (Dacre and Mackey, 1999, p59). It is essential that in evaluating there is knowledge of traditions and awareness of history and culture, as well as a body of knowledge of subject and understanding of craft.

There is further agreement, then, that reflection should not be a mechanistic exercise, but rather, a means of deepening understanding of self in relation to differing contexts eg others' perceptions, environment, occasion. When focusing on the development of collaborative skills, it is examples of this sort of reflective process which we have attempted to illustrate by our case studies. The reflection here goes beyond a mirror's reflection to a pro-active, multiple perspective reflection in which learning is viewed as interaction between changing contexts.

27.4   Case study 1.
Central School of Speech and Drama (CSSD)

Within the CI class on the BA (Hons) Acting course at CSSD, one way in which students experience multiple perspectives is by frequently changing partners. It is taught in a careful way so that the touch is impersonal - it has respect and sensitivity but contact with a body part is made and the necessary support for the body is provided. The students develop the ability to fall and allow others to fall before catching them. Within the work is complicité and a discovery of individuals within the group through movement. It has a powerful effect on group dynamics within the session demanding professional behaviour. In CI, students learn that trying to control someone else is futile. If they try to do so by, for example, pre-empting how someone else will react, the improvisation is unproductive and a stalemate will occur physically. As the classes continue, physical inhibitions even in their most subtle forms, such as someone constantly in the support role, lose their hold and the physical and mental liberation is apparent in most participants. The students thank each other after each improvisation and realise that they have learned something from each different partner. Even if initially the student's desire to move in a certain way has had to be relinquished because the partner's movement simply did not accommodate a preconceived idea, s/he is encouraged to surprise him/herself. On reflection of the experience of this physical dialogue the student often acknowledges how important it is to be open to the unexpected - an aspect of the learning process which cannot be underestimated.

Learning about each other through touch and a Contact Improvisation is a concentrated and often extreme physical encounter which need not be applied exclusively in the Performing Arts. In its most basic form, it has much to offer the non-performer and the technique may be applied in other disciplines where it is desirable to establish a sense of group identity and trust before embarking on any collaborative work. Allowing for a few moments of silence to reflect on the Contact Improvisation experience before moving into the next exercise enables the student to recognise the reflective process in the body. At a later stage s/he may try to express something of the experience in words if this is appropriate for deeper understanding and assessments such as peer feedback and self-reflection.

The following two case studies, drawn from the project's first year research, illustrate quite different ways in which reflection can be incorporated into the assessment of group work.

27.5   Case Study 2. School of Media, Music and Performance, University of Salford

Multimedia theatre is a project whose "assessment strategy reflects the aims of the module to encourage students to apply theoretical understanding to practical experimentation and is therefore designed to reward ideas and creativity alongside critical reflection and contextualisation". The critical analysis and evaluation of the piece created by the group as well as the supporting documentation detailing original ideas for additional scenes/sequences for the development and extension of the piece "offer each student the opportunity to express their personal vision and understanding of the group-devised piece and enable individual students to be rewarded for the quality of their understanding and ideas (Smart, 2001).

Asking students to suggest ideas for the development of the piece rather than to identify their contributions to what already exists, enables the assessor to distinguish the depth of student engagement with concepts and the originality and creativity of their own ideas. Students suggesting further creative ideas, which are appropriate in the context of the presentation, are likely to have been fully involved in the generation of the group-based work. There is also a space for those whose ideas were perhaps not used or who disagreed with the decisions of the group to express their opinions in an analytical context within the evaluation of the piece. Thus the assessor is able to reward aspects of intellectual and creative process that were perhaps unseen.

It was widely reported that objectivity and self-reflexivity are often under-developed in students and that there may be difficulties with the critical contextualisation of students' practical ideas (Bryan, 2001). This example shows a most effective way of extrapolating what levels of cognitive skills and critical reflexivity have been employed by an individual in the creative group process and assessing these specifically. It exemplifies Guile and Griffiths' (2001) Connective Model, which describes an ideal relationship between academic and practical learning. Although their model is devised for work experience, its focus on the need for students to make links between experiential and theoretical learning is equally valid for performing artists and other disciplines where the development of 'boundary crossing' skills is seen as important.

27.6   Case Study 3. School of Media, Music and Performance, University of Salford

Video projects are assessed through working notebook, reflective critical self-assessment and individual viva voce. Reflection is assessed through the critical self-assessment and the viva voce supports assessment of both process and reflection with equal weighting. Peer assessment questionnaires provide clarity of the whole picture of the marking and also frame how the observation and reflection might work. The combination is deemed effective as peer assessment encourages them to face and justify personal problems. If there has been a personal issue raised by one student with another and this is repeated by others, then there is a basis to the statements. The log books are read before the viva and thus personal performance can be related to the whole group and awareness checked. Students can be honest in the viva and in their log books about their individual contribution. However, there is still the issue of criticising peers, or indeed friends, which is acknowledged in most forms of peer assessment (Smart, 2001).

27.7   Case Study 4, School of Dance and Theatre, Bretton Hall (amalgamated with University of Leeds since 2001)

A set of criteria or protocols is defined for actors' logs and work-files, a different one for performance, and the results of the two conflated. Dramaturgs record and evaluate rehearsal processes, rehearsal outcomes and performance effectiveness. This provides an informal reviewing and assessment of their peers. Third level actors who undertake a directing project are encouraged to keep evaluative journals that informally assess the progress of their first and second level acting colleagues within the rehearsal and performance process. These are often anonymised and currently do not contribute to formal profiling of the first and second-level actors (Johnson, 2001).

Our research indicates that when peer assessment can be incorporated into the formal assessment strategy, students tend to take the process more seriously. It also conveys a powerful message to students that their critical judgement is valued by tutors and within the institution (Bryan, 2001).

The following case study illustrates a common problem ensuring that the collaborative process is really the focus for assessment.

27.8   Case Study 5, Drama Department, University of Ulster

In a large number of modules reflection on the process of working together is assessed through reflective logs and, in some cases, written essays or examinations. Such reflection is vital in the process of learning from experience. However, there are two dangers here. In assessing their abilities to reflect through these forms, there is a danger that the represented process comes to stand for the actual experience. Students who are effective at reading the rules of the game engage in post-hoc rationalisations and descriptions, which may be far from their actual experiences or contribution at the time. Here, the ability to reflect insightfully may take precedence over the actual engagement at the time, which is the crucial element of collaboration. Furthermore, by using written means to assess collaborative practical working, there is the danger that such forms favour skills of articulacy rather than collaboration. The issue of 'fairness' under the QAA definition is called into question: 'a fair assessment method is one that rewards only the attributes being measured' (Cook, R. 2000) QAA Code of Practice – quality and standards in HE. on line.

Alerting tutors of a difficult process in the logs or module evaluation may be too late to address the situation and the effect of some students' non-participation cannot be redressed for the other members of the group (Maguire, 2001).

In a situation like this, Moon's suggestion of combining both individual and group reflection could help to ensure that the collaborative process remains the focus for attention

Although group vivas have proved to be both cost effective and of particular benefit to the learning process (Crème, 1999; Moon, 1999; Snaith, 2001), we encountered few examples of group vivas being used as a method of summative assessment.

A notable exception was found at Anglia Polytechnic University, where the English department applies a universal ten percent accreditation for students' seminar contributions. In this instance, not only are clear criteria made explicit from the beginning of any course, students are also guided through various exercises on how to participate effectively in seminars. This example demonstrates sound learning objectives (eg learning to function effectively in a group discussion) being inextricably linked with the mode of assessment (Snaith, 2001). It also conveys a powerful message to the students that considered talking, listening and responding to each other is valued by the whole department.

27.9 Conclusion

Since it is known that assessment is a powerful motivator of student learning, we can no longer ignore the learning potential of assessing collaboration. Our case studies provide ample evidence that performing arts students do acquire complex team skills. Perhaps the time to foreground collaborative skills, to define them and to understand their importance is during the reflective process, once they have experienced the potency of group working.

It is argued here that students need a structured frame of reference which is rooted within the specific context for reflection to be both useful and empowering. Effective reflection, therefore, includes a knowledge, and eventually possession, of appropriate critical vocabulary so that students become empowered to express themselves within a group situation.

In order to achieve this, the learning space needs to be safe so that the potency of group dynamics can be fully explored.

References

Adair, J (1989). Effective team building, London, Gower. In O'Sullivan, T, Rice, J, Rogers, S and Saunders, C (1996) *Successful Group Work*, London: Kogan Page and De Montfort University.

Adkins, J (2000). Contact Connection (a national newsletter about contact improvisation), Issue **19**.

Bainbridge Cohen, B. (1993). *Sensing Feeling and Action, the Experiential Anatomy of Body-Mind Centering.* Contact Editions.

Barnett, R (1977). The Limitations of Competence. In Moon, J (1999) *Reflection in Learning & Professional Development.* Kogan Page.

Barnett, R (1990). *The Idea of Higher Education.* Buckingham: SRHE and Open University Press.

Belbin, RM (1981). *Management teams - why they succeed or fail.* London: Butterworth.

Heinemann in O'Sullivan, T, Rice, J, Rogers, S and Saunders, C (1996). *Successful Group Work.* London: Kogan Page and De Montford University.

Boud, D and Walker, D (1998). Promoting Reflection in Professional Courses: the challenge of context. *Studies in Higher Education,* **23**(2), 191–206.

Brockbank, A and McGill, I (1998). *Facilitating Reflective Learning in Higher Education.* Buckingham: SRHE and Open University Press.

Brown, S (1999). Institutional Strategies for Assessment. In Brown, S and Glasner A (Eds), *Assessment Matters in Higher Education: Choosing and Using Diverse Approaches.* Buckingham: SRHE and Open University Press.

Bryan, C, (in press). Assessing Group Practice, HEFCE Project Paper.

Cowan, J (1998). *On Becoming an Innovative University Teacher,* Buckingham: SRHE and Open University Press.

Cowan, J (2002). Facilitating development through varieties of reflection, article on ILTHE Members' Resource: URL at http://www.ilt.ac.uk

Crème, P (1999). New forms of student and assessment in social anthropology: research through practice at the University of Sussex, National Network in Teaching and Learning Anthropology FDTL Project 1997 - 1998.

Dacre, K & Mackey, S (1999). Self-interpreting Animals: action research and the reflective drama journal. *Research in Drama Education,* **4**(1), Carfax. p.59.

Foucault, M (1980). The Eye of Power: In Power/Knowledge: Selected Interviews and other writings 1972-1977 (Ed), Colin Gordon trans. Colin Gordon, Leo Marshall, John Mepham, Kate Soper, Brighton: Harvest Press.

Hutchinson, DJ & Allen, KW (1997). The reflection integration model: A process for facilitating reflective learning. *The Teacher Educator* **32**, 226–234.

Kember, D, Jones, A, Loke, A, McKay, J, Sinclair, K, Tse, H, Webb, C, Weng, F, Wong, M & Yeung, E (1999). Determining the level of reflective thinking from students' written journals using a coding scheme based on the work of Mezirow. *International Journal of Lifelong Education* **18**, 18–30.

Green, D (2001). Assessing Group Practice, unpublished project report.

Guile, D & Griffiths, T (2001). Learning Through Work Experience. *Journal of Education in Work,* **14** (1), 113–131.

Jacques, D (2001). *Learning in Groups,* (3rd Edn), first published in 1984, London: Kogan Page.

Johnson, W (2001). Assessing Group Practice, unpublished project report.

Maguire, T (2001). Assessing Group Practice, unpublished project report.

Maclellan, E (1999). Reflective Commentaries: what do they say about learning? *Educational Action Research,* **7**(3), 433–449.

Moon, J (1999). *Reflection in Learning & Professional Development.* Kogan Page.

O'Sullivan, T, Rice, J, Rogers, S and Saunders, C (1996). *Successful Group Work.* London: Kogan Page and De Montford University.

Schön, D (1987). *Educating the Reflective Practitioner.* San Francisco: Jossey-Bass Inc.

Taylor, R (1992). *Visual Arts Education*. The Falmer Press.

Tuckman and Jenson (1977). Stages of Small Group Development Revisited. *Groups and Organisational Studies*, **2** 419–427.

Smart, J (2001). Assessing Group Practice, unpublished project report

Snaith, A (2001). Conversations and seminars. In Stott, R, Young, T, and Bryan, C (Eds), *Speaking your Mind: Oral Presentation and Seminar Skills*, pp 6-28. Longman.

28 Assessing in triplicate

Jackie Smart[1] and Steve Dixon[2]

1 King Alfred's College, Winchester, 2 University of Salford

Key words: academic, art, assessment, collaborative, creativity, criticality, discourse, Foucault, process, product, professional.

The original and full version of this paper was published as The Discourse of Assessment: language and value in the assessment of group practice in the performing arts in the journal, Arts and Humanities in Higher Education: an international journal of theory, research and practice, Vol. 1 no.2, (Eds. Ellie Chambers, Jan Parker & Marshall Gregory) pp 185 - 204. It is reproduced here by permission of Sage Publications, Thousand Oaks, London and New Delhi.

28.1   Introduction

In this paper, we will be examining ways in which the language and structures used in assessing undergraduate collaborative practice in the performing arts convey ideas of value. Our methodology draws on discourse theories deriving from the work of Michel Foucault. Discourse analysis examines the different ideologies, cultural perspectives and political positions at play within texts in order to expose the underlying values they inscribe. Our suggestion is that much assessment of group performance in Higher Education takes place at the intersection between several discourses including what we will term 'The Academy', 'Professional Theatre' and 'Art'. We propose that the uneasy dialogue between these discourses, as they express themselves through assessment, results from the sometimes contradictory values they espouse. Our aim is to identify discourse conflicts experienced by students and staff and to trace the roots of these conflicts through their inscription in the choice of themes and language used in assessment criteria.

As an illustration of how our understanding of a word can change depending on the discourse in which it is articulated, let's look at the word 'assessment' itself. To assess is commonly understood to mean to evaluate: to value. The act of assessing student practical work commonly requires the assessor to attribute 'value' to the performance and to articulate it in numerical terms. Value implies a common currency by which a product or service is measured: what it's worth. This understanding of the meaning of 'value' implies market-related criteria for assessment, something we might associate with the 'professional' discourse we have identified. Within the educational arena however, would these be the kind of criteria we would wish to apply? Under the generic heading 'collaborative skills', for example, value may be accorded to skills such as listening, ability to compromise or ability to lead, but criteria such as 'ability to cut corners', 'ability to manipulate others' or 'ruthlessness' are never seen. Within the discourse and practice of 'Professional Theatre' (as well as in many other professional and business fields) the latter attributes may enable a student to succeed as effectively as the former, yet it would be considered inappropriate and reactionary to include them within an educational setting. The question arises, is worth being attributed solely to those skills or knowledges embedded within the learning outcomes or, by implication, also to particular human qualities or characteristics which may be accounted more morally creditable than others?

28.2   Presentation: ideology as pedagogy in assessment criteria

The choice of assessment criteria, and the language used to express them reflect the ideological and cultural value systems at the core of Foucault's discourse theory. Our research into the choice of language used in criteria for group performance work reveals diverse approaches and institutional emphases. These can be divided into three general types of criteria which can be readily mapped against the distinct belief systems we have outlined: 'The Academy', 'Professional Theatre' and 'Art'.

Criteria reflecting what are perceived as traditional 'Academic' values concentrated on the evaluation of students' understanding and analysis of the performance process and context. Common words here included: understanding; analysis; research; interpretation; contextualisation; evaluation. Criteria emphasising the 'Art' discourse primarily focused on creativity and experimentation and adopted words such as: imagination; innovation; aesthetics; design; creativity; exploration; experimentation; risk. 'Professional Theatre' oriented criteria emphasised technical skills and specific aspects of performance delivery: characterisation; control; confidence; concentration; dynamics; spontaneity; expression; stage presence; individuality.

We found that the widest variety of language was applied to professional skills-based criteria, where criteria were commonly sub-divided to focus very specifically on particular aspects of technique. For example, one criterion for acting such as 'characterisation' may be sub-divided to highlight its constituent parts: physicalisation; vocalisation; credibility; development; psychology, depth; tempo-rhythm. Each of these may be further subdivided; for example we found 'physicalisation' broken down into many criteria such as: physical control; physical expression; balance; relaxation; articulation. Each of these may be subdivided again until we move fractally towards infinity.

A fundamental factor acknowledged by the Assessing Group Practice consortium is the complexity and fallibility of the term 'assessment' itself when applied to performance. The arts intend to provoke and affect us emotionally and subconsciously as well as intellectually and consciously. Therefore, if when we assess performance we attempt not to feel in order to remain objective, precisely what, why and how are we assessing?

28.3   Environment: The Academy and Professional Theatre

In Britain, prior to 1992, there was a marked differentiation between the academic world of the university, which consciously associated itself with a purity of intellectual endeavour, and the more vocational and technical world of the Polytechnic, which was more closely allied to training for a professional working life. Although this is changing, courses in dance, drama and performance still often sit somewhat uneasily on the line between the intellectual and the vocational.

The Benchmarking Statement for Dance, Drama & Performance (DDP) produced by the Quality Assurance Agency for Higher Education[1], addresses this tension in several ways.

One of the first things the Statement does is to make the reader aware of the diversity of provision, from the conservatoire, where the focus is on training the professional practitioner, to those institutions which place greater emphasis on "the pursuit of scholarship and research." Despite acknowledging this range, the Statement leaves us in no doubt that the practical and technical skills needed by the professional practitioner will not be valued on their own. It asserts that

> Within DDP, learning and teaching will be closely related, through a variety of
> approaches that… cohere… around the integration of practice and theory. (p 6)

How is this integration to be achieved? The Statement describes experiential learning as "a key principle of study" and refers us to such concepts as "embodied knowledge" and "practice as research".

In terms of assessment too, the Statement places emphasis on the interrelationship of practical and intellectual engagement. Students aspiring to good grades should demonstrate knowledge and understanding through "creative and intelligent engagement," while in subject skills', they should "engage creatively and critically" with a whole variety of processes and entities. We get a clear message then that only certain types of practice, those that can be theorised, are valued within The Academy. The Academic discourse is privileged and appropriate creativity within the subject field is still largely defined as that which emerges from a critical sensibility.

Despite the emphasis placed on collaborative learning and on 'learning through doing' in group contexts, it is not until the third section, "generic and graduate skills", that we find any reference to group work. Individual achievement, we may conclude, is still located above the collaborative and inter-personal skills related to effective group practice.

28.4   Collaboration: the student and the group

It is extremely important to remember that the social dynamic in which students become involved with their peers is absolutely central to their university experience. It is very often the case that a group of students working on a performance project will also be socialising or indeed living together. Supervising tutors on a project are rarely party to all the complex inter-personal negotiations which students undergo during a project, but a university education is, for the student, an holistic experience in which it can be very difficult indeed to disentangle the demands of personal, social and educational discourses.

28.5   Case studies

The following case studies are drawn from group practical assessments which took place in the School of Media, Music and Performance at the University of Salford, where there is a conscious emphasis on providing an education which will enable graduates to go on to work in professional performance and production areas.

Case study 1:   *Production Manager, Level 3 Video Drama Project, BA (Hons)*
Media and Performance.

The assessment for this module represents some of the difficulties inherent in combining 'academic', 'professional' and 'artistic' discourses. On one level, the module is designed to provide a 'professional' level experience for final year students. On another, it is designed to be an 'academic' expression of the students' capacity to apply their theoretical understanding of contemporary media performance in original and creative ways.

Students work collaboratively, each on a specified role (director, actor, editor etc). A staff supervisor attends three days of the video shoot in order to observe the students in action and each student is required to submit a working notebook and a reflective critical self-assessment.

There are generic criteria applicable to all participants, which place heavy emphasis on 'professionalism'. The Production Manager's individual brief includes, amongst other instructions, the following:

- Monitor crew performance and as far as possible ensure completion of tasks on schedule

- Delegate responsibilities not covered by role criteria listed in other crew grades

- Act effectively as the final arbitrator to resolve disputes and enforce discipline where appropriate.

During an interview, one student who took on this Production Manager role expressed the opinion that the criteria involved her in a power relationship with her peers which, while appropriate to a professional production manager, was problematic in terms of her status as a fellow student. Her ability to monitor, delegate and arbitrate, for example, depended very much on whether other members of the group would accept her authority. Her grade was therefore dependent on her ability to impose this authority on those she considered friends. In attempting to fulfil the requirements of her role she tried to create a distance between her personal and professional identities but she found this reduced her sense of ownership of the group production. This feeling was exacerbated by the lack of creative input her role allowed, which also limited the range of criteria on which she could be assessed. She did not believe that tutors valued the organisational and collaborative aspects of the project as highly as the creative elements and, since the complex power relations involved in her role remained hidden, she believed that her attempts to deal with them could not be given due credit.

On this module, the academic rigour expected of a final year degree module is located within the students' creative practice and ability to critically reflect on that practice, but where a student has not played a specifically creative role, it is difficult to establish the meaning that 'criticality' has. In reflecting on her role as Production Manager, this student was being asked to think and speak critically about the complex human relations, interactions and negotiations that took place between her and her peers, a process which necessitated significant juggling of the discourses of 'professionalism' and 'friendship'.

While teamwork skills are presented as highly valued in the assignment brief, grades are awarded on an individual basis. This raises the perennial question of how much teamwork is actually 'worth'. There is also the problem of the translation of action into words. The contribution the production manager has made to the 'document' which is the video drama production itself is relatively intangible because it is concerned with process rather than product. The amount of time the supervisor can spend on set is limited so that much of the student's contribution can only be expressed after the event in her written and oral commentaries.

The next case study concerns a project in which similar difficulties emerged, and documents the way staff attempted to resolve them.

Case Study 2:   Level 2, One Act Play, BA (Hons) Performing Arts

In this Year 2 module, students work in small groups with one taking the role of director. As with all project work at Salford, normal timetabled classes are suspended so that the students can rehearse their production full-time, to mirror professional practice.

In response to student concerns about the assessment of the module, a formal, anonymous, system of peer assessment was introduced into this module in 2001. Each student was asked to complete a form on which they graded their peers on aspects including:

- Organisation and time-management skills
- Commitment to the rehearsal process
- Practical engagement with the rehearsal process
- Creative engagement with the rehearsal process
- Communicative and inter-personal skills

At a training session held to introduce students to this new model, staff and students worked together to interpret these criteria by translating them into specific questions. This was an illuminating exercise which highlighted a wide range of possible interpretations and inherent 'discourses'. Students argued, for example, about how time-management differed from commitment and about what differentiated a practical from a creative contribution. A debate took place about what constituted 'communicative skills' and which of these were most valuable within the process of rehearsing a play. The peer assessment form was then redrafted to reflect the issues raised, and represented a mixture of student and staff contributions, as the following example illustrates:

> *How would you rate this person's creative contribution to the rehearsal process?*
>
> Did they contribute ideas which were used in the performance? (student suggestion)
>
> Did they contribute ideas and, if so, were those ideas relevant and effective? (tutor's amendment)
>
> Did they engage with the ideas of others (student suggestion)
>
> and did they help to develop these in useful and appropriate ways?(tutor's addition)

One factor this process exposes is what we consider to be a fallacious assumption that students and staff share a mutual understanding of criteria and language commonly applied to the assessment of group work. It is important to realise that while assessment criteria may be expressed in broad or generic terms, those engaged in a practical collaborative process are concerned with concrete activities and need to understand the process by which these are translated into marks.

Case Study 3:   *Level 1 Performance Workshop Projects, BA (Hons) Performing Arts; BA (Hons) Media and Performance; HND Physical Theatre and Dance; and HND Performing Arts (Media Performance).*

The final case study considers the notion of 'appropriateness' of assessment terminology in relation to the specific demands of the theatre-art study undertaken and relates this to a method of continuous self-assessment, which can be effective in facilitating students' engagement with the assessment process as an aid to learning.

Mixed groups of first year performance students from different courses engage in an intensive three-week project, with a workshop performance at the end. The assessment of the projects is weighted towards process and the assessment of process is undertaken by the workshop leader. Generic criteria provide a framework for assessment of the module but individual tutors are free to adapt these.

The case study concerns a workshop project focusing on Contact Improvisation: an improvisational dance form where partners retain physical contact with one another. The kinds of movement involved constitute a challenge to the conventional vocabulary and grammar of dance. There are no steps or routines to learn, and the main skill required in both rehearsal and performance is a developed ability to 'listen to' and understand the language of one's own body and the bodies of others. In this context, the project tutor adapted the generic assignment brief to reflect his perspective on the philosophy of the subject field.

Students on all the projects are asked to keep a working notebook recording and analysing their experience of the workshop project in terms of the skills, concepts and approaches addressed. On the first day of the Contact Improvisation workshop, the project tutor, Malcolm Manning gave the students a list of eight questions to act as a starting point for the notebook:

1. How do I learn?

2. What helps me to relax?

3. What does being present mean to me?

4. To what extent do I feel comfortable in my own body?

5. How does this affect my ability to work with someone else's body?

6. To what extent can I bring the answers to these questions into my movement?

7. How do I imagine applying what I am learning to my University life/other lives?

8. What do I feel most like saying about the workshop?

During each session, Malcolm gave students time to write down answers to these questions so that they could see if and how these changed as the project progressed. He told them that at the end of the workshop they would use their answers as a basis for assessing their process for themselves. Students had some initial difficulties with this approach, but, as the workshop progressed the questions began to make more sense to them. They found they could relate them to the activities they were undertaking and they began to develop a sense of group cohesion based around their shared experience of the difficulties of this new way of learning.

What surprised both students and tutors was how coherent an explanation of the principles and processes of Contact Improvisation was provided by the accumulated answers to the questions. Despite having felt lost and unsure of 'what the tutor wanted us to say' at the start of the process, the students reported that they found the approach effective in prompting them to think hard about the meaning of what they were doing each day. They described the experience as liberating and empowering because it both sought out their personal and inter-personal responses to the project and acknowledged them as valuable.

The success of this approach to assessment lay partly in a specificity of assessment design directly related to and integrated with the particular study undertaken, and partly in its reconstruction of students' ideas of what assessment is for. Contact Improvisation takes the form of a subjective experiential process and thus it is very difficult to construct a critical analysis of it 'after the fact'. The more subjective form of writing that students were asked to engage in here was akin to the movement form they were involved in studying and the mode of continuous self-assessment 'made sense' to the students in that it actively encouraged ongoing reflection upon what they were experiencing and learning.

26.6   Conclusions

It remains only for us to identify the key conclusions of this study. One is that in the discourses both of The Academy and of Professional Theatre, the assessment of collaborative practice currently appears to privilege the achievement of the individual over that of the group. This can mean that the group work recognised throughout the sector as being central to theatre and dance education actually takes place in an atmosphere of competition. Those who display the ability to create productive group working environments may gain only modest credit and perceive this as unfair.

A parallel conclusion is the relative under-valuation of process in the assessment of practical work, a factor which conflicts with the high value accorded to process within contemporary Art discourses. Often, students can only gain credit for process by means of their ability to translate it into a traditional format deemed 'appropriate' within the discourse of 'The Academy'. They must be able to critically articulate their creativity and interpersonal skills in a verbal or written form 'after the fact'. It is important to recognise that this approach fundamentally changes the nature of the experiential exercise and wholly removes it from the group context in which it took place.

Modes of self and peer assessment at HE level represent one way of reformulating the balance between teaching and learning. Such methods can be said to be particularly appropriate to performance studies in that they provide a means of according value to aspects of the creative process which may remain unseen by staff assessors. They can also function to reposition students as a self-critical 'audience' as well as initiators of their work, enabling an investment in assessment as learning process rather than product evaluation. However, care needs to be taken both to recognise the delicate position such strategies place the student in, and to ensure that they do not simply reproduce similar 'do it then talk about it' models.

We need to remember that the most effective assessment strategies will be inherently related to the nature of the study undertaken and this may mean paying closer attention to the relative numerical values ascribed to academic, artistic and professional elements. It is not necessary for every assignment to provide opportunities to assess everything that is valued in Higher Education. Perhaps there are forms of creativity that need not be critical, kinds of skill that are not knowledge-based, kinds of learning that do not carry 'economic' worth, but are nonetheless of value.

It is axiomatic that we speak most confidently in a language we feel we own. If our aim as educators is to enable students to become independent learners, and if we accept that assessment is part of the learning experience, then it becomes necessary to develop a language for assessment which students can feel they own, and can thus speak with confidence and authority. If the rebalancing of the educational equation in favour of learning rather than teaching is to be achieved, it seems appropriate to involve students in discussing and negotiating the terms by which their achievements will be valued. Students must be at the genesis of these new shared languages of learning and assessment.

[1]2002, Quality Assurance Agency for Higher Education. Available online at www.qaa.ac.uk

29 'The show must go on!' group formation and affectivity: some considerations for group work from higher education performing arts programmes.

Tom Maguire
University of Ulster

Keywords: Group formation; assessment; performing arts

Abstract

Despite the centrality of group work in the practices of the performing arts within the educational and industrial settings, little research has been hitherto undertaken into the processes of group working within these disciplines in the higher education sector. Based on literature in related disciplines and research within the Assessing Group Practice project, this paper examines some considerations to be addressed in the processes of group formation. Evidence is presented of the desirability of groups which are heterogeneous since group members have to both manage the achievement of tasks and maintain the group itself; processes which require a range of skills, aptitudes and behaviours. Notwithstanding this evidence, there appears less emphasis within the United Kingdom's higher education performing arts sector on such group maintenance roles due to the predominance of task roles associated with or derived from processes of theatrical production. Nonetheless, it is argued that the ways in which groups are formed, the first stage in the group maintenance process, will have a direct impact on the tasks achieved, the experience of group work and the learning which results. The variety of ways in which groups are formed is then examined. This includes formed, compulsory and natural groups. This argument rests on the claim that the alignment between the needs and values of individuals and those of the groups of which they are members has a large effect as a motivating factor. Group cohesion is presented as a key indicator of such alignment. Moreover, many of the problems associated with group work, such as low or late attendance, superficial co-operation or other forms of sabotage, may be avoided if such a motivational context can be created. A number of examples of effective practice from across the sector are presented to support this. Based on these examples, it is suggested that election and selection are important processes in ensuring such group cohesion, individual motivation, and deeper engagement with group tasks. These are particularly pertinent within the performing arts since they are embedded within many of the theatrical processes which are used routinely already.

29.1   Introduction

It is a commonplace assumption that group work is a central part of the experience of the performing arts within higher education despite the diversity of practices which fall under this heading. From complicity between participants in a workshop to the collaboratively devised performance or the hierarchical structuring of a quasi-professional production process, students form and are formed by a range of group situations as part of the performing arts disciplines.[1] Surprisingly, given this central place which group work occupies, there has been little research into the specific dimensions of the experience of students working together in the performing arts and the effects this might have on their learning. Thus, despite the richness which dramatic processes are seen to offer in the development of group work in a number of other settings (see for example Hickson 1995; Jennings 1986) and perceived difficulties in deploying groups as a learning strategy which is assessed, group work appears to be taken for granted and uninterrogated within the performing arts in higher education.

Uniquely, the Assessing Group Practice project, sets out to disseminate effective practice within the United Kingdom context, and this paper is the result of the collaboration of project consortium members and initial research undertaken under the auspices of the project into group work within drama and related programmes across the United Kindgdom.[2] In this paper I wish to identify some key considerations which might be taken into account in the planning and implementation of group work. I have focused on one specific process associated with group work, group formation, as an area in which these considerations are operational with particular force.

29.2   Groupwork factors

By contrast with performing arts education, much has been written on the ways in which individuals come together in groups within the fields of management (Adair 1986; Belbin 1981 , Boyle 1997); social work and therapy (Doel and Sawdon 1999; Heap 1977; Vernelle 1994); and education more generally (Gibbs 1994; Hertz-Lazarowitz and Miller 1992). In reviewing such literature on group working, it is clear that in all spheres in which it is used, it is regarded as a complex and multi-faceted activity. Factors influencing its procedures and outcomes in one formulation include the type of group member, the purpose of the group and the type of group (Whitaker, cited in Barnes et al 1999: 5). For work groups (see Douglas 1983: 111ff), the task defines the purpose of the group and achievement of the task assumes a high priority in evaluating the effectiveness of the group. The influence of Belbin's group role preferences which focus on task-related roles has even pervaded much education literature (cf. Belbin 1981 and Gibbs 1995, for example). Yet even in the literature on work groups, there is a consensus around the importance of maintaining a balance between the achievement of the task and the maintenance and development of the individual members of the group and the group as a whole: 'Groups are not only there to carry out tasks – they provide you with a series of opportunities to grow as a person' (Adair 1986:13). Within social work practice, Heap identifies these two dimensions with specific group types, while acknowledging that they may in fact be complementary elements within a single group:

> certain groups – usually informal and rather homogeneous – come into being in order to provide emotional satisfaction for members. Others – usually more formally constituted and relatively heterogeneous – come together in order to explore explicit goals. The former are called psyche groups and the latter are socio groups. The success of these groups may be registered respectively by how enjoyable are the former and how effective are the latter   (1977: 23)

Within education, O'Donnell and Dansereau formulate these dimensions in their acronym CAMS: 'Group interactions involve complex combinations of the cognitive/motor (C), affective (A), metacognitive (M) and social (S) activities of the learners involved' (1992: 124). The importance of addressing all these dimensions is assumed in the rest of this paper.

29.3   Work groups in the performing arts

In much of the group work in the performing arts, it is easy to identify facets of work groups or project teams. Adair identifies the following key characteristics of work groups:

> Have a common task (or a common set of individual tasks) which tend to be explicit
>
> Relationships are functional
>
> Groups exist to work on tasks
>
> Leadership tends to go with competence
>
> Work groups are often temporary
>
> (1986: 5-6)

These would appear to be characteristic of a number of models of group work on practical projects across the discipline. So, for example at Liverpool John Moores University, final year students undertaking a module in Directing work with first year undergraduates to produce performances through which they are assessed. In a number of other institutions, such as Central School of Speech and Drama and the University of Leeds, it is common practice for students working on different modules or programmes of study to combine to participate in production projects which mimic the processes and roles of the theatre industry. At Liverpool Hope, final year students may work together on independent projects which are specified through the use of individual learning agreements against which the individual and group are assessed. In these, students may indicate specific roles and tasks for which they have responsibility.

In all these contexts, the functional aspects of collaboration, particularly where students are staging performance work, indicate what Heap calls the 'dominance' of roles associated with the task over group building and maintenance roles which are 'recessive' (1977:23).[3] The ultimate test in performing arts is that the 'show must go on', yet we ignore at our peril Slavin's observation that *'learning is completely different from 'group' productivity'* (1992: 150) [italics in original]. In the rest of this paper, I shall explore the processes through which students come into groups as one aspect of the student experience of group work. These processes both manifest and affect student motivation within a group and consequently what the individual student may learn and what the whole group may achieve. The method here is to use theoretical and research perspectives to explain the success of particular processes as perceived by practitioners.

29.4   Group formation processes

In forming groups, Millis and Cottell caution that

> In general, groups should be heterogeneous, should not isolate minority students or women, and should be chosen by the instructor. The groups should be large enough to provide sufficient resources for the group to function but not so large that scheduling out-of-class activities or students "hiding" becomes a problem. [1998: online]

The brevity and clarity of such advice, while extremely useful, conceals the complexity of the processes involved in group formation, particularly for students within higher education. Three broad processes by which groups might be formed are identified by Heap: compulsory, formed, or natural (Heap 1977: 27ff). Briefly then, compulsory groups are where: 'Some agency, external to the group, forms a group by the exercise of authority… It should be noted that compulsory membership does not rule out common purpose… compulsion may in fact sometimes even intensify the experience of common purpose' (Heap 1977: 27). Formed groups too 'are frequently formed by external initiative, the members have some choice. In a sense they select themselves, since they may accept or refuse the invitation of the sponsor... A sufficient number choose to accept this offer, and a viable group is formed' (Heap 1977: 28). Natural groups 'arise spontaneously... Without external initiative or compulsion, the members simply 'come together' through circumstances which often seem to involve a large element of chance' (Heap 1977: 8).

Students in higher education are, of course, members of multiple groups, each of which may be formed by one or more of the processes above. Where students are grouped in compulsory modules or assigned membership of a class by the exigencies of time-tabling, these would appear to be compulsory groups. Formed groups occur on optional modules; on projects or activities for which students audition or apply; or through student clubs or societies. It should be noted that in some of these instances, students are primarily applying to take part in an activity, rather than to associate with particular other students. Heap describes difficulties which might arise thus: 'Unforeseeable negative responses to others, and the numerous intangible obstacles to interaction are more likely to manifest themselves in formed than in natural groups. The formed group assumes that bonds will develop on the basis of certain similarities between members' (Heap 1977 : 32). Not only are students members of multiple groups, but the processes interact to influence the student's experience of and engagement with each. Friendships occur between students on compulsory modules; such compulsory groups may take place within a broader process of a formed group, since the student has applied to join a particular programme of study; formed groups may arise within natural groups when particular tasks are set; students may be compelled to work together on modules they have elected to take. So group formation may be an unstable and fluid process.

29.5   Individual needs and group membership

While this fluidity is inevitable, it is important to recognise that membership of any group makes demands on the individual in return for satisfying some of the individual's needs, and these needs may have a particular intensity for students as they enter higher education. The bonds which tie an individual to a group may depend therefore on the place of the needs being met in the individual's hierarchy of need, together with the predictability and reliability of those bonds. Entry into higher education may separate the individual student from the variety of 'primary groups' (Heap 1977: 21) which have provided a range of support hitherto, particularly where the student is moving away from home or long-term relationships forged previously. The student in this situation has a range of powerful and compelling emotional and psychological needs to meet in making transitions into and through the various levels of higher education. However, large student cohorts, semesterisation and modularisation, for example, may mean that a student is faced with new relationships in a series of compulsory or formed groups on a bi-annual cycle in the course of the programme. Such circumstances, where group membership is unstable or transitory, may well militate against the satisfaction of compelling emotional and psychological needs within work groups arising within the programme. When needs are not met within any specific group, the student has a number of courses of action. According to Douglas,

> If there are alternative sources of need satisfaction available, for example, other groups, then, if there are no restrictions on movement, when the pressure to conform becomes too great it will tend to reduce an individual's level of satisfaction for his or her group below the point where these alternative sources become more attractive... where

members cannot move… psychological withdrawal may be one method of coping, but others, much more disruptive and designed to change the situation, are equally likely. (1983: 44)

Furthermore, students are faced with demands from the range of groups to which they belong, and may be faced with reconciling conflicts between their needs and these demands from different sources.[4] Again, such reconciliation may occur at the expense of groups which meet fewer or less important needs. This may explain some of the difficulties arising for students working together. They may have different needs and motivations in approaching their tasks or may be giving that task greater or less priority in dealing with the demands of multiple group membership. If membership of more stable or long-lasting formal and informal psyche groups outside the programme satisfies primary needs, membership of a work group on the programme will receive less priority.

29.6   Individual needs and group membership

So, students, consciously or subconsciously select where their efforts are placed and to what they will commit themselves. Such selections will have a direct impact on the work groups in which they are placed, and crucially the other students with whom they will work. There are a number of implications which derive from this in considering how groups might be assessed. The first of these concerns the relationship between individual learning and group productivity. As Slavin points out, 'learning is completely different from "group" productivity' (1992: 150). How do assessment regimes judge the former while at the same time rewarding the latter? Secondly, if the ways in which groups are formed and develop affect the learning of individual students, what can tutors do to ensure effective learning in groups? The answer may well lie in the development of group cohesiveness. Adair argues that

> The cohesiveness of a group is determined by the strength of the bonds that bind the individual parts together into a unified whole. This property is related to other more traditional concepts such as morale and team spirit. Cohesiveness, the strength of attraction of the group for its members, is also linked to the degree of interest commitment to the common task. It is sometimes referred to as the 'we-feeling' of a group.
> (1986:19)

The more demands that tasks make on individuals, the greater the cohesiveness required. Both compulsory and formed groups may achieve this 'we-feeling' through specific group-building processes. Compulsory groups do have a harder task to achieve it, however. Although Heap's description is of a social work group, the features outlines correspond with unsuccessful groups in any higher education setting:

> The aggression aroused by compulsion may of course be expressed in other ways than uncooperative silence. It may simply come directly into the open. It may also lead to indirect forms of sabotage such as low or late attendance ostensibly caused by sickness, or by other duties or by "forgetting". A more subtle and common form of sabotage is that of apparent but very superficial cooperation.
> (Heap 1977:30)

By contrast, natural groups by definition have a sense of group cohesion just by coming together. Natural grouping may therefore be seen as a highly effective process to ensure both group cohesion and individual learning. Natural groupings derive from elective processes of group formation. These research findings and theoretical findings appear to indicate that election and selection are effective strategies in group formation by aiding group cohesion, individual motivation and, consequently, individual learning.

29.7   Creating a motivating context: election and selection

In our Assessing Group Practice survey, it was found that election in practice was reported as having a crucial role in developing successful groups which combined aspects of both natural groups and work teams in their functionality and success. Highly motivated students perceived that such groups met a number of their most important needs. Where students elect into the group and into the scheme of work that requires them to work together in the first instance, there seems to be a higher degree of bond and commitment to the group. Individuals who are compelled to work together in groups (particularly those which are then expected to exercise some sort of independence) function together less successfully.

Thus, compelling students to work together without any attention to selecting them according to their needs, abilities or motivations may well inhibit the learning of each individual within the group. Both the under-motivated and the highly-motivated can be adversely affected by the experience of each other. Although Johnson and Johnson's description of things that go wrong in groups utilises a distinction between able and less able, its features can be related to the under- and highly-motivated too:

> Less able members sometimes "leave it to George" to complete the group's tasks, thus creating a free-rider effect (Kerr & Bruun 1983) whereby group members expend decreasing amounts of efforts and just go through the teamwork motions. At the same time, the more able group members may expend less effort in an attempt to avoid the sucker effect of doing all the work (Kerr, 1983). High-ability group members may be deferred to and may take over the important leadership roles in ways that benefit them at the expense of the other group members (the rich-get-richer effect)   (1992: 178)

The importance of election as a manifestation of motivation is key from early within the recruitment process. In a programme where students are highly focused and for which entry is by interview or audition through which student talents, abilities and needs are matched to the demands of the programme, students are also more likely to form natural groups which may focus around the tasks of the discipline at an earlier stage. This is not to promote the highly vocational single honours programme above others (particularly combined degrees) but to point out that group work in such circumstances can often rely on shared motivations and expectations about the issues and processes involved. Thus, highly focused and/or selective programmes may draw individuals together into 'natural groups' whose constituency coincides with the focus required. This feature may hold also for elements within programmes for which entry is selective or which are particularly specialised: such as in a Theatre-in-Education module at Liverpool Hope, or a strand of community theatre modules at University of Ulster or linked Directing modules at Liverpool John Moores.

Once on a programme students may find themselves encountering a variety of methods for the formation of groups: self-selection from within a module cohort; self-selection for entry into a module (students effectively only take the module if they have a viable group beforehand); vetted self-selection (albeit with a light hand) to ensure a degree of fairness between groups; or by tutor allocation. By and large, on the programmes surveyed, most groups were formed by self-selection and this appears to be a key factor in ensuring that students retain responsibility for the relationships into which they will enter.

29.8 Addressing The limitations of election

Of course election or self-selection may merely replace one set of problems, concerning group cohesiveness, with another to do with group achievement, as Gibbs points out:

> If groups are allowed to form themselves there will be groups of friends together. This will improve interaction and co-operation but may mitigate against rigour, self-discipline or being able to tackle difficult group problems. It will also tend to produce groups of good students and a rump of poor students no group wants as members. This may open you up to accusations of unfairness.
> (1995: 8)

This is borne out by one student's comments: "When students pick their own groups you will end up with your friends – you may not be hard working and it is easy to tell your friends that you're not doing that or you'll not be there, but you don't want to let strangers down". This comment by a second year, BA Humanities Combined student at the University of Ulster contrasts with that of a second year Theatre Studies student who noted that: "You know who you can work well with".

Mistaking personal solidarity for success has been identified as one difficulty when students' reflections on their work have been assessed. However, while Gibbs' point is well-made in a general context, it might be worth noting that it may have limited applicability in the performing arts, due to particular practices within the disciplines. These may be grouped as rehearsal; public presentation; and vertical grouping. These practices foster the creation of strong reference groups which Douglas notes 'have been called 'invisible committees' and appear to act as a standard against which an individual measures his or her performance' (1983: 48). In the performing arts such reference groups are made visible.

29.8.1 Rehearsal

The concept of rehearsal is not unique to the performing arts, but it is central to them. For example, a staff or student director will coach student actors, giving feedback and support which identifies the qualities and deficiencies of the work in hand. Indeed, part of the skill of the director is to address both the emotional and psychological needs of the actor in encountering the demands of the task. It is also common practice that where a student is directing, s/he will be observed in the rehearsal room and given feedback and guidance on the management of that process as it unfolds. Rehearsal allows the opportunity for experimentation, risk-taking and the creation of a secure environment in which the group has to reconcile its task with the needs of the individual members.

29.8.2 Public presentation

Secondly, the public nature of the outputs of group activities itself forces recognition of the academic community's standards for rigour. Critical audiences, especially of peers, can form potent reference groups in such circumstances. Frequently, groups will be required to demonstrate work in progress which is subject to critical feedback by peers or a tutor, so that rigour is demanded and standards set and monitored. In public performance, there are few hiding places.

29.8.3   Vertical grouping

Moreover, while Gibbs notes that, 'In work contexts teams seldom select their own membership, and it may be more realistic to allocate students randomly' (1995: 8) in the performing arts professions, the project nature of much production work actually does allow team members to select one another. Furthermore, auditioning and other selection processes help to assure group members of a shared motivation and commitment. Where student groups cut across divisions between year groups (vertical grouping), there is an opportunity to pass on such standards from cohort to cohort. The success of vertical group formation appears to rest on a high level of intrinsic motivation from all concerned, a culture of 'professionalism' (students adopting quasi-professional roles), and a differentiation of roles and assessment regimes according to the different stages of the individuals involved. This seemed to be most effective in those programmes or elements of programmes with a high degree of vocational orientation (directing, theatre practice, performance skills). Vertical group formation may also have a high return in creating the social glue which is a key component in enabling students to make the transition from one level of the programme to another, establishing and maintaining the particular ethos and culture of the subject area, and developing transformation of knowledge as students themselves take on the roles of mentors / peer tutors or role models for aspirant first years. This last point should be stressed since where there is no formal training in particular competencies/skills/behaviours associated with group working, good role models may form an invaluable educational support.

29.9   Conclusions

The argument here, then, has been that motivation to learn through working with other students is contingent upon an alignment of the needs and values of the individual as a whole with the needs and values of the other members of the group (together with the values demanded by the task structure and the values recognised in the reward structure). In utilising groups, lecturers should be aware of the potential difficulties which arise when this alignment is not present. It is argued from the evidence of practitioners that selection and election may support effective working by enhancing and drawing on student motivation. The difficulties which might arise from such processes are addressed by specific practices of the performing arts around rehearsal, public performance and vertical group formation. Moreover, these practices appear to reinforce awareness of the affective dimensions of group working at the same time as they focus on the tasks being undertaken. Clearly in these aspects, there are some effective practices within the performing arts which other disciplines might wish to adopt and adapt.

Notes:

1.   This is, not of course, a complete survey of the ways in which students work together in the performing arts. Students will often collaborate on smaller or more discrete tasks than complete production work, particularly within workshop settings or in seminar discussions.
2.   Assessing Group Practice See Introduction to these three consortium papers or for further details visit the project website http://assessing-groupwork.ulst.ac.uk/.
3.   One notable exception to this is a module in Creative Group Processes at University of Ulster in which students work together as an end in itself rather than as a means to a public performance. It is no coincidence, however, that the module co-ordinator for this module is himself a dramatherapist with a broad range of experience in therapeutic and community drama practices.

4.   An additional inhibitor is the necessity which students increasingly experience of engaging in employment to support their studies.

Bibliography

Adair, J, (1986). *Effective Teambuilding: How to Make a Winning Team*. London: Pan.

Belbin, RM (1981). *Management Teams*. London: Heinemann.

Barnes, B, Ernst, S and Hyde, K, (1999). *An Introduction to Groupwork: A Group-Analytic Perspective*. Basingstoke: Macmillan.

Boyle, R, (1997). *Team-based Working*. Dublin: Institute of Public Administration.

Doel, M and Sawdon, C, (1999). *The Essential Groupworker: Teaching and Learning Creative Groupwork*. London: Jessica Kingsley.

Douglas, T, (1983). *Groups: Understanding People Gathered Together*. London: Tavistock Publications.

Gibbs, G, (1995). *Learning in Teams: A Tutor Guide*, (Rev ed). Oxford: Oxford Centre for Staff and Learning Development.

Heap, K, (1977). *Group Theory for Social Workers: An Introduction*. Oxford: Pergamon Press.

Hickson, A, (1995). *Creative Action Methods in Groupwork*. Bicester: Winslow Press.

Quality Assurance Agency for Higher Education (1998). Q0 14/98 Subject Overview Report: Quality Assessment of Drama, Dance and Cinematics, 1996-1998 [online]. Available from: http://www.qaa.ac.uk/revreps/subjrev/All/qo14-98.pdf . Accessed 5/7/2001.

(2201).Draft Benchmarking Statements For Consultation: Dance, Drama And Performance Arts [online]. Available from http://www.qaa.ac.uk/crntwork/benchmark/phase2/dance.pdf. Accessed 25/8/01.

Jennings, S, (1986). *Creative Drama in Groupwork*. Bicester: Winslow Press.

Johnson, DW and Johnson, RT (1992). Positive Interdependence: Key to Effective Co-operation. In Hertz-Lazarowitz, R and Miller, N, 1992 *Interaction in Co-operative Groups. The Theoretical Anatomy of Group Learning*, pp 174–199. Cambridge: CUP.

Millis, BJ, and Cottell, PG, Jr (1998). Co-operative learning for higher education faculty, American Council on Education, Series on Higher Education. Phoenix: The Oryx Press,. AZ, cited in National Institute for Science Education (1997). Doing CL [online]. Available from http://www.wcer.wisc.edu/nise/cl1/CL/doingcl/choogrp.htm. Accessed 5/7/01.

O' Donnell, AM and Dansereau, DF (1992). Scripted Co-operation in Student Dyads: A Method for Analyzing and Enhancing Academic Learning and Performance. In Hertz-Lazarowitz, R and Miller, N, *Interaction in Co-operative Groups. The Theoretical Anatomy of Group Learning*, pp120–141. Cambridge: CUP.

Slavin, RE (1992). When and Why Does Co-operative Learning Increase Achievement? Theoretical and Empirical Perspectives. In Hertz-Lazarowitz, R and Miller, N, *Interaction in Co-operative Groups. The Theoretical Anatomy of Group Learning*, pp145–173. Cambridge.

Vernelle, B (1994). *Understanding and Using Groups*. London: Whiting and Birch.

Sue Clegg and Philip Garrahan
Sheffield Hallam University

The New Labour Government in the UK has emphasised the importance of developing highly skilled 'knowledge' workers as part of its strategy for enhancing competitiveness. ts target for higher education is to increase the participation rate to 50% by 2010. This strategy is not unique to the UK, but represents a considerable challenge given the historically low levels of participation in higher education in Britain. Widening participation has progressed unevenly in different institutions; case studies of particular sites are therefore particularly valuable. The symposium presents two papers reporting on research and policy from Sheffield Hallam University. The University continually commissions units, such as the Learning and Teaching Institute and the Student Services Centre, to undertake research projects, collecting and interpreting data to inform policy making. The challenges of widening participation can only be addressed by looking critically at institutional practices and exploring the full implications of diversity.

The major success of widening participation has been the increased proportion of women entering higher education. Gender dynamics have received considerable research and policy attention. However, other areas, particularly increased ethnic diversity and the inclusive policies for students with disabilities, have received relatively little attention. The papers in the symposium focus on the experiences and challenges of ethnic diversity and disability. All the work is supported by the University as part of its commitment to grounding learning and teaching developments in an ongoing cycle of research and of encouraging staff in Schools to reflect on practice.

A number of projects concerned with diversity have been commissioned, including work on the experiences of ethnic minority students, and work on the role of admissions tutors in widening participation. In the symposium, we presented two papers dealing with different aspects of the challenges of diversity. The first paper reports on a small study of a group of academics, faced with larger classes and a more diverse student group. From the initial framing of the issues facing them in terms of student motivation, it became evident that some staff were drawing on broader racialising discourses to identify particular groups of students as a 'problem'. The second paper looks at research into disabled students' experiences. This research was initiated in response to demands from disabled students for more accessible and equitable assessment practices. For inclusion to be meaningful in meeting the needs of disabled students it must extend beyond a reactive approach and be embedded in the whole learning experience.

Case studies can offer insight into the complex mechanisms and inter-play of meanings involved in the aspiration of embracing diversity. The papers in the symposium are aimed at opening debates on the basis of analyses of local contexts as well as broader trends. The symposium provided participants with an opportunity to reflect on their own experiences and debate strategies which can contribute to the creation of a more inclusive and democratic higher education.

30 Racialising discourses and critical reflection in the academy

---

Sadie Parr, Sue Clegg and Stephen Wan[1]
Sheffield Hallam University

30.1   Introduction

In the 1960s and 1970s universities had student numbers in the hundreds; today most universities number above 15,000 (McNair, 1997). These changes mark a move from an elite to a semi-mass higher education system (Scott, 1997) in which students from non-traditional backgrounds have become better represented. Reflecting these changes, equal opportunities discourses and policies have made their mark on the higher education agenda. However, questions of ethnicity and 'race' have been under-theorised; antiracism as both an anti-oppressive discourse and strategy has not been addressed (Neal, 1995). The liberal ethos of the university underpins this dearth of engagement with issues of racism and antiracism. This ethos masks a reality in which staff and students bring to the university identities shaped by social forces operating outside of academia and, in turn, the university reflects and reproduces attitudes and beliefs prevalent in wider society.

The paper reports on a small piece of research that sought to investigate lecturers' perceptions that level-one undergraduate students lack motivation. During in depth intervies, a number of lecturers – as part of their dialogue about Asian students, as a 'problematic'. These racialised discourses seemed to have been triggered by the circumstances in which lecturers find themselvez: the dramatic rise in student numbers: a corresponding change in the student profile of universities: and a reduction in unit funding.

We argue that our observations highlight the fact that the university is no ivory tower immune from the structures and processes that affect the wider society. Accordingly, we argue for antiracist strategies and initiatives that compel the academy to confront and challenge its central values and ideals if widening participation and diversity are to be genuinely embraced.

30.2   The politics of 'whiteness': racism in the everyday

A growing collection of school ethnographies indicate that racism is an oppressive force that operates in the minutiae of everyday practices and expectations:

> racism is commonplace and routine; in studies of primary and secondary schools alike, teachers' notions of 'race' and ethnicity have important consequences for the lives of all students. (Gillborn, 1998, p.12).

There is no reason why we should not expect to find racialising practices operating in a similar way within the higher education sector. Yet, in contrast with the debates that have been had with regard to racism in the compulsory sector (Gillborn, 1990, 1998; Troyna & Williams, 1986; Troyna, 1993; Troyna & Hatcher, 1992), there has been a worrying absence of work that pays attention to issues of racism within higher education. There are notable exceptions (see Modood and Fenton's work, 1999 and Modood and Shiner, 2002) but these are few, and even fewer studies have paid attention to the less tangible, more subtle processes of racialisation that Gillborn (1998, p. 11) calls the "the operation of racism as a daily oppressive force".

This observation has been echoed by John Bird (1996) and, more recently in the Anti-Racist Toolkit developed by the Centre for Ethnicity and Race Studies (CERS) at Leeds University. They argue that the rationality and liberality of the 'ivory tower' appear to have acted successfully to mask masculinity and whiteness. Academia is discursively projected as a site of dis-interested rationality, a place where racial discrimination can have no part. The university, however, is not isolated from wider social forces: its traditions and systems are neither neutral and objective, nor sacrosanct. Universities are constructed in ways that privilege and benefit certain kinds of people. They are premised on a normative 'whiteness', albeit one crossed by class and gender dynamics.

Many writers have analysed how the historical legacy of colonialism and imperialism create the conditions under which those considered non-white are racialised, and how the authority of whiteness retains a degree of invisibility:

> Whiteness constitutes and demarcates ideas, feelings, social practices, cultural formations, and systems of intelligibility that are identified with or attributed to white people and which are invested in by white people as 'white'. Whiteness is also a refusal to acknowledge how white people are implicated in certain social relations of privilege and relations of domination and subordination (McLaren & Torres, 1999, p. 56)

Whiteness is a position of privilege from which others are differentiated; it is an invisible norm that informs and moulds racism. The 'whiteness' of the university goes unnoticed and unacknowledged in its manifestations in the everyday.

In the antiracist toolkit – designed to assist institutions in the process of anti-racist and 'race' equality planning and action – the authors advocate the need for a research agenda that moves beyond a focus on admissions to courses and pass rates, or on appointments and career progression, and looks towards more subtle, less overt racist practices that are manifest in seemingly disinterested, even mundane practices, policies and processes. Among other things, this entails problematising and destabilising notions such as talent, ability, motivation, and excellence:

> We have to question what 'excellence in education' means and whether performance can be measured by something more than income to the HEI [Higher Education Institution], low dropout rates, degree results, graduate access to job market and research ratings (CERS, 2002, p. 21)

Our research attempts to contribute to these debates. We found evidence of racialised thinking when we were not looking for it, when the issue being researched had already been framed as a learning and teaching problem. Below we describe the study and begin to unpack the research participants' narratives on student motivation.

30.3   The study

Sheffield Hallam University is a large post-1992 English university with approximately 24,000 students. The university is one of the group which pride themselves on widening participation and a commitment to learning and teaching (THES, 2002). It has been successful in increasing enrolments from minority ethnic groups: at the end of 2000, 15.3% of students (undergraduate and postgraduate) were from minority groups. The school in which the research took place has successfully attracted students from minority groups, and in 2001 less than 75% of its students recorded themselves as ethnically white.

Staff in all schools have been encouraged to identify learning and teaching issues and to use central resources, including research assistance support, to help them improve practice (Clegg et al, 2001). As part of this general strategy one school, which has very large first year groups, invited two of the researchers to help them look at a problem that they had identified as involving poor student motivation. It was agreed that it would be useful to talk to staff working on first year modules to establish their views on what the issues were and that a semi-structured interview would be the most appropriate instrument. The aim was to try to establish how staff framed the learning and teaching issues and that the questioning should not, therefore, begin with assumptions about the motivation of first year students. The interviews took an open approach but probed for views about:

- how staff understood student motivation

- their views on the motivation of their first year students

- what factors were felt to impact on motivation

- whether some groups of students were more motivated than others

- what if any strategies the staff member had adopted to enhance / tackle students' motivation

The interviews were conducted by two researchers, who were both young and relatively junior in the academic hierarchy, in the staff member's own space. The context was, therefore, conducive to encouraging staff to be open about their views. A total of 12 in-depth interviews with 13 staff were carried out; one of the interviews was with two members of staff who chose to be interviewed together. The interviews were not recorded but detailed notes were made, including verbatim quotes. Transcripts were produced after each interview and numbered to preserve anonymity. Feedback was given to the project commissioner in the form of a written summary and the researchers' concerns about the representation of issues as 'an Asian problem' were openly discussed. Rather than challenging the interpretation, he seemed to assent to the description, accepting the representation of the 'problem' in terms of racialised categories as apparently descriptively neutral. The researchers have presented the data and their concerns at an open seminar designed to engage a broader layer of staff from across the university in debating how 'problems' may become racialised.

30.3.1 The case study data

We have chosen to organise the presentation of the data around a number of themes, which emerged from the analysis. Our interest in the analysis was in exploring how individuals framed and described their experiences. We have, therefore, put the verbatim quotations into the context in which the individuals concerned expressed themselves, and attempted to describe the logics individual staff were using. All the references to 'an' or 'the' 'Asian problem' were unprompted and we have been careful in the analysis to stay close to the descriptive context in which claims were being made. We were particularly mindful of distinguishing whether individuals thought there were problems 'for' students or 'of' students, and have been careful to avoid over-interpretation by not attributing beliefs to individual staff beyond those they described. Most of the staff interviewed were in contact with the same students, as they were directly involved in delivering core modules. Their different understandings of students' motivation and attendance patterns cannot, therefore, be reduced to a set of factual claims about the students since contradictory claims were being made by different members of staff about the same students. Rather, the analysis is looking at the categories through which individual tutor's own experience is lived.

30.3.2   Then and now

Staff used different rhetorical devices with which to describe their experiences. One of the most powerful appeared to be a narrative of 'then' and 'now', whereby current experiences were made sense of in terms of a remembered or projected past. These comparisons over time were used to order tutors' views on current students. In the interview, which took place with two women staff members, there was a detailed discussion of the sorts of students that the course was now dealing with. Both the women had considerable experience of teaching in higher education: 19 years and 21 years. They resisted the idea of a 'glorious past' [5] but, nonetheless, were agreed that 'the proportion of students at the bottom has increased' [5], using a combination of low student marks and attendance as their definition of the 'bottom'. The explanation offered was that this was due to the expansion in higher education and students studying in higher education who 'would not have traditionally gone to university' [5]. One of the two women raised issues about whether these students really were students, or rather 'playing at being students' [5], since some students stayed on at university but did not bother turning up to lectures or engaging with the course they were enrolled on. In the interview, the two women assumed 'an Asian problem' [5] of low attendance and achievement.

Similarly, another male tutor made comparisons by looking backwards over time. He recalled his own experiences as a student 15 to 20 years ago, when he felt that 'the culture was very different in higher education' [2]. Like the women described above, his views appeared to reflect values about being a real student. He believed that a substantial proportion of the first year students 'do not respect learning' [2] or the value of knowledge, or indeed respect 'the tutor or each other' [2]. He asked, rhetorically, that if they did not respect the tutor, 'why should they listen to me?' [2]. He believed the 'kids' of today are completely different from the university entrants that staff were used to. Reflecting on his own life, he felt that as an 18 year old in the 1960s he had much more in common with the 18 year olds of the 1930s, than he has with the 18 year olds of the late 1990s and today. This tutor was also pessimistic about the students' achievements, which he attributed to school level – 'GCSEs are awful' [2] (the standard UK qualification taken at 16 years), and GNVQ qualifications (a newer vocational qualification) consist of 'trivial practical exercises' [2]. His negative framing of 'then' and 'now' in terms of declining standards was in turn associated with 'Muslim students' [2], who he particularly mentioned in terms of low, or less valuable qualifications.

This narrative of then and now was not always given a negative twist in relation to characteristics of students. One member of staff, who had been teaching for eight years, refused the framing of the 'problem' in terms of either student motivation or particular groups of students. His narrative was primarily organised around comparisons between different structures or processes: class sizes were smaller 'then'; 'now' his lectures are 'anywhere up to 300 students' [3] and his tutorial groups are 25, with some students receiving no tutorial support. Other staff were focused on structural changes in higher education, for example: the impact of modularisation on the student experience. One member of staff described students as having to 'jump through more hoops' [1]. It was clear that this comment was made in reference to the interviewee's perception that students were under increasing multiple pressures 'now'; with finance, faster paced delivery, and new pressures of skill requirements, that students did not have back 'then', when he was a student.

30.3.3   Contested views of motivation

The original framing of the project was in terms of motivation, but, as in the organisation of the narratives above there were individual differences in whether and how staff thought about motivation. One male member of staff with considerable teaching experience felt that a number of students were not motivated when they arrive at university. He described how staff had examined records of first year assessments and attendance – 'motivation is strongly linked to attendance' [9] – in an attempt to identify which 'subgroups' were not performing. He identified one particular sub-group who he claimed were unmotivated, 'young, Asian males' [9]. He felt this had become a noticeable trend over the last two or three years, and that in the current year it was 'obvious' that 'there is an Asian group that hasn't engaged'' [9]. For this tutor there was an almost complete overlap between motivational problems and his capacity to label the group of students as Asian. His logic was very close to the two women interviewed together, who were similarly convinced that poor motivation as evidenced by a lack of attendance and low grades was a particular problem with Asian (male) students. The apparently factual nature of the claims, which are important to the participants in the claim of the 'obviousness' of the connections, began to unravel in the joint interview when the two women began to graph the connections between marks and attendance. The women had circled the 'Asian' students with a red pen, only to admit that to their surprise there appeared to be no particular trend or difference between them and the non-Asian students.

Another member of staff consciously distanced himself from the idea of the 'Asian' problem. He made the comment that some of his colleagues seem to think 'a certain ethnic group' [7] are the unmotivated students and was keen to distance himself from this belief. Instead, he felt that if this particular student group were unmotivated one year it was merely 'coincidental' [7]. Tutors who did not employ the ascription of the 'Asian problem' were also much more cautious about claiming a general motivational problem. A male member of staff with 29 years of experience challenged the taken-for-granted nature of motivation. He claimed that 'motivation' was not a 'lucid thing' [1] and was difficult to measure. He talked about the fact that there is a 'perception of low student motivation levels' [1], rather than there being an actual reduction in motivation levels. His view was simply that student expectations had changed, and he recalled that 20-30 years ago, students having to work part-time was virtually unheard of. He said that absence from attending classes is often mistaken by staff for a lack of student motivation, but that he believed that low attendance could usually be explained by the different social pressures that students now have to deal with. He firmly believed that students are motivated to study, and that staff perceptions of student motivation are too easily swayed by what they observe 'superficially' [1]. His reasoning depended on attributing different meanings to the fact of non-attendance. His analysis of non-attendance drew attention to the changing circumstances of students rather than the attributes of students.

30.3.4   Good behaviour

The most striking element in the racialised accounts of the problems staff felt they faced is that it focused on ideas about what constitutes appropriate behaviour for students. These judgements rely on behaviour codes which Asian male students were deemed to transgress.

These accounts were sometimes based on quite complex chains of reasoning. For example, one tutor felt the problem could be engendered by the strong parental influence that he thought is placed on 'young Asian males' [9] to go to university. He felt that they may be pushed into going to university and that when they arrive they do not want to work but rather experience the freedom that university offers: 'There isn't a strong grip on them' and they are suddenly 'allowed to do what they want.' [9]. As well as their behaviour, as students, being problematic he wondered about 'a lack of respect for female lecturers' [9], which suggests that he believes that there are appropriate gender as well as authority norms.

The difficulties some staff appear to face with behaviour is illustrated by one lecturer, who believed that there was a major problem in first year classes. He described scenarios in which students would attend classes, but find them playing around with mobile phones or using email for social purposes. He said he was loathed to treat the students as children because they were young adults, but that he has asked some students to leave lectures and tutorials because they were disruptive. This tutor associated particular groups of students with poor and declining standards from areas such as Bradford and East Midlands and schools with many students scraping through with two A-levels, (the traditional exam-based 'gold standard' in English schools) at grade E (a low grade), or groups of students and their 'mates' [2], holding GNVQ qualifications (a newer vocational route for post-16 year students). It was clear in the context of the interview that the East Midlands and Bradford were meant to be recognisable as areas with high proportions of 'Muslims' [2]. This tutor also felt that there were constraints on his own actions. He felt that despite his attempts to motivate and engage students he had largely failed and that the standard of student work had declined. However, he felt that he was not allowed to fail more students. He claimed that if he tried to fail the number of students that he truly believed should fail, external examiners would question the failure rates. Failing students meant ultimately losing students whilst on their course and hence the associated income. He felt that students were aware of this, and knew they would not be failed, and hence 'played the game' [2].

It was clear from the interviews that the 'Asian problem' and the ways it was associated with 'behaviour' were organised around a discourse of masculinity. It was male students who were being described and this was taken as self evident in the descriptions of the problems. Although not as explicit, it is highly likely from the contexts of description that staff are taking for granted that these are first generation university entrants whose parents have not experienced higher education. Moreover, it seems likely from the use of the term 'Muslim' interchangeably with 'Asian' and the references to locality that staff are distinguishing between these Asian males and other Asians from, say, Indian Hindu backgrounds. When we describe the accounts as racialised we are, therefore, aware of the need to deconstruct the complex web of meaning that such racialising practices involve, and that this is likely to entail class location as well as masculinity.

30.3.5   Agency

Nearly all the tutors interviewed described how they had tried to adapt their teaching strategies and tried to innovate. For example, the male tutor described above, who had experienced problems with difficult student behaviour, tried to innovate but felt his attempts were a failure. His sense of personal agency and of the scope for change was extremely muted. He described the possibility of using more active group work, but claimed 'some would just sit there and not do much' [9] and that the problem with group work was that it allowed some students to 'coast' [9]. This pessimistic stance appeared to be a characteristic of the staff who attributed the problems as being the property of students and in particular identified an 'Asian problem'. Other staff, who looked to structural pressures of changing students' finances and the pressures of students working, were less likely to blame attendance on motivation. Large class sizes and less contact time appear to be dealt with in terms of these broader elements of the tutors' interpretative framework, and some tutors appeared to be more able to cope. Across the interviews it appeared that problems either become racialised, or become issues that were addressed within a learning and teaching framework. Staff who did not engage with racialising categories appeared much more able to confront the changes to their working patterns and deal with them without externalising the problems onto the students, whether in the form of 'motivation' or declining 'qualification'.

One member of staff, who had recently been on a course for new staff members, organised his interview mostly in terms of the experiments he had been trying with 'real world' problems and 'fuzzy problems' [6] more suited to the sorts of judgements made in industry. He said that the new staff course he was taking helped in dealing with students with 'diverse backgrounds' [6]. His staff course had allowed him to learn about different models of teaching and to discuss teaching and learning issues. Interestingly this member of staff, reversing the norm, welcomed newer qualifications and found that the traditional exam based 'A' levels did not prepare students for problem based learning. He clearly experienced high levels of personal agency, and while he described the difficulties of students working and debt he did not see the students themselves as problems. The problems were something students faced rather than problem students. It is this latter move that seems associated with the racialisation of 'problems', particularly with attendance and behaviour. While all the staff interviewed appeared to share the perception that large classes, lectures, and lack of student financial support were major issues, how they dealt with the perceived consequences, as we have shown, varied widely.

30.4   Reflections on the findings

At this point in the paper we want to use the case study as a stepping off point into a broader consideration of some issues we believe the case study highlights.

30.4.1 Racialised thinking

In the interviews, behavioural norms associated with the 'traditional (or "real") student' and assumptions about academic preparedness/potential fed into narratives about student motivation that distinguished Asian students. Behavioural 'problems' became related in a deterministic way to cultural factors attributed to Asian male students and they were perceived to not possess the cultural capital necessary for success and inclusion at university. Asian male students were also perceived as being more likely to possess a qualification that was demarcated as not adequately preparing students for academia. Using the criteria of qualifications to differentiate between individuals may, albeit unwittingly, disadvantage some minority groups (CERS, 2002).

Racialised thinking renders discrimination (and the whiteness on which it is based) less recognisable: notions of maintaining objective, neutral standards framed the lecturer's arguments. The unembarrassed tone in which an 'Asian problem' was described also suggested that the participants deemed the meanings of the label self-evident and we had no basis, therefore, for believing that any of the participants felt themselves to be racist. The lecturers seemed to assume that because Asian students really are a problem they were not being racist because racial prejudice is based upon ignorance and myth (see Bird, 1996 for similar observations). Moreover, the context of the interviews seemed driven by a desire for improving practice: the staff group was clearly concerned with the nature of the student experience and wanted to make constructive changes.

It seems that although the student body is now more diverse, minority students are only legitimately 'included' when they conform to the expectations of the traditional, middle class, and 'white' academic. In our study, rather than responding to diversity through teaching and learning initiatives, Asian men were seen to own 'problems' and so they themselves became a problem. They became what Callinicos (1993) refers to as ready-made scapegoats: a process enabled by the implicit 'whiteness' on which the university survives and which works "as an unmarked marker of others' differentness" (Frankenburg, 1993, p. 198). Those with the appropriate social and linguistic resources are deemed more motivated.

Some authors have attempted to expand the discussion of participation and inclusion by distinguishing between 'cultural diversity' and 'cultural difference' (Bhabha 1990, Edwards, 2000). Bhabha (1990) argues that the dominant liberal tradition accepts that cultures are diverse and that, in some sense, the diversity of cultures is a good and positive thing and ought to be encouraged.

> It is commonplace of a plural, democratic societies to say that they can encourage and accommodate cultural diversity (Bhabha, 1990, p. 208)

This acceptance, however, disguises the ways in which this 'cultured' and 'civilised' attitude is based on the ability of Western societies "to appreciate cultures in a kind of musee imaginaire; as though one should be able to collect and appreciate them" (Bhabha (1990, p. 208). However, such an imaginary world leaves 'civilised' values untouched, and limits the ways in which cultural difference might act as a challenge to the dominant norms. For Bhabha such thinking is evident in the endorsement of policies of widening participation:

> cultural diversity becomes the bedrock of multicultural educational policy in this country. There are two problems with it: one is the very obvious one that, although there is an entertainment and encouragement of cultural diversity, there is also a corresponding containment of it. A transparent norm is constituted, a norm given by the host society or dominant culture, which says that 'these other cultures are fine, but we must be able to locate them within our own grid.' This is what I mean by a creation of cultural diversity and a containment of cultural difference. (Bhabha, 1990, p. 208)

The idea that people can be welcomed into the university as long as they obey the often unwritten rules of the game, 'our own grid', is identified by Bird (1996) as one of the ways in which higher education institutions have been able to claim that they do not discriminate.

30.4.2   Policy Responses

While we are not claiming the perceptions uncovered in our research are representative, the research does highlight the need for a reflexive awareness within universities. By doing so, we can begin to challenge the ways in which 'problems' are framed in terms of racialising categories.

To do this, we argue for research agenda that interrogates 'race' and ethnicity in a bid to inform progressive policy decisions. As Bird asserts: "it is as dangerous to assume that there is prejudice and discrimination as to reject their existence outright" (1996, p. 79). We need empirical evidence both that there is prejudice and discrimination, and what the nature of that prejudice and discrimination is. If racialised attitudes are institutionalised within a particular culture, before anything may be changed, that culture needs to be fully understood. This can only be done through reflective and critical research.

This will not be easy. There is some resistance to opening up these issues to debate. There was, for example, some unease about discussing our findings internally, and we were accused of over-interpreting the data. Moreover, when we opened up the discussion some staff moved immediately to an acceptance that there must be a factual 'Asian problem' of attendance, although we presented no data which could suggest this could be the case, and indeed we explicitly resisted this framing. As McLaren and Torres (1999) argue:

> 'Unfortunately, the continued use of 'race' in educational research, whether intentional or not, upholds a definition of 'race' as a causal factor. In other words, significance and meaning are attributed to phenotypical features, rather than the historical, social and discursive production of the processes of racialization.' (McLaren & Toress, 1999, p. 47)

The idea of 'race' as causal is deeply embedded, and at the seminar other members of staff from different areas began comparisons with different groups of students they had encountered including 'Asian girls'. We would take this as further evidence of the depths of common sense racialised thinking, which fails to recognise the position from which it is arguing.

30.5   Conclusion

It is striking that discussion about the meaning of increased diversity and widening participation for mainstream practices in higher education is only just beginning. Unless we as practitioners are willing to engage in debate, explore the racialised nature of the academy, and challenge its whiteness, the containment of cultural difference will persist. Without critical reflexivity the 'whiteness' of the academy will go unnoticed and uncommented. In turn, the widening participation agenda will falter. Rather than leading to a valuing of diversity it will increase underlying tensions as some staff seek to blame diversity for the broader ills of the higher education system. Research programmes are necessary in order to both broaden our understanding of the processes and structures of racism, and in turn, enable well-founded and effective anti-racist policy making that informs all aspects of the learning and teaching experience.

References

Bhabha, H (1990). The Third Space, Rutherford, J (Ed), *Identity: Community, Culture, Difference,* London: Lawrence and Wishart.

Bird, J (1996). *Black Students in Higher Education: Rhetorics and Realitie,* Buckingham: SRHE and Open University Press.

Callinicos, A (1993). *Race and Class,* London: Bookmark.

Centre for Ethnicity and Racism Studies (CERS) (2002). Building the Antiracist University: A toolkit: http://www.leeds.ac.uk/cers/toolkit/toolkit.htm

Frankenberg, R (1993). The Social Construction of Whiteness: White Women, *Race Matters* Minnesota: The University of Minnesota Press.

Gillborn, D (1990). *'Race', Ethnicity and Education,* London: Unwin and Hyman.

Gillborn, D (1998). Race and Ethnicity in Compulsory Schooling. In Modood, T & Acland, T (Eds), *Race and Higher Education,* London: Policy Studies Institute.

Mclaren, P & Torres, R (1999). Racism and Multicultural Education: Rethinking 'Race' and 'Whiteness'. In Late Capitalism. May, S (Ed), *Critical Multiculturalism: Rethinking Multicultural Education and Antiracist Educatio*, London and Philadelphia: Falmer Press.

McNair, S (1997). Changing Frameworks and Qualifications. In Coffield, F, & Williamson, B (Eds), *Repositioning higher education*. Buckingham: SRHE and Open University Press.

Modood, T (1998). Ethnic Minorities Drive for Qualifications. In Modood, T & Acland, T, (Eds), *Race and Higher Education*, London: Policy Studies Institute.

Modood, T & Shiner, M (2002). Help or Hindrance? Higher Education and three Routes to Ethnic Equality. *British Journal of Sociology of Education*, **23**(2).

Neal, S (1995). Antiracist Discourses and Initiatives in Higher Education in Griffiths, M and Troyna, B (Eds), *Antiracism, Culture and Social Justice in Education*, Stoke on Trent: Trentham Books.

Scott, C (1997). Changing ideas of the university, in Smith E, & Webster, F (Eds), *The Postmodern university? Contested Visions of Higher Education and Society*, Buckingham: SRHE and Open University.

THES, (2002). Scaling the heights, January 18.
http://www.thesis.co.uk/archive/story.asp?id=81535&state_value=Archive

Troyna, B (1993). *Racism and Education: A comprehensive introductio*, Sydney: Unwin and Hyman.

Troyna, B & Williams, J (1986). *Racism, Education and the State*, London: Croom Helm.

Troyna, B & Hatcher, R (1992). *Racism in Children's lives: A study of mainly White Primary Schools*, London: Routledge.

Notes

1   A fuller version of this paper has been accepted for publication in Teaching in Higher Education and will appear 2003.

31 Striving for genuine inclusion – academic assessment and disabled students

Madeleine Freewood and Len Spriggs
Sheffield Hallam University

Keywords;   Disabled students, academic assessment, compensation, inclusion.

Overview

Provision in Higher Education for disabled students has previously tended to focus on improving physical access or welfare support, however there is a growing recognition that genuine inclusion also means revisiting the curriculum to ensure learning, teaching and assessment are themselves accessible (Adams 2000). This is both recognised and reinforced by the Disability Discrimination Act, Part IV (HMSO 2001).

Thus it is no longer adequate to regard the requirements of disabled students as in some way peripheral or outside those of the larger student body. Ad hoc responses to personal adjustments have to be replaced by the mainstreaming of practice and procedure in a strategic way. This means ownership of disability issues needs to extend beyond the remit of a core specialised number of staff and be embedded in both teaching practice and university policy (McCarthy & Hurst 2001).

In recognition of this, a two-year research project is being undertaken at Sheffield Hallam University to evaluate the disabled student experience of academic assessment, with a view to establishing and disseminating university-wide good practice in this area.

This paper reports on the preliminary findings of the research drawn, using data elicited from semi-structured interviews with students, academic and administrative staff and staff from central departments such as Registry. In particular it focuses on how staff perceptions of disability, rather than pedagogic decisions, are often used to inform judgements of how disabled students should be assessed.

31.1   Introduction

Research indicates that assessment adjustments for disabled students in UK Higher Education (HE) have tended in the past to be ad hoc or laissez-faire (Earle, Adams and French 1999; Konur 2002) rather than strategic. This type of approach is no longer appropriate if institutions are to adhere to policy initiatives such as the Quality Assurance Agency (QAA) Code of Practice – Students with Disabilities (1999) and the Special Educational Needs and Disability Act (SENDA) 2001, which amends the Disability Discrimination Act (DDA) 1995. Both of these incorporate a clear focus on learning, teaching and assessment, representing what Adams (2001) argues is the need for "a cultural shift in the way institutions respond to the requirements of disabled students".

Achieving this will necessarily involve a recognition that support services need to increasingly work "alongside academic staff in considering [disabled] students' learning needs, including course design and delivery" (p17; 2001). This means making a conscious effort to extend ownership of disability issues beyond the traditional small core of specialised 'support' staff, and embed them in both teaching practice and university policy.

Sheffield Hallam University (SHU) has an established service supporting disabled students and is well placed to address the needs of a diverse student population. Ways to engender a shared ownership of disability issues are being explored by the Disabled Student Support Team (DSST) in a number of key areas. These include running accredited disability modules, strategies to extend and embed staff disability training and a two year action research oriented project which is exploring disabled students' experience of academic assessment to inform the production of university guidelines.

31.2   Methodological considerations

The findings reported here are taken from data gathered in the first stage of the ongoing research project: a series of 26 semi-structured qualitative interviews with University staff (academic and administrative) and disabled students. This initial stage of the research was concerned with identifying key issues relating to academic assessment for further exploration. To this end, the researcher elected to conduct a series of one-to-one qualitative interviews with members of University staff and disabled students, adopting a 'feminist perspective' which asserts 'the personal subjective experience' as a legitimate area of research (Morris, 1991, p6).

Disability studies have been critical of research projects which have failed to involve or benefit disabled people, and as such have often acted to disempower them (Finkelstein 1992, Coles 2001). It was therefore regarded as fundamental to include a key role for disabled students in this project.

The student sample included deaf/hearing impaired students, dyslexic students, physically and visually impaired students, and a student with mental health difficulties. They were either invited or self-selected to take part in interview. However, while it was considered important to include students with a range of impairments in the sample so as to incorporate a diverse set of student experiences in the research, the focus of the interviews was on 'disabling environments' within the context of teaching, learning and assessment, as opposed to an individual's impairment. This was in accord with the Social Model of Disability (Oliver 1996), which challenges the view of disability as 'a personal medical tragedy', locating the disabling aspects associated with a person's 'impairment' in society and being due to their treatment by that society.

In interview, the researcher adopted an "egalitarian research agenda" as advocated by Duckett and Pratt (2001), which involves aligning the methodology to a "person-centred approach" (p819) and actively trying to challenge the traditional power dynamic between researcher and participant. This was considered particularly important within an HE context when interviewing students because there can be a tendency for this power dynamic to be reinforced by the hierarchies already inherent in a university setting.

The context of the HE environment was also important when considering student involvement in the project. A clear balance had to be struck between actively involving students in the project while guarding against the danger of exploiting the student group by taking too much time away from study, in a way not expected of their non-disabled peers. The researcher has thus considered it important to let all student participants define their own parameters in relation to the time they can devote to the research. Students have been kept informed of the progress of the research with opportunities for further (optional) involvement, thus allowing students to prioritise these alongside other university commitments.

Like the student sample, the staff sample was made up of participants either invited or self-selected and the interview format followed a similar structure to those of the student interviews. Again the focus for the interview was the support structures in place to facilitate the assessment of disabled students, rather than discussion of individual student's impairments. However, the views of some staff, reflecting dominant popular discourses around disability, were based on assumptions more in line with a medical or individual model of disability than the Social Model. As a result, a number of staff acted throughout their interview to re-focus discussion onto what they perceived to be an individual student's 'deficits'. This emphasis had the effect of framing assessment adjustments or alternative assessments as a form of 'compensation'.

The role of the researcher in this context was complex. Whilst adhering to the Social Model, the views which staff expressed were important data in understanding how staff comprehended the precepts of external drivers such as the DDA Part IV (SENDA) and QAA as well as institutional recommendations concerning good practice. For example Konur comments that while staff might adhere to such recommendations, their attitude to implementation of such, impacts on how students experience them. The example he gives involves staff attitudes to assessment adjustments. While they may be sanctioned at an institutional level, the environment in which students sit such assessments is affected if, on a personal level, staff "see every application for the provision of assessment adjustments by disabled students as an example of 'fraud'" [p149].

Thus the researcher trod an ideological and moral tight-rope between, on the one hand, allowing staff to have the space to express views ideologically opposed to the research paradigm but, on the other, seeking not to reinforce or legitimise any stereotypes of disabled people as presented in interview.

Finally, as outlined above, during the student interviews the researcher aimed to address issues around power dynamics. Within HE the Research Assistant is often regarded as a 'novice academic' therefore when the researcher interviewed staff in many cases this power dynamic was reversed. This was compounded, the researcher believed, by both her age and gender. However, being the 'less powerful' partner in the interview, led the researcher to feel, she was perceived as non-threatening, leading to an environment where staff felt they could 'get things off their chest' without having to be too concerned about the views of the listener. This was also facilitated by the guarantee of anonymity.

31.3   Findings and discussion

Student and staff interview transcripts have been analysed separately to identify common themes. These themes have been grouped and are presented below.

In many ways it is self-evident that academic assessments take place in a particular context. The effect of this, however, is that neither staff nor students see academic assessment as a separate issue that can be discussed without reference to this context. Indeed, the research data suggests that understandings of this context frame their perceptions of assessment. Academic assessment is thus more than simply about measuring outcomes. For example, views on employability, graduate identity, the model of disability drawn on, and their level of disability awareness, can all impact on, academics' positions regarding assessment methods. Similarly, students' relationships with tutors, views about the programme of study and what it means to be a university student, as well as past educational experiences impact on how they approach and undertake assessment. This paper will explore further some of these themes.

31.4   Exploring the notion of 'compensation'

While it is important to recognise that all students will have different learning styles and difficulties, and that there is no simple division of the needs of disabled students on one side and non-disabled students on the other, it is also important to recognise that particular groups will experience specific and explicit inequalities.

There is, for example, a distinct difference between the student who is nervous going into an exam and a student with mental health difficulties for whom the stress of an exam causes specific and medically recognised difficulties that will significantly influence their performance in that assessment. Similarly, this deaf student made the following comment in interview:

> The lecturer objected to [me asking] for notes and OHPs in advance, he said it wasn't fair, that I had an advantage over the hearing students, [but] non-deaf students for example can record the information in the lecture they don't have to sit there and listen, or they can select what information they want to record for themselves. I don't have that option.

The rationale for assessment adjustments and alternative assessments is to remove specific barriers of this type so that disabled students can be judged equally against their peers. Assessment adjustments recommended at SHU include separate accommodation, use of assistive technology, lengthened time to complete assessments and marking written work for content and accuracy rather than grammatical structure and written expression. Alternative assessments are negotiated between academic members of staff, the DSST and the disabled student.

In interview, staff were asked to comment about assessment adjustments and alternative assessments, both in terms of how they were organised in their School and the impact they might have on course design, writing of marking criteria, learning outcomes etc. What soon became apparent was the model of disability that staff drew upon greatly impacted on their response to this question. Where staff conceptualised the disabled student in a medical or individual model of disability there was a tendency to reframe assessment adjustments as being about compensation for a student's impairment as opposed to the intention of creating parity with their non-disabled peers. When this occurred discussion then focused on who truly deserved this kind of compensation, what kind of proof is needed regarding this, who is qualified to judge this proof etc. In this context any student not deemed to be deserving was by implication fraudulent and would be seen as 'trying it on' or 'playing psychological games'.

Commentators such as Earle and Sharp [2000] have similarly expressed reservations about what they term 'compensatory forms of assessment' [p543]. They make the legitimate argument that assessments taken by disabled students must test exactly the same skills and knowledge as those taken by their non-disabled peers. The educational argument about how this is best achieved is obscured, however, by a tendency to re-focus discussion on individual students' impairments. In this context it is interesting to note that the fear expressed by Earle and Sharp and by staff in interviews, that disabled students are advantaged by assessment adjustments, is not equal to the fear that disabled students could be disadvantaged by the current assessment method! By not considering this, assessment of disabled students becomes more about assessing their ability to assimilate into the status quo, as can be seen illustrated below where a member of staff refers to assessment method and outcome interchangeably. In the following quote, therefore, assessment experience and assessment purpose become perceived as one and the same thing:

> Because they are having longer they don't sit with the main bulk of the students, so the examination experience is actually different. They are generally more comfortable rooms, they're generally warmer rooms, they're generally quieter rooms, if you imagine 300 people in the main hall here on level 6 compared with 5 students in a classroom with carpets and very comfortable chairs and larger tables, so the student can spread out, they can make nice – you know, cushions on the chairs rather than plastic chairs up in the main hall, tables that don't, because it's on a carpeted floor the tables are steady whereas in the main hall the table wobbles.

This perception of the experience of separate accommodation not only contrasts with the description provided by other staff and students, but the ability of a student to be able to negotiate an inadequate table becomes regarded as part of the assessment process by which a student should be judged. The educational discussion about parity and equity, what skills are and should be assessed and how they are being marked becomes lost by a refocusing of discussion in terms of the fraudulent disabled student. This in itself raises concern about what impact notions of this kind have on decisions made by academics when marking disabled student's assessments and awarding grades.

The view expressed above by one member of staff can however be contrasted with the comments below in which the members of staff are discussing the purpose of an assessment, rather than the individual:

> No I don't see anything wrong in giving them room, erm, I don't see anything wrong in giving any student room to be honest provided that they are not going to use an external source for finding answers. It's the speed with which people think that we are marking then and I'm not always sure that that is a good idea. It's not an exam then, it's a race.

> If that different method brings out the same kind of level of performance as the students who do the standard thing of going in and sitting the exams then I don't see any problem with that I really don't and that's been my attitude to open book exams say. [Referring to a specific module where students are assessed by open book exams.] It's not a memory test so it meant that we could set an exam that wasn't just a memory test but asked them to apply what they learned.

The following quote further highlights the role perceptions of a student's impairment, rather than pedagogic decisions, can play when judgements are made about how disabled students should be assessed.

> I suppose of course, it would be a different example if people perceive it differently, perhaps unjustly, but if you had a student who was physically unable to write in any form, quadriplegia or something like that, I think people would accept that then. But a dyslexic student who could write but was disadvantaged by having to write, the subject group might still say we'd rather you wrote because that is the activity that is central, and we'll make allowances. But I can see that from a student point of view that might not be such an attractive proposition.

The aim of the quality agenda, with its emphasis on defining learning outcomes and assessment criteria, is to make explicit what skills are being assessed and how. However, this masks the types of judgements that are being made by individuals when marking assessed work, as one member of staff comments when discussing assessing disabled students: "Where the nature of the problem is understood something can be worked out". What this notion often assumes is that there is a set of shared meanings about how to 'work something out' when in fact there appears a wide variety of academic opinion and experience. Furthermore 'working it out' has the potential to be ad hoc rather than strategic. Indeed, some staff held a misunderstanding that they should tailor assessments to make them easier for disabled students, which is as damaging as not recognising where barriers may exist in current assessment methods.

On the whole, consensus was expressed in staff interviews in line with the comments made by this academic:

> Making the exam different [for a disabled student] is a different ball game, it's just how different, in what respect is it different, that would need to be discussed. You can't have somebody doing manufacturing engineering at whatever level if they are doing something other than manufacturing; [if] there's an academic parallel... then fine.

But what this means in practice is more complex. This complexity should not be avoided but addressed in discussing how we ensure equity of experience for students when undertaking academic assessments, including discussion in relation to which issues are generic and what issues are subject specific. For example, the implications for assessing a student orally rather than by a written exam on an English literature module were discussed with a member of staff in one interview. While he considered it possible to devise an appropriate marking scheme for an oral exam using the same questions as the written exam but applying a different set of criteria to it, the tutor was concerned that it raised the issue of whether it was acceptable to have an English degree graduate who did not have a "certain level of writing skills". The tutor suggested that it would be possible to argue that "the student could still be very skilled at constructing arguments, [and] organising material".

What this reinforces is that views on assessment are also mediated by other notions such as employability, graduate identity and key skills. This is not surprising considering the market driven nature of the HE sector. Indeed, some staff clearly saw themselves as gatekeepers to licensed professions and this was used to inform judgements about assessing disabled students. Yet these notions are particularly nebulous and open to a myriad of personal interpretations. There was a clear danger that staff were drawing on outmoded views about disabled people in the workplace to inform decisions about implementing assessment adjustments, or the use of alternative assessments.

It is, therefore, very important to ensure that learning outcomes, assessment criteria and curricula design are informed by a shared understanding of the relevant pedagogic issues. Focusing on an individual model leads to discussion infused by assumptions and stereotypes about what staff think disabled students are capable of, with students cast either in the role of attempted frauds or tragic victims in need of compensation. This necessarily involves a cultural shift away from seeing disabled students as separate from other students, with educational needs that must be dealt with outside of the rest of the curriculum.

31.5   Incorporating the student experience

Data from the student interviews revealed that very often disabled students did not have access to, or a full understanding of, university structures and the rules and regulations governing assessment. This is probably no different from non-disabled students but has a particular impact on disabled students. There are two issues here. Firstly, consideration has to be given to the physical and cognitive accessibility of rules and regulations outlined in module/course guides and the student handbook to ensure that their format is not prohibiting access to any student group. The second issue is more complex and relates to students' relationships with their tutors. As we might expect, it is generally an accepted practice that students do not question the assessment method chosen by their tutor or how work is marked. Even where some negotiation around assessment takes place students are necessarily called on to put their trust in procedures which are in place as well as the judgement of the marker. However where staff regard assessment adjustments or alternative assessments as add-on and an 'individual' issue rather than a curriculum design issue this relationship of trust can be placed under stress.

It is currently standard practice in SHU for disabled students to be consulted via what is termed the 'Higher Education Study Aids and Study Strategies Assessment' (HESASS) process about their access and support requirements for their chosen course. Based on these requirements individual student 'Learning Contracts' are then drawn up. Knowing when certain requirements on their Learning Contracts are being met is obvious to students, for example, where a student's Learning Contract asks that students receive a hard copy of OHPs in advance of a lecture. However other requirements, particularly those related to marking work, are not so obvious. For example, dyslexic students were not always clear whether their work was being marked for content and context rather than grammatical accuracy, or even how this requirement has been interpreted by a member of staff. In fact there was a feeling that this process was potentially ad hoc rather than strategic and embedded in practice. This student comments about this when discussing assessment by oral presentations:

> I don't know if the tutor knows if I get up that I am the one... I don't know whether they know when they're watching my presentation [and taking my Learning Contract requirements] into consideration.

Where there is this type of student concern there is little or no space for student staff dialogue around the issue, and students who raise their concerns risk being labelled as a 'problem'. Thus pedagogic issues which should have been resolved at curriculum design stage can potentially evolve into being understood as a personal issue where staff feel their professional judgement is being questioned and students feel their needs are being ignored. This can be illustrated further when looking at the contradictory representations of disabled students found in staff interviews. On the one hand staff regarded disabled students as passive and dependent (ie in need of compensation), and on the other as over-demanding. For the student this is a difficult position to mediate; the choice can be between not raising an issue or being seen as demanding.

The student comment below illustrates this further:

> Last semester I had a visiting lecturer and I explained that I had a Learning Contract etc. and everything seemed fine, but for eight weeks the person refused to give me any OHPs etc. and I just had to cope. But then I went up to the head of the department to complain and I explained about the visiting lecturer, the lecturer was quite difficult to lip-read he used to speak with no pause, it was just one constant stream of speech, so it was quite difficult... everybody was just really confused and didn't understand what this lecturer was saying, which meant that my interpreter had to ask for information before hand and this lecturer was getting quite shirty about it. It was a difficult situation, and I was quite worried because I thought I don't really want to end up in a situation where I end up failing my essay.

The juxtaposition of the dependent and the demanding disabled student is often further complicated when tutors fail to realise the power dynamics that exist between disabled student and member of staff, particularly in any discussion of assessment. As one student commented: "I'm still really quite embarrassed about it and like when I have to go and tell my tutors it really takes my nerves and things like that." The same student who made this comment went on to describe trying to arrange a private moment with a tutor to discuss issues related to assessment:

> I did go to see him [module tutor]…and I said I had a Learning Contract and he had five minutes with me or something stood up in this room with loads of people which I was quite upset about, because I was like 'I've got a learning contract' [spoken softly] and I'm trying to keep it quiet, as well as listen to what he was saying and he says well it just doesn't make sense and stuff like that.

This focus on the 'problem' disabled student works to divert attention away from learning, teaching and assessment practice. This can be illustrated in students' varying experience of group work. Groupwork tends to be an issue that excites student opinion generally. However, for disabled students there appear to be particular issues about design, support and implementation of the groupwork process that can turn a potentially valuable experience into a painful and negative one.

It is worth contrasting the experiences of several students here. The first example involves a blind student being set, as part of a group task, an exercise that involved visual measurements. Not only was this a completely inaccessible exercise but the student was forced into a position of reliance on his peers, skewing the whole group-working interaction.

The second example is that of a deaf student who is a British Sign Language user. The student is on a course with a larger number of students and does not know his peers very well. Where group work assessments had taken place over a semester this had on the whole been a positive experience. However at the time of interview, he had a tutorial where students were expected to complete a different group activity each week, working in a different group each time. In this case the student commented that the hearing students did not want him in their group, he did not "fit in" and had to "force" himself on a group. For this reason he often chose to miss this particular tutorial.

The first example is clearly that of a poorly designed assessment, which has the additional effect of acting to isolate the student within his group by preventing him from being able to contribute in any way. The second example is interesting in that while it might be considered one of the learning outcomes of groups to negotiate roles and responsibilities and work out difficulties, the format of group interaction is acting to significantly disadvantage this student solely because of his deafness. This is an issue of awareness for students and staff and a problem with how the activity is designed. A further illustration of this was presented by a dyslexic student who commented that he needs to have time to plan and carry out his work. While time management impacts on all students in a group work activities, if students in his group don't pull their weight and leave it all until the last minute he is doubly penalised.

The final example is that of a student with mental health difficulties. On assigning the groups the course tutor met with the student group to discuss planning and organising the group assignment. In this context the student and tutor were able to discuss with the other members of the group issues relating to her mental health difficulties. The student knew that the tutor was aware of her difficulties and was provided with a safe and supportive environment to discuss group working roles with her peers. This was regarded by the student as a positive experience.

This case study demonstrates how the tendency to problematise the disabled student rather than locating the difficulty in assessment design and implementation circumnavigates the pedagogic discussion that needs to take place about best practice in accessible group work design. Furthermore it can easily lead to ad hoc decisions based on tutor perceptions of disabled students placing undue stress on the tutor student relationship, as students are forced into a position of non-participation or making requests for additional information relating to inaccessible practice in a way non-disabled students do not experience. This can be seen as representative of a range of assessment methods.

31.6   Conclusion

As outlined in the introduction and reinforced by interview data, mainstreaming genuine inclusion, in relation to academic assessment, involves facilitating a change in culture in the UK Higher Education sector. This means challenging a laissez faire culture of assessing disabled students, often informed by a discourse of 'compensation' rather than equity, which has been prevalent in recent years.

Changing the culture necessarily involves exploration and development of a shared set of understandings around the educational issues involved, an unpacking of the curriculum and the assumptions it is founded on, so that what has been termed the "conspiracy of the normal" (Hammond and Steffani, 2001) can be seen. This will enable new and different choices to be made relating to the development of effective teaching and learning strategies. Furthermore, this debate needs to be embedded in the process of curriculum design, rather than seen only as the remit of disability specialists or as part of disability awareness sessions. Achieving this means extending ownership of disability issues to all players in Higher Education and creating new partnerships.

Finally, thought needs to be given as to how to provide an opportunity for disabled students to feed back their experiences in a constructive way which is not prone to interpretation as either fraudulent or over-demanding. While individual disabled students will have specific requirements that will have to be met, this needs to be seen in the context of an educational debate rather than a compensation model, as the latter can lead to undue stress being placed on the tutor – student relationship and inequitable decisions relating to academic assessment being made.

References

Adams, M (2001). Changing the Culture: Addressing the needs of disabled students, *Update on Inclusion*, **3**, Spring 2001, p17.

Coles, J (2001). The Social Model of Disability: what does it mean for practice in services for people with learning difficulties? *Disability & Society*, **16**(4), 501–510.

Duckett, P & Pratt, R (2001). The Researched Opinions on Research: visually impaired people and visual impairment, *Disability & Society*, **16**(6), 815–835.

Earle, Adams & French (1999). A national survey of assessment practices in higher education: special provisions for students with disabilities and learning difficulties, *The SKILL Journal*, **65**, 22–24. London.

Earle and Sharp (2000). Disability and Assessment in the UK: should we compensate disabled students? *Teaching in Higher Education*, **5**(4) 541–545.

Finkelstein, V (1992). Setting Future Agendas, Researching Disability: setting the agenda for change, National Conference - 1 June, 1992.

Hammond and Stefani, (2001). Moving Towards an Inclusive Curriculum at the Glasgow School of Art, *The SKILL Journal*, **71**, 3–10. London.

Her Majesty's Stationery Office (HMSO) (1995). *Disability Discrimination Act 1995* [Online] UK, London. HMSO. Last accessed on August 2002 at URL: http://www.hmso.gov.uk/acts/acts1995/1995050.htm

Konur, O (2002). Assessment of Disabled Students in Higher Education: current public issues, *Assessment and Evaluation in Higher Education*, **27**(2), 131–152.

McCarthy, D & Hurst A (2001). A Briefing on Assessing Disabled Students, *The LTSN Generic Centre Assessment Series Guides*, Series no. 8, LTSN York.

Morris, J (1991). *Pride Against Prejudice*, The Women's Press.

Oliver, (1996). *Understanding Disability: From Theory to Practice* Basingstoke: Macmillan and St. Martin's Press.

Quality Assurance Agency (1999). Code of Practice for the assurance of the academic quality and standards in higher education: Students with disabilities. [Online]. Last accessed August 2002 at URL: http://www.qaa.ac.uk/public/cop/copswd/cop_disab.pdf

Peter Ashworth

Sheffield Hallam University, UK

If academic malpractice is increasing among students this is a practical worry, of course. But it also presents a phenomenon of immense research interest. The consideration of academic malpractice makes the researcher aware of so many other features of the academy.

Academic malpractice relates to the question of what education is taken by students to be for. Malpractice relates also to the meaning of assessment. The meaning of authority is also implicated. And what about the question of the status of the text, and the issue of individual originality? Both are essential components of plagiarism and some of the other forms of malpractice.

It cannot be over-stated how bound up in culture and history these things are. Consider the very idea of plagiarism. It assumes, I think without question,

- The individual ownership of intellectual work

- Personal authorship, creativity or originality

- The view that knowledge has a history; and past authors must be acknowledged

All these things are (as we might say) implicated in a certain Western, modernist epistem? We should not be caught unawares, then, by the fact that students from other cultures find it puzzling not to be allowed to put forwards expert writing by a renowned authority as their answer to an essay or exam question. Why on earth not?

It also ought not to surprise us that even students of Western background have to be carefully acculturated into what can be seen as the quaint local norms of the academy. This precaution is not always thoroughly taken – or the issue is not seen as acculturation, but as discipline.

Three papers on these matters, then.

Jude Carroll points out that it is unusual for tutors' time, energy and interest to be sufficiently great to discover and pursue plagiarists. How should they do what is necessary without the task becoming disproportionate? In other words, what is most cost effective? She describes relevant features of induction, electronic detection, disciplinary procedure, and course design. The paper discusses how tutors might prioritise activities which are effective and relatively trouble-free.

Becoming aware that students were cheating with regard to problem based learning (PBL) in medicine, Barbara Cogdell, Bob Matthew and Craig Gray used interviews, and an extended version of the Franklyn-Stokes and Newstead (1995) questionnaire about student cheating, with the addition of some items specifically aimed at malpractice in PBL. It became plain that activities in which 'corners were cut' in PBL sessions were very general and students did not seem to regard them as cheating. But such activities as obtaining last year's objectives before a PBL brainstorming session seriously conflict with the aims of a PBL course.

Finally, Madeleine Freewood, Ranald Macdonald and Peter Ashworth discuss the findings of an in-depth interview study of the meaning of plagiarism for students, based on earlier work (Ashworth, Bannister & Thorne 1997). They found that student understandings of plagiarism are very varied, and these understandings are not always addressed by official guidance. Interestingly, plagiarism was taken by students as either theft of text or theft of ideas, producing quite distinct attitudes and behaviour.

The conclusion of all three papers is that the issue is not just to police malpractice, but to ensure that there is a shared understanding between staff and students about such things as plagiarism. Student acculturation into the academy is needed.

References

Ashworth, P, Bannister, P and Thorne, P (1997). Guilty in whose eyes? University students' perceptions of cheating and plagiarism in academic work and assessment. *Studies in Higher Education* **22** 187-203

Franklyn-Stokes, A and Newstead, SE (1995). Undergraduate cheating: who does what and why? *Studies in Higher Education* **20** 159-172

32 Deterring student plagiarism: where best to start?

Jude Carroll

Oxford Brookes University

Abstract

In the last few years, universities across the world have moved from brief entries in their student handbooks about plagiarism to, in some cases, a more complex and comprehensive approach which combines a number of different actions and procedures. This new, more holistic, approach may be more effective at deterring and detecting plagiarism. It probably arose in response to worries about increasing student copying which could threaten the integrity and value of university awards. Instead of just telling students "you must not plagiarise", many universities are now creating complex web sites. Articles and books full of advice for tutors on deterring plagiarism have also appeared.

However, a holistic approach to plagiarism still rests largely on individual academics, often acting alone or sometimes in co-operation with close colleagues. When tutors seek advice, they encounter dozens of ideas from how to design out easy options and how to inform/teach their students through to ways of detecting and punishing offenders. Most admit they could and possibly should do all these things and more. Yet their time is limited, their energy finite and their personal professional aspirations may be in conflict with actions and attention needed to pursue offenders. Advice on plagiarism now needs to focus on which interventions and actions seem to have the most impact with a view to offering guidance to individuals and to their institutions on how best to begin.

This paper notes the literature on effective interventions and adds observations and evaluation data collected over 24 months in a medium-sized UK university. It describes small-scale studies on induction; comments on the introduction of electronic detection, reports on one aspect linked to implementing a new disciplinary procedure and offers one example of how course design decreased copying between students. It then offers suggestions and recommendations for anyone wishing to address the growing worry about plagiarism in student work on where they might start.

32.1 Introduction

When Franklyn-Stokes and Newstead published a paper on student cheating in 1995, they commented on the "curious lack of previous work on cheating in the UK" (p 159) and on staff who were "at the very least somewhat naïve about the extent and nature of cheating" (p 170). Seven years later in 2002, the picture is very different. There is a growing perception in both the UK and in English-speaking countries that cheating in general and plagiarism in particular have increased. Academics fear that cheating levels might already be high (Bull et al, 2001). In academic papers, in the media and in most staff common rooms, worries are shared that the wide availability of resources on the internet, especially in English, may mean it will become ever easier for students to pass off work that is not their own. Many studies report the worry that students who currently do not cheat face ever stronger temptations to do so (Whitely and Keith-Spiegel, 2002). However, there is now no lack of advice and information on many aspects of plagiarism.

Useful taxonomies have evolved that classify and define student cheating behaviours (ibid, 2002). Other research looks at students in particular and documents:

- frequency of cheating behaviour (eg McCabe, 2002)

- student motivation and rationale for their plagiarism (eg Bannister and Ashworth, 1998; Harris, 2001, Whitley and Keith-Spiegel, 2002)

- the academic skills students need and/or lack to avoid plagiarism (eg Wilhoit, 1994; Gajadhar, 1998; Wahrer, 2002)

- students' self-management and organisation (eg Roig and de Tommasso, 1995)

- and the special needs of particular groups such as international students (Wilson, 1997).

Alongside this student-focused work, other studies have considered academic staff, documenting for example their understanding of what constitutes plagiarism (eg Walker, 1998; Evans, 2000). Some studies describe what cues academics use to detect plagiarism (eg Bull et al, 2001; Hinchliffe, 1999) their motivations for acting or ignoring student cheating (eg Whitley and Keith-Spiegel, 2002) and the tariffs tutors set for specific instances of plagiarism (eg Walker, 1998; Carroll, in press). Accessing any of these publications will demonstrate a large and growing bibliography of resources and information.

Not surprisingly, as information about plagiarism grew, so too did the literature offering guidance and advice. Students can access dozens of sites such as the University of Indiana site at http://education.indiana.edu/~frick/plagiarism/ (July 2002) which includes an on-line quiz that allows students to check their understanding. The University of Alberta site at http://www.library.ualberta.ca/guides/plagiarism/ (July, 2002) is one of the student sites which frequently suggests others, as is the University of California at Davis http://sja.ucdavis.edu/avoid.htm#guidelines (July, 2002). Most student sites cover definitions of plagiarism (and some define collusion); most provide instruction on the skills needed to avoid accusations of both plagiarism and collusion. A few explain the values and beliefs underpinning academic rules on citation and explain why acknowledging others' ideas and work is important such as the site created at LeMoyne College on http://www.lemoyne.edu/library/plagiarism.htm (July 2002).

Advice to academics is also plentiful. Any quick search of the web or an academic index will reveal articles on-line and in print offering guidance on designing tasks that make plagiarism less likely such as the often-cited advice by Harris (2000 2 lots of 2001 in ref, no 2000) on student research papers. See also Boehm (1998) and McKenzie (1998). Other authors concentrate on spotting plagiarism (eg Hinchliffe, 1999; Fain and Bates, 2001), on using electronic detection strategies and web-based searching for the student's sources (eg Harris, 2001) and on appropriate punishment (Walker, 1998). Much of this advice is now gathered together in comprehensive handbooks (Carroll and Appleton, 2001; Carroll, 2002; Harris, 2001; Whitley and Keith-Spiegel, 2002) which list the dozens of different actions and interventions that academics are advised to take which may help deter students from plagiarism and/or detect it if and when they have plagiarised. Taken together, this holistic approach is recommended as an alternative to "catch-and-punish" tactics where the institution waits until the student offends then punishes him or her for doing so.

However, whilst a multi-faceted approach may be the most appropriate and the most valid, it may also be a stumbling block to addressing plagiarism. Because most actions against plagiarism are taken at the level of an individual academic, they must compete with a multitude of other demands on academic time and attention. Faced with too many alternatives or actions, with too many demanding suggestions and too much choice, inaction may seem the most tempting option. Academics need ideas on where best to start and how best to channel their energies. Several small-scale studies at Oxford Brookes University offer some insight into this matter.

32.2   The impact of induction sessions

In most Higher Education institutions, student handbooks and course guides include statements about plagiarism and cheating but there is little evidence that students either read or heed this advice. As a result, many HEIs offer additional guidance during induction programmes but here again, evidence on effectiveness is sparse. To check the impact of induction guidance on plagiarism, a 15-minute presentation was included in the induction programme for 100 first-year students at Oxford Brookes University in September 2001. The session included a definition of plagiarism and encouragement to cite other sources to enhance their marks. It finished with a short exercise on distinguishing between acceptable and unacceptable academic writing. Students were contacted at the end of their first year (June 2002) and asked about the session via a seven-question email questionnaire. Twenty students (20%) responded saying they had attended the session. Question 2 asked for a definition of plagiarism, and all respondents offered almost verbatim one or more aspects of the definition provided in the session which was Passing off someone else's work as your own, intentionally or unintentionally, for your own benefit. Fourteen mentioned giving credit to others' "work", six mentioned "words" and four included "ideas and theories" in the aspects requiring citation.

Question 3 asked how they had acted on the information in the briefing. All referred to adopting standard citation rules, attentive note taking, and "being careful in my choice of words" although one commented that, in ten months at university, the need to cite others "has not arisen in my [field of study] yet". Asked to comment on the session, exactly half the comments were positive ("clear", "useful", "just the right length", "reassuring") and half were negative ("confusing", "worrying", "too long"). All respondents thought the session should be repeated in the following year's induction programme, including three students who said (paradoxically) that induction was an inappropriate time for this information. 20% suggested that a repeated session should be shorter than 15 minutes.

The survey, though small, confirms that an induction session is relatively ineffective for conveying information with 50% of those responding describing the session as "confusing" but very effective at generating strong feelings. Even ten months later, 8 of the 20 remembered the session as "worrying" and one suggested that next time, the presenter should "try not to make it so intimidating". The belief that an even shorter session would be appropriate, presumably reverting to the handbook approach ("Don't plagiarise") could have several interpretations: perhaps it reflects the understandable wish to focus on other matters at the start of a programme or it might show a lack of awareness of the issue. Finally, it could mean students would rather not consider such things at all.

This feedback shows that short induction sessions do offer a reasonable return for the academic effort involved and would be a useful starting point. Should academics choose to use this approach, it would seem advisable to offer clear, limited information to lessen student "confusion", and to follow up a brief presentation with opportunities for further information and discussion (or even, as one student suggested, handouts). It would not, however, be justified to view an induction session on its own as an effective deterrent for plagiarism.

32.3   Designing out copying opportunities

Much of the advice offered to academic staff concerns ways of designing out easy cheating opportunities for students. (See, for example Harris, 2001; Carroll, 2002) Suggestions range from the obvious such as developing new tasks and assessment requirements each time the course is repeated to using assessment methods other than essays which are much more available on line (eg McDowell and Brown, 2001). The impact of adopting a course-design approach to deterring plagiarism is relatively untested, its justification resting largely on common sense and face validity. Here, the argument is that such an approach might offer large benefits for relatively little time and effort and offers a small case study which seems to support this claim.

In May 2001, a team of three lecturers and a staff developer met for one day to consider how a one-year Foundation Art course might be revised. One issue under discussion was the problem of copying in practical workshops designed to teach practical skills such as working in 3-D, photography and working with wood. In previous years students were assigned a group then rotated through six different workshops. Students quickly began using the previous groups' work as a template for their own, often giving tutors many identical solutions to that workshop's brief. This was acceptable in that students were using the practical skills which were the explicit purpose of the workshops but tutors wanted to stop inadvertently condoning copying, and instead encourage creativity. Within an hour, they devised a method of creating project briefs whereby students would pull five objects from a pool of thirty at the start of each workshop period and the resulting collection then became the brief. In this example, forty minutes of tutor effort (though they still had the challenge of selecting thirty objects which would be interchangeable and effective) would result in considerably more student effort as each group devised their own solution(s) to a novel and unpredictable problem. The team believed this should solve the problem although evidence on its effectiveness is not yet available. If it does, they will have reduced an 80% copying rate to 0% with less than three hours' academic input.

It may be that other courses could significantly diminish plagiarism opportunities for a large number of students with a similar small investment of time and thinking, even perhaps resulting in more student learning at the same time. Based on this example, it would seem a good place to encourage anyone to begin taking action against plagiarism and collusion.

32.4   Detection of student plagiarism: specialist officers

Another way academics can use their time to protect the integrity of academic awards is by detecting and punishing students who plagiarise. Tutors can take the traditional route and investigate individual pieces of student work if and when they arouse suspicion. More recently, some tutors have begun using electronic programmes designed to screen all student work for copying. Screening programmes can either look for collusion within a cohort in a package such as CopyCatch (see http://www.copycatch.freeserve.co.uk/vocalyse.htm) or search for cut-and-paste plagiarism from internet sources on programmes such as Turnitin (see http://www.turnitin.com) that will search the web for documents similar to the one submitted. A variety of data on the time required to do both types of detection was collected over 18 months at Oxford Brookes University and subsequently inspected for patterns and trends (Carroll, in press).

In April 2002, 30 minute interviews were conducted by the author with 15 specialist officers charged with investigating and dealing with plagiarism cases at Oxford Brookes University. These academics, known as Academic Misconduct Officers or AMOs, were appointed in 2000 by the university as part of a revision of procedures for dealing with academic misconduct amongst students. Each school appointed a senior member of staff to the AMO role with the larger schools appointing two, making a total of 17. AMOs were made responsible for all actions once an individual academic had alerted them of a case (or cases) of possible student misconduct. AMO duties included investigating the case, interviewing the student, and recommending further action. Action by the AMO could either be a referral to the university's full disciplinary procedure or AMOs could assign a punishment in line with university guidelines and criteria. The AMO system was developed to encourage academic staff to detect and report plagiarism without the possible worry about the time required to pursue a case because anecdotal evidence from tutors showed this worry about time to be a key factor in under-reporting plagiarism. Interviews after 18 months of operation of this new approach with 15 of the 17 AMOs provided an opportunity to evaluate the scheme as a whole. The full report on the findings was reported to appropriate university committees; only data relevant to time is offered here.

According to the interviews, investigation of individual cases varied greatly in length. The shortest lasted a few seconds following a Google search; the longest reported involved an important piece of postgraduate work and collusion within a cohort learning at a distance requiring a full week's work. The general view of AMOs was that a case of possible plagiarism usually required a day's work to assemble. In some cases, it was the reporting academic's time that was used for investigation and in others, the AMO's. A further two hours of AMO time was commonly needed to interview the student and arrive at a recommendation as to further action. In a third of the cases reported for the previous 18 months, the student proceeded to a full university disciplinary panel with the remaining two-thirds of cases being dealt with by AMOs. In the latter cases, the AMO assigned a punishment using agreed tariffs. For the purpose of the AMO review, AMOs were asked to report only the time needed to refer students to disciplinary panels or to apply 'fast-track' penalties.

AMO interviews revealed that 150 cases were considered by AMOs in the previous 18 months, some of which proved not to be plagiarism. However, all cases, regardless of the outcome were seen as equally time-consuming, making the total equivalent to 150 days' work. The Oxford Brookes Personnel Department assumes 215 working days per year for an academic member of staff when discussing academic workloads. This means that assembling cases for plagiarism required roughly the equivalent of half a full-time post when calculated pro rata over 18 months in a medium-sized UK university of 10,000 students. This calculation does not include the considerable time spent meeting and discussing tariffs and criteria necessary for fair and consistent 'fast-tracking' of punishments nor the resources necessary for the formal disciplinary hearings.

Comments as to whether this is an effective use of academic time are probably not helpful as this work must be done to support academic policies and procedures. However, data on time requirements can be useful to managers and academic planners for realistic support and planning for roles such as those performed by AMOs at Oxford Brookes.

32.5 Detection of student plagiarism: individual academic's efforts

A second source of information on the time involved for detection emerged from tracking an individual academic who became interested in electronic detection. The author met with her over one year then reviewed the information for comments on how she had used her time.

This particular academic became interested in plagiarism when she joined a working party at Oxford Brookes charged with rewriting the disciplinary procedures (see above). She subsequently acquired and learned to use a software package, called CopyCatch, for detecting collusion and/or copying between students (see above and http://www.copycatch.freeserve.co.uk/vocalyse.htm). She needed two hours to become acquainted with the package, considerably shorter than the times mentioned in a national study of electronic detection carried out by the Joint Information Systems Committee (JISC) in 2001 (see http://www.jiscpas.ac.uk for information and Chester, 2001 for a full project report). In the JISC study, tutors took much longer; in this case, her high levels of competence and confidence in using C&IT made this a simple task.

Once she knew how to use the package, she also found it straightforward to screen students as they were already required to submit work electronically and most were as technically adept as their tutor. She was able to screen 250 first-year students' work for collusion (ie copying from others in the cohort) in 30 minutes and took a shorter time to screen 50 postgraduate student scripts. Again, this experience was dissimilar to that reported in a previous study of electronic screening (Chester, 2001) which found that staff encountered significant time requirements and administrative difficulties in screening student cohorts. In the 2001 study, this "hassle" was the most important factor in deterring staff from using electronic detection. In contrast, this case shows that screening can be a relatively straightforward task once the infrastructure is in place and the academic suitably inclined and skilled. This relatively small allocation of time does not, however, show that electronic screening is effective unless the effort also deters cheating.

In the Brookes example, the lecturer did not find any collusion in the undergraduate group, a finding which parallels that of the JISC study (Chester, 2001) where screening with the students' prior knowledge revealed little large-scale cheating. In this case, the lecturer explained the finding by commenting, "It was the first term of a first year class; I would not have expected them to be cheating anyway". She did not believe students acted differently because of the screening and noted that assessment tasks had already been changed the year before to deter copying. However, after she told them that all their work would be checked, fifteen students (out of 200+) approached her individually to discuss worries about cheating by fellow first-year students in other classes which was being ignored or overlooked by the lecturers concerned. These students were distressed that others were "getting away with it". Many felt their own marks would suffer as a result but none were willing to disclose information on individual 'cheaters'. The lecturer commented she felt 'overwhelmed' by the students' disclosures.

As an aside, the same lecturer taught this cohort of students in a compulsory module on study skills in the following term, delivering two lectures on using the library, referencing and plagiarism. On that occasion, no students used the opportunity to discuss any matters concerning other students. She commented, "When it impinged on their marks, they got involved. When they were treating it [plagiarism] as an academic subject, nobody approached me".

When asked to speculate as to the overall impact of electronic detection, this lecturer did not see the equivalent of one or two days of her time over the previous year spent on electronic detection as having any impact on undergraduate students' emerging values or on their behaviour regarding plagiarism. She believed it had a negative impact on students' ideas as to how effectively the university managed student cheating.

The same lecturer used CopyCatch to screen for collusion in a postgraduate cohort where the students were relatively well known to her (ie she supervised all their practical sessions). When she told them their work would be screened, two delegations totaling 11 students (equivalent to a fifth of the cohort) came to her office. She described them as "vociferous" and made clear they regarded her actions as constituting a lack of trust in their integrity. Nevertheless, she persisted and one serious case of two students colluding with each other (out of 50 scripts) emerged. Neither 'colluder' had been in the 'delegations' and both were referred to the University's discipline process. When the lecturer was asked by the author as to why she thought these two students ignored the warning about screening, the lecturer said, "It's habit. They are not worried about being caught and feel even if they are, so what?" Her explanation is supported by Whitley and Keith-Spiegel's review of the literature (2002) which found a strong relationship between current cheating behaviour and "having cheated in the past" (p 31). When asked to review the effectiveness of electronic screening in the case of postgraduates, the lecturer saw it as relatively undemanding in terms of her time or energy. She planned to continue to use the CopyCatch programme but would take more care in future to discuss the matter with students. She saw little evidence of electronic screening changing how students behaved but as she was personally committed to policing student work in order to guard the value of academic awards, she believed it to be a good use of her time. She was also keen to support the students who did not cheat. If other lecturers felt similarly committed, this case does support the value of using time in screening but only with sufficient technical support.

Finally, tracking this lecturer produced evidence on how and to what effect she developed and enhanced her skills at web searching to identify the source of student material that might be plagiarised once suspicion had been aroused. She explored a range of web detection tools and read relevant guides such as Robert Harris' The Plagiarism Handbook (2001) which offers extensive advice on searching the Web, taking about a week of her time over 12 months to do so. She used these reactive detection skills in four cases of suspected plagiarism, taking between two and six hours per case for a total of about 20 hours' work. Once again, it is likely that her previous C&IT skills meant she was aware of the capacities and organisation of internet resources and could conduct the searches with some confidence and speed; others may have needed considerably more time for the same results. In all four cases, she then produced a report and handed the case over to the AMO who operated as described in the previous paragraphs.

Despite expressing satisfaction in successful detection in three of the four cases and strong evidence in the fourth, she sees little benefit in spending time this way for individual academics. She commented, "Where's the payoff? There is none". Whilst this might be true at the individual level, the school's record on pursuing and punishing plagiarism is significant in that fear of detection remains a key deterrent for students (Freewood, 2001).

32.6   Effective use of time in detection

By reviewing the above information on detection, it is possible to support the widely heard anecdotal evidence that detecting and dealing with individual cases of plagiarism is time consuming. However, it may not be the most effective use of academic time. Compare, for example, the time it took for the lecturer described above to locate the original sources in one case of plagiarism with a lecturer in a separate initiative who developed and ran a 90-minute workshop teaching 50 students the academic writing skills necessary to avoid plagiarism – though those 50 newly-skilled students might be more inclined to apply their knowledge if they have a sense that someone is keeping an eye on their efforts! However, both these examples and the JISC study have shown that "keeping an eye" has negative as well as positive effects on the relationship between lecturers and students. (Chester, 2001; Carroll, in press).

32.7 Recommendations arising from one institution's efforts on plagiarism

It may not always be possible to influence how and in what form individuals or institutions address the issue of student plagiarism. One person's curiosity, interests and skills or an institution's needs and opportunities may be what triggers actions. However, whenever possible, it may be useful to consider how best to channel time and effort in pursuit of the most benefit.

- **On course design:** It seems likely that time spent redesigning courses to remove opportunities for plagiarism will have the most widespread and lasting effect.

- **On teaching the skills:** Time spent teaching students will probably have a greater impact than that devoted to finding and punishing individual instances of cheating.

- **On electronic detection:** Enthusiasm for electronic detection seems to be growing and can only be encouraged when the JISC launches a national electronic detection service, an intention they announced in July 2002 (see http://www.jiscpas.ac.uk for more information). Small scale studies support the call for academic staff to monitor the time spent on detection as we cannot yet show it benefits student learning and because it proves to be very time consuming. Any efforts at electronic detection need to be supported by the best use of technology and by (at a minimum) access to appropriately skilled IT specialists.

- **On workload planning:** Managers need to include the responsibilities of roles such as that undertaken by Academic Misconduct Officers at Oxford Brookes. Workload planning should make realistic provision for the time required to police and protect academic regulations.

- **On informing students**: Steps need to be taken to inform students about detection activities in a sensitive way, stressing academic values rather than a "catch and punish" mentality

32.8 A final word

This paper considered individual interventions designed to deter plagiarism; however, the case for the holistic approach remains. It is difficult to see that any one action on its own will have the desired effect of discouraging cheaters, reassuring the majority who work for their grades, and safe guarding the integrity of academic awards. Yet even an integrated approach must start somewhere.

References

Bannister, P and Ashworth, P (1998). Four good reasons for cheating and plagiarism. In Rust, C (Ed), *Improving Student Learning: Improving Students as Learners*, pp 233 – 241, Oxford: Oxford Centre for Staff and Learning Development.

Boehm, D (1998). Well-designed Assignments: A third solution, http://www.svsu.edu/~dboehm/Assignments.htm (July 2002)

Bull, J, Collins, C, Coughlin, E and Sharpe, D (2001). Technical Review of Plagiarism Detection Software Report. http://www.jisc.ac.uk/pub01/luton.pdf (July 2002)

Carroll, J and Appleton, J (2001). Plagiarism: a good practice guide, http://www.jisc.ac.uk/pub01.brookes.pdf (July, 2002)

Carroll, J (2002). *A Handbook for Deterring Plagiarism in Higher Education,* Oxford: Oxford Centre for Staff and Learning Development.

Carroll, J (in press) A review of the Academic Misconduct Officers role in managing student plagiarism.

Chester, G (2001). Plagiarism Detection, and Prevention: final report of the JISC electronic plagiarism detection project, http://www.jisc.ac.uk/pub01/plagiarism_final.pdf (July 2002)

Evans, J (2000). The new plagiarism in Higher Education: from selection to reflection, http://www.warwick.ac.uk/ETS/interactions/vol4no2/evans.html (July 2002)

Fain, M and Bates, P (2001). Cheating 101: Paper Mills and You http://www.coastal.edu/library/papermil.htm

Franklyn-Stokes and Newstead (1995). Undergraduate Cheating: who does what and why, *Studies in Higher Education*, **20**(2) 159-172.

Freewood, M (2001). Student perceptions of plagiarism: a research project, Sheffield Hallam University Plagiarism and Inappropriate Collusion Steering Group

Gajadhar, J (1998). Issues in plagiarism for the new millennium: an assessment odyssey, http://ultibase.rmit.edu.au/Articles/dec98/gajad1.htm (July 2002)

Harris, R (2001). Antiplagiarism strategies in research papers, http://www.virtualsalt.com/antiplag.htm (July 2002)

Harris, R (2001). *The Plagiarism Handbook,* Los Angeles: Pyrczak Publishing.

Hinchliffe, L (1999). Cut and paste plagiarism: preventing, detecting and tracking on line plagiarism, http://alexia.lis.uiuc.edu/~janicke/plagiary.htm (July, 2002)

Hinchliffe, L (2000). Can the computer identify plagiarism? *The CATalyst*, February 5-6, Centre for the Advancement of Teaching, Illinois State University

McCabe, D (2002). CAI research, http://academicintegrity.org/cai_research.asp (July 2002)

McDowell, L and Brown, S (2001). Assessing students: cheating and plagiarism, http://www.ilt.ac.uk (July, 2002: restricted access to ILT members only)

McKenzie, J (1998). The new plagiarism: seven antidotes to prevent highway robbery in an electronic age, http://www.fno.org/may98/cov98may.html (July 2002)

Roig, M and de Tommaso, L (1995). Are college cheating and plagiarism related to academic procrastination? *Psychological Reports, * **77**, 691-698.

Wahrer, S (2002). Plagiarism: avoiding the greatest academic sin, http://www.bgsu.edu/offices/acen/writerslab/handouts/plagiarism.pdf (July 2002)

Walker, J (1998). Student plagiarism in universities: what are we doing about it? *Higher Education Research and Development*, **17**(1), 89-106.

Whitley, B and Keith-Spiegel, P (2002). *Academic Dishonesty: An Educator's Guide*, London: Lawrence Erlbaum Associates.

Wilhoit, S (1994). Helping students avoid plagiarism *College Teaching*, **42**(4), 161-164.

Wilson, K (1997). Wording it up: plagiarism and the interdiscourse of international students. Paper given to the annual conference, Higher Education Research and Development Society of Australia, Adelaide, 8-11 July.

33 Why simply policing plagiarism is not the answer.

Madeleine Freewood, Ranald Macdonald and Peter Ashworth
Sheffield Hallam University

Keywords: plagiarism, internet, academic integrity, student experience

Overview

Increasing use of the internet has strengthened academic concern with plagiarism. In response to this, a whole range of commercial electronic detection packages have been developed and there has been a proliferation of research and academic guidance on how to identify and punish plagiarism. Less research has been carried out on the meaning of plagiarism to students however.

Based on our earlier work (Ashworth, Bannister & Thorne 1997), twelve semi-structured interviews were undertaken with undergraduates students studying a broad range of subjects. These reveal that student understandings of plagiarism are varied, and their concerns are not always addressed by official guidance. In particular, students tend to regard plagiarism as either theft of text or theft of ideas, with very different resultant attitudes and behaviour.

Findings such as this indicate that mere policing is not the solution. More work needs to be done to ensure that there is a shared understanding between staff and students about plagiarism and its relationship to scholarship and originality.

33.1   Introduction

Interest in cheating behaviours has led to a number of research studies being undertaken to try and quantify type and frequency of such 'academic mis-conduct', (eg Norton et al, 2001). At the same time, and in response to the perception of an increase in levels of cheating, numerous guides for tutors offering advice on how to identify and punish cheating behaviours, and plagiarism in particular, have been compiled. Many of these are available online (eg Harris, 2000). These types of publication assume a shared understanding of the sort of behaviour that constitutes cheating in higher education, and the negative impact behaviour of this kind is thought to have on the values inherent in academia. However while it is widely understood that cheating and plagiarism are wrong, Carroll and Appleton comment that actually defining what constitutes cheating and plagiarism proves more difficult. They recommend "institutions should invest time and energy into reaching consensus on defining breaches of academic regulations" (Carroll & Appleton, 2001: p16) before disseminating them widely to academics and students.

Whitely & Keith-Spiegel (2002: p17) give the following typology of academic dishonesty. The first four are from Pavela (1978); the remainder are their own.

- **Cheating** - intentionally using or attempting to use unauthorised materials, information or study aids in any academic exercise

- **Fabrication** - intentional and unauthorised falsification or invention of any information or citation in an academic exercise

- **Plagiarism** - deliberate adoption or reproduction of ideas or words or statements of another person as one's own without acknowledgement

- **Facilitating academic dishonesty** - helping someone offend in the above ways

- **Misrepresentation** - giving false information concerning an academic exercise such as a false excuse for missing a deadline

- **Failure to contribute to a collaborative project**

- **Sabotage** - involves hindering others

One of the characteristics that makes plagiarism different from other forms of cheating is the elevated status and culturally specific meaning given to it in in Higher Education (HE), as is discussed below:

> In another quite separable domain but within the same broad cultural base, that of newspaper and broadcast journalism, Bell (1991) has also argued that what might be called plagiarism in academic contexts is viewed as common daily practice in putting out the daily news. Little of what appears in print, according to Bell, is likely to have followed principles of attribution held so dear within academic contexts. (Scollon 1995: p2)

This can be further illustrated by contrasting the above example with this extract from the University of Edinburgh's Guidelines for Faculties on the Avoidance of Plagiarism. It states that:

> Cheating and plagiarism are academic offences… Plagiarism attacks the fundamental principles of scholarship and the foundations upon which the academic community rests. (University of Edinburgh, 1999)

Thus whilst all cheating behaviours are regarded as academically and often morally wrong, plagiarism can be seen to be held in particularly low esteem, because it is regarded an as attack on core academic values.

Ensuring students understand plagiarism can be regarded therefore not just as a skills based or dissemination activity but as an enculturation task. For students to fully appreciate what plagiarism is and why it will be punished they need to possess not just a clear understanding of what constitutes plagiarism, or the skills needed to avoid it, but also to understand why it is imbued with this particular status.

33.2   Method

Research into student perceptions of plagiarism was commissioned by Sheffield Hallam University's (SHU) Plagiarism and Collusion Steering Group. The group, which includes membership from Schools, Student Services Centre, the Students' Union, the Learning and Teaching Institute and Academic Registry, has been charged with re-drafting the university regulations relating to plagiarism and collusion which are currently under review.

In line with Carroll & Appleton's (2001) good practice recommendation about defining plagiarism, as described in the introduction, the formation of this group was to support discussion and agreement about a university definition of plagiarism. To inform this discussion and to formulate recommendations about dissemination of an agreed institutional definition, the group felt it was necessary to explore student views of plagiarism. Building on previous work into student perceptions of cheating conducted at SHU (Ashworth et al, 1997) the method used was intended to elicit how plagiarism appears from the perspective of the student.

Twelve semi-structured interviews were carried out with undergraduate students, chosen at random from a range of courses and including mature and international students. Designed to be informal in setting, the format of the interview did not pre-suppose that plagiarism was wrong, either morally or academically, and invited students to describe their understanding of plagiarism and different kinds of scenarios in which it might take place. In addition, as students would be aware that the university considers the act of plagiarism to be a serious academic offence, it was regarded as important that students felt they were in a safe environment where they could speak confidentially to the researcher and where anonymity was assured.

In keeping with the methodology of the previous SHU work into cheating, interviews were analysed separately "themes common to the students, or issues which – though responded to in different ways – were widely recognised by the students ,were noted" (Ashworth et al, 1997: pp 189-90). These themes have been grouped and are presented in the findings section below.

33.3   Findings

The findings have been summarised under five main headings. These are:

- Defining plagiarism
- Views on whether plagiarism is wrong
- Prevention
- Detection
- Punishment

33.3.1   Defining plagiarism

All students interviewed were familiar with the term 'plagiarism' and when asked to define it there was a universal consensus that it involved 'copying' without proper acknowledgement. However, when students were asked how they had come to this understanding and in what circumstances plagiarism might occur, this straight-forward definition was placed under increasing stress

Primarily confusion related to two key areas of understanding. The first of these was a skills issue. Students recognised that plagiarism was about copying text, however they also understood that copying in certain contexts (e.g. a referenced quote) was not only regarded as acceptable but positively encouraged, being regarded as 'good' academic practice. This confusion can be seen illustrated by the following comment: "as long as you put the author in the bibliography then it seems OK to copy".

The second area of confusion related to students extending the definition of plagiarism to incorporate the copying of ideas. This definition led to a fear of accidental plagiarism: "I think there's gotta be an element of naivety about some cases ... you've got stuff in your head you can't source".

The subject students were studying also had an impact on how they defined and understood plagiarism. Students studying subjects which had a strong reliance on coursework / essay based assessments, such as English, Education Studies or Environmental Conservation, were particularly prone to confusion over whether plagiarism was the copying of text or ideas. This appeared to be rooted in an understanding that to make a valuable contribution to the subject area students were expected to demonstrate originality by building on the existing canon but felt uncertain about quite what skills are needed to do this. There was a tension between students being aware that they were being asked to create something original often based on the analysis of secondary sources, and the fact that many first and second year students feel like novices, so rely heavily on a steer from their tutors or information found in books and journals.

This can be illustrated by comparing two separate comments made by the same student: "... especially the English course the whole point is to make you own decisions, maybe on other courses it isn't quite so central that you come up with your own ideas" and when referring to using material from the internet "just because it sounds good to you doesn't mean it's either right or correct."

In contrast, a Computing student described that in programming, copying of external sources cannot be accidental – there is either a right or wrong answer, and you are either correct or not. In this area, however, either deliberate or unwitting collusion can lead students to copy from one another. When asked if he considered plagiarism wrong, this particular student replied: "if you need help and your friend helps you and puts some of their work in it, it can help you understand what you did wrong and help you improve yourself."

33.3.2   Views on whether plagiarism is wrong

Answers to the question whether or not plagiarism was wrong fell along a continuum, often mediated by the extent to which students felt plagiarism could occur inadvertently. At one end of the spectrum there were those who felt plagiarism was a deliberate act that could never be justified. However, other answers were affected by the degree of sympathy students felt for the plagiarist, taking into consideration why they might be tempted to plagiarise and how it could occur by accident.

> Everyone does plagiarism for a number of reasons, some students might fall behind, they might not understand their work so it's an act of desperation on their part; other students they are just downright lazy.

Only one student responded to this question by saying they did not believe plagiarism was wrong. Her reason for this was that:

> ...whatever you're doing you're relying on your experience of life or whatever, um, sometimes you have to rely on other people's experiences to consolidate your point of view.

This particular view was mediated by the student's subject background, Fine Art, which involves studying in an environment where students are encouraged to work in a studio, to share ideas and to "look at other artists all the time". She continued: "postmodernism is basically copying, where do you draw the line between it being plagiarism and an actual art movement?"

However, the student did go on to distinguish different types of copying. Behaviour which involved an older student "blatantly" copying a first year's work would be an unacceptable form of plagiarism and should be recognised as such by tutors.

The supremacy of published books, journals or other external sources was upheld by many students. As such, copying from friends was often regarded as distinct from copying from published sources. In one way it was regarded as less serious because it was potentially more likely to happen by accident - through sharing ideas, working together or helping a friend. A number of students commented on the influence of peer networks on plagiarism, bending to peer pressure because you are "weak willed" or do not want to refuse to help a "desperate" friend.

There was also scope for students to be accidentally involved in aiding plagiarism through an abuse of trust by a friend who may borrow notes or their essay to read. Although opinions varied on the extent to which the person lending the notes should be punished for the other's plagiarism, it was generally considered that this form of plagiarism was worse than working together because it ultimately involved an abuse of trust and could lead to an 'innocent' party getting into trouble.

Interestingly, the authority given to a published text or the views of the tutor was not on the whole extended to material on the internet, which was regarded by many as an unreliable source. Thus, while a number of students commented on the perceived ease with which one could copy and paste from internet sites, material on the internet was seen to lack academic rigour and so often not worth copying. Students who copied from the Internet were similar to those who deliberately copied off other students, looking for a quick fix either because of laziness or poor time management.

Group work was the other area in which it was felt that plagiarism could occur, primarily in two main ways - if there is a lazy person that you have to help out so the group mark doesn't suffer, or if the group contains a dominant person who pressures others in adopting their views. Most students, however, felt that deliberate plagiarism was a solitary practice, usually committed in the run up to a deadline or because of pressures to succeed.

33.3.3   Prevention

The role and influence of the tutor was seen as particularly important. Students were aware that in terms of its values, university was distinct from their previous educational experiences or the workplace: "You can get away with a whole lot of things at secondary school, just completely copying." The understanding that being at university means meeting a different set of expectations leads students to rely heavily on their tutor to indicate what is acceptable behaviour. And the closer to their course such information was the better. Generic information provided in institutional documents about avoiding plagiarism (eg the Student Handbook) was regarded as secondary to course booklets or material prepared by the tutor. The views expressed by a student's tutor (particularly as the marker of their work) were highly rated. This was accompanied by a strong belief in the expert status of the tutor.

How the tutor responds to acts of plagiarism also appeared important in preventing further acts of plagiarism occurring in the future. One third year student related the experience of being caught plagiarising in the first year. The tutor, by helping him to understand not just that it was wrong but why it was wrong, enabled him to come to understand the value of his own work, to use quotes critically and generate his own ideas from the text.

33.3.4 Detection

Perceptions of the success of detection (and types of detection) were again often based on the view of the tutor as expert. While students acknowledged that tutors differ in terms of the rigor with which they mark work, many still believed in the ability of the lecturer to detect copied work: "The tutors, they know the books, they know the ideas, they know the people, they can tell when it's been rejigged and rehashed, they're not gonna miss it".

This view contrasted with the perception of the effectiveness of electronic detection software. A number of students thought the likelihood that such software would be effective was not very high and considered that while internet detection sounds "more official" tutors are just as, if not more, likely to find plagiarism. Only the two computing students were more confident in the ability of software to find out similarities in student work.

By contrast, the non-computing students, and particularly those who wrote a lot of course-work essays or were assessed by portfolio, were uncomfortable with the idea of a computer being used to read their work. They valued the fact the tutor read and commented on their work; the idea of any of this process being automated was unpleasant and for some smacked of "big brother".

> If it was more fact based or if it was less opinion and more figure work or something I don't know, but I mean no a computer wouldn't be able to read the words and know what they meant, they just read the words.

This view of the tutor as expert can lead to a real sense of disillusionment if the tutors fail to detect plagiarism. Students felt that tutors worked very hard and had a lot of marking so perhaps an occasional incidence of plagiarism would slip through the net but they felt that if tutors were ignoring plagiarism or did not take it seriously, they would feel personally let down:

> You have to be seen to be doing something because it's pretty demoralising. It seems to us, or it seems to me that the tutors are a bit lazy, sometimes it seems like they just don't give a stuff and you think if you don't give a stuff then I won't give a stuff.

33.3.5 Punishment

In line with the view that plagiarism could be defined simply as copying without acknowledgement, within the interviews there was a collective characterisation of the type of student who would plagiarise. They were malevolent, deliberate in their wrong-doing and, above all lazy, the word used most frequently to describe this sort of person. This student should be caught and, most importantly, punished, sometimes severely by being thrown off the course, more usually by being made to do their assessment over and over again until they got it right without the aid of cheating. However, when the interviewees moved from the conceptual to the lived experience of being a student and talked about things that had happened to them, their friends and people on their course, almost without exception this image of the plagiarist was problematised.

In a single interview students could be seen to switch between varying views of plagiarism: plagiarism as the unacknowledged copying of text, as the unacknowledged copying of ideas, 'plagiarism' as a legitimate strategy (helping a friend, bettering oneself, appropriate within the subject area) or malicious act. This interplay then acted to frame how they considered plagiarism should be punished and enforced and whose responsibility plagiarism was.

That tutors should act when they detected plagiarism was agreed on by all students interviewed. This action should not be the same in every circumstance however; where there were skills based deficiencies these need to be addressed; punishment should also be accompanied with an understanding of why plagiarism is wrong. Tutors who did not act were characterised as "liars" capable of "hollow threats". The fact that students now pay course fees also influenced students' views in this area. Condoning or failing to act meant the student was not receiving value for money for their degree.

33.4   Discussion

The findings suggest that where plagiarism was understood to mean the unacknowledged copying of text, students were more likely to focus on the importance of the university responsibility to teach correct referencing techniques. Part of this responsibility was to ensure that individual tutors be consistent and clear about what these techniques were and how they should be presented.

In relation to punishment, a moral tone was often adopted, as the unacknowledged copying of text was regarded as tantamount to theft. Once a student was made aware of correct referencing methods, any copying of text without using these methods was regarded as an intentional act and the likelihood of plagiarising by accident was seen as slight. Once the offence of plagiarism had been committed, it was considered that the role of the university was to catch and punish the plagiarist so as to maintain academic standards. It was feared that where the university did not do this, the value of a degree was lessened. It acted to devalue the effort put into work by the 'truthful' or 'conscientious' student and could create a culture which would lead other students to cheat deliberately as a means to succeed.

Where plagiarism was understood to mean the unacknowledged copying of ideas, the possibility of plagiarising by accident was a real concern. As a result, views on how to punish the plagiarist dealt very much with trying to establish the circumstances in which plagiarism took place and to what extent it was a deliberate act. Furthermore, where students regarded the definition of plagiarism as incorporating the copying of ideas, it followed that in order not to plagiarise, all academic work must include 'original' thought. For undergraduate students, who often regarded themselves as the novice and their tutor or a publication as the authority or expert on their subject, this perceived pressure to come up with original ideas, combined with the fear of accidentally plagiarising ideas, could be very confusing, as the following extracts demonstrate. Indeed, as the second of these two comments suggest, this confusion could lead, oddly, to a tendency to over-rely on published work.

> At the end of the day in my first year I'm not going to have anything to say about my course that anyone probably hasn't said at the turn of the century. So I mean it's difficult not to say what someone else hasn't said before but it might as well come out of your own head.

> There are that many opinions out there that at some stage somebody has most likely thought of it already before you've thought of it, so it puts me off wanting to come up with any original comments, because I have a feeling that if I said something original they will say somebody else has said this before you so why haven't you acknowledged them for it… it's a bit worrying about trying to come with something original.

That originality can be gained by comparing and contrasting existing arguments to reach new conclusions is missing from this first year student's understanding. Thus the feeling that academia and the values upon which it rests somehow demand originality, without a full understanding of how this is judged or can be achieved, is a serious source of difficulty for some students.

Similarly, this understanding of plagiarism and originality shaped the way students regarded collusion and copying from peers. When plagiarism was considered to be the unacknowledged copying of ideas, the process by which an idea discussed in a group becomes 'your own' and is therefore no longer plagiarism could be confusing. Referring to a situation whereby a student has read an idea in a book and has discussed it with another student over coffee, one interviewee stated:

> I would imagine it's so diluted [the original idea] by the time it's gone through two or three different minds it's gotta be diluted to the point that you're not actually plagiarising, you're sharing ideas.

One student expressed surprise at the idea that copying from peers could be plagiarism:

> I know that's plagiarism but I never thought of plagiarism in those terms I thought it was more copying academic work, you know people who've had their work published rather than copying from a friend or someone on your course.

This view represents a resurfacing of a belief of the undergraduate student as a novice not capable of originality. A number of students saw copying from a friend as a foolish strategy that would lead you to getting the 'wrong' answer. It is also interesting to note that the comments above regarding group-work consider the threat of plagiarism resulting from the copying of an idea from a book through discussion.

In this context, plagiarism (as either the copying of text or ideas) could be regarded by students as a 'strategy to learn', as a means of aping the necessary academic style or language of academia. Thus the way information was presented in journals, books and on websites was used by a number of students as a template for their own work, and they remained unsure about whether this was in fact plagiarism or not:

> How I write an essay is I take a book and literally just copy the structure of it, reword the quotes or whatever, use different sources for it, but basically I would just copy the structure and no-one has ever picked me up on that at all and that's how I write essays, that's how I do it…

This mimicry of academic style and language was extended by some students to view 'plagiarism' of this kind as a means of navigating through the university system.

> I think basically, plagiarism is a way of bettering what you know, if it gets you into the next semester and it gets you into the next year on the course then that's a way of learning and maybe that's the wrong way, but when you have no real knowledge of something… then it's a way of learning.

Furthermore, as part of this it is recognised that the importance of plagiarism seems reduced outside of a HE environment. One student saw particular well respected writers as plagiarising the ideas of others (through pastiche, drawing on existing traditions etc) and appearing to get away with it:

> If somebody of that ilk and in that situation in life gets away with plagiarism why should a first year who's basically trying to better themselves, go on to better things, be punished?

Similarly, the quote from the Fine Art students in the findings section about postmodernism represents a similar confusion. Students experienced a lack of clarity about how one type of behaviour is regarded as a grave misconduct, while apparently equivalent behaviour in respected members of the academic/educated community is regarded as acceptable.

As a result of this confusion, the successful use of academic sounding language and through this process the loss of the novice persona was regarded as a positive and credible use of 'plagiarism' (sounding like the published texts by using their words, painting in the style of a well known artist, etc). A 'worthy' or 'well intentioned' act of plagiarism to 'better' oneself was regarded as distinct from the ill intentioned and deliberate or malicious act of plagiarism.

It is interesting to compare these comments with the 'rules of the game' tactics presented by Norton et al who, in their 2001 study, explored not only the cheating behaviours of undergraduate students in UK HE but the deliberate strategies students employed to elicit the highest marks possible – 'the rules of the game'. Of the 24 'rules of the game' items listed by Norton et al, three tactics are particularly interesting in this context. These strategies are having "used big words / technical terms / jargon to impress your lecturer; tried to reflect your lecturer's opinions / views / style as closely as possible; chosen an essay title nearest to the lecturer's subject or research area." While they are deliberate strategies, the motivation may be less than simply malevolent. Rather, it is possible to interpret them as attempts by the 'novice' student to replicate the wider academic values which they understand they need to adopt to be part of the academic culture, but as yet do not have skills to fully understand quite what these elusive values are. They can thus only try and copy what they think are markers of these values.

The reasons these types of strategies or behaviours are considered either plagiaristic or strategic by students is because they are aware that some attempt at fraud is taking place. The fraud however is the effort to be part of the academic culture, to espouse academic values without fully knowing what they really are. This can be evidenced by the reply of one of the students in interview when asked how plagiarism is explained to students: "they keep that wisdom to themselves!"

In these terms it is interesting that many of the students thought the punishment for plagiarism should be that students are made to do the assignment again and again until they get it right: "you should have to go away and rethink and redo it, that's important, and learn from it, learn from the process". What is it here that is considered important for students to learn from the process - the skills alone or also a better sense of academic values?

33.5   Conclusion

Without exception, all students were able to say that plagiarism involved unacknowledged copying, yet further probing of this understanding revealed a high level of confusion which in some cases ends up increasing the likelihood of students plagiarising. Nor is it simply a skills based issue. The research findings demonstrate that undergraduate students see themselves very much as novices in the academic world. They understand that there are values and expectations, and that University is somehow different to other realms of experience (the workplace, School or college). Plagiarism, cannot therefore, just be discussed in terms of penalties or skills, but must also be seen in terms of the role it plays in academic culture. As the research findings indicate, the role of the tutor in this process is highly valued by the student, much more than a simple fear of punishment. Students look to the tutors to provide the guidance to signpost the values of scholarship and nature of originality.

Reducing cases of plagiarism needs to focus away from simply a policing and punishment model to a more holistic approach. Such an approach needs to be based on an institutionally agreed and widely understood definition of plagiarism, that individual academics agree with. This has to be disseminated, not just in a generic document such as the student handbook alongside a few lines stressing the penalties for transgression, but via course specific material explaining it in terms of the student's specific subject area. Secondly, pedagogic measures to 'design out' plagiarism opportunities (Carroll and Appleton, 2001) need to occur alongside instruction on referencing skills, appropriate use of secondary sources etc. Finally, through discussion with their tutors students need to be enabled to reach an understanding of why plagiarism is wrong and what it means in their own academic context.

References

Ashworth, PD, Bannister, P and Thorne, P (1997). Guilty in whose eyes? University students' perceptions of cheating and plagiarism in academic work and assessment. *Studies in Higher Education*, **22**, 87-203

Carroll, J and Appleton, J (2001). Plagiarism – A good practice guide (online), Joint Information Systems Committee, last accessed on 8th May 2002 at URL http://www.jisc.ac.uk/pub01/brookes.pdf

Harris, R (2000). Anti-plagiarism Strategies for Research Papers Vanguard (online) University of Southern California, last accessed on 8th May 2002 at URL http://www.sccu.edu/Faculty/R_Harris/antiplag.htm

Norton, LS, Tilley, AJ, Franklyn-Stokes, A and Newstead, SE (2001). The Pressures of Assessment in Undergraduate Courses and their Effect on Student Behaviours *Assessment & Evaluation in Higher Education*, **26**, 269 –284

Pavela G (1978). Judicial review of academic decision-making after Horowitz. *School Law Journal*, **55** (8), 55-75

Scollon, R (1995). Plagiarism and Ideology: Identity in intercultural discourse. *Language in Society*, **24**, 1-28

University of Edinburgh – Registry (1999). Guidelines for Faculties on the Avoidance of Plagiarism (on-line), University of Edinburgh. Last accessed 16th August 2002 at URL: http://www.registry.ed.ac.uk/staff/Examinations/facultiesandplagiarism.htm

Whitley, BE and Keith-Spiegel P (2002). *Academic Dishonesty: An Educator's Guide*, London: Lawrence Erlbaum Associates.

34 Academic cheating: an investigation of medical students' views of cheating on a problem based learning course.

Barbara Cogdell, Bob Matthew and Craig Gray

University of Glasgow

34.1 Introduction

Listening to our colleagues we might be mistaken into thinking that cheating is a new phenomenon: "It would never have happened when we were students." This impression has been generated by high profile scandals reported in the press, such as the cases of large numbers of computer science students caught cheating at the Universities of Glasgow (Times Higher Education Supplement (THES) 3/9/99) and Edinburgh (THES 20/8/99 and 27/8/99). Other recent reports of cheating include medical students at St Andrews (THES 24/7/98), a final year student at the Royal Free and University College London Medical School (Smith 2000), social science students at University of Wales, Cardiff (THES 19/12/97) and even the student union president at the University of Oxford (THES 11/9/98).

However cheating is not new. As long ago as 1941, Drake wrote an article entitled "Why students cheat". It also occurs all over the world, eg Germany (Rost and Wild 1994) and Russia (Poltorak 1995). However most of the literature on cheating comes from the United States. It ranges from websites warning against electronic plagiarism (Halstead-Nussloch et al 1995 and Ryan), details of medical students cheating (Baldwin et al 1996) to investigations of whether honour codes in institutions influence the amount of cheating that occurs (McCabe and Trevino 1993). A newspaper report in 1994 (THES 2/12/94) claims that on US college campuses cheating is rampart and rising. The most audacious cheating scheme that we came across made use of the different time zones across the States (THES 15/11/96). A team of test-takers sat the Graduate Management Admission Test and the Graduate Record Exam in New York City. They memorised the questions and then sent the answers to candidates sitting the same tests three hours later in Los Angeles.

Various factors have contributed to the possible increase in cheating. There have been huge increases in student numbers leading to a decreased staff-student ratio. This means that the staff are unlikely to know the true abilities of all the students that they teach. Methods of assessment have changed to more continuous assessment with less work being done under exam conditions. The advent of new technology is also having a profound effect. Stored computer files have been used to cheat in exams (THES 11/9/98); Bristol University has admitted that they find it difficult to police the use of graphical calculators in exams (THES 13/8/99); four Scottish universities are changing their regulations in order to prevent the use of mobile phones in exams (Tait 2001); cutting and pasting material from websites into course-work is common place (THES 16/7/99) and even complete essays may be downloaded from the Internet (Clayton 1997).

The initial impetus for this study of academic honesty occurred when one of the authors discovered that three groups of students (seven students) had submitted identical answers to problems in a "take-home" test which was part of their continuous-assessment course-work. One group of students claimed that they had done the work collaboratively, while in another case the students were flat mates and one student had happened to find the other's work lying in their flat. The student who had done the original work had had no idea that the work had been copied. Another incident happened later in the year when a student was found to have a mobile phone in an exam with a text-message with answers to some of the exam questions. These incidents led us to consider just what is cheating in the academic sense, how widespread is it and what should be done to prevent it occurring.

We found two detailed studies of cheating amongst British students and we used these as a basis for our study. Franklyn-Stokes and Newstead (1995) did a study using a questionnaire, while Ashworth, Bannister and Thorne (1997) interviewed students.

34.2 Outline of the problem based learning course for medical students at the University of Glasgow

As well as revealing the attitudes of medical students towards cheating, our study turned out to reveal some important insights into how students behave when using a problem based learning (PBL) approach. Therefore we will give a brief description of how this method of teaching medical students is used in the University of Glasgow. Instead of conventional lectures, tutorials and practical classes in separate subjects such as biochemistry, physiology and anatomy, the students learn from a series of scenarios or short stories about medical conditions or illnesses. All the different aspects of a topic are studied in an integrated fashion, so if the topic of the scenario was a man having a heart attack, students would learn about the normal function of the heart, its anatomy, pharmacology and associated societal risks for cardio-vascular disease. The underlying principle of the PBL approach is that the students not only learn the required facts but that they also learn a method of problem solving. The idea is to equip them with a technique which they can use throughout their subsequent careers.

The students meet at PBL sessions in groups of eight to ten, twice a week with a member of staff who acts as a facilitator rather than as a teacher. The students first read through the scenario. They then "brainstorm", where they as a group discuss everything that they already know about the topic of the scenario. The brainstorming serves two purposes: it reviews what the students already know and lays a foundation for further learning, and secondly it reveals any gaps in their knowledge. At the end of the brainstorming the students produce a number of questions which they will use to focus their individual self-directed learning over the next three or four days. They use various resources such as text books, journals and websites to answer their questions. Associated with the PBL sessions are some practical classes and lectures, but these are purely provided as additional resources. The first hour of the next PBL session is spent with the students feeding back their answers to the questions to the rest of the group. In the second hour the process begins again with a new scenario.

34.3 Methods

A semi-structured group interview (Robson 1994) was conducted with five medical students. The students were four females and one male, and were either in their third or fourth years at university. The interview was based on questions that we had prepared earlier (see Appendix 1). It was recorded and a transcript was made. The open coding method of Strauss and Corbin (1990) was used to identify concepts and categorise the information in the interview. The study by Dearnley and Matthew (2000) was used as a guide for doing the open coding.

After the interview the students were asked to complete a questionnaire. Another nine medical students from the same years of study were also given the questionnaire. The questionnaire (see Tables 34.1 and 34.2) consisted of 20 statements describing behaviours taken from the questionnaire used by Franklyn-Stokes and Newstead (1995). We also added the following four statements which referred specifically to the PBL method of learning used at the University of Glasgow.

- Reading course work submitted by students from previous years and using their ideas (statement 7)

- Using notes from previous students in PBL sessions instead of doing your own notes (statement 11)

- Obtaining last year's objectives before a PBL brainstorming session (statement 16)

- Not contributing to PBL sessions (statement 22)

Beside each statement in the questionnaire were two boxes, one for seriousness and the other for frequency. In these boxes the students were asked to mark each behaviour first according to how serious an offence they considered it to be using a five point scale, where 1 was equal to "not at all serious" and 5 was equal to "extremely serious". Secondly they were asked to give an estimate of a percentage value for what they thought the frequency of each behaviour among students in their current class and in the previous year of study. For this they were asked to use a percentage scale where 0% was "nobody did it" and 100% was "everybody did it at least once".

34.4   Results

34.4.1   Interview

The main 'concept' of the interview was cheating. Analysis of what the students said, in particular regarding their definition of cheating, gave three categories into which cheating could be divided. These categories are 'Institutional role', 'Moral aspects' and 'Peer influences'. Two of these categories could be further broken down into sub-categories (see Figure 34.1).

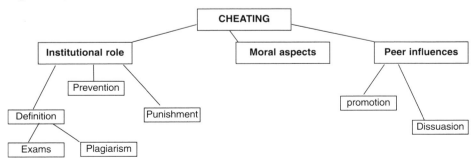

Figure 34.1   Key themes and their subcategories

Institutional role

The institution in this case is the university, but it could equally well be an exam board or a school. Technically, cheating is whatever the university decides is cheating. The students recognised this and said that cheating is

> something you're not allowed to do by the university

Apart from actually specifying what is cheating, the university has two other important roles with regard to cheating namely preventing students cheating and punishment of those students caught cheating. Hence we have added 'Definition', 'Prevention' and 'Punishment' as sub-categories to the Institutional role in Figure 34.1.

The interview also revealed two quite distinct types of cheating behaviours which were viewed quite differently by the students, namely cheating in 'Exams' and 'Plagiarism'. For example they say:

> if you copied the person next to you – a big chunk of their exam question, we would all say, 'Oh that is cheating, that is really bad'. But you see people sitting in the computer cluster – 'Oh that's a good point'.

And:

> You do see people copying chunks of paragraphs for essays, an introductory paragraph and we never thought that was cheating.

The university has specific policies on both these cheating behaviours so we have included them as separate sub-categories under 'Definition'.

Prevention: the measures that the university takes to prevent cheating must have an effect on how much cheating occurs, e.g. the rigorous enforcement of exam procedures. Initially the university should have a policy to inform students what they are allowed to do and what they are not allowed to do. In the case of exams the students knew exactly what the regulations were and so had a clear picture of what constituted cheating in exams:

> taking information into the exam that you shouldn't have or copying from someone else in the exam.

However in the case of plagiarism the situation was not so clear. They knew what plagiarism was but the differences between copying, getting ideas, quoting, redrafting, collaboration, group-work and paraphrasing were not always obvious. Although they do conclude that:

> it's not cheating if you reference it

They also mentioned other practices that influence the occurrence of cheating such as provision of formulae in exams and the wiping of memories of graphic calculators. They also recognised situations where the university had changed its policy to prevent future cheating.

Punishment: Prevention might also be achieved by punishment of offenders if they are caught. However the students were rather hazy about what the punishments might actually be. This was true both of what the university policy for dealing with cheaters is and of what happened to students who had cheated. They were able to recount in detail several instances of cheating, but in each case they were unable to say what ultimately happened to the offenders.

Moral aspects

The students were quite clear about how they should define cheating in the academic sense. They definitely felt that cheating was immoral as witnessed by their statements that cheating was:

> morally not very right
>
> something that gives you an unfair advantage over somebody else
>
> using any dishonest means for your own personal gain

They realised that moral aspects alone would not prevent cheating. There were also some things that they might view as ethically unacceptable but without the university classifying them as cheating then they were not cheating.

Peer influences

The pressure of other students can have a great effect on whether cheating occurs or not. Peers can both encourage and discourage cheating, so we have divided peer influences into the sub-categories 'Promotion' and 'Dissuasion'.

Promotion: peer pressure can promote cheating in a number of ways. The students mentioned the following:

- Students may cheat to impress their colleagues:

   kids who just cheated because it was fun and it was cruel to take in your book and put it on your desk and to cheat, and we mean, it doesn't really matter that they cheat because, it sounds condescending, but they go and they cheat and they still come out with the same grade they would have got anyway because they were cheating for a laugh to show off.

- They may feel sorry for other students who are having difficulties:

   They were passing notes to their friends who weren't quite as clever and they got caught.

- Collaboration may lead to cheating. One of the examples of cheating was an extreme case of this:

   One had written the first part of the essay and the other person had written the second half, both put the same thing in together.

- The view that 'it is wrong to inform on others', would make cheating easier:

   we would hate [ourselves] if we did that and they got thrown off the course or whatever and even if they had cheated.

Dissuasion: cheating may also be discouraged by peer pressure such as concern over what others would think of them:

> If I'm sitting looking over someone's shoulder or something we know if they look at me, they'll say 'Ah ha you're pure bad'.

There is also the feeling that it is not right to gain an advantage over others, as already mentioned.Other students might inform on them or do something unpleasant to them:

> If they got me in trouble we would very very quickly grass them up.

34.5   Questionnaire

A comparison of the answers to the questionnaire with those found by Franklyn-Stokes and Newstead (1995) gives a positive correlation for both frequency and seriousness (Tables 32.1 and 32.2 and Figures 32.2 and 32.3). This correlation was highly significant in both cases (Frequency: $r = 0.87$, $N = 20$, $p < 0.0005$ Pearson product-moment correlation; rho = 0.90, N=20, $p < 0.005$ Spearman's rank correlation) (Seriousness: $r = 0.88$, $N = 20$, $p < 0.0005$ Pearson product-moment correlation; rho = 0.88, N=20, $p < 0.005$ Spearman's rank correlation). This shows that although our sample was small our findings are likely to be valid. It also indicates that our findings for medical students were similar to their findings for other groups of students.

In order to compare our results with those of Franklyn-Stokes and Newstead (1995) it was necessary to turn the scales into average marks as this was the way that they analysed their data. Technically this is not a good way to summarise data as the scales are not necessarily linear, but it is commonly done and is convenient.

Statements (table 34.1)	Average 'seriousness' mark out of 5	Data from Franklyn-Stokes & Newstead	Order from Franklyn Stokes & Newstead
16. Obtaining last year's objectives before a PBL . brainstorming session	1.57	N/a	N/a
11. Using notes from previous student in PBL . sessions instead of doing own notes	1.64	N/a	N/a
22. Not contributing to PBL sessions.	1.69	N/a	N/a
7. Reading coursework submitted by students . from years and using their ideas	2.00	N/a	N/a
3. Fabricating references or a bibliography.	2.07	2.97	1
10. Continuing to write in an examination after the invigilator has asked the candidates to stop writing.	2.07	3.02	2
15. Not contributing fair share to group work.	2.50	3.95	8
18. Paraphrasing material from another source without acknowledging the original author.	2.93	3.35	3
1. Allowing own course work to be copied by another student.	3.00	3.44	4
17. Ensuring the availability of books or journal articles.in the library by deliberately mis-shelving them so that other students cannot find them, or by cutting out the relevant article or chapter.	3.14	4.75	13
23. Submitting a piece of coursework as an individual piece of work when it has actually been written jointly with another student.	3.23	4.11	10
5. Copying another student's coursework with their knowledge.	3.50	3.5	5
6. Lying about medical or other circumstances to get an extended deadline or exemption from a piece of work.	3.57	3.94	7
14. Inventing data (ie entering non-existent results. into the database).	3.64	3.52	6

Table 34.1   Statements ranked according to seriousness

Statements (table 34.1 continued)	Average 'seriousness' mark out of 5	Data from Franklyn-Stokes & Newstead	Order from Franklyn Stokes & Newstead
24. Doing another student's course work for them.	3.69	4.32	11
21. Altering data (eg adjusting data to obtain a . significant result).	3.77	3.97	9
4. Lying about medical or other circumstances to get . special consideration by examiners (eg the Examination Board take a more lenient view of results; extra time to complete the examination).	4.00	4.86	14
8. Submitting coursework from an outside source (eg a former student offers to sell pre-prepared essays; 'essay banks' on the web)	4.29	4.64	12
12. Copying another student's coursework without their knowledge.	4.36	5.42	17
13. Illicitly gaining advance information about contents of an examination paper.	4.57	5.43	18
19. Copying from a neighbour during an examination . without them realising.	4.77	5.36	16
2. Taking unauthorised material into an examination. (eg cribs).	4.79	5.45	
19			
20. Premeditated collusion between two or more students to communicate answers to each other during an examination (eg using mobile phones).	4.92	5.28	15
9. A student taking an examination for someone else or having someone else take an examination for them.	5.00	5.78	20

Table 34.1   Statements ranked according to seriousness
(Statement numbers refer to their order in the questionnaire)

Statements (table 34.2)	Average frequency mark (%)	Data from Franklyn-Stokes & Newstead	Order from Franklyn Stokes & Newstead
9. A student taking an examination for someone else or having someone else take an examination for them.	0.11	2.39	1
2. Taking unauthorised material into an examination . (eg cribs)	0.61	8.24	4
20. Premeditated collusion between two or more students to communicate answers to each other during an examination (eg using mobile phones)	1.55	8.02	3
8. Submitting coursework from an outside source (eg a former student offers to sell pre-prepared essays; ' essay banks' on the web)	4.21	18.39	8

Statements (table 34.2 continued)		Average frequency mark (%)	Data from Franklyn-Stokes & Newstead	Order from Franklyn Stokes & Newstead
13.	Illicitly gaining advance information about contents of . an examination paper	4.43	7.53	2
19.	Copying from a neighbour during an examination without them realising.	6.15	14.27	5
12.	Copying another student's coursework without their knowledge.	10.36	14.48	6
23.	Doing another student's course work for them.	12.20	15.37	7
4.	Lying about medical or other circumstances to get . special consideration by examiners (eg the Examination Board take a more lenient view of results; extra time to complete the examination)	12.71	18.97	9
6.	Lying about medical or other circumstances to get an extended deadline or exemption from a piece of work.	18.43	39.89	12
14.	Inventing data (ie entering non-existent results into the database).	25.29	47.24	17
24.	Submitting a piece of coursework as an individual piece of work when it has actually been written jointly with another student	27.60	24.11	10
5.	Copying another student's coursework with . their knowledge	27.71	46.6	16
17.	Ensuring the availability of books or journal articles in the library by deliberately mis-shelving them so that other students cannot find them, or by cutting out the relevant article or chapter.	29.71	34.67	11
21.	Altering data (eg adjusting data to obtain a . significant result)	36.10	42.93	15
1.	Allowing own course work to be copied by another student.	36.14	40.41	13
7.	Reading coursework submitted by students from years . and using their ideas	48.36	N/a	N/a
11.	Using notes from previous student in PBL sessions . instead of doing own notes	57.14	N/a	N/a
18.	Paraphrasing material from another source without acknowledging the original author.	59.64	57.32	20
3.	Fabricating references or a bibliography.	61.79	47.78	18
10.	Continuing to write in an examination after the . invigilator has asked the candidates to stop writing	62.43	42.5	14
15.	Not contributing fair share to group work.	63.57	51.29	19
22.	Not contributing to PBL sessions.	67.00		
16.	Obtaining last year's objectives before a PBL brainstorming session.	73.21		

Table 34.2   Statements ranked according to reported frequency

The scales we used were not exactly the same as those used by Franklyn-Stokes and Newstead (1995). For seriousness we used a five point scale whereas they used a six point scale. With hindsight we realise it would have been better to use a 6 point scale for comparison purposes. A five point scale is the one we normally use in other questionnaires. However if the end point of the scale we used is made the same as that of the scale used by Franklyn-Stokes and Newstead then the points on the graph are scattered closely around a line with a 45 degree slope (Figure 34.2). Close inspection shows that seven points lie above the line while 13 are below. This shows that our students possibly considered some of the activities to be more serious than the students of Franklyn-Stokes and Newstead considered them to be. However to prove this would need a larger sample size.

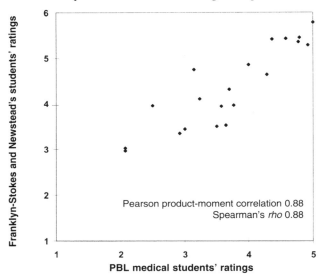

Figure 34.2   Comparison of our data for PBL medical students' ratings of seriousness of cheating with those of Franklyn-Stokes and Newstead (1995)

Our values for frequency differ more from those of the Franklyn-Stokes and Newstead study than the values for seriousness. Most of the points on the frequency graph (Figure 34.3) lie above the diagonal. This shows that our students considered all these activities to occur less frequently than did the students of Franklyn-Stokes and Newstead study. This might be just the result of the scales used in answering the questionnaire. Franklyn-Stokes and Newstead asked their respondents to mark on a line with endpoints of 0% and 100% what percentage of students undertook each activity, while we asked them to give a numerical value for percentage. On the other hand it might indicate a difference in behaviour of medical students with less frequent cheating. An interesting aspect is that the four activities with the highest reported frequencies of occurrence were thought to occur more frequently by our students than by those of Franklyn-Stokes and Newstead (Table 34.2). These activities were:

18. Paraphrasing material without acknowledging the original author

3. Fabricating references or bibliography

10. Continuing to write in an examination after the invigilator has asked the candidates to stop writing

15. Not contributing fair share to group work.

Our students reported frequencies around 60% for these activities which would indicate that that the majority of students would find it acceptable to do these.

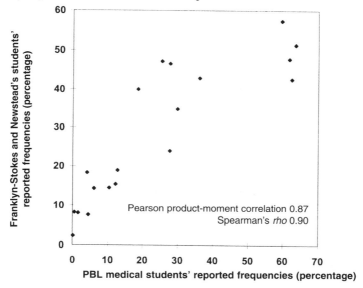

Figure 34.3   Comparison of our data for PBL medical students' reported frequencies of cheating with those of Franklyn-Stokes and Newstead (1995)

It is to be expected that the more seriously the students perceive a cheating activity the less frequently it occurs. This was indeed the case and there was a good inverse linear relationship between the frequency and ratings for seriousness (Figure 34.4). This correlation was highly significant (r = -0.95, N = 24, p < 0.0005 Pearson product-moment correlation; rho = -0.94, N=24, p < 0.005 Spearman's rank correlation). This also agrees with the findings of Franklyn-Stokes and Newstead.

Looking at our data for frequency it seems that the reported frequencies for the different cheating activities can be divided into three distinct groups (we have drawn thicker lines on Table 34.2 showing these three groups of activities). One group consisted of statements about behaviours which are considered to occur very infrequently. These are mostly connected with examinations. Those behaviours associated with plagiarism are more frequent. This is consistent with what was said in the interview.

The four statements (7, 11, 16 and 22 shaded in the tables) which applied solely to medical students have been plotted as open squares on the graph of Figure 34.4. These behaviours are all considered to be very frequent and not very serious. Hence approximately three quarters of the students had on some occasion seen last year's objectives before a PBL brainstorming session. Considering there are eight or nine students in each PBL group then it would probably follow that at least one of the students in each group had seen last year's objectives beforehand.

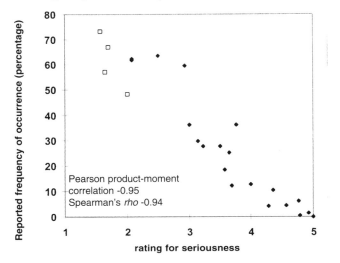

Figure 34.4   Reported frequencies plotted against ratings of seriousness of cheating.
The open squares represent the four statements which refer to behaviours
associated with the PBL course.

34.5   Discussion

Franklyn-Stokes and Newstead (1995) extended their study to ask whether the students being
questioned had done any of the cheating activities and if the actual frequencies corresponded
well with the perceived frequencies found in the first part of their study. As our results for
their questions correlated well with theirs, it is reasonable to conclude that the perceived
frequencies of the four activities relating to PBL teaching reflects their actual occurrence. All
these activities seemed so widespread that obviously the students did not really consider them
as cheating. Indeed if you refer back to their definition of cheating you might be able to make
the case that the activities of statements 11, 16 and 23 are not cheating. There are no university
rules against them and the students' moral definition that cheating gains an unfair advantage
also does not apply. The only person that would ultimately suffer is the student undertaking
the activity. However there is considerable conflict between these activities and what the PBL
course is trying to achieve. Knowing the objectives before the brainstorming session distorts
the activity and would prevent true exploration of all the possible outcomes from a scenario.
It would also have a negative effect on the others in the group if students do not contribute
equally to the brainstorming and feedback parts of a PBL session. Even using the notes of
previous students defeats the aims of PBL. Our findings indicate that perhaps some attempt
should be made to alter the order and content of the scenarios of a PBL course from one year
to the next. If the occurrence of these PBL related activities is as widespread as suggested by
our results, there would surely be the impression that students were performing better in their
PBL in successive years. The first year of the course would have been at a 'disadvantage'.
However, whether this would translate to better exam results is debatable.

It would definitely have been interesting to investigate the nature of these activities further
by asking more about PBL in the interview with the students. Unfortunately we handed out

the questionnaire after the interview so we did not realise that the students thought these activities occurred so frequently and that they rated them as so unimportant.

The results from the interview agreed well with those of Ashworth, Bannister and Thorne (1997), although theirs was a more detailed study. Their students were studying a range of disciplines, but not medicine, and most of them were mature students. Our findings agreed with theirs as regards the strong moral basis to the students' views and that students found the concept of plagiarism confusing.

In the interview the students mention one extra form of cheating that is not in the questionnaire. This is cheating to get into medical school. This type of cheating is probably only relevant to medical students and a few other distinct groups of students as there is not so much pressure for entry into other courses.

Recently the BMJ published an anonymous letter about a medical student who had taken the Oxford Medical Dictionary into one of her final exams (Smith, 2000). This provoked quite a heated on-line correspondence over the next few weeks with a total of 101 replies from 95 respondents (Davies, 2001). Many thought that the student had been cheating and so should have been punished considerably more severely than she had been. However several replies questioned the nature of the examination system and whether it truly measured the sort of skills required by newly qualified doctors today. The question was also raised whether we should expect medical students to behave differently from other groups of students (Glick, 2001). The results from our study would suggest that they behave very similarly to other groups of students. This also agrees with the results of a questionnaire given to Dundee medical students which found that some students reported engaging in dishonest behaviour (Rennie and Crosby, 2001). Perhaps our results are not surprising as at Glasgow applicants for medical school are not screened for their integrity. Glick (2001) discusses whether and how applicants should be tested for ethical maturity, and also emphasises that medical ethics should be taught throughout the medical curriculum.

So what can be done to prevent cheating? Although we did not ask specific questions about prevention it was clear from the interview that the students would benefit from more explicit descriptions of what is cheating and what the punishment would be. In America many universities have honour codes and a national code of ethics is being implemented (McCabe and Trevino 1993 and THES 24/7/98). Recently the Educational Testing Service and the Advertising Council (1999) launched a national public service advertising campaign aimed at discouraging academic cheating. So far in Britain there have been no calls for national anti-cheating policies. However suggestions for dealing with plagiarism have been given by Clive Williams (1993) and Wolverhampton University launched an anti-plagiarism poster campaign (THES 20/1/95 and 14/4/95). A very detailed report with many practical suggestions on how to prevent plagiarism occurring has been written by Carroll and Appleton (2001) of Oxford Brookes University. Technical ways to deal with electronic plagiarism are now available. Academics at Birmingham University have devised a program called Copycatch that looks at linguistic styles (THES 16/7/99) while Glasgow University's computing science department has written software based on techniques used for comparing gene sequences (THES 3/9/99) to detect cheating. An American company will check manuscripts for any matches found on the Internet or their own databases (iParadigms inc.). However these plagiarism checks will only work if the students' work is submitted in electronic form. Another solution is to do all assessments under examination conditions.

We have plans to extend this study to a larger group of students to see if our pilot study accurately reflects the views of most medical students. We will include students entering their first year as this would enable us to investigate whether their views and behaviours change during their years of study. We also aim to give a similar questionnaire to the facilitators and follow this with a staff workshop to discuss the issues that have arisen from our study. We hope this will lead to an increased awareness and improved practices in the method of monitoring the students' behaviour on a PBL course. This should help ensure that the PBL process is not undermined by students trying to take shortcuts with their learning process.

References

Ashworth, P, Bannister, P and Thorne, P (1997). Guilty in whose eyes? University students' perceptions of cheating and plagiarism in academic work and assessment. *Studies in Higher Education* **22**, 187–203.

Baldwin, DC, Daugherty, SR, Rowley, BD and Schwarz, MD (1996). *Academic Medicine* **71**, 267–273.

Clegg, F (1982). *Simple Statistics*. Cambridge: Cambridge University Press.

Davies, S (2001). Cheating at medical school: Summary of rapid responses. *British Medical Journal* **322**, p296.

Dearnley, C and Matthew, B (2000). A group of nurses experience open learning: exploring the impact. *Open Learning* **15**, 191–206.

Drake, CA (1941). Why Students cheat. *Journal of Higher Education* **12**, 418–420.

Franklyn-Stokes, A and Newstead, SE (1995). Undergraduate cheating: who does what and why? *Studies in Higher Education* **20**, 159–172.

Glick, SM (2001). Cheating at Medical School. *British Medical Journal* **322**, p250–251.

McCabe, DL and Trevino, LK (1993). Academic Dishonesty. *Journal of Higher Education* **64**, 522–538.

Poltorak, Y (1995). Cheating behaviour among students of four Moscow institutes. *Higher Education* **30**, 225–246.

Robson, Colin (1994). *Real world research: A resource for social scientists and practitioner-researchers*. Oxford: Blackwell.

Rennie, SC and Crosby, JR (2001). Are "tomorrow's doctors" honest? Questionnaire study exploring medical students' attitutudes and reported behaviour on academic misconduct. *British Medical Journal* **322**, 274–275.

Rost, DH and Wild, KP (1994). Cheating and achievement-avoidance at school: components and assessment. *British Journal of Educational Psychology* **64**, 119–132.

Smith, R (2000). Cheating at Medical School. *British Medical Journal* **321**, p398.

Strauss, A and Corbin, J (1990). *Basics of qualitative research*. London: Sage Publications.

Williams, C (1993). Plagiarism: The need for an institutional policy. *Education Today* **43**, 22–25.

Newspapers

Tait, Mike (16/2/2001) Universities ban the phone cheats. *Metro*

The Times Higher Education Supplement:

	Cheating students difficult to detect.	13/8/99
Baty, P.	Prospering cheats on the up.	19/12/97
Baty, P.	Student cheat forces a review.	1/9/98
Cornwell, T.	Cheating racket used time zones.	15/11/96
Hodges, L.	Cheating rears its ugly head.	2/12/94
Marcus, J.	Honesty code to stop cheats.	24/7/98
Parlour, J.	Thou shalt honour thy sources.	14/4/95
Targett, S.	Poster campaign warns against plagiarism.	20/1/95
Utley, A.	Techno cheats bedevil sector.	16/7/99
Wojtas, O.	Medicine under fire at St Andrews.	4/7/98
Wojtas, O.	Edinburgh draws a fine line between cheating and copying.	20/8/99
Wojtas, O.	Accused students claim they 'cooperated' not collaborated.	27/8/99
Wojtas, O.	tudents asked for cheat alert.	3/9/99

Websites

bmj.com eLetters for Smith (2000). www.bmj.com/cgi/eletters/321/7258/39

Carroll, J. and Appleton, J. (2001). Plagiarism: a good practice guide.
www.jisc.ac.uk/pub01/luton.pdf

Clayton, M. (1997). Term papers at the click of a mouse. The Christian Science Monitor
www.csmonitor.com/durable/1997/10/27/feat/learning.1.htm

The Educational Testing Service and the Advertising Council campaign against cheating
(1999). www.nocheating.org

Halstead-Nussloch, R., Harbot, B. and Murphy, M. (1995). Plagiarism
www.sct.edu/sct/departments/cs/classes/gshpla.htm

iParadigms inc. (1999-2000). www.plagiarism.org

Ryan, J., Student plagiarism in an online world
www.asee.org/prism/december/html/student_plagiarism_in_an_onlin.htm

Appendix 1: Interview

The following questions were used as the basis for the interview:

1. Please define the term cheating. What is meant by cheating in an undergraduate university degree course?

2. Were you aware of any cheating on your course during the last year? We are not asking for any names, just a description of the incidents.

3. How do you think cheating should be dealt with?

Prompts

-   What should happen to someone who hands in a piece of work copied from a friend?

-   Should anything happen to the friend?

-   Should the punishment be the same if they are caught for a second time?

-   When should they be sent down?

Suppose you had a friend whose mother was seriously ill and had missed a week of the course. She asks to copy your assignment or else she will be given no credit for the course. Do you let her? Having copied your work she gets an A for the module and you only get a B. How would you feel? You both want to study the same honours subject. There are limited places and only the best students get in. She is accepted and you are not. Would this change your answer to the previous question? Would you do anything?

The enhancing teaching-learning environments in undergraduate courses project

Keith Trigwell
University of Oxford

The Enhancing Teaching-Learning Environments (ETL) project, which started in January 2001, is seeking to develop subject-specific conceptual frameworks to guide institutional, faculty or departmental development of teaching-learning environments. The frameworks will seek to integrate findings from research both with the professional knowledge of academic staff and with national and institutional criteria describing high quality teaching and learning. By working collaboratively with departmental partners, we are exploring ways of enhancing the system-wide capacity for research-based practice. The project is funded by the Economic and Social Research Council as part of the UK-wide Teaching and Learning Research Programme (TLRP). The programme as a whole is intended to strengthen the research base informing the quality of teaching and learning in the UK. It is committed to pursuing useful research and seeks to involve teachers very directly in the ongoing work of the project.

Members of the ETL project team are based in three centres, at Edinburgh, Durham and Coventry Universities. We aim to work collaboratively with up to twenty partner departments in five contrasting subject areas: biosciences, economics, electronic engineering, history, and media and communications. The departments have been chosen to provide good coverage of academic disciplines and professional areas and a variety of traditional and innovative teaching-learning environments. The project team will support its partner departments in reviewing the effectiveness of their undergraduate teaching in two course settings and in identifying new ways of encouraging high-quality learning in their respective subject areas.

The various outputs of the project will be brought together and diffused by means of an integrated dissemination strategy which combines web-accessible resources with printed materials and collaborative workshops and seminars. The aim will be to assist those responsible for modules, courses and programmes of study to monitor, review and enhance the efficacy of teaching-learning environments by deploying data gathering and analytic tools which are evidence-based and have clear conceptual underpinnings. Our project extends over four years, until at least December 2004.

The papers presented at the symposium discussed some of the initial findings emerging during the first year of the research. As the project has got under way the research team have begun to explore a range of theoretical perspectives that might help in the development of subject-specific conceptual frameworks. These include 'constructive alignment', 'ways of thinking and practising in the subject area' and 'action poetry' – discussed by McCune and Reimann in the first paper; and 'threshold concepts' and 'troublesome knowledge'- considered by Meyer and Land in the second paper. Symposium participants engaged in a lively discussion of these findings and of the wider work of the project. This was a very useful opportunity for the presenters and for other members of the project team present at the session. We were able to draw on participants' wide range of expertise to feed ideas into the ongoing work of the project.

35 The enhancing teaching-learning environments in undergraduate courses project: some initial reflections and observations

Velda McCune and Nicola Reimann

Universities of Edinburgh and Durham

Abstract

This paper will provide a brief overview of the Enhancing Teaching-Learning Environments in Undergraduate Courses (ETL) project, but will focus mainly on some of the provisional findings and conceptualisations emerging from the first year of the research. One of the project aims is to develop subject-specific frameworks and tools to aid academic staff in the development of their courses and to encourage high quality student learning. This paper addresses our emerging ideas about three key concerns that will inform the development of these frameworks and tools. We will begin by offering a perspective on high quality learning in higher education. This will be followed by a discussion of how we might conceptualise teaching-learning environments and their effects on students' learning. Finally, we will introduce some key ideas about communication and discourse in the project.

35.1   Introduction

This paper provides an introduction to some of the ongoing work of the ETL project and offers a necessarily limited and provisional view of some of the principal concepts which underpin that work. In the first section of the paper, we provide a brief description of the ongoing data collection and analysis. This is followed by a discussion of how we might conceptualise high quality learning in different subject areas. Some members of the team are making use of the notion of ways of thinking and practising in the subject area, as a means of encompassing all of the different facets which might form part of a definition of high quality learning. Others have begun to focus more narrowly on particular aspects of students' knowledge and understanding. As seen, for example, in the discussion of threshold concepts and troublesome knowledge presented in the paper by Erik Meyer and Ray Land in this symposium.

The next part of the paper considers teaching-learning environments – the complex interacting set of contextual factors which may influence a student's learning on a particular course unit or module. This sense of the teaching-learning environment of a course unit as being an interacting system ties in well with John Biggs' notion of constructive alignment, a concept we have made use of since the beginning of the project. The final part of the paper focuses on issues of language and communication relevant to our work with colleagues in the five subject areas and more generally to the dissemination of our findings.

As space is limited – and given that the authors of this paper are most involved in the work being carried out in the biological sciences and economics – the examples given in the remainder of this paper draw on these two subject areas. The ideas presented here do, however, draw on the work of the whole ETL project team and on the advice of our subject advisors, international consultants, and colleagues in our partner departments.

35.2   Ongoing data collection and analysis

The pilot work carried out in the first year of the project began with a survey of teaching quality assessment reports from thirty-seven highly-rated departments (Cousin and Hounsell, 2002). The reports were chosen so as to be broadly representative of the range of institutions currently offering undergraduate-level courses in the five subject areas in focus in the project. Subsequently, telephone interviews were carried out with staff from twenty highly-rated departments. Ongoing discussions with our subject advisors, and a literature review, have helped us to make sense of those findings, and to develop our emerging understanding of teaching and learning in those areas.

The second phase of the project is currently in progress and involves working with colleagues in up to twenty departments across the five subject areas. Typically, the work in each department will begin with an investigation of the teaching-learning environments in two course units or modules, using both qualitative and quantitative methodologies. One of these course units is usually in the first year of undergraduate study and one in the third or fourth year. The findings from this initial work in each setting will then be discussed with course teams and, in some contexts, a 'collaborative initiative' will be developed. This 'collaborative initiative' will be some change to the course unit, which is designed by the course team and ETL researchers to have a positive impact on the quality of the students' learning. Where such a change is made, it is then evaluated. (More details of this work can be found on the project web site at http://www.ed.ac.uk/etl.)

Deep approach	Surface approach
The intention to understand ideas for yourself Making links between topics Relating what is learned to the wider world Looking for patterns and underlying principles Checking evidence and relating it to conclusions Examining logic and argument cautiously and critically Becoming actively interested in the course content	The intention to cope minimally with course requirements Studying without reflecting on purpose or strategy Treating the course as unrelated bits of knowledge Memorising without understanding Accepting ideas without questioning them
Monitoring studying	**Organisation and effort in studying**
Keeping your studies well focused Monitoring understanding and addressing any problems Monitoring and developing generic skills Monitoring and enhancing the quality of work produced	Organising your studies Managing time and effort effectively Maintaining concentration

Table 35.1   Current conceptualisation of approaches to learning and studying in the project (Based partly on Entwistle, 1997 p 19)

35.3 High quality learning and ways of thinking and practising

One way of exemplifying the nature of high quality learning, is through the literature on students' approaches to learning and studying. The approaches describe qualitatively different ways of learning and studying which students may choose to adopt. Differences in students' approaches can be related to learning outcomes in higher education (Biggs, 1999; Entwistle, 1997, 1998; Marton and Säljö, 1997; Prosser and Trigwell, 1999). Table 35.1 provides an overview of the current conceptualisation of approaches to learning and studying within the ETL project. The deep approach, monitoring studying and organisation and effort in studying might all be seen as aspects of high quality learning in higher education.

It is important to be aware that the approaches are necessarily simplifications of the complexities of high quality learning. The wider literature and early findings from the ETL project suggest some ways in which the description of high quality learning might be extended. Some of these aspects of students' learning seem more generic, whilst others are obviously tied in with students' experiences of coming to terms with particular subject areas, hence the term ways of thinking and practising in the subject area.

Figure 35.1 presents our tentative initial model for ways of thinking and practising in the biosciences based on ten telephone interviews carried out in the first phase of the project (Hounsell and McCune, 2002).

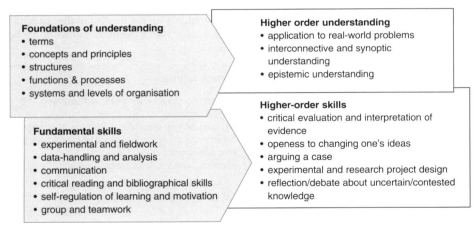

Figure 35.1   Aspects of ways of thinking and practising in biology

In this analysis we identified, firstly, some aspects of the forms of understanding that students might be expected to develop over the course of their degree. We divided these into foundations of understanding and higher order understanding. The former might include an understanding of concepts, principles, functions and processes. The latter encompasses, for example, 'interconnective and synoptic understanding' – where students try to grasp patterns of relationships or to take a broad holistic view of the subject – and 'epistemic understanding' – where students begin to understand the nature and origins of knowledge in the biosciences. The second main part of Figure 35.1 refers to the skills, techniques or competences that students might develop. Again higher order skills are seen as building on fundamental skills and these are both interconnected with students' developing understanding.

From this model, and the wider literature, it seems clear that ways of thinking and practising in the subject area may include a broad range of aspects. Figure 35.1 focuses mainly on knowledge, understanding and skills, but the literature also suggests the need for attention to the ways in which students monitor and regulate their learning, which are interconnected with their aims and goals (Beaty, Gibbs and Morgan, 1997; Pintrich et al 1993; Vermunt, 1998). The ways of thinking and practising that students develop may also involve coming to terms with particular language, beliefs, values and ways of acting (Anderson, 1997; Becher and Trowler, 2001; Hounsell, 1988, 1997; Lave and Wenger, 1999; Perry, 1988; Ramsden, 1997).

How ways of thinking and practising may be conceptualised in a wider range of subject areas, and the extent of its usefulness as a concept, will emerge gradually throughout the project. There are obviously some potential difficulties with its use, one of which is its very breadth. Ways of thinking and practising potentially brings together so many aspects of students' learning, that it can be very difficult to define. It also merges what might be seen as more generic aspects with themes which seem more subject-specific. In practise, however, there may be considerable overlap between the two. Further, it is likely to prove problematic to explore ways of thinking and practising in diverse, or contested, or multi-disciplinary subject areas. There are, however, indications in the findings from the first phase of the project, that it may prove to have a useful organisational function.

35.4   Teaching-learning environments and constructive alignment

There is now a considerable body of research on the effects that students' perceptions of teaching-learning environments have on their learning, and we will not attempt a full review here. This body of literature suggests that a broad range of influences should be considered, when attempting to understand a particular course unit or module within the ETL project. These include workload, teaching and student support and the effects of assessment and feedback (see for example, Anderson, 1997; Biggs, 1999; Entwistle, 1998; Hounsell, 1997; Prosser and Trigwell, 1999; Vermunt, 1995; Weinstein, Husman and Dierking, 2000; Ramsden, 1997). Much of this literature considers the effects of teaching-learning environments on students' general approaches to learning and studying. We must also be aware, within the ETL project, of how students' experiences might affect the development of their ways of thinking and practising in particular subject areas. One possibility in that regard, is that students may learn much about disciplinary cultures in a tacit manner, alongside more explicit teaching (Anderson, 1997; Becher and Trowler, 2001; Hounsell, 1988; Lave and Wenger, 1999; Sambell and McDowell, 1998).

In Biggs' work, constructive alignment refers to the extent to which all the different aspects of the teaching-learning environment work in harmony to elicit high quality learning (Biggs, 1996). As we have reflected on the use of constructive alignment as a model for understanding teaching-learning environments within the ETL project, we have begun to develop our ideas about what it might mean for us in different contexts. We have also considered what points we should bring to the fore when discussing the concept with departmental partners. For example, in writing on this topic for colleagues in the biological sciences, we have taken care to point out that we do not see constructive alignment as all or nothing. In other words, we do not expect that it will be possible to have complete alignment, nor do we consider there to be any one right way to achieve alignment. Instead, we have suggested that there would be a range of possible ways in which a degree of alignment could be achieved in a given setting, depending on the very real constraints imposed on staff in higher education and on the nature of the high quality learning sought by staff and students (Hounsell and McCune, 2002).

It seems from our initial analyses, that constructive alignment can provide useful perspectives on our findings. For example, in the telephone interviews from the first phase of the project, we were able to tentatively identify some aspects of constructive alignment in the course units under discussion. We grouped these aspects into five themes, firstly, alignment to students, which addresses how an environment may be aligned to what may sometimes be a diverse group of students. This has been an important theme in our project discussions. One example is given in the following extract, which relates to how the curriculum progresses as students become more experienced in the subject area.

> In the first year most of the material would be non-controversial, it would be relatively straightforward textbook information. In the second year we are beginning to open up the debate… we would introduce them to… presenting both sides of the case so they are now beginning to get the difference between an accepted view and where, how you inform the particular debate… And then in the third year… the idea that they will be dealing with loose ends is something else that we are very keen on, that they move away from the idea that we understand everything about a subject to making sure that they have got the core knowledge and then dealing with all of the areas which are not understood…

The next two themes from our analysis of the biosciences telephone interviews were alignment of teaching-learning strategies and alignment of assessment. These referred to instances where staff discussed how these two aspects of their courses supported desired ways of thinking and practising. Alignment of learning support included instances where the support provided to students was described as supporting high quality learning. Finally, alignment of course organisation and management referred to extracts focused on broader systems-level issues of course organisation (Hounsell and McCune, 2002).

35.5   Communication with departmental partners

Pedagogical change and academic development form one strand of inquiry within ETL. The possibility of change and the processes through which it can be achieved are to a large extent dependent on communication and within this strand we are therefore concerned with finding appropriate ways of communicating about learning and teaching, with a view to enabling change. In order to explore suitable ways of communicating about learning and teaching, we need to explore, on the one hand, the ways in which our departmental partners talk about learning and teaching and the ways in which they conceptualise pedagogic phenomena. On the other hand, we have to increase our awareness of the discourses we employ ourselves and in which the project is embedded. We also need to determine which kinds of language are most conducive to bringing about change.

35.6   Action poetry

In their work which focuses on putting knowledge into action, David Perkins and Daniel Wilson draw attention to the importance of what they call "action poetry". The concept of action poetry has been conceived as one possible way of bridging the gap which exists when people have access to useable knowledge, but are unable to put it into action when they are required to make changes in real life. "Good action poetry is simply language about what to do that is simple, memorable and to the point" (Perkins & Wilson, in press: 3). It evokes "mental snapshots that make the idea actionable in real time and stressful situations." (ibid). The idea of action poetry is reflected in certain concepts which ETL is trying to develop. The notion of threshold concepts for instance, has been conceived with this general approach in mind. As good action poetry, the term is expressive and employs metaphor which makes it immediately accessible.

However, when communicating about learning and teaching in higher education, there is much more to consider than using language which helps people to put knowledge into action. It is the complexity and multiplicity of the discourses involved which is the main issue here. Whenever academics talk about learning and teaching in their respective disciplines, that discourse contains traces of many other discourses, each of which evokes specific connotations and conceptual frameworks as well as emotional reactions. Discourse layer upon layer needs to be peeled back and understood, in order to make sense of the way in which specific ways of talking about teaching and learning can either promote or prevent change.

35.7   The discourse of the disciplines

There are clear links between disciplines and pedagogy (Hativa and Marincovich, 1995, Becher and Trowler, 2001) and the discipline-specific nature of high quality learning is one of the main foci of ETL. Reviews of the learning and teaching literature in the five subject areas have brought out the distinct influence of disciplinary discourses on the ways in which academics reflect upon pedagogic issues. One of the striking features characterising the economics education literature, for instance, is the way in which pedagogy is conceptualised in economic categories and economic terminology. Course design is regarded as an economic problem (Johnston, McDonald and Williams, 2001) and new instructional methods are evaluated according to their opportunity costs and cost-effectiveness (Blecha, 1999). There are numerous examples in the literature of economists reflecting upon the "opportunity cost" of a pedagogic innovation and the allocation of "scarce resources", much in the same way, one might assume, in which economic problems would be discussed.

> The issue here is opportunity cost – there are too many topics in econometrics that must be covered to allow time for teaching students programming skills.
> (Kennedy, 2001:119, our emphasis, VM & NR)

> The chapter concludes with… a brief assessment of the opportunity cost of using this approach.
> (Watts, 1998: 185-6, our emphasis, VM & NR)

> The second lesson is how scarce, and hence how valuable, the time of students is.
> (Hansen and Jackson, 1996; our emphasis, VM & NR)

This economic perspective on teaching and learning also has its limitations as Dolton, Klein and Weir (1994) illustrate. When conducting a cost-benefit analysis of a peer tutoring project, they totally omit to evaluate the less quantifiable gains in student learning.

35.8   The discourse of managerialism and quality assurance

Over the past decade or so major shifts have taken place in British higher education institutions (Becher and Trowler, 2001, Henkel, 1997). Among other features, these are characterised by a substantial growth of managerialism (Becher and Trowler, 2001: 1-22).

Within university institutions this has meant the development of corporate strategies, strong central management teams, a proliferation of cross-institutional support units concerned with quality assurance, teaching and learning, staff development and so on. The result has been to shift the focus away from the academic department in terms of initiatives and to impose greater scrutiny of the department's documents, practices and policies from the centre... Increasingly departments and academics are expected to meet corporately determined standards. (Becher and Trowler, 2001: 11)

Developments of this kind have considerable implications for learning and teaching in higher education and the related discourse. If academics are made to describe their teaching-learning practices and environments in the terms and categories provided and prescribed by the centre, disciplinary differences are likely to become less visible and teaching-learning environments are likely to become, or at least to appear, more streamlined within the process. In what way this may be the case needs to be investigated within the framework of ETL. Highly standardised institutional documents such as module descriptors/proformas, for instance, which have to be produced for validation purposes, require academics to integrate terms such as "intended learning outcomes", "learning and teaching strategies" and "level descriptors" into their vocabulary. Several of these terms have their origins in the educational literature, in particular in the literature on student learning which is central to ETL. However, although there is an overlap between the discourse of research on student learning and that of managerialism and quality assurance, this does not necessarily imply that the gap between research and practice is already starting to be bridged.

The integration of certain lexical items into lecturers' standard vocabulary is borne out by some of the data which has been collected so far. In conversations with the ETL team and in formal interviews staff have, as a matter of course, used terms like "transferable skills", "flexible learning" and "formative" and "summative" assessment. The following excerpt from a focus group with staff in economics illustrates this phenomenon:

> Lecturer 1: There is a separation between the formative and the summative, an absolute separation. And the summative may take the form of 100% exam...
>
> Focus group moderator: Right.
>
> Lecturer 1: ...or it may take a mixed mode, a summative assignment plus an examination. Some odd variation of that. But in essence those are the distinctions. The confusion you had came from the summative essay where it would have been a mixed mode summative assessment.
>
> Focus group moderator: And that would have been an essay which is set in the course of the year.
>
> Lecturer 2: Yes
>
> Lecturer 1: Well, it is set for submission typically at the end of the year anyway. So it's just we are getting two forms, two pieces of work to assess at the end of the year.

It has been stressed in the literature that the distinction between formative and summative assessment is not clear-cut (Rowntree, 1977: 122, Brown, Bull and Pendlebury, 1997: 251, Yorke, in press: 3). This unspecific, catch-all nature of such terms makes them unsuitable as good action poetry. The above quotation shows that these terms can be so vague that we do not know what exactly people refer to when they employ them.

Within a higher education system characterised by managerialism, talking to and with academics about, for instance, the alignment of the teaching-learning environment to learning outcomes carries the risk of evoking connotations of executive directives and collusion with institutional management. Many academics are familiar with these terms, but it may be that they are not necessarily regarded as vehicles which help them to think about and improve pedagogic practice, but as unwanted bureaucratic tools which are used to exert control and whose relevance is external to academics' own concerns and interests. If we want to be successful in our attempts to enhance teaching and learning environments, we have to be aware of these connotations and perhaps avoid using such loaded terms altogether. We also have to be aware of the many possible meanings of a concept such as "learning outcomes". When this term is used by academics, it may be unclear whether they refer to what has been put on paper in order to fulfil the requirements of, say validation panels or QAA assessors, or to what they genuinely want their students to learn – or whether it is a mixture of both. Many of the documents in which academics refer to learning and teaching, such as module and course handbooks, may have been written with quality assessors as the prime audience in mind, although, on the surface, they are geared towards students. As a consequence of quality assurance and quality control, academics might find it difficult to talk about learning and teaching without feeling inspected. Compare the following extracts from a focus group carried out for the ETL project, offset against sections taken from the relevant QAA report. The overlap of language is striking.

from focus group:

> I think probably the first thing we do is to offer a portfolio of well designed degree courses that cover the core, what we perceive to be the core elements of economics.

from QAA report:

> The curricula offered by the Department are effective in meeting a diverse range of students' interests. This is achieved at undergraduate level through a portfolio of programmes .....

from focus group:

> And then we provide them with a quite a wide range of options that give them opportunities to pursue their own particular interest within the subject.

from QAA report:

> The reviewers found ample evidence confirming the achievement of the aim to provide coherent and progressive curricula that also allow students on the economics programmes considerable flexibility in selecting module options to suit their interests.

from focus group:

> The programmes are progressive, there is clear progression between the different years, starting at obviously at an introductory level, but taking the student through to, you know, quite an advanced level in terms of developments within the subject.

from QAA report

> A recent reconstruction of the undergraduate programme sought to assure clear progression in all the degrees.

35.9   The discourse of the ETL project

While we are trying to find ways of communicating about learning and teaching which address discipline-specific concerns as well as crossing disciplinary boundaries, the discourse of ETL itself has its origin in a particular discipline, namely education and, more specifically, in the student learning literature. This literature has generated its own conceptual and methodological frameworks and an increasing number of academic staff have encountered concepts such as deep and surface approaches to learning, in the context of initial university teacher training courses and via organisations such as Institute of Learning and Teaching[1]. However, even if they are familiar with some of these concepts, staff from other disciplinary backgrounds may not have a firm grasp on all aspects involved. Many of these terms and categories are now widely utilised within higher education, but as pointed out above, this can also be a disadvantage due to their close connection with managerialism.

A considerable proportion of the terms ETL uses may still be alien or problematic to academics from the five disciplines we are investigating. We have to be aware, for instance, of the way in which colleagues from other disciplines might react to the term constructive alignment, due to its connection both with managerialism and with constructivism. Another example is the term "intervention" which was originally employed to refer to the changes to the teaching-learning environments which are going to be negotiated, implemented and evaluated as part of the collaboration between ETL and our partner departments. Our increasing awareness of the connotations of imposition and experimentation which the term "intervention" is likely to evoke, has resulted in the decision to replace it with "collaborative initiative".

As we are trying to capture and verbalise our own emerging insights and findings, some of the terms we use within ETL draw less on existing lexical items and jargon. Ways of thinking and practising and threshold concepts are examples of such terms. In addition to substantiating and validating these categories against the data, one of our tasks must be to investigate how useful they are when communicating with our departmental partners and in what way they can contribute to bringing about change.

35.10   Conclusion

During the first year of the project, the ETL team have begun to develop a set of concepts which we hope will helpfully inform our ongoing collaboration with departmental partners to further develop the teaching-learning environments in their course units. There is still, however, considerable work to be done to refine these initial perspectives. Some members of the team have expanded our initial perspectives on high-quality learning in their work on ways of thinking and practising in the subject area. Whilst there is already a considerable body of literature in the area of teaching-learning environments in higher education, we are only beginning to understand how constructive alignment might be understood in different contexts. It may be that alignment to students will become an important issue in this regard. The concepts set out in this paper will eventually develop to form part of the basis of subject-specific tools and conceptual frameworks which can be used more widely to enhance teaching-learning environments.

For pedagogic change to be successful, we will need to be sensitive towards language and communication. We are operating in a field which is characterised by a multiplicity of discourses: the discourse of the disciplines ETL is investigating, the discourse of managerialism and quality assurance, the discourse of education in general and that of student learning research, in which the discourse of the project is rooted, in particular. Each one of these discourses evokes specific connotations and it is important to be aware of them, if we want to communicate about learning and teaching as well as instigating change. A way forward, however, has been to develop our own action poetry which deliberately distances itself from the pitfalls of the discourses discussed above. Ways of thinking and practising and threshold concepts are examples of our emerging action poetry. This action poetry must be conducive to putting ideas into action, accessible and mutually comprehensible, whilst avoiding oversimplification. Our action poetry must be sensitive to discipline-specific and context-specific variation and, if at all possible, avoid terms and categories taken from other discourses which are already loaded with layers of meaning. Most importantly, collecting data about the processes and results of communicating with our project partners has to be an integral part of our research strategy.

Acknowledgements

The ideas being developed in the ETL project are a product not only of the whole project team, but also of our subject advisors, international consultants, and colleagues in our collaborating departments. Researchers on the project team, besides the authors, are Charles Anderson, Liz Beaty, Adrian Bromage, Glynis Cousin, Kate Day, Noel Entwistle, Dai Hounsell, Jenny Hounsell, Ray Land, Erik Meyer and Jennifer Nisbet. Hilary Tait was also involved in the early stages of the project.

References

Anderson, C (1997). Enabling and shaping understanding through tutorials. In Marton, F, Hounsell, DJ and Entwistle, NJ (Eds), *The experience of learning*, (2nd Edn), pp 184–197. Edinburgh: Scottish Academic Press.

Beaty, L, Gibbs, G and Morgan, A (1997). Learning orientations and study contracts. In Marton, F, Hounsell, DJ and Entwistle, NJ (Eds), *The experience of learning*, (2nd Edn), 72–88. Edinburgh: Scottish Academic Press,.

Becher, T and Trowler, PR (2001). *Academic tribes and territories. Intellectual enquiry and the culture of disciplines,* (2nd Edn). Buckingham & Philadelphia: SRHE and Open University Press.

Biggs, JB (1996). Enhancing teaching through constructive alignment. *Higher Education,* **32**, 347–364.

Biggs, JB (1999). *Teaching for quality learning at university,* Buckingham: SRHE and Open University Press.

Blecha, B (1999). Instructional effectiveness, the web, and economics. *Social Science Computer Review,* **17**(3), 275–288.

Brown, G, Bull, J and Pendlebury, M (1997). *Assessing student learning in higher education,* London and New York: Routledge.

Cousin, G and Hounsell, D (2002). Characteristics of teaching-learning environments awarded high ratings in teaching quality assessments, Universities of Edinburgh, Coventry and Durham: Enhancing Teaching-Learning Environments in Undergraduate Courses (ETL) Project, Occasional Reports, 1.

Dolton, P Klein, D and Weir, I (1994). The economic evaluation of peer counselling in facilitating computer use in higher education. *Education Economics,* **2**(3), 313–326.

Entwistle, NJ (1997). Contrasting perspectives on learning. In Marton, F, Hounsell, D and Entwistle, NJ (Eds), *The experience of learning,* (2nd Edn), pp 3–22. Edinburgh: Scottish Academic Press.

Entwistle, NJ (1998). Improving teaching through research in student learning. In Forest, JJF (Ed), *University teaching international perspectives*, New York and London: Garland Publishing.

Hansen, WL and Jackson, M (1996). Total quality improvement in the classroom. *Quality in Higher Education*, **2**(3), 211–217.

Hativa, N, and Marincovich, M (Eds), (1995). *Disciplinary differences in teaching and learning: Implications for practice*, San Francisco, CA: Jossey-Bass.

Henkel, M (1997). Academic values and the university as corporate enterprise. *Higher Education Quarterly*, **51**(2), 134-143.

Hounsell, D (1988). Towards an anatomy of academic discourse: meaning and context in the undergraduate essay. In Säljö, R (Ed), *The written world: studies in literate thought and action*, pp161–177. Berlin: Springer Verlag.

Hounsell, D (1997). Contrasting conceptions of essay writing. In Marton, F, Hounsell, DJ and Entwistle, NJ (Eds), *The experience of learning*, (2nd Edn), pp 106–125. Edinburgh: Scottish Academic Press.

Hounsell, D and McCune, V (2002). Teaching-learning environments in undergraduate biology: initial perspectives and findings. Universities of Edinburgh, Coventry and Durham: Enhancing Teaching-Learning Environments in Undergraduate Courses (ETL) Project, Occasional Reports, 2.

Johnston, C, McDonald, I and Williams, R (2001). The scholarship of teaching economics. *Journal of Economic Education*, **32**(3), 195–201.

Kennedy, PE (2001). Bootstrapping student understanding of what is going on in econometrics. *Journal of Economic Education*, **32**(2), 110–123.

Lave, J and Wenger, E (1999). Learning and pedagogy in communities of practice. In Leach, J and Moon, B (Eds), *Learners and Pedagogy*, pp 22–31. London: Paul Chapman Publishing in association with OUP.

Marton, F and Säljö, R (1997). Approaches to learning. In Marton, F, Hounsell, DJ and Entwistle, NJ (Eds), *The Experience of Learning*, (2nd Edn), pp 39–58. Edinburgh: Scottish Academic Press.

Perkins, D and Wilson, D (in press) Knowledge into action. *Knowledge Directions: The Journal of the Institute of Knowledge Management*.

Perry, WG (1988). Different worlds in the same classroom. In Ramsden, P (Ed), *Improving learning: new perspectives*, pp 145–161. London: Kogan Page.

Pintrich, PR, Smith, DAF, Garcia, T and McKeachie, WJ (1993). Reliability and predictive validity of the Motivated Strategies for Learning Questionnaire (MSLQ). *Educational and Psychological Measurement*, **53**, 801–813.

Prosser, M, and Trigwell, K (1999). *Understanding learning and teaching: the experience in higher education*. Buckingham: SRHE and Open University Press.

Ramsden, P (1997). The context of learning in academic departments. In Marton, F, Hounsell, DJ and Entwistle, NJ (Eds), *The experience of learning*, (2nd Edn). Edinburgh: Scottish Academic Press.

Rowntree, D (1977). *Assessing students. How shall we know them?* London, New York, Hagerstown and San Francisco: Harper & Row.

Sambell, K and McDowell, L (1998). The construction of the hidden curriculum. *Assessment and Evaluation in Higher Education*, **23**, 391–402.

Vermunt, JD (1995). Process-oriented instruction in learning and thinking strategies. *European Journal of Psychology of Education*, **10**, 325–349.

Vermunt, JD (1998). The regulation of constructive learning processes. *British Journal of Educational Psychology*, **68**, 149–71.

Watts, M (1998). Using literature and drama in undergraduate economics courses. In Becker, WE and Watts, M (Eds), *Teaching economics to undergraduates. Alternatives to chalk and talk*, pp 185–207. Cheltenham, UK, Northampton, MA, USA: Edward Elgar.

Weinstein, CE, Husman, J, and Dierking, DR (2000). Self-regulation interventions with a focus on learning strategies. In Boekaerts, M, Pintrich, PR and Zeidner, M (Eds), *Handbook of self-regulation*, pp 727–747. London: Academic Press.

Yorke, M (in press). Formative assessment in higher education: Moves towards theory and the enhancement of pedagogic practice. *Higher Education*

Notes

1   Professional body for all who teach and support learning in UK higher education.

36 Threshold concepts and troublesome knowledge: linkages to ways of thinking and practising within the disciplines

Jan HF Meyer[1] and Ray Land[2]

1 University of Durham 2 Coventry University

Abstract

This paper arises from ongoing research undertaken by the Economics team of the ESRC/ TLRP Project 'Enhancing Teaching and Learning Environments' (ETL)[1]. This forms part of the large scale ESRC Teaching and Learning Research Programme Phase 2. ETL is seeking to identify factors leading to high quality learning environments within five disciplinary contexts across a range of HE institutions. Meyer's notion of a threshold concept was introduced into project discussions on learning outcomes as a particular basis for differentiating between core learning outcomes that represent 'seeing things in a new way' and those that do not. A threshold concept is thus seen as something distinct within what university teachers would typically describe as 'core concepts'. Furthermore, threshold concepts may represent, or lead to, what Perkins (1999) describes as 'troublesome knowledge' – knowledge that is conceptually difficult, counter-intuitive or 'alien'. The paper attempts to define characteristics of threshold concepts and, in the light of Perkins' work, to indicate correspondences between the notion of threshold concepts and that of 'troublesome knowledge.'

36.1   Introduction

A threshold concept can be considered as akin to a portal, opening up a new and previously inaccessible way of thinking about something. It represents a transformed way of understanding, or interpreting, or viewing something without which the learner cannot progress. As a consequence of comprehending a threshold concept there may thus be a transformed internal view of subject matter, subject landscape, or even world view. This transformation may be sudden or it may be protracted over a considerable period of time, with the transition to understanding proving troublesome. Such a transformed view or landscape may represent how people 'think' in a particular discipline, or how they perceive, apprehend, or experience particular phenomena within that discipline (or more generally). It might, of course, be argued, in a critical sense, that such transformed understanding leads to a privileged or dominant view and therefore a contestable way of understanding something. This would give rise to discussion of how threshold concepts come to be identified and prioritised in the first instance. However, first we require examples.

A simple illustrative example can be taken from the kitchen. Cooking is fundamentally a process of using heat (in various degrees and sources) to effect desired outcomes. In physics one encounters the concept of heat transfer and its mathematical formalisation (as an equation) that represents heat transfer as a function of something called the temperature gradient. It is not necessary to have a sophisticated understanding of physics to have this principle quite simply illustrated. Imagine that you have just poured two identical hot cups of tea (ie they are at the same temperature) and you have milk to add. You want to cool down one cup of tea as quickly as possible because you are in a hurry to drink it. You add the milk to the first cup immediately, wait a few minutes and then add an equal quantity of milk to the second cup. At this point which cup of tea will be cooler, and why? (Answer is the second cup because in the initial stages of cooling it is hotter than the first cup with the milk in it and it therefore loses more heat because of the steeper temperature gradient.) When the physics of heat transfer is thus basically grasped by people in terms of things specific to what goes on in the kitchen, it will fundamentally alter how they perceive this aspect of cooking, and they might consequently even filter out what to look for (the signified!) when they watch the better class of television cookery programmes; for example, a focus on the pots and pans that are selected by the chef in context (the heat source in relation to the cooking process to be applied as a function of time and its regulation to the ingredients) rather than simply on the ingredients and, superficially, the 'method'. So it could be said that, as a stand alone example, heat transfer or, more precisely, controlling the rate of heat transfer, is a threshold concept in cookery because it alters the way in which you think about cooking. And, in the special case where barbecuing is the method of cooking (where heat transfer is via radiation) you also have to take into account the inverse square law, which explains why so many people find barbecuing a 'troublesome' notion. We shall return to the notion of troublesomeness later.

36.2   Threshold concepts and troublesome knowledge within subject disciplines

Our discussions with practitioners in a range of more formal disciplinary contexts in higher education have led us to conclude that a threshold concept can of itself inherently represent what Perkins (1999) refers to as troublesome knowledge – knowledge that is 'alien', or counter-intuitive or even intellectually absurd at face value. It increasingly appears that a threshold concept may on its own constitute, or in its application lead to, such troublesome knowledge.

36.2.1

From a student perspective let us consider some examples from pure mathematics, firstly that of a complex number – a number that is formally defined as consisting of a 'real' and an 'imaginary' component and which is simply expressed in symbolic (abstract) terms as x + iy, where x and y are real numbers (simply put, the numbers we all deal with in the 'real' world; numbers we can for example count on our fingers), and i is the square root of minus 1 ($\sqrt{-1}$). In other words i is a number which when squared (multiplied by itself) equals minus one (-1). So a complex number consists of a real part (x), and a purely imaginary part (iy). The idea of the imaginary part in this case is, in fact, absurd to many people and beyond their intellectual grasp as an abstract entity. But although complex numbers are apparently absurd intellectual artefacts they are the gateway to the conceptualization and solution of problems in the pure and applied sciences that could not otherwise be considered.

In pure mathematics the concept of a 'limit' is a threshold concept; it is the gateway to mathematical analysis and constitutes a fundamental basis for understanding some of the foundations and application of other branches of mathematics such as differential and integral calculus. Limits, although not inherently troublesome in the same immediate sense as complex numbers, lead in their application to examples of troublesome knowledge. The limit as x tends to zero of the function $f(x)=(\text{sine } x)/x$ is in fact one (1), which is counter - intuitive. In the simple (say, geometric), imagining of this limit is the ratio of two entities (the sine of x, and x) both of which independently tend to zero as x tends to zero and which are also (an irrelevant point, but a conceptual red herring if the threshold concept of a limit is not understood) respectively equal to zero when x equals zero. So the troublesome knowledge here then (based on mathematical proof) is that something which is getting infinitesimally small divided by something else doing the same thing is somehow approaching one in the limiting case.

That mathematicians themselves are aware of issues that surround threshold concepts is evident from the work of Artigue (2001 p 211) who refers to a 'a theory of epistemological obstacles' and, by way of summary, gives as a first example of such obstacles:

> …the everyday meaning of the word 'limit, which induces resistant conceptions of the limit as a barrier or as the last term of a process, or tends to restrict convergence to monotonic convergence…

The idea is then developed by way of more complex examples that, as forms of knowledge, 'epistemological obstacles' constitute 'resistant difficulties' for students.

36.2.2

Within literary and cultural studies the concept of signification can prove problematic, even 'subversive' in that it undermines previous beliefs, and leads to troublesome knowledge insofar as the non-referentiality of language is seen to uncover the limits of truth claims. For example, the recognition (through grasping the notion of signification) that all systems of meaning function like signifiers within a language, (that is, that terms derive meaning from their relationship to each other, rather than in any direct empirical relationship with a 'reality') leads on to an understanding that there are no positive terms. Hence the basis of many systems of meaning, including positivist science and the basis of many religious and moral systems, falls into question. This can be a personally disturbing and disorienting notion leading to hesitancy or even resistance in learners. Other aspects of post-structuralist practice such as techniques of deconstruction for analysing literary texts (with a strong emphasis on the ironic, the contradictory, the ludic) often appear counter-intuitive, looking for absences, or what is not there, in order to gain insights into how the text is currently structured by a prevailing set of (occluded or tacit) values or priorities.

36.2.3

One final illustrative example from Economics will suffice, again from the student perspective. The concept of opportunity cost has been put forward as one of many examples of a threshold concept in the study of Economics. Martin Shanahan (2002) of the University of South Australia assesses the transformative effect of this concept as follows:

> 'Opportunity cost is the evaluation placed on the most highly valued of the rejected alternatives or opportunities' (Eatwell *et al*, 1998 Vol 3, p 719). Fundamental to the discipline of economics is the issue of choice: choosing between scarce resources or alternatives. Economists are interested in how individuals, groups, organisations, and societies make choices, particularly when faced with the reality that resources and alternatives are limited. No-one can have everything, and in most cases the 'constraints' faced by the chooser can be quite severe and binding. People choose, for example, how to allocate their time, their work or leisure; firms choose between different methods of

production and combinations of inputs; societies choose between different legal regimes, levels of exports or imports etc. Fundamental to the economic way of approaching the issue of choice is how to compare choices. Thus 'The concept of opportunity cost (or alternative cost) expresses the basic relationship between scarcity and choice' (Eatwell *et al*, ibid); for this reason it is a fundamental (or threshold) concept in Economics.

Thus opportunity cost captures the idea that choices can be compared, and that every choice (including not choosing) means rejecting alternatives. A student who has a good grasp of this concept has moved a long way toward breaking out of a framework of thinking that sees choices as predetermined, or unchangeable. They have also moved toward seeing 'two sides' of every choice, and in looking beyond immediate consequences, and even just monetary 'costs' towards a more abstract way of thinking.

Thus to quote Eatwell *et al* for a final time (ibid), 'Opportunity cost, the value placed on the rejected option by the chooser, is the obstacle to choice; it is that which must be considered, evaluated and ultimately rejected before the preferred option is chosen. Opportunity cost in any particular choice is, of course, influenced by prior choices that have been made, but with respect to this choice itself, opportunity cost is choice-influencing rather than choice-influenced' (Emphasis in original). Thus, if 'accepted' by the individual student as a valid way of interpreting the world, it fundamentally changes their way of thinking about their own choices, as well as serving as a tool to interpret the choices made by others. (Shanahan, 2002)

36.3.   Characteristics of a threshold concept

A threshold concept is thus seen as something distinct within what university teachers would typically describe as 'core concepts'. A core concept is a conceptual 'building block' that progresses understanding of the subject; it has to be understood but it does not necessarily lead to a qualitatively different view of subject matter. So, for example, the concept of gravity – the idea that any two bodies attract one another with a force that is proportional to the product of their masses and inversely proportional to the distance between them – represents a threshold concept, whereas the concept of a centre of gravity does not, although the latter is a core concept in many of the applied sciences.

Our discussions with practitioners in a range of disciplinary areas have led us to conclude that a threshold concept, across a range of subject contexts, is likely to be:

a.   *Transformative*, in that, once understood, its potential effect on student learning and behaviour, is to occasion a significant shift in the perception of a subject, or part thereof. In certain powerful instances, such as the comprehension of specific politico-philosophical insights (for example, aspects of Marxist, feminist or post-structuralist analysis) the shift in perspective may lead to a transformation of personal identity, a reconstruction of subjectivity. In such instances transformed perspective is likely to involve an affective component – a shift in values, feeling or attitude. In this regard there are correspondences with Mezirow's (1978) work on 'perspective transformation'. A threshold concept may also involve a performative element. Sproull (2002) points out how the gaining of aquatic confidence in Sports Science students leads to a dramatically enhanced appreciation of water as a sporting and exploratory environment. This would be an interesting example of an enactive concept in Bruner's sense (Bruner, 1966).

b. Probably *irreversible*, in that the change of perspective occasioned by acquisition of a threshold concept is unlikely to be forgotten, or will be unlearned only by considerable effort. As a conveniently graphical metaphor, the post-lapsarian state of Adam and Eve after their expulsion from Eden illustrates how new (in this case dangerous) knowledge radically transforms their landscape as they pass through the threshold from innocence to experience (new understanding). They gain freedom, responsibility and autonomy, though this is not a comfortable transition. As they look back to the Gate at the East of Eden their return across the threshold is barred by Cherubim 'and a flaming sword which turned every way' (Genesis 3:24) to prevent return to the tree of knowledge. Respondents within our study have pointed to the difficulty experienced by expert practitioners looking back across thresholds they have personally long since crossed and attempting to understand (from their own transformed perspective) the difficulties faced from (untransformed) student perspectives.

c *Integrative*; that is, it exposes the previously hidden interrelatedness of something. Note that if we re-examine the earlier example of opportunity cost from the novice perspective we may observe that while it satisfies (a) and (b) above, it may not be integrative. Davies (2002) provides the following useful insight:
One way of seeking to identify a threshold concept in economics might be to examine discourse on social and economic policy between economists and non-economists. We might infer that a powerful, integrative, idea used by an economist but not by a colleague from another discipline is characteristic of a community of practice rather than a general level of education. For example, Adnett and Davies (2002) show how non-economists have tended to view parental quest for a 'good education' for their children as a simple zero-sum game whereas an economist would anticipate some supply-side responses and peer effects within and beyond school which make the prediction of game outcomes far more difficult. An economist is working here with a concept of general equilibrium which is not a typical feature of educated common-sense. Ideas like this may be thought troublesome not only because their integrative nature makes them difficult to learn, but also because they make the world appear a more problematic and troublesome place.
Davies (op cit) also reminds us, in a salutary fashion, that 'any threshold concept can only integrate so much'.

d. Possibly often (though not necessarily always) bounded in that any conceptual space will have terminal frontiers, bordering with thresholds into new conceptual areas. It might be that such boundedness in certain instances serves to constitute the demarcation between disciplinary areas, to define academic territories:
Within the field of Cultural Studies a threshold concept that has to be understood early is the breakdown of the barrier between high and popular culture. This is fundamental to the Cultural Studies approach. This is a significant departure from practice in English Literature where that concept not only doesn't really exist but if it did (ie if you crossed that threshold) it would undermine the discipline of Eng Lit itself. (Bayne, 2002).
Another respondent to the project (ETL Respondent 2) informed us that where students encountered severe conceptual difficulty such areas of the curriculum were quietly dropped. In this sense the conceptual thresholds served to trim the parameters of the curriculum.

e. Potentially (and possibly inherently) troublesome, for the reasons discussed below.

36.4 Forms of troublesome knowledge: 'When troubles come they come not single spies...'

The notion of a threshold concept might remain merely an interesting issue of cognitive organisation and perspective were it not for the strong indication from our data that such concepts often prove problematic or 'troublesome' for learners. Kennedy's discussion of the concept of 'sampling distribution' in Econometrics appears to identify one such threshold concept that is possibly 'troublesome' for students.

> Upon completion of introductory statistics courses, the majority of students do not understand the basic logic of classical statistics as captured in the concept of repeated samples and a sampling distribution. They know how to do mechanical things such as compute a sample variance, run a regression, and test a hypothesis, but they do not have a feel for the 'big picture'. They have learned a bunch of techniques, but to them they are just that, a bunch of techniques, and they know they can pass the course by remembering how these techniques work. They view statistics as a branch of mathematics because it uses mathematical formulas, so they look at statistics through a mathematical lens. What they are missing is the statistical lens through which to view the world, allowing this world to make sense. The concept of sampling distribution is this statistical lens. My own experience discovering this lens was a revelation, akin to the experience I had when I put on my first pair of eyeglasses – suddenly everything was sharp and clear. (Kennedy, 1998 p142)

Given the centrality of such concepts within sequences of learning and curricular structures their troublesomeness for students assumes significant pedagogical importance. How might we best assist our students to gain understanding of such concepts? What might account for the variation in student facility to cope (or not) with these learning thresholds?

Perkins (1999) has defined troublesome knowledge as that which appears counter-intuitive, alien (emanating from another culture or discourse), or incoherent (discrete aspects are unproblematic but there is no organising principle). He suggests that knowledge might be troublesome for different reasons.

36.4.1 Ritual knowledge

Ritual knowledge, suggests Perkins (1999), has 'a routine and rather meaningless character'. It feels, he argues, 'like part of a social or an individual ritual: how we answer when asked such-and-such, the routine that we execute to get a particular result'.

> Names and dates often are little more than ritual knowledge. So are routines in arithmetic...such as the notorious 'invert and multiply' to divide fractions. Whereas inert knowledge needs more active use, ritual knowledge needs more meaningfulness (of course, knowledge can be both inert and ritualised). (Perkins, 1999 p 7)

Diagrams which are extensively used in Economics to represent complex relationships may well provide an example of the kind of ritualised knowledge that Perkins identifies here. Though students may have learned with some facility how to plot and represent economic relationships, and may well be able to explain the diagrammatic representation of a model, they may not understand the mathematical functional complexity that lies behind the representation.

36.4.2   Inert knowledge

Inert knowledge, suggests Perkins, 'sits in the mind's attic, unpacked only when specifically called for by a quiz or a direct prompt but otherwise gathering dust'. He cites passive vocabulary - words that are understood but not used actively – as a simple example.

> Unfortunately, considerable knowledge that we would like to see used actively proves to be inert. Students commonly learn ideas about society and self in history and social studies but make no connections to today's events or family life. Students learn concepts in science but make little connection to the world around them. Students learn techniques in math but fail to connect them to everyday applications or to their science studies (op cit,1999 p 8).

This failure to connect may well relate back to the integrative characteristic of threshold concepts. As Davies (op cit) pointed out:

> 'Integration' is troublesome because you need to acquire the bits before you can integrate, but once you've got the bits you need to be persuaded to see them in a different way.

Sproull (2002) provides an example of how students find difficulty both in integrating and in making connections between conceptually difficult topics and 'the world around them'. He reports the way in which metabolism acts as a troublesome threshold concept within Exercise Physiology. The function of metabolism, as presented within a standard course text on Exercise Physiology, apparently proves troublesome for Sports Science students who are often unable to make integrative understandings with the sports-related knowledge, activities and practices that they encounter elsewhere in their programme. In this sense their knowledge of metabolism remains 'inert'. As a bridging device to foster integrative understandings Sproull uses an autobiographical work on running by a Cambridge scientist (Newsholme and Leech, 1985) to scaffold and make accessible the concept of metabolism in a sporting context, which then has the transformative potential to open up the understanding of these students in crucial ways in relation to the ways in which human bodies perform in sporting contexts.   In this way the inert, superficial, mimetic use of the language of a threshold concept becomes enlivened.

36.4.3   Conceptually difficult knowledge

Perkins argues that conceptually difficult knowledge is encountered as troublesome in all curricula but perhaps particularly in mathematics and science. A mix of misimpressions from everyday experience (objects slow down automatically), reasonable but mistaken expectations (heavier objects fall faster), and the strangeness and complexity of scientists' views of the matter (Newton's laws; such concepts as velocity as a vector, momentum, and so on) stand in the way. The result is often a mix of misunderstandings and ritual knowledge: Students learn the ritual responses to definitional questions and quantitative problems, but their intuitive beliefs and interpretations resurface in quantitative modelling and in outside-of-classroom contexts.

> I think data analysis is very, very difficult... You pick up an empirical piece of analysis. There is an immense amount of work involved in getting your head round the data, deciding on the correct estimation techniques – you know, will the estimation techniques actually match to the theory you are trying to test? And I think this is just an incredibly difficult thing to teach undergraduates. The more I think about it – the more difficult I think that is (ETL Respondent 1).

Another colleague wondered whether there might be a difference between the relative difficulties of subjects according to their use of threshold concepts, in particular the degree of integration required. He cited as an example the perceived contrast in conceptual difficulty between Economics and Business Studies in the UK 'A' Level curriculum (Davies, 2002).

36.4.4   Alien knowledge

Perkins characterises 'foreign' or 'alien' knowledge as that which 'comes from a perspective that conflicts with our own. Sometimes the learner does not even recognize the knowledge as foreign' (op cit, p9). A threshold concept that is counter-intuitive for many novice Physics students is the idea, formalised in Newton's second law of motion, that a force acting on a body produces acceleration rather than simply velocity or 'motion'. Formally put, Newton's second law states that force equals mass times acceleration. That this is 'troublesome knowledge' is reflected in the difficulty that students have in answering a question along the following lines: If a car is travelling along a road at a constant speed (ie velocity, or rate of change of displacement with respect to time, is constant over time) then what is the resultant force acting on the car? (Answer is zero.) McCloskey (1983, cited in Perkins, op cit) makes a similar point about understanding objects in motion, arguing that 'Learners find it hard to accept that objects in motion will continue at the same rate in the same direction unless some force, such as friction or gravity, impedes them. They find it hard to believe that heavier objects fall at the same rate as lighter ones, air resistance aside'.

36.4.5   Tacit knowledge

Perkins suggests that there might be other sources of troublesomeness in knowledge, emanating perhaps from the complexity of the knowledge, its seeming inconsistency or paradoxical nature or because it contains subtle distinctions, such as that between weight and mass. He invites further categories, one of which (not mentioned by Perkins) we would identify as tacit knowledge, that which remains mainly personal and implicit (Polanyi, 1958) at a level of 'practical consciousness' (Giddens, 1984) though its emergent but unexamined understandings are often shared within a specific community of practice (Wenger, 1998).

Manning (2002) provides an example from Music of such a tacit threshold concept, which students within Western musical traditions find troublesome.

> Students who study the art and practice of Western music learn from very early on the concept of equal temperament, that is the basic notion of the musical octave and its division thereof into what is perceived as twelve equal steps in terms of pitch. Thus the interval between two adjacent notes on the keyboard, known as a semitone is logarithmically always the same, no matter what pairing is selected. This process of learning, however, is for the most part implicit, and it is rare indeed for either teacher or student to study this concept in any depth at primary or secondary level. The notion of keys, both major and minor, the function of harmony, and the principles of modulation are thus introduced without any real regard for the reasons why equal temperament has been so axiomatic for the development of classical music, from the 17th century to the present day.

> Some elements of doubt as to the robustness of this seemingly all-embracing concept may become apparent to more observant students, but it is rare that explanations are either sought or offered. Those who sing in choirs might, for example, notice that a well-tuned chord does not quite accord to the corresponding intervals produced by conventional keyboard instruments and that problems of intonation can prove

particularly acute in the case of unaccompanied vocal works that modulate through many keys. It might also occur to string players that the established practice of tuning strings in 'perfect' fifths, such that no beating can be detected when adjacent strings are played simultaneously, also differs from the equivalent keyboard intervals. In the main, however, these discrepancies are merely accommodated within the overall framework of equal temperament.

What is interesting about Manning's account is how it shows that the source of troublesomeness might often be a compounding of the different kinds of knowledge discussed above. 'When troubles come,' Shakespeare warned us, 'they come not single spies, but in battalions' (Hamlet Act 4 Sc 5, ll.83-84). The troublesomeness Manning identifies with students' understanding of equal temperament in music compounds both tacit knowledge and alien knowledge, where what appears counter-intuitive in new knowledge is over-ridden by existing tacit understanding.

> As the study of music becomes increasingly multicultural, possible clues as to the existence of other tuning systems are sometimes encountered, but the tendency to Westernise such cultures in terms of popular music once again asserts the dominance of equal temperament. The chance hearing, perhaps, of an Indonesian gamelan orchestra may lead a student to observe that the gongs appear to be 'out of tune', but it is rare indeed that they recognise the significance of alternative tuning systems in the development of other musical genres in Asia and beyond.

> Thus it is that an understanding of tuning methodologies and their evolution through history and across the world becomes a threshold concept for an advanced understanding of pitch organisation in music. This aspect of music study will be encountered by tertiary level students in the context of: i) the study of late renaissance and early baroque Western music, when the evolution of harmonic structures necessitated the development of tuning systems that could sustain modulation to more remote keys, ii) the study of ethnomusicology, and iii) the manipulation of timbre in the context of electroacoustic music. Recognition that the structure and organisation of music involves acoustic principles that not only are concerned with the different timbres of instrumental and electronic sources but also their associated tuning systems elevates the analysis of music and modes of composition to new levels of understanding of the processes involved (ibid).

36.4.6   Troublesome language

Language itself, as used within any academic discipline, can be another source of conceptual troublesomeness. Specific discourses have developed within disciplines to represent (and simultaneously privilege) particular understandings and ways of seeing and thinking. Such discourses distinguish individual communities of practice and are necessarily less familiar to new entrants to such discursive communities or those peripheral to them (Wenger, 2000). The discursive practices of a given community may render previously 'familiar' concepts strange and subsequently conceptually difficult. The use of the term 'culture' within first year Social Anthropology, for example, is reported as problematic in this way (Knottenbelt, 2002). Moreover, the inherently arbitrary and non-referential nature of language compounds conceptual difficulty through obliging those seeking to teach or clarify concepts to deploy further terms, metaphors and concepts in an endless play of signification (Derrida, 1978). 'There is no concept which exists outside systems of thought and language; there is no concept which is not involved in the infinite play of meaning. In order to function socially we do make temporary determinations of meaning but meaning itself is never determinate' (Land and Bayne, 1999). Eagleton (1983) points out that language:

> instead of being a well-defined, clearly demarcated structure containing symmetrical units of signifiers and signifieds, now begins to look much more like a sprawling limitless web where there is a constant interchange and circulation of elements, where none of the elements is absolutely definable and where everything is caught up and traced through by everything else.

As an example of such conceptual difficulty, Hodgkin (2002), discussing education in the visual arts, reports the difficulty of understanding the concept of 'art' itself, locating the concept 'somewhere in the gap that exists between history, scholarship and the feeling of being on the edge of tears'. Reimann (2002) draws attention to the particularly problematic (and complex) example of foreign language learning, where language is also the content.

> If 'foreign' knowledge is troublesome, will learning foreign languages, including knowledge and insights about foreign cultures ('otherness'), always be troublesome? Does this perhaps contribute to the reputation of languages as difficult subjects? Also, in foreign language learning, issues of content and of language merge. The language is the content. Students get very disconcerted when they come across ways of expressing familiar concepts in a different way, for example numbers. Surely saying eighty-four is more 'natural' – better than quatre-vingt-quatre or vierundachtzig? Is this particularly troublesome?

Here we see the notion of alien knowledge compounded with the inherently problematic nature of language itself – another instance of troubles coming not as single spies.

36.5   Ways of thinking and practising (WTP)

Threshold concepts would seem to be more readily identified within disciplinary contexts where there is a relatively greater degree of consensus on what constitutes a body of knowledge (for example, Mathematics, Physics, Medicine). However within areas where there is not such a clearly identified body of knowledge it might still be the case that what the ETL project team (McCune and Reimann, 2003) have come to encapsulate in the term ways of thinking and practising (WTP) also constitutes a crucial threshold function in leading to a transformed understanding. A participant within our project identified the threshold function of a way of thinking and practising within the teaching of Economics:

> we have to instil in students a kind of acceptance of modelling which is quite fundamental to the way in which we approach most of our analysis... we want our students to start to think about problems, issues. You get them to formulate, if not explicitly at least implicitly, some kind of formal analytical structure or model that simplifies things but then allows someone to think through a problem in a very structured way. That's something fundamental I think (ETL Respondent 3).

Another participant from a large modern English university offered a similar view:

> Within Economics I sense that sometimes students see abstract models as abstract models and don't see the link between them and the real world, so that students would be quite happy talking about problems of inflation, unemployment and so on, but as soon as you say 'Good, let's have a look at the model', they sort of switch off. They think that's a completely separate issue. 'I don't want to do the model, I just want to talk about inflation or unemployment.' So the idea that models which look abstract – can be

looked at abstractly – actually talk about the real world, perhaps that is a crucial factor. I mean they tend to put models into one box and then the discussion about the policy issues in another box. They don't necessarily see that the two must be linked. Perhaps that's a threshold issue… (ETL Respondent 4).

And finally we may consider an extract from a book on the teaching of undergraduate Economics:

When the dust settles, most students leave the introductory course never having fully grasped the essence of microeconomics. Thus the opportunity cost concept, so utterly central to our understanding of what it means to think like an economist, is but one among hundreds of other concepts that go by in a blur. (Frank, 1998 p14) [emphasis added].

36.6   Conclusion

The intention of this paper has been to open up discussion of threshold concepts as an important but problematic factor in the design of effective learning environments within disciplines and to indicate the linkages to ways of thinking and practising within these disciplines. It is our contention that where threshold concepts exist within curricula there is a likelihood, owing to their powerful transformative effects, that they may prove troublesome for students. Difficulty in understanding threshold concepts may leave the learner in a state of liminality (Latin limen – 'threshold'), a suspended state in which understanding approximates to a kind of mimicry or lack of authenticity. Palmer (2001), in a discussion of liminality and hermeneutics, reminds us that the insights gained when the learner crosses the threshold might also be unsettling, involving a sense of loss:

The truth or insight may be a pleasant awakening or rob one of an illusion; the understanding itself is morally neutral. The quicksilver flash of insight may make one rich or poor in an instant. (Palmer, 2001 p 4)

A further significant issue is that threshold concepts might be interpreted as part of a 'totalising' or colonising view of the curriculum. Such a view would point to the effects of power relations within curricula with threshold concepts serving to provide a measure, and exert a 'normalising' function in the Foucaldian sense (Foucault, 1979, 1980). Whose threshold concepts then becomes a salient question. These are non-trivial concerns and merit further consideration.

These issues notwithstanding, conversations with colleagues in various disciplines have confirmed that the idea of a threshold concept remains a powerful one to the extent even of being used to benchmark curricula. It appears, however, that threshold concepts are more readily identifiable in some disciplines (such as Physics) than in others (such as History). Wherever present they constitute an obvious, and perhaps neglected, focus for evaluating teaching strategies and learning outcomes. The present study has drawn primarily from the perspectives of teachers in higher education. A research question is also opened up on the degree to which threshold concepts, as perceived by teachers, are experienced by students, and with what variation. If it is accepted that these threshold concepts represent experiential entities in the minds of students to what extent can they be constructively aligned? Might threshold concepts usefully provide a micro-perspective for examining learning environments? These questions will form the basis of a subsequent paper drawing on the perspectives of students in higher education.

References

Adnett, N and Davies, P (2000). Education as a positional good: implications for market-based reforms of state schooling. *British Journal of Educational Studies*, **50**(2), 189-202.

Artigue, M (2001).What can we learn from educational research at the university level? In Holton, D (Ed), *The teaching and learning of mathematics at university level*, Dordrecht: Kluwer Academic Publishers.

Bayne, S (2002). *Personal communication with the authors,* Edinburgh: Queen Margaret University College.

Bruner, J (1966). *Toward a Theory of Instruction*, Cambridge MA: Harvard University Press.

Davies, P (2002). Personal communication with the authors, University of Staffordshire.

Derrida, J (1978). Structure, sign and play in the discourse of the human sciences. Cited in Lodge, D (Ed), (1988) *Modern Criticism and Theory*, London: Longman.

Eagleton, T (1983). *Literary Theory: an introduction*, Oxford: Blackwell.

Eatwell, J, Milgate, M and Newman, P (Eds), (1998). *The New Palgrave. A Dictionary of Economics*, London: Macmillan.

Foucault, M (1979). *Discipline and Punish: the birth of the prison*, Harmondsworth: Penguin.

Foucault, M (1980). *Power/Knowledge,* New York: Pantheon.

Frank, RH (1998). Some thoughts on the micro principles course. In Walstad, WB and Saunders, P (Eds), *Teaching Undergraduate Economics: A handbook for instructors*, Chapter 2, 13-20. Boston: Irwin / McGraw-Hill.

Giddens, A (1984). *The Constitution of Society*, Cambridge: Polity Press.

Hodgkin, H (2002). Annual Edinburgh Festival Lecture, University of Edinburgh.

Kennedy, P (1998). Using Monte Carlo studies for teaching econometrics. In Becker, W and Watts, M (Eds), *Teaching economics to undergraduates. Alternatives to chalk and talk*, Cheltenham, Northampton / Mass: Edward Elgar.

Knottenbelt, M (2002). Personal communication with the authors, University of Edinburgh.

Land R, and Bayne, S (1999. Computer-mediated learning, synchronicity and the metaphysics of presence. In Collis, B and Oliver, R (Eds), ED-MEDIA 1999, *Proceedings of 11th Annual World Conference on Educational Multimedia, Hypermedia & Telecommunications, American Association for the Advancement of Computing in Education,* Charlottesville,VA.

Manning, P (2002). Personal communication with the authors, University of Durham.

Mezirow, J (1978). Perspective transformation. *Adult Education*, **28**(2), 100-109.

McCloskey, M (1983). Naive theories of motion. In Gentner, D and Stevens, AL (Eds), *Mental models,* Hillsdale, NJ: Erlbaum, cited in Perkins (1999). (p. 299324).

McCune, V and Reimann, N (2002). The Enhancing Teaching-Learning Environments in Undergraduate Courses Project: Some Initial Reflections and Observations, In Rust C (Ed) *Improving Student Learning Theory and Practice – 10 years on*, (this volume, Chapter 35). Oxford: Oxford Centre for Staff and Learning Development.

Newsholme, E and Leech, T (1985). *Runner: Energy and Endurance*, (4th Edn). New Jersey, Oxford, London: Walter L Meagher.

Palmer, RE (2001). The Liminality of Hermes and the Meaning of Hermeneutics, MacMurray College, http://www.mac.edu/~rpalmer/liminality.html Last Modified May 29, 2001

Perkins, D (1999). *The Many Faces of Constructivism, Educational Leadership*, **57**(3), November

Polanyi, M (1958). *Personal Knowledge*, London: Routledge.

Reimann, N (2002). Personal communication with the authors, University of Durham.

Shanahan, M (2002). Personal communication with the authors, University of South Australia.

Sproull, J (2002). Personal communication with authors, University of Edinburgh.

Wenger, E (2000). *Communities of Practice*, Cambridge: Cambridge University Press.

Acknowledgements

This chapter was prepared as part of the work of the Enhancing Teaching-Learning Environments in Undergraduate Courses project, which is funded by the Teaching and Learning Research Programme of the Economic and Social Research Council (http://www.tlrp.org). The project is being undertaken by a team drawn from the Universities of Coventry, Durham and Edinburgh. At the time of writing, members of the project team were Charles Anderson, Liz Beaty, Adrian Bromage, Glynis Cousin, Kate Day, Noel Entwistle, Dai Hounsell, Jenny Hounsell, Ray Land, Velda McCune, Erik Meyer and Nicola Reimann. Further information about the project is available on its website (http://www.ed.ac.uk/etl).

Notes

1   ESRC Teaching and Learning Research Programme Project No L139251099